Ceph: Designing and Implementing Scalable Storage Systems

Design, implement, and manage software-defined storage solutions that provide excellent performance

Michael Hackett
Vikhyat Umrao
Karan Singh
Nick Fisk
Anthony D'Atri
Vaibhav Bhembre

BIRMINGHAM - MUMBAI

Ceph: Designing and Implementing Scalable Storage Systems

Copyright © 2019 Packt Publishing

First Published: January 2019

Production Reference: 1290119

Published by Packt Publishing Ltd.
Livery Place, 35 Livery Street
Birmingham, B3 2PB, U.K.

ISBN 978-1-78829-541-3

www.packtpub.com

`mapt.io`

Mapt is an online digital library that gives you full access to over 5,000 books and videos, as well as industry-leading tools to help you plan your personal development and advance your career. For more information, please visit our website.

Why Subscribe?

- Spend less time learning and more time coding with practical eBooks and Videos from over 4,000 industry professionals

- Improve your learning with Skill Plans built especially for you

- Get a free eBook or video every month

- Mapt is fully searchable

- Copy and paste, print, and bookmark content

Packt.com

Did you know that Packt offers eBook versions of every book published, with PDF and ePub files available? You can upgrade to the eBook version at `www.packt.com` and as a print book customer, you are entitled to a discount on the eBook copy. Get in touch with us at `customercare@packtpub.com` for more details.

At `www.packt.com`, you can also read a collection of free technical articles, sign up for a range of free newsletters, and receive exclusive discounts and offers on Packt books and eBooks.

Contributors

About the Authors

Michael Hackett is a storage and SAN expert in customer support. He has been working on Ceph and storage-related products for over 12 years. Michael is currently working at Red Hat, based in Massachusetts, where he is a principal software maintenance engineer for Red Hat Ceph and the technical product lead for the global Ceph team.

Vikhyat Umrao has been working on software-defined storage technology, with specific expertise in Ceph Unified Storage. He has been working on Ceph for over 3 years now and in his current position at Red Hat, he focuses on the support and development of Ceph to solve Red Hat Ceph storage customer issues and upstream reported issues.

Karan Singh is a certified professional for technologies like OpenStack, NetApp and Oracle Solaris. He is currently working as a System Specialist of Storage and Cloud Platform for CSC - IT Center for Science Ltd, focusing all his energies on providing IaaS cloud solutions based on OpenStack and Ceph and building economic multi-petabyte storage system using Ceph.

Nick Fisk is an IT specialist with a strong history in enterprise storage. Throughout his career, he worked in a variety of roles and mastered several technologies. Over the years, he has deployed several clusters. He spends time in the Ceph community, helping others and improving certain areas of Ceph.

Anthony D'Atri's career in system administration spans from laptops to vector supercomputers. He has brought his passion for fleet management and server components to bear on a holistic yet, detailed approach to deployment and operations. Anthony worked for three years at Cisco using Ceph as a petabyte-scale object and block backend to multiple OpenStack clouds.

Vaibhav Bhembre is a systems programmer working currently as a technical lead for cloud storage products at DigitalOcean. From helping to scale dynamically generated campaign sends to over million users at a time, to architecting a cloud-scale compute and storage platform, Vaibhav has years of experience writing software across all layers of the stack.

Packt Is Searching for Authors Like You

If you're interested in becoming an author for Packt, please
visit `authors.packtpub.com` and apply today. We have worked with thousands of
developers and tech professionals, just like you, to help them share their insight with the
global tech community. You can make a general application, apply for a specific hot topic
that we are recruiting an author for, or submit your own idea.

Table of Contents

Preface

This Learning Path takes you through the basics of Ceph all the way to gain an in-depth understanding of its advanced features. You'll gather skills to plan, deploy, and manage your Ceph cluster. After an introduction to the Ceph architecture and its core projects, you'll be able to set up a Ceph cluster and learn how to monitor its health, improve its performance, and troubleshoot any issues.

By following the step-by-step approach of this Learning Path, you'll learn how Ceph integrates with OpenStack, Glance, Manila, Swift, and Cinder. With knowledge of federated architecture and CephFS, you'll use Calamari and VSM to monitor the Ceph environment. In the upcoming chapters, you'll study the key areas of Ceph, including BlueStore, erasure coding, and cache tiering. More specifically, you'll discover what they can do for your storage system. In the concluding chapters, you will develop applications that use Librados and distributed computations with shared object classes, and see how Ceph and its supporting infrastructure can be optimized. By the end of this Learning Path, you'll have the practical knowledge of operating Ceph in a production environment.

Who This Book Is For

If you are a developer, system administrator, storage professional, or cloud engineer who wants to understand how to deploy a Ceph cluster, this Learning Path is ideal for you. It will help you discover ways in which Ceph features can solve your data storage problems. Basic knowledge of storage systems and GNU/Linux will be beneficial.

What This Book Covers

Chapter 1, *Ceph - Introduction and Beyond*, covers an introduction to Ceph, gradually moving toward RAID and its challenges, and a Ceph architectural overview. Finally, we will go through Ceph installation and configuration.

Chapter 2, *Working with Ceph Block Device*, covers an introduction to the Ceph Block Device and provisioning of the Ceph block device. We will also go through RBD snapshots and clones, as well as implementing a disaster-recovery solution with RBD mirroring.

Chapter 3, *Working with Ceph and Openstack*, covers configuring Openstack clients for use with Ceph, as well as storage options for OpenStack using cinder, glance, and nova.

Chapter 4, *Working with Ceph Object Storage,* covers a deep dive into Ceph object storage, including RGW setup and configuration, S3, and OpenStack Swift access. Finally, we will set up RGW with the Hadoop S3A plugin.

Chapter 5, *Working with Ceph Object Storage Multi-Site v2,* helps you to deep dive into the new Multi-site v2, while configuring two Ceph clusters to mirror objects between them in an object disaster recovery solution.

Chapter 6, *Working with the Ceph Filesystem,* covers an introduction to CephFS, deploying and accessing MDS and CephFS via kerenel, FUSE, and NFS-Ganesha.

Chapter 7, *Operating and Managing a Ceph Cluster,* covers Ceph service management with systemd, and scaling up and scaling down a Ceph cluster. This chapter also includes failed disk replacement and upgrading Ceph infrastructures.

Chapter 8, *Ceph under the Hood,* explores the Ceph CRUSH map, understanding the internals of the CRUSH map and CRUSH tunables, followed by Ceph authentication and authorization. This chapter also covers dynamic cluster management and understanding Ceph PG. Finally, we create the specifics required for specific hardware.

Chapter 9, *The Virtual Storage Manager for Ceph,* speaks about Virtual Storage Manager (VSM), covering it's introduction and architecture. We will also go through the deployment of VSM and then the creation of a Ceph cluster, using VSM to manage it.

Chapter 10, *More on Ceph,* covers Ceph benchmarking, Ceph troubleshooting using admin socket, API, and the ceph-objectstore tool. This chapter also covers the deployment of Ceph using Ansible and Ceph memory profiling. Furthermore, it covers health checking your Ceph cluster using Ceph Medic and the new experimental backend Ceph BlueStore.

Chapter 11, *Deploying Ceph,* is a no-nonsense step-by-step instructional chapter on how to set up a Ceph cluster. This chapter covers the ceph-deploy tool for testing and goes onto covering Ansible. A section on change management is also included, and it explains how this is essential for the stability of large Ceph clusters.

Chapter 12, *BlueStore,* explains that Ceph has to be able to provide atomic operations around data and metadata and how filestore was built to provide these guarantees on top of standard filesystems. We will also cover the problems around this approach. The chapter then introduces BlueStore and explains how it works and the problems that it solves. This will include the components and how they interact with different types of storage devices. We will also have an overview of key-value stores, including RocksDB, which is used by BlueStore. Some of the BlueStore settings and how they interact with different hardware configurations will be discussed.

Chapter 13, *Erasure Coding for Better Storage Efficiency*, covers how erasure coding works and how it's implemented in Ceph, including explanations of RADOS pool parameters and erasure coding profiles. A reference to the changes in the Kraken release will highlight the possibility of append-overwrites to erasure pools, which will allow RBDs to directly function on erasure-coded pools. Performance considerations will also be explained. This will include references to BlueStore, as it is required for sufficient performance. Finally, we have step-by-step instructions on actually setting up erasure coding on a pool, which can be used as a mechanical reference for sysadmins.

Chapter 14, *Developing with Librados*, explains how Librados is used to build applications that can interact directly with a Ceph cluster. It then moves onto several different examples of using Librados in different languages to give you an idea of how it can be used, including atomic transactions.

Chapter 15, *Distributed Computation with Ceph RADOS Classes*, discusses the benefits of moving processing directly into the OSD to effectively perform distributed computing. It then covers how to get started with RADOS classes by building simple ones with Lua. It then covers how to build your own C++ RADOS class into the Ceph source tree and conduct benchmarks against performing processing on the client versus the OSD.

Chapter 16, *Tiering with Ceph*, explains how RADOS tiering works in Ceph, where it should be used, and its pitfalls. It takes you step-by-step through configuring tiering on a Ceph cluster and finally covers the tuning options to extract the best performance for tiering. An example using Graphite will demonstrate the value of being able to manipulate captured data to provide more meaningful output in graph form.

Chapter 17, *Troubleshooting*, explains how although Ceph is largely autonomous in taking care of itself and recovering from failure scenarios, in some cases, human intervention is required. We'll look at common errors and failure scenarios and how to bring Ceph back to full health by troubleshooting them.

Chapter 18, *Disaster Recovery*, covers situations when Ceph is in such a state that there is a complete loss of service or data loss has occurred. Less familiar recovery techniques are required to restore access to the cluster and, hopefully, recover data. This chapter arms you with the knowledge to attempt recovery in these scenarios.

Chapter 19, *Operations and Maintenance*, is a deep and wide inventory of day to day operations. We cover management of Ceph topologies, services, and configuration settings as well as, maintenance and debugging.

Chapter 20, *Monitoring Ceph*, a comprehensive collection of commands, practices, and dashboard software to help keep a close eye on the health of Ceph clusters.

Chapter 21, *Performance and Stability Tuning*, provides a collection of Ceph, networks, filesystems, and underlying operating system settings to optimize cluster performance and stability. Benchmarking of cluster performance is also explored.

To Get the Most out of This Book

This book requires that you have enough resources to run the whole Ceph lab environment. The minimum hardware or virtual requirements are as follows:

- CPU: 2 cores
- Memory: 8 GB RAM
- Disk space: 40 GB

The various software components required to follow the instructions in the chapters are as follows:

- VirtualBox 4.0 or higher (https://www.virtualbox.org/wiki/Downloads)

- GIT (http://www.git-scm.com/downloads)

- Vagrant 1.5.0 or higher (https://www.vagrantup.com/downloads.html)

- CentOS operating system 7.0 or higher (http://wiki.centos.org/Download)

- Ceph software Jewel packages Version 10.2.0 or higher (http://ceph.com/resources/downloads/)

- S3 Client, typically S3cmd (http://s3tools.org/download)

- Python-swift client

- NFS Ganesha

- Ceph Fuse

- CephMetrics (https://github.com/ceph/cephmetrics)

- Ceph-Medic (https://github.com/ceph/ceph-medic)

- Virtual Storage Manager 2.0 or higher (https://github.com/01org/virtual-storagemanager/releases/tag/v2.1.0)

- Ceph-Ansible (`https://github.com/ceph/ceph-ansible`)

- OpenStack RDO (`http://rdo.fedorapeople.org/rdo-release.rpm`)

Download the Example Code Files

You can download the example code files for this book from your account at `www.packt.com`. If you purchased this book elsewhere, you can visit `www.packt.com/support` and register to have the files emailed directly to you.

You can download the code files by following these steps:

1. Log in or register at `www.packt.com`.
2. Select the **SUPPORT** tab.
3. Click on **Code Downloads & Errata**.
4. Enter the name of the book in the **Search** box and follow the onscreen instructions.

Once the file is downloaded, please make sure that you unzip or extract the folder using the latest version of:

- WinRAR/7-Zip for Windows
- Zipeg/iZip/UnRarX for Mac
- 7-Zip/PeaZip for Linux

The code bundle for the book is also hosted on GitHub at `https://github.com/PacktPublishing/Ceph-Designing-and-Implementing-Scalable-Storage-Systems`. In case there's an update to the code, it will be updated on the existing GitHub repository.

We also have other code bundles from our rich catalog of books and videos available at `https://github.com/PacktPublishing/`. Check them out!

Conventions Used

In this book, you will find a number of text styles that distinguish between different kinds of information. Here are some examples of these styles and an explanation of their meaning. Code words in text, database table names, folder names, filenames, file extensions, pathnames, dummy URLs, user input, and Twitter handles are shown as follows: "Verify the `installrc` file" A block of code is set as follows:

```
AGENT_ADDRESS_LIST="192.168.123.101 192.168.123.102 192.168.123.103"
        CONTROLLER_ADDRESS="192.168.123.100"
```

Any command-line input or output is written as follows:

```
vagrant plugin install vagrant-hostmanager
```

New terms and **important words** are shown in bold. Words that you see on the screen, for example, in menus or dialog boxes, appear in the text like this: "It has probed OSDs 1 and 2 for the data, which means that it didn't find anything it needed. It wants to try and pol OSD 0, but it can't because the OSD is down, hence the message as **starting or marking this osd lost may let us proceed appeared**."

Warnings or important notes appear like this.

Tips and tricks appear like this.

Get in Touch

Feedback from our readers is always welcome.

General feedback: If you have questions about any aspect of this book, mention the book title in the subject of your message and email us at customercare@packtpub.com.

Errata: Although we have taken every care to ensure the accuracy of our content, mistakes do happen. If you have found a mistake in this book, we would be grateful if you would report this to us. Please visit www.packt.com/submit-errata, selecting your book, clicking on the Errata Submission Form link, and entering the details.

Piracy: If you come across any illegal copies of our works in any form on the Internet, we would be grateful if you would provide us with the location address or website name. Please contact us at copyright@packt.com with a link to the material.

If you are interested in becoming an author: If there is a topic that you have expertise in and you are interested in either writing or contributing to a book, please visit authors.packtpub.com.

Reviews

Please leave a review. Once you have read and used this book, why not leave a review on the site that you purchased it from? Potential readers can then see and use your unbiased opinion to make purchase decisions, we at Packt can understand what you think about our products, and our authors can see your feedback on their book. Thank you!

For more information about Packt, please visit packt.com.

Ceph - Introduction and Beyond

In this chapter, we will cover the following recipes:

- Ceph – the beginning of a new era
- RAID – the end of an era
- Ceph – the architectural overview
- Planning a Ceph deployment
- Setting up a virtual infrastructure
- Installing and configuring Ceph
- Scaling up your Ceph cluster
- Using Ceph clusters with a hands-on approach

Introduction

Ceph is currently the hottest **software-defined storage** (**SDS**) technology and is shaking up the entire storage industry. It is an open source project that provides unified software-defined solutions for *block*, *file*, and *object* storage. The core idea of Ceph is to provide a distributed storage system that is massively scalable and high performing with no single point of failure. From the roots, it has been designed to be highly scalable (up to the *exabyte* level and beyond) while running on general-purpose commodity hardware.

Ceph is acquiring most of the traction in the storage industry due to its open, scalable, and reliable nature. This is the era of cloud computing and software-defined infrastructure, where we need a storage backend that is purely software-defined and, more importantly, cloud-ready. Ceph fits in here very well, regardless of whether you are running a public, private, or hybrid cloud.

Today's software systems are very smart and make the best use of commodity hardware to run gigantic-scale infrastructures. Ceph is one of them; it intelligently uses commodity hardware to provide enterprise-grade robust and highly reliable storage systems.

Ceph has been raised and nourished with the help of the Ceph upstream community with an architectural philosophy that includes the following:

- Every component must scale linearly
- There should not be any single point of failure
- The solution must be software-based, open source, and adaptable
- The Ceph software should run on readily available commodity hardware
- Every component must be self-managing and self-healing wherever possible

The foundation of Ceph lies in objects, which are its building blocks. Object storage such as Ceph is the perfect provision for current and future needs for unstructured data storage. Object storage has its advantages over traditional storage solutions; we can achieve platform and hardware independence using object storage. Ceph plays meticulously with objects and replicates them across the cluster to avail reliability; in Ceph, objects are not tied to a physical path, making object location independent. This flexibility enables Ceph to scale linearly from the petabyte to the *exabyte* level.

Ceph provides great performance, enormous scalability, power, and flexibility to organizations. It helps them get rid of expensive proprietary storage silos. Ceph is indeed an enterprise-class storage solution that runs on commodity hardware; it is a low-cost yet feature-rich storage system. Ceph's universal storage system provides block, file, and object storage under one hood, enabling customers to use storage as they want.

In the following section, we will learn about Ceph releases.

Ceph is being developed and improved at a rapid pace. On July 3, 2012, Sage announced the first LTS release of Ceph with the code name Argonaut. Since then, we have seen 12 new releases come up. Ceph releases are categorized as **Long Term Support (LTS)**, and stable releases and every alternate Ceph release are LTS releases. For more information, visit https://Ceph.com/category/releases/.

Ceph release name	Ceph release version	Released On
Argonaut	V0.48 (LTS)	July 3, 2012
Bobtail	V0.56 (LTS)	January 1, 2013
Cuttlefish	V0.61	May 7, 2013
Dumpling	V0.67 (LTS)	August 14, 2013
Emperor	V0.72	November 9, 2013
Firefly	V0.80 (LTS)	May 7, 2014
Giant	V0.87.1	Feb 26, 2015
Hammer	V0.94 (LTS)	April 7, 2015
Infernalis	V9.0.0	May 5, 2015
Jewel	V10.0.0 (LTS)	Nov, 2015
Kraken	V11.0.0	June 2016
Luminous	V12.0.0 (LTS)	Feb 2017

Here is a fact: Ceph release names follow an alphabetic order; the next one will be an *M* release. The term *Ceph* is a common nickname given to pet octopuses and is considered a short form of *Cephalopod*, which is a class of marine animals that belong to the mollusk phylum. Ceph has octopuses as its mascot, which represents Ceph's highly parallel behavior, similar to octopuses.

Ceph – the beginning of a new era

Data storage requirements have grown explosively over the last few years. Research shows that data in large organizations is growing at a rate of 40 to 60 percent annually, and many companies are doubling their data footprint each year. IDC analysts have estimated that worldwide, there were 54.4 exabytes of total digital data in the year 2000. By 2007, this reached 295 exabytes, and by 2020, it's expected to reach 44 zettabytes worldwide. Such data growth cannot be managed by traditional storage systems; we need a system such as Ceph, which is distributed, scalable and most importantly, economically viable. Ceph has been specially designed to handle today's as well as the future's data storage needs.

Software-defined storage – SDS

SDS is what is needed to reduce TCO for your storage infrastructure. In addition to reduced storage cost, SDS can offer flexibility, scalability, and reliability. Ceph is a true SDS solution; it runs on commodity hardware with no vendor lock-in and provides low cost per GB. Unlike traditional storage systems, where hardware gets married to software, in SDS, you are free to choose commodity hardware from any manufacturer and are free to design a heterogeneous hardware solution for your own needs. Ceph's software-defined storage on top of this hardware provides all the intelligence you need and will take care of everything, providing all the enterprise storage features right from the software layer.

Cloud storage

One of the drawbacks of a cloud infrastructure is the storage. Every cloud infrastructure needs a storage system that is reliable, low-cost, and scalable with a tighter integration than its other cloud components. There are many traditional storage solutions out there in the market that claim to be cloud-ready, but today, we not only need cloud readiness, but also a lot more beyond that. We need a storage system that should be fully integrated with cloud systems and can provide lower TCO without any compromise to reliability and scalability. Cloud systems are software-defined and are built on top of commodity hardware; similarly, it needs a storage system that follows the same methodology, that is, being software-defined on top of commodity hardware, and Ceph is the best choice available for cloud use cases.

Ceph has been rapidly evolving and bridging the gap of a true cloud storage backend. It is grabbing the center stage with every major open source cloud platform, namely OpenStack, CloudStack, and OpenNebula. Moreover, Ceph has succeeded in building up beneficial partnerships with cloud vendors such as Red Hat, Canonical, Mirantis, SUSE, and many more. These companies are favoring Ceph big time and including it as an official storage backend for their cloud OpenStack distributions, thus making Ceph a red-hot technology in cloud storage space.

The OpenStack project is one of the finest examples of open source software powering public and private clouds. It has proven itself as an end-to-end open source cloud solution. OpenStack is a collection of programs, such as Cinder, Glance, and Swift, which provide storage capabilities to OpenStack. These OpenStack components require a reliable, scalable, and all in one storage backend such as Ceph. For this reason, OpenStack and Ceph communities have been working together for many years to develop a fully compatible Ceph storage backend for the OpenStack.

Cloud infrastructure based on Ceph provides much-needed flexibility to service providers to build *Storage-as-a-Service* and *Infrastructure-as-a-Service* solutions, which they cannot achieve from other traditional enterprise storage solutions as they are not designed to fulfill cloud needs. Using Ceph, service providers can offer low-cost, reliable cloud storage to their customers.

Unified next-generation storage architecture

The definition of unified storage has changed lately. A few years ago, the term *unified storage* referred to providing file and block storage from a single system. Now because of recent technological advancements, such as *cloud computing*, *big data*, and *the internet of Things*, a new kind of storage has been evolving, that is, object storage. Thus, all storage systems that do not support object storage are not really unified storage solutions. True unified storage is like Ceph; it supports blocks, files, and object storage from a single system.

In Ceph, the term *unified storage* is more meaningful than what existing storage vendors claim to provide. It has been designed from the ground up to be future-ready, and it's constructed such that it can handle enormous amounts of data. When we call Ceph *future ready*, we mean to focus on its object storage capabilities, which is a better fit for today's mix of unstructured data rather than blocks or files.

Everything in Ceph relies on intelligent objects, whether it's block storage or file storage. Rather than managing blocks and files underneath, Ceph manages objects and supports block-and-file-based storage on top of it. Objects provide enormous scaling with increased performance by eliminating metadata operations. Ceph uses an algorithm to dynamically compute where the object should be stored and retrieved from.

The traditional storage architecture of SAN and NAS systems is very limited. Basically, they follow the tradition of controller high availability; that is, if one storage controller fails, it serves data from the second controller. But, what if the second controller fails at the same time, or even worse if the entire disk shelf fails? In most cases, you will end up losing your data. This kind of storage architecture, which cannot sustain multiple failures, is definitely what we do not want today. Another drawback of traditional storage systems is their data storage and access mechanism. They maintain a central lookup table to keep track of metadata, which means that every time a client sends a request for a read or write operation, the storage system first performs a lookup in the huge metadata table, and after receiving the real data location, it performs the client operation. For a smaller storage system, you might not notice performance hits, but think of a large storage cluster—you would definitely be bound by performance limits with this approach. This would even restrict your scalability.

Ceph does not follow this traditional storage architecture; in fact, the architecture has been completely reinvented. Rather than storing and manipulating metadata, Ceph introduces a newer way: the CRUSH algorithm. CRUSH stands for **Controlled Replication Under Scalable Hashing**. Instead of performing a lookup in the metadata table for every client request, the CRUSH algorithm computes on demand where the data should be written to or read from. By computing metadata, the need to manage a centralized table for metadata is no longer there. Modern computers are amazingly fast and can perform a CRUSH lookup very quickly; moreover, this computing load, which is generally not too much, can be distributed across cluster nodes, leveraging the power of distributed storage. In addition to this, CRUSH has a unique property, which is infrastructure awareness. It understands the relationship between various components of your infrastructure and stores your data in a unique failure zone, such as a disk, node, rack, row, and data center room, among others. CRUSH stores all the copies of your data such that it is available even if a few components fail in a failure zone. It is due to CRUSH that Ceph can handle multiple component failures and provide reliability and durability.

The CRUSH algorithm makes Ceph self-managing and self-healing. In the event of component failure in a failure zone, CRUSH senses which component has failed and determines the effect on the cluster. Without any administrative intervention, CRUSH self-manages and self-heals by performing a recovering operation for the data lost due to failure. CRUSH regenerates the data from the replica copies that the cluster maintains. If you have configured the Ceph CRUSH map in the correct order, it makes sure that at least one copy of your data is always accessible. Using CRUSH, we can design a highly reliable storage infrastructure with no single point of failure. This makes Ceph a highly scalable and reliable storage system that is future-ready. CRUSH is covered more in detail in `Chapter 8, Ceph Under the Hood`.

RAID – the end of an era

The RAID technology has been the fundamental building block for storage systems for years. It has proven successful for almost every kind of data that has been generated in the last 3 decades. But all eras must come to an end, and this time, it's RAID's turn. These systems have started showing limitations and are incapable of delivering to future storage needs. In the course of the last few years, cloud infrastructures have gained strong momentum and are imposing new requirements on storage and challenging traditional RAID systems. In this section, we will uncover the limitations imposed by RAID systems.

RAID rebuilds are painful

The most painful thing in a RAID technology is its super-lengthy rebuild process. Disk manufacturers are packing lots of storage capacity per disk. They are now producing an extra-large capacity of disk drives at a fraction of the price. We no longer talk about 450 GB, 600 GB, or even 1 TB disks, as there is a larger capacity of disks available today. The newer enterprise disk specification offers disks up to 4 TB, 6 TB, and even 10 TB disk drives, and the capacities keep increasing year by year.

Think of an enterprise RAID-based storage system that is made up of numerous 4 TB or 6 TB disk drives. Unfortunately, when such a disk drive fails, RAID will take several hours and even up to days to repair a single failed disk. Meanwhile, if another drive fails from the same RAID group, then it would become a chaotic situation. Repairing multiple large disk drives using RAID is a cumbersome process.

RAID spare disks increases TCO

The RAID system requires a few disks as hot spare disks. These are just free disks that will be used only when a disk fails; else, they will not be used for data storage. This adds extra cost to the system and increases TCO. Moreover, if you're running short of spare disks and immediately a disk fails in the RAID group, then you will face a severe problem.

RAID can be expensive and hardware dependent

RAID requires a set of identical disk drivers in a single RAID group; you would face penalties if you change the disk size, rpm, or disk type. Doing so would adversely affect the capacity and performance of your storage system. This makes RAID highly choosy about the hardware.

Also, enterprise RAID-based systems often require expensive hardware components, such as RAID controllers, which significantly increases the system cost. These RAID controllers will become single points of failure if you do not have many of them.

The growing RAID group is a challenge

RAID can hit a dead end when it's not possible to grow the RAID group size, which means that there is no scale-out support. After a point, you cannot grow your RAID-based system, even though you have money. Some systems allow the addition of disk shelves but up to a very limited capacity; however, these new disk shelves put a load on the existing storage controller. So, you can gain some capacity but with a performance trade-off.

The RAID reliability model is no longer promising

RAID can be configured with a variety of different types; the most common types are RAID5 and RAID6, which can survive the failure of one and two disks, respectively. RAID cannot ensure data reliability after a two-disk failure. This is one of the biggest drawbacks of RAID systems.

Moreover, at the time of a RAID rebuild operation, client requests are most likely to starve for I/O until the rebuild completes. Another limiting factor with RAID is that it only protects against disk failure; it cannot protect against a failure of the network, server hardware, OS, power, or other data center disasters.

After discussing RAID's drawbacks, we can come to the conclusion that we now need a system that can overcome all these drawbacks in performance and cost-effective way. The Ceph storage system is one of the best solutions available today to address these problems. Let's see how.

For reliability, Ceph makes use of the data replication method, which means it does not use RAID, thus overcoming all the problems that can be found in a RAID-based enterprise system. Ceph is a software-defined storage, so we do not require any specialized hardware for data replication; moreover, the replication level is highly customized by means of commands, which means that the Ceph storage administrator can manage the replication factor of a minimum of one and a maximum of a higher number, totally depending on the underlying infrastructure.

In an event of one or more disk failures, Ceph's replication is a better process than RAID. When a disk drive fails, all the data that was residing on that disk at that point of time start recovering from its peer disks. Since Ceph is a distributed system, all the data copies are scattered on the entire cluster of disks in the form of objects, such that no two object's copies should reside on the same disk and must reside in a different failure zone defined by the CRUSH map. The good part is that all the cluster disks participate in data recovery. This makes the recovery operation amazingly fast with the least performance problems. Furthermore, the recovery operation does not require any spare disks; the data is simply replicated to other Ceph disks in the cluster. Ceph uses a weighting mechanism for its disks, so different disk sizes is not a problem.

In addition to the replication method, Ceph also supports another advanced way of data reliability: using the erasure-coding technique. Erasure-coded pools require less storage space compared to replicated pools. In erasure-coding, data is recovered or regenerated algorithmically by erasure code calculation. You can use both the techniques of data availability, that is, replication as well as erasure-coding, in the same Ceph cluster but over different storage pools. We will learn more about the erasure-coding technique in the upcoming chapters.

Ceph – the architectural overview

The Ceph internal architecture is pretty straightforward, and we will learn about it with the help of the following diagram:

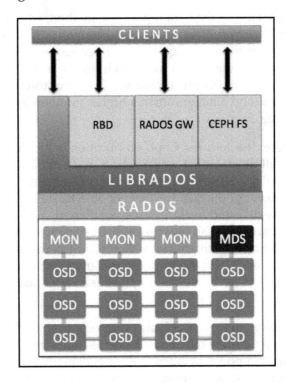

- **Ceph monitors (MON)**: Ceph monitors track the health of the entire cluster by keeping a map of the cluster state. They maintain a separate map of information for each component, which includes an OSD map, MON map, PG map (discussed in later chapters), and CRUSH map. All the cluster nodes report to monitor nodes and share information about every change in their state. The monitor does not store actual data; this is the job of the OSD.
- **Ceph object storage device (OSD)**: As soon as your application issues a write operation to the Ceph cluster, data gets stored in the OSD in the form of objects.

This is the only component of the Ceph cluster where actual user data is stored, and the same data is retrieved when the client issues a read operation. Usually, one OSD daemon is tied to one physical disk in your cluster. So in general, the total number of physical disks in your Ceph cluster is the same as the number of OSD daemons working underneath to store user data on each physical disk.

- **Ceph metadata server (MDS)**: The MDS keeps track of file hierarchy and stores metadata only for the CephFS filesystem. The Ceph block device and RADOS gateway do not require metadata; hence, they do not need the Ceph MDS daemon. The MDS does not serve data directly to clients, thus removing the single point of failure from the system.
- **RADOS**: The **Reliable Autonomic Distributed Object Store (RADOS)** is the foundation of the Ceph storage cluster. Everything in Ceph is stored in the form of objects, and the RADOS object store is responsible for storing these objects irrespective of their data types. The RADOS layer makes sure that data always remains consistent. To do this, it performs data replication, failure detection, and recovery, as well as data migration and rebalancing across cluster nodes.
- **librados**: The librados library is a convenient way to gain access to RADOS with support to the PHP, Ruby, Java, Python, C, and C++ programming languages. It provides a native interface for the Ceph storage cluster (RADOS) as well as a base for other services, such as RBD, RGW, and CephFS, which are built on top of librados. Librados also supports direct access to RADOS from applications with no HTTP overhead.
- **RADOS block devices (RBDs)**: RBDs, which are now known as the Ceph block device, provide persistent block storage, which is thin-provisioned, resizable, and stores data striped over multiple OSDs. The RBD service has been built as a native interface on top of librados.
- **RADOS gateway interface (RGW)**: RGW provides object storage service. It uses librgw (the Rados Gateway Library) and librados, allowing applications to establish connections with the Ceph object storage. The RGW provides RESTful APIs with interfaces that are compatible with Amazon S3 and OpenStack Swift.
- **CephFS**: The Ceph filesystem provides a POSIX-compliant filesystem that uses the Ceph storage cluster to store user data on a filesystem. Like RBD and RGW, the CephFS service is also implemented as a native interface to librados.
- **Ceph manager**: The *Ceph manager* daemon (ceph-mgr) was introduced in the Kraken release, and it runs alongside monitor daemons to provide additional monitoring and interfaces to external monitoring and management systems.

Planning a Ceph deployment

A Ceph storage cluster is created on top of the commodity hardware. This commodity hardware includes industry-standard servers loaded with physical disk drives that provide storage capacity and some standard networking infrastructure. These servers run standard Linux distributions and Ceph software on top of them. The following diagram helps you understand the basic view of a Ceph cluster:

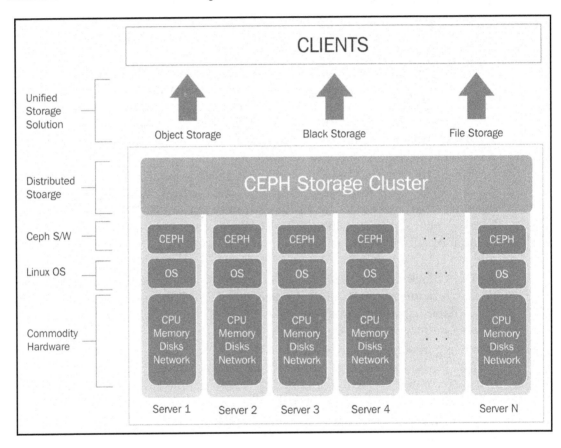

As explained earlier, Ceph does not have a very specific hardware requirement. For the purpose of testing and learning, we can deploy a Ceph cluster on top of virtual machines. In this section and in the later chapters of this book, we will be working on a Ceph cluster that is built on top of virtual machines. It's very convenient to use a virtual environment to test Ceph, as it's fairly easy to set up and can be destroyed and recreated anytime. It's good to know that a virtual infrastructure for the Ceph cluster should not be used for a production environment, and you might face serious problems with this.

Setting up a virtual infrastructure

To set up a virtual infrastructure, you will require open source software, such as Oracle VirtualBox and Vagrant, to automate virtual machine creation for you. Make sure you have the software installed and working correctly on your host machine. The installation processes of the software are beyond the scope of this book; you can follow their respective documentation in order to get them installed and working correctly.

Getting ready

You will need the following software to get started:

- **Oracle VirtualBox**: This is an open source virtualization software package for host machines based on x86 and AMD64/Intel64. It supports Microsoft Windows, Linux, and Apple macOS X host operating systems. Make sure it's installed and working correctly. More information can be found at `https://www.virtualbox.org`.

  Once you have installed VirtualBox, run the following command to ensure the installation was successful:

  ```
  # VBoxManage --version
  ```

  ```
  [vumrao@ceph-jewel ~]$
  [vumrao@ceph-jewel ~]$ VBoxManage --version
  5.1.26r117224
  [vumrao@ceph-jewel ~]$
  ```

- **Vagrant**: This is software meant for creating virtual development environments. It works as a wrapper around virtualization software, such as VirtualBox, VMware, KVM, and so on. It supports the Microsoft Windows, Linux, and Apple macOS X host operating systems. Make sure it's installed and working correctly. More information can be found at `https://www.vagrantup.com/`. Once you have installed Vagrant, run the following command to ensure the installation was successful:

  ```
  # vagrant --version
  ```

  ```
  [vumrao@ceph-jewel ~]$
  [vumrao@ceph-jewel ~]$ vagrant --version
  Vagrant 1.9.1
  [vumrao@ceph-jewel ~]$
  ```

- **Git**: This is a distributed revision control system and the most popular and widely adopted version control system for software development. It supports Microsoft Windows, Linux, and Apple macOS X operating systems. Make sure it's installed
  and working correctly. More information can be found at `http://git-scm.com/`.

  Once you have installed Git, run the following command to ensure the installation was successful:

  ```
  # git --version
  ```

  ```
  [vumrao@ceph-jewel ~]$
  [vumrao@ceph-jewel ~]$ git --version
  git version 2.13.3
  [vumrao@ceph-jewel ~]$
  ```

How to do it...

Once you have installed the mentioned software, we will proceed with virtual machine creation:

1. `git clone` Ceph-Designing-and-Implementing-Scalable-Storage-Sytems repository to your VirtualBox host machine:

   ```
   $ git clone
   https://github.com/PacktPublishing/Ceph-Designing-and-Implementing-Scalable
   -Storage-Systems
   ```

2. Under the directory, you will find `vagrantfile`, which is our Vagrant configuration file that basically instructs VirtualBox to launch the VMs that we require at different stages of this book. Vagrant will automate the VM's creation, installation, and configuration for you; it makes the initial environment easy to set up:

```
$ cd Ceph-Designing-and-Implementing-Scalable-Storage-Systems ; ls -l
```

—

3. Next, we will launch three VMs using Vagrant; they are required throughout this chapter:

```
$ vagrant up ceph-node1 ceph-node2 ceph-node3
```

If the default Vagrant provider is not set to VirtualBox, set it to VirtualBox. To make it permanent, it can be added to user `.bashrc` file:
```
# export VAGRANT_DEFAULT_PROVIDER=virtualbox
# echo $VAGRANT_DEFAULT_PROVIDER
```

4. Run `vagrant up ceph-node1 ceph-node2 ceph-node3`.
5. Check the status of your virtual machines:

```
$ vagrant status ceph-node1 ceph-node2 ceph-node3
```

The username and password that Vagrant uses to configure virtual machine is `vagrant`, and Vagrant has `sudo` rights. The default password for the root user is `vagrant`.

6. Vagrant will, by default, set up hostnames as `ceph-node<node_number>` and IP address subnet as `192.168.1.X` and will create three additional disks that will be used as OSDs by the Ceph cluster. Log in to each of these machines one by one and check whether the hostname, networking, and additional disks have been set up correctly by Vagrant:

```
$ vagrant ssh ceph-node1
$ ip addr show
$ sudo fdisk -l
$ exit
```

7. Vagrant is configured to update `hosts` file on the VMs. For convenience, update the `/etc/hosts` file on your host machine with the following content:

```
192.168.1.101 ceph-node1
192.168.1.102 ceph-node2
192.168.1.103 ceph-node3
```

8. Update all the three VM's to the latest CentOS release and reboot to the latest kernel.

9. Generate root SSH keys for `ceph-node1` and copy the keys to `ceph-node2` and `ceph-node3`. The password for the root user on these VMs is `vagrant`. Enter the root user password when asked by the `ssh-copy-id` command and proceed with the default settings:

```
$ vagrant ssh ceph-node1
$ sudo su -
# ssh-keygen
# ssh-copy-id root@ceph-node1
# ssh-copy-id root@ceph-node2
# ssh-copy-id root@ceph-node3
```

```
[root@ceph-node1 ~]#
[root@ceph-node1 ~]# ssh-copy-id root@ceph-node2
The authenticity of host 'ceph-node2 (192.168.1.102)' can't be established.
ECDSA key fingerprint is af:2a:a5:74:a7:0b:f5:5b:ef:c5:4b:2a:fe:1d:30:8e.
Are you sure you want to continue connecting (yes/no)? yes
/bin/ssh-copy-id: INFO: attempting to log in with the new key(s), to filter out any that are already installed
/bin/ssh-copy-id: INFO: 1 key(s) remain to be installed -- if you are prompted now it is to install the new keys
root@ceph-node2's password:

Number of key(s) added: 1

Now try logging into the machine, with:   "ssh 'root@ceph-node2'"
and check to make sure that only the key(s) you wanted were added.

[root@ceph-node1 ~]#
```

10. Once the SSH keys are copied to `ceph-node2` and `ceph-node3`, the root user from `ceph-node1` can do an `ssh` login to VMs without entering the password:

```
# ssh ceph-node2 hostname
# ssh ceph-node3 hostname
```

```
[root@ceph-node1 ~]#
[root@ceph-node1 ~]# ssh ceph-node2 hostname
ceph-node2
[root@ceph-node1 ~]# ssh ceph-node3 hostname
ceph-node3
[root@ceph-node1 ~]#
```

11. Enable ports that are required by the Ceph MON, OSD, and MDS on the operating system's firewall. Execute the following commands on all VMs:

```
# firewall-cmd --zone=public --add-port=6789/tcp --permanent
# firewall-cmd --zone=public --add-port=6800-7100/tcp --permanent
# firewall-cmd --reload
# firewall-cmd --zone=public --list-all
```

```
[root@ceph-node1 ~]#
[root@ceph-node1 ~]# firewall-cmd --zone=public --add-port=6789/tcp --permanent
success
[root@ceph-node1 ~]# firewall-cmd --zone=public --add-port=6800-7100/tcp --permanent
success
[root@ceph-node1 ~]# firewall-cmd --reload
success
[root@ceph-node1 ~]# firewall-cmd --zone=public --list-all
public (active)
  target: default
  icmp-block-inversion: no
  interfaces: enp0s3 enp0s8
  sources:
  services: dhcpv6-client ssh
  ports: 6789/tcp 6800-7100/tcp
  protocols:
  masquerade: no
  forward-ports:
  sourceports:
  icmp-blocks:
  rich rules:

[root@ceph-node1 ~]#
```

12. Install and configure NTP on all VMs:

```
# yum install ntp ntpdate -y
# ntpdate pool.ntp.org
# systemctl restart ntpdate.service
# systemctl restart ntpd.service
# systemctl enable ntpd.service
# systemctl enable ntpdate.service
```

Installing and configuring Ceph

To deploy our first Ceph cluster, we will use the `ceph-ansible` tool to install and configure Ceph on all three virtual machines. The `ceph-ansible` tool is a part of the Ceph project, which is used for easy deployment and management of your Ceph storage cluster. In the previous section, we created three virtual machines with CentOS 7, which have connectivity with the internet over NAT, as well as private host-only networks.

We will configure these machines as Ceph storage clusters, as mentioned in the following diagram:

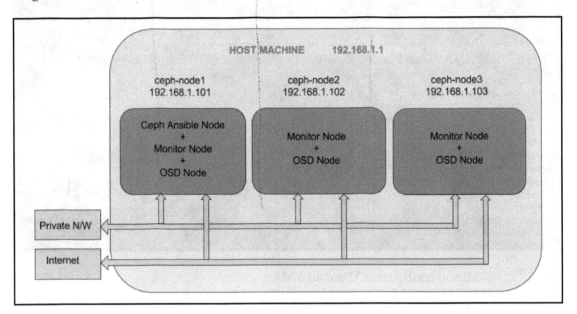

Creating the Ceph cluster on ceph-node1

We will first install Ceph and configure `ceph-node1` as the Ceph monitor and the Ceph OSD node. Later recipes in this chapter will introduce `ceph-node2` and `ceph-node3`.

How to do it...

Copy `ceph-ansible` package on `ceph-node1` from the `Ceph-Cookbook-Second-Edition` directory.

1. Use `vagrant` as the password for the root user:

   ```
   # cd Ceph-Designing-and-Implementing-Scalable-Storage-Systems
   # scp ceph-ansible-2.2.10-38.g7ef908a.el7.noarch.rpm root@ceph-node1:/root
   ```

2. Log in to `ceph-node1` and install `ceph-ansible` on `ceph-node1`:

   ```
   [root@ceph-node1 ~]#
   yum install ceph-ansible-2.2.10-38.g7ef908a.el7.noarch.rpm -y
   ```

   ```
   Running transaction
     Installing : python-passlib-1.6.5-2.el7.noarch
     Installing : ansible-2.3.2.0-2.el7.noarch
     Installing : ceph-ansible-2.2.10-38.g7ef908a.el7.noarch
     Verifying  : ansible-2.3.2.0-2.el7.noarch
     Verifying  : ceph-ansible-2.2.10-38.g7ef908a.el7.noarch
     Verifying  : python-passlib-1.6.5-2.el7.noarch

   Installed:
     ceph-ansible.noarch 0:2.2.10-38.g7ef908a.el7

   Dependency Installed:
     ansible.noarch 0:2.3.2.0-2.el7                              python-passlib.noarch 0:1.6.5-2.el7
   ```

3. Update the Ceph hosts to `/etc/ansible/hosts`:

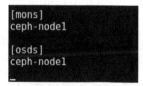

   ```
   [mons]
   ceph-node1

   [osds]
   ceph-node1
   ```

4. Verify that Ansible can reach the Ceph hosts mentioned in `/etc/ansible/hosts`:

```
[root@ceph-node1 ~]#
[root@ceph-node1 ~]# ansible all -m ping
ceph-node1 | SUCCESS => {
    "changed": false,
    "ping": "pong"
}
[root@ceph-node1 ~]#
```

5. Create a directory under the root home directory so Ceph Ansible can use it for storing the keys:

```
[root@ceph-node1 ~]#
[root@ceph-node1 ~]# mkdir ceph-ansible-keys
[root@ceph-node1 ~]#
```

6. Create a symbolic link to the Ansible `group_vars` directory in the `/etc/ansible/` directory:

```
[root@ceph-node1 ~]#
[root@ceph-node1 ~]# ln -s /usr/share/ceph-ansible/group_vars /etc/ansible/group_vars
[root@ceph-node1 ~]#
```

7. Go to `/etc/ansible/group_vars` and copy an `all.yml` file from the `all.yml.sample` file and open it to define configuration options' values:

```
[root@ceph-node1 ~]#
[root@ceph-node1 ~]# cd /etc/ansible/group_vars
[root@ceph-node1 group_vars]# cp all.yml.sample all.yml
[root@ceph-node1 group_vars]# vim all.yml
[root@ceph-node1 group_vars]#
```

8. Define the following configuration options in `all.yml` for the latest jewel version on CentOS 7:

```
fetch_directory: ~/ceph-ansible-keys
centos_package_dependencies:
  - python-pycurl
  - hdparm
  - epel-release
  - python-setuptools
  - libselinux-python
ceph_origin: 'upstream' # or 'distro' or 'local'
ceph_stable: true # use ceph stable branch
ceph_stable_release: jewel # ceph stable release
ceph_stable_redhat_distro: el7
cephx: true
monitor_interface: enp0s8
journal_size: 2048 # OSD journal size in MB
public_network: 192.168.1.0/24
cluster_network: 192.168.1.0/24
osd_mkfs_type: xfs
osd_mkfs_options_xfs: -f -i size=2048
osd_mount_options_xfs: noatime,largeio,inode64,swalloc
```

9. Go to /etc/ansible/group_vars and copy an osds.yml file from the osds.yml.sample file and open it to define configuration options' values:

```
[root@ceph-node1 group_vars]#
[root@ceph-node1 group_vars]# cp osds.yml.sample osds.yml
[root@ceph-node1 group_vars]# vim osds.yml
[root@ceph-node1 group_vars]# _
```

10. Define the following configuration options in osds.yml for OSD disks; we are co-locating an OSD journal in the OSD data disk:

```
devices:
  - /dev/sdb
  - /dev/sdc
  - /dev/sdd
journal_collocation: true
```

11. Go to /usr/share/ceph-ansible and add retry_files_save_path option in ansible.cfg in the [defaults] tag:

```
[root@ceph-node1 ~]#
[root@ceph-node1 ~]# cd /usr/share/ceph-ansible
[root@ceph-node1 ceph-ansible]# vim ansible.cfg
[root@ceph-node1 ceph-ansible]# cat ansible.cfg | grep retry_files_save
retry_files_save_path = ~/
[root@ceph-node1 ceph-ansible]#
```

12. Run Ansible playbook in order to deploy the Ceph cluster on `ceph-node1`:

To run the playbook, you need `site.yml`, which is present in the same path: `/usr/share/ceph-ansible/`. You should be in the `/usr/share/ceph-ansible/` path and should run following commands:

```
# cp site.yml.sample site.yml
# ansible-playbook site.yml
```

```
[root@ceph-node1 ceph-ansible]#
[root@ceph-node1 ceph-ansible]# cp site.yml.sample site.yml
[root@ceph-node1 ceph-ansible]# ansible-playbook site.yml
[DEPRECATION WARNING]: docker is kept for backwards compatibility but usage is discouraged. The module documentation details page may explain more about this rationale.
This feature will be removed in a future
release. Deprecation warnings can be disabled by setting deprecation_warnings=False in ansible.cfg.

PLAY [mons,agents,osds,mdss,rgws,nfss,restapis,rbdmirrors,clients,mgrs] ***********************************************************
```

Once playbook completes the Ceph cluster installation job and plays the recap with `failed=0`, it means `ceph-ansible` has deployed the Ceph cluster, as shown in the following screenshot:

```
PLAY RECAP ***********************************************************************
ceph-node1                 : ok=126   changed=24    unreachable=0    failed=0

[root@ceph-node1 ceph-ansible]#
[root@ceph-node1 ceph-ansible]# ceph -s
    cluster 8e396f0b-81ba-4a79-8bf2-7d29be9de05b
     health HEALTH_WARN
            64 pgs degraded
            64 pgs undersized
            too few PGs per OSD (21 < min 30)
     monmap e1: 1 mons at {ceph-node1=192.168.1.101:6789/0}
            election epoch 3, quorum 0 ceph-node1
     osdmap e13: 3 osds: 3 up, 3 in
            flags sortbitwise,require_jewel_osds
      pgmap v24: 64 pgs, 1 pools, 0 bytes data, 0 objects
            101816 kB used, 55163 MB / 55262 MB avail
                  64 undersized+degraded+peered
[root@ceph-node1 ceph-ansible]# ceph osd tree
ID WEIGHT  TYPE NAME        UP/DOWN REWEIGHT PRIMARY-AFFINITY
-1 0.05278 root default
-2 0.05278     host ceph-node1
 0 0.01759         osd.0         up  1.00000          1.00000
 1 0.01759         osd.1         up  1.00000          1.00000
 2 0.01759         osd.2         up  1.00000          1.00000
[root@ceph-node1 ceph-ansible]#
```

You have all three OSD daemons and one monitor daemon up and running in `ceph-node1`.

Here's how you can check the Ceph jewel release installed version. You can run the `ceph -v` command to check the installed ceph version:

```
[root@ceph-node1 ceph-ansible]#
[root@ceph-node1 ceph-ansible]# ceph -v
ceph version 10.2.9 (2ee413f77150c0f375ff6f10edd6c8f9c7d060d0)
[root@ceph-node1 ceph-ansible]#
```

Scaling up your Ceph cluster

At this point, we have a running Ceph cluster with one MON and three OSDs configured on `ceph-node1`. Now we will scale up the cluster by adding `ceph-node2` and `ceph-node3` as MON and OSD nodes.

How to do it...

A Ceph storage cluster requires at least one monitor to run. For high availability, a Ceph storage cluster relies on an odd number of monitors and more than one, for example, 3 or 5, to form a quorum. It uses the Paxos algorithm to maintain quorum majority. You will notice that your Ceph cluster is currently showing HEALTH_WARN; this is because we have not configured any OSDs other than `ceph-node1`. By default, the data in a Ceph cluster is replicated three times, that too on three different OSDs hosted on three different nodes.

Since we already have one monitor running on `ceph-node1`, let's create two more monitors for our Ceph cluster and configure OSDs on `ceph-node2` and `ceph-node3`:

1. Update the Ceph hosts `ceph-node2` and `ceph-node3` to `/etc/ansible/hosts`:

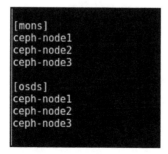

```
[mons]
ceph-node1
ceph-node2
ceph-node3

[osds]
ceph-node1
ceph-node2
ceph-node3
```

2. Verify that Ansible can reach the Ceph hosts mentioned in
   `/etc/ansible/hosts`:

```
[root@ceph-node1 ceph-ansible]#
[root@ceph-node1 ceph-ansible]# ansible all -m ping
ceph-node3 | SUCCESS => {
    "changed": false,
    "ping": "pong"
}
ceph-node2 | SUCCESS => {
    "changed": false,
    "ping": "pong"
}
ceph-node1 | SUCCESS => {
    "changed": false,
    "ping": "pong"
}
[root@ceph-node1 ceph-ansible]#
```

3. Run Ansible playbook in order to scale up the Ceph cluster on `ceph-node2` and
   `ceph-node3`:

```
[root@ceph-node1 ceph-ansible]#
[root@ceph-node1 ceph-ansible]# ansible-playbook site.yml
[DEPRECATION WARNING]: docker is kept for backwards compatibility but usage is discouraged. The module documentation details page may explain more about this rationale.
This feature will be removed in a future
release. Deprecation warnings can be disabled by setting deprecation_warnings=False in ansible.cfg.

PLAY [mons,agents,osds,mdss,rgws,nfss,restapis,rbdmirrors,clients,mgrs] ********************************************************

TASK [check for python2] ******************************************************************************************************
ok: [ceph-node3]
ok: [ceph-node2]
ok: [ceph-node1]
```

Once playbook completes the ceph cluster scaleout job and plays the recap with `failed=0`, it means that the Ceph ansible has deployed more Ceph daemons in the cluster, as shown in the following screenshot.

You have three more OSD daemons and one more monitor daemon running in `ceph-node2` and three more OSD daemons and one more monitor daemon running in `ceph-node3`. Now you have total nine OSD daemons and three monitor daemons running on three nodes:

```
PLAY RECAP ***********************************************************************************************************************
ceph-node1                    : ok=123   changed=2    unreachable=0    failed=0
ceph-node2                    : ok=119   changed=4    unreachable=0    failed=0
ceph-node3                    : ok=120   changed=4    unreachable=0    failed=0

[root@ceph-node1 ceph-ansible]# ceph -s
    cluster 8e396f0b-81ba-4a79-8bf2-7d29be9de05b
     health HEALTH_WARN
            too few PGs per OSD (21 < min 30)
     monmap e3: 3 mons at {ceph-node1=192.168.1.101:6789/0,ceph-node2=192.168.1.102:6789/0,ceph-node3=192.168.1.103:6789/0}
            election epoch 10, quorum 0,1,2 ceph-node1,ceph-node2,ceph-node3
     osdmap e34: 9 osds: 9 up, 9 in
            flags sortbitwise,require_jewel_osds
      pgmap v64: 64 pgs, 1 pools, 0 bytes data, 0 objects
            302 MB used, 161 GB / 161 GB avail
                  64 active+clean
[root@ceph-node1 ceph-ansible]# ceph osd tree
ID WEIGHT  TYPE NAME          UP/DOWN REWEIGHT PRIMARY-AFFINITY
-1 0.15834 root default
-2 0.05278     host ceph-node1
 0 0.01759         osd.0          up  1.00000          1.00000
 1 0.01759         osd.1          up  1.00000          1.00000
 2 0.01759         osd.2          up  1.00000          1.00000
-3 0.05278     host ceph-node3
 3 0.01759         osd.3          up  1.00000          1.00000
 5 0.01759         osd.5          up  1.00000          1.00000
 7 0.01759         osd.7          up  1.00000          1.00000
-4 0.05278     host ceph-node2
 4 0.01759         osd.4          up  1.00000          1.00000
 6 0.01759         osd.6          up  1.00000          1.00000
 8 0.01759         osd.8          up  1.00000          1.00000
[root@ceph-node1 ceph-ansible]# ceph osd pool set rbd pg_num 128
set pool 0 pg_num to 128
[root@ceph-node1 ceph-ansible]# ceph osd pool set rbd pgp_num 128
set pool 0 pgp_num to 128
[root@ceph-node1 ceph-ansible]# ceph -s
    cluster 8e396f0b-81ba-4a79-8bf2-7d29be9de05b
     health HEALTH_OK
     monmap e3: 3 mons at {ceph-node1=192.168.1.101:6789/0,ceph-node2=192.168.1.102:6789/0,ceph-node3=192.168.1.103:6789/0}
            election epoch 10, quorum 0,1,2 ceph-node1,ceph-node2,ceph-node3
     osdmap e38: 9 osds: 9 up, 9 in
            flags sortbitwise,require_jewel_osds
      pgmap v77: 128 pgs, 1 pools, 0 bytes data, 0 objects
            306 MB used, 161 GB / 161 GB avail
                 128 active+clean
[root@ceph-node1 ceph-ansible]#
```

4. We were getting a `too few PGs per OSD` warning and because of that, we increased the default RBD pool PGs from 64 to 128. Check the status of your Ceph cluster; at this stage, your cluster is healthy. PGs - placement groups are covered in detail in `Chapter 8`, *Ceph Under the Hood*.

Using the Ceph cluster with a hands-on approach

Now that we have a running Ceph cluster, we will perform some hands-on practice to gain experience with Ceph using some basic commands.

How to do it...

Below are some of the common commands used by Ceph admins:

1. Check the status of your Ceph installation:

   ```
   # ceph -s or # ceph status
   ```

2. Check Ceph's health detail:

   ```
   # ceph health detail
   ```

3. Watch the cluster health:

   ```
   # ceph -w
   ```

4. Check Ceph's monitor quorum status:

   ```
   # ceph quorum_status --format json-pretty
   ```

5. Dump Ceph's monitor information:

   ```
   # ceph mon dump
   ```

6. Check the cluster usage status:

   ```
   # ceph df
   ```

7. Check the Ceph monitor, OSD, pool, and placement group stats:

   ```
   # ceph mon stat
   # ceph osd stat
   # ceph osd pool stats
   # ceph pg stat
   ```

8. List the placement group:

   ```
   # ceph pg dump
   ```

9. List the Ceph pools in detail:

   ```
   # ceph osd pool ls detail
   ```

10. Check the CRUSH map view of OSDs:

    ```
    # ceph osd tree
    ```

11. Check Ceph's OSD usage:

    ```
    # ceph osd df
    ```

12. List the cluster authentication keys:

    ```
    # ceph auth list
    ```

These were some basic commands that you learned in this section. In the upcoming chapters, you will learn advanced commands for Ceph cluster management.

Working with Ceph Block Device

In this chapter, we will cover the following recipes:

- Configuring Ceph client
- Creating Ceph Block Device
- Mapping Ceph Block Device
- Resizing Ceph RBD
- Working with RBD snapshots
- Working with RBD clones
- Disaster recovery replication using RBD mirroring
- Configuring pools for RBD mirroring with one way replication
- Configuring image mirroring
- Configuring two-way mirroring
- Recovering from a disaster!

Introduction

Once you have installed and configured your Ceph storage cluster, the next task is performing storage provisioning. Storage provisioning is the process of assigning storage space or capacity to physical or virtual servers, either in the form of block, file, or object storage. A typical computer system or server comes with a limited local storage capacity that might not be enough for your data storage needs.

Storage solutions such as Ceph provide virtually unlimited storage capacity to these servers, making them capable of storing all your data and making sure that you do not run out of space. Using a dedicated storage system instead of local storage gives you the much-needed flexibility in terms of scalability, reliability, and performance.

Ceph can provision storage capacity in a unified way, which includes block, filesystem, and object storage. The following diagram shows storage formats supported by Ceph, and depending on your use case, you can select one or more storage options:

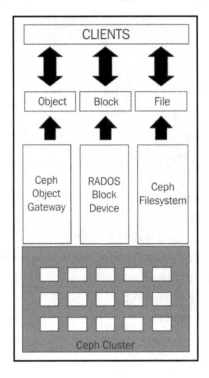

We will discuss each of these options in detail in this book, but in this chapter, we will focus on Ceph block storage.

The **Ceph Block Device**, formerly known as **RADOS Block Device**, provides reliable, distributed, and high-performance block storage disks to clients. A RADOS Block Device makes use of the `librbd` library and stores a block of data in sequential form striped over multiple OSDs in a Ceph cluster. RBD is backed by the RADOS layer of Ceph, thus every block device is spread over multiple Ceph nodes, delivering high performance and excellent reliability. RBD has native support for Linux kernel, which means that RBD drivers are well integrated with the Linux kernel since the past few years. In addition to reliability and performance, RBD also provides enterprise features such as full and incremental snapshots, thin provisioning, Copy-On-Write cloning, dynamic resizing, and so on. RBD also supports in-memory caching, which drastically improves its performance:

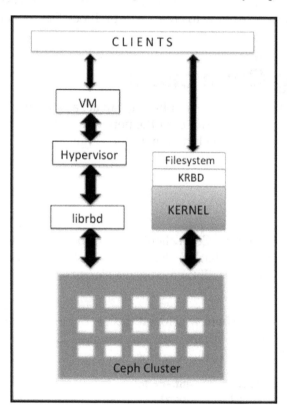

Industry-leading open source hypervisors, such as KVM and Xen, provide full support to RBD and leverage its features on their guest virtual machines. Other proprietary hypervisors, such as VMware and Microsoft Hyper-V will be supported very soon. There has been a lot of work going on in the community to support these hypervisors. The Ceph Block Device provides full support to cloud platforms such as OpenStack, CloudStack, as well as others. It has been proven successful and feature-rich for these cloud platforms. In OpenStack, you can use the Ceph Block Device with Cinder (block) and Glance (imaging) components. Doing so, you can spin thousands of **virtual machines** (**VMs**) in very little time, taking advantage of the Copy-On-Write feature of the Ceph Block Storage.

All these features make RBD an ideal candidate for cloud platforms such as OpenStack and CloudStack. We will now learn how to create a Ceph Block Device and make use of it.

Configuring Ceph client

Any regular Linux host (RHEL or Debian-based) can act as a Ceph client. The client interacts with the Ceph storage cluster over the network to store or retrieve user data. Ceph RBD support has been added to the Linux mainline kernel, starting with 2.6.34 and later versions.

How to do it...

As we did earlier, we will set up a Ceph client machine using Vagrant and VirtualBox. We will use the same `Vagrantfile` that we cloned in the last chapter i.e. Chapter 1, *Ceph - Introduction and Beyond*. Vagrant will then launch a CentOS 7.3 virtual machine that we will configure as a Ceph client:

1. From the directory where we cloned the `Ceph-Designing-and-Implementing-Scalable-Storage-Systems` GitHub repository, launch the client virtual machine using Vagrant:

```
$ vagrant status client-node1
$ vagrant up client-node1
```

2. Log in to `client-node1` and update the node:

```
$ vagrant ssh client-node1
$ sudo yum update -y
```

The username and password that Vagrant uses to configure virtual machines is `vagrant`, and Vagrant has `sudo` rights. The default password for the root user is `vagrant`.

3. Check OS and kernel release (this is optional):

```
# cat /etc/centos-release
# uname -r
```

4. Check for RBD support in the kernel:

```
# sudo modprobe rbd
```

```
[root@client-node1 ~]# cat /etc/centos-release
CentOS Linux release 7.3.1611 (Core)
[root@client-node1 ~]# uname -r
3.10.0-514.26.2.el7.x86_64
[root@client-node1 ~]# modprobe rbd
[root@client-node1 ~]# echo $?
0
[root@client-node1 ~]#
```

5. Allow `ceph-node1` monitor machine to access `client-node1` over SSH. To do this, copy root SSH keys from `ceph-node1` to `client-node1` Vagrant user. Execute the following commands from `ceph-node1` machine until otherwise specified:

```
## Log in to the ceph-node1 machine
$ vagrant ssh ceph-node1
$ sudo su -
# ssh-copy-id vagrant@client-node1
```

Provide a one-time Vagrant user password, that is, `vagrant`, for `client-node1`. Once the SSH keys are copied from `ceph-node1` to `client-node1`, you should able to log in to `client-node1` without a password.

6. Using Ansible, we will create the `ceph-client` role which will copy the Ceph configuration file and administration `keyring` to the client node. On our Ansible administration node, `ceph-node1`, add a new section `[clients]` to the `/etc/ansible/hosts` file:

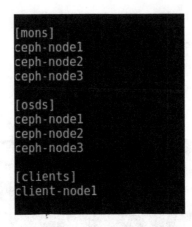

```
[mons]
ceph-node1
ceph-node2
ceph-node3

[osds]
ceph-node1
ceph-node2
ceph-node3

[clients]
client-node1
```

7. Go to the `/etc/ansible/group_vars` directory on `ceph-node1` and create a copy of `clients.yml` from the `clients.yml.sample`:

```
# cp clients.yml.sample clients.yml
```

You can instruct the ceph-client to create pools and clients by updating the `clients.yml` file. By uncommenting the `user_config` and setting to true you have the ability to define customer pools and client names altogether with Cephx capabilities.

8. Run the Ansible playbook from `ceph-node1`:

```
root@ceph-node1 ceph-ansible # ansible-playbook site.yml
```

```
PLAY RECAP ***********************************************************
*****
ceph-node1                  : ok=124   changed=2    unreachable=0    failed=0

ceph-node2                  : ok=118   changed=2    unreachable=0    failed=0

ceph-node3                  : ok=119   changed=2    unreachable=0    failed=0

client-node1                : ok=40    changed=13   unreachable=0    failed=0

[root@ceph-node1 ceph-ansible]#
```

9. On `client-node1` check and validate that the `keyring` and `ceph.conf` file were populated into the `/etc/ceph` directory by Ansible:

```
[root@client-node1 ~]# cd /etc/ceph
[root@client-node1 ceph]# ls
ceph.client.admin.keyring  ceph.conf  ceph.d  rbdmap
[root@client-node1 ceph]#
```

10. On `client-node1` you can validate that the Ceph client packages were installed by Ansible:

```
[root@client-node1 ceph]# rpm -qa |grep ceph
ceph-fuse-10.2.9-0.el7.x86_64
python-cephfs-10.2.9-0.el7.x86_64
ceph-selinux-10.2.9-0.el7.x86_64
ceph-base-10.2.9-0.el7.x86_64
libcephfs1-10.2.9-0.el7.x86_64
ceph-common-10.2.9-0.el7.x86_64
[root@client-node1 ceph]#
```

11. The client machine will require Ceph keys to access the Ceph cluster. Ceph creates a default user, client.admin, which has full access to the Ceph cluster and Ansible copies the client.admin key to client nodes. It's not recommended to share client.admin keys with client nodes. A better approach is to create a new Ceph user with separate keys and allow access to specific Ceph pools. In our case, we will create a Ceph user, client.rbd, with access to the RBD pool. By default, Ceph Block Devices are created on the RBD pool:

```
[root@ceph-node1 ~]# ceph auth get-or-create client.rbd mon 'allow r' osd
'allow class-read object_prefix rbd_children, allow rwx pool=rbd'
[client.rbd]
        key = AQC7fbBZb9p/MxAAJiWeI+3RrokobUgTy7wNIQ==
[root@ceph-node1 ~]# 
```

12. Add the key to client-node1 machine for client.rbd user:

```
[root@ceph-node1 ~]# ceph auth get-or-create client.rbd | ssh vagrant@clie
nt-node1 sudo tee /etc/ceph/ceph.client.rbd.keyring
vagrant@client-node1's password:
[client.rbd]
        key = AQC7fbBZb9p/MxAAJiWeI+3RrokobUgTy7wNIQ==
[root@ceph-node1 ~]# 
```

13. By this step, client-node1 should be ready to act as a Ceph client. Check the cluster status from the client-node1 machine by providing the username and secret key:

```
# cat /etc/ceph/ceph.client.rbd.keyring >> /etc/ceph/keyring
### Since we are not using the default user client.admin we
need to supply username that will connect to the Ceph cluster
# ceph -s --name client.rbd
```

```
[root@client-node1 ~]# cat /etc/ceph/ceph.client.rbd.keyring >> /etc/ceph/
keyring
[root@client-node1 ~]# ceph -s --name client.rbd
    cluster f90d2a73-29b1-4c81-b598-cd3a74541833
    health HEALTH_OK
    monmap e1: 3 mons at {ceph-node1=10.19.1.101:6789/0,ceph-node2=10.19.
1.102:6789/0,ceph-node3=10.19.1.103:6789/0}
            election epoch 6, quorum 0,1,2 ceph-node1,ceph-node2,ceph-node
3
    osdmap e30: 9 osds: 9 up, 9 in
            flags sortbitwise,require_jewel_osds
    pgmap v59: 128 pgs, 1 pools, 690 bytes data, 4 objects
            307 MB used, 161 GB / 161 GB avail
                128 active+clean
[root@client-node1 ~]# 
```

Creating Ceph Block Device

Up to now, we have configured Ceph client, and now we will demonstrate creating a Ceph Block Device from the `client-node1` machine.

How to do it...

1. Create a RADOS Block Device named `rbd1` of size 10240 MB:

   ```
   # rbd create rbd1 --size 10240 --name client.rbd
   ```

2. There are multiple options that you can use to list RBD images:

   ```
   ## The default pool to store block device images is "rbd",
      you can also specify the pool name with the rbd
      command using -p option:
   # rbd ls --name client.rbd
   # rbd ls -p rbd --name client.rbd
   # rbd list --name client.rbd
   ```

3. Check the details of the RBD image:

```
# rbd --image rbd1 info --name client.rbd
```

```
[root@client-node1 ~]# rbd create rbd1 --size 10240 --name client.rbd
[root@client-node1 ~]# rbd ls --name client.rbd
rbd1
[root@client-node1 ~]# rbd --image rbd1 info --name client.rbd
rbd image 'rbd1':
        size 10240 MB in 2560 objects
        order 22 (4096 kB objects)
        block_name_prefix: rbd_data.110e238e1f29
        format: 2
        features: layering, exclusive-lock, object-map, fast-diff, deep-fl
atten
        flags:
[root@client-node1 ~]#
```

Mapping Ceph Block Device

Now that we have created a block device on a Ceph cluster, in order to use this block device, we need to map it to the client machine. To do this, execute the following commands from the `client-node1` machine.

How to do it...

1. Map the block device to the `client-node1`:

```
# rbd map --image rbd1 --name client.rbd
```

```
[root@client-node1 ~]# rbd map --image rbd1 --name client.rbd
rbd: sysfs write failed
RBD image feature set mismatch. You can disable features unsupported by th
e kernel with "rbd feature disable".
In some cases useful info is found in syslog - try "dmesg | tail" or so.
rbd: map failed: (6) No such device or address
```

 Notice the mapping of the images has failed due to a feature set mismatch!

2. With Ceph Jewel the new default format for RBD images is 2 and Ceph Jewel default configuration includes the following default Ceph Block Device features:
   - `layering`: layering support
   - `exclusive-lock`: exclusive locking support
   - `object-map`: object map support (requires `exclusive-lock`)
   - `deep-flatten`: snapshot flatten support
   - `fast-diff`: fast diff calculations (requires `object-map`)

   Using the **krbd (kernel rbd)** client on `client-node1` we will be unable to map the block device image on CentOS kernel 3.10 as this kernel does not support `object-map`, `deep-flatten` and `fast-diff` (support was introduced in kernel 4.9). In order to work around this we will disable the unsupported features, there are several options to do this:

   - Disable the unsupported features dynamically (this is the option we will be using):

     ```
     # rbd feature disable rbd1
         exclusive-lock object-map
         deep-flatten fast-diff
     ```

   - When creating the RBD image initially utilize the `--image-feature layering` option with the `rbd create` command which will only enable the layering feature:

     ```
     # rbd create rbd1 --size 10240
         --image-feature layering
         --name client.rbd
     ```

   - Disable the feature in the Ceph configuration file:

     ```
     rbd_default_features = 1
     ```

All these features work for the user-space RBD client librbd.

```
[root@client-node1 ~]# rbd feature disable rbd1 exclusive-lock object-
map deep-flatten fast-diff
[root@client-node1 ~]# rbd --image rbd1 info --name client.rbd
rbd image 'rbd1':
        size 10240 MB in 2560 objects
        order 22 (4096 kB objects)
        block_name_prefix: rbd_data.1128238e1f29
        format: 2
        features: layering
        flags:
[root@client-node1 ~]# 
```

3. Retry mapping the block device with the unsupported features now disabled:

```
# rbd map --image rbd1 --name client.rbd
```

4. Check the mapped block device:

```
rbd showmapped --name client.rbd
```

```
[root@client-node1 ~]# rbd map --image rbd1 --name client.rbd
/dev/rbd0
[root@client-node1 ~]# rbd showmapped --name client.rbd
id pool image snap device
0  rbd  rbd1  -    /dev/rbd0
[root@client-node1 ~]# 
```

5. To make use of this block device, we should create a filesystem on this and mount it:

```
# fdisk -l /dev/rbd0
# mkfs.xfs /dev/rbd0
# mkdir /mnt/ceph-disk1
# mount /dev/rbd0 /mnt/ceph-disk1
# df -h /mnt/ceph-disk1
```

```
[root@client-node1 ~]# fdisk -l /dev/rbd0

Disk /dev/rbd0: 10.7 GB, 10737418240 bytes, 20971520 sectors
Units = sectors of 1 * 512 = 512 bytes
Sector size (logical/physical): 512 bytes / 512 bytes
I/O size (minimum/optimal): 4194304 bytes / 4194304 bytes

[root@client-node1 ~]# mkfs.xfs /dev/rbd0
meta-data=/dev/rbd0              isize=512    agcount=17, agsize=162816 bl
ks
         =                       sectsz=512   attr=2, projid32bit=1
         =                       crc=1        finobt=0, sparse=0
data     =                       bsize=4096   blocks=2621440, imaxpct=25
         =                       sunit=1024   swidth=1024 blks
naming   =version 2              bsize=4096   ascii-ci=0 ftype=1
log      =internal log           bsize=4096   blocks=2560, version=2
         =                       sectsz=512   sunit=8 blks, lazy-count=1
realtime =none                   extsz=4096   blocks=0, rtextents=0
[root@client-node1 ~]# mkdir /mnt/ceph-disk1
[root@client-node1 ~]# mount /dev/rbd0 /mnt/ceph-disk1
[root@client-node1 ~]# df -h /mnt/ceph-disk1
Filesystem      Size  Used Avail Use% Mounted on
/dev/rbd0        10G   33M   10G   1% /mnt/ceph-disk1
[root@client-node1 ~]#
```

6. Test the block device by writing data to it:

dd if=/dev/zero of=/mnt/ceph-disk1/file1 count=100 bs=1M

```
[root@client-node1 ~]# dd if=/dev/zero of=/mnt/ceph-disk1/file1 count=100
bs=1M
100+0 records in
100+0 records out
104857600 bytes (105 MB) copied, 1.18044 s, 88.8 MB/s
[root@client-node1 ~]# df -h /mnt/ceph-disk1
Filesystem      Size  Used Avail Use% Mounted on
/dev/rbd0        10G  133M  9.9G   2% /mnt/ceph-disk1
[root@client-node1 ~]#
```

7. To map the block device across reboots, we will need to create and configure a services file:

   1. Create a new file in the `/usr/local/bin` directory for mounting and unmounting and include the following:

```
# cd /usr/local/bin
# vim rbd-mount
```

```
#!/bin/bash

# Pool name where block device image is stored
export poolname=rbd

# Disk image name
export rbdimage=rbd1

# Mounted directory
export mountpoint=/mnt/ceph-disk1

# Image mount/unmount and pool are passed from the systemd service as
arguments
# Are we are mounting or unmounting
if [ "$1" == "m" ]; then
   modprobe rbd
   rbd feature disable $rbdimage exclusive-lock object-map fast-diff d
eep-flatten
   rbd map $rbdimage --id rbd --keyring /etc/ceph/ceph.client.rbd.keyr
ing
   mkdir -p $mountpoint
   mount /dev/rbd/$poolname/$rbdimage $mountpoint
fi
if [ "$1" == "u" ]; then
   umount $mountpoint
   rbd unmap /dev/rbd/$poolname/$rbdimage
fi
~
```

   2. Save the file and make it executable:

```
# sudo chmod +x rbd-mount
```

This can be done automatically by grabbing the `rbd-mount` script from the `Ceph-Designing-and-Implementing-Scalable-Storage-Systems` repository and making it executable:

```
# wget https://raw.githubusercontent.com/PacktPublishing/
  Ceph-Designing-and-Implementing-Scalable-Storage-
Systems/Module_1/master/
     rbdmap -O /usr/local/bin/rbd-mount
# chmod +x /usr/local/bin/rbd-mount
```

3. Go to the `systemd` directory and create the service file, include the following in the file `rbd-mount.service`:

```
# cd /etc/systemd/system/
# vim rbd-mount.service
```

```
[Unit]
Description=RADOS block device mapping for $rbdimage in pool $poolname"
Conflicts=shutdown.target
Wants=network-online.target
After=NetworkManager-wait-online.service
[Service]
Type=oneshot
RemainAfterExit=yes
ExecStart=/usr/local/bin/rbd-mount m
ExecStop=/usr/local/bin/rbd-mount u
[Install]
WantedBy=multi-user.target
~
~
```

This can be done automatically by grabbing the service file from the `Ceph-Designing-and-Implementing-Scalable-Storage-Systems/Chapter02` repository:

```
# wget https://raw.githubusercontent.com/PacktPublishing/
    Ceph-Designing-and-Implementing-Scalable-Storage-
Systems/Chapter02/rbd-mount.service
```

4. After saving the file and exiting Vim, reload the `systemd` files and enable the `rbd-mount.service` to start at boot time:

```
# systemctl daemon-reload
# systemctl enable rbd-mount.service
```

8. Reboot `client-node1` and verify that block device `rbd0` is mounted to `/mnt/ceph-disk1` after the reboot:

```
root@client-node1 # reboot -f
# df -h
```

```
[root@client-node1 system]# df -h
Filesystem               Size  Used Avail Use% Mounted on
/dev/mapper/centos-root  6.7G  1.7G  5.1G  25% /
devtmpfs                 234M     0  234M   0% /dev
tmpfs                    245M     0  245M   0% /dev/shm
tmpfs                    245M  4.3M  241M   2% /run
tmpfs                    245M     0  245M   0% /sys/fs/cgroup
/dev/sda1                497M  193M  305M  39% /boot
/dev/rbd0                 10G  133M  9.9G   2% /mnt/ceph-disk1
tmpfs                     49M     0   49M   0% /run/user/0
[root@client-node1 system]#
```

Resizing Ceph RBD

Ceph supports thin provisioned block devices, which means that the physical storage space will not get occupied until you begin storing data on the block device. The Ceph Block Device is very flexible; you can increase or decrease the size of an RBD on the fly from the Ceph storage end. However, the underlying filesystem should support resizing. Advance filesystems such as XFS, Btrfs, EXT, ZFS, and others support filesystem resizing to a certain extent. Please follow filesystem specific documentation to know more about resizing.

XFS does not currently support shrinking, Btrfs, and ext4 do support shrinking but should be done with caution!

How to do it...

To increase or decrease the Ceph RBD image size, use the `--size <New_Size_in_MB>` option with the `rbd resize` command, this will set the new size for the RBD image:

1. The original size of the RBD image that we created earlier was 10 GB. We will now increase its size to 20 GB:

   ```
   # rbd resize --image rbd1 --size 20480 --name client.rbd
   # rbd info --image rbd1 --name client.rbd
   ```

   ```
   [root@client-node1 system]# rbd resize --image rbd1 --size 20480 --name cl
   ient.rbd
   Resizing image: 100% complete...done.
   [root@client-node1 system]# rbd info --image rbd1 --name client.rbd
   rbd image 'rbd1':
           size 20480 MB in 5120 objects
           order 22 (4096 kB objects)
           block_name_prefix: rbd_data.110e238e1f29
           format: 2
           features: layering, exclusive-lock
           flags:
   [root@client-node1 system]#
   ```

2. Grow the filesystem so that we can make use of increased storage space. It's worth knowing that the filesystem resize is a feature of the OS as well as the device filesystem. You should read filesystem documentation before resizing any partition. The XFS filesystem supports online resizing. Check system messages to know the filesystem size change (you will notice `df -h` shows the original `10G` size even though we resized, as the filesystem still see's the original size):

```
# df -h
# lsblk
# dmesg | grep -i capacity
# xfs_growfs -d /mnt/ceph-disk1
```

```
[root@client-node1 system]# df -h
Filesystem                  Size  Used Avail Use% Mounted on
/dev/mapper/centos-root     6.7G  1.7G  5.1G  25% /
devtmpfs                    234M     0  234M   0% /dev
tmpfs                       245M     0  245M   0% /dev/shm
tmpfs                       245M  4.3M  241M   2% /run
tmpfs                       245M     0  245M   0% /sys/fs/cgroup
/dev/sda1                   497M  193M  305M  39% /boot
/dev/rbd0                    10G  133M  9.9G   2% /mnt/ceph-disk1
tmpfs                        49M     0   49M   0% /run/user/0
[root@client-node1 system]# lsblk
NAME             MAJ:MIN RM  SIZE RO TYPE MOUNTPOINT
sda                8:0    0    8G  0 disk
├─sda1             8:1    0  500M  0 part /boot
└─sda2             8:2    0  7.5G  0 part
  ├─centos-swap  253:0    0  820M  0 lvm  [SWAP]
  └─centos-root  253:1    0  6.7G  0 lvm  /
sr0               11:0    1 1024M  0 rom
rbd0             252:0    0   20G  0 disk /mnt/ceph-disk1
[root@client-node1 system]# dmesg |grep -i capacity
[    9.783649] rbd: rbd0: capacity 10737418240 features 0x5
[ 1882.993946] rbd0: detected capacity change from 10737418240 to 214748364
80
[root@client-node1 system]# xfs_growfs -d /mnt/ceph-disk1
meta-data=/dev/rbd0              isize=512    agcount=17, agsize=162816 blk
s
         =                       sectsz=512   attr=2, projid32bit=1
         =                       crc=1        finobt=0 spinodes=0
data     =                       bsize=4096   blocks=2621440, imaxpct=25
         =                       sunit=1024   swidth=1024 blks
naming   =version 2              bsize=4096   ascii-ci=0 ftype=1
log      =internal               bsize=4096   blocks=2560, version=2
         =                       sectsz=512   sunit=8 blks, lazy-count=1
realtime =none                   extsz=4096   blocks=0, rtextents=0
data blocks changed from 2621440 to 5242880
[root@client-node1 system]# df -h
Filesystem                  Size  Used Avail Use% Mounted on
/dev/mapper/centos-root     6.7G  1.7G  5.1G  25% /
devtmpfs                    234M     0  234M   0% /dev
tmpfs                       245M     0  245M   0% /dev/shm
tmpfs                       245M  4.3M  241M   2% /run
tmpfs                       245M     0  245M   0% /sys/fs/cgroup
/dev/sda1                   497M  193M  305M  39% /boot
/dev/rbd0                    20G  134M   20G   1% /mnt/ceph-disk1
tmpfs                        49M     0   49M   0% /run/user/0
[root@client-node1 system]#
```

Working with RBD snapshots

Ceph extends full support to snapshots, which are point-in-time, read-only copies of an RBD image. You can preserve the state of a Ceph RBD image by creating snapshots and restoring the snapshot to get the original data.

If you take a snapshot of an RBD image while I/O is in progress to the image the snapshot may be inconsistent. If this occurs you will be required to clone the snapshot to a new image for it to be mountable. When taking snapshots it is recommended to cease I/O from the application to the image before taking the snapshot. This can be done by customizing the application to issue a freeze before a snapshot or can manually be done using the `fsfreeze` command (man page for `fsfreeze` details this command further).

How to do it...

Let's see how a snapshot works with Ceph:

1. To test the snapshot functionality of Ceph, let's create a file on the block device that we created earlier:

   ```
   # echo "Hello Ceph This is snapshot test"
     > /mnt/ceph-disk1/snapshot_test_file
   ```

   ```
   [root@client-node1 system]# echo "Hello Ceph This is snapshot test" > /mnt
   /ceph-disk1/snapshot_test_file
   [root@client-node1 system]# ls -l /mnt/ceph-disk1
   total 102404
   -rw-r--r-- 1 root root 104857600 Sep  7 03:50 file1
   -rw-r--r-- 1 root root        33 Sep  7 05:10 snapshot_test_file
   [root@client-node1 system]# cat /mnt/ceph-disk1/snapshot_test_file
   Hello Ceph This is snapshot test
   [root@client-node1 system]#
   ```

2. Create a snapshot for the Ceph Block Device. Syntax for the same is as follows:

   ```
   # rbd snap create <pool name>/<image name>@<snap name>
   # rbd snap create rbd/rbd1@snapshot1
   ```

3. To list the snapshots of an image, use the following syntax:

   ```
   # rbd snap ls <pool name>/<image name>
   # rbd snap ls rbd/rbd1
   ```

```
[root@client-node1 system]# rbd snap create rbd/rbd1@snapshot1 --name clie
nt.rbd
[root@client-node1 system]# rbd snap ls rbd/rbd1 --name client.rbd
SNAPID NAME            SIZE
     4 snapshot1 20480 MB
[root@client-node1 system]# █
```

4. To test the snapshot restore functionality of Ceph RBD, let's delete files from the filesystem:

   ```
   # rm -f /mnt/ceph-disk1/*
   ```

5. We will now restore the Ceph RBD snapshot to get back the files that we deleted in the last step. Please note that a rollback operation will overwrite the current version of the RBD image and its data with the snapshot version. You should perform this operation carefully. The syntax is as follows:

   ```
   # rbd snap rollback <pool-name>/<image-name>@<snap-name>
   # umount /mnt/ceph-disk1
   # rbd snap rollback rbd/rbd1@snapshot1 --name client.rbd
   ```

    Prior to the rollback operation, the filesystem was unmounted to validate a refreshed filesystem state after the rollback.

6. Once the snapshot rollback operation is completed, remount the Ceph RBD filesystem to refresh the filesystem state. You should be able to get your deleted files back:

   ```
   # mount /dev/rbd0 /mnt/ceph-disk1
   # ls -l /mnt/ceph-disk1
   ```

```
[root@client-node1 ~]# ls -l /mnt/ceph-disk1
total 102400
-rw-r--r-- 1 root root 104857600 Sep  7 05:50 file1
-rw-r--r-- 1 root root         0 Sep  7 05:52 snapshot_test_file
[root@client-node1 ~]# rm -f /mnt/ceph-disk1/*
[root@client-node1 ~]# ls -l /mnt/ceph-disk1
total 0
[root@client-node1 ~]# umount /mnt/ceph-disk1
[root@client-node1 ~]# rbd snap rollback rbd/rbd1@snapshot1 --name client.rbd
Rolling back to snapshot: 100% complete...done.
[root@client-node1 ~]# mount /dev/rbd0 /mnt/ceph-disk1
[root@client-node1 ~]# ls -l /mnt/ceph-disk1
total 102400
-rw-r--r-- 1 root root 104857600 Sep  7 05:50 file1
-rw-r--r-- 1 root root         0 Sep  7 05:52 snapshot_test_file
[root@client-node1 ~]# █
```

7. You are also able to rename snapshots if you so choose. The syntax is as follows:

```
#rbd snap rename <pool-name>/<image-name>@<original-snapshot-
name> <pool-name>/<image-name>@<new-snapshot-name>
# rbd snap rename rbd/rbd1@snapshot1 rbd/rbd1@snapshot1_new
```

8. When you no longer need snapshots, you can remove a specific snapshot using the following syntax. Deleting the snapshot will not delete your current data on the Ceph RBD image:

```
# rbd snap rm <pool-name>/<image-name>@<snap-name>
# rbd snap rm rbd/rbd1@snapshot1 --name client.rbd
```

9. If you have multiple snapshots of an RBD image and you wish to delete all the snapshots with a single command, then use the `purge` subcommand. The syntax is as follows:

```
# rbd snap purge <pool-name>/<image-name>
# rbd snap purge rbd/rbd1 --name client.rbd
```

Working with RBD clones

Ceph supports a very nice feature for creating **Copy-On-Write** (**COW**) clones from RBD snapshots. This is also known as *snapshot layering* in Ceph. Layering allows clients to create multiple instant clones of Ceph RBD. This feature is extremely useful for cloud and virtualization platforms such as OpenStack, CloudStack, Qemu/KVM, and so on. These platforms usually protect Ceph RBD images containing an OS/VM image in the form of a snapshot. Later, this snapshot is cloned multiple times to spawn new virtual machines/instances. Snapshots are read-only, but COW clones are fully writable; this feature of Ceph provides a greater level of flexibility and is extremely useful in cloud platforms. In the later chapters, we will discover more on COW clones for spawning OpenStack instances:

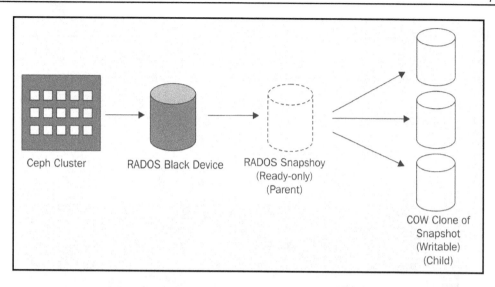

Ceph Cluster   RADOS Black Device   RADOS Snapshoy (Ready-only) (Parent)   COW Clone of Snapshot (Writable) (Child)

Every cloned image (child image) stores references of its parent snapshot to read image data. Hence, the parent snapshot should be protected before it can be used for cloning. At the time of data writing on the COW cloned image, it stores new data references to itself. COW cloned images are as good as RBD. They are quite flexible like RBD, which means that they are writable, resizable, and support snapshots and further cloning.

In Ceph RBD, images are of two types: format-1 and format-2. The RBD snapshot feature is available on both types, that is, in format-1 as well as in format-2 RBD images. However, the layering feature (the COW cloning feature) is available only for the RBD image with format-2. The default RBD image format in Jewel is format-2.

How to do it...

To demonstrate RBD cloning, we will intentionally create an RBD image (specifying the layering feature) then create and protect its snapshot, and finally, create COW clones out of it:

1. Create an RBD image with `layering` feature specified and check it's details:

   ```
   # rbd create rbd2 --size 10240
     --image-feature layering --name client.rbd
   # rbd info --image rbd2 --name client.rbd
   ```

   ```
   [root@client-node1 ~]# rbd create rbd2 --size 10240 --image-feature layering --na
   me client.rbd
   [root@client-node1 ~]# rbd info --image rbd2 --name client.rbd
   rbd image 'rbd2':
           size 10240 MB in 2560 objects
           order 22 (4096 kB objects)
           block_name_prefix: rbd_data.373e2ae8944a
           format: 2
           features: layering
           flags:
   [root@client-node1 ~]#
   ```

2. Create a snapshot of this RBD image:

   ```
   # rbd snap create rbd/rbd2@snapshot_for_cloning
     --name client.rbd
   ```

3. To create a COW clone, protect the snapshot. This is an important step, we should protect the snapshot because if the snapshot gets deleted, all the attached COW clones will be destroyed:

   ```
   # rbd snap protect rbd/rbd2@snapshot_for_cloning
     --name client.rbd
   ```

4. Next, we will create a cloned RBD image, specifying the `layering` feature, using this snapshot. The syntax is as follows:

   ```
   # rbd clone <pool-name>/<parent-image-name>@<snap-name>
     <pool-name>/<child_image-name>
     --image-feature <feature-name>
   # rbd clone rbd/rbd2@snapshot_for_cloning rbd/clone_rbd2
     --image-feature layering --name client.rbd
   ```

5. Creating a clone is a quick process. Once it's completed, check the new image information. You will notice that its parent pool, image, and snapshot information will be displayed:

   # rbd info rbd/clone_rbd2 --name client.rbd

   The clients do not always provide equivalent functionality, for example, the fuse client supports `client-enforced` quotas while the kernel client does not:

```
[root@client-node1 ~]# rbd snap create rbd/rbd2@snapshot_for_cloning --name clien
t.rbd
[root@client-node1 ~]# rbd snap protect rbd/rbd2@snapshot_for_cloning --name clie
nt.rbd
[root@client-node1 ~]# rbd clone rbd/rbd2@snapshot_for_cloning rbd/clone_rbd2 --i
mage-feature layering --name client.rbd
[root@client-node1 ~]# rbd info rbd/clone_rbd2 --name client.rbd
rbd image 'clone_rbd2':
        size 10240 MB in 2560 objects
        order 22 (4096 kB objects)
        block_name_prefix: rbd_data.37483d1b58ba
        format: 2
        features: layering
        flags:
        parent: rbd/rbd2@snapshot_for_cloning
        overlap: 10240 MB
[root@client-node1 ~]#
```

6. You also have the ability to list children of a snapshot. To list the children of a snapshot execute the following:

   # rbd children rbd/rbd2@snapshot_for_cloning

   We now have a cloned RBD image that is dependent on it's parent image. To split this cloned image from it's parent snapshot we will need to flatten the image which would require copying all the data from the parent snapshot image to the clone. Flattening may take awhile to complete and depends on the size of the parent snapshot image. One the cloned image is flattened there is no longer a relationship between the parent snapshot and the RBD clone. Please note that a flattened image will contain all information from the snapshot and will use more space than a clone.

7. To initiate the flattening process, use the following:

   # rbd flatten rbd/clone_rbd2 --name client.rbd
   # rbd info --image clone_rbd2 --name client.rbd

After the completion of the flattening process, if you check image information, you will notice that the parent image/snapshot name is not present and the clone is independent:

```
[root@client-node1 ~]# rbd flatten rbd/clone_rbd2 --name client.rbd
Image flatten: 100% complete...done.
[root@client-node1 ~]# rbd info --image clone_rbd2 --name client.rbd
rbd image 'clone_rbd2':
        size 10240 MB in 2560 objects
        order 22 (4096 kB objects)
        block_name_prefix: rbd_data.37483d1b58ba
        format: 2
        features: layering
        flags:
[root@client-node1 ~]#
```

If the `deep-flatten` feature is enabled on an image the image clone is dissociated from its parent by default.

8. You can also remove the parent image snapshot if you no longer require it. Before removing the snapshot, you first have to unprotect it:

    # **rbd snap unprotect rbd/rbd2@snapshot_for_cloning
    --name client.rbd**

9. Once the snapshot is unprotected, you can remove it:

    # **rbd snap rm rbd/rbd2@snapshot_for_cloning --name client.rbd**

Disaster recovery replication using RBD mirroring

RBD mirroring is an asynchronous replication of RBD images between multiple Ceph clusters. RBD mirroring validates a point-in-time consistent replica of any change to an RBD image, including snapshots, clones, read and write IOPS and block device resizing. RBD mirroring can run in an active+active setup or an active+passive setup. RBD mirroring utilizes the RBD journaling and exclusive lock features which enables the RBD image to record all changes to the image in order of which they occur. These features validate that a crash-consistent copy of the remote image is available locally. Before mirroring can be enabled on a Ceph cluster the journaling feature must be enabled on the RBD image.

The daemon responsible for ensuring point-in-time consistency from one Ceph cluster to the other is the `rbd-mirror` daemon. Depending on your chosen type of replication the rbd-mirror daemon runs on either a single cluster or an each participating in the mirroring:

- **One way replication**: Data is mirrored from a primary site to secondary site. RBD mirror runs only on secondary site.
- **Two-way replication**: Active-Active configuration. Data is mirrored from a primary site to secondary site and mirrored back from a primary site to secondary site. RBD mirror runs on both primary and secondary sites.

Since we store the RBD images on both local and remote pools it is best practices to ensure the CRUSH hierarchy backing the mirrored pool is the same speed, size and type media. Also, proper bandwidth should be allocated between sites to handle the mirroring traffic.

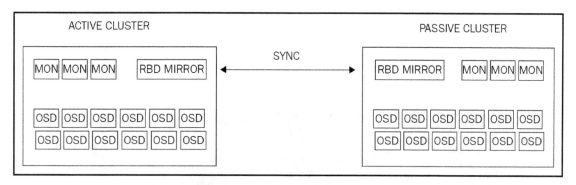

How to do it...

For this recipe, we will be configuring a second Ceph cluster with Ceph nodes `ceph-node5`, `ceph-node6`, and `ceph-node7`. The previous `Chapter 1`, *Ceph – Introduction and Beyond*, can be referenced for setting up your second Ceph cluster using Ansible with nodes 5, 6, and 7 taking the place of 1, 2, and 3 in the recipes, some highlights, and changes that must be made before running the playbook on the secondary cluster are below:

1. Your `/etc/ansible/hosts` file from each of your Ansible configuration nodes (`ceph-node1` and `ceph-node5`) should look as follows:

   ```
   #Primary site (ceph-node1):
    [mons]
    ceph-node1
    ceph-node2
    ceph-node3
   ```

```
[osds]
ceph-node1
ceph-node2
ceph-node3
#Secondary site (ceph-node5):
[mons]
 ceph-node5
 ceph-node6
 ceph-node7
 [osds]
 ceph-node5
 ceph-node6
 ceph-node7
```

2. Your cluster will require a distinct name, the default cluster naming is ceph. Since our primary cluster is named ceph our secondary cluster must be named something different. For this recipe, we will name the secondary cluster as backup. We will need to edit the all.yml file on ceph-node5 to reflect this change prior to deploying by commenting out cluster and renaming backup:

```
root@ceph-node5 group_vars # vim all.yml
```

```
##########
# GENERAL #
##########

fetch_directory: ~/ceph-ansible-keys

# The 'cluster' variable determines the name of the cluster.
# Changing the default value to something else means that you will
# need to change all the command line calls as well, for example if
# your cluster name is 'foo':
# "ceph health" will become "ceph --cluster foo health"
#
# An easier way to handle this is to use the environment variable CEPH_ARGS
# So run: "export CEPH_ARGS="--cluster foo"
# With that you will be able to run "ceph health" normally
cluster: backup
```

It is possible to mirror RBD images between two clusters of the same name this requires changing the name of one of the clusters in the /etc/sysconfig/ceph file to a name other then Ceph and then creating a symlink to the ceph.conf file.

3. Run Ansible to install the second Ceph cluster with the distinct name of backup:

```
root@ceph-node5 ceph-ansible # ansible-playbook site.yml
```

4. When the playbook competes set the Ceph environment variable to use cluster name of backup:

```
# export CEPH_ARGS="--cluster backup"
```

5. In each of the clusters create a pool called data, this pool will be mirrored between the sites:

```
root@ceph-node1 # ceph osd pool create data 64
root@ceph-node5 # ceph osd pool create data 64
```

6. Create the user client.local on the ceph Ceph cluster and give it a rwx access to data pool:

```
root@ceph-node1 # ceph auth get-or-create client.local
mon 'allow r' osd 'allow class-read object_prefix rbd_children,
allow rwx pool=data' -o /etc/ceph/ceph.client.local.keyring
--cluster ceph
```

7. Create the user client.remote on the backup cluster and give it a rwx access to data pool:

```
root@ceph-node5 # ceph auth get-or-create client.remote
mon 'allow r' osd 'allow class-read object_prefix rbd_children,
allow rwx pool=data' -o /etc/ceph/backup.client.remote.keyring
--cluster backup
```

8. Copy the Ceph configuration file from each of the clusters into the /etc/ceph directory of the corresponding peer cluster:

```
root@ceph-node1 # scp /etc/ceph/ceph.conf
root@ceph-node5:/etc/ceph/ceph.conf
root@ceph-node5 # scp /etc/ceph/backup.conf
root@ceph.node1:/etc/ceph/backup.conf
```

9. Copy the keyrings for the user `client.local` and `client.remote` from each of the clusters into the `/etc/ceph` directory of the corresponding peer cluster:

```
root@ceph-node1 # scp /etc/ceph/ceph.client.local.keyring
root@ceph-node5:/etc/ceph/ceph.client.local.keyring
root@ceph-node5 # scp /etc/ceph/backup.client.remote.keyring
root@ceph-node1:/etc/ceph/backup.client.remote.keyring
```

We now have two Ceph clusters, with a `client.local` and a `client.remote` user, copies of their peer `ceph.conf` file in the `etc/ceph` directory and keyrings for the corresponding users on each peer cluster. In the next recipe we will configure mirroring on the data pool.

Configuring pools for RBD mirroring with one way replication

RBD mirroring is configured by enabling it on a pool basis in a primary and secondary Ceph cluster. There are two modes that can be configured with RBD mirroring depending on what level of data you choose to mirror. Note that the enabled RBD mirroring configuration must be the same per pool on primary and secondary clusters.

- **Pool mode**: Any image in a pool with journaling enabled is mirrored to the secondary cluster.
- **Image mode**: Only specifically chosen images with mirroring enabled will be mirrored to the secondary cluster. This requires the image to have mirroring enabled for it.

How to do it...

Before any data can be mirrored from the Ceph cluster to the `backup` cluster we first need install the `rbd-mirror` daemon on the `backup` cluster, enable mirroring on the data pool and then add a peer cluster to the pool:

1. On `ceph-node5` in the `backup` cluster install and configure the `rbd-mirror`. The client ID of remote (our user) is what the `rbd-mirror` daemon will use:

```
root@ceph-node5 # yum install -y rbd-mirror
                # systemctl enable ceph-rbd-mirror.target
                # systemctl enable ceph-rbd-mirror@remote
                # systemctl start ceph-rbd-mirror@remote
```

2. Enable mirroring of the whole pool named data in cluster `ceph`. The syntax is as follows:

```
              # rbd mirror pool enable <pool> <mode>
root@ceph-node1 # rbd mirror pool enable data pool
```

3. Enable mirroring of the whole pool named `rbd` in the cluster `backup`:

```
root@ceph-node5 # rbd mirror pool enable data pool
```

4. For the `rbd-mirror` daemon to discover it's peer cluster, we now must register the peer to the pool. We will need to add the `ceph` cluster as a peer to the `backup` cluster. The syntax is as follows:

```
              # rbd mirror pool peer add <pool>
                <client-name@cluster-name>
root@ceph-node5 # rbd mirror pool peer add
                data client.local@ceph
```

5. Next, we will validate the peer relationship between the pools and the cluster. The syntax is as follows:

```
              # rbd mirror pool info <pool>
root@ceph-node5 # rbd mirror pool info rbd
```

```
[root@ceph-node5 ceph-ansible]# rbd mirror pool info data
Mode: pool
Peers:
  UUID                                    NAME CLIENT
  a786a03b-f91a-46e3-a053-93c1f5adc324 ceph client.local
[root@ceph-node5 ceph-ansible]#
```

Mirroring is now enabled at the pool level for pool data in the `ceph` and `backup` clusters and a pool peer is configured for the data pool in the cluster `backup`.

6. Review the data pool in each cluster and see there are currently no RBD images in either site. Once verified we will create three new RBD images in the data pool with `exclusive-lock` and journaling enabled and watch them sync to the secondary `backup` cluster:

```
# rbd ls data
# rbd create image-1 --size 1024 --pool data
  --image-feature exclusive-lock,journaling
```

1. Pool mirrors can be polled for a status of the images as they sync to the `backup` cluster:

   # rbd mirror pool status data

   ```
   [root@ceph-node1 ceph]# rbd -p data ls
   [root@ceph-node1 ceph]# rbd create image-1 --size 1024 --pool data --image-feature exclusive-lock,journ
   aling
   [root@ceph-node1 ceph]# rbd create image-2 --size 1024 --pool data --image-feature exclusive-lock,journ
   aling
   [root@ceph-node1 ceph]# rbd create image-3 --size 1024 --pool data --image-feature exclusive-lock,journ
   aling
   [root@ceph-node1 ceph]# rbd -p data ls
   image-1
   image-2
   image-3
   ```

2. Viewing the remote site for before and after on the `data` pool:

   ```
   [root@ceph-node5 ceph-ansible]# rbd -p data ls
   [root@ceph-node5 ceph-ansible]# rbd -p data ls
   image-1
   image-2
   image-3
   ```

3. Viewing the image sync status on the remote site:

   ```
   [root@ceph-node5 ceph-ansible]# rbd mirror pool status data
   health: WARNING
   images: 3 total
       3 syncing
   ```

4. Viewing the healthy state of the journal replaying the image on the remote site:

   ```
   [root@ceph-node5 ceph-ansible]# rbd mirror pool status data
   health: OK
   images: 3 total
       3 replaying
   ```

   Replaying is the image state we want to see as this means the `rbd-mirror` daemon sees the images in sync and is replaying the journals for any changes to the images that need to be sync.

7. We will now delete the three images from the `ceph` cluster and watch as they are removed from the `backup` cluster:

```
# rbd rm -p data image-<num>
```

```
[root@ceph-node1 ceph]# rbd rm -p data image-1
Removing image: 100% complete...done.
[root@ceph-node1 ceph]# rbd rm -p data image-2
Removing image: 100% complete...done.
[root@ceph-node1 ceph]# rbd rm -p data image-3
Removing image: 100% complete...done.
[root@ceph-node1 ceph]# rbd ls -p data
[root@ceph-node1 ceph]#
```

8. Viewing the `pool` status to validate the images are removed from the remote site:

```
# rbd mirror pool status data
```

```
[root@ceph-node5 ceph-ansible]# rbd mirror pool status data
health: OK
images: 0 total
```

If at any point and time you choose to disable mirroring on a pool this can be done via the `rbd mirror peer remove` and `rbd mirror pool disable` commands for the chosen pool. Please note when mirroring is disabled for a pool you also disable mirroring on any images residing in the pool.

Following is the syntax for removing mirroring:

1. To remove peer:

```
# rbd mirror peer remove <pool-name> <peer-uuid>
```

2. To remove mirroring on pool:

```
# rbd mirror pool disable <pool>
```

Configuring image mirroring

Image mirroring can be used when you choose to only want to mirror a specific subset of images and not an entire pool. The next recipe we will enable mirroring on a single image in the data pool and not mirror the other two images in the pool. This recipe requires you to have completed step 1 - step 9 in *Disaster recovery replication using RBD mirroring* recipe and have `rbd-mirror` running on backup site:

How to do it...

1. Create three images in the `ceph` cluster as we did in the previous recipe:

   ```
   # rbd create image-1 --size 1024 --pool data
     --image-feature exclusive-lock,journaling
   ```

2. Enable image mirroring on the data pool on the `ceph` and `backup` clusters:

   ```
   # rbd mirror pool enable data image
   ```

3. Add `ceph` cluster as a peer to `backup` cluster:

   ```
   root@ceph-node5 # rbd mirror pool peer add
                    data client.local@ceph
   ```

4. Validate that peer is successfully added:

   ```
   # rbd mirror pool info
   ```

```
[root@ceph-node5 ceph-ansible]# rbd mirror pool enable data image
[root@ceph-node5 ceph-ansible]# rbd mirror pool peer add data client.local
@ceph
7a5c3404-02bf-4b94-8944-f0b733d47473
[root@ceph-node5 ceph-ansible]# rbd mirror pool info
Mode: pool
Peers:
  UUID                                      NAME CLIENT
  4204c228-643f-4e3d-a206-0e07aff355ea ceph client.rbd
```

5. In the `ceph` cluster, enable image mirroring on `image-1`, `image-2` and `image-3` will not be mirrored:

   root@ceph-node1 # rbd mirror image enable data/image-1

   ```
   [root@ceph-node1 ceph]# rbd mirror pool enable data image
   [root@ceph-node1 ceph]# rbd mirror image enable data/image-1
   Mirroring enabled
   [root@ceph-node1 ceph]# rbd ls -p data
   image-1
   image-2
   image-3
   [root@ceph-node1 ceph]#
   ```

6. Check mirror status in `backup` cluster to verify single image being mirrored:

   # rbd mirror pool status

7. Check the image status in the `backup` cluster to validate the statue of this image and that image being mirrored is `image-1`:

   # rbd mirror image status data/image-1

   ```
   [root@ceph-node5 ceph-ansible]# rbd mirror pool status data
   health: OK
   images: 1 total
       1 replaying
   [root@ceph-node5 ceph-ansible]# rbd mirror image status data/image-1
   image-1:
     global_id:   712afcbe-4514-4a6c-89ef-0eef74766f66
     state:       up+replaying
     description: replaying, master_position=[object_number=3, tag_tid=2, ent
   ry_tid=3], mirror_position=[object_number=3, tag_tid=2, entry_tid=3], entr
   ies_behind_master=0
     last_update: 2017-09-10 06:10:55
   [root@ceph-node5 ceph-ansible]#
   ```

Configuring two-way mirroring

Two-way mirroring requires a `rbd-mirror` daemon running on both clusters, the primary and the secondary. With two way mirroring it is possible to mirror data or images from the primary site to a secondary site, and the secondary site can mirror data or images back to the primary site.

We will not be demoing this configuration in this book at it is very similar to the one-way configuration, but we will highlight the changes needed for two way replication at the pool level, these steps are covered in the one-way replication recipe.

How to do it...

1. Both clients must have the `rbd-mirror` installed and running:

   ```
   # yum install rbd-mirror
   # systemctl enable ceph-rbd-mirror.target
   # systemctl enable ceph-rbd-mirror@<client-id>
   # systemctl start ceph-rbd-mirror@<client-id>
   ```

2. As with one way mirroring, both clients must have copies of the respective cluster configuration files and keyrings for client users for the mirrored pools.

3. The pools to be replicated must have mirroring enabled at the pool or image level in *both* clusters:

   ```
   # rbd mirror pool enable <pool> <replication type>
   # rbd mirror pool enable <pool> <replication type>
   ```

4. Validate that mirroring has been successfully enabled:

   ```
   # rbd mirror pool status data
   ```

5. The pools to be replicated must have a peer registered for mirroring in *both* clusters:

   ```
   # rbd mirror pool peer add <pool>
     client.<user>@<primary cluster name>
   # rbd mirror pool peer add <pool>
     client.<user>@<secondary cluster name>
   ```

See also

For more information, please refer to: `http://docs.ceph.com/docs/master/rbd/rbd-mirroring/`.

Recovering from a disaster!

The following recipes will show how to fail over to the mirrored data on the `backup` cluster after the primary cluster `ceph` has encountered a disaster and how to failback once the `ceph` cluster has recovered. There are two methods for failover when dealing with a disaster:

- **Orderly**: Failover after an orderly shutdown. This would be a proper shutdown of the cluster and demotion and promotion of the image.
- **Non-orderly**: Failover after a non-orderly shutdown. This would be a complete loss of the primary cluster. In this case, the failback would require a resynchronizing of the image.

How to do it...

1. How to properly failover after an orderly shutdown:
   - Stop all client's that are writing to the primary image
   - Demote the primary image located on the `ceph` cluster:

     ```
     # rbd mirror image demote data/image-1
     ```

   - Promote the non-primary image located on the `backup` cluster:

     ```
     # rbd-mirror image promote data/image-1
     ```

   - Validate image has become primary on the `backup` cluster:

     ```
     # rbd mirror image status data/image-1
     ```

   - Resume client access to the image:

```
[root@ceph-node1 ceph]# rbd mirror image demote data/image-1
Image demoted to non-primary
[root@ceph-node1 ceph]#
```

```
[root@ceph-node5 ceph-ansible]# rbd mirror image promote data/image-1
Image promoted to primary
[root@ceph-node5 ceph-ansible]# rbd mirror image status data/image-1
image-1:
  global_id:   712afcbe-4514-4a6c-89ef-0eef74766f66
  state:       up+stopped
  description: remote image is non-primary or local image is primary
  last_update: 2017-09-10 06:35:25
[root@ceph-node5 ceph-ansible]#
```

2. How to properly failover after a non-orderly shutdown:
    - Validate that the primary cluster is in a down state
    - Stop all client access to the `ceph` cluster that accesses the primary image
    - Promote the non-primary image using the FORCE option on the `backup` cluster, as the demotion cannot be propagated to the down `ceph` cluster:

    ```
    # rbd-mirror image promote data/image-1
    ```

    - Resume client access to the peer image

3. How to failback from a disaster:
    - If there was a non-orderly shutdown on the `ceph` cluster then demote the old primary image on the `ceph` cluster once it returns:

    ```
    # rbd mirror image demote data/image-1
    ```

    - Resynchronize the image *only* if there was a non-orderly shutdown:

    ```
    # rbd mirror image resync data/image-1
    ```

    - Validate that the re-synchronization has completed and image is in up+replaying state:

    ```
    # rbd mirror image status data/image-1
    ```

    - Demote the secondary image on the `backup` cluster:

    ```
    # rbd mirror image demote data/image-1
    ```

    - Promote the formerly primary image on `ceph` cluster:

    ```
    # rbd mirror image promotion data/image-1
    ```

3
Working with Ceph and OpenStack

In this chapter we will cover the following recipes:

- Ceph – the best match for OpenStack
- Setting up OpenStack
- Configuring OpenStack as Ceph clients
- Configuring Glance for Ceph backend
- Configuring Cinder for Ceph backend
- Configuring Nova to boot instances from Ceph RBD
- Configuring Nova to attach Ceph RBD

Introduction

OpenStack is an open source software platform for building and managing public and private cloud infrastructure. It is being governed by an independent, non-profit foundation known as *The OpenStack Foundation*. It has the largest and the most active community, which is backed by technology giants such as HP, Red Hat, Dell-EMC, Cisco, IBM, Rackspace, and many more.

OpenStack's idea for a cloud is that it should be simple to implement and massively scalable.

OpenStack is considered as the cloud operating system where users are allowed to instantly deploy hundreds of virtual machines in an automated way. It also provides an efficient way of hassle-free management of these machines. OpenStack is known for its dynamic scale up, scale out, and distributed architecture capabilities, making your cloud environment robust and future-ready. OpenStack provides an enterprise-class **Infrastructure-as-a-Service (IaaS)** platform for all your cloud needs. As shown in the following high-level diagram, OpenStack is made up of several different software components that work together to provide cloud services:

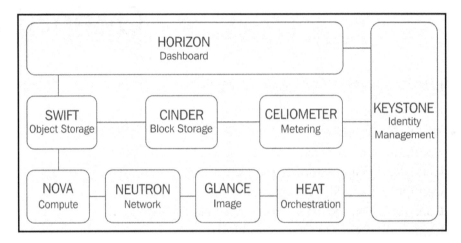

Out of all these components, in this chapter, we will focus on Cinder and Glance, which provide block storage and image services respectively. For more information on OpenStack components, please visit http://www.openstack.org/.

Ceph – the best match for OpenStack

OpenStack adoption continues to rise at an incredible rate, and it is incredibly popular as it's based on software-defined on a wide range, whether it's computing, networking, or even storage. And when you talk about storage for OpenStack, Ceph will get all the attention. An OpenStack user survey, conducted in April 2017, showed Ceph dominating the block storage driver market with a whopping 65% usage, 41% higher (Source - https:/ /www.openstack.org/assets/survey/April2017SurveyReport.pdf) than the next storage driver.

Ceph provides the robust, reliable storage backend that OpenStack was looking for. Its seamless integration with OpenStack components such as Cinder, Glance, Nova, and Keystone provides an all-in-one cloud storage backend for OpenStack. Here are some key benefits that make Ceph the best match for OpenStack:

- Ceph provides an enterprise-grade, feature-rich storage backend at a very low cost per gigabyte, which helps to keep the OpenStack cloud deployment price down

- Ceph is a unified storage solution for block, file, or object storage for OpenStack, allowing applications to use storage as they need

- Ceph provides advance block storage capabilities for OpenStack clouds, which includes the easy and quick spawning of instances, as well as the backup and cloning of VMs

- It provides default persistent volumes for OpenStack instances that can work like traditional servers, where data will not flush on rebooting the VMs

- Ceph supports OpenStack in being host-independent by supporting VM migrations, scaling up storage components without affecting VMs

- It provides a snapshot feature to OpenStack volumes, which can also be used as a means of backup

- Ceph's *copy-on-write* cloning feature provides OpenStack to spin up several instances at once, which helps the provisioning mechanism function faster

- Ceph supports rich APIs for both Swift and S3 object storage interfaces

The Ceph and OpenStack communities continue to work to make the integration more seamless and to make use of new features as they emerge.

OpenStack is a modular system that has a unique component for a specific set of tasks. There are several components that require a reliable storage backend, such as Ceph and extend full integration to it, as shown in the following diagram:

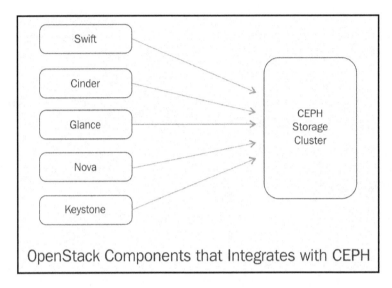

OpenStack Components that Integrates with CEPH

Each of these components uses Ceph in their own way to store block devices and objects. The majority of cloud deployment based on OpenStack and Ceph use the Cinder, Glance, and the Swift integrations with Ceph. Keystone integration is used when you need S3-compatible object storage on the Ceph backend. Nova integration allows boot from Ceph volume capabilities for your OpenStack instances.

Setting up OpenStack

OpenStack setup and configuration is beyond the scope of this book, however, for ease of demonstration, we will use a virtual machine that is preinstalled with the OpenStack RDO Juno release. If you like, you can also use your own OpenStack environment and can perform Ceph integration.

How to do it...

In this recipe, we will demonstrate setting up a preconfigured OpenStack environment using Vagrant and accessing it via CLI and GUI:

1. Launch `openstack-node1` using `vagrantfile` as we did for Ceph nodes in the last chapter i.e. Chapter 2, *Working with Ceph Block Device*. Make sure that you are on the host machine and are under the `Ceph-Designing-and-Implementing-Scalable-Storage-Systems` repository before bringing up `openstack-node1` using Vagrant:

   ```
   # cd Ceph-Designing-and-Implementing-Scalable-Storage-Systems
   # vagrant up openstack-node1
   ```

2. Log in to the OpenStack node with the following `vagrant` command:

   ```
   # vagrant status openstack-node1
   $ vagrant ssh openstack-node1
   ```

3. We assume that you have some knowledge of OpenStack and are aware of its operations. We will source the `keystone_admin` file, which has been placed under `/root`, and to do this, we need to switch to root:

   ```
   $ sudo su -
   $ source keystonerc_admin
   ```

   We will now run some native OpenStack commands to make sure that OpenStack is set up correctly. Please note that some of these commands do not show any information since this is a fresh OpenStack environment and does not have instances or volumes created:

   ```
   # nova list
   # cinder list
   # glance image-list
   ```

```
[root@os-node1 ~]# source keystonerc_admin
[root@os-node1 ~(keystone_admin)]# nova list
+----+------+--------+------------+-------------+----------+
| ID | Name | Status | Task State | Power State | Networks |
+----+------+--------+------------+-------------+----------+
+----+------+--------+------------+-------------+----------+
[root@os-node1 ~(keystone_admin)]# cinder list
+----+--------+--------------+------+-------------+----------+-------------+
| ID | Status | Display Name | Size | Volume Type | Bootable | Attached to |
+----+--------+--------------+------+-------------+----------+-------------+
+----+--------+--------------+------+-------------+----------+-------------+
[root@os-node1 ~(keystone_admin)]# glance image-list
+--------------------------------------+--------+-------------+------------------+----------+--------+
| ID                                   | Name   | Disk Format | Container Format | Size     | Status |
+--------------------------------------+--------+-------------+------------------+----------+--------+
| 5c261af7-9388-44ad-a8ce-f9ebdad2e5cb | cirros | qcow2       | bare             | 13200896 | active |
+--------------------------------------+--------+-------------+------------------+----------+--------+
[root@os-node1 ~(keystone_admin)]# 
```

4. You can also log into the OpenStack horizon web interface
   (`https://192.168.1.111/dashboard`) using the username `admin` and the
   password `vagrant`:

5. After logging in, the **Overview** page opens:

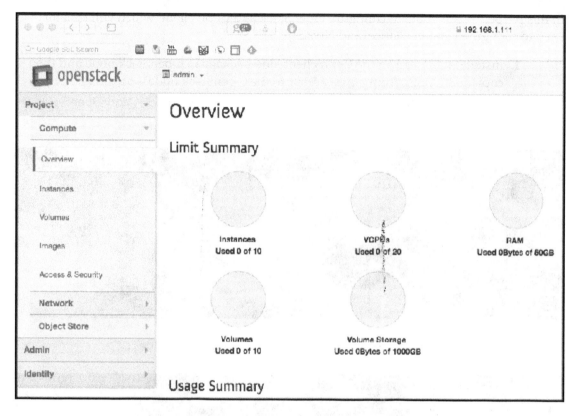

OpenStack Dashboard Overview

Configuring OpenStack as Ceph clients

OpenStack nodes should be configured as Ceph clients in order to access the Ceph cluster. To do this, install Ceph packages on OpenStack nodes and make sure it can access the Ceph cluster.

How to do it...

In this recipe, we are going to configure OpenStack as a Ceph client, which will be later used to configure Cinder, Glance, and Nova:

1. Install `ceph-common` the Ceph client-side package in OpenStack node and then copy `ceph.conf` from `ceph-node1` to the OpenStack node – `os-nod1`.

2. Create an SSH tunnel between the monitor node `ceph-node1` and OpenStack `os-node1`:

```
[root@ceph-node1 group_vars]#
[root@ceph-node1 group_vars]# ssh-copy-id root@os-node1
/usr/bin/ssh-copy-id: INFO: Source of key(s) to be installed: "/root/.ssh/id_rsa.pub"
The authenticity of host 'os-node1 (192.168.1.111)' can't be established.
ECDSA key fingerprint is SHA256:LKEJvMiROJpoHqwTWm1X8kuT9Mg1jkfXE6WjQ4MrogU.
ECDSA key fingerprint is MD5:af:2a:a5:74:a7:0b:f5:5b:ef:c5:4b:2a:fe:1d:30:8e.
Are you sure you want to continue connecting (yes/no)? yes
/usr/bin/ssh-copy-id: INFO: attempting to log in with the new key(s), to filter out any that are already installed
/usr/bin/ssh-copy-id: INFO: 1 key(s) remain to be installed -- if you are prompted now it is to install the new keys
root@os-node1's password:

Number of key(s) added: 1

Now try logging into the machine, with:    "ssh 'root@os-node1'"
and check to make sure that only the key(s) you wanted were added.

[root@ceph-node1 group_vars]#
```

3. Copy the Ceph repository file from `ceph-node1` to `os-node1`:

```
[root@ceph-node1 group_vars]#
[root@ceph-node1 group_vars]# scp /etc/yum.repos.d/ceph_stable.repo os-node1:/etc/yum.repos.d/.
ceph_stable.repo
[root@ceph-node1 group_vars]#
```

4. Install `ceph-common` package in `os-node1`:

```
[root@os-node1 ~(keystone_admin)]#
[root@os-node1 ~(keystone_admin)]# yum install ceph-common -y
Loaded plugins: fastestmirror, priorities
base
ceph_stable
```

5. Once it completes, you will have the following message:

6. Copy `ceph.conf` from `ceph-node1` to `os-node1`:

```
[root@ceph-node1 group_vars]#
[root@ceph-node1 group_vars]# scp /etc/ceph/ceph.conf os-node1:/etc/ceph/
ceph.conf
[root@ceph-node1 group_vars]#
```

7. Create Ceph pools for Cinder, Glance, and Nova from monitor node `ceph-node1`. You may use any available pool, but it's recommended that you create separate pools for OpenStack components:

```
# ceph osd pool create images 128
# ceph osd pool create volumes 128
# ceph osd pool create vms 128
```

```
[root@ceph-node1 ceph]# ceph osd pool create images 128
pool 'images' created
[root@ceph-node1 ceph]# ceph osd pool create volumes 128
pool 'volumes' created
[root@ceph-node1 ceph]# ceph osd pool create vms 128
pool 'vms' created
[root@ceph-node1 ceph]# ceph osd lspools
0 rbd,1 images,2 volumes,3 vms,
[root@ceph-node1 ceph]#
```

We have used 128 as PG number for these three pools. For the PG calculation, for your pools, you can use Ceph PGcalc tool `http://ceph.com/pgcalc/`.

8. Set up client authentication by creating a new user for Cinder and Glance:

```
# ceph auth get-or-create client.cinder mon 'allow r' osd
    'allow class-read object_prefix rbd_children, allow rwx
pool=volumes,
        allow rwx pool=vms, allow rx pool=images'

# ceph auth get-or-create client.glance mon 'allow r' osd
    'allow class-read object_prefix rbd_children, allow rwx
pool=images'
```

```
[root@ceph-node1 ~]#
[root@ceph-node1 ~]# ceph auth get-or-create client.cinder mon 'allow r' osd 'allow class-read object_prefix rbd_children, allow rwx pool=volumes, allow rwx pool=vms, allow rx pool=images'
[client.cinder]
        key = AQAjOclZx/d5IxAAA007JU1PaQXfrqin6fPPnQ==
[root@ceph-node1 ~]# ceph auth get-or-create client.glance mon 'allow r' osd 'allow class-read object_prefix rbd_children, allow rwx pool=images'
[client.glance]
        key = AQAwOclZwet1MRAAi5ER7wKOeWj7YmMqK8zC1w==
[root@ceph-node1 ~]#
```

9. Add the keyrings to `os-node1` and change their ownership:

```
# ceph auth get-or-create client.glance |
    ssh os-node1 sudo tee /etc/ceph/ceph.client.glance.keyring
# ssh os-node1 sudo chown glance:glance
    /etc/ceph/ceph.client.glance.keyring
# ceph auth get-or-create client.cinder |
    ssh os-node1 sudo tee /etc/ceph/ceph.client.cinder.keyring
# ssh os-node1 sudo chown cinder:cinder
    /etc/ceph/ceph.client.cinder.keyring
```

```
[root@ceph-node1 ~]#
[root@ceph-node1 ~]# ceph auth get-or-create client.glance | ssh os-node1 sudo tee /etc/ceph/ceph.client.glance.keyring
[client.glance]
        key = AQAwOclZwet1MRAAi5ER7wKOeWj7YmMqK8zC1w==
[root@ceph-node1 ~]# ssh os-node1 sudo chown glance:glance /etc/ceph/ceph.client.glance.keyring
[root@ceph-node1 ~]# ceph auth get-or-create client.cinder | ssh os-node1 sudo tee /etc/ceph/ceph.client.cinder.keyring
[client.cinder]
        key = AQAjOclZx/d5IxAAA007JU1PaQXfrqin6fPPnQ==
[root@ceph-node1 ~]# ssh os-node1 sudo chown cinder:cinder /etc/ceph/ceph.client.cinder.keyring
```

10. The `libvirt` process requires accessing the Ceph cluster while attaching or detaching a block device from Cinder. We should create a temporary copy of the `client.cinder` key that will be needed for the Cinder and Nova configuration later in this chapter:

```
# ceph auth get-key client.cinder |
    ssh os-node1 tee /etc/ceph/temp.client.cinder.key
```

11. At this point, you can test the previous configuration by accessing the Ceph cluster from `os-node1` using the `client.glance` and `client.cinder` Ceph users.

    Log in to `os-node1` and run the following commands:

    ```
    $ vagrant ssh openstack-node1
    $ sudo su -
    # ceph -s --id glance
    # ceph -s --id cinder
    ```

    ```
    [root@os-node1 ~]# ceph -s --id glance
        cluster 585ce77b-476c-4f52-b147-93fe9424eb2a
        health HEALTH_OK
        monmap e1: 3 mons at {ceph-node1=192.168.1.101:6789/0,ceph-node2=192.168.1.102:6789/0,ceph-node3=192.168.1.103:6789/0}
            election epoch 6, quorum 0,1,2 ceph-node1,ceph-node2,ceph-node3
        osdmap e90: 9 osds: 9 up, 9 in
            flags sortbitwise,require_jewel_osds
        pgmap v2566: 600 pgs, 15 pools, 4161 bytes data, 183 objects
            352 MB used, 161 GB / 161 GB avail
                600 active+clean
    [root@os-node1 ~]#
    [root@os-node1 ~]#
    [root@os-node1 ~]# ceph -s --id cinder
        cluster 585ce77b-476c-4f52-b147-93fe9424eb2a
        health HEALTH_OK
        monmap e1: 3 mons at {ceph-node1=192.168.1.101:6789/0,ceph-node2=192.168.1.102:6789/0,ceph-node3=192.168.1.103:6789/0}
            election epoch 6, quorum 0,1,2 ceph-node1,ceph-node2,ceph-node3
        osdmap e90: 9 osds: 9 up, 9 in
            flags sortbitwise,require_jewel_osds
        pgmap v2566: 600 pgs, 15 pools, 4161 bytes data, 183 objects
            352 MB used, 161 GB / 161 GB avail
                600 active+clean
    [root@os-node1 ~]#
    ```

12. Finally, generate UUID, then create, define, and set the secret key to `libvirt` and remove temporary keys:

    1. Generate a UUID by using the following command:

       ```
       # cd /etc/ceph
       # uuidgen
       ```

    2. Create a `secret` file and set this UUID number to it:

       ```
       cat > secret.xml <<EOF
       <secret ephemeral='no' private='no'>
       <uuid>e279566e-bc97-46d0-bd90-68080a2a0ad8</uuid>
       <usage type='ceph'>
       <name>client.cinder secret</name>
       </usage>
       </secret>
       EOF
       ```

Make sure that you use your own UUID generated for your environment.

```
[root@os-node1 ceph]#
[root@os-node1 ceph]# cd /etc/ceph/
[root@os-node1 ceph]# uuidgen
e279566e-bc97-46d0-bd90-68080a2a0ad8
[root@os-node1 ceph]# cat > secret.xml << EOF
> <secret ephemeral='no' private='no'>
>   <uuid>e279566e-bc97-46d0-bd90-68080a2a0ad8</uuid>
>   <usage type='ceph'>
>     <name>client.cinder secret</name>
>   </usage>
> </secret>
> EOF
[root@os-node1 ceph]#
```

3. Define the secret and keep the generated secret value safe. We will require this secret value in the next steps:

   # virsh secret-define --file secret.xml

```
[root@os-node1 ceph]#
[root@os-node1 ceph]# virsh secret-define --file secret.xml
Secret e279566e-bc97-46d0-bd90-68080a2a0ad8 created

[root@os-node1 ceph]# _
```

4. Set the secret value that was generated in the last step to `virsh` and delete temporary files. Deleting the temporary files is optional; it's done just to keep the system clean:

```
# virsh secret-set-value
--secret e279566e-bc97-46d0-bd90-68080a2a0ad8
--base64 $(cat temp.client.cinder.key) &&
rm temp.client.cinder.key secret.xml
# virsh secret-list
```

```
[root@os-node1 ceph]#
[root@os-node1 ceph]# virsh secret-define --file secret.xml
Secret e279566e-bc97-46d0-bd90-68080a2a0ad8 created

[root@os-node1 ceph]#
[root@os-node1 ceph]# virsh secret-set-value --secret e279566e-bc97-46d0-bd90-68080a2a0ad8 --base64 $(cat temp.client.cinder.key) && rm temp.client.cinder.key secret.xml
Secret value set

rm: remove regular file 'temp.client.cinder.key'? y
rm: remove regular file 'secret.xml'? y
[root@os-node1 ceph]#
[root@os-node1 ceph]# virsh secret-list
 UUID                                  Usage
--------------------------------------------------------------
 e279566e-bc97-46d0-bd90-68080a2a0ad8  ceph client.cinder secret

[root@os-node1 ceph]#
```

Configuring Glance for Ceph backend

We have completed the configuration required from the Ceph side. In this recipe, we will configure the OpenStack Glance to use Ceph as a storage backend.

How to do it...

This recipe talks about configuring the Glance component of OpenStack to store virtual machine images on Ceph RBD:

1. Log in to `os-node1`, which is our Glance node, and edit `/etc/glance/glance-api.conf` for the following changes:
    1. Under the `[DEFAULT]` section, make sure that the following lines are present:

        ```
        default_store=rbd
        show_image_direct_url=True
        ```

2. Execute the following command to verify entries:

```
# cat /etc/glance/glance-api.conf |
egrep -i "default_store|image_direct"
```

```
[root@os-node1 ceph]# cat /etc/glance/glance-api.conf | egrep -i "default_store|image_direct"
default_store=rbd
show_image_direct_url=True
[root@os-node1 ceph]#
```

3. Under the `[glance_store]` section, make sure that the following lines are present under RBD store options:

```
stores = rbd
rbd_store_ceph_conf=/etc/ceph/ceph.conf
rbd_store_user=glance
rbd_store_pool=images
rbd_store_chunk_size=8
```

4. Execute the following command to verify the previous entries:

```
# cat /etc/glance/glance-api.conf |
egrep -v "#|default" | grep -i rbd
```

```
[root@os-node1 ceph]# cat /etc/glance/glance-api.conf | egrep -v "#|default" | grep -i rbd
stores = rbd
rbd_store_ceph_conf=/etc/ceph/ceph.conf
rbd_store_user=glance
rbd_store_pool=images
rbd_store_chunk_size=8
[root@os-node1 ceph]#
```

2. Restart the OpenStack Glance services:

```
# service openstack-glance-api restart
```

3. Source the `keystonerc_admin` file for OpenStack and list the Glance images:

```
# source /root/keystonerc_admin
# glance image-list
```

```
[root@os-node1 ~]# source /root/keystonerc_admin
[root@os-node1 ~(keystone_admin)]# glance image-list
+--------------------------------------+--------+-------------+------------------+----------+--------+
| ID                                   | Name   | Disk Format | Container Format | Size     | Status |
+--------------------------------------+--------+-------------+------------------+----------+--------+
| 5c261af7-9388-44ad-a8ce-f9ebdad2e5cb | cirros | qcow2       | bare             | 13200896 | active |
+--------------------------------------+--------+-------------+------------------+----------+--------+
[root@os-node1 ~(keystone_admin)]#
```

4. Download the cirros image from the internet, which will later be stored in Ceph:

```
# wget http://download.cirros-cloud.net/0.3.1/cirros-0.3.1-
  x86_64-disk.img
```

5. Add a new Glance image using the following command:

```
# glance image-create --name cirros_image --is-public=true
  --disk-format=qcow2 --container-format=bare
    < cirros-0.3.1-x86_64-disk.img
```

```
[root@os-node1 ~(keystone_admin)]#
[root@os-node1 ~(keystone_admin)]# glance image-create --name cirros_image --is-public=true --disk-format=qcow2 --container-format=bare < cirros-0.3.1-x86_64-disk.img
+------------------+--------------------------------------+
| Property         | Value                                |
+------------------+--------------------------------------+
| checksum         | d972013792949d0d3ba628fbe8685bce     |
| container_format | bare                                 |
| created_at       | 2017-09-25T18:00:49                  |
| deleted          | False                                |
| deleted_at       | None                                 |
| disk_format      | qcow2                                |
| id               | b1c39f06-5330-4b04-ae0f-0b1d5e901e5b |
| is_public        | True                                 |
| min_disk         | 0                                    |
| min_ram          | 0                                    |
| name             | cirros_image                         |
| owner            | c9f87abe43ea49239313565ca74ebaa0     |
| protected        | False                                |
| size             | 13147648                             |
| status           | active                               |
| updated_at       | 2017-09-25T18:00:50                  |
| virtual_size     | None                                 |
+------------------+--------------------------------------+
[root@os-node1 ~(keystone_admin)]#
```

6. List the Glance images using the following command; you will notice there are now two Glance images:

   # glance image-list

```
[root@os-node1 ~(keystone_admin)]#
[root@os-node1 ~(keystone_admin)]# glance image-list
+--------------------------------------+--------------+-------------+------------------+----------+--------+
| ID                                   | Name         | Disk Format | Container Format | Size     | Status |
+--------------------------------------+--------------+-------------+------------------+----------+--------+
| 5c261af7-9388-44ad-a8ce-f9ebdad2e5cb | cirros       | qcow2       | bare             | 13200896 | active |
| b1c39f06-5330-4b04-ae0f-0b1d5e901e5b | cirros_image | qcow2       | bare             | 13147648 | active |
+--------------------------------------+--------------+-------------+------------------+----------+--------+
[root@os-node1 ~(keystone_admin)]#
```

7. You can verify that the new image is stored in Ceph by querying the image ID in the Ceph images pool:

   # rbd -p images ls --id glance
   # rbd info images/<image name> --id glance

```
[root@os-node1 ~(keystone_admin)]#
[root@os-node1 ~(keystone_admin)]# rbd -p images ls --id glance
b1c39f06-5330-4b04-ae0f-0b1d5e901e5b
[root@os-node1 ~(keystone_admin)]# rbd info images/b1c39f06-5330-4b04-ae0f-0b1d5e901e5b --id glance
rbd image 'b1c39f06-5330-4b04-ae0f-0b1d5e901e5b':
        size 12839 kB in 2 objects
        order 23 (8192 kB objects)
        block_name_prefix: rbd_data.278a23b69012
        format: 2
        features: layering
        flags:
[root@os-node1 ~(keystone_admin)]#
```

8. Since we have configured Glance to use Ceph for its default storage, all the Glance images will now be stored in Ceph. You can also try creating images from the OpenStack horizon dashboard:

9. Finally, we will try to launch an instance using the image that we have created earlier:

```
# nova boot --flavor 1 --image b1c39f06-5330-4b04-ae0f-0b1d5e901e5b vm1
```

```
[root@os-node1 ~(keystone_admin)]#
[root@os-node1 ~(keystone_admin)]# nova boot --flavor 1 --image b1c39f06-5330-4b04-ae0f-0b1d5e901e5b vm1
+--------------------------------------+----------------------------------------------------------+
| Property                             | Value                                                    |
+--------------------------------------+----------------------------------------------------------+
| OS-DCF:diskConfig                    | MANUAL                                                   |
| OS-EXT-AZ:availability_zone          | nova                                                    |
| OS-EXT-SRV-ATTR:host                 | -                                                       |
| OS-EXT-SRV-ATTR:hypervisor_hostname  | -                                                       |
| OS-EXT-SRV-ATTR:instance_name        | instance-00000001                                       |
| OS-EXT-STS:power_state               | 0                                                       |
| OS-EXT-STS:task_state                | scheduling                                              |
| OS-EXT-STS:vm_state                  | building                                                |
| OS-SRV-USG:launched_at               | -                                                       |
| OS-SRV-USG:terminated_at             | -                                                       |
| accessIPv4                           |                                                         |
| accessIPv6                           |                                                         |
| adminPass                            | 265PXYcotdev                                            |
| config_drive                         |                                                         |
| created                              | 2017-09-25T18:53:05Z                                    |
| flavor                               | m1.tiny (1)                                             |
| hostId                               |                                                         |
| id                                   | cee98754-de7b-440d-b20c-10e2620e8217                    |
| image                                | cirros_image (b1c39f06-5330-4b04-ae0f-0b1d5e901e5b)     |
| key_name                             | -                                                       |
| metadata                             | {}                                                      |
| name                                 | vm1                                                     |
| os-extended-volumes:volumes_attached | []                                                      |
| progress                             | 0                                                       |
| security_groups                      | default                                                 |
| status                               | BUILD                                                   |
| tenant_id                            | c9f87abe43ea49239313565ca74ebaa0                        |
| updated                              | 2017-09-25T18:53:05Z                                    |
| user_id                              | 58e7a4c12d4f44ed865b2bf8ddf2f8f4                        |
+--------------------------------------+----------------------------------------------------------+
```

10. You can check with the Nova list command:

```
[root@os-node1 ~(keystone_admin)]#
[root@os-node1 ~(keystone_admin)]# nova list
+--------------------------------------+------+--------+------------+-------------+----------------------+
| ID                                   | Name | Status | Task State | Power State | Networks             |
+--------------------------------------+------+--------+------------+-------------+----------------------+
| cee98754-de7b-440d-b20c-10e2620e8217 | vm1  | ACTIVE | -          | Running     | public=172.24.4.227  |
+--------------------------------------+------+--------+------------+-------------+----------------------+
[root@os-node1 ~(keystone_admin)]#
```

While you are adding new Glance images or creating an instance from the Glance image stored on Ceph, you can check the IO on the Ceph cluster by monitoring it and using the `# watch ceph -s` command.

Configuring Cinder for Ceph backend

The Cinder program of OpenStack provides block storage to virtual machines. In this recipe, we will configure OpenStack Cinder to use Ceph as a storage backend. OpenStack Cinder requires a driver to interact with the Ceph Block Device. On the OpenStack node, edit the `/etc/qinder/cinder.conf` configuration file by adding the code snippet given in the following section.

How to do it...

In the last recipe, we learned to configure Glance to use Ceph. In this recipe, we will learn to use the Ceph RBD with the Cinder service of OpenStack:

1. Since in this demonstration we are not using multiple backend cinder configurations, comment the `enabled_backends` option from the `/etc/cinder/cinder.conf` file:

2. Navigate to the options defined in `cinder.volume.drivers.rbd` section of the `/etc/cinder/cinder.conf` file and add the following (replace the secret UUID with your environments value):

   ```
   volume_driver = cinder.volume.drivers.rbd.RBDDriver
   rbd_pool = volumes
   rbd_user = cinder
   rbd_secret_uuid = e279566e-bc97-46d0-bd90-68080a2a0ad8
   rbd_ceph_conf = /etc/ceph/ceph.conf
   rbd_flatten_volume_from_snapshot = false
   rbd_max_clone_depth = 5
   rbd_store_chunk_size = 4
   rados_connect_timeout = -1
   glance_api_version = 2
   ```

3. Execute the following command to verify the previous entries:

```
# cat /etc/cinder/cinder.conf | egrep "rbd|rados|version" |
  grep -v "#"
```

```
[root@os-node1 ~(keystone_admin)]#
[root@os-node1 ~(keystone_admin)]# cat /etc/cinder/cinder.conf | egrep "rbd|rados|version" | grep -v "#"
volume_driver = cinder.volume.drivers.rbd.RBDDriver
rbd_pool = volumes
rbd_user = cinder
rbd_secret_uuid = e279566e-bc97-46d0-bd90-68080a2a0ad8
rbd_ceph_conf = /etc/ceph/ceph.conf
rbd_flatten_volume_from_snapshot = false
rbd_max_clone_depth = 5
rbd_store_chunk_size = 4
rados_connect_timeout = -1
glance_api_version = 2
[root@os-node1 ~(keystone_admin)]#
```

4. Comment `enabled_backend=lvm` option in `/etc/cinder/cinder.conf`:

```
[root@os-node1 ~(keystone_admin)]#
[root@os-node1 ~(keystone_admin)]# cat /etc/cinder/cinder.conf | grep enabled_backend
#enabled_backends=<None>
#enabled_backends=lvm
[root@os-node1 ~(keystone_admin)]#
```

5. Restart the OpenStack Cinder services:

```
# service openstack-cinder-volume restart
```

6. Source the `keystone_admin` files for OpenStack:

```
# source /root/keystonerc_admin
# cinder list
```

7. To test this configuration, create your first Cinder volume of 2 GB, which should now be created on your Ceph cluster:

```
# cinder create --display-name ceph-volume01
  --display-description "Cinder volume on CEPH storage" 2
```

```
[root@os-node1 ~]# source /root/keystonerc admin
[root@os-node1 ~(keystone_admin)]# cinder list
+----+--------+--------------+------+-------------+----------+-------------+
| ID | Status | Display Name | Size | Volume Type | Bootable | Attached to |
+----+--------+--------------+------+-------------+----------+-------------+
+----+--------+--------------+------+-------------+----------+-------------+
[root@os-node1 ~(keystone_admin)]# cinder create --display-name ceph-volume01 --display-description "Cinder volume on CEPH storage" 2
+---------------------+--------------------------------------+
|       Property      |                Value                 |
+---------------------+--------------------------------------+
|     attachments     |                  []                  |
|  availability_zone  |                 nova                 |
|       bootable      |                false                 |
|      created_at     |      2017-09-25T19:47:42.488505      |
| display_description |     Cinder volume on CEPH storage    |
|     display_name    |            ceph-volume01             |
|      encrypted      |                False                 |
|          id         | 7443e2b6-0674-4950-9371-49094a1702a7 |
|       metadata      |                  {}                  |
|         size        |                  2                   |
|     snapshot_id     |                 None                 |
|     source_volid    |                 None                 |
|        status       |               creating               |
|     volume_type     |                 None                 |
+---------------------+--------------------------------------+
[root@os-node1 ~(keystone_admin)]#
```

8. Check the volume by listing the Cinder and Ceph volumes pool:

   # cinder list

```
[root@os-node1 ~(keystone_admin)]#
[root@os-node1 ~(keystone_admin)]# cinder list
+--------------------------------------+-----------+--------------+------+-------------+----------+-------------+
|                  ID                  |  Status   | Display Name | Size | Volume Type | Bootable | Attached to |
+--------------------------------------+-----------+--------------+------+-------------+----------+-------------+
| 7443e2b6-0674-4950-9371-49094a1702a7 | available | ceph-volume01 |  2   |    None     |  false   |             |
+--------------------------------------+-----------+--------------+------+-------------+----------+-------------+
[root@os-node1 ~(keystone_admin)]#
```

   # rbd -p volumes ls --id cinder

   **# rbd info volumes/volume-7443e2b6-0674-4950-9371-49094a1702a7
   --id cinder**

```
[root@os-node1 ~(keystone_admin)]#
[root@os-node1 ~(keystone_admin)]# rbd -p volumes ls --id cinder
volume-7443e2b6-0674-4950-9371-49094a1702a7
[root@os-node1 ~(keystone_admin)]# rbd info volumes/volume-7443e2b6-0674-4950-9371-49094a1702a7 --id cinder
rbd image 'volume-7443e2b6-0674-4950-9371-49094a1702a7':
        size 2048 MB in 512 objects
        order 22 (4096 kB objects)
        block_name_prefix: rbd_data.2ad7f3d9bcfab
        format: 2
        features: layering
        flags:
[root@os-node1 ~(keystone_admin)]#
```

9. Similarly, try creating another volume using the OpenStack horizon dashboard.

Configuring Nova to boot instances from Ceph RBD

In order to boot all OpenStack instances into Ceph, that is, for the *boot-from-volume* feature, we should configure an ephemeral backend for Nova. To do this, edit /etc/nova/nova.conf on the OpenStack node and perform the following changes.

How to do it...

This recipe deals with configuring Nova to store the entire virtual machines on the Ceph RBD:

1. Navigate to the [libvirt] section and add the following:

   ```
   inject_partition=-2
   images_type=rbd
   images_rbd_pool=vms
   images_rbd_ceph_conf=/etc/ceph/ceph.conf
   rbd_user=cinder
   rbd_secret_uuid= e279566e-bc97-46d0-bd90-68080a2a0ad8
   ```

2. Verify your changes:

   ```
   # cat /etc/nova/nova.conf|egrep "rbd|partition" | grep -v "#"
   ```

   ```
   [root@os-node1 ~(keystone_admin)]#
   [root@os-node1 ~(keystone_admin)]# cat /etc/nova/nova.conf|egrep "rbd|partition" | grep -v "#"
   inject_partition=-2
   images_type=rbd
   images_rbd_pool=vms
   images_rbd_ceph_conf=/etc/ceph/ceph.conf
   rbd_user=cinder
   rbd_secret_uuid=e279566e-bc97-46d0-bd90-68080a2a0ad8
   [root@os-node1 ~(keystone_admin)]#
   ```

3. Restart the OpenStack Nova services:

```
# service openstack-nova-compute restart
```

4. To boot a virtual machine in Ceph, the Glance image format must be RAW. We will use the same cirros image that we downloaded earlier in this chapter and convert this image from the QCOW to the RAW format (this is important). You can also use any other image, as long as it's in the RAW format:

```
# qemu-img convert -f qcow2 -O raw cirros-0.3.1-x86_64-disk.img
cirros-0.3.1-x86_64-disk.raw
```

5. Create a Glance image using a RAW image:

```
# glance image-create --name cirros_raw_image
  --is-public=true --disk-format=raw
  --container-format=bare < cirros-0.3.1-x86_64-disk.raw
```

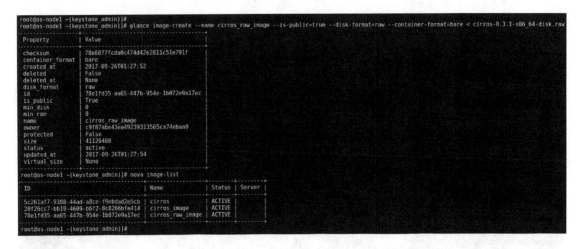

6. To test the boot from the Ceph volume feature, create a bootable volume:

```
# nova image-list
# cinder create --image-id 78e1fd35-aa65-447b-954e-1b072e9a17ec
               --display-name cirros-ceph-boot-volume 1
```

7. List Cinder volumes to check if the bootable field is true:

```
# cinder list
```

```
[root@os-node1 ~(keystone_admin)]# cinder list
+--------------------------------------+-----------+------------------------+------+-------------+----------+-------------+
|                  ID                  |  Status   |      Display Name      | Size | Volume Type | Bootable | Attached to |
+--------------------------------------+-----------+------------------------+------+-------------+----------+-------------+
| 21bb3f31-6f9e-4d26-9afd-5eec3f450034 | available |      ceph-volume01     |  2   |     None    |  false   |             |
| d3a3eb50-6b3a-4a93-b90c-b17d01e10b64 | available | cirros-ceph-boot-volume|  1   |     None    |  true    |             |
+--------------------------------------+-----------+------------------------+------+-------------+----------+-------------+
[root@os-node1 ~(keystone_admin)]#
[root@os-node1 ~(keystone_admin)]# rbd info volumes/volume-d3a3eb50-6b3a-4a93-b90c-b17d01e10b64 --id cinder
rbd image 'volume-d3a3eb50-6b3a-4a93-b90c-b17d01e10b64':
        size 1024 MB in 256 objects
        order 22 (4096 kB objects)
        block_name_prefix: rbd_data.35a5f72c334e2
        format: 2
        features: layering
        flags:
        parent: images/78e1fd35-aa65-447b-954e-1b072e9a17ec@snap
        overlap: 40162 kB
[root@os-node1 ~(keystone_admin)]#
```

8. Now, we have a bootable volume, which is stored on Ceph, so let's launch an instance with this volume:

   1. We have a known issue with qemu-kvm package which is causing nova boot to fail:

      ```
      Log - "libvirtError: internal error: process exited
      while connecting to monitor: ... Unknown protocol"
      ```

2. We have the following packages installed in the `os-node1` VM which have this issue:

```
qemu-kvm-1.5.3-60.el7_0.11.x86_64
qemu-kvm-common-1.5.3-60.el7_0.11.x86_64
qemu-img-1.5.3-60.el7_0.11.x86_64
```

3. Please upgrade the `qemu-kvm`, `qemu-kvm-common` and `qemu-img` packages:

```
$ yum update qemu-kvm qemu-img -y
```

4. It will install the following packages:

```
qemu-kvm-common-1.5.3-141.el7_4.2.x86_64
qemu-kvm-1.5.3-141.el7_4.2.x86_64
qemu-img-1.5.3-141.el7_4.2.x86_64
```

```
Updated:
  qemu-img.x86 64 10:1.5.3-141.el7 4.2                                    qemu-kvm.x86_64 10:1.5.3-141.el7 4.2
```

```
# nova boot --flavor 1 --block_device_mapping
  vda=d3a3eb50-6b3a-4a93-b90c-b17d01e10b64::0
--image 78e1fd35-aa65-447b-954e-1b072e9a17ec
  vm2_on_ceph
--block_device_mapping vda = <cinder bootable
volume id >
--image = <Glance image associated with the bootable
  volume>
```

```
[root@os-node1 ~(keystone_admin)]#
[root@os-node1 ~(keystone_admin)]# nova boot --flavor 1 --block_device_mapping vda=d3a3eb50-6b3a-4a93-b90c-b17d01e10b64 --image 78e1fd35-aa65-447b-954e-1b072e9a17ec vm2_on_ceph
+-------------------------------------+----------------------------------------------------+
| Property                            | Value                                              |
+-------------------------------------+----------------------------------------------------+
| OS-DCF:diskConfig                   | MANUAL                                             |
| OS-EXT-AZ:availability_zone         | nova                                               |
| OS-EXT-SRV-ATTR:host                | -                                                  |
| OS-EXT-SRV-ATTR:hypervisor_hostname | -                                                  |
| OS-EXT-SRV-ATTR:instance_name       | instance-00000033                                  |
| OS-EXT-STS:power_state              | 0                                                  |
| OS-EXT-STS:task_state               | scheduling                                         |
| OS-EXT-STS:vm_state                 | building                                           |
| OS-SRV-USG:launched_at              | -                                                  |
| OS-SRV-USG:terminated_at            | -                                                  |
| accessIPv4                          |                                                    |
| accessIPv6                          |                                                    |
| adminPass                           | gAtgzhu2or9T                                       |
| config_drive                        |                                                    |
| created                             | 2017-09-26T03:32:57Z                               |
| flavor                              | m1.tiny (1)                                         |
| hostId                              |                                                    |
| id                                  | 45c2f1a6-80ce-4ff4-8adf-237de30ca332               |
| image                               | cirros_raw_image (78e1fd35-aa65-447b-954e-1b072e9a17ec) |
| key_name                            | -                                                  |
| metadata                            | {}                                                 |
| name                                | vm2_on_ceph                                        |
| os-extended-volumes:volumes attached| [{"id": "d3a3eb50-6b3a-4a93-b90c-b17d01e10b64"}]   |
| progress                            | 0                                                  |
| security_groups                     | default                                            |
| status                              | BUILD                                              |
| tenant_id                           | c9f87abe43ea49239313565ca74ebaa0                   |
| updated                             | 2017-09-26T03:32:57Z                               |
| user_id                             | 58e7a4c12d4f44ed865b2bf8ddf2f8f4                   |
+-------------------------------------+----------------------------------------------------+
```

9. Finally, check the instance status:

```
# nova list
```

```
[root@os-node1 ~(keystone_admin)]#
[root@os-node1 ~(keystone_admin)]# nova list
+--------------------------------------+-------------+--------+------------+-------------+-----------------------+
| ID                                   | Name        | Status | Task State | Power State | Networks              |
+--------------------------------------+-------------+--------+------------+-------------+-----------------------+
| 45c2f1a6-80ce-4ff4-8adf-237de30ca332 | vm2_on_ceph | ACTIVE | -          | Running     | public=172.24.4.231   |
+--------------------------------------+-------------+--------+------------+-------------+-----------------------+
[root@os-node1 ~(keystone_admin)]#
```

10. At this point, we have an instance running from a Ceph volume. Let's do a boot from image:

```
# nova boot --flavor 1
         --image 78e1fd35-aa65-447b-954e-1b072e9a17ec
         vm1_on_ceph
```

```
[root@os-node1 ~(keystone_admin)]# nova boot --flavor 1 --image 78e1fd35-aa65-447b-954e-1b072e9a17ec vm1_on_ceph
+--------------------------------------+---------------------------------------------------------------+
| Property                             | Value                                                         |
+--------------------------------------+---------------------------------------------------------------+
| OS-DCF:diskConfig                    | MANUAL                                                         |
| OS-EXT-AZ:availability_zone          | nova                                                          |
| OS-EXT-SRV-ATTR:host                 | -                                                             |
| OS-EXT-SRV-ATTR:hypervisor_hostname  | -                                                             |
| OS-EXT-SRV-ATTR:instance_name        | instance-00000034                                            |
| OS-EXT-STS:power_state               | 0                                                            |
| OS-EXT-STS:task_state                | scheduling                                                   |
| OS-EXT-STS:vm_state                  | building                                                     |
| OS-SRV-USG:launched_at               | -                                                            |
| OS-SRV-USG:terminated_at             | -                                                            |
| accessIPv4                           |                                                              |
| accessIPv6                           |                                                              |
| adminPass                            | e2onrYJVs6Yh                                                 |
| config_drive                         |                                                              |
| created                              | 2017-09-26T03:50:54Z                                         |
| flavor                               | m1.tiny (1)                                                  |
| hostId                               |                                                              |
| id                                   | 31000c20-5847-48eb-b2e3-6b681f5df46c                        |
| image                                | cirros_raw_image (78e1fd35-aa65-447b-954e-1b072e9a17ec)     |
| key_name                             | -                                                            |
| metadata                             | {}                                                           |
| name                                 | vm1_on_ceph                                                 |
| os-extended-volumes:volumes_attached | []                                                           |
| progress                             | 0                                                            |
| security_groups                      | default                                                      |
| status                               | BUILD                                                        |
| tenant_id                            | c9f87abe43ea49239313565ca74ebaa0                            |
| updated                              | 2017-09-26T03:50:55Z                                         |
| user_id                              | 58e7a4c12d4f44ed865b2bf8ddf2f8f4                            |
+--------------------------------------+---------------------------------------------------------------+
[root@os-node1 ~(keystone_admin)]#
```

11. Finally, check the instance status:

    ```
    # nova list
    ```

```
[root@os-node1 ~(keystone_admin)]#
[root@os-node1 ~(keystone_admin)]# nova list
+--------------------------------------+-------------+--------+------------+-------------+------------------------+
| ID                                   | Name        | Status | Task State | Power State | Networks               |
+--------------------------------------+-------------+--------+------------+-------------+------------------------+
| 31000c20-5847-48eb-b2e3-6b681f5df46c | vm1_on_ceph | ACTIVE | -          | Running     | public=172.24.4.232    |
| 45c2f1a6-80ce-4ff4-8adf-237de30ca332 | vm2_on_ceph | ACTIVE | -          | Running     | public=172.24.4.231    |
+--------------------------------------+-------------+--------+------------+-------------+------------------------+
[root@os-node1 ~(keystone_admin)]# _
```

12. Check if the instance is stored in Ceph:

```
[root@os-node1 ~(keystone_admin)]#
[root@os-node1 ~(keystone_admin)]# nova list
+--------------------------------------+-------------+--------+------------+-------------+------------------------+
| ID                                   | Name        | Status | Task State | Power State | Networks               |
+--------------------------------------+-------------+--------+------------+-------------+------------------------+
| 31000c20-5847-48eb-b2e3-6b681f5df46c | vm1_on_ceph | ACTIVE | -          | Running     | public=172.24.4.232    |
| 45c2f1a6-80ce-4ff4-8adf-237de30ca332 | vm2_on_ceph | ACTIVE | -          | Running     | public=172.24.4.231    |
+--------------------------------------+-------------+--------+------------+-------------+------------------------+
[root@os-node1 ~(keystone_admin)]#
[root@os-node1 ~(keystone_admin)]# rbd -p vms ls --id cinder
31000c20-5847-48eb-b2e3-6b681f5df46c_disk
[root@os-node1 ~(keystone_admin)]# rbd info vms/31000c20-5847-48eb-b2e3-6b681f5df46c_disk --id cinder
rbd image '31000c20-5847-48eb-b2e3-6b681f5df46c_disk':
        size 1024 MB in 256 objects
        order 22 (4096 kB objects)
        block_name_prefix: rbd_data.3a1e1238e1f29
        format: 2
        features: layering, exclusive-lock, object-map, fast-diff, deep-flatten
        flags:
[root@os-node1 ~(keystone_admin)]#
```

Configuring Nova to attach Ceph RBD

In order to attach the Ceph RBD to OpenStack instances, we should configure the Nova component of OpenStack by adding the RBD user and UUID information that it needs to connect to the Ceph cluster. To do this, we need to edit /etc/nova/nova.conf on the OpenStack node and perform the steps that are given in the following section.

How to do it...

The Cinder service that we configured in the last recipe creates volumes on Ceph, however, to attach these volumes to OpenStack instances, we need to configure Nova:

1. We have already configured the following options to enable volume attachment:

   ```
   rbd_user=cinder
   rbd_secret_uuid= e279566e-bc97-46d0-bd90-68080a2a0ad8
   ```

2. To test this configuration, we will attach the Cinder volume to an OpenStack instance. List the instance and volumes to get the ID:

   ```
   # nova list
   # cinder list
   ```

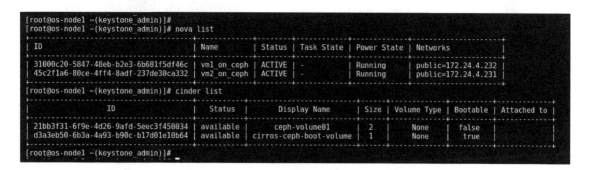

3. Attach the volume to the instance:

   ```
   # nova volume-attach 31000c20-5847-48eb-b2e3-6b681f5df46c
   21bb3f31-6f9e-4d26-9afd-5eec3f450034
   # cinder list
   ```

Working with Ceph Object Storage

4

In this chapter, we will cover the following recipes:

- Understanding Ceph object storage
- RADOS Gateway standard setup, installation, and configuration
- Creating the radosgw user
- Accessing the Ceph object storage using the S3 API
- Accessing the Ceph object storage using the Swift API
- Integrating RADOS Gateway with OpenStack Keystone
- Integrating RADOS Gateway with Hadoop S3A plugin

Introduction

Object-based storage has been getting a lot of industry attention as organizations are looking for flexibility for their enormous data. Object storage is an approach to store data in the form of objects rather than traditional files and blocks, and each object stores data, metadata, and a unique identifier. In this chapter, we will understand the object storage part of Ceph and gain practical knowledge by configuring the Ceph RADOS Gateway.

Understanding Ceph object storage

Object storage cannot be directly accessed by an operating system as a disk of a filesystem. Rather, it can only be accessed via API at the application level. Ceph is a distributed object storage system that provides an object storage interface via the Ceph object gateway, also known as the **RADOS Gateway (RGW)** interface, which has been built on top of the Ceph RADOS layer. The RGW uses librgw (RADOS Gateway Library) and librados, allowing applications to establish a connection with the Ceph object storage. The RGW provides applications with a RESTful S3 / Swift-compatible API interface to store data in the form of objects in the Ceph cluster. Ceph also supports multitenant object storage, accessible via RESTful API. In addition to this, the RGW also supports Ceph Admin APIs that can be used to manage the Ceph storage cluster using native API calls.

The librados software libraries are very flexible and can allow user applications to directly access the Ceph storage cluster via C, C++, Java, Python, and PHP bindings. Ceph object storage also has multisite capabilities, that is, it provides solutions for disaster recovery.

The following image represents a Ceph object storage:

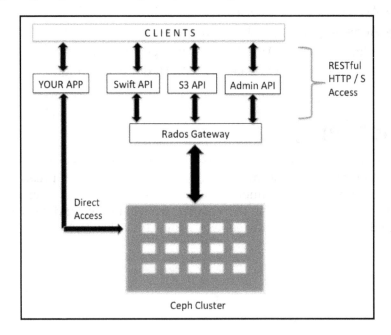

RADOS Gateway standard setup, installation, and configuration

For a production environment, it's recommended that you configure the RGW on a physical, dedicated machine. However, if your object storage workload is not too much, you can consider using any of the monitor machines as an RGW node. The RGW is a separate service that externally connects to a Ceph cluster and provides object storage access to its clients. In a production environment, it's recommended that you run more than one instance of the RGW, masked by a **Load Balancer**, as shown in the following diagram:

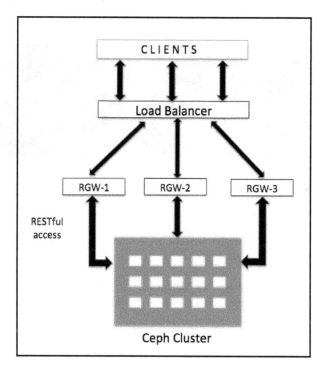

Starting with the Firefly release of Ceph, a new RGW frontend had been introduced: Civetweb, which is a lightweight standalone web server. Civetweb has been embedded directly into the `ceph-radosgw` service, making the Ceph object storage service deployment quicker and easier.

In the following recipes, we will demonstrate the RGW configuration using Civetweb on a virtual machine that will interact with the same Ceph cluster that we have created in `Chapter 1`, *Ceph – Introduction and Beyond*.

Setting up the RADOS Gateway node

To run the Ceph object storage service, we should have a running Ceph cluster and the RGW node should have access to the Ceph network.

Like you should have it as you created in `Chapter 1`, *Ceph – Introduction and Beyond* with following Ceph status:

```
[root@ceph-node2 ~]#
[root@ceph-node2 ~]# ceph -s
    cluster 585ce77b-476c-4f52-b147-93fe9424eb2a
     health HEALTH_OK
     monmap e1: 3 mons at {ceph-node1=192.168.1.101:6789/0,ceph-node2=192.168.1.102:6789/0,ceph-node3=192.168.1.103:6789/0}
            election epoch 4, quorum 0,1,2 ceph-node1,ceph-node2,ceph-node3
     osdmap e36: 9 osds: 9 up, 9 in
            flags sortbitwise,require_jewel_osds
      pgmap v80: 128 pgs, 1 pools, 0 bytes data, 0 objects
            307 MB used, 161 GB / 161 GB avail
                 128 active+clean
[root@ceph-node2 ~]#
```

How to do it...

As demonstrated in the earlier chapters, we will boot up a virtual machine using Vagrant and configure that as our RGW node:

1. Launch `rgw-node1` using `vagrantfile`, as we have done for Ceph nodes in `Chapter 1`, *Ceph – Introduction and Beyond*. Make sure you are on the host machine and under the `Ceph-Designing-and-Implementing-Scalable-Storage-Systems` repository before bringing up `rgw-node1` using Vagrant:

   ```
   # cd Ceph-Designing-and-Implementing-Scalable-Storage-Systems
   # vagrant up rgw-node1
   ```

2. Once `rgw-node1` is up, check the Vagrant status, and log into the node:

```
$ vagrant status rgw-node1
```

```
$ vagrant ssh rgw-node1
```

3. Upgrade to the latest CentOS 7.4, you can use the following command:

```
$ sudo yum update -y
```

4. Check if `rgw-node1` can reach the Ceph cluster nodes:

```
# ping ceph-node1 -c 3
# ping ceph-node2 -c 3
# ping ceph-node3 -c 3
```

5. Verify the localhost file entries, hostname, and FQDN for `rgw-node1`:

```
# cat /etc/hosts | grep -i rgw
# hostname
# hostname -f
```

```
[vagrant@rgw-node1 ~]$
[vagrant@rgw-node1 ~]$ cat /etc/hosts | grep -i rgw
127.0.0.1        rgw-node1.cephcookbook.com        rgw-node1
192.168.1.106 rgw-node1.cephcookbook.com rgw-node1
[vagrant@rgw-node1 ~]$ hostname
rgw-node1.cephcookbook.com
[vagrant@rgw-node1 ~]$ hostname -f
rgw-node1.cephcookbook.com
[vagrant@rgw-node1 ~]$
```

Installing and configuring the RADOS Gateway

The previous recipe was about setting up a virtual machine for RGW. In this recipe, we will learn to set up the `ceph-radosgw` service on this node.

How to do it...

1. To install and configure the Ceph RGW, we will use the ceph-ansbile from ceph-node1, which is our ceph-ansible and one of the monitor node. Log in to the ceph-node1 and perform the following commands:
   1. Make sure that the ceph-node1 can reach the rgw-node1 over the network by using the following command:

      ```
      # ping rgw-node1 -c 1
      ```

   2. Allow ceph-node1 a password-less SSH login to rgw-node1 and test the connection.

 The root password for rgw-node1 is the same as earlier, that is, vagrant.
   ```
   # ssh-copy-id rgw-node1
   # ssh rgw-node1 hostname
   ```

2. Add rgw-node1 to the ceph-ansible hosts file and test the Ansible ping command:

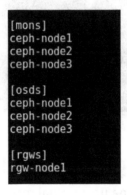

```
[mons]
ceph-node1
ceph-node2
ceph-node3

[osds]
ceph-node1
ceph-node2
ceph-node3

[rgws]
rgw-node1
```

```
# ansible all -m ping
```

```
[root@ceph-node1 ~]#
[root@ceph-node1 ~]# ansible all -m ping
ceph-node1 | SUCCESS => {
    "changed": false,
    "ping": "pong"
}
ceph-node3 | SUCCESS => {
    "changed": false,
    "ping": "pong"
}
rgw-node1 | SUCCESS => {
    "changed": false,
    "ping": "pong"
}
ceph-node2 | SUCCESS => {
    "changed": false,
    "ping": "pong"
}
[root@ceph-node1 ~]#
```

3. Update `all.yml` file to install and configure the Ceph RGW in the VM `rgw-node1`:

    ```
    [root@ceph-node1 ceph-ansible]# cd /usr/share/
                                    ceph-ansible/group_vars/
    [root@ceph-node1 group_vars]# vim all.yml
    ```

4. Enable the `radosgw_civetweb_port` and `radosgw_civetweb_bind_ip` option. In this book, `rgw-node1` has IP `192.168.1.106` and we are using port `8080`:

```
[root@ceph-node1 group_vars]#
[root@ceph-node1 group_vars]# cat all.yml | egrep 'radosgw_civetweb_port|radosgw_civetweb_bind_ip'
radosgw_civetweb_port: 8080
radosgw_civetweb_bind_ip: 192.168.1.106 # when using ipv6 enclose with brackets: "[{{ ansible_default_ipv6.address }}]"
#radosgw_civetweb_options: "port={{ radosgw_civetweb_bind_ip }}:{{ radosgw_civetweb_port }} num_threads={{ radosgw_civetweb_num_threads }}"
[root@ceph-node1 group_vars]#
```

5. Change the directory back to `/usr/share/ceph-ansible` and then run the playbook, it will install and configure the RGW in `rgw-node1`:

```
$ cd ..
$ ansible-playbook site.yml
```

```
[root@ceph-node1 group_vars]# cd ..
[root@ceph-node1 ceph-ansible]# ansible-playbook site.yml
[DEPRECATION WARNING]: docker is kept for backwards compatibility but usage is discouraged.
This feature will be removed in a future
 release. Deprecation warnings can be disabled by setting deprecation_warnings=False in ansi

PLAY [mons,agents,osds,mdss,rgws,nfss,restapis,rbdmirrors,clients,mgrs] *******************

TASK [check for python2] *****************************************************************
ok: [ceph-node3]
ok: [rgw-node1]
ok: [ceph-node2]
ok: [ceph-node1]
```

6. Once `ceph-ansible` finishes the installation and configuration, you will have the following recap output:

```
PLAY RECAP *******************************************************************************
ceph-node1                 : ok=127   changed=6    unreachable=0    failed=0
ceph-node2                 : ok=121   changed=6    unreachable=0    failed=0
ceph-node3                 : ok=122   changed=6    unreachable=0    failed=0
rgw-node1                  : ok=46    changed=14   unreachable=0    failed=0

[root@ceph-node1 ceph-ansible]#
```

7. Once it completes, you will have the `radosgw` daemon running in `rgw-node1`:

```
[root@rgw-node1 ~]#
[root@rgw-node1 ~]# ps -ef | grep rados
ceph      3558     1  0 22:27 ?        00:00:00 /usr/bin/radosgw -f --cluster ceph --name client.rgw.rgw-node1 --setuser ceph --setgroup ceph
root      3771  1149  0 22:31 pts/0    00:00:00 grep --color=auto rados
[root@rgw-node1 ~]#
```

8. And you will notice in the following screenshot that we now have more pools which got created for RGW:

```
[root@ceph-node2 ~]# ceph -s
    cluster 585ce77b-476c-4f52-b147-93fe9424eb2a
     health HEALTH_OK
     monmap e1: 3 mons at {ceph-node1=192.168.1.101:6789/0,ceph-node2=192.168.1.102:6789/0,ceph-node3=192.168.1.103:6789/0}
            election epoch 6, quorum 0,1,2 ceph-node1,ceph-node2,ceph-node3
     osdmap e74: 9 osds: 9 up, 9 in
            flags sortbitwise,require_jewel_osds
      pgmap v205: 176 pgs, 7 pools, 1588 bytes data, 171 objects
            317 MB used, 161 GB / 161 GB avail
                 176 active+clean
[root@ceph-node2 ~]# ceph osd pool ls
rbd
.rgw.root
default.rgw.control
default.rgw.data.root
default.rgw.gc
default.rgw.log
default.rgw.users.uid
```

9. The Civetweb web server that is embedded into the `radosgw` daemon should now be running on the specified port, `8080`:

```
[root@rgw-node1 ~]#
[root@rgw-node1 ~]# netstat -tnlp | grep radosgw
tcp        0      0 192.168.1.106:8080      0.0.0.0:*           LISTEN      3558/radosgw
[root@rgw-node1 ~]#
```

10. You will have the following entries related to this RGW in `rgw-node1` VM `/etc/ceph/ceph.conf`:

```
[client.rgw.rgw-node1]
host = rgw-node1
keyring = /var/lib/ceph/radosgw/ceph-rgw.rgw-node1/keyring
rgw socket path = /tmp/radosgw-rgw-node1.sock
log file = /var/log/ceph/ceph-rgw-rgw-node1.log
rgw data = /var/lib/ceph/radosgw/ceph-rgw.rgw-node1
rgw frontends = civetweb port=192.168.1.106:8080 num_threads=100
rgw resolve cname = False
```

Creating the radosgw user

To use the Ceph object storage, we should create an initial Ceph object gateway user for the S3 interface and then create a subuser for the Swift interface.

How to do it...

Following steps will help you to create `radosgw` user:

1. Make sure that the `rgw-node1` is able to access the Ceph cluster:

   ```
   # ceph -s -k /var/lib/ceph/radosgw/ceph-rgw.rgw-node1/keyring
     --name client.rgw.rgw-node1
   ```

2. Create a RADOS Gateway user for the S3 access:

   ```
   # radosgw-admin user create --uid=pratima
     --display-name="Pratima Umrao"
     --email=pratima@cephcookbook.com
     -k /var/lib/ceph/radosgw/ceph-rgw.rgw-node1/keyring
     --name client.rgw.rgw-node1
   ```

```json
{
    "user_id": "pratima",
    "display_name": "Pratima Umrao",
    "email": "pratima@cephcookbook.com",
    "suspended": 0,
    "max_buckets": 1000,
    "auid": 0,
    "subusers": [],
    "keys": [
        {
            "user": "pratima",
            "access_key": "7L0HXU1F6DK9RTB8HK8M",
            "secret_key": "kNcVjuMUWxnNv3enKDCHGAkZu5oeYqKKbjiUKfSI"
        }
    ],
    "swift_keys": [],
    "caps": [],
    "op_mask": "read, write, delete",
    "default_placement": "",
    "placement_tags": [],
    "bucket_quota": {
        "enabled": false,
        "max_size_kb": -1,
        "max_objects": -1
    },
    "user_quota": {
        "enabled": false,
        "max_size_kb": -1,
        "max_objects": -1
    },
    "temp_url_keys": []
}
```

3. The values keys (`access_key`) and the keys (`secret_key`) would be required later in this chapter for access validation.

4. To use Ceph object storage with the Swift API, we need to create a Swift subuser on the Ceph RGW:

```
# radosgw-admin subuser create --uid=pratima
  --subuser=pratima:swift --access=full
  -k /var/lib/ceph/radosgw/ceph-rgw.rgw-node1/keyring
  --name client.rgw.rgw-node1
```

```
{
    "user_id": "pratima",
    "display_name": "Pratima Umrao",
    "email": "pratima@cephcookbook.com",
    "suspended": 0,
    "max_buckets": 1000,
    "auid": 0,
    "subusers": [
        {
            "id": "pratima:swift",
            "permissions": "full-control"
        }
    ],
    "keys": [
        {
            "user": "pratima",
            "access_key": "7L0HXU1F6DK9RTB8HK8M",
            "secret_key": "kNcVjuMUWxnNv3enKDCHGAkZu5oeYqKKbjiUKfSI"
        }
    ],
    "swift_keys": [
        {
            "user": "pratima:swift",
            "secret_key": "whUTYlKFeKvKO59O6wFOANoyoH37SUJEjBD9cQmH"
        }
    ],
    "caps": [],
    "op_mask": "read, write, delete",
    "default_placement": "",
    "placement_tags": [],
    "bucket_quota": {
        "enabled": false,
        "max_size_kb": -1,
        "max_objects": -1
    },
    "user_quota": {
        "enabled": false,
        "max_size_kb": -1,
        "max_objects": -1
    },
    "temp_url_keys": []
}
```

See also...

The *Accessing the Ceph object storage using the Swift API* recipe.

Accessing the Ceph object storage using S3 API

Amazon Web Services offer **Simple Storage Service** (**S3**) that provides storage through web interfaces such as REST. Ceph extends its compatibility with S3 through the RESTful API. S3 client applications can access Ceph object storage based on access and secret keys. S3 also requires a DNS server in place as it uses the virtual host bucket naming convention, that is, `<object_name>.<RGW_Fqdn>`.

How to do it...

Perform the following steps to configure DNS on the `rgw-node1` node. If you have an existing DNS server, you can skip the DNS configuration and use your DNS server.

Configuring DNS

1. Install bind packages on the `ceph-rgw` node:

   ```
   # yum install bind* -y
   ```

2. Edit `/etc/named.conf` and add information for IP addresses, IP range, and zone, which are mentioned as follows. You can match the changes from the author's version of the `named.conf` file provided with this book:

   ```
   listen-on port 53 { 127.0.0.1;192.168.1.106; };
   ### Add DNS IP ###
   allow-query { localhost;192.168.1.0/24; };
   ### Add IP Range ###
   ```

```
options {
        listen-on port 53 { 127.0.0.1;192.168.1.106; };   ### Add DNS IP ###
        listen-on-v6 port 53 { ::1; };
        directory       "/var/named";
        dump-file       "/var/named/data/cache_dump.db";
        statistics-file "/var/named/data/named_stats.txt";
        memstatistics-file "/var/named/data/named_mem_stats.txt";
        allow-query     { localhost;192.168.1.0/24; };    ### Add IP Range ###
```

```
### Add new zone for the domain cephcookbook.com before EOF ###
zone "cephcookbook.com" IN {
type master;
file "db.cephcookbook.com";
allow-update { none; };
};
```

```
### Add new zone for domain cephcookbook.com before EOF  ###
zone "cephcookbook.com" IN {
type master;
file "db.cephcookbook.com";
allow-update { none; };
};
include "/etc/named.rfc1912.zones";
include "/etc/named.root.key";
```

3. Create the zone file /var/named/db.cephcookbook.com, with the following content:

```
@ 86400 IN SOA cephcookbook.com. root.cephcookbook.com. (
20091028 ; serial yyyy-mm-dd
10800 ; refresh every 15 min
3600 ; retry every hour
3600000 ; expire after 1 month +
86400 ); min ttl of 1 day
@ 86400 IN NS cephbookbook.com.
@ 86400 IN A 192.168.1.106
* 86400 IN CNAME @
```

```
[root@rgw-node1 named]#
[root@rgw-node1 named]# cat /var/named/db.cephcookbook.com
@ 86400 IN SOA cephcookbook.com. root.cephcookbook.com. (
20091028 ; serial yyyy-mm-dd
10800 ; refresh every 15 min
3600 ; retry every hour
3600000 ; expire after 1 month +
86400 ); min ttl of 1 day
@ 86400 IN NS cephbookbook.com.
@ 86400 IN A 192.168.1.106
* 86400 IN CNAME @
[root@rgw-node1 named]#
```

4. Edit `/etc/resolve.conf` and add the following content on top of the file:

```
search cephcookbook.com
nameserver 192.168.1.106
```

```
[root@rgw-node1 named]# cat /etc/resolv.conf
# Generated by NetworkManager
search cephcookbook.com
nameserver 192.168.1.106
search redhat.com cephcookbook.com
nameserver 10.0.2.3
[root@rgw-node1 named]#
```

5. Start the named service:

```
# systemctl start named.service
```

6. Test the DNS configuration files for any syntax errors:

```
# named-checkconf /etc/named.conf
# named-checkzone cephcookbook.com
              /var/named/db.cephcookbook.com
```

```
[root@rgw-node1 named]#
[root@rgw-node1 named]# named-checkconf /etc/named.conf
[root@rgw-node1 named]# named-checkzone cephcookbook.com /var/named/db.cephcookbook.com
zone cephcookbook.com/IN: loaded serial 20091028
OK
[root@rgw-node1 named]#
```

7. Test the DNS server:

```
# dig rgw-node1.cephcookbook.com
# nslookup rgw-node1.cephcookbook.com
```

Configuring the s3cmd client

To access Ceph object storage via the S3 API, we should configure the client machine with s3cmd as well as the DNS client settings. Perform the following steps to configure the s3cmd client machine:

1. Bring up the `client-node1` virtual machine using Vagrant. This virtual machine will be used as a client machine for S3 object storage.

2. Go to the `Ceph-Designing-and-Implementing-Scalable-Storage-Systems` repository directory and run the following command:

```
$ vagrant up client-node1
$ vagrant ssh client-node1
```

3. Upgrade the `client-node1` to the latest CentOS 7.4:

```
$ sudo yum update -y
$reboot
$ vagrant ssh client-node1
```

4. Install the `bind-utils` package:

```
# yum install bind-utils -y
```

5. On the `client-node1` machine, update `/etc/resolve.conf` with the DNS server entries on top of the file:

```
search cephcookbook.com
nameserver 192.168.1.106
```

6. Test the DNS settings on the `client-node1`:

```
# dig rgw-node1.cephcookbook.com
# nslookup rgw-node1.cephcookbook.com
```

7. `client-node1` should be able to resolve all the subdomains for `rgw-node1.cephcookbook.com`:

```
# ping mj.rgw-node1.cephcookbook.com -c 1
# ping anything.rgw-node1.cephcookbook.com -c 1
```

Configure the S3 client (s3cmd) on client-node1

Following commands are used for configuring `s3cmd` on the `client-node1`:

1. Install `s3cmd` using the following command:

```
# yum install s3cmd -y
```

2. Configure `s3cmd` by providing the `access_key` and `secret_key` of the user, `pratima`, which we created earlier in this chapter. Execute the following command and follow the prompts:

```
# s3cmd --configure
```

```
[root@client-node1 ~]#
[root@client-node1 ~]# s3cmd --configure

Enter new values or accept defaults in brackets with Enter.
Refer to user manual for detailed description of all options.

Access key and Secret key are your identifiers for Amazon S3. Leave them empty for using the env variables.
Access Key: 7L0HXU1F6DK9RTB8HK8M
Secret Key: kNcVjuMUWxnNv3enKDCHGAkZu5oeYqKKbjiUKfSI
Default Region [US]:

Encryption password is used to protect your files from reading
by unauthorized persons while in transfer to S3
Encryption password:
Path to GPG program [/bin/gpg]:

When using secure HTTPS protocol all communication with Amazon S3
servers is protected from 3rd party eavesdropping. This method is
slower than plain HTTP, and can only be proxied with Python 2.7 or newer
Use HTTPS protocol [Yes]: no

On some networks all internet access must go through a HTTP proxy.
Try setting it here if you can't connect to S3 directly
HTTP Proxy server name:

New settings:
  Access Key: 7L0HXU1F6DK9RTB8HK8M
  Secret Key: kNcVjuMUWxnNv3enKDCHGAkZu5oeYqKKbjiUKfSI
  Default Region: US
  Encryption password:
  Path to GPG program: /bin/gpg
  Use HTTPS protocol: False
  HTTP Proxy server name:
  HTTP Proxy server port: 0

Test access with supplied credentials? [Y/n] n

Save settings? [y/N] y
Configuration saved to '/root/.s3cfg'
[root@client-node1 ~]#
```

The `s3cmd --configure` command will create `/root/.s3cfg`.

3. Edit this file for the RGW host details. Modify `host_base` and `host_bucket`, as shown. Make sure these lines do not have trailing spaces at the end:

```
host_base = rgw-node1.cephcookbook.com:8080
host_bucket = %(bucket).rgw-node1.cephcookbook.com:8080
```

```
[root@client-node1 ~]#
[root@client-node1 ~]# cat .s3cfg | egrep "access_key|secret_key|host_base|host_bucket"
access_key = 7L0HXU1F6DK9RTB8HK8M
host_base = rgw-node1.cephcookbook.com:8080
host_bucket = %(bucket).rgw-node1.cephcookbook.com:8080
secret_key = kNcVjuMUWxnNv3enKDCHGAkZu5oeYqKKbjiUKfSI
[root@client-node1 ~]#
```

4. Finally, we will create buckets and put objects into them:

```
# s3cmd mb s3://first-bucket
# s3cmd ls
# s3cmd put /etc/hosts s3://first-bucket
# s3cmd ls s3://first-bucket
```

```
[root@client-node1 ~]#
[root@client-node1 ~]# s3cmd mb s3://first-bucket
Bucket 's3://first-bucket/' created
[root@client-node1 ~]# s3cmd ls
2017-09-24 22:53  s3://first-bucket
[root@client-node1 ~]#
[root@client-node1 ~]# s3cmd put /etc/hosts s3://first-bucket
upload: '/etc/hosts' -> 's3://first-bucket/hosts'  [1 of 1]
 789 of 789   100% in    1s    538.43 B/s  done
[root@client-node1 ~]#
[root@client-node1 ~]# s3cmd ls s3://first-bucket
2017-09-24 22:53       789   s3://first-bucket/hosts
[root@client-node1 ~]#
```

Accessing the Ceph object storage using the Swift API

Ceph supports RESTful API that is compatible with the basic data access model of the Swift API. In the last section, we covered accessing the Ceph cluster via the S3 API; in this section, we will learn to access it via the Swift API.

How to do it...

To use Ceph object storage with the Swift API, we need the Swift sub-user and secret keys that we created earlier in this chapter. This user information will then be passed using the Swift CLI tool in order to access the Ceph object storage:

1. On the `client-node1`, a virtual machine installs the Python Swift client:

```
# easy_install pip
# pip install --upgrade setuptools
# pip install --upgrade python-swiftclient
```

2. Get the swift sub-user and secret keys from the RGW node:

```
# radosgw-admin user info --uid pratima
-k /var/lib/ceph/radosgw/ceph-rgw.rgw-node1/keyring
--name client.rgw.rgw-node1
```

3. Access Ceph object storage by listing the default bucket:

```
# swift -A http://192.168.1.106:8080/auth/1.0
-U pratima:swift
-K whUTYlKFeKvKO5906wFOANoyoH37SUJEjBD9cQmH list
```

4. Add a new bucket, `second-bucket`:

```
# swift -A http://192.168.1.106:8080/auth/1.0
-U pratima:swift
-K whUTYlKFeKvKO5906wFOANoyoH37SUJEjBD9cQmH post second-bucket
```

5. List the buckets; it should show the new `second-bucket` as well:

```
# swift -A http://192.168.1.106:8080/auth/1.0
-U pratima:swift
-K whUTYlKFeKvKO5906wFOANoyoH37SUJEjBD9cQmH list
```

```
[root@client-node1 ~]#
[root@client-node1 ~]# swift -A http://192.168.1.106:8080/auth/1.0 -U pratima:swift -K whUTYlKFeKvKO5906wFOANoyoH37SUJEjBD9cQmH list
first-bucket
[root@client-node1 ~]# swift -A http://192.168.1.106:8080/auth/1.0 -U pratima:swift -K whUTYlKFeKvKO5906wFOANoyoH37SUJEjBD9cQmH post second-bucket
[root@client-node1 ~]# swift -A http://192.168.1.106:8080/auth/1.0 -U pratima:swift -K whUTYlKFeKvKO5906wFOANoyoH37SUJEjBD9cQmH list
first-bucket
second-bucket
[root@client-node1 ~]#
```

Integrating RADOS Gateway with OpenStack Keystone

Ceph can be integrated with the OpenStack identity management service, *Keystone*. With this integration, the Ceph RGW is configured to accept Keystone tokens for user authority. So, any user who is validated by Keystone will get rights to access the RGW.

How to do it...

Execute the following command on your `openstack-node1`, unless otherwise specified:

1. Configure OpenStack to point to the Ceph RGW by creating the service and its endpoints:

   ```
   # keystone service-create --name swift --type object-store
   --description "ceph object store"
   ```

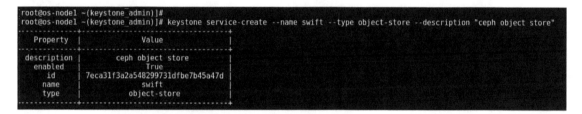

   ```
   # keystone endpoint-create --service-id
   6614554878344bbeaa7fec0d5dccca7f --publicurl
   http://192.168.1.106:8080/swift/v1 --internalurl
   http://192.168.1.106:8080/swift/v1 --adminurl
   http://192.168.1.106:8080/swift/v1 --region RegionOne
   ```

2. Get the Keystone admin token, which will be used for the RGW configuration:

   ```
   # cat /etc/keystone/keystone.conf | grep -i admin_token
   ```

3. Create a directory for certificates:

```
# mkdir -p /var/ceph/nss
```

4. Generate OpenSSL certificates:

```
# openssl x509 -in /etc/keystone/ssl/certs/ca.pem
-pubkey|certutil -d /var/ceph/nss -A -n ca -t "TCu,Cu,Tuw"
# openssl x509 -in /etc/keystone/ssl/certs/signing_cert.pem
-pubkey | certutil -A -d /var/ceph/nss -n signing_cert
-t "P,P,P"
```

```
[root@os-node1 ~(keystone_admin)]# cat /etc/keystone/keystone.conf | grep -i admin_token
#admin_token=ADMIN
admin_token=f72adb0238d74bb885005744ce526148
[root@os-node1 ~(keystone_admin)]#
[root@os-node1 ~(keystone_admin)]# mkdir -p /var/ceph/nss
[root@os-node1 ~(keystone_admin)]# openssl x509 -in /etc/keystone/ssl/certs/ca.pem -pubkey|certutil -d /var/ceph/nss -A -n ca -t "TCu,Cu,Tuw"
Notice: Trust flag u is set automatically if the private key is present.
[root@os-node1 ~(keystone_admin)]#
[root@os-node1 ~(keystone_admin)]# openssl x509 -in /etc/keystone/ssl/certs/signing_cert.pem -pubkey | certutil -A -d /var/ceph/nss -n signing_cert -t "P,P,P"
[root@os-node1 ~(keystone_admin)]# ls -l /var/ceph/nss/
total 76
-rw------- 1 root root 65536 Sep 26 07:19 cert8.db
-rw------- 1 root root 16384 Sep 26 07:19 key3.db
-rw------- 1 root root 16384 Sep 26 07:19 secmod.db
[root@os-node1 ~(keystone_admin)]#
```

5. Create the `/var/ceph/nss` directory on `rgw-node1`:

```
# mkdir -p /var/ceph/nss
```

6. From `openstack-node1`, copy OpenSSL certificates to `rgw-node1`. If you are logging in for the first time, you will get an SSH confirmation; type `yes` and then type the root password, which is `vagrant` for all the machines:

```
# scp /var/ceph/nss/* rgw-node1:/var/ceph/nss
```

7. Update `/etc/ceph/ceph.conf` on `rgw-node1` with the following entries under the `[client.rgw.rgw-node1]` section:

```
rgw keystone url = http://192.168.1.111:5000
rgw keystone admin token = f72adb0238d74bb885005744ce526148
rgw keystone accepted roles = admin, Member, swiftoperator
rgw keystone token cache size = 500
rgw keystone revocation interval = 60
rgw s3 auth use keystone = true
nss db path = /var/ceph/nss
```

`rgw keystone url` must be the Keystone management URL that can be gotten from the `# keystone endpoint-list` command. `rgw keystone admin token` is the token value that we saved in *step 2* of this recipe.

8. Finally, restart the `ceph-radosgw` service:

   ```
   # systemctl restart ceph-radosgw.target
   ```

9. Now, to test the Keystone and Ceph integration, switch back to `openstack-node1` and run the basic Swift commands, and it should not ask for any user keys:

   ```
   # export OS_STORAGE_URL=http://192.168.1.106:8080/swift/v1
   # swift list
   # swift post swift-test-bucket
   # swift list
   ```

```
[root@os-node1 ~(keystone_admin)]#
[root@os-node1 ~(keystone_admin)]# export OS_STORAGE_URL=http://192.168.1.106:8080/swift/v1
[root@os-node1 ~(keystone_admin)]# swift list
[root@os-node1 ~(keystone_admin)]# swift post swift-test-bucket
[root@os-node1 ~(keystone_admin)]# swift list
swift-test-bucket
[root@os-node1 ~(keystone_admin)]# swift stat swift-test-bucket
                      Account: v1
                    Container: swift-test-bucket
                      Objects: 0
                        Bytes: 0
                     Read ACL:
                    Write ACL:
                      Sync To:
                     Sync Key:
                Accept-Ranges: bytes
             X-Storage-Policy: default-placement
 X-Container-Bytes-Used-Actual: 0
                  X-Timestamp: 1506400950.36066
                   X-Trans-Id: tx00000000000000000000c-0059c9dabf-4405b-default
                 Content-Type: text/plain; charset=utf-8
[root@os-node1 ~(keystone_admin)]#
```

10. Let us verify if the container `swift-test-bucket` got created in the RGW:

```
[root@rgw-node1 ~]#
[root@rgw-node1 ~]# radosgw-admin bucket list -k /var/lib/ceph/radosgw/ceph-rgw.rgw-node1/keyring --name client.rgw.rgw-node1
[
    "first-bucket",
    "swift-test-bucket",
    "second-bucket"
]
[root@rgw-node1 ~]#
```

Integrating RADOS Gateway with Hadoop S3A plugin

For data analytics applications that require **Hadoop Distributed File System (HDFS)** access, the Ceph object gateway can be accessed using the Apache S3A connector for Hadoop. The S3A connector is an open source tool that presents S3 compatible object storage as an HDFS file system with HDFS file system read and write semantics to the applications while data is stored in the Ceph object gateway.

Ceph object gateway Jewel version 10.2.9 is fully compatible with the S3A connector that ships with Hadoop 2.7.3.

How to do it...

You can use `client-node1` to configure Hadoop S3A client.

1. Install Java packages in the `client-node1`:

    ```
    # yum install java* -y
    ```

    ```
    Installed:
      java-1.6.0-openjdk.x86_64 1:1.6.0.41-1.13.13.1.el7_3
      java-1.6.0-openjdk-devel.x86_64 1:1.6.0.41-1.13.13.1.el7_3
      java-1.6.0-openjdk-src.x86_64 1:1.6.0.41-1.13.13.1.el7_3
      java-1.7.0-openjdk-accessibility.x86_64 1:1.7.0.151-2.6.11.1.el7_4
      java-1.7.0-openjdk-devel.x86_64 1:1.7.0.151-2.6.11.1.el7_4
      java-1.7.0-openjdk-javadoc.noarch 1:1.7.0.151-2.6.11.1.el7_4
      java-1.8.0-openjdk.x86_64 1:1.8.0.144-0.b01.el7_4
      java-1.8.0-openjdk-accessibility-debug.x86_64 1:1.8.0.144-0.b01.el7_4
      java-1.8.0-openjdk-demo.x86_64 1:1.8.0.144-0.b01.el7_4
      java-1.8.0-openjdk-devel.x86_64 1:1.8.0.144-0.b01.el7_4
      java-1.8.0-openjdk-headless.x86_64 1:1.8.0.144-0.b01.el7_4
      java-1.8.0-openjdk-javadoc.noarch 1:1.8.0.144-0.b01.el7_4
      java-1.8.0-openjdk-javadoc-zip.noarch 1:1.8.0.144-0.b01.el7_4
      java-1.8.0-openjdk-src.x86_64 1:1.8.0.144-0.b01.el7_4
      java-atk-wrapper.x86_64 0:0.30.4-5.el7
      java-dirq-javadoc.noarch 0:1.8-1.el7
      java-oauth-javadoc.noarch 0:20100601-13.el7
      java_cup-javadoc.noarch 1:0.11a-16.el7
      javacc.noarch 0:5.0-10.el7
      javacc-javadoc.noarch 0:5.0-10.el7
      javacc-maven-plugin.noarch 0:2.6-17.el7
      javamail.noarch 0:1.4.6-8.el7
      javapackages-tools.noarch 0:3.4.1-11.el7
      javaparser-javadoc.noarch 0:1.0.11-3.el7
      javassist-javadoc.noarch 0:3.16.1-10.el7
      javawriter.noarch 0:2.5.1-4.el7
    ```

2. Download the Hadoop `.tar` file from `https://archive.apache.org/dist/hadoop/core/hadoop-2.7.3/hadoop-2.7.3.tar.gz`:

```
[root@client-node1 ~]# wget https://archive.apache.org/dist/hadoop/core/hadoop-2.7.3/hadoop-2.7.3.tar.gz
--2017-09-27 05:25:52--  https://archive.apache.org/dist/hadoop/core/hadoop-2.7.3/hadoop-2.7.3.tar.gz
Resolving archive.apache.org (archive.apache.org)... 163.172.17.199
Connecting to archive.apache.org (archive.apache.org)|163.172.17.199|:443... connected.
HTTP request sent, awaiting response... 200 OK
Length: 214092195 (204M) [application/x-gzip]
Saving to: 'hadoop-2.7.3.tar.gz'

100%[==================================================================================>]

2017-09-27 05:26:44 (4.03 MB/s) - 'hadoop-2.7.3.tar.gz' saved [214092195/214092195]

[root@client-node1 ~]#
```

3. Extract the Hadoop `.tar` file:

   # tar -xvf hadoop-2.7.3.tar.gz

```
[root@client-node1 ~]#
[root@client-node1 ~]# cd hadoop-2.7.3
[root@client-node1 hadoop-2.7.3]# ll
total 116
drwxr-xr-x 2 root root  4096 Aug 18  2016 bin
drwxr-xr-x 3 root root    19 Aug 18  2016 etc
drwxr-xr-x 2 root root   101 Aug 18  2016 include
drwxr-xr-x 3 root root    19 Aug 18  2016 lib
drwxr-xr-x 2 root root  4096 Aug 18  2016 libexec
-rw-r--r-- 1 root root 84854 Aug 18  2016 LICENSE.txt
-rw-r--r-- 1 root root 14978 Aug 18  2016 NOTICE.txt
-rw-r--r-- 1 root root  1366 Aug 18  2016 README.txt
drwxr-xr-x 2 root root  4096 Aug 18  2016 sbin
drwxr-xr-x 4 root root    29 Aug 18  2016 share
[root@client-node1 hadoop-2.7.3]#
```

4. Add the following in the `.bashrc` file:

```
export JAVA_HOME=/usr/lib/jvm/jre-1.8.0-openjdk
export
PATH=/usr/local/sbin:/usr/local/bin:/usr/sbin:/usr/bin:/root/
                                bin:/root/hadoop-2.7.3/bin
```

```
[root@client-node1 ~]#
[root@client-node1 ~]# cat .bashrc | grep export
export JAVA_HOME=/usr/lib/jvm/jre-1.8.0-openjdk
export PATH=/usr/local/sbin:/usr/local/bin:/usr/sbin:/usr/bin:/root/bin:/root/hadoop-2.7.3/bin
[root@client-node1 ~]#
```

5. Update the `/root/hadoop-2.7.3/etc/hadoop/core-site.xml` file with the following details. Add the RGW node IP and Port and we have the RGW user `pratima` as the access key and secret key.

```
<!-- Put site-specific property overrides in this file. -->

<configuration>

<!-- RGW node IP and Port. -->

<property>
  <name>fs.s3a.endpoint</name>
  <value>192.168.1.106:8080</value>
</property>

<!-- RGW user pratima access key. -->

<property>
  <name>fs.s3a.access.key</name>
  <value>7L0HXU1F6DK9RTB8HK8M</value>
</property>

<!-- RGW user pratima secret key. -->

<property>
  <name>fs.s3a.secret.key</name>
  <value>kNcVjuMUWxnNv3enKDCHGAkZu5oeYqKKbjiUKfSI</value>
</property>

<property>
  <name>fs.s3a.buffer.dir</name>
  <value>${hadoop.tmp.dir}/s3a</value>
</property>

<property>
  <name>test.fs.s3a.encryption.enabled</name>
  <value>false</value>
</property>

<property>
  <name>fs.s3a.connection.ssl.enabled</name>
  <value>false</value>
</property>

<property>
  <name>fs.s3a.multipart.size</name>
  <value>104857600</value>
</property>

<!-- necessary for Hadoop to load our filesystem driver -->
<property>
  <name>fs.s3a.impl</name>
  <value>org.apache.hadoop.fs.s3a.S3AFileSystem</value>
</property>

</configuration>
```

6. You can now upload a file using the `hadoop distcp` command to your RGW
   `first-bucket`:

   # **hadoop distcp /root/anaconda-ks.cfg s3a://first-bucket/**

   You will have initial map logs in the command line:

```
[root@client-node1 ~]# hadoop distcp /root/anaconda-ks.cfg s3a://first-bucket/

17/09/27 05:41:45 INFO tools.DistCp: Input Options: DistCpOptions{atomicCommit=false, syncFolder=false, deleteMissing=false, ignoreFailures=false, m
'uniformsize', sourceFileListing=null, sourcePaths=[/root/anaconda-ks.cfg], targetPath=s3a://first-bucket/, targetPathExists=true, preserveRawXattrs
17/09/27 05:41:45 INFO Configuration.deprecation: session.id is deprecated. Instead, use dfs.metrics.session-id
17/09/27 05:41:45 INFO jvm.JvmMetrics: Initializing JVM Metrics with processName=JobTracker, sessionId=
17/09/27 05:41:51 INFO Configuration.deprecation: io.sort.mb is deprecated. Instead, use mapreduce.task.io.sort.mb
17/09/27 05:41:51 INFO Configuration.deprecation: io.sort.factor is deprecated. Instead, use mapreduce.task.io.sort.factor
17/09/27 05:41:51 INFO jvm.JvmMetrics: Cannot initialize JVM Metrics with processName=JobTracker, sessionId= - already initialized
17/09/27 05:41:51 INFO mapreduce.JobSubmitter: number of splits:1
17/09/27 05:41:51 INFO mapreduce.JobSubmitter: Submitting tokens for job: job_local967237231_0001
17/09/27 05:41:51 INFO mapreduce.Job: The url to track the job: http://localhost:8080/
17/09/27 05:41:51 INFO tools.DistCp: DistCp job-id: job_local967237231_0001
17/09/27 05:41:51 INFO mapreduce.Job: Running job: job_local967237231_0001
17/09/27 05:41:51 INFO mapred.LocalJobRunner: OutputCommitter set in config null
17/09/27 05:41:51 INFO output.FileOutputCommitter: File Output Committer Algorithm version is 1
17/09/27 05:41:51 INFO mapred.LocalJobRunner: OutputCommitter is org.apache.hadoop.tools.mapred.CopyCommitter
17/09/27 05:41:52 INFO mapred.LocalJobRunner: Waiting for map tasks
17/09/27 05:41:52 INFO mapred.LocalJobRunner: Starting task: attempt_local967237231_0001_m_000000_0
17/09/27 05:41:52 INFO output.FileOutputCommitter: File Output Committer Algorithm version is 1
17/09/27 05:41:52 INFO mapred.Task:  Using ResourceCalculatorProcessTree : [ ]
17/09/27 05:41:52 INFO mapred.MapTask: Processing split: file:/tmp/hadoop-root/mapred/staging/root1557284174/.staging/_distcp-1998956257/fileList.se
17/09/27 05:41:52 INFO output.FileOutputCommitter: File Output Committer Algorithm version is 1
17/09/27 05:41:52 INFO mapreduce.Job: Job job_local967237231_0001 running in uber mode : false
17/09/27 05:41:52 INFO mapreduce.Job:  map 0% reduce 0%
17/09/27 05:41:57 INFO mapred.CopyMapper: Copying file:/root/anaconda-ks.cfg to s3a://first-bucket/anaconda-ks.cfg
17/09/27 05:42:01 INFO mapred.LocalJobRunner: Copying file:/root/anaconda-ks.cfg to s3a://first-bucket/anaconda-ks.cfg > map
17/09/27 05:42:01 INFO mapreduce.Job:  map 0% reduce 0%
17/09/27 05:42:15 INFO mapred.RetriableFileCopyCommand: Creating temp file: s3a://first-bucket/.distcp.tmp.attempt_local967237231_0001_m_000000_0
17/09/27 05:42:19 INFO mapred.LocalJobRunner: 100.0% Copying file:/root/anaconda-ks.cfg to s3a://first-bucket/anaconda-ks.cfg [815.0B/815.0B] > map
17/09/27 05:42:22 INFO mapred.LocalJobRunner: 100.0% Copying file:/root/anaconda-ks.cfg to s3a://first-bucket/anaconda-ks.cfg [815.0B/815.0B] > map
17/09/27 05:43:09 INFO mapred.LocalJobRunner: 100.0% Copying file:/root/anaconda-ks.cfg to s3a://first-bucket/anaconda-ks.cfg [815.0B/815.0B] > map
```

Once it will finish the upload, you will have the following logs:

```
File System Counters
        FILE: Number of bytes read=130262
        FILE: Number of bytes written=416919
        FILE: Number of read operations=0
        FILE: Number of large read operations=0
        FILE: Number of write operations=0
        S3A: Number of bytes read=0
        S3A: Number of bytes written=815
        S3A: Number of read operations=14
        S3A: Number of large read operations=0
        S3A: Number of write operations=3
Map-Reduce Framework
        Map input records=1
        Map output records=0
        Input split bytes=157
        Spilled Records=0
        Failed Shuffles=0
        Merged Map outputs=0
        GC time elapsed (ms)=22
        Total committed heap usage (bytes)=16564224
File Input Format Counters
        Bytes Read=235
File Output Format Counters
        Bytes Written=8
org.apache.hadoop.tools.mapred.CopyMapper$Counter
        BYTESCOPIED=815
        BYTESEXPECTED=815
        COPY=1
[root@client-node1 ~]#
```

7. Now you can verify if the `anaconda-ks.cfg` file got uploaded to the `first-bucket`

5
Working with Ceph Object Storage Multi-Site v2

In this chapter, we will cover the following recipes:

- Functional changes from Hammer federated configuration
- RGW multi-site v2 requirement
- Installing the Ceph RGW multi-site v2 environment
- Configuring Ceph RGW multi-site v2
- Testing user, bucket, and object sync between master and secondary sites

Introduction

A single zone configuration typically consists of one zone group, containing one zone and one or more RGW instances, where you may load balance gateway client requests between instances. In a single zone configuration, typically, multiple gateway instances point to a single Ceph storage cluster. With the Jewel release, Ceph supports several multi-site configuration options for the Ceph Object Gateway:

- **Zone**: In a zone, one or more Ceph Object Gateways are logically grouped.
- **Zone group**: A zone group is a container of multiple zones. In a multi-site configuration there should be a master zone group. All the changes to configurations are handled by the master zone group.
- **Realm**: A realm can have multiple zone groups. It allows separation of the zone groups themselves between clusters. There can be multiple realms for having different configurations in the same cluster.

- **Period**: Every realm has a corresponding current period. Each period is a container of an epoch and an unique id. A period holds the current state of configuration of the zone groups and object storage strategies. Each period's commit operation, as well as any configuration change for a non-master zone, will increment the period's epoch.

Following is the diagrammatic representation of zone configuration:

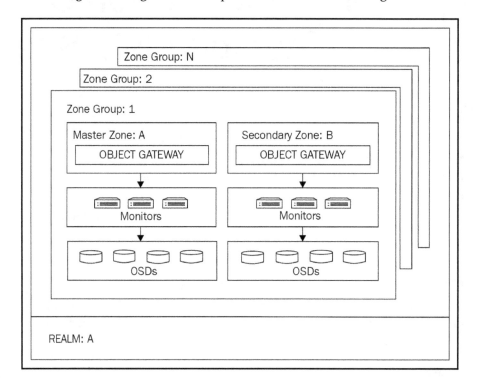

Functional changes from Hammer federated configuration

In Jewel, you can configure each Ceph Object Gateway to work in an active-active zone configuration, allowing for writes to non-master zones.

The multi-site configuration is stored within a container known as a realm. It stores zones, zone groups, and a time period with multiple epochs for tracking changes to the configuration. In Jewel, the `ceph-radosgw` daemons handle the synchronization by eliminating the need for a separate synchronization agent. Also, the new approach to synchronization allows the Ceph Object Gateway to operate with an active-active configuration instead of active-passive.

RGW multi-site v2 requirement

In this recipe, you need a minimum of two Ceph clusters and a minimum of two object gateways (one for each Ceph cluster). This is a minimum requirement for RGW multi-site.

This recipe assumes two Ceph object Gateway servers, named `us-east-1` and `us-west-1`, with two respective Ceph clusters.

In a multi-site configuration, a master zone group and a master zone are required. Additionally, each zone group requires a master zone. Zone groups may have one or more secondary, or non-master, zones.

In this recipe, the `us-east-1` host will serve as the master zone of the master zone group; the `us-west-1` host will serve as the secondary zone of the master zone group.

Installing the Ceph RGW multi-site v2 environment

You need to install two clusters, and on each cluster, you need to install a minimum of one RGW daemon for client I/O and for RGW replication.

How to do it...

In this recipe, we will use the `ceph-node1`, `ceph-node2`, and `ceph-node3` VMs for the first cluster, and in this cluster, we will use the `us-east-1` VM for the RGW node. In the second cluster, we will use the `ceph-node4`, `ceph-node5`, and `ceph-node5` VMs for cluster nodes and the `us-west-1` VM for the RGW node.

You should use Chapter 1, *Ceph – Introduction and Beyond*, for installing both clusters and Chapter 4, *Working with Ceph Object Storage*, for installing RGW nodes in both clusters:

1. Bring up all eight VMs with the help of the vagrant up command:

    ```
    $ vagrant up ceph-node1 ceph-node2 ceph-node3 ceph-node4 ceph-node5
    ceph-node6 us-east-1 us-west-1
    ```

2. Once all VMs come up, log in and update to CentOS release 7.4 and then reboot to CentOS 7.4:

    ```
    # vagrant ssh <vm-name>
    #sudo su -
    # yum update -y
    # reboot
    ```

    You should configure firewall settings and NTP settings, as given in Chapter 1, *Ceph – Introduction and Beyond*, in all the nodes used in the multi-site configuration.

Create the primary cluster and primary RGW node us-east-1:

1. Install the ceph-ansible and ansible package, as given in Chapter 1, *Ceph – Introduction and Beyond*, and then update /etc/ansible/hosts for cluster 1 VMs:

    ```
    [mons]
    ceph-node1
    ceph-node2
    ceph-node3

    [osds]
    ceph-node1
    ceph-node2
    ceph-node3

    [rgws]
    us-east-1
    ```

2. You should copy the ceph-node1 ssh key to all cluster 1 nodes, including RGW node us-east-1.

3. Update `all.yml` and `osds.yml` and other Ansible configuration files, as given in `Chapter 1`, *Ceph – Introduction and Beyond*. For the `us-east-1` RGW node, you should enable the following options in `all.yml`:

```
radosgw_civetweb_port: 8080
radosgw_civetweb_bind_ip: 192.168.1.107
```

4. After this configuration, you should run the `ansible-playbook` to install cluster 1 with the `us-east-1` RGW node:

   ansible-playbook site.yml

5. Once the `ansible-playbook` finishes installing the cluster, you will have the following cluster running; please notice the monitor names:

```
[root@ceph-node1 ~]#
[root@ceph-node1 ~]# ceph -s
    cluster 15e6d769-958f-412d-bd98-67a3852263cd
     health HEALTH_OK
     monmap e1: 3 mons at {ceph-node1=192.168.1.101:6789/0,ceph-node2=192.168.1.102:6789/0,ceph-node3=192.168.1.103:6789/0}
            election epoch 12, quorum 0,1,2 ceph-node1,ceph-node2,ceph-node3
     osdmap e42: 9 osds: 9 up, 9 in
            flags sortbitwise,require_jewel_osds
      pgmap v177: 112 pgs, 7 pools, 1588 bytes data, 171 objects
            313 MB used, 161 GB / 161 GB avail
                 112 active+clean
[root@ceph-node1 ~]#
```

Create the secondary cluster and primary RGW node `us-west-1`:

1. Install the `ceph-ansible` and `ansible` package, as given in `Chapter 1`, *Ceph – Introduction and Beyond*, and then update `/etc/ansible/hosts` for the cluster 2 VMs:

```
[mons]
ceph-node4
ceph-node5
ceph-node6

[osds]
ceph-node4
ceph-node5
ceph-node6

[rgws]
us-west-1
```

   You should copy the `ceph-node4` ssh key to all cluster 2 nodes, including the RGW node `us-west-1`.

2. Update `all.yml` and `osds.yml` and other Ansible configuration files, as given in Chapter 1, *Ceph – Introduction and Beyond*. For the `us-west-1` RGW node, you should enable the following options in `all.yml`:

```
radosgw_civetweb_port: 8080
radosgw_civetweb_bind_ip: 192.168.1.108
```

3. After this configuration, you should run the `ansible-playbook` to install cluster 1 with the `us-west-1` RGW node:

   ansible-playbook site.yml

4. Once the ansible-playbook finishes installing the cluster, you will have the following cluster running; please notice the monitor names:

```
[root@ceph-node4 ~]#
[root@ceph-node4 ~]# ceph -s
    cluster 5234b0c8-d7a2-4ae1-b06d-14d3238e705f
     health HEALTH_OK
     monmap e1: 3 mons at {ceph-node4=192.168.1.104:6789/0,ceph-node5=192.168.1.115:6789/0,ceph-node6=192.168.1.116:6789/0}
            election epoch 8, quorum 0,1,2 ceph-node4,ceph-node5,ceph-node6
     osdmap e62: 9 osds: 9 up, 9 in
            flags sortbitwise,require_jewel_osds
      pgmap v160: 112 pgs, 7 pools, 1588 bytes data, 171 objects
            313 MB used, 161 GB / 161 GB avail
                 112 active+clean
[root@ceph-node4 ~]#
```

Configuring Ceph RGW multi-site v2

In the following sections, you will be configuring the master zone and secondary zone for RGW active-active multi-site; this means you can write data on both of the sites and it will be replicated to the other site cluster. Metadata operations like user creation should only be performed on the primary site.

How to do it...

We will use the following steps to configure the RGW multi-site v2 master zone and the secondary zone:

Configuring a master zone

All RADOS Gateways in a multi-site v2 configuration will get their configuration from a `radosgw` daemon on a node within the master zone group and master zone. To configure your RADOS Gateways in a multi-site v2 configuration, you need to choose a `radosgw` instance to configure the master zone group and master zone. You should be using the `us-east-1` RGW instance to configure your master zone:

1. Create an RGW keyring in the `/etc/ceph` path and check if you are able to access the cluster with user RGW Cephx:

   ```
   # cp /var/lib/ceph/radosgw/ceph-rgw.us-east-1/
     keyring /etc/ceph/ceph.client.rgw.us-east-1.keyring
   # cat /etc/ceph/ceph.client.rgw.us-east-1.keyring
   # ceph -s --id rgw.us-east-1
   ```

   ```
   [root@us-east-1 ~]#
   [root@us-east-1 ~]# cp /var/lib/ceph/radosgw/ceph-rgw.us-east-1/keyring /etc/ceph/ceph.client.rgw.us-east-1.keyring
   [root@us-east-1 ~]# cat /etc/ceph/ceph.client.rgw.us-east-1.keyring
   [client.rgw.us-east-1]
        key = AQBXLstZpee7KhAAYhfn2S59EY5FH+XP5G8Jpg==
   [root@us-east-1 ~]#
   [root@us-east-1 ~]#
   [root@us-east-1 ~]# ceph -s --id rgw.us-east-1
       cluster 15e6d769-958f-412d-bd98-67a3852263cd
        health HEALTH_OK
        monmap e1: 3 mons at {ceph-node1=192.168.1.101:6789/0,ceph-node2=192.168.1.102:6789/0,ceph-node3=192.168.1.103:6789/0}
               election epoch 16, quorum 0,1,2 ceph-node1,ceph-node2,ceph-node3
        osdmap e50: 9 osds: 9 up, 9 in
               flags sortbitwise,require_jewel_osds
         pgmap v1680: 112 pgs, 7 pools, 1588 bytes data, 171 objects
               346 MB used, 161 GB / 161 GB avail
                    112 active+clean
   [root@us-east-1 ~]#
   ```

   Now you should be able to use this RGW Cephx user to run `radosgw-admin` commands in cluster 1.

2. Create the RGW multi-site v2 realm. Run the following command in the `us-east-1` RGW node to create a realm:

   ```
   # radosgw-admin realm create --rgw-realm=cookbookv2
                                --default --id rgw.us-east-1
   ```

   ```
   [root@us-east-1 ~]#
   [root@us-east-1 ~]# radosgw-admin realm create --rgw-realm=cookbookv2 --default --id rgw.us-east-1
   2017-09-28 00:23:11.899968 7f9f6aa259c0  1 error read_lastest_epoch .rgw.root:periods.12f916f0-3ce8-4f6c-ad8c-e08a6e0cfad8.latest_epoch
   {
       "id": "9a66b241-eda4-4577-b5d5-aaf3d259168f",
       "name": "cookbookv2",
       "current_period": "12f916f0-3ce8-4f6c-ad8c-e08a6e0cfad8",
       "epoch": 1
   }

   [root@us-east-1 ~]#
   ```

You can ignore the error message given in the preceding screenshot; it will be fixed in the future release of Jewel. It is a known issue; it is not an error, but an information message declared as an error message. This will not cause any issues in configuring RGW multi-site v2.

3. Create a master zone group. An RGW realm must have at least one RGW zone group, which will serve as the master zone group for the realm.

   Run the following command in the `us-east-1` RGW node to create a master zone group:

```
# radosgw-admin zonegroup create --rgw-zonegroup=us
  --endpoints=http://us-east-1.cephcookbook.com:8080
  --rgw-realm=cookbookv2 --master --default
  --id rgw.us-east-1
```

```
{
    "id": "f5152481-422f-4ae5-a75d-7eaeae5c2b60",
    "name": "us",
    "api_name": "us",
    "is_master": "true",
    "endpoints": [
        "http:\/\/us-east-1.cephcookbook.com:8080"
    ],
    "hostnames": [],
    "hostnames_s3website": [],
    "master_zone": "",
    "zones": [],
    "placement_targets": [],
    "default_placement": "",
    "realm_id": "9a66b241-eda4-4577-b5d5-aaf3d259168f"
}
```

4. Create a master zone. An RGW zone group must have at least one RGW zone. Run the following command in the `us-east-1` RGW node to create a master zone:

```
# radosgw-admin zone create --rgw-zonegroup=us
--rgw-zone=us-east-1 --master --default
--endpoints=http://us-east-1.cephcookbook.com:8080
--id rgw.us-east-1
```

```json
{
    "id": "286299f7-73eb-4da3-96ae-f0c6a0288d09",
    "name": "us-east-1",
    "domain_root": "us-east-1.rgw.data.root",
    "control_pool": "us-east-1.rgw.control",
    "gc_pool": "us-east-1.rgw.gc",
    "log_pool": "us-east-1.rgw.log",
    "intent_log_pool": "us-east-1.rgw.intent-log",
    "usage_log_pool": "us-east-1.rgw.usage",
    "user_keys_pool": "us-east-1.rgw.users.keys",
    "user_email_pool": "us-east-1.rgw.users.email",
    "user_swift_pool": "us-east-1.rgw.users.swift",
    "user_uid_pool": "us-east-1.rgw.users.uid",
    "system_key": {
        "access_key": "",
        "secret_key": ""
    },
    "placement_pools": [
        {
            "key": "default-placement",
            "val": {
                "index_pool": "us-east-1.rgw.buckets.index",
                "data_pool": "us-east-1.rgw.buckets.data",
                "data_extra_pool": "us-east-1.rgw.buckets.non-ec",
                "index_type": 0
            }
        }
    ],
    "metadata_heap": "",
    "realm_id": "9a66b241-eda4-4577-b5d5-aaf3d259168f"
}
```

5. Remove default zone group and zone information from cluster 1:

```
# radosgw-admin zonegroup remove --rgw-zonegroup=default
--rgw-zone=default --id rgw.us-east-1
# radosgw-admin zone delete --rgw-zone=default
--id rgw.us-east-1
# radosgw-admin zonegroup delete --rgw-zonegroup=default
--id rgw.us-east-1
```

Finally, update the period with the new us zone group and us-east-1 zone which will be used for multi-site v2:

```
# radosgw-admin period update --commit --id rgw.us-east-1
```

6. Remove the RGW default pools:

```
[root@us-east-1 ~]#
[root@us-east-1 ~]# rados lspools --id rgw.us-east-1
rbd
.rgw.root
default.rgw.control
default.rgw.data.root
default.rgw.gc
default.rgw.log
default.rgw.users.uid
[root@us-east-1 ~]#
```

```
# for i in `ceph osd pool ls --id rgw.us-east-1 |
grep default.rgw`; do ceph osd pool delete $i $i
--yes-i-really-really-mean-it --id rgw.us-east-1; done
```

```
[root@us-east-1 ~]#
[root@us-east-1 ~]# for i in `ceph osd pool ls --id rgw.us-east-1 | grep default.rgw`; do ceph osd pool delete $i $i --yes-i-really-really-mean-it --id rgw.us-east-1; done
pool 'default.rgw.control' removed
pool 'default.rgw.data.root' removed
pool 'default.rgw.gc' removed
pool 'default.rgw.log' removed
pool 'default.rgw.users.uid' removed
[root@us-east-1 ~]#
```

7. Create an RGW multi-site v2 system user. In the master zone, create a system user to establish authentication between multi-site `radosgw` daemons:

```
# radosgw-admin user create --uid="replication-user"
  --display-name="Multisite v2 replication user"
  --system --id rgw.us-east-1
```

```
{
    "user_id": "replication-user",
    "display_name": "Multisite v2 replication user",
    "email": "",
    "suspended": 0,
    "max_buckets": 1000,
    "auid": 0,
    "subusers": [],
    "keys": [
        {
            "user": "replication-user",
            "access_key": "ZYCDNTEASHKREV4X9BUJ",
            "secret_key": "4JbC4OC4vC6fy6EY6Pfp8rPZMrpDnYmETZxNyyu9"
        }
    ],
    "swift_keys": [],
    "caps": [],
    "op_mask": "read, write, delete",
    "system": "true",
    "default_placement": "",
    "placement_tags": [],
    "bucket_quota": {
        "enabled": false,
        "max_size_kb": -1,
        "max_objects": -1
    },
    "user_quota": {
        "enabled": false,
        "max_size_kb": -1,
        "max_objects": -1
    },
    "temp_url_keys": []
}
```

 Make a note of the access key and secret key for the system user named `"replication-user"` because you need to use the same access key and secret key in the secondary zone.

8. Finally, update the period with this system user information:

```
# radosgw-admin zone modify --rgw-zone=us-east-1
  --access-key=ZYCDNTEASHKREV4X9BUJ
  --secret=4JbC4OC4vC6fy6EY6Pfp8rPZMrpDnYmETZxNyyu9
  --id rgw.us-east-1
# radosgw-admin period update --commit --id rgw.us-east-1
```

9. You also need to update the `[client.rgw.us-east-1]` section of `ceph.conf` with the `rgw_zone=us-east-1` option:

```
[client.rgw.us-east-1]
rgw_zone = us-east-1
host = us-east-1
keyring = /var/lib/ceph/radosgw/ceph-rgw.us-east-1/keyring
rgw socket path = /tmp/radosgw-us-east-1.sock
log file = /var/log/ceph/ceph-rgw-us-east-1.log
rgw data = /var/lib/ceph/radosgw/ceph-rgw.us-east-1
rgw frontends = civetweb port=192.168.1.107:8080 num_threads=100
rgw resolve cname = False
```

10. Restart the `us-east-1` RGW daemon:

```
#  systemctl restart ceph-radosgw.target
```

Configuring a secondary zone

In RGW, multi-site zones replicate all data within a zone group to ensure that each zone has the same set data. In this section, you will be configuring the secondary zone. You should be using the `us-west-1` RGW instance to configure your secondary zone:

1. Create an RGW keyring in the `/etc/ceph` path and check if you are able to access the cluster with user RGW Cephx:

```
# cp /var/lib/ceph/radosgw/ceph-rgw.us-west-1/
keyring /etc/ceph/ceph.client.rgw.us-west-1.keyring
# cat /etc/ceph/ceph.client.rgw.us-west-1.keyring
# ceph -s --id rgw.us-west-1
```

```
[root@us-west-1 ~]#
[root@us-west-1 ~]# cp /var/lib/ceph/radosgw/ceph-rgw.us-west-1/keyring /etc/ceph/ceph.client.rgw.us-west-1.keyring
[root@us-west-1 ~]#
[root@us-west-1 ~]# cat /etc/ceph/ceph.client.rgw.us-west-1.keyring
[client.rgw.us-west-1]
        key = AQCTNstZZAeuDBAA3Njk/HvQMsnhBlgOFwmgAQ==
[root@us-west-1 ~]#
[root@us-west-1 ~]# ceph -s --id rgw.us-west-1
    cluster 5234b0c8-d7a2-4ae1-b06d-14d3238e705f
     health HEALTH_OK
     monmap e1: 3 mons at {ceph-node4=192.168.1.104:6789/0,ceph-node5=192.168.1.115:6789/0,ceph-node6=192.168.1.116:6789/0}
            election epoch 16, quorum 0,1,2 ceph-node4,ceph-node5,ceph-node6
     osdmap e71: 9 osds: 9 up, 9 in
            flags sortbitwise,require_jewel_osds
      pgmap v1367: 112 pgs, 7 pools, 1588 bytes data, 171 objects
            344 MB used, 161 GB / 161 GB avail
                 112 active+clean
[root@us-west-1 ~]#
```

You should be running the following steps in the secondary site RGW node `us-west-1`:

2. First of all, you need to pull the RGW realm.

   You need to use the RGW endpoint URL path and the access key and secret key of the master zone in the master zone group to pull the realm to the secondary zone RGW node:

   ```
   # radosgw-admin realm pull
   --url=http://us-east-1.cephcookbook.com:8080
   --access-key=ZYCDNTEASHKREV4X9BUJ
   --secret=4JbC4OC4vC6fy6EY6Pfp8rPZMrpDnYmETZxNyyu9
   --id rgw.us-west-1
   ```

   ```
   {
       "id": "9a66b241-eda4-4577-b5d5-aaf3d259168f",
       "name": "cookbookv2",
       "current_period": "e4844523-625e-4ce3-a0b9-c4e7635a8cf0",
       "epoch": 2
   }
   ```

3. As this is the default realm for this RGW multi-site setup, you need to make it default:

   ```
   # radosgw-admin realm default --rgw-realm=cookbookv2
                                 --id rgw.us-west-1
   ```

4. You need to pull the period from the master site, because you need to get the latest version of the zone group and zone configurations for the realm:

   ```
   # radosgw-admin period pull
   --url=http://us-east-1.cephcookbook.com:8080
   --access-key=ZYCDNTEASHKREV4X9BUJ
   --secret=4JbC4OC4vC6fy6EY6Pfp8rPZMrpDnYmETZxNyyu9
   --id rgw.us-west-1
   ```

5. Create a secondary zone. Your secondary zone RGW node is `us-west-1` and you need to run the following command in the secondary zone RGW node `us-west-1`:

```
# radosgw-admin zone create --rgw-zonegroup=us
  --rgw-zone=us-west-1 --access-key=ZYCDNTEASHKREV4X9BUJ
  --secret=4JbC4OC4vC6fy6EY6Pfp8rPZMrpDnYmETZxNyyu9
  --endpoints=http://us-west-1.cephcookbook.com:8080
  --id rgw.us-west-1
```

```json
{
    "id": "66dbedf3-1068-43c9-bc63-e4daea1fab17",
    "name": "us-west-1",
    "domain_root": "us-west-1.rgw.data.root",
    "control_pool": "us-west-1.rgw.control",
    "gc_pool": "us-west-1.rgw.gc",
    "log_pool": "us-west-1.rgw.log",
    "intent_log_pool": "us-west-1.rgw.intent-log",
    "usage_log_pool": "us-west-1.rgw.usage",
    "user_keys_pool": "us-west-1.rgw.users.keys",
    "user_email_pool": "us-west-1.rgw.users.email",
    "user_swift_pool": "us-west-1.rgw.users.swift",
    "user_uid_pool": "us-west-1.rgw.users.uid",
    "system_key": {
        "access_key": "ZYCDNTEASHKREV4X9BUJ",
        "secret_key": "4JbC4OC4vC6fy6EY6Pfp8rPZMrpDnYmETZxNyyu9"
    },
    "placement_pools": [
        {
            "key": "default-placement",
            "val": {
                "index_pool": "us-west-1.rgw.buckets.index",
                "data_pool": "us-west-1.rgw.buckets.data",
                "data_extra_pool": "us-west-1.rgw.buckets.non-ec",
                "index_type": 0
            }
        }
    ],
    "metadata_heap": "",
    "realm_id": "9a66b241-eda4-4577-b5d5-aaf3d259168f"
}
```

6. Remove the default zone from the secondary site, as you are not using it:

```
# radosgw-admin zone delete --rgw-zone=default
                            --id rgw.us-west-1
```

7. Finally, update the period on the secondary site:

```
# radosgw-admin period update --commit
  --id rgw.us-west-1
```

8. Remove the RGW default pools:

```
# for i in `ceph osd pool ls --id rgw.us-west-1 |
  grep default.rgw`; do ceph osd pool delete $i $i
  --yes-i-really-really-mean-it --id rgw.us-west-1; done
```

```
[root@us-west-1 ~]# for i in `ceph osd pool ls --id rgw.us-west-1 | grep default.rgw`; do ceph osd pool delete $i $i --yes-i-really-really-mean-it --id rgw.us-west-1; done
pool 'default.rgw.control' removed
pool 'default.rgw.data.root' removed
pool 'default.rgw.gc' removed
pool 'default.rgw.log' removed
pool 'default.rgw.users.uid' removed
[root@us-west-1 ~]#
[root@us-west-1 ~]#
[root@us-west-1 ~]#
[root@us-west-1 ~]# rados lspools --id rgw.us-west-1
rbd
.rgw.root
us-west-1.rgw.control
us-west-1.rgw.data.root
us-west-1.rgw.gc
us-west-1.rgw.log
[root@us-west-1 ~]#
```

9. You also need to update the `[client.rgw.us-west-1]` section of `ceph.conf` with the `rgw_zone=us-west-1` option:

```
[client.rgw.us-west-1]
rgw_zone = us-west-1
host = us-west-1
keyring = /var/lib/ceph/radosgw/ceph-rgw.us-west-1/keyring
rgw socket path = /tmp/radosgw-us-west-1.sock
log file = /var/log/ceph/ceph-rgw-us-west-1.log
rgw data = /var/lib/ceph/radosgw/ceph-rgw-us-west-1
rgw frontends = civetweb port=192.168.1.108:8080 num_threads=100
rgw resolve cname = False
```

10. Then, restart the `us-west-1` RGW daemon:

```
# systemctl restart ceph-radosgw.target
```

With this, you have both the master and secondary site up and running with active-active asynchronous replication, and now you can check the synchronization status on both of the sites.

Checking the synchronization status

The following commands will be used for checking the status between the master zone and the secondary zone:

1. Cluster 1 master zone `us-east-1` synchronization status:

```
# radosgw-admin sync status --id rgw.us-east-1
```

```
          realm 9a66b241-eda4-4577-b5d5-aaf3d259168f (cookbookv2)
      zonegroup f5152481-422f-4ae5-a75d-7eaeae5c2b60 (us)
           zone 286299f7-73eb-4da3-96ae-f0c6a0288d09 (us-east-1)
  metadata sync no sync (zone is master)
      data sync source: 66dbedf3-1068-43c9-bc63-e4daea1fab17 (us-west-1)
                        syncing
                        full sync: 0/128 shards
                        incremental sync: 128/128 shards
                        data is caught up with source
```

2. Cluster 2 secondary zone `us-west-1` synchronization status:

```
# radosgw-admin sync status --id rgw.us-west-1
```

```
        realm 9a66b241-eda4-4577-b5d5-aaf3d259168f (cookbookv2)
    zonegroup f5152481-422f-4ae5-a75d-7eaeae5c2b60 (us)
         zone 66dbedf3-1068-43c9-bc63-e4daea1fab17 (us-west-1)
metadata sync syncing
              full sync: 0/64 shards
              incremental sync: 64/64 shards
              metadata is caught up with master
    data sync source: 286299f7-73eb-4da3-96ae-f0c6a0288d09 (us-east-1)
                      syncing
                      full sync: 0/128 shards
                      incremental sync: 128/128 shards
                      data is caught up with source
```

Testing user, bucket, and object sync between master and secondary sites

By this time, you should have configured RGW multi-site V2. In this recipe, you will test user, bucket, and object synchronization between the master and secondary sites.

How to do it...

We will use the following commands for testing user, bucket, and object sync between the master and secondary zones:

1. Let's create an s3 user in the master site and check if it gets synced to the secondary site. You should run the following commands in the master site RGW node us-east-1:

   ```
   # radosgw-admin user create --uid=pratima
                               --display-name="Pratima Umrao"
                               --id rgw.us-east-1
   ```

```
{
    "user_id": "pratima",
    "display_name": "Pratima Umrao",
    "email": "",
    "suspended": 0,
    "max_buckets": 1000,
    "auid": 0,
    "subusers": [],
    "keys": [
        {
            "user": "pratima",
            "access_key": "AH6X7HQWBGT8TB8K1P62",
            "secret_key": "bL6TUS8wOmW1h4ViIMUmJz1JwYRXxaFaPcVTXt9k"
        }
    ],
    "swift_keys": [],
    "caps": [],
    "op_mask": "read, write, delete",
    "default_placement": "",
    "placement_tags": [],
    "bucket_quota": {
        "enabled": false,
        "max_size_kb": -1,
        "max_objects": -1
    },
    "user_quota": {
        "enabled": false,
        "max_size_kb": -1,
        "max_objects": -1
    },
    "temp_url_keys": []
}
```

2. Check the number of users in the master site:

```
# radosgw-admin metadata list user --id rgw.us-east-1
```

```
[
    "pratima",
    "replication-user"
]
```

3. Let's verify that the user "pratima" got synced to the secondary site. You should run the following commands in the secondary site RGW node us-west-1:

```
# radosgw-admin metadata list user --id rgw.us-west-1
```

```
[
    "pratima",
    "replication-user"
]
```

```
# radosgw-admin user info --uid=pratima --id rgw.us-west-1
```

```
{
    "user_id": "pratima",
    "display_name": "Pratima Umrao",
    "email": "",
    "suspended": 0,
    "max_buckets": 1000,
    "auid": 0,
    "subusers": [],
    "keys": [
        {
            "user": "pratima",
            "access_key": "AH6X7HQWBGT8TB8K1P62",
            "secret_key": "bL6TUS8wOmW1h4ViIMUmJz1JwYRXxaFaPcVTXt9k"
        }
    ],
    "swift_keys": [],
    "caps": [],
    "op_mask": "read, write, delete",
    "default_placement": "",
    "placement_tags": [],
    "bucket_quota": {
        "enabled": false,
        "max_size_kb": -1,
        "max_objects": -1
    },
    "user_quota": {
        "enabled": false,
        "max_size_kb": -1,
        "max_objects": -1
    },
    "temp_url_keys": []
}
[root@us-west-1 ~]#
```

We will use the s3cmd application in both sites to create the buckets and upload the objects to these buckets and see if the buckets and objects are getting synced on both the sites.

4. Install and configure s3cmd at the master site us-east-1 node:

```
[root@us-east-1 ~]#
[root@us-east-1 ~]# yum install s3cmd -y
Loaded plugins: fastestmirror
base
ceph_stable
epel/x86_64/metalink
extras
updates
Loading mirror speeds from cached hostfile
 * base: mirrors.rit.edu
 * epel: mirror.math.princeton.edu
 * extras: mirror.cogentco.com
 * updates: mirrors.cmich.edu
Resolving Dependencies
--> Running transaction check
---> Package s3cmd.noarch 0:1.6.1-1.el7 will be installed
--> Processing Dependency: python-magic for package: s3cmd-1.6.1-1.el7.noarch
--> Processing Dependency: python-dateutil for package: s3cmd-1.6.1-1.el7.noarc
--> Running transaction check
---> Package python-dateutil.noarch 0:1.5-7.el7 will be installed
---> Package python-magic.noarch 0:5.11-33.el7 will be installed
--> Finished Dependency Resolution

Dependencies Resolved

================================================================================
 Package                                          Arch
================================================================================
Installing:
 s3cmd                                            noarch
```

5. Configure s3cmd at the master site in the us-east-1 RGW node:

```
[root@us-east-1 ~]# s3cmd --configure

Enter new values or accept defaults in brackets with Enter.
Refer to user manual for detailed description of all options.

Access key and Secret key are your identifiers for Amazon S3. Leave them empty for using the env variables.
Access Key: AH6X7HQWBGT8TB8K1P62
Secret Key: bL6TUS8wOmW1h4ViIMUmJz1JwYRXxaFaPcVTXt9k
Default Region [US]:

Encryption password is used to protect your files from reading
by unauthorized persons while in transfer to S3
Encryption password:
Path to GPG program [/bin/gpg]:

When using secure HTTPS protocol all communication with Amazon S3
servers is protected from 3rd party eavesdropping. This method is
slower than plain HTTP, and can only be proxied with Python 2.7 or newer
Use HTTPS protocol [Yes]: No

On some networks all internet access must go through a HTTP proxy.
Try setting it here if you can't connect to S3 directly
HTTP Proxy server name:

New settings:
  Access Key: AH6X7HQWBGT8TB8K1P62
  Secret Key: bL6TUS8wOmW1h4ViIMJmJz1JwYRXxaFaPcVTXt9k
  Default Region: US
  Encryption password:
  Path to GPG program: /bin/gpg
  Use HTTPS protocol: False
  HTTP Proxy server name:
  HTTP Proxy server port: 0

Test access with supplied credentials? [Y/n] n

Save settings? [y/N] y
Configuration saved to '/root/.s3cfg'
[root@us-east-1 ~]# _
```

6. Update .s3cfg file options host_base and host_bucket with the master site RGW node hostname us-east-1.cephcookbook.com:

```
[root@us-east-1 ~]#
[root@us-east-1 ~]# cat .s3cfg | egrep "host_base|host_bucket"
host_base = us-east-1.cephcookbook.com:8080
host_bucket = %(bucket).us-east-1.cephcookbook.com:8080
[root@us-east-1 ~]#
```

7. Install and configure s3cmd at the secondary site `us-west-1` node:

```
[root@us-west-1 ~]#
[root@us-west-1 ~]# yum install s3cmd -y
Loaded plugins: fastestmirror
base
ceph_stable
epel/x86_64/metalink
epel
extras
updates
(1/8): base/7/x86_64/group_gz
(2/8): ceph_stable/x86_64/primary_db
(3/8): base/7/x86_64/primary_db
(4/8): epel/x86_64/updateinfo
(5/8): epel/x86_64/group_gz
(6/8): extras/7/x86_64/primary_db
(7/8): epel/x86_64/primary_db
(8/8): updates/7/x86_64/primary_db
Determining fastest mirrors
 * base: mirror.linux.duke.edu
 * epel: fedora-epel.mirrors.tds.net
 * extras: mirror.vtti.vt.edu
 * updates: centos.localmsp.org
Resolving Dependencies
--> Running transaction check
---> Package s3cmd.noarch 0:1.6.1-1.el7 will be installed
--> Processing Dependency: python-magic for package: s3cmd-1.6.1-1.el7.noarch
--> Processing Dependency: python-dateutil for package: s3cmd-1.6.1-1.el7.noarch
--> Running transaction check
---> Package python-dateutil.noarch 0:1.5-7.el7 will be installed
---> Package python-magic.noarch 0:5.11-33.el7 will be installed
--> Finished Dependency Resolution

Dependencies Resolved

===============================================================================
 Package                                                      Arch
===============================================================================
Installing:
 s3cmd                                                        noarch
```

8. Configure s3cmd at the secondary site in the `us-west-1` RGW node:

```
[root@us-west-1 ~]#
[root@us-west-1 ~]# s3cmd --configure

Enter new values or accept defaults in brackets with Enter.
Refer to user manual for detailed description of all options.

Access key and Secret key are your identifiers for Amazon S3. Leave them empty for using the env variables.
Access Key: AH6X7HQWBGT8TB8K1P62
Secret Key: bL6TUS8wOmW1h4ViIMUmJz1JwYRXxaFaPcVTXt9k
Default Region [US]:

Encryption password is used to protect your files from reading
by unauthorized persons while in transfer to S3
Encryption password:
Path to GPG program [/bin/gpg]:

When using secure HTTPS protocol all communication with Amazon S3
servers is protected from 3rd party eavesdropping. This method is
slower than plain HTTP, and can only be proxied with Python 2.7 or newer
Use HTTPS protocol [Yes]: no

On some networks all internet access must go through a HTTP proxy.
Try setting it here if you can't connect to S3 directly
HTTP Proxy server name:

New settings:
  Access Key: AH6X7HQWBGT8TB8K1P62
  Secret Key: bL6TUS8wOmW1h4ViIMUmJz1JwYRXxaFaPcVTXt9k
  Default Region: US
  Encryption password:
  Path to GPG program: /bin/gpg
  Use HTTPS protocol: False
  HTTP Proxy server name:
  HTTP Proxy server port: 0

Test access with supplied credentials? [Y/n] n

Save settings? [y/N] y
Configuration saved to '/root/.s3cfg'
[root@us-west-1 ~]#
```

9. Update .s3cfg file options host_base and host_bucket with the master site RGW node hostname us-west-1.

```
[root@us-west-1 ~]#
[root@us-west-1 ~]# cat .s3cfg | egrep "host_base|host_bucket"
host_base = us-west-1.cephcookbook.com:8080
host_bucket = %(bucket).us-west-1.cephcookbook.com:8080
[root@us-west-1 ~]#
```

10. Create the `test-bucket-master` and `upload: '/etc/hosts'` object in the bucket `test-bucket-master`:

```
[root@us-east-1 ~]# s3cmd mb s3://test-bucket-master
Bucket 's3://test-bucket-master/' created

[root@us-east-1 ~]# s3cmd ls
2017-09-28 03:45  s3://test-bucket-master

[root@us-east-1 ~]# radosgw-admin bucket list --id rgw.us-east-1
[
    "test-bucket-master"
]

[root@us-east-1 ~]# s3cmd put /etc/hosts s3://test-bucket-master
upload: '/etc/hosts' -> 's3://test-bucket-master/hosts'  [1 of 1]
 800 of 800   100% in    1s    560.59 B/s  done

[root@us-east-1 ~]# s3cmd ls s3://test-bucket-master
2017-09-28 03:46        800   s3://test-bucket-master/hosts
[root@us-east-1 ~]#
```

11. You can now check in the secondary site that the bucket and objects are synced:

```
[root@us-west-1 ~]#
[root@us-west-1 ~]# radosgw-admin bucket list --id rgw.us-west-1
[
    "test-bucket-master"
]
[root@us-west-1 ~]# s3cmd ls
2017-09-28 03:45  s3://test-bucket-master

[root@us-west-1 ~]# s3cmd ls s3://test-bucket-master
2017-09-28 03:46        800   s3://test-bucket-master/hosts
[root@us-west-1 ~]#
```

12. Now you can do the opposite to check the active-active replication; for this, you need to create the `test-bucket-secondary` and `upload: '/root/anaconda-ks.cfg'` objects in the bucket `test-bucket-secondary` at the secondary RGW node `us-west-1`:

```
[root@us-west-1 ~]#
[root@us-west-1 ~]# s3cmd mb s3://test-bucket-secondary
Bucket 's3://test-bucket-secondary/' created

[root@us-west-1 ~]# s3cmd ls
2017-09-28 03:45  s3://test-bucket-master
2017-09-28 03:56  s3://test-bucket-secondary

[root@us-west-1 ~]# s3cmd put /root/anaconda-ks.cfg s3://test-bucket-secondary
upload: '/root/anaconda-ks.cfg' -> 's3://test-bucket-secondary/anaconda-ks.cfg'  [1 of 1]
 815 of 815   100% in    0s    59.05 kB/s  done

[root@us-west-1 ~]# s3cmd ls s3://test-bucket-secondary
2017-09-28 03:56       815   s3://test-bucket-secondary/anaconda-ks.cfg
[root@us-west-1 ~]#
```

13. You can now check in the master site that the bucket `test-bucket-secondary`
    and `anaconda-ks.cfg` objects are synced:

```
[root@us-east-1 ~]# radosgw-admin bucket list --id rgw.us-east-1
[
    "test-bucket-master",
    "test-bucket-secondary"
]
[root@us-east-1 ~]#

[root@us-east-1 ~]# s3cmd ls
2017-09-28 03:45  s3://test-bucket-master
2017-09-28 03:56  s3://test-bucket-secondary

[root@us-east-1 ~]# s3cmd ls s3://test-bucket-secondary
2017-09-28 03:56       815   s3://test-bucket-secondary/anaconda-ks.cfg
[root@us-east-1 ~]#
```

You can see that the bucket `test-bucket-secondary` and `anaconda-ks.cfg` objects are
synced to the master site `us-east-1`. This is the behavior of active-active replication.

6
Working with the Ceph Filesystem

In this chapter, we will cover the following recipes:

- Understanding the Ceph Filesystem and MDS
- Deploying Ceph MDS
- Accessing Ceph FS through kernel driver
- Accessing Ceph FS through FUSE client
- Exporting the Ceph Filesystem as NFS
- Ceph FS – a drop-in replacement for HDFS

Introduction

The Ceph Filesystem, also known as Ceph FS, is a POSIX-compliant filesystem that uses the Ceph storage cluster to store user data. Ceph FS supports the native Linux kernel driver, which makes Ceph FS highly adaptive across any flavor of the Linux OS. In this chapter, we will cover the Ceph Filesystem in detail, including its deployment, understanding the kernel driver and FUSE.

Understanding the Ceph Filesystem and MDS

The Ceph Filesystem offers the POSIX-compliant distributed filesystem of any size that uses Ceph RADOS to store its data. To implement the Ceph Filesystem, you need a running Ceph storage cluster and at least one Ceph **Metadata Server (MDS)** to manage its metadata and keep it separated from data, which helps in reducing complexity and improves reliability. The following diagram depicts the architectural view of Ceph FS and its interfaces:

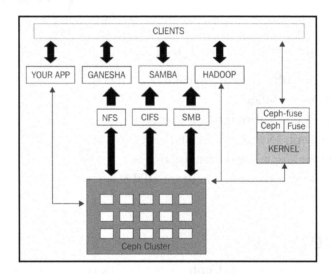

The `libcephfs` libraries play an important role in supporting its multiple client implementations. It has the native Linux kernel driver support, and thus clients can use native filesystem mounting, for example, using the mount command. It has tight integration with SAMBA and support for CIFS and SMB. Ceph FS extends its support to **Filesystem in USErspace (FUSE)** using `cephfuse` modules. It also allows direct application interaction with the RADOS cluster using the `libcephfs` libraries. Ceph FS is gaining popularity as a replacement for Hadoop HDFS. Previous versions of HDFS only supported the single name node, which impacts its scalability and creates a single point of failure; however, this has been changed in the current versions of HDFS. Unlike HDFS, Ceph FS can be implemented over multiple MDS in an active-active state, thus making it highly scalable, high performing, and with no single point of failure.

Ceph MDS is required only for the Ceph FS; other storage methods' block and object-based storage does not require MDS services. Ceph MDS operates as a daemon, which allows the client to mount a POSIX filesystem of any size. MDS does not serve any data directly to the client; data serving is done only by the OSD. MDS provides a shared coherent filesystem with a smart caching layer, hence drastically reducing reads and writes. It extends its benefits towards dynamic subtree partitioning and a single MDS for a piece of metadata. It is dynamic in nature; daemons can join and leave, and the takeover to failed nodes is quick.

MDS does not store local data, which is quite useful in some scenarios. If an MDS daemon dies, we can start it up again on any system that has cluster access. The Metadata Server's daemons are configured as active or passive. The primary MDS node becomes active and the rest will go into *standby*. In the event of primary MDS failure, the second node takes charge and is promoted to active. For even faster recovery, you can specify that a standby node should follow one of your active nodes, which will keep the same data in memory to pre-populate the cache.

Jewel (v10.2.0) is the first Ceph release to include stable Ceph FS code and fsck/repair tools, although multiple active MDS is running safely, and snapshots are still experimental. Ceph FS development continues to go at a very fast pace, and we can expect it to be fully production-ready in the Luminous release. For your non-critical workloads, you can consider using Ceph FS with single MDS and no snapshots.

In the coming sections, we will cover recipes for configuring both kernel and FUSE clients. Which client you choose to use is based on your use case. But the FUSE client is the easiest way to get up-to-date code, while the kernel client will often give better performance. Also, the clients do not always provide equivalent functionality; for example, the FUSE client supports client-enforced quotas while the kernel client does not.

Deploying Ceph MDS

To configure the Metadata Server for the Ceph Filesystem, you should have a running Ceph cluster. In the earlier chapters, we learned to deploy the Ceph storage cluster using Ansible; we will use the same cluster and Ansible for the MDS deployment.

How to do it...

Deploying an MDS server through `ceph-ansible` is quite easy, let's review the steps on how this is done:

1. Using Ansible from `ceph-node1`, we will deploy and configure MDS on `ceph-node2`. On our Ansible configuration node `ceph-node1`, add a new section `[mdss]` to the `/etc/ansible/hosts` file:

```
#ceph-cookbook

[mons]
ceph-node1
ceph-node2
ceph-node3

[osds]
ceph-node1
ceph-node2
ceph-node3

[clients]
client-node1

[mdss]
ceph-node2
```

2. Navigate to the Ansible configuration directory on `ceph-node1`, `/usr/share/ceph-ansible`:

   root@ceph-node1 # cd /usr/share/ceph-ansible

3. Run the Ansible playbook to deploy the MDS on `ceph-node2`:

   # ansible-playbook site.yml

4. Once the playbook completes successfully, you can validate that the MDS is up and active, that we have created two pools, cephfs_data and cephfs_metadata, and that the Ceph Filesystem was created successfully:

```
# ceph mds stat
# ceph osd pool ls
# ceph fs ls
```

```
[root@ceph-node1 ceph]# ceph mds stat
e5: 1/1/1 up {0=ceph-node2=up:active}
[root@ceph-node1 ceph]# ceph osd pool ls
rbd
cephfs_data
cephfs_metadata
[root@ceph-node1 ceph]# ceph fs ls
name: cephfs, metadata pool: cephfs_metadata, data pools: [cephfs_data ]
[root@ceph-node1 ceph]#
```

5. It's recommended that you don't share client.admin user keyring with Ceph clients, so we will create a user client.cephfs on the Ceph cluster and will allow this user access to the Ceph FS pools, then we will transfer the keyring we created to client-node1:

```
root@ceph-node1 # ceph auth get-or-create client.cephfs
                       mon 'allow r'
mds 'allow r, allow rw path=/' osd 'allow rw pool=cephfs_data'
-o ceph.client.cephfs.keyring
```

```
[root@ceph-node1 ceph]# ceph auth get-or-create client.cephfs mon 'allow r' mds 'allow r, allow rw path=/' osd 'allow rw
pool=cephfs_data' -o ceph.client.cephfs.keyring
[root@ceph-node1 ceph]#
```

```
root@client-node1 # scp root@ceph-node1:/etc/ceph/
ceph.client.cephfs.keyring /etc/ceph/ceph.client.cephfs.keyring
root@client-node1 cat /etc/ceph/client.cephfs.keyring
```

```
[root@client-node1 ceph]# scp root@ceph-node1:/etc/ceph/ceph.client.cephfs.keyring /etc/
ceph/ceph.client.cephfs.keyring
root@ceph-node1's password:
ceph.client.cephfs.keyring                         100%   64     0.1KB/s   00:00
[root@client-node1 ceph]# cat /etc/ceph/ceph.client.cephfs.keyring
[client.cephfs]
        key = AQAimbFZAFAVOBAAsKsSAO9rtD9+dVWoj0CDDA==
[root@client-node1 ceph]#
```

Accessing Ceph FS through kernel driver

Native support for Ceph has been added in the Linux kernel 2.6.34 and the later versions. In this recipe, we will demonstrate how to access Ceph FS through the Linux kernel driver on `client-node1`.

How to do it...

In order for our client to have access to Ceph FS, we need to configure the client for accessing the cluster and mounting Ceph FS. Let's review how this is done:

1. Check your client's Linux kernel version:

   root@client-node1 # uname -r

2. Create a mount point directory in which you want to mount the filesystem:

   # mkdir /mnt/cephfs

3. Get the keys for the `client.cephfs` user, which we created in the last section. Execute the following command from the Ceph monitor node to get the user keys:

   # ceph auth get-key client.cephfs

4. Mount Ceph FS using the native Linux mount call with the following syntax:

   Syntax: # `mount -t ceph <monitor _IP:Monitor_port>:/ <mount_point_name> -o name=admin,secret=<admin_user_key>`

   # mount -t ceph ceph-node1:6789:/ /mnt/cephfs
   -o name=cephfs,secret=AQAimbFZAFAVOBAAsksSA09rtD9+dVWoj0CDDA==

```
[root@client-node1 ceph]# uname -r
3.10.0-514.26.2.el7.x86_64
[root@client-node1 ceph]# mkdir /mnt/cephfs
[root@client-node1 ceph]# ceph auth get-key client.cephfs
AQAimbFZAFAVOBAAsKsSA09rtD9+dVWoj0CDDA==[root@client-node1 ceph]#
[root@client-node1 ceph]# mount -t ceph ceph-node1:6789:/ /mnt/cephfs -o name=cephfs,sec
ret=AQAimbFZAFAVOBAAsKsSA09rtD9+dVWoj0CDDA==
[root@client-node1 ceph]# df -h /mnt/cephfs
Filesystem          Size  Used Avail Use% Mounted on
10.19.1.101:6789:/  162G  1.1G  161G   1% /mnt/cephfs
[root@client-node1 ceph]#
```

5. To mount Ceph FS more securely and avoid the admin key being visible in the command history, store the admin `keyring` as plain text in a separate file and use this file as a mount option for `secretkey`:

```
# echo AQAimbFZAFAVOBAAsksSA09rtD9+dVWoj0CDDA==
  > /etc/ceph/cephfskey
# mount -t ceph ceph-node1:6789:/ /mnt/cephfs
-o name=cephfs,secretfile=/etc/ceph/cephfskey
```

6. To allow the Ceph FS mount during the OS startup, add the following lines in the `/etc/fstab` file on `client-node1`:

Syntax: `<Mon_ipaddress>:<Monitor_port>:/ <mount_point>`
`<filesystem_name>`
`[name=username,secret=secretkey|secretfile=/<path/to/secretfile`
`],[{mount.options}]`

```
# echo "ceph-node1:6789:/ /mnt/cephfs ceph
  name=cephfs,secretfile=/etc/ceph/
      cephfskey,_netdev,noattime 0 0" >>
  /etc/fstab
```

Use the `_netdev` option to ensure that the filesystem is mounted after the networking subsystem to prevent networking issues.

7. `umount` and `mount` the Ceph FS again to validate clean mount:

```
# umount /mnt/cephfs
# mount /mnt/cephfs
```

```
[root@client-node1 ceph]# echo "ceph-node1:6789:/ /mnt/cephfs ceph name=cephfs,secretfil
e=/etc/ceph/cephfskey,_netdev,noatime 0 0" >> /etc/fstab
[root@client-node1 ceph]# cat /etc/fstab |grep -i cephfs
ceph-node1:6789:/ /mnt/cephfs ceph name=cephfs,secretfile=/etc/ceph/cephfskey,_netdev,no
atime 0 0
[root@client-node1 ceph]# umount /mnt/cephfs
[root@client-node1 ceph]# mount /mnt/cephfs
[root@client-node1 ceph]# df -h /mnt/cephfs
Filesystem          Size  Used Avail Use% Mounted on
10.19.1.101:6789:/  162G  1.1G  161G   1% /mnt/cephfs
[root@client-node1 ceph]#
```

8. Perform some I/O on the Ceph Filesystem and then `umount` it:

   ```
   # dd if=/dev/zero of=/mnt/cephfs/file1 bs=1M count=1024
   # umount /mnt/cephfs
   ```

   ```
   [root@client-node1 ceph]# dd if=/dev/zero of=/mnt/cephfs/file1 bs=1M count=1024
   1024+0 records in
   1024+0 records out
   1073741824 bytes (1.1 GB) copied, 14.8411 s, 72.3 MB/s
   [root@client-node1 ceph]# ls -l /mnt/cephfs/file1
   -rw-r--r-- 1 root root 1073741824 Sep  7 22:58 /mnt/cephfs/file1
   [root@client-node1 ceph]# umount /mnt/cephfs
   [root@client-node1 ceph]#
   ```

Accessing Ceph FS through FUSE client

The Ceph Filesystem is natively supported by the LINUX kernel; however, if your host is running on a lower kernel version or if you have any application dependency, you can always use the FUSE client for Ceph to mount Ceph FS.

How to do it...

Let's review how to configure FUSE client for access to the Ceph cluster and mounting Ceph FS:

1. Validate that the Ceph FUSE package is installed on the machine `client-node1` (Ansible installs this as part of the client packages):

   ```
   # rpm -qa |grep -i ceph-fuse
   ```

2. Validate that the Ceph FS `keyring` file is created `client-node1` in `/etc/ceph/ceph.client.cephfs.keyring`, with the following contents (note your key will be different from the example):

   ```
   [root@client-node1 ceph]# cat /etc/ceph/ceph.client.cephfs.keyring
   [client.cephfs]
           key = AQAimbFZAFAVOBAAsKsSA09rtD9+dVWoj0CDDA==
   [root@client-node1 ceph]#
   ```

3. Mount Ceph FS using the FUSE client:

```
# ceph-fuse --keyring /etc/ceph/ceph.client.cephfs.keyring
           --name client.cephfs -m ceph-node1:6789 /mnt/cephfs
```

```
[root@client-node1 ceph]# ceph-fuse --keyring /etc/ceph/ceph.client.cephfs.keyring --nam
e client.cephfs -m ceph-node1:6789 /mnt/cephfs
ceph-fuse[4923]: starting ceph client
2017-09-07 23:18:46.778884 7fc873eedec0 -1 init, newargv = 0x7fc87f0f2a20 newargc=11
ceph-fuse[4923]: starting fuse
Aborted
[root@client-node1 ceph]# df -h /mnt/cephfs
Filesystem      Size  Used Avail Use% Mounted on
ceph-fuse       162G  4.1G  158G   3% /mnt/cephfs
[root@client-node1 ceph]#
```

4. To mount Ceph FS at OS boot, add the following lines to the `/etc/fstab` file on the `client-node1`:

```
# echo "id=cephfs,keyring=ceph.client.cephfs.keyring /mnt/cephfs
  fuse.ceph defaults 0 0 _netdev" >> /etc/fstab
# umount /mnt/cephfs
# mount /mnt/cephfs
```

```
[root@client-node1 ceph]# echo "id=cephfs,keyring=ceph.client.cephfs.keyring /mn
t/cephfs fuse.ceph defaults 0 0 _netdev" >> /etc/fstab
[root@client-node1 ceph]# umount /mnt/cephfs
[root@client-node1 ceph]# mount /mnt/cephfs
ceph-fuse[5062]: starting ceph client
2017-09-07 23:28:46.885160 7fe9fe11fec0 -1 init, newargv = 0x7fea09c4e1c0 newarg
c=13
ceph-fuse[5062]: starting fuse
[root@client-node1 ceph]# df -h /mnt/cephfs
Filesystem      Size  Used Avail Use% Mounted on
ceph-fuse       162G  4.1G  158G   3% /mnt/cephfs
[root@client-node1 ceph]#
```

Exporting the Ceph Filesystem as NFS

The **Network Filesystem** (**NFS**) is one of the most popular shareable filesystem protocols that can be used with every Unix-based system. Unix-based clients that do not understand the Ceph FS type can still access the Ceph Filesystem using NFS. To do this, we would require an NFS server in place that can re-export Ceph FS as an NFS share. NFS-Ganesha is an NFS server that runs in user space and supports the Ceph FS **File System Abstraction Layer** (**FSAL**) using `libcephfs`.

In this recipe, we will demonstrate creating `ceph-node1` as an NFS-Ganesha server and exporting Ceph FS as an NFS and mounting it on the `client-node1`.

How to do it...

Let's walk-through the steps to utilize `client-node1` as an NFS-Ganesha server to export Ceph FS as NFS:

1. On `ceph-node1`, install the packages required for `nfs-ganesha`:

   # sudo yum install -y nfs-utils nfs-ganesha

2. Since this is a test setup, disable the firewall. For the production setup, you might consider enabling the required ports over a firewall, which is generally `2049`:

   # systemctl stop firewalld; systemctl disable firewalld

3. Enable the `rpc` services required by NFS:

   # systemctl start rpcbind; systemctl enable rpcbind
   # systemctl start rpc-stat.d.service

4. Create the NFS-Ganesha configuration file, `/etc/ganesha.conf`, with the following content:

```
[root@ceph-node1 ceph]# cat /etc/ganesha.conf
EXPORT
{
    Export_ID = 1;
    Path = "/";
    Pseudo = "/";
    Access_Type = RW;
    SecType = "none";
    NFS_Protocols = "3";
    Squash = No_Root_Squash;
    Transport_Protocols = TCP;

    FSAL {
            Name = CEPH;
    }
}
[root@ceph-node1 ceph]#
```

5. Finally, start the NFS Ganesha daemon by providing the `ganesha.conf` file that we created in the last step. You can verify the exported NFS share using the `showmount` command:

```
# ganesha.nfsd -f /etc/ganesha.conf -L /var/log/ganesha.log -N
NIV_DEBUG
      # showmount -e
```

```
[root@ceph-node1 ceph]# ganesha.nfsd -f /etc/ganesha.conf -L /var/log/ganesha.log -N NIV_DEBU
G
[root@ceph-node1 ceph]# ps -ef |grep -i nfs
root      23674     1  0 23:50 ?        00:00:00 ganesha.nfsd -f /etc/ganesha.conf -L /var
/log/ganesha.log -N NIV_DEBUG
root      23705 22638  0 23:51 pts/1    00:00:00 grep --color=auto -i nfs
[root@ceph-node1 ceph]#
```

Let's recall the steps that we have taken: `ceph-node2` has been configured as Ceph MDS, and `ceph-node1` has been configured as the NFS-Ganesha server. Next, in order to mount the NFS share on the client machines, we just need to install the NFS client packages and mount the share exported by `ceph-node1`, as shown next:

Install the NFS client packages on `client-node1` and `mount`:

```
root@client-node1 # yum install -y nfs-utils
                  # mkdir /mnt/cephfs
                  # mount -o rw,noatime 10.19.1.101:/ /mnt/cephfs
```

```
[root@client-node1 mnt]# mount -o rw,noatime 10.19.1.101:/ /mnt/cephfs
[root@client-node1 mnt]# df -h /mnt/cephfs
Filesystem       Size  Used Avail Use% Mounted on
10.19.1.101:/       0     0     0    -  /mnt/cephfs
[root@client-node1 mnt]#
```

Ceph FS – a drop-in replacement for HDFS

Hadoop is a programming framework that supports the processing and storage of large data sets in a distributed computing environment. The Hadoop core includes the analytics MapReduce engine and the distributed file system known as **Hadoop Distributed File System (HDFS)**, which has several weaknesses that are listed as follows:

- It had a single point of failure until the recent versions of HDFS

- It isn't POSIX compliant

- It stores at least three copies of data

- It has a centralized name server resulting in scalability challenges

The Apache Hadoop project and other software vendors are working independently to fix these gaps in HDFS.

The Ceph community has done some development in this space, and it has a filesystem plugin for Hadoop that possibly overcomes the limitations of HDFS and can be used as a drop-in replacement for it. There are three requirements for using Ceph FS with HDFS; they are as follows:

- Running the Ceph cluster

- Running the Hadoop cluster

- Installing the Ceph FS Hadoop plugin

The Hadoop and HDFS implementation are beyond the scope of this book; however, in this section, we will superficially discuss how Ceph FS can be used in conjunction with HDFS. Hadoop clients can access Ceph FS through a Java-based plugin named hadoop-cephfs.jar. The two-java classes that follow are required to support Hadoop connectivity to Ceph FS.

- libcephfs.jar: This file should be placed in /usr/share/java/, and the path should be added to HADOOP_CLASSPATH in the Hadoop_env.sh file.

- libcephfs_jni.so: This file should be added to the LD_LIBRARY_PATH environment parameter and placed in /usr/lib/hadoop/lib. You should also soft link it to /usr/lib/hadoop/lib/native/Linux-amd64-64/libcephfs_jni.so.

In addition to this, the native Ceph FS client must be installed on each node of the Hadoop cluster. For more of the latest information on using Ceph FS for Hadoop, please visit the official Ceph documentation at http://ceph.com/docs/master/cephfs/hadoop, and Ceph GitHub at https://github.com/ceph/cephfs-hadoop.

7
Operating and Managing a Ceph Cluster

In this chapter, we will cover the following recipes:

- Understanding Ceph service management
- Managing the cluster configuration file
- Running Ceph with SYSTEMD
- Scale-up versus scale-out
- Scaling out your Ceph cluster
- Scaling down your Ceph cluster
- Replacing a failed disk in the Ceph cluster
- Upgrading your Ceph cluster
- Maintaining a Ceph cluster

Introduction

At this point, I'm sure you are pretty confident in Ceph cluster deployment, provisioning, as well as monitoring. In this chapter, we will cover standard topics such as Ceph service management. We will also cover advanced topics such as scaling up your cluster using ceph-ansible by adding OSD and MON nodes and finally, upgrading the Ceph cluster followed by some maintenance operations.

Understanding Ceph service management

Every component of Ceph, whether it's MON, OSD, MDS, or RGW, runs as a service on top of an underlying operating system. As a Ceph storage administrator, you should know about the Ceph services and how to operate them. As per Red Hat based distributions, Ceph daemons are managed as a traditional systemd manager service. Each time you start, restart, and stop Ceph daemons (or your entire cluster), you must specify at least one option and one command. You may also specify a daemon type or a daemon instance. The general syntax for this is as follows:

```
systemctl [options...] command [service name...]
```

The `systemctl` options include:

- `--help` or `-h`: Prints a short help text
- `--all` or `-a`: When listing units, show all loaded units, regardless of their state
- `--signal` or `-s`: When used will kill, choose which signal to send to the selected process
- `--force` or `-f`: When used with enable, overwrites any existing conflicting symlinks
- `--host` or `-h`: Execute an operation on a remote host

The `systemctl` commands include the following:

- `status`: Shows status of the daemon
- `start`: Starts the daemon
- `stop`: Stops the daemon

- `restart`: Stops and then starts the daemon
- `kill`: Kills the specified daemon
- `reload`: Reloads the config file without interrupting pending operations
- `list-units`: Lists known units managed by systemd
- `condrestart`: Restarts if the service is already running
- `enable`: Turns the service on for the next boot or other triggering event
- `disable`: Turns the service off for the next boot or other triggering event
- `is-enabled`: Used to check whether a service is configured to start or not in the current environment

`systemctl` can target the following Ceph service types:

- `ceph-mon`
- `ceph-osd`
- `ceph-mds`
- `ceph-radosgw`

Managing the cluster configuration file

If you are managing a large cluster, it's good practice to keep your cluster configuration file (`/etc/ceph/ceph.conf`) updated with information about cluster MONs, OSDs, MDSs, and RGW nodes. With these entries in place, you can manage all your cluster services from a single node.

How to do it...

`ceph-ansible` manages all aspects of the ceph configuration file that we will be using to update our cluster configuration. In order to achieve this, we will be updating the Ceph configuration file using the `ceph_conf_overrides` section of the `/etc/ansible/group_vars/all.yml` file and will be adding the details of all MON, OSD, and MDS nodes. Ansible supports the same sections as the Ceph configuration file: `[global]`, `[mon]`, `[osd]`, `[mds]`, `[rgw]`, and so on.

Adding monitor nodes to the Ceph configuration file

Since we have three monitor nodes, add their details to the `ceph_conf_overrides` section of the `all.yml` file:

1. In `ceph-node1` in the `/usr/share/ceph-ansible/group_vars` directory, edit the `ceph_conf_overrides` section of the `all.yml` to reflect the three monitors in the cluster:

```
###################
# CONFIG OVERRIDE #
###################

# Ceph configuration file override.
# This allows you to specify more configuration options
# using an INI style format.
# The following sections are supported: [global], [mon], [osd], [mds], [rgw]
#
# Example:
# ceph_conf_overrides:
#    global:
#       foo: 1234
#       bar: 5678
#
ceph_conf_overrides:
   mon:
      mon data: /var/lib/ceph/mon/$cluster-$id
   mon.ceph-node1:
      host: ceph-node1
      mon addr: ceph-node1:6789
   mon.ceph-node2:
      host: ceph-node2
      mon addr: ceph-node2:6789
   mon.ceph-node3:
      host: ceph-node3
      mon addr: ceph-node3:6789
```

2. Save the updated `all.yml` file and re-run the playbook from the `/usr/share/ceph-ansible` directory:

    # ansible-playbook site.yml

3. Validate that the Ceph configuration file has properly updated the monitor nodes in the cluster by viewing the `/etc/ceph/ceph.conf` file:

```
[mon]
        mon data = /var/lib/ceph/mon/$cluster-$id
[mon.ceph-node1]
        host = ceph-node1
        mon addr = ceph-node1:6789
[mon.ceph-node2]
        host = ceph-node2
        mon addr = ceph-node2:6789
[mon.ceph-node3]
        host = ceph-node3
        mon addr = ceph-node3:6789
```

 The spacing and format of the `all.yml` file needs to be exactly as seen in the screenshot and example or else when the ansible-playbook is run, it will error out due to improper format.

Adding an MDS node to the Ceph configuration file

As in the monitors, let's add MDS node details to the `/etc/ceph/ceph.conf` file from `ceph-node1` using Ansible:

1. On `ceph-node1` in the `/usr/share/ceph-ansible/group_vars` directory, edit the `ceph_conf_overrides` section of the `all.yml` to reflect the MDS nodes details. As with the monitors, please be careful with the formatting of the file or the running of the playbook will fail with a formatting error:

```
ceph_conf_overrides:
  mon:
    mon data: /var/lib/ceph/mon/$cluster-$id
  mon.ceph-node1:
    host: ceph-node1
    mon addr: ceph-node1:6789
  mon.ceph-node2:
    host: ceph-node2
    mon addr: ceph-node2:6789
  mon.ceph-node3:
    host: ceph-node3
    mon addr: ceph-node3:6789

  mds.ceph-node2:
    host: ceph-node2
```

2. Save the updated `all.yml` file and re-run the playbook from the `/usr/share/ceph-ansible` directory:

```
# ansible-playbook site.yml
```

3. Validate that the Ceph configuration file updated the MDS node in the cluster by viewing the `/etc/ceph/ceph.conf` file:

```
[mds]

[mds.ceph-node2]
        host = ceph-node2
```

Adding OSD nodes to the Ceph configuration file

Now, let's add the OSD nodes details to the `/etc/ceph/ceph.conf` file from `ceph-node1` using Ansible:

1. On `ceph-node1` in the `/usr/share/ceph-ansible/group_vars` directory, edit the `ceph_conf_overrides` section of the `all.yml` to reflect the OSD nodes details. As with the monitors, please be careful with the formatting of the file or the running of the playbook will fail with a formatting error:

```
ceph_conf_overrides:
  mon:
      mon data: /var/lib/ceph/mon/$cluster-$id
  mon.ceph-node1:
    host: ceph-node1
    mon addr: ceph-node1:6789
  mon.ceph-node2:
    host: ceph-node2
    mon addr: ceph-node2:6789
  mon.ceph-node3:
    host: ceph-node3
    mon addr: ceph-node3:6789

  mds.ceph-node2:
    host: ceph-node2

  osd:
      osd data: /var/lib/ceph/osd/$cluster-$id
      osd journal: /var/lib/ceph/osd/$cluster-$id/journal
  osd.0:
    host: ceph-node1
  osd.1:
    host: ceph-node1
  osd.2:
    host: ceph-node1
  osd.3:
    host: ceph-node2
  osd.4:
    host: ceph-node2
  osd.5:
    host: ceph-node2
  osd.6:
    host: ceph-node3
  osd.7:
    host: ceph-node3
  osd.8:
    host: ceph-node3
```

2. Save the updated `all.yml` file and re-run the playbook from the `/usr/share/ceph-ansible` directory:

```
# ansible-playbook site.yml
```

3. Validate that the Ceph configuration file properly updated the OSD nodes in the cluster by viewing the `/etc/ceph/ceph.conf` file:

```
[osd]
        osd data = /var/lib/ceph/osd/$cluster-$id
        osd journal = /var/lib/ceph/osd/$cluster-$id/journal
[osd.0]
        host = ceph-node1
[osd.1]
        host = ceph-node1
[osd.2]
        host = ceph-node1
[osd.3]
        host = ceph-node2
[osd.4]
        host = ceph-node2
[osd.5]
        host = ceph-node2
[osd.6]
        host = ceph-node3
[osd.7]
        host = ceph-node3
[osd.8]
        host = ceph-node3
```

Running Ceph with systemd

Ceph process management is done through the systemd service. Systemd is a replacement for the UNIX System V systems (**SYSVINIT**). The general syntax for managing Ceph daemons using systemd is `systemctl [options] {command} {service/target}`.

How to do it...

Let's have a detailed look at managing Ceph daemons using systemd:

Starting and stopping all daemons

To start or stop all Ceph daemons, perform the following set of commands.

Let's see how to start and stop all Ceph daemons:

1. To start all Ceph services on a particular node, execute the systemd manager for the Ceph unit with the `start` command. This command will start all Ceph services that you have deployed for this node:

   ```
   # systemctl start ceph.target
   ```

2. To stop all Ceph services on one particular node, execute the systemd manager for the Ceph unit using the `stop` command. This command will stop all Ceph services that you have deployed for this node:

   ```
   # systemctl stop ceph\*.service ceph\*.target
   ```

3. To start/stop all Ceph services on a remote host, execute the systemd manager with the `-H` option (specifying the remote hostname) with the `start` or `stop` command on the Ceph unit.

4. To start all Ceph services for `ceph-node2` from `ceph-node1` use the following command:

   ```
   root@ceph-node1 # systemctl -H ceph-node2 start ceph.target
   ```

5. To stop all Ceph services for `ceph-node2` from `ceph-node1` use the following command:

   ```
   root@ceph-node1 # systemctl -H ceph-node2 stop ceph\*.service
   ceph\*.target
   ```

 Since your `ceph.conf` file has all of your Ceph hosts defined and your current node can `ssh` to all those other nodes you can use the `-H` option to start and stop all Ceph services for a particular host from another remote host. The `ceph.conf` file should be identical in all the nodes.

Querying systemd units on a node

To list the Ceph systemd units on a Ceph node, perform the following set of commands.

Let's see how to determine which Ceph services are running on a particular node. This can be helpful to determine the location of which OSD or MON services are running on a certain node:

1. To list all the Ceph systemd units on a node, execute the systemd manager for the Ceph service/target using the `status` command. This command will display all active services/targets systemd has loaded:

   # systemctl status ceph*.service ceph*.target

2. To list the status on a particular Ceph service, execute the systemd manager for the specified Ceph service using the `status` command. To check the status of `mon.0` issue:

   root@ceph-node1 # systemctl status ceph-mon@ceph-node1

   To check the status of `osd.1` issue:

   root@ceph-node1 # systemctl status ceph-osd@1

3. To list all the systemd units on a particular node from a remote host, execute the systemd manager with the `-H` option (specifying the remote hostname) using the `status` command. This command will display all active services/targets systemd has loaded on a remote host. To check all systemd units on `ceph-node2` from `ceph-node1` issue:

   root@ceph-node1 # systemctl -H ceph-node2 status ceph*.service ceph*.target

4. To list the status on a particular Ceph service on a remote host, execute the systemd manager with the `-H` option (specifying the remote hostname), using the `status` command. To check the status of `mon.1` from `ceph-node1` issue:

   root@ceph-node1 # systemctl -H ceph-node2 status ceph-mon@ceph-node2

Starting and stopping all daemons by type

To start or stop all Ceph daemons by their types, perform the following set of commands:

Starting daemons by type:

1. To start the Ceph monitor daemons on localhost, execute the systemd manager with the `start` command followed by the daemon type:

   ```
   # systemctl start ceph-mon.target
   ```

2. To start the Ceph monitor daemon on a remote host, execute the same command with the `-H` option and the specified hostname. To start `mon.1` from `ceph-node1` issue:

   ```
   root@ceph-node1 # systemctl -H ceph-node2 start ceph-mon.target
   ```

3. Similarly, you can start daemons of other types, that is `osds`, `mds`, and `ceph-radosgw` by issuing:

   ```
   # systemctl start ceph-osd.target
   # systemctl start ceph-mds.target
   # systemctl start ceph-radosgw.target
   ```

Stopping daemons by type:

1. To stop the Ceph monitor daemons on a localhost, execute the systemd manager with the `stop` command followed by the daemon type:

   ```
   # systemctl stop ceph-mon.target
   ```

2. To stop the Ceph monitor daemon on a remote host, execute the same command with the `-H` option and the specified hostname. To stop `mon.1` from `ceph-node1` issue:

   ```
   root@ceph-node1 # systemctl -H ceph-node2 stop ceph.mon.target
   ```

3. Similarly, you can stop daemons of other types, that is `osds`, `mds`, and `ceph-radosgw` by issuing:

   ```
   # systemctl stop ceph-osd.target
   # systemctl stop ceph-mon.target
   # systemctl stop ceph-radosgw.target
   ```

Starting and stopping a specific daemon

To start or stop a specific Ceph daemon, perform the following set of commands:

Starting a specific daemon by instance:

To start a specific daemon on a local host, execute the systemd manager with the `start` command followed by the `{daemon_type}@{id/hostname}`, for example:

1. Start the `mon.0` daemon:

    ```
    root@ceph-node1 # systemctl start ceph-mon@ceph-node1
    ```

2. Similarly, you can start other daemons and their instances:

    ```
    root@ceph-node1 # systemctl start ceph-osd@1
    root@ceph-node1 # systemctl -H ceph-node2 start ceph-mon@ceph-node2
    root@rgw-node1 # systemctl stop ceph-radosgw@rgw-node1
    ```

Stopping a specific daemon by instance:

To stop a specific daemon on the local host, execute the systemd manager with the `stop` command followed by the `{daemon_type}@{id/hostname}`, for example:

1. Stop the `mon.0` daemon:

    ```
    root@ceph-node1 # systemctl stop ceph-mon@ceph-node1
    ```

2. Similarly, you can stop other daemons and their instances:

    ```
    root@ceph-node1 # systemctl stop ceph-osd@1
    root@ceph-node1 # systemctl -H ceph-node2 stop ceph-mon@ceph-node2</kbd>
    root@rgw-node1 # systemctl start ceph-radosgw@rgw-node1
    ```

Scale-up versus scale-out

When you are building up a storage infrastructure, scalability is one of the most important design aspects. The storage solution that you have chosen for your infrastructure should be scalable enough to accommodate your future data needs. Usually, a storage system starts with small to medium capacity and grows gradually into a large storage solution.

Traditional storage systems were based on scale-up design and were limited by a certain storage capacity. If you try to expand these storage systems over a certain limit, you might need to compromise the performance, reliability, and availability. The scale-up design methodology for storage involves adding disk resources to the existing controller systems, which becomes a bottleneck for performance, capacity, and manageability when it reaches a certain level.

On the other hand, scale-out design focuses on adding entire new devices containing disks, CPU, memory, and other resources to the existing storage cluster. With this type of design, you don't face the challenges that have been seen in scale-up design; it rather benefits from linear performance improvement. The following diagram explains the scale-up and scale-out design of a storage system:

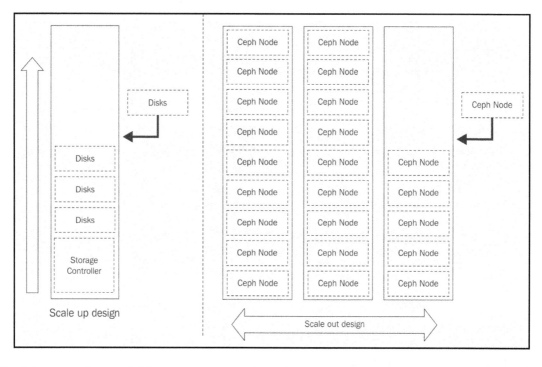

Ceph is a seamless scalable storage system based on scale-out design, where you can add a compute node with a bunch of disks to an existing Ceph cluster and extend your storage system to a larger storage capacity.

Scaling out your Ceph cluster

From the roots, Ceph has been designed to grow from a few nodes to several hundreds, and it's supposed to scale on the fly without any downtime. In this recipe, we will dive deep into the Ceph scale-out feature by adding MON, OSD, MDS, and RGW nodes.

How to do it...

Scaling out a Ceph cluster is important as the need for increased capacity in the cluster grows. Let's walk through expanding several areas of the Ceph cluster:

Adding the Ceph OSD

Adding an OSD node to the Ceph cluster is an online process. To demonstrate this, we require a new virtual machine named `ceph-node4` with three disks that will act as OSDs. This new node will then be added to our existing Ceph cluster.

Run the following commands from `ceph-node1` until otherwise specified from any other node:

1. Create a new node, `ceph-node4`, with three disks (OSD). You can follow the process of creating a new virtual machine with disks and the OS configuration, as mentioned in the *Setting up a virtual infrastructure* recipe in `Chapter 1`, *Ceph – Introduction and Beyond*, and make sure `ceph-node1` can ssh into `ceph-node4`. Before adding the new node to the Ceph cluster, let's check the current OSD tree. As shown in the following screenshot, the cluster has three nodes and a total of nine OSDs:

   ```
   # ceph osd tree
   ```

   ```
   [root@ceph-node1 ~]# ceph osd tree
   ID WEIGHT  TYPE NAME              UP/DOWN REWEIGHT PRIMARY-AFFINITY
   -1 0.15834 root default
   -2 0.05278     host ceph-node1
    0 0.01759         osd.0              up  1.00000          1.00000
    1 0.01759         osd.1              up  1.00000          1.00000
    2 0.01759         osd.2              up  1.00000          1.00000
   -3 0.05278     host ceph-node3
    3 0.01759         osd.3              up  1.00000          1.00000
    4 0.01759         osd.4              up  1.00000          1.00000
    5 0.01759         osd.5              up  1.00000          1.00000
   -4 0.05278     host ceph-node2
    6 0.01759         osd.6              up  1.00000          1.00000
    7 0.01759         osd.7              up  1.00000          1.00000
    8 0.01759         osd.8              up  1.00000          1.00000
   ```

2. Update the `/etc/ansible/hosts` file with `ceph-node4` under the `[osds]` section:

```
[mons]
ceph-node1
ceph-node2
ceph-node3

[osds]
ceph-node1
ceph-node2
ceph-node3
ceph-node4
```

3. Verify that Ansible can reach the newly added `ceph-node4` mentioned in `/etc/ansible/hosts`:

root@ceph-node1 # ansible all -m ping

```
[root@ceph-node1 ~]# ansible all -m ping
ceph-node2 | SUCCESS => {
    "changed": false,
    "ping": "pong"
}
ceph-node3 | SUCCESS => {
    "changed": false,
    "ping": "pong"
}
ceph-node4 | SUCCESS => {
    "changed": false,
    "ping": "pong"
}
ceph-node1 | SUCCESS => {
    "changed": false,
    "ping": "pong"
}
```

4. List the available devices of `ceph-node4` to be used as OSD's (sdb, sdc, and sdd):

root@ceph-node4 # lsblk

```
[root@ceph-node4 vagrant]# lsblk
NAME            MAJ:MIN RM   SIZE RO TYPE MOUNTPOINT
sda               8:0    0    8G  0 disk
├─sda1            8:1    0  500M  0 part /boot
└─sda2            8:2    0  7.5G  0 part
  ├─centos-swap 253:0    0  820M  0 lvm  [SWAP]
  └─centos-root 253:1    0  6.7G  0 lvm  /
sdb               8:16   0   20G  0 disk
sdc               8:32   0   20G  0 disk
sdd               8:48   0   20G  0 disk
sr0              11:0    1 1024M  0 rom
```

5. Review the `osds.yml` file on `ceph-node1` and validate that it lists the specified `devices` corresponding to the storage devices on the OSD node `ceph-node4` and that `journal_collocation` is set to `true`:

```
devices:
  - /dev/sdb
  - /dev/sdc
  - /dev/sdd
journal_collocation: true
```

6. Run the Ansible playbook to deploy the OSD node `ceph-node4` with three OSDs from the `/usr/share/ceph-ansible` directory:

root@ceph-node1 ceph-ansible # ansible-playbook site.yml

```
PLAY RECAP **********************************************************************
ceph-node1                 : ok=123  changed=2   unreachable=0   failed=0
ceph-node2                 : ok=117  changed=2   unreachable=0   failed=0
ceph-node3                 : ok=118  changed=2   unreachable=0   failed=0
ceph-node4                 : ok=60   changed=16  unreachable=0   failed=0
```

7. As soon as you add new OSDs to the Ceph cluster, you will notice that the Ceph cluster starts rebalancing the existing data to the new OSDs. You can monitor rebalancing using the following command; after a while, you will notice that your Ceph cluster becomes stable:

 # watch ceph -s

```
Every 2.0s: ceph -s                                          Fri Aug 18 00:17:29 2017

    cluster f05098c5-b187-43ef-bd58-03c8567620d5
     health HEALTH_OK
     monmap e3: 3 mons at {ceph-node1=192.168.1.101:6789/0,ceph-node2=192.168.1.102:6789/0,ceph-node3=19
2.168.1.103:6789/0}
            election epoch 50, quorum 0,1,2 ceph-node1,ceph-node2,ceph-node3
     osdmap e180: 12 osds: 12 up, 12 in
            flags sortbitwise,require_jewel_osds
      pgmap v479: 128 pgs, 1 pools, 0 bytes data, 0 objects
            440 MB used, 215 GB / 215 GB avail
                 128 active+clean
```

8. Once the addition of the OSDs for `ceph-node4` completes successfully, you will notice the cluster's new storage capacity:

rados df

```
[root@ceph-node1 ceph-ansible]# rados df
pool name              KB      objects      clones    degraded    unfound         rd       rd
KB        wr        wr KB
rbd                     0            0           0           0          0          0
0         0          0
    total used     450992            0
    total avail 225906016
    total space 226357008
```

ceph df

9. Check the OSD tree; it will give you a better understanding of your cluster. You should notice the new OSDs under `ceph-node4`, which have been recently added:

ceph osd tree

```
[root@ceph-node1 ceph-ansible]# ceph osd tree
ID WEIGHT  TYPE NAME              UP/DOWN REWEIGHT PRIMARY-AFFINITY
-1 0.21112 root default
-2 0.05278     host ceph-node1
 0 0.01759         osd.0              up  1.00000          1.00000
 1 0.01759         osd.1              up  1.00000          1.00000
 2 0.01759         osd.2              up  1.00000          1.00000
-3 0.05278     host ceph-node3
 3 0.01759         osd.3              up  1.00000          1.00000
 4 0.01759         osd.4              up  1.00000          1.00000
 5 0.01759         osd.5              up  1.00000          1.00000
-4 0.05278     host ceph-node2
 6 0.01759         osd.6              up  1.00000          1.00000
 7 0.01759         osd.7              up  1.00000          1.00000
 8 0.01759         osd.8              up  1.00000          1.00000
-5 0.05278     host ceph-node4
 9 0.01759         osd.9              up  1.00000          1.00000
10 0.01759         osd.10             up  1.00000          1.00000
11 0.01759         osd.11             up  1.00000          1.00000
```

10. This command outputs some valuable information such as OSD weight, any reweight that may be set, primary affinity that is set, which Ceph node hosts which OSD, and the UP/DOWN status of an OSD.

Just now, we learned how to add a new node to the existing Ceph cluster. It's a good time to understand that as the number of OSDs increases, choosing the right value for the PG becomes more important because it has a significant influence on the behavior of the cluster. Increasing the PG count on a large cluster can be an expensive operation. I encourage you to take a look at http://docs.ceph.com/docs/master/rados/operations/placement-groups/#choosing-the-number-of-placement-groups for any updated information on **Placement Groups (PGs)**.

Adding the Ceph MON

In an environment where you have deployed a large Ceph cluster, you might want to increase your monitor count. Like in an OSD, adding new monitors to the Ceph cluster is an online process. In this recipe, we will configure ceph-node4 as a monitor node.

Since this is a test Ceph cluster, we will add ceph-node4 as the fourth monitor node. However, in the production setup, you should always have an *odd number* of monitor nodes in your Ceph cluster in order to form a quorum:

1. Update the /etc/ansible/hosts file with ceph-node4 under the [mons] section:

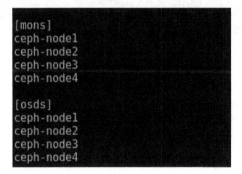

```
[mons]
ceph-node1
ceph-node2
ceph-node3
ceph-node4

[osds]
ceph-node1
ceph-node2
ceph-node3
ceph-node4
```

2. Run the Ansible playbook to deploy the new MON on `ceph-node4`:

```
root@ceph-node1 ceph-ansible # ansible-playbook site.yml
```

```
PLAY RECAP ***********************************************************************
ceph-node1                 : ok=127  changed=6   unreachable=0    failed=0
ceph-node2                 : ok=121  changed=6   unreachable=0    failed=0
ceph-node3                 : ok=121  changed=6   unreachable=0    failed=0
ceph-node4                 : ok=122  changed=13  unreachable=0    failed=0
```

3. Once `ceph-node4` is configured as a monitor node, check the ceph status to see the cluster status. Please note that `ceph-node4` is your new monitor node:

```
[root@ceph-node1 ceph-ansible]# ceph -s
    cluster f05098c5-b187-43ef-bd58-03c8567620d5
     health HEALTH_OK
     monmap e4: 4 mons at {ceph-node1=192.168.1.101:6789/0,ceph-node2=192.168.1.102:6789/0,ceph-node3=19
2.168.1.103:6789/0,ceph-node4=192.168.1.104:6789/0}
            election epoch 58, quorum 0,1,2,3 ceph-node1,ceph-node2,ceph-node3,ceph-node4
     osdmap e207: 12 osds: 12 up, 12 in
            flags sortbitwise,require_jewel_osds
      pgmap v565: 128 pgs, 1 pools, 0 bytes data, 0 objects
            448 MB used, 215 GB / 215 GB avail
                 128 active+clean
```

4. Check the Ceph monitor status and notice `ceph-node4` as the new Ceph monitor:

```
[root@ceph-node1 ceph-ansible]# ceph mon stat
e4: 4 mons at {ceph-node1=192.168.1.101:6789/0,ceph-node2=192.168.1.102:6789/0,ceph-node3=192.168.1.103:
6789/0,ceph-node4=192.168.1.104:6789/0}, election epoch 58, quorum 0,1,2,3 ceph-node1,ceph-node2,ceph-no
de3,ceph-node4
```

There's more...

For an object storage use case, you will have to deploy the Ceph RGW component using Ansible, and to make your object storage service highly available and performing, you should deploy more than one instance of the Ceph RGW. A Ceph object storage service can easily scale from one to several nodes of RGW using Ansible.

The following diagram shows how multiple RGW instances can be deployed and scaled to provide the **High-Availability (HA)** object storage service:

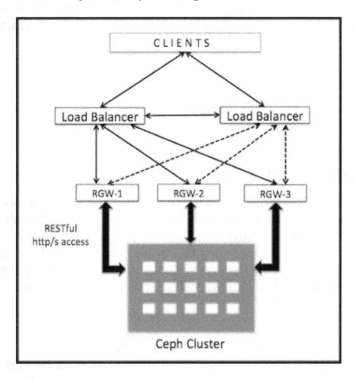

Scaling RGW is the same as adding additional RGW nodes with Ansible; please refer to the *Installing Rados Gateway* recipe in `Chapter 4`, *Working with Ceph Object Storage*, to add more RGW nodes to your Ceph environment.

Scaling down your Ceph cluster

One of the most important features of a storage system is its flexibility. A good storage solution should be flexible enough to support its expansion and reduction without causing any downtime to the services. Traditional storage systems have limited flexibility; the expansion and reduction of such systems is a tough job. Sometimes, you feel locked with storage capacity and that you cannot perform changes as per your needs.

Ceph is an absolutely flexible storage system that supports on-the-fly changes to storage capacity, whether expansion or reduction. In the last recipe, we learned how easy it is to scale out a Ceph cluster. In this recipe, we will scale down a Ceph cluster, without any impact on data accessibility, by removing `ceph-node4` from the Ceph cluster.

How to do it...

Since removing an OSD node is not currently supported in ceph-ansible, let's follow the next set of steps to do this manually.

Removing the Ceph OSD

Before proceeding with the cluster size reduction, scaling it down, or removing the OSD node, make sure that the cluster has enough free space to accommodate all the data present on the node you are planning to move out. The cluster should not be at its full ratio, which is the percentage of used disk space in an OSD. So, as best practice, do not remove the OSD or OSD node without considering the impact on the full ratio. At the current time of writing this book Ceph-Ansible does not support scaling down of the Ceph OSD nodes in a cluster and this must be done manually.

1. As we need to scale down the cluster, we will remove `ceph-node4` and all of its associated OSDs out of the cluster. Ceph OSDs should be set out so that Ceph can perform data recovery. From any of the Ceph nodes, take the OSDs out of the cluster:

```
# ceph osd out osd.9
# ceph osd out osd.10
# ceph osd out osd.11
```

```
[root@ceph-node1 ~]# ceph osd out osd.9
marked out osd.9.
[root@ceph-node1 ~]# ceph osd out osd.10
marked out osd.10.
[root@ceph-node1 ~]# ceph osd out osd.11
marked out osd.11.
[root@ceph-node1 ~]#
```

2. As soon as you mark an OSD out of the cluster, Ceph will start rebalancing the cluster by migrating the PGs out of the OSDs that were made out to other OSDs inside the cluster. Your cluster state will become unhealthy for some time, but it will be good for the server data to clients. Based on the number of OSDs removed, there might be some drop in cluster performance until the recovery time is complete. You can throttle the backfill and recovery as covered in this chapter in throttle backfill and recovery section.

   Once the cluster is healthy again, it should perform as usual:

   ```
   # ceph -s
   ```

```
root@ceph-node4 ~]# ceph -s
    cluster f05098c5-b187-43ef-bd58-03c8567620d5
     health HEALTH_WARN
            37 pgs peering
     monmap e4: 4 mons at {ceph-node1=192.168.1.101:6789/0,ceph-node2=192.168.1.102:6789/0,ceph-node3=192
168.1.103:6789/0,ceph-node4=192.168.1.104:6789/0}
            election epoch 60, quorum 0,1,2,3 ceph-node1,ceph-node2,ceph-node3,ceph-node4
     osdmap e255: 12 osds: 12 up, 9 in
            flags sortbitwise,require_jewel_osds
      pgmap v664: 128 pgs, 1 pools, 0 bytes data, 0 objects
            349 MB used, 161 GB / 161 GB avail
                 87 active+clean
                 32 peering
                  5 remapped+peering
                  4 activating
```

Here, you can see that the cluster is in the recovery mode but at the same time is serving data to clients. You can observe the recovery process using the following:

```
# ceph -w
```

```
2017-08-18 01:37:21.513877 mon.0 [INF] from='client.? 192.168.1.101:0/1982323814' entity='client.admin' c
md=[{"prefix": "osd out", "ids": ["osd.11"]}]: dispatch
2017-08-18 01:37:21.936129 mon.0 [INF] from='client.? 192.168.1.101:0/1982323814' entity='client.admin' c
md='[{"prefix": "osd out", "ids": ["osd.11"]}]': finished
2017-08-18 01:37:22.010637 mon.0 [INF] osdmap e268: 12 osds: 12 up, 9 in
2017-08-18 01:37:22.077412 mon.0 [INF] pgmap v802: 128 pgs: 18 remapped+peering, 29 peering, 81 active+cl
ean; 0 bytes data, 354 MB used, 161 GB / 161 GB avail
2017-08-18 01:37:22.199150 mon.0 [INF] osdmap e269: 12 osds: 12 up, 9 in
2017-08-18 01:37:22.221990 mon.0 [INF] pgmap v803: 128 pgs: 18 remapped+peering, 29 peering, 81 active+cl
ean; 0 bytes data, 354 MB used, 161 GB / 161 GB avail
```

3. As we have marked osd.9, osd.10, and osd.11 as out of the cluster, they will not participate in storing data, but their services are still running. Let's stop these OSDs:

   ```
   root@ceph-node1 # systemctl -H ceph-node4 stop ceph-osd.target
   ```

Once the OSDs are down, check the OSD tree; you will observe that the OSDs are down and out:

```
# ceph osd tree
```

```
[root@ceph-node1 ~]# ceph osd tree
ID  WEIGHT   TYPE NAME           UP/DOWN REWEIGHT PRIMARY-AFFINITY
-1  0.21112  root default
-2  0.05278      host ceph-node1
 0  0.01759          osd.0            up  1.00000          1.00000
 1  0.01759          osd.1            up  1.00000          1.00000
 2  0.01759          osd.2            up  1.00000          1.00000
-3  0.05278      host ceph-node3
 3  0.01759          osd.3            up  1.00000          1.00000
 4  0.01759          osd.4            up  1.00000          1.00000
 5  0.01759          osd.5            up  1.00000          1.00000
-4  0.05278      host ceph-node2
 6  0.01759          osd.6            up  1.00000          1.00000
 7  0.01759          osd.7            up  1.00000          1.00000
 8  0.01759          osd.8            up  1.00000          1.00000
-5  0.05278      host ceph-node4
 9  0.01759          osd.9          down        0          1.00000
10  0.01759          osd.10         down        0          1.00000
11  0.01759          osd.11         down        0          1.00000
```

4. Now that the OSDs are no longer part of the Ceph cluster, let's remove them from the CRUSH map:

```
# ceph osd crush remove osd.9
# ceph osd crush remove osd.10
# ceph osd crush remove osd.11
```

```
[root@ceph-node1 ~]# ceph osd crush remove osd.9
removed item id 9 name 'osd.9' from crush map
[root@ceph-node1 ~]# ceph osd crush remove osd.10
removed item id 10 name 'osd.10' from crush map
[root@ceph-node1 ~]# ceph osd crush remove osd.11
removed item id 11 name 'osd.11' from crush map
[root@ceph-node1 ~]#
```

5. As soon as the OSDs are removed from the CRUSH map, the Ceph cluster becomes healthy. You should also observe the OSD map; since we have not removed the OSDs, it will still show 12 OSDs, 9 UP, and 9 IN:

```
# ceph -s
```

```
[root@ceph-node1 ~]# ceph -s
    cluster f05098c5-b187-43ef-bd58-03c8567620d5
     health HEALTH_OK
     monmap e4: 4 mons at {ceph-node1=192.168.1.101:6789/0,ceph-node2=192.168.1.102:6789/0,ceph-node3=192
.168.1.103:6789/0,ceph-node4=192.168.1.104:6789/0}
            election epoch 64, quorum 0,1,2,3 ceph-node1,ceph-node2,ceph-node3,ceph-node4
     osdmap e293: 12 osds: 9 up, 9 in
            flags sortbitwise,require_jewel_osds
      pgmap v1052: 128 pgs, 1 pools, 0 bytes data, 0 objects
            361 MB used, 161 GB / 161 GB avail
                 128 active+clean
```

6. Remove the OSD authentication keys:

```
# ceph auth del osd.9
# ceph auth del osd.10
# ceph auth del osd.11
```

```
[root@ceph-node1 ~]# ceph auth del osd.9
updated
[root@ceph-node1 ~]# ceph auth del osd.10
updated
[root@ceph-node1 ~]# ceph auth del osd.11
updated
```

7. Finally, remove the OSD and check your cluster status; you should observe 9 OSDs, 9 UP, and 9 IN, and the cluster health should be OK:

```
# ceph osd rm osd.9
# ceph osd rm osd.10
# ceph osd rm osd.11
```

```
[root@ceph-node1 ~]# ceph osd rm osd.9
removed osd.9
[root@ceph-node1 ~]# ceph osd rm osd.10
removed osd.10
[root@ceph-node1 ~]# ceph osd rm osd.11
removed osd.11
[root@ceph-node1 ~]#
```

8. To keep your cluster clean, perform some housekeeping; as we have removed all the OSDs from the CRUSH map, `ceph-node4` does not hold any items. Remove `ceph-node4` from the CRUSH map; this will remove all the traces of this node from the Ceph cluster:

```
# ceph osd crush remove ceph-node4
```

```
[root@ceph-node1 ~]# ceph osd crush remove ceph-node4
removed item id -5 name 'ceph-node4' from crush map
```

9. Once the OSD node has been removed from the cluster and the CRUSH map, a final validation of the Ceph status should be done to verify HEALTH_OK:

```
# ceph -s
```

```
[root@ceph-node1 ~]# ceph -s
    cluster f05098c5-b187-43ef-bd58-03c8567620d5
     health HEALTH_OK
     monmap e4: 4 mons at {ceph-node1=192.168.1.101:6789/0,ceph-node2=192.168.1.102:6789/0,ceph-node3=192
.168.1.103:6789/0,ceph-node4=192.168.1.104:6789/0}
            election epoch 64, quorum 0,1,2,3 ceph-node1,ceph-node2,ceph-node3,ceph-node4
     osdmap e297: 9 osds: 9 up, 9 in
            flags sortbitwise,require_jewel_osds
      pgmap v1082: 128 pgs, 1 pools, 0 bytes data, 0 objects
            362 MB used, 161 GB / 161 GB avail
                 128 active+clean
```

10. To complete removal of `ceph-node4` from the cluster, update the `/etc/ansible/hosts` file on `ceph-node1` and remove `ceph-node4` from the `[osds]` section so the next time the playbook is run it will not redeploy `ceph-node4` as an OSD node:

```
[mons]
ceph-node1
ceph-node2
ceph-node3
ceph-node4

[osds]
ceph-node1
ceph-node2
ceph-node3
```

Removing the Ceph MON

Removing a Ceph MON is generally not a very frequently required task. When you remove monitors from a cluster, consider that Ceph monitors use the PAXOS algorithm to establish consensus about the master cluster map. You must have a sufficient number of monitors to establish a quorum for consensus on the cluster map. In this recipe, we will learn how to remove the `ceph-node4` monitor from the Ceph cluster. At the current time of writing this book, ceph-ansible does not support scaling down of Ceph MON nodes in a cluster and this must be done manually.

1. Check the monitor status:

   ```
   # ceph mon stat
   ```

   ```
   [root@ceph-node1 ceph-ansible]# ceph mon stat
   e4: 4 mons at {ceph-node1=192.168.1.101:6789/0,ceph-node2=192.168.1.102:6789/0,ceph-node3=192.168.1.103:6
   789/0,ceph-node4=192.168.1.104:6789/0}, election epoch 64, quorum 0,1,2,3 ceph-node1,ceph-node2,ceph-node
   3,ceph-node4
   ```

2. Stop the monitor service on `ceph-node4`:

   ```
   root@ceph-node1 # systemctl -H ceph-node4 stop ceph-mon.target
   ```

3. Remove the monitor from the cluster:

   ```
   # ceph mon remove ceph-node4
   ```

   ```
   [root@ceph-node1 ceph-ansible]# ceph mon remove ceph-node4
   removing mon.ceph-node4 at 192.168.1.104:6789/0, there will be 3 monitors
   ```

4. Check to see that your monitors have left the quorum:

    ```
    # ceph quorum_status --format json-pretty
    ```

```
[root@ceph-node1 ceph-ansible]# ceph quorum_status --format json-pretty
{
    "election_epoch": 70,
    "quorum": [
        0,
        1,
        2
    ],
    "quorum_names": [
        "ceph-node1",
        "ceph-node2",
        "ceph-node3"
    ],
    "quorum_leader_name": "ceph-node1",
    "monmap": {
        "epoch": 5,
        "fsid": "f05098c5-b187-43ef-bd58-03c8567620d5",
        "modified": "2017-08-18 02:33:32.706251",
        "created": "2017-08-17 17:21:11.831589",
        "mons": [
            {
                "rank": 0,
                "name": "ceph-node1",
                "addr": "192.168.1.101:6789\/0"
            },
            {
                "rank": 1,
                "name": "ceph-node2",
                "addr": "192.168.1.102:6789\/0"
            },
            {
                "rank": 2,
                "name": "ceph-node3",
                "addr": "192.168.1.103:6789\/0"
            }
        ]
    }
}
```

5. Update the `/etc/ansible/hosts` file and remove `ceph-node4` from the
   `[mons]` section so `ceph-node4` is not redeployed as a mon and the `ceph.conf`
   file is properly updated:

```
[mons]
ceph-node1
ceph-node2
ceph-node3

[osds]
ceph-node1
ceph-node2
ceph-node3
```

6. You can choose to back up the monitor data on `ceph-node4` or remove it. To
   back it up, you can create a removed directory and move the data there:

   ```
   # mkdir /var/lib/ceph/mon/removed
   # mv /var/lib/ceph/mon/ceph-ceph-node4
   /var/lib/ceph/mon/removed/ceph-ceph-node4
   ```

7. If you choose not to back up the monitor data, then remove the monitor data on
   `ceph-node4`:

   ```
   # rm -r /var/lib/ceph/mon/ceph-ceph-node4
   ```

8. Re-run the Ansible playbook to update the `ceph.conf` on all the nodes in the
   cluster to complete the removal of monitor `ceph-node4`:

   ```
   root@ceph-node1 # ansible-playbook site.yml
   ```

9. Finally, check the monitor status; the cluster should have three monitors:

```
[root@ceph-node1 ceph-ansible]# ceph mon stat
e5: 3 mons at {ceph-node1=192.168.1.101:6789/0,ceph-node2=192.168.1.102:6789/0,ceph-node3=192.168.1.103:6
789/0}, election epoch 70, quorum 0,1,2 ceph-node1,ceph-node2,ceph-node3
```

Replacing a failed disk in the Ceph cluster

A Ceph cluster can be made up of 10 to several thousand physical disks that provide storage capacity to the cluster. As the number of physical disks increases for your Ceph cluster, the frequency of disk failures also increases. Hence, replacing a failed disk drive might become a repetitive task for a Ceph storage administrator. In this recipe, we will learn about the disk replacement process for a Ceph cluster.

How to do it...

These steps will walk you through the proper replacement process of a Ceph OSD:

1. Let's verify cluster health; since this cluster does not have any failed disk status, it would be HEALTH_OK:

   ```
   # ceph status
   ```

   ```
   [root@ceph-node1 ceph-ansible]# ceph status
       cluster f05098c5-b187-43ef-bd58-03c8567620d5
        health HEALTH_OK
        monmap e5: 3 mons at {ceph-node1=192.168.1.101:6789/0,ceph-node2=192.168.1.102:6789/0,ceph-node3=192
   .168.1.103:6789/0}
            election epoch 70, quorum 0,1,2 ceph-node1,ceph-node2,ceph-node3
        osdmap e311: 9 osds: 9 up, 9 in
            flags sortbitwise,require_jewel_osds
         pgmap v1118: 128 pgs, 1 pools, 0 bytes data, 0 objects
            353 MB used, 161 GB / 161 GB avail
                 128 active+clean
   ```

2. Since we are demonstrating this exercise on virtual machines, we need to forcefully fail a disk by bringing `ceph-node1` down, detaching a disk, and powering up the VM. Execute the following commands from your HOST machine:

   ```
   # VBoxManage controlvm ceph-node1 poweroff
   # VBoxManage storageattach ceph-node1 --storagectl "SATA" --
   port 1 --device 0 --type hdd --medium none
   # VBoxManage startvm ceph-node1
   ```

The following screenshot will be your output:

```
teeri:ceph-cookbook ksingh$ VBoxManage  controlvm ceph-node1 poweroff
0%...10%...20%...30%...40%...50%...60%...70%...80%...90%...100%
teeri:ceph-cookbook ksingh$
teeri:ceph-cookbook ksingh$ VBoxManage storageattach ceph-node1 --storagectl "SATA" --port 1 --device 0 --type hdd --medium none
teeri:ceph-cookbook ksingh$ VBoxManage startvm ceph-node1
Waiting for VM "ceph-node1" to power on...
VM "ceph-node1" has been successfully started.
teeri:ceph-cookbook ksingh$
```

3. Now `ceph-node1` contains a failed disk, `osd.0`, which should be replaced:

   # **ceph osd tree**

```
[root@ceph-node1 ~]# ceph osd tree
ID WEIGHT  TYPE NAME           UP/DOWN REWEIGHT PRIMARY-AFFINITY
-1 0.15834 root default
-2 0.05278     host ceph-node1
 0 0.01759         osd.0         down  1.00000          1.00000
 1 0.01759         osd.1         up    1.00000          1.00000
 2 0.01759         osd.2         up    1.00000          1.00000
-3 0.05278     host ceph-node3
 3 0.01759         osd.3         up    1.00000          1.00000
 4 0.01759         osd.4         up    1.00000          1.00000
 5 0.01759         osd.5         up    1.00000          1.00000
-4 0.05278     host ceph-node2
 6 0.01759         osd.6         up    1.00000          1.00000
 7 0.01759         osd.7         up    1.00000          1.00000
 8 0.01759         osd.8         up    1.00000          1.00000
```

   # **ceph -s**

```
[root@ceph-node1 ~]# ceph -s
    cluster f05098c5-b187-43ef-bd58-03c8567620d5
     health HEALTH_WARN
            50 pgs stuck unclean
            1/9 in osds are down
     monmap e5: 3 mons at {ceph-node1=192.168.1.101:6789/0,ceph-node2=192.168.1.102:6789/0,ceph-node3=192
.168.1.103:6789/0}
            election epoch 78, quorum 0,1,2 ceph-node1,ceph-node2,ceph-node3
     osdmap e336: 9 osds: 8 up, 9 in; 50 remapped pgs
            flags sortbitwise,require_jewel_osds
      pgmap v1209: 128 pgs, 1 pools, 0 bytes data, 0 objects
            321 MB used, 143 GB / 143 GB avail
                  78 active+clean
                  41 active+remapped
                   9 active
```

You will also notice that osd.0 is DOWN. However, in the ceph osd tree it's still showing a weight of 1.00000 meaning it is still marked as IN. As long as its status is marked IN, the Ceph cluster will not trigger data recovery for this drive. A further look into the ceph -s shows us an osdmap of 9 osds: 8 up, 9 in. By default, the Ceph cluster takes 300 seconds to mark a down disk as OUT and then triggers data recovery. The reason for this timeout is to avoid unnecessary data movements due to short-term outages, for example, server reboot. One can increase or even decrease this timeout value if you prefer.

4. You should wait 300 seconds to trigger data recovery, or else you can manually mark the failed OSD as OUT:

   ```
   # ceph osd out osd.0
   ```

5. As soon as the OSD is marked OUT, the Ceph cluster will initiate a recovery operation for the PGs that were hosted on the failed disk. You can watch the recovery operation using the following command:

   ```
   # ceph status
   ```

6. Let's now remove the failed disk OSD from the Ceph CRUSH map:

   ```
   # ceph osd crush rm osd.0
   ```

7. Delete the Ceph authentication keys for the OSD:

   ```
   # ceph auth del osd.0
   ```

8. Finally, remove the OSD from the Ceph cluster:

   ```
   # ceph osd rm osd.0
   ```

   ```
   [root@ceph-node1 ~]# ceph osd crush rm osd.0
   removed item id 0 name 'osd.0' from crush map
   [root@ceph-node1 ~]# ceph auth del osd.0
   updated
   [root@ceph-node1 ~]# ceph osd rm osd.0
   removed osd.0
   [root@ceph-node1 ~]#
   ```

9. Since one of your OSDs is unavailable, the cluster health will not be OK, and the cluster will be performing recovery. Nothing to worry about here; this is a normal Ceph operation. Once the recovery operation is complete, your cluster will attain HEALTH_OK:

```
# ceph -s
# ceph osd stat
```

```
[root@ceph-node1 ~]# ceph -s
    cluster f05098c5-b187-43ef-bd58-03c8567620d5
     health HEALTH_OK
     monmap e5: 3 mons at {ceph-node1=192.168.1.101:6789/0,ceph-node2=192.168.1.102:6789/0,ceph-node3=192
.168.1.103:6789/0}
            election epoch 78, quorum 0,1,2 ceph-node1,ceph-node2,ceph-node3
     osdmap e343: 8 osds: 8 up, 8 in
            flags sortbitwise,require_jewel_osds
      pgmap v1238: 128 pgs, 1 pools, 0 bytes data, 0 objects
            324 MB used, 143 GB / 143 GB avail
                 128 active+clean
[root@ceph-node1 ~]# ceph osd stat
     osdmap e343: 8 osds: 8 up, 8 in
            flags sortbitwise,require_jewel_osds
[root@ceph-node1 ~]#
```

10. At this point, you should physically replace the failed disk with the new disk on your Ceph node. These days, almost all the servers and server OS support disk hot swapping, so you will not require any downtime for disk replacement.

11. Since we are simulating this on a virtual machine, we need to power off the VM, add a new disk, and restart the VM. Once the disk is inserted, make a note of its OS device ID:

```
# VBoxManage controlvm ceph-node1 poweroff
# VBoxManage storageattach ceph-node1 --storagectl "SATA" --
port 1 --device 0 --type hdd --medium ceph-node1_disk2.vdi
# VBoxManage startvm ceph-node1
```

12. Before adding the new disk back into the cluster, we will zap the disk to validate it is in a clean state:

```
root@ceph-node1 # ceph-disk zap /dev/sdb
```

13. View the device to validate that partitions were cleared with zap:

```
# lsblk
```

```
[root@ceph-node1 ceph-ansible]# lsblk
NAME               MAJ:MIN RM   SIZE RO TYPE MOUNTPOINT
sda                    8:0   0    8G  0 disk
├─sda1                 8:1   0  500M  0 part /boot
└─sda2                 8:2   0  7.5G  0 part
  ├─centos-swap      253:0   0  820M  0 lvm  [SWAP]
  └─centos-root      253:1   0  6.7G  0 lvm  /
sdb                    8:16  0   20G  0 disk
sdc                    8:32  0   20G  0 disk
├─sdc1                 8:33  0   18G  0 part /var/lib/ceph/osd/ceph-1
└─sdc2                 8:34  0    2G  0 part
sdd                    8:48  0   20G  0 disk
├─sdd1                 8:49  0   18G  0 part /var/lib/ceph/osd/ceph-2
└─sdd2                 8:50  0    2G  0 part
sr0                   11:0   1 1024M  0 rom
```

14. Add the new disk into the cluster using the `ceph-disk prepare` command:

```
root@ceph-node1 # ceph-disk --setuser ceph --setgroup ceph
prepare --fs-type xfs /dev/sdb
```

The `ceph-disk` prepare command does all the manual work of creating the OSD, the OSD key, authentication, placing the OSD in the CRUSH map, and so on:

```
[root@ceph-node1 ceph-ansible]# ceph-disk --setuser ceph --setgroup ceph prepare --fs-type xfs /dev/sdb
The operation has completed successfully.
The operation has completed successfully.
meta-data=/dev/sdb1              isize=2048   agcount=4, agsize=1179583 blks
         =                       sectsz=512   attr=2, projid32bit=1
         =                       crc=1        finobt=0, sparse=0
data     =                       bsize=4096   blocks=4718331, imaxpct=25
         =                       sunit=0      swidth=0 blks
naming   =version 2              bsize=4096   ascii-ci=0 ftype=1
log      =internal log           bsize=4096   blocks=2560, version=2
         =                       sectsz=512   sunit=0 blks, lazy-count=1
realtime =none                   extsz=4096   blocks=0, rtextents=0
Warning: The kernel is still using the old partition table.
The new table will be used at the next reboot.
The operation has completed successfully.
```

15. Check the device after the prepare completes to validate that the OSD directory is mounted:

    ```
    # lsblk
    ```

```
[root@ceph-node1 ceph-ansible]# lsblk
NAME              MAJ:MIN RM  SIZE RO TYPE MOUNTPOINT
sda                  8:0    0    8G  0 disk
├─sda1               8:1    0  500M  0 part /boot
└─sda2               8:2    0  7.5G  0 part
  ├─centos-swap    253:0    0  820M  0 lvm  [SWAP]
  └─centos-root    253:1    0  6.7G  0 lvm  /
sdb                  8:16   0   20G  0 disk
├─sdb1               8:17   0   18G  0 part /var/lib/ceph/osd/ceph-0
└─sdb2               8:18   0    2G  0 part
sdc                  8:32   0   20G  0 disk
├─sdc1               8:33   0   18G  0 part /var/lib/ceph/osd/ceph-1
└─sdc2               8:34   0    2G  0 part
sdd                  8:48   0   20G  0 disk
├─sdd1               8:49   0   18G  0 part /var/lib/ceph/osd/ceph-2
└─sdd2               8:50   0    2G  0 part
sr0                 11:0    1 1024M  0 rom
```

16. Once the `ceph-disk prepare` command completes, the OSD will be added to the cluster successfully and Ceph will perform a backfilling operation and will start moving PGs from secondary OSDs to the new OSD. The recovery operation might take a while, but after it, your Ceph cluster will be HEALTH_OK again:

    ```
    # ceph -s
    # ceph osd stat
    ```

```
[root@ceph-node1 ceph-ansible]# ceph -s
    cluster f05098c5-b187-43ef-bd58-03c8567620d5
     health HEALTH_OK
     monmap e5: 3 mons at {ceph-node1=192.168.1.101:6789/0,ceph-node2=192.168.1.102:6789/0,ceph-node3=192
.168.1.103:6789/0}
            election epoch 86, quorum 0,1,2 ceph-node1,ceph-node2,ceph-node3
     osdmap e368: 9 osds: 9 up, 9 in
            flags sortbitwise,require_jewel_osds
      pgmap v1317: 128 pgs, 1 pools, 0 bytes data, 0 objects
            378 MB used, 161 GB / 161 GB avail
                 128 active+clean
[root@ceph-node1 ceph-ansible]# ceph osd stat
     osdmap e368: 9 osds: 9 up, 9 in
            flags sortbitwise,require_jewel_osds
```

Upgrading your Ceph cluster

One of the several reasons for the greatness of Ceph is that almost all the operations on a Ceph cluster can be performed online, which means that your Ceph cluster is in production and serving clients, and you can perform administrative tasks on the cluster without downtime. One of these operations is upgrading the Ceph cluster version.

Since the first chapter, we have been using the Jewel release of Ceph. We will be demonstrating upgrading the Ceph cluster version from Jewel to Kraken using the Ansible `rolling_update.yml` playbook located in the `/usr/share/ceph-ansible/infrastructure-playbooks` directory. The `rolling_update.yml` playbook fully automates the Ceph cluster upgrade process.

Ansible upgrades the Ceph nodes in the following order, one at a time:

- Monitor nodes
- OSD nodes
- MDS nodes
- Ceph RadosGW nodes
- All other Ceph client nodes

During the upgrade, Ansible will also set the `noout`, `noscrub`, and `nodeep-scrub` flags on the cluster to prevent any unnecessary data movement on the cluster and overhead from scrubbing. Ansible also has built-in checks during the upgrade which will check cluster PG states and will not move forward if the cluster encounters an issue.

Once you upgrade a Ceph daemon, you cannot downgrade it. It's very much recommended to refer to the release-specific sections at `http://docs.ceph.com/docs/master/release-notes/` to identify release-specific procedures for upgrading the Ceph cluster.

How to do it...

In this recipe, we will upgrade our Ceph cluster, which is running on the Jewel release (10.2.9), to the latest stable Kraken (11.2.1) release:

1. On `ceph-node1` navigate to the `/usr/share/ceph-ansible/group_vars/all.yml` file and change the `ceph_stable_release` from Jewel to Kraken:

```
# COMMUNITY VERSION
ceph_stable: true # use ceph stable branch
#ceph_mirror: http://download.ceph.com
#ceph_stable_key: https://download.ceph.com/keys/release.asc
ceph_stable_release: kraken # ceph stable release
#ceph_stable_repo: "{{ ceph_mirror }}/debian-{{ ceph_stable_release }}"
```

2. On `ceph-node1` navigate to the `/usr/share/ceph-ansible/group_vars/all.yml` file and uncomment and change the `upgrade_ceph_packages` from `False` to `True`:

```
# This variable determines if ceph packages can be updated.  If False, the
# package resources will use "state=present".  If True, they will use
# "state=latest".
upgrade_ceph_packages: True
```

3. Copy the `rolling_update.yml` from the infrastructure-playbooks directory to the `/usr/share/ceph-ansible` directory:

```
# cp /usr/share/ceph-ansible/infrastructure-
playbooks/rolling_update.yml /usr/share/ceph-ansible
```

4. Run the `rolling_update.yml` playbook:

```
# ansible-playbook rolling_update.yml
```

5. Once the playbook completes, validate the new running Ceph version on our Ceph nodes using `ceph tell`:

```
# ceph tell mon.* version
# ceph tell osd.* version
```

```
[root@ceph-node1 ceph]# ceph tell mon.* version
mon.ceph-node1: ceph version 11.2.1 (e0354f9d3b1eea1d75a7dd487ba8098311be38a7)
mon.ceph-node2: ceph version 11.2.1 (e0354f9d3b1eea1d75a7dd487ba8098311be38a7)
mon.ceph-node3: ceph version 11.2.1 (e0354f9d3b1eea1d75a7dd487ba8098311be38a7)
[root@ceph-node1 ceph]# ceph tell osd.* version
osd.0: {
    "version": "ceph version 11.2.1 (e0354f9d3b1eea1d75a7dd487ba8098311be38a7)"
}
osd.1: {
    "version": "ceph version 11.2.1 (e0354f9d3b1eea1d75a7dd487ba8098311be38a7)"
}
osd.2: {
    "version": "ceph version 11.2.1 (e0354f9d3b1eea1d75a7dd487ba8098311be38a7)"
}
osd.3: {
    "version": "ceph version 11.2.1 (e0354f9d3b1eea1d75a7dd487ba8098311be38a7)"
}
osd.4: {
    "version": "ceph version 11.2.1 (e0354f9d3b1eea1d75a7dd487ba8098311be38a7)"
}
osd.5: {
    "version": "ceph version 11.2.1 (e0354f9d3b1eea1d75a7dd487ba8098311be38a7)"
}
osd.6: {
    "version": "ceph version 11.2.1 (e0354f9d3b1eea1d75a7dd487ba8098311be38a7)"
}
osd.7: {
    "version": "ceph version 11.2.1 (e0354f9d3b1eea1d75a7dd487ba8098311be38a7)"
}
osd.8: {
    "version": "ceph version 11.2.1 (e0354f9d3b1eea1d75a7dd487ba8098311be38a7)"
```

6. Running `ceph -v` will also show the newly upgraded Kraken (11.2.1) running on the Ceph cluster:

```
# ceph -v
```

```
[root@ceph-node1 ceph]# ceph -v
ceph version 11.2.1 (e0354f9d3b1eea1d75a7dd487ba8098311be38a7)
```

Running the `rolling_update.yml` playbook will prompt a question: *Are you sure you want to upgrade the cluster?*. Once a *Yes* reply is entered, Ansible will kick off the upgrade; this is your last chance to abort the upgrade!

Maintaining a Ceph cluster

Being a Ceph storage admin, maintaining your Ceph cluster will be one of your top priorities. Ceph is a distributed system that is designed to grow from tens of OSDs to several thousands of them. One of the key things required to maintain a Ceph cluster is to manage its OSDs. In this recipe, we will cover Ceph sub commands for OSDs and PGs that will help you during cluster maintenance and troubleshooting.

How to do it...

To understand the need for these commands better, let's assume a scenario where you want to add a new node to your production Ceph cluster. One way is to simply add the new node with several disks to the Ceph cluster, and the cluster will start backfilling and shuffling the data on to the new node. This is fine for a test cluster.

However, the situation becomes very critical when it comes to a production setup, where you should use some of the `ceph osd` subcommands/flags, which are mentioned as follows, before adding a new node to the cluster, such as `noin`, `nobackfill`, and so on. This is done so that your cluster does not immediately start the backfilling process when the new node comes in. You can then unset these flags during non-peak hours, and the cluster will take its time to rebalance:

1. The usages of these flags are as simple as set and unset. For example, to set a flag, use the following command lines:

```
# ceph osd set <flag_name>
# ceph osd set noout
# ceph osd set nodown
# ceph osd set norecover
```

2. Now to unset the same flags, use the following command lines:

```
# ceph osd unset <flag_name>
# ceph osd unset noout
# ceph osd unset nodown
# ceph osd unset norecover
```

How it works...

We will now learn what these flags are and why they are used:

- noout: This forces the Ceph cluster to not mark any OSD as out of the cluster, irrespective of its status. It makes sure all the OSDs remain inside the cluster.
- nodown: This forces the Ceph cluster to not mark any OSD down, irrespective of its status. It makes sure all the OSDs remain UP and none of them DOWN.
- noup: This forces the Ceph cluster to not mark any down OSD as UP. So, any OSD that is marked DOWN can only come UP after this flag is unset. This also applies to new OSDs that are joining the cluster.
- noin: This forces the Ceph cluster to not allow any new OSD to join the cluster. This is quite useful if you are adding several OSDs at once and don't want them to join the cluster automatically.
- norecover: This forces the Ceph cluster to not perform cluster recovery.
- nobackfill: This forces the Ceph cluster to not perform backfilling. This is quite useful when you are adding several OSDs at once and don't want Ceph to perform automatic data placement on the new node.
- norebalance: This forces the Ceph cluster to not perform cluster rebalancing.
- noscrub: This forces Ceph to not perform OSD scrubbing.
- nodeep-scrub: This forces Ceph to not perform OSD deep scrubbing.

Throttle the backfill and recovery:

If you want to add the new OSD node in production peak hours or non-peak hours and you want to have the least impact in client IO as compared to Ceph data rebalance - recovery and backfill IO due to new OSD new. You can throttle the backfill and recovery with the help of following commands:

- Set `osd_max_backfills = 1` option to throttle the backfill threads. You can add this in ceph.conf [osd] section and you can also set it dynamically with the following command:

  - `# ceph tell osd.* injectargs '--osd_max_backfills 1'`

- Set `osd_recovery_max_active = 1` option to throttle the recovery threads. You can add this in ceph.conf [osd] section and you can also set it dynamically with the following command:

  - `# ceph tell osd.* injectargs '--osd_recovery_max_active 1'`

- Set `osd_recovery_op_priority = 1` option to lower the recovery priority. You can add this in ceph.conf [osd] section and you can also set it dynamically with the following command:

  - `# ceph tell osd.* injectargs '--osd_recovery_op_priority 1'`

With the Jewel release of Ceph, there are two additional flags that are enabled by default when a Ceph cluster is installed at Jewel. If the cluster was upgraded from a version prior to Jewel (Hammer for example) these flags can be enabled:

- `sortbitwise`: The `sortbitwise` flag indicates that objects are sorted in a bitwise fashion. The old sort order `nibblewise`, was an historical artifact of filestore that is simply inefficient with the current version of Ceph. Bitwise sort order makes operations that require listing objects, like backfill and scrubbing, a bit more efficient:

  ```
  # ceph osd set sortbitwise
  ```

- `require_jewel_osds`: This flag prevents any pre-Jewel OSDs from joining the Ceph cluster. The purpose of this flag is to prevent an OSD from joining the cluster that will not support features that the Jewel code supports leading to possible OSD flapping and cluster issues:

  ```
  # ceph osd set require_jewel_osds
  ```

Setting the `sortbitwise` flag is a disruptive change as each PG must go through peering and each client must re-send inflight requests. There is no data movement in the cluster from setting this flag. Also note that ALL OSD's in the cluster must be running Jewel prior to setting this flag.

In addition to these flags, you can also use the following commands to repair OSDs and PGs:

- `ceph osd repair`: This performs repairing on a specified OSD.
- `ceph pg repair`: This performs repairing on a specified PG. Use this command with caution; based on your cluster state, this command can impact user data if not used carefully.
- `ceph pg scrub`: This performs scrubbing on a specified PG.
- `ceph deep-scrub`: This performs deep-scrubbing on specified PGs.

The Ceph CLI is quite powerful for end-to-end cluster management. You can get more information at `http://docs.ceph.com/docs/master/rados/man/`.

d manager service. Each time you start, restart, and stop Ceph daemons (or your entire cluster), you must specify at least one option and one command. You may also specify a daemon type or a daemon instance. The general syntax for this is as follows:

```
systemctl [options...] command [service name...]
```

The `systemctl` options include:

- `--help` or `-h`: Prints a short help text
- `--all` or `-a`: When listing units, show all loaded units, regardless of their state
- `--signal` or `-s`: When used will kill, choose which signal to send to the selected process
- `--force` or `-f`: When used with enable, overwrite any existing conflicting symlinks
- `--host` or `-h`: Execute an operation on a remote host

The `systemctl` commands include the following:

- `status`: Shows status of the daemon
- `start`: Starts the daemon
- `stop`: Stops the daemon
- `restart`: Stops and then starts the daemon
- `kill`: Kills the specified daemon
- `reload`: Reloads the config file without interrupting pending operations
- `list-units`: List known units managed by systemd
- `condrestart`: Restarts if the service is already running
- `enable`: Turns the service on for the next boot or other triggering event
- `disable`: Turns the service off for the next boot or other triggering event
- `is-enabled`: Used to check whether a service is configured to start or not in the current environment

`systemctl` can target the following Ceph service types:

- `ceph-mon`
- `ceph-osd`
- `ceph-mds`
- `ceph-radosgw`

8
Ceph under the Hood

In this chapter, we will cover the following recipes:

- Ceph scalability and high availability
- Understanding the CRUSH mechanism
- CRUSH map internals
- CRUSH tunables
- Ceph cluster map
- High availability monitors
- Ceph authentication and authorization
- I/O path from a Ceph client to a Ceph cluster
- Ceph placement group
- Placement group states
- Creating Ceph pools on specific OSDs

Introduction

In this chapter, we will take a deep dive into the internal workings of Ceph by understanding its features such as scalability, high availability, authentication, and authorization. We will also cover CRUSH map, which is one of the most important parts of the Ceph cluster. Finally, we will go through dynamic cluster management and the custom CRUSH map settings for Ceph pools.

Ceph scalability and high availability

To understand Ceph scalability and high availability, let's first talk about the architecture of traditional storage systems. Under this architecture, to store or retrieve data, clients talk to a centralized component known as a controller or gateway. These storage controllers act as a single point of contact for a client's request. The following diagram illustrates this situation:

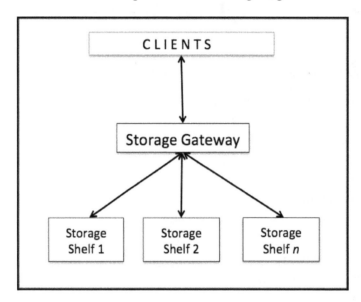

This storage gateway, which acts as a single point of entry to storage systems, also becomes the single point of failure. This also imposes a limit on scalability and performance while a single point of failure is being introduced, such that the whole system goes down if the centralized component goes down.

Ceph does not follow this traditional storage architecture; it has been totally reinvented for the next-generation of storage. Ceph eliminates the centralized gateway by enabling the clients to interact with the Ceph OSD daemons directly. The following diagram illustrates how clients connect to the Ceph cluster:

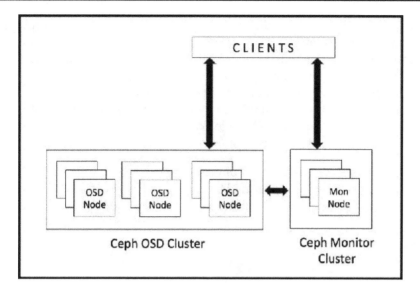

The Ceph OSD daemons create objects and their replicas on other Ceph nodes to ensure data safety and high availability. A cluster of monitors is used by Ceph to eliminate centralization and to ensure high availability. Ceph uses an algorithm called **Controlled Replication Under Scalable Hashing** (**CRUSH**). With the help of CRUSH, a client on demand calculates where the data should be written to or read from. In the following recipe, we will examine the details of the Ceph CRUSH algorithm.

Understanding the CRUSH mechanism

When it comes to data storage and management, Ceph uses the CRUSH algorithm, which is an intelligent data distribution mechanism of Ceph. As we discussed in the last recipe, traditional storage systems use a central metadata/index table to know where the user's data is stored. Ceph, on the other hand, uses the CRUSH algorithm to deterministically compute where the data should be written to or read from. Instead of storing metadata, CRUSH computes metadata on demand, thus removing the need for a centralized server/gateway or broker. It empowers Ceph clients to compute metadata, also known as *CRUSH lookup*, and communicates with OSDs directly.

For a read/write operation to Ceph clusters, clients first contact a Ceph monitor and retrieve a copy of the cluster map, which is inclusive of five maps, namely the monitor, OSD, MDS, and CRUSH and PG maps; we will cover these maps later in this chapter. These cluster maps help clients know the state and configuration of the Ceph cluster. Next, the data is converted to objects using an object name and pool names/IDs. This object is then hashed with the number of PGs to generate a final PG within the required Ceph pool. This calculated PG then goes through a CRUSH lookup function to determine the primary, secondary, and tertiary OSD locations to store or retrieve data.

Once the client gets the exact OSD ID, it contacts the OSDs directly and stores the data. All of these compute operations are performed by the clients; hence, they do not affect the cluster performance. The following diagram illustrates the entire process:

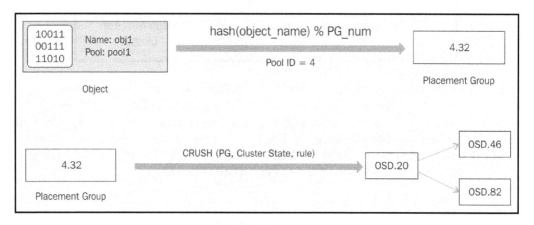

CRUSH map internals

To know what is inside a CRUSH map, and for easy editing, we need to extract and decompile it to convert it into a human-readable form. The following diagram illustrates this process:

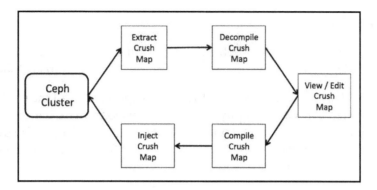

The change to the Ceph cluster by the CRUSH map is dynamic, that is, once the new CRUSH map is injected into the Ceph cluster, all the changes will come into effect immediately, on the fly.

How to do it...

We will now take a look at the CRUSH map of our Ceph cluster:

1. Extract the CRUSH map from any of the monitor nodes:

   ```
   # ceph osd getcrushmap -o crushmap_compiled_file
   ```

2. Once you have the CRUSH map, decompile it to convert it into a human-readable/editable form:

   ```
   # crushtool -d crushmap_compiled_file
              -o crushmap_decompiled_file
   ```

   At this point, the output file, crushmap_decompiled_file, can be viewed/edited in your favorite editor. In the next recipe, we will learn how to perform changes to the CRUSH map.

3. Once the changes are done, you should compile these changes:

   ```
   # crushtool -c crushmap_decompiled_file -o newcrushmap
   ```

4. Finally, inject the newly compiled CRUSH map into the Ceph cluster:

   ```
   # ceph osd setcrushmap -i newcrushmap
   ```

How it works...

Now that we know how to edit the Ceph CRUSH map, let's understand what's inside the CRUSH map. A CRUSH map file contains four main sections; they are as follows:

- **Devices**: This section of the CRUSH map keeps a list of all the OSD devices in your cluster. The OSD is a physical disk corresponding to the ceph-osd daemon. To map the PG to the OSD device, CRUSH requires a list of OSD devices. This list of devices appears in the beginning of the CRUSH map to declare the device in the CRUSH map. The following is the sample device list:

```
# devices
device 0 osd.0
device 1 osd.1
device 2 osd.2
device 3 osd.3
device 4 osd.4
device 5 osd.5
device 6 osd.6
device 7 osd.7
device 8 osd.8
```

- **Bucket types**: This defines the types of buckets used in your CRUSH hierarchy. Buckets consist of a hierarchical aggregation of physical locations (for example, rows, racks, chassis, hosts, and so on) and their assigned weights. They facilitate a hierarchy of nodes and leaves, where the node bucket represents a physical location and can aggregate other nodes and leaves buckets under the hierarchy. The leaf bucket represents the ceph-osd daemon and its underlying physical device. The following table lists the default bucket types:

Number	CRUSH Bucket	Description
0	**OSD**	An OSD daemon (for example, osd.1, osd.2, and so on).
1	**Host**	A host name containing one or more OSDs.
2	**Rack**	A computer rack containing one or more hosts.
3	**Row**	A row in a series of racks.
4	**Room**	A room containing racks and rows of hosts.
5	**Data Center**	A physical data center containing rooms.
6	**Root**	This is the beginning of the bucket hierarchy.

CRUSH also supports custom bucket type creation. These default bucket types can be deleted and new types can be introduced as per your needs.

- **Bucket instances**: Once you define bucket types, you must declare bucket instances for your hosts. A bucket instance requires the bucket type, a unique name (string), a unique ID expressed as a negative integer, a weight relative to the total capacity of its item, a bucket algorithm (straw, by default), and the hash (0, by default, reflecting the CRUSH hash rjenkins1). A bucket may have one or more items, and these items may consist of other buckets or OSDs. The item should have a weight that reflects the relative weight of the item. The general syntax of a bucket type looks as follows:

```
[bucket-type] [bucket-name] {
id [a unique negative numeric ID]
weight [the relative capacity the item]
alg [ the bucket type: uniform | list | tree | straw |straw2]
hash [the hash type: 0 by default]
item [item-name] weight [weight]
}
```

We will now briefly cover the parameters used by the CRUSH bucket instance:

- bucket-type: It's the type of bucket, where we must specify the OSD's location in the CRUSH hierarchy.
- bucket-name: A unique bucket name.
- id: The unique ID, expressed as a negative integer.

- weight: Ceph writes data evenly across the cluster disks, which helps in performance and better data distribution. This forces all the disks to participate in the cluster and make sure that all cluster disks are equally utilized, irrespective of their capacity. To do so, Ceph uses a weighting mechanism. CRUSH allocates weights to each OSD. The higher the weight of an OSD, the more physical storage capacity it will have. A weight is a relative difference between device capacities. We recommend using 1.00 as the relative weight for a 1 TB storage device. Similarly, a weight of 0.5 would represent approximately 500 GB, and a weight of 3.00 would represent approximately 3 TB.

- alg: Ceph supports multiple algorithm bucket types for your selection. These algorithms differ from each other on the basis of performance and reorganizational efficiency. Let's briefly cover these bucket types:

  - uniform: The uniform bucket can be used if the storage devices have exactly the same weight. For non-uniform weights, this bucket type should not be used. The addition or removal of devices in this bucket type requires the complete reshuffling of data, which makes this bucket type less efficient.

  - list: The list buckets aggregate their contents as linked lists and can contain storage devices with arbitrary weights. In the case of cluster expansion, new storage devices can be added to the head of a linked list with minimum data migration. However, storage device removal requires a significant amount of data movement. So, this bucket type is suitable for scenarios under which the addition of new devices to the cluster is extremely rare or non-existent. In addition, list buckets are efficient for small sets of items, but they may not be appropriate for large sets.

- `tree`: The `tree` buckets store their items in a binary tree. It is more efficient than list buckets because a bucket contains a larger set of items. Tree buckets are structured as a weighted binary search tree with items at the leaves. Each interior node knows the total weight of its left and right subtrees and is labeled according to a fixed strategy. The `tree` buckets are an all-around boon, providing excellent performance and decent reorganization efficiency.

- `straw`: To select an item using `list` and `tree` buckets, a limited number of hash values need to be calculated and compared by weight. They use a divide and conquer strategy, which gives precedence to certain items (for example, those at the beginning of a list). This improves the performance of the replica placement process, but it introduces moderate reorganization when bucket contents change due to addition, removal, or re-weighting.

The `straw` bucket type allows all items to compete fairly against each other for replica placement. In a scenario where removal is expected and reorganization efficiency is critical, `straw` buckets provide optimal migration behavior between subtrees. This bucket type allows all items to fairly compete against each other for replica placement through a process analogous to a draw of straws.

- `straw2`: This is an improved `straw` bucket that correctly avoids any data movement between items A and B, when neither A's nor B's weights are changed. In other words, if we adjust the weight of item C by adding a new device to it, or by removing it completely, the data movement will take place to or from C, never between other items in the bucket. Thus, the `straw2` bucket algorithm reduces the amount of data migration required when changes are made to the cluster.

- `hash`: Each bucket uses a hash algorithm. Currently, Ceph supports `rjenkins1`. Enter `0` as your hash setting to select `rjenkins1`.

- `item`: A bucket may have one or more items. These items may consist of node buckets or leaves. Items may have a weight that reflects the relative weight of the item.

The following screenshot illustrates the CRUSH bucket instance. Here, we have three host bucket instances. These host bucket instances consist of OSDs buckets:

```
# buckets
host ceph-node1 {
        id -2           # do not change unnecessarily
        # weight 0.053
        alg straw
        hash 0  # rjenkins1
        item osd.0 weight 0.018
        item osd.1 weight 0.018
        item osd.2 weight 0.018
}
host ceph-node3 {
        id -3           # do not change unnecessarily
        # weight 0.053
        alg straw
        hash 0  # rjenkins1
        item osd.3 weight 0.018
        item osd.5 weight 0.018
        item osd.7 weight 0.018
}
host ceph-node2 {
        id -4           # do not change unnecessarily
        # weight 0.053
        alg straw
        hash 0  # rjenkins1
        item osd.4 weight 0.018
        item osd.6 weight 0.018
        item osd.8 weight 0.018
}
root default {
        id -1           # do not change unnecessarily
        # weight 0.158
        alg straw
        hash 0  # rjenkins1
        item ceph-node1 weight 0.053
        item ceph-node3 weight 0.053
        item ceph-node2 weight 0.053
}
```

- **Rules**: The CRUSH maps contain CRUSH rules that determine the data placement for pools. As the name suggests, these are the rules that define the pool properties and the way data gets stored in the pools. They define the replication and placement policy that allows CRUSH to store objects in a Ceph cluster. The default CRUSH map contains a rule for default pools, that is, rbd. The general syntax of a CRUSH rule looks as follows:

```
rule <rulename>
{
ruleset <ruleset>
type [ replicated | erasure ]
min_size <min-size>
max_size <max-size>
step take <bucket-type>
step [choose|chooseleaf] [firstn] <num> <bucket-type>
step emit
}
```

We will now briefly cover these parameters used by the CRUSH rule:

- ruleset: An integer value; it classifies a rule as belonging to a set of rules.
- type: A string value; it's the type of pool that is either replicated or erasure coded.
- min_size: An integer value; if a pool makes fewer replicas than this number, CRUSH will not select this rule.
- max_size: An integer value; if a pool makes more replicas than this number, CRUSH will not select this rule.
- step take: This takes a bucket name and begins iterating down the tree.
- step choose firstn <num> type <bucket-type>: This selects the number (N) of buckets of a given type, where the number (N) is usually the number of replicas in the pool (that is, pool size):
  - If num == 0, select N buckets
  - If num > 0 && < N, select num buckets
  - If num < 0, select N − num buckets

For example: step choose firstn 1 type row

In this example, num=1, and let's suppose the pool size is 3, then CRUSH
will evaluate this condition as 1 > 0 && < 3. Hence, it will select 1
row type bucket.

- step chooseleaf firstn <num> type <bucket-type>: This
  first selects a set of buckets of a bucket type, and then chooses the
  leaf node from the subtree of each bucket in the set of buckets. The
  number of buckets in the set (N) is usually the number of replicas
  in the pool:

  - If num == 0, select N buckets
  - If num > 0 && < N, select num buckets
  - If num < 0, select N - num buckets

For example: step chooseleaf firstn 0 type row

In this example, num=0, and let's suppose the pool size is 3, then
CRUSH will evaluate this condition as 0 == 0, and then select a row
type bucket set, such that the set contains three buckets. Then it will
choose the leaf node from the subtree of each bucket. In this way,
CRUSH will select three leaf nodes.

- step emit: This first outputs the current value and empties the
  stack. This is typically used at the end of a rule, but it may also be
  used to form different trees in the same rule.

CRUSH tunables

In Ceph, developers calculate the placement of data by making an enhancement to the
CRUSH algorithm. Developers have introduced a series of CRUSH tunable options to
support the change in behavior. These options control the improved variation or legacy of
the algorithm that is used. Both Ceph servers and clients must support the new version of
CRUSH for using new tunables.

Hence, Ceph developers have named CRUSH tunable profiles in the name of the Ceph
version in which they were introduced. For example, the Firefly release supports the firefly
tunables that will not work with the older clients. The ceph-osd and ceph-mon will
prevent older clients from connecting to the cluster, as soon as a given set of tunables are
changed from the legacy default behavior. These old clients do not support the new
CRUSH features.

For more information, please visit `http://docs.ceph.com/docs/jewel/rados/operations/crush-map/#tunables`.

The evolution of CRUSH tunables

In the following section, we will explain the evolution of the CRUSH tunables.

Argonaut – legacy

Using the legacy CRUSH tunable Argonaut is fine behavior for some clusters as long as a large amount of OSD's have not been marked out of the cluster as this can cause issues with properly rebalancing data when OSD's are marked out.

Bobtail – CRUSH_TUNABLES2

The Bobtail profile fixes several CRUSH issues:

- In CRUSH hierarchies with a smaller number of devices in buckets, such as a host leaf bucket with one OSDs - three OSDs under it, the PGs may get mapped to less than the desired number of replica
- In larger Ceph clusters with several hierarchy layers (`row`, `rack`, `host`, `osd`) it is possible that a small amount of PGs could get mapped to less than the desired amount of OSDs
- If an OSD gets marked out in Bobtail, the data usually gets rebalanced to nearby OSDs in the bucket instead of across the entire CRUSH hierarchy

The following are the new tunables:

- `choose_local_tries`: The number of local retries is given by this tunable. The legacy and optimal values are 2 and 0, respectively.
- `choose_local_fallback_tries`: The legacy and optimal values are 5 and 0, respectively.
- `choose_total_tries`: The total number of attempts required for an item to be chosen. Legacy value was 19. Further testing has shown that this is too low of a value and the more appropriate value for a typical cluster is 50. For very large clusters, a bigger value might be necessary to properly choose an item.

- chooseleaf_descend_once: Either a recursive chooseleaf attempt will retry, or will only try once and allow the original placement to retry. The default and optimal values of legacy are 0 and 1, respectively:
    - **Migration impact**: A moderate amount of data movement is triggered if we move from Argonaut version to Bobtail version. We will have to be cautious on a cluster that is already populated with data.

Firefly – CRUSH_TUNABLES3

The Firefly profile resolves an issue where the chooseleaf CRUSH rule behavior, which is responsible for PG mappings, will come up with too few results when too many OSDs have been marked out of the cluster and will not be able to map the PG.

The following are the new tunables:

- chooseleaf_vary_r: If a recursive chooseleaf attempt starts with a non-zero value of r, based on the number of attempts parent has already made. The default value of legacy is 0, but with such a value, CRUSH is sometimes not able to find a mapping, which can lead to PGs in an unmapped state. The optimal value (in terms of computational cost and correctness) is 1:
    - **Migration impact**: For the existing clusters that have lots of existing data, changing from 0 to 1 will cause a lot of data to move; a value of 4 or 5 will allow CRUSH to find a valid mapping, but it will make less data move.
- straw_calc_version: This tunable resolves an issue when there were items in the CRUSH map with a weight of 0 or a mix of different weights in straw buckets. This would lead CRUSH to distribute data incorrectly throughout the cluster. Old is preserved by the value 0, broken internal weight calculation; behavior is fixed by the value 1:
    - **Migration impact**: Move to the straw_calc_version 1 tunable and then adjust a straw bucket (add, remove, or reweight an item, or use the reweight-all command) triggers a small to moderate amount of data movement if the cluster has hit one of the problematic conditions. This tunable option is special because it has absolutely no impact concerning the required kernel version in the client side.

Hammer – CRUSH_V4

The Hammer tunable profile does not affect the mapping of existing CRUSH maps simply by changing the profile and requires manual manipulation of the CRUSH map by enabling a new `straw` bucket type on CRUSH buckets:

- `straw2`: The `straw2` bucket resolves several initial limitations of the original `straw` bucket algorithm. The major change is that with the initial `straw` buckets, changing the weight of a bucket item would lead to multiple PG mapping changes of other bucket items outside the item that was actually reweighted. `straw2` will allow only changing mappings to or from the bucket that was actually reweighted:
    - **Migration impact**: Changing a bucket type from `straw` to `straw2` will result in a fairly small amount of data movement, depending on how much the bucket item weights vary from each other. When all the weights are same, no data will move, and when item weights vary considerably there will be more movement.

Jewel – CRUSH_TUNABLES5

The Jewel profile will improve CRUSH's overall behavior by limiting the number PG mapping changes when an OSD is marked out of the cluster.

The following is the new tunable:

- `chooseleaf_stable`: A recursive `chooseleaf` attempt will use a better value for an inner loop that greatly reduces the number of mapping changes when an OSD is marked out. The legacy value is `0`, while the new value of `1` uses the new approach:
    - `Migration impact`: Changing this value on an existing cluster will result in a very large amount of data movement as almost every PG mapping is likely to change

Ceph and kernel versions that support given tunables

Following are the Ceph and kernel versions that support given tunables:

Tunables	Ceph and kernel versions that support given tunables
CRUSH_TUNABLES	Argonaut series, v0.48.1 or recent version v0.49 or greater Linux kernel version v3.6 or recent (for the file system and RBD kernel clients)
CRUSH_TUNABLES2	v0.55 or recent, including Bobtail series (v0.56.x) Linux kernel version v3.9 or recent (for the filesystem and RBD kernel clients)
CRUSH_TUNABLES3	v0.78 (Firefly) or recent version CentOS 7.1, Linux kernel version v3.15 or recent (for the filesystem and RBD kernel clients)
CRUSH_V4	v0.94 (Hammer) or recent CentOS 7.1, Linux kernel version v4.1 or recent (for the filesystem and RBD kernel clients)
CRUSH_TUNABLES5	v10.2.0 (Jewel) or recent CentOS 7.3, Linux kernel version v4.5 or recent (for the filesystem and RBD kernel clients)

Warning when tunables are non-optimal

Ceph clusters will issue a health warning if the current running CRUSH tunables are not optimal for the current running Ceph version starting at v0.74.

In order to remove this warning from the Ceph cluster you can adjust the tunables on the existing cluster. Adjusting the CRUSH tunables will result in some data movement (possibly as much as 10% of the data on the cluster). This is the obviously preferred route to take, but care should be taken on a production cluster as any movement of data may affect the current cluster performance.

You can enable optimal tunables with:

```
ceph osd crush tunables optimal
```

If you begin to see issues with performance due to the load from the data movement on the cluster caused by the rebalance from the tunables change or if you run into a client compatibility issue (old kernel `cephfs` or `rbd` clients, or prebobtail `librados` clients) you can switch back to legacy tunables with:

```
ceph osd crush tunables legacy
```

A few important points

An adjustment to a CRUSH tunable will result in the shift of some PGs between storage nodes. If the Ceph cluster contains a large amount of data already, be prepared that there may be a good amount of PG movement with a CRUSH tunable change.

Monitor and OSD daemons will start and each daemon will require the new enabled CRUSH features of each new connection as they receive the updated maps. Any client that is already connected to the cluster will be grandfathered in; this will lead to unwanted behaviors if the clients (kernel version, Ceph version) do not support the newly enabled features. If you choose to set your CRUSH tunables to optimal, please verify that all Ceph nodes and clients are running the same version:

- If your CRUSH tunables are set to a value that is not legacy, then reverted back to default value the OSD daemons will not be required to support the feature. Please note that the OSD peering process does require reviewing and comprehending old maps, so you should not run old versions of Ceph if the cluster had previously used a non-legacy CRUSH tunable, even if the latest maps were reverted to legacy default values. It is very important to validate that all OSDs are running the same Ceph version.
  The simplest way to adjust the CRUSH tunables is by changing to a known profile. Those are:

    - `legacy`: The `legacy` profile gives the legacy behavior from Argonaut and previous versions
    - `argonaut`: The `argonaut` profile gives the legacy values that are supported by the original Argonaut release
    - `bobtail`: The values that are supported by the Bobtail release are given by the `bobtail` profile
    - `firefly`: The values that are supported by Firefly release are given by the `firefly` profile
    - `hammer`: The values that are supported by the Hammer release are given by the `hammer` profile

- `jewel`: The values that are supported by the Jewel release are given by the `jewel` profile
- `optimal`: The `optimal` profile gives the best/optimal values of the current Ceph version
- `default`: The default values of a new cluster is given by `default` profile

You can select a profile on a running cluster with the following command:

```
ceph osd crush tunables {PROFILE}
```

Note that this may result in some data movement.

You can check the current profile on a running cluster with the following command:

```
ceph osd crush show-tunables
```

```
[vagrant@ceph-node3 ~]$
[vagrant@ceph-node3 ~]$ sudo ceph osd crush tunables optimal
adjusted tunables profile to optimal
[vagrant@ceph-node3 ~]$ sudo ceph osd crush show-tunables
{
    "choose_local_tries": 0,
    "choose_local_fallback_tries": 0,
    "choose_total_tries": 50,
    "chooseleaf_descend_once": 1,
    "chooseleaf_vary_r": 1,
    "chooseleaf_stable": 1,
    "straw_calc_version": 1,
    "allowed_bucket_algs": 54,
    "profile": "jewel",
    "optimal_tunables": 1,
    "legacy_tunables": 0,
    "minimum_required_version": "jewel",
    "require_feature_tunables": 1,
    "require_feature_tunables2": 1,
    "has_v2_rules": 0,
    "require_feature_tunables3": 1,
    "has_v3_rules": 0,
    "has_v4_buckets": 0,
    "require_feature_tunables5": 1,
    "has_v5_rules": 0
}
[vagrant@ceph-node3 ~]$
```

Ceph cluster map

Ceph monitors are responsible for monitoring the health of the entire cluster as well as maintaining the cluster membership state, state of peer nodes, and cluster configuration information. The Ceph monitor performs these tasks by maintaining a master copy of the cluster map. The cluster map includes monitor maps, OSD maps, the PG map, the CRUSH map, and the MDS map. All these maps are collectively known as *cluster maps*. Let's take a quick look at the functionality of each map:

- **Monitor map**: It holds end-to-end information about the monitor node, which includes the Ceph cluster ID, monitor hostname, and IP address with the port number. It also stores the current epoch for map creation and last changed time too. You can check your cluster's monitor map by executing the following:

  ```
  # ceph mon dump
  ```

- **OSD map**: It stores some common fields, such as cluster ID, epoch for OSD map creation and last changed, and information related to pools, such as pool names, pool ID, type, replication level, and PGs. It also stores OSD information such as count, state, weight, last clean interval, and OSD host information. You can check your cluster's OSD maps by executing the following:

  ```
  # ceph osd dump
  ```

- **PG map**: It holds the PG version, timestamp, last OSD map epoch, full ratio, and near full ratio information. It also keeps track of each PG ID, object count, state, state stamp, up and acting OSD sets, and finally, the scrub details. To check your cluster PG map, execute the following:

  ```
  # ceph pg dump
  ```

- **CRUSH map**: It holds information on your clusters devices, buckets, failure domain hierarchy, and the rules defined for the failure domain when storing data. To check your cluster CRUSH map, execute the following:

  ```
  # ceph osd crush dump
  ```

- **MDS map**: This stores information on the current MDS map epoch, map creation and modification time, data and metadata pool ID, cluster MDS count, and the MDS state. To check your cluster MDS map, execute the following:

  ```
  # ceph mds dump
  ```

High availability monitors

The Ceph monitor does not store and serve data to clients; it serves updated cluster maps to clients as well as to other cluster nodes. Clients and other cluster nodes periodically check with monitors for the most recent copies of cluster maps. The Ceph monitor must be contacted by Ceph clients for obtaining the most recent copy of the cluster map before they can read or write data.

A Ceph storage cluster can operate with a single monitor, however, this introduces the risk of a single point of failure to the cluster; that is, if the monitor node goes down, Ceph clients cannot read or write data. To overcome this, a typical Ceph cluster consists of a cluster of Ceph monitors. A multi-monitored Ceph architecture develops quorum and provides consensus for distributed decision-making in clusters by using the Paxos algorithm. The monitor count in your cluster should be an odd number; the bare minimum requirement is one monitor node, and the recommended count is three. Since a monitor operates in the quorum, more than half of the total monitor nodes should always be available to prevent split-brain problems. Out of all the cluster monitors, one of them operates as the leader. The other monitor nodes are entitled to become leaders if the leader monitor is unavailable. A production cluster must have at least three monitor nodes to provide high availability.

Ceph authentication and authorization

In this recipe, we will cover the authentication and authorization mechanism used by Ceph. Users are either individuals or system actors such as applications, which use Ceph clients to interact with the Ceph storage cluster daemons. The following diagram illustrates this flow:

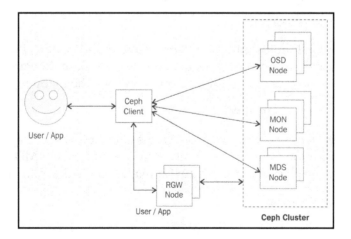

Ceph provides two authentication modes. They are as follows:

- `none`: With this mode, any user can access the Ceph cluster without authentication. This mode is disabled by default. Cryptographic authentication, which includes encrypting and decrypting user keys, has some computational costs. You can disable the Ceph authentication if you are very sure that your network infrastructure is secure, the clients/Ceph cluster nodes have established trust, and you want to save some computation by disabling authentication. However, this is not recommended, and you might be at risk of a man-in-the-middle attack. Still, if you are interested in disabling the Ceph authentication, you can do it by adding the following parameters in the global section of your Ceph configuration file on all the nodes, followed by the Ceph service restart:

```
auth cluster required = none
auth service required = none
auth client required = none
```

- `cephx`: Ceph provides its Cephx authentication system to authenticate users and daemons in order to identify users and protect against man-in-the-middle attacks. The Cephx protocol works similar to Kerberos to some extent and allows clients to access the Ceph cluster. It's worth knowing that the Cephx protocol does not do data encryption. In a Ceph cluster, the Cephx protocol is enabled by default. If you have disabled Cephx by adding the preceding `auth` options to your cluster configuration file, then you can enable Cephx in two ways. One is to simply remove all `auth` entries from the cluster configuration file, which are `none`, or you can explicitly enable Cephx by adding the following options in the cluster configuration file and restarting the Ceph services:

```
auth cluster required = cephx
auth service required = cephx
auth client required = cephx
```

Now that we have covered the different authentication modes of Ceph, let's understand how authentication and authorization works within Ceph.

Ceph authentication

To access the Ceph cluster, an actor/user/application invokes the Ceph client to contact the cluster's monitor node. Usually, a Ceph cluster has more than one monitor, and a Ceph client can connect to any monitor node to initiate the authentication process. This multimonitor architecture of Ceph removes a single point of failure situation during the authentication process.

To use Cephx, an administrator, that is, `client.admin`, must create a user account on the Ceph cluster. To create a user account, the `client.admin` user invokes the `ceph auth get-or-create key` command. The Ceph authentication subsystem generates a username and a secret key, stores this information on the Ceph monitor, and returns the user's secret key to the `client.admin` user that has invoked the user creation command. The Ceph sys-admin should share this username and secret key with the Ceph client that wants to use the Ceph storage service in a secure manner. The following diagram visualizes this entire process:

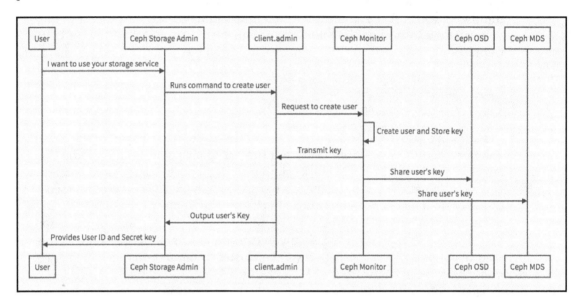

In the last recipe, we learned the process of user creation and how a user's secret keys are stored across all the cluster nodes. We will now examine how users are authenticated by Ceph and allowed access to cluster nodes.

In order to access the Ceph cluster, the client first contacts the Ceph monitor node and passes only its username. The Cephx protocol works in such a way that both parties are able to prove to each other that they have a copy of the key without actually revealing it. This is the reason that a client only sends its username, but not its secret key.

The session key for the user is generated by the monitor is encrypted with the secret key associated with that user. The encrypted session key is transmitted by the monitor back to the client. The client then decrypts the payload with its key to retrieve the session key. This session key remains valid for that user for the current session.

Using the session key, the client requests for a ticket from the Ceph monitor. The Ceph monitor verifies the session key and then generates a ticket, encrypted with the user's secret key, and transmits this to the user. The client decrypts the ticket and uses it to sign requests to OSDs and metadata servers throughout the cluster.

The ongoing communications between the Ceph nodes and the client are authenticated by the Cephx protocol. Each message sent between the Ceph nodes and the client, post the initial authentication, is signed using a ticket that the metadata nodes, OSDs, and monitors verify with their shared secret key. Cephx tickets do expire, so an attacker cannot use an expired ticket or session key to gain access to the Ceph cluster. The following diagram illustrates the entire authentication process that has been explained here:

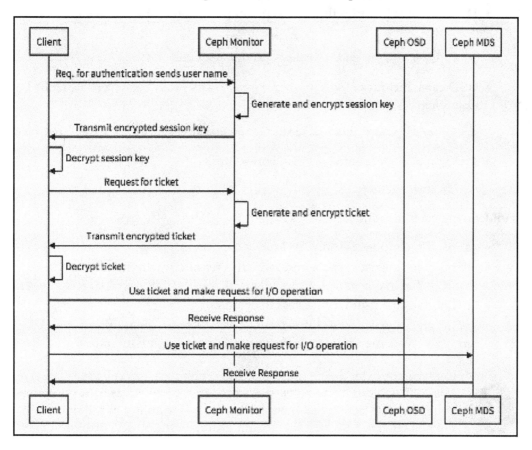

Ceph authorization

In the last recipe, we covered the authentication process used by Ceph. In this recipe, we will examine its authorization process. Once a user is authenticated, he is authorized for different types of access, activities, or roles. Ceph uses the term capabilities, which is abbreviated to caps. Capabilities are the rights a user gets that define the level of access they have to operate the cluster. The capability syntax looks as follows:

```
{daemon-type} 'allow {capability}' [{daemon-type} 'allow {capability}']
```

A detailed explanation of capability syntax is as follows:

- **Monitor caps**: Includes the r, w, x, parameters, and allow profiles {cap}. For example:

  ```
  mon 'allow rwx' or mon 'allow profile osd'
  ```

- **OSD caps**: Includes r, w, x, class-read, class-write, and profile OSD. For example:

  ```
  osd 'allow rwx' or osd 'allow class-read, allow rwx pool=rbd'
  ```

- **MDS caps**: Only requires allow. For example:

  ```
  mds 'allow'
  ```

Let's understand each capability:

- allow: This implies rw only for MDS.
- r: This gives the user read access, which is required with the monitor to read CRUSH maps.
- w: This gives the user write access to objects.
- x: This gives the user the ability to call class methods, including read and write, and also, the rights to perform auth operations on monitors.

Ceph can be extended by creating shared object classes called Ceph classes. Ceph can load .so classes stored in the OSD class dir. For a class, you can create new object methods that have the ability to call native methods in the Ceph object store, for example, the objects that you have defined in your class can call native Ceph methods such as read and write.

- `class-read`: This is a subset of x that allows users to call class read methods.
- `class-write`: This is a subset of x that allows users to call class write methods.
- `*`: This gives users full permission (r, w, and x) on a specific pool as well as to execute admin commands.
- `profile osd`: This allows users to connect as an OSD to other OSDs or monitors. Used for the OSD heartbeat traffic and status reporting.
- `profile mds`: This allows users to connect as an MDS to other MDSs.
- `profile bootstrap-osd`: This allows users to bootstrap an OSD. For example, `ceph-deploy` and `ceph-disk` tools use the client.bootstrap-osd user, which has permission to add keys and bootstrap an OSD.
- `profile bootstrap-mds`: This allows the user to bootstrap the metadata server. For example, the `ceph-deploy` tool uses the `client.bootstrap-mds` user to add keys and bootstrap the metadata server.

A user can be the individual user of an application, such as cinder/nova in the case of OpenStack. Creating users allows you to control what can access your Ceph storage cluster, its pools, and the data within the pools. In Ceph, a user should have a type, which is always client, and an ID, which can be any name. So, a valid username syntax in Ceph is `TYPE.ID`, that is, `client.<name>`, for example, `client.admin` or `client.cinder`.

How to do it...

In the following recipe, we will discuss more Ceph user management by running some commands:

1. To list the users in your cluster, execute the following command:

   ```
   # ceph auth list
   ```

   The output of this command shows that for each daemon type, Ceph creates a user with different capabilities. It also lists the `client.admin` user, which is the cluster admin user.

2. To retrieve a specific user, for example, `client.admin`, execute the following:

   ```
   # ceph auth get client.admin
   ```

   ```
   [vagrant@ceph-node3 ~]$
   [vagrant@ceph-node3 ~]$ sudo ceph auth get client.admin
   exported keyring for client.admin
   [client.admin]
           key = AQDyj4ZZZBISKhAAnOlJYPyttbcDUBde0pIvfg==
           caps mds = "allow *"
           caps mon = "allow *"
           caps osd = "allow *"
   [vagrant@ceph-node3 ~]$
   ```

3. Create a user, `client.rbd`:

   ```
   # ceph auth get-or-create client.rbd
   ```

   ```
   [vagrant@ceph-node3 ~]$
   [vagrant@ceph-node3 ~]$ sudo ceph auth get-or-create client.rbd
   [client.rbd]
           key = AQCabZhZusKJMxAAAHh4TP+XDVzy48T7ulxnhw==
   [vagrant@ceph-node3 ~]$
   ```

   This will create the user, `client.rbd`, with no capabilities, and a user with no caps is of no use.

4. Add capabilities to the `client.rbd` user and list the user's capabilities:

   ```
   [vagrant@ceph-node3 ~]$
   [vagrant@ceph-node3 ~]$ sudo ceph auth caps client.rbd mon 'allow r' osd 'allow rwx pool=rbd'
   updated caps for client.rbd
   [vagrant@ceph-node3 ~]$ sudo ceph auth get client.rbd
   exported keyring for client.rbd
   [client.rbd]
           key = AQCabZhZusKJMxAAAHh4TP+XDVzy48T7ulxnhw==
           caps mon = "allow r"
           caps osd = "allow rwx pool=rbd"
   [vagrant@ceph-node3 ~]$
   ```

I/O path from a Ceph client to a Ceph cluster

Let's have a quick recap of how clients access the Ceph cluster. To perform a write operation with the Ceph cluster, the client gets the latest copy of the cluster map from the Ceph monitor (if they do not have it already). The cluster map provides information about the Ceph cluster layout. Then the client writes/reads the object, which is stored on a Ceph pool. The pool selects OSDs based on the CRUSH ruleset for that pool. The following diagram illustrates this entire process:

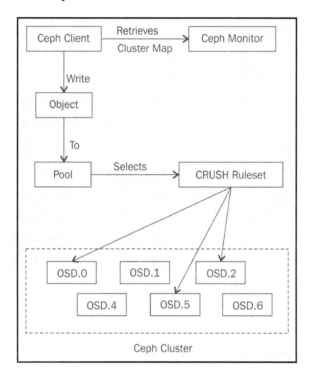

Now, let's understand the process of data storage inside the Ceph cluster. Ceph stores data in logical partitions known as pools. These pools hold multiple PGs, which in turn hold objects. Ceph is a true distributed storage system in which each object is replicated and stored across different OSDs each time. This mechanism has been explained with the help of the following diagram, in which we have tried to present how objects get stored in the Ceph cluster:

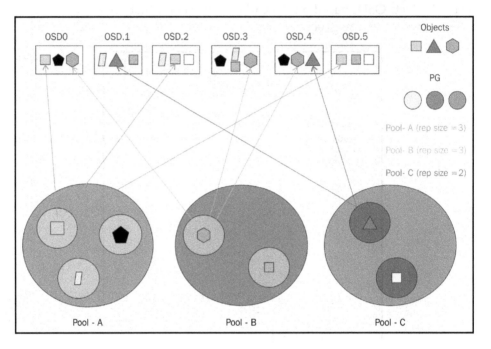

Ceph Placement Group

A **Placement Group** (**PG**) is a logical collection of objects that are replicated on OSDs to provide reliability in a storage system. Depending on the replication level of a Ceph pool, each PG is replicated and distributed on more than one OSD of a Ceph cluster. You can consider a PG as a logical container holding multiple objects, such that this logical container is mapped to multiple OSDs:

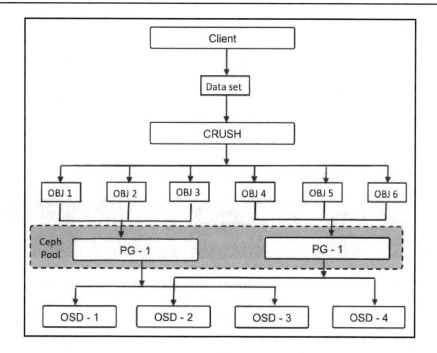

The PGs are essential for the scalability and performance of a Ceph storage system. Without PGs, it will be difficult to manage and track tens of millions of objects that are replicated and spread over hundreds of OSDs. The management of these objects without a PG will also result in a computational penalty. Instead of managing every object individually, a system has to manage the PGs with numerous objects. This makes Ceph a more manageable and less complex system.

Each PG requires some system resources, as they have to manage multiple objects. The number of PGs in a cluster should be meticulously calculated, and this is discussed later in this book. Usually, increasing the number of PGs in your cluster rebalances the OSD load. A recommended number of PGs per OSD is 50 to 100, to avoid high resource utilization on the OSD node. As the amount of data on a Ceph cluster increases, you might need to tune the cluster by adjusting the PG counts. When devices are added to or removed from a cluster, CRUSH manages the relocation of PGs in the most optimized way.

Now, we have understood that a Ceph PG stores its data on multiple OSDs for reliability and high availability. These OSDs are referred to as primary, secondary, tertiary, and so on, and they belong to a set known as the acting set for that PG. For each PG acting set, the first OSD is primary and the latter are secondary and tertiary.

How to do it...

To understand this better, let's find out the acting set for a PG from our Ceph cluster:

1. Add a temporary object with name `hosts` to a pool `rbd`:

   ```
   # rados put -p rbd hosts /etc/hosts
   ```

2. Check the PG name for object `hosts`:

   ```
   # ceph osd map rbd hosts
   ```

```
[vagrant@ceph-node3 ~]$
[vagrant@ceph-node3 ~]$ sudo rados put -p rbd hosts /etc/hosts
[vagrant@ceph-node3 ~]$ sudo ceph osd map rbd hosts
osdmap e67 pool 'rbd' (0) object 'hosts' -> pg 0.ea1b298e (0.e) -> up ([2,4,3], p2) acting ([2,4,3], p2)
[vagrant@ceph-node3 ~]$
```

If you observe the output, Placement Group (`0.e`) has an up set `[2,4,3]` and an acting set `[2,4,3]`. So, here `osd.2` is the primary OSD, and `osd.4` and `osd.3` are secondary and tertiary OSDs. The primary OSD is the only OSD that entertains write operations from clients. When it comes to read, by default it also comes from the primary OSD; however, we can change this behavior by setting up read affinity.

The OSD's that are up remains in the up set, as well as the acting set. Once the primary OSD is down, it is first removed from the up set and then from the acting set. The secondary OSD is then promoted to become the primary OSD. Ceph recovers PGs of the failed OSD to a new OSD and then adds it to the up and acting sets to ensure high availability. In a Ceph cluster, an OSD can be the primary OSD for some PGs, while at the same time, it can be the secondary or tertiary OSD for other PGs.

Placement Group states

Ceph PGs may exhibit several states based on what's happening inside the cluster at that point in time. To know the state of a PG, you can see the output of the command `ceph status`. In this recipe, we will cover these different states of PGs and understand what each state actually means:

- **Creating**: The PG is being created. This generally happens when pools are being created or when PGs are increased for a pool.
- **Active**: All PGs are active, and requests to the PG will be processed.

- **Clean**: All objects in the PG are replicated the correct number of times.
- **Down**: A replica with necessary data is down, so the PG is offline (down).
- **Replay**: The PG is waiting for clients to replay operations after an OSD has crashed.
- **Splitting**: The PG is being split into multiple PGs. Usually, a PG attains this state when PGs are increased for an existing pool. For example, if you increase the PGs of a pool rbd from 64 to 128, the existing PGs will split, and some of their objects will be moved to new PGs.
- **Scrubbing**: The PG is being checked for inconsistencies.
- **Degraded**: Some objects in the PG are not replicated as many times as they are supposed to be.
- **Inconsistent**: The PG replica is not consistent. For example, there is the wrong size of object, or objects are missing from one replica after recovery is finished.
- **Peering**: The PG is undergoing the peering process, in which it's trying to bring the OSDs that store the replicas of the PG into agreement about the state of the objects and metadata in the PG.
- **Repair**: The PG is being checked, and any inconsistencies found will be repaired (if possible).
- **Recovering**: Objects are being migrated/synchronized with replicas. When an OSD goes down, its contents may fall behind the current state of other replicas in the PGs. So, the PG goes into a recovering state and objects will be migrated/synchronized with replicas.
- **Backfill**: When a new OSD joins the cluster, CRUSH will reassign PGs from existing OSDs in the cluster to the newly added OSD. Once the backfilling is complete, the new OSD will begin serving requests when it is ready.
- **Backfill-wait**: The PG is waiting in line to start backfill.
- **Incomplete**: A PG is missing a necessary period of history from its log. This generally occurs when an OSD that contains needed information fails or is unavailable.
- **Stale**: The PG is in an unknown state—the monitors have not received an update for it since the PG mapping changed. When you start your cluster, it is common to see the stale state until the peering process completes.
- **Remapped**: When the acting set that services a PG changes, the data migrates from the old acting set to the new acting set. It may take some time for a new primary OSD to service requests. So, it may ask the old primary OSD to continue to service requests until the PG migration is complete. Once data migration completes, the mapping uses the primary OSD of the new acting set.

The following are two more new PG states that were added in jewel release for the snapshot trimming feature:

- `snaptrim`: The PGs are currently being trimmed
- `snaptrim_wait`: The PGs are waiting to be trimmed

Creating Ceph pools on specific OSDs

A Ceph cluster typically consists of several nodes having multiple disk drives. And, these disk drives can be of mixed types. For example, your Ceph nodes might contain disks of the types SATA, NL-SAS, SAS, SSD, or even PCIe, and so on. Ceph provides you with the flexibility to create pools on specific drive types. For example, you can create a high performing SSD pool from a set of SSD disks, or you can create a high capacity, low-cost pool using the SATA disk drives.

In this recipe, we will understand how to create a pool named `ssd-pool` backed by SSD disks, and another pool named `sata-pool`, which is backed by SATA disks. To achieve this, we will edit CRUSH maps and make the necessary configurations.

The Ceph cluster that we deployed and have played around with in this book is hosted on virtual machines and does not have real SSD disks backing it. Hence, we will be assuming we have a few virtual disks as SSD disks for learning purposes. There will be no change if you are performing this exercise on a real SSD disk-based Ceph cluster.

For the following demonstration, let's assume that `osd.0`, `osd.3`, and `osd.6` are SSD disks, and we would be creating an SSD pool on these disks. Similarly, let's assume `osd.1`, `osd.5`, and `osd.7` are SATA disks, which would be hosting the SATA pool.

How to do it...

Let's begin the configuration:

1. Get the current CRUSH map and decompile it:

   ```
   # ceph osd getcrushmap -o crushmapdump
   # crushtool -d crushmapdump -o crushmapdump-decompiled
   ```

   ```
   [vagrant@ceph-node3 ~]$
   [vagrant@ceph-node3 ~]$ sudo ceph osd getcrushmap -o crushmapdump
   got crush map from osdmap epoch 67
   [vagrant@ceph-node3 ~]$ sudo crushtool -d crushmapdump -o crushmapdump-decompiled
   [vagrant@ceph-node3 ~]$ ls -l crushmapdump-decompiled
   -rw-r--r-- 1 root root 1476 Aug 19 20:35 crushmapdump-decompiled
   [vagrant@ceph-node3 ~]$
   ```

2. Edit the `crushmapdump-decompiled` CRUSH map file and add the following section after the `root` default section:

   ```
   root ssd {
           id -5
           alg straw
           hash 0
           item osd.0 weight 0.010
           item osd.3 weight 0.010
           item osd.6 weight 0.010
   }

   root sata {
           id -6
           alg straw
           hash 0
           item osd.1 weight 0.010
           item osd.4 weight 0.010
           item osd.7 weight 0.010
   }
   ```

3. Create the CRUSH rule by adding the following rules under the `rule` section of the CRUSH map, and then save and exit the file:

```
rule ssd-pool {
        ruleset 1
        type replicated
        min_size 1
        max_size 10
        step take ssd
        step chooseleaf firstn 0 type osd
        step emit
}

rule sata-pool {
        ruleset 2
        type replicated
        min_size 1
        max_size 10
        step take sata
        step chooseleaf firstn 0 type osd
        step emit
}
```

4. Compile and inject the new CRUSH map in the Ceph cluster:

```
# crushtool -c crushmapdump-decompiled -o crushmapdump-compiled
```

```
# ceph osd setcrushmap -i crushmapdump-compiled
```

 Add the `osd_crush_update_on_start=false` option in either the `[global]` or `[osd]` section of `ceph.conf` in all the OSD nodes so in future if any OSD nodes or OSD's will be restarted they will use custom CRUSH map and will not update it back to default.

5. Once the new CRUSH map has been applied to the Ceph cluster, check the OSD tree view for the new arrangement, and notice the `ssd` and `sata` root buckets:

```
# ceph osd tree
```

```
[root@ceph-node1 ~]# ceph osd tree
ID WEIGHT  TYPE NAME          UP/DOWN REWEIGHT PRIMARY-AFFINITY
-6 0.02998 root sata
 1 0.00999     osd.1              up  1.00000          1.00000
 4 0.00999     osd.4              up  1.00000          1.00000
 7 0.00999     osd.7              up  1.00000          1.00000
-5 0.02998 root ssd
 0 0.00999     osd.0              up  1.00000          1.00000
 3 0.00999     osd.3              up  1.00000          1.00000
 6 0.00999     osd.6              up  1.00000          1.00000
-1 0.09000 root default
-3 0.03000     host ceph-node2
 3 0.00999         osd.3          up  1.00000          1.00000
 4 0.00999         osd.4          up  1.00000          1.00000
 5 0.00999         osd.5          up  1.00000          1.00000
-4 0.03000     host ceph-node3
 6 0.00999         osd.6          up  1.00000          1.00000
 7 0.00999         osd.7          up  1.00000          1.00000
 8 0.00999         osd.8          up  1.00000          1.00000
-2 0.03000     host ceph-node1
 1 0.00999         osd.1          up  1.00000          1.00000
 2 0.00999         osd.2          up  1.00000          1.00000
 0 0.00999         osd.0          up  1.00000          1.00000
[root@ceph-node1 ~]#
```

6. Create and verify the `ssd-pool`.

 Since this is a small cluster hosted on virtual machines, we will create these pools with a few PGs.

1. Create the `ssd-pool`:

   ```
   # ceph osd pool create ssd-pool 8 8
   ```

2. Verify the `ssd-pool`; notice that the `crush_ruleset` is 0, which is by default:

   ```
   # ceph osd dump | grep -i ssd
   ```

```
[root@ceph-node1 ~]# ceph osd pool create ssd-pool 8 8
pool 'ssd-pool' created
[root@ceph-node1 ~]# ceph osd dump | grep -i ssd
pool 45 'ssd-pool' replicated size 3 min_size 2 crush_ruleset 0 object_hash rjenkins pg_num 8 pgp_num 8
last_change 4446 flags hashpspool stripe_width 0
[root@ceph-node1 ~]#
```

3. Let's change the `crush_ruleset` to 1 so that the new pool gets created on the SSD disks:

```
# ceph osd pool set ssd-pool crush_ruleset 1
```

4. Verify the pool and notice the change in `crush_ruleset`:

```
# ceph osd dump | grep -i ssd
```

```
[root@ceph-node1 ~]# ceph osd pool set ssd-pool crush_ruleset 1
set pool 45 crush_ruleset to 1
[root@ceph-node1 ~]# ceph osd dump | grep -i ssd
pool 45 'ssd-pool' replicated size 3 min_size 2 crush_ruleset 1 object_hash rjenkins pg_num 8 pgp_num 8
last_change 4448 flags hashpspool stripe_width 0
[root@ceph-node1 ~]# _
```

7. Similarly, create and verify `sata-pool`:

```
[root@ceph-node1 ~]# ceph osd pool create sata-pool 8 8
pool 'sata-pool' created
[root@ceph-node1 ~]# ceph osd dump | grep -i sata
pool 46 'sata-pool' replicated size 3 min_size 2 crush_ruleset 0 object_hash rjenkins
pg_num 8 pgp_num 8 last_change 4450 flags hashpspool stripe_width 0
[root@ceph-node1 ~]#
[root@ceph-node1 ~]# ceph osd pool set sata-pool crush_ruleset 2
set pool 46 crush_ruleset to 1
[root@ceph-node1 ~]#
[root@ceph-node1 ~]# ceph osd dump | grep -i sata
pool 46 'sata-pool' replicated size 3 min_size 2 crush_ruleset 2 object_hash rjenkins
pg_num 8 pgp_num 8 last_change 4452 flags hashpspool stripe_width 0
[root@ceph-node1 ~]#
```

8. Let's add some objects to these pools:

1. Since these pools are new, they should not contain any objects, but let's verify this by using the `rados` list command:

```
# rados -p ssd-pool ls
```

```
# rados -p sata-pool ls
```

2. We will now add an object to these pools using the `rados put` command. The syntax would be `rados -p <pool_name> put <object_name> <file_name>`:

```
# rados -p ssd-pool put dummy_object1 /etc/hosts
# rados -p sata-pool put dummy_object1 /etc/hosts
```

3. Using the `rados` list command, list these pools. You should get the object names that we stored in the last step:

```
# rados -p ssd-pool ls
# rados -p sata-pool ls
```

```
[root@ceph-node1 ~]# rados -p ssd-pool ls
[root@ceph-node1 ~]# rados -p sata-pool ls
[root@ceph-node1 ~]#
[root@ceph-node1 ~]# rados -p ssd-pool put dummy_object1 /etc/hosts
[root@ceph-node1 ~]# rados -p sata-pool put dummy_object1 /etc/hosts
[root@ceph-node1 ~]#
[root@ceph-node1 ~]# rados -p ssd-pool ls
dummy_object1
[root@ceph-node1 ~]# rados -p sata-pool ls
dummy_object1
[root@ceph-node1 ~]#
```

9. Now, the interesting part of this entire section is to verify that the objects are getting stored on the correct set of OSDs:

1. For the `ssd-pool`, we have used the OSDs 0, 3, and 6. Check the `osd map` for `ssd-pool` using the syntax `ceph osd map <pool_name> <object_name>`:

```
# ceph osd map ssd-pool dummy_object1
```

2. Similarly, check the object from sata-pool:

```
# ceph osd map sata-pool dummy_object1
```

```
[root@ceph-node1 ~]# ceph osd map ssd-pool dummy_object1
osdmap e4455 pool 'ssd-pool' (45) object 'dummy_object1' -> pg 45.71968e96 (45.6) -> up ([3,0,6], p3) acting ([3,0,6], p3)
[root@ceph-node1 ~]#
[root@ceph-node1 ~]# ceph osd map sata-pool dummy_object1
osdmap e4455 pool 'sata-pool' (46) object 'dummy_object1' -> pg 46.71968e96 (46.6) -> up ([1,7,4], p1) acting ([1,7,4], p1)
[root@ceph-node1 ~]#
```

As shown in the preceding screenshot, the object that is created on `ssd-pool` is actually stored on the OSDs set [3, 0, 6], and the object that is created on `sata-pool` gets stored on the OSDs set [1, 7, 4]. This output was expected, and it verifies that the pool that we created uses the correct set of OSDs as we requested. This type of configuration can be very useful in a production setup, where you would like to create a fast pool based on SSDs only, and a medium/slower performing pool based on spinning disks.

The Virtual Storage Manager
for Ceph

9

In this chapter, we will cover the following recipes:

- Understanding the VSM architecture
- Setting up the VSM environment
- Getting ready for VSM
- Installing VSM
- Creating a Ceph cluster using VSM
- Exploring the VSM dashboard
- Upgrading the Ceph cluster using VSM
- VSM roadmap
- VSM resources

Introductionc

The **Virtual Storage Manager** (**VSM**) is software originally initiated and developed by Intel for Ceph cluster management; it was later open sourced by Intel under the Apache 2.0 License. Ceph comes with the `ceph-deploy` CLI tool for cluster deployment, and it also provides a rich CLI for cluster management. VSM, on the other hand, provides a web-based user interface to simplify the creation and management of Ceph clusters. By using the VSM GUI Ceph cluster, the operator can monitor overall cluster health, manage cluster hardware and storage capacity, as well as attach the Ceph storage pools to the OpenStack Cinder.

VSM is developed in Python using OpenStack Horizon as its base for the application framework. It has the familiar look and feel of OpenStack Horizon for both software developers and OpenStack administrators. Some of the key features of VSM include the following:

- A web-based user interface for easy administration of the Ceph cluster
- It better organizes and manages the server and storage devices
- It aids the Ceph cluster's deployment and scale up by adding the MON, OSD, and MDS nodes
- It aids the Ceph cluster component and capacity monitoring
- It is beneficial to the overall cluster and individual node performance monitoring
- It allows the creation of erasure coded and cache tier pools
- It assists in creating and attaching pools to the OpenStack Cinder
- It brings the multiuser management interface to Ceph cluster
- It allows for the upgrading of the Ceph cluster

Understanding the VSM architecture

In this recipe, we will quickly go through the architecture of VSM, which consists of the following components:

The VSM controller

VSM is a web-based application that is typically hosted on a controller machine, which is referred to as a VSM controller node. You can use a dedicated physical or virtual server that can act as a VSM controller node. The VSM controller software is the core component of VSM that connects to the Ceph cluster through VSM agents. The VSM controller gathers all the data coming from VSM agents and monitors the Ceph cluster. For operations such as cluster creation, pool creation, and so on, the VSM controller sends instructions to VSM agents to perform the required operation. As shown in the following diagram, Ceph administrators/operators connect to the VSM controller node via HTTPs or APIs, and they can use VSM software. The VSM controller node also connects to the OpenStack controller to configure OpenStack to use Ceph. In addition to the web user interface service, the VSM controller also hosts MariaDB and RabbitMQ.

The VSM agent

The VSM agent is a process that runs on all Ceph cluster nodes. The job of the VSM agent is to send server configuration, cluster health/status information, as well as performance data to the VSM controller. The VSM agent uses the server manifest file to identify the VSM controller node, authenticate against it, and determine server configuration.

The following diagram illustrates the interaction of different VSM components with each other as well as with the OpenStack infrastructure and VSM operators:

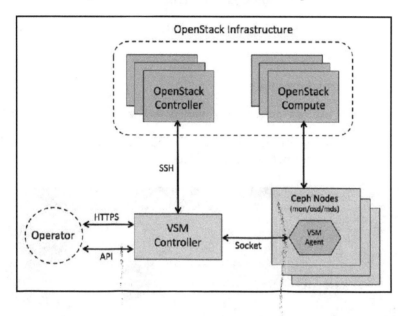

Setting up the VSM environment

In order to use VSM, you are required to build the Ceph cluster using VSM. VSM version 2.2.0 can control or manage the existing Ceph cluster (import the existing Ceph cluster). In this recipe, we will use Vagrant to launch four virtual machines named `vsm-controller`, `vsm-node1`, `vsm-node2`, and `vsm-node3`. The `vsm-controller` virtual machine will act as the VSM controller node and `vsm-node1`, `vsm-node2`, and `vsm-node3` will act as VSM agent nodes running the Ceph cluster.

How to do it...

Perform the following steps for setting up the VSM environment:

1. The `Vagrantfile` for launching the VSM virtual machines is available on the `Ceph-Designing-and-Implementing-Scalable-Storage-Systems` GitHub repository. Clone this repository, if you have not already done so:

   ```
   $ git clone git@github.com:PacktPublishing/Ceph-Designing-and-
   Implementing-Scalable-Storage-Systems.git
   ```

2. `Vagrantfile` for launching the VSM nodes is located on the `vsm` directory:

   ```
   $ cd vsm
   ```

3. Launch the virtual machines:

   ```
   $ vagrant up vsm-controller vsm-node1 vsm-node2 vsm-node3
   ```

4. Once the virtual machines are launched, you should have four virtual machines running with proper networking in place:

   ```
   [vumrao@ceph-jewel vsm]$
   [vumrao@ceph-jewel vsm]$ vagrant status
   Current machine states:

   vsm-node1                 running (virtualbox)
   vsm-node2                 running (virtualbox)
   vsm-node3                 running (virtualbox)
   vsm-controller            running (virtualbox)

   This environment represents multiple VMs. The VMs are all listed
   above with their current state. For more information about a specific
   VM, run `vagrant status NAME`.
   [vumrao@ceph-jewel vsm]$
   ```

To log in to these VMs, use `cephuser` as both the username and password. For a root login, the password is `vagrant`. Vagrant automates the networking between these VMs with the following details:

```
192.168.123.100 vsm-controller
192.168.123.101 vsm-node1
192.168.123.102 vsm-node2
192.168.123.103 vsm-node3
```

Getting ready for VSM

In the last recipe, we preconfigured virtual machines using Vagrant; they are to be used with VSM. In this recipe, we will learn about the preflight configuration that is needed on these VMs so that it can be used with VSM.

Please note that by using Vagrant, we have done most of this preflight configuration using the shell script file, `Ceph-Designing-and-Implementing-Scalable-Storage-Systems/vsm/post-deploy.sh`, present in the GitHub repository that we cloned in the last recipe. You might not want to repeat these first four steps as Vagrant already performed them. We are explaining these steps here so that you can learn what Vagrant did in the background.

How to do it...

Use the following steps to configure the VSM environment:

1. Create the user, `cephuser`, on all the nodes that will be used for VSM deployment. For simplicity, we will set the password of this user as `cephuser`. You can always use a username of your choice. Also, provide `sudo` rights to this user:

   ```
   # useradd cephuser
   # echo 'cephuser:cephuser' | chpasswd
   # echo "cephuser ALL=(ALL) NOPASSWD: ALL" >>
    /etc/sudoers
   ```

2. Ensure that the NTP is configured:

   ```
   # systemctl stop ntpd
   # systemctl stop ntpdate
   # ntpdate 0.centos.pool.ntp.org > /dev/null 2> /dev/null
   # systemctl start ntpdate
   # systemctl start ntpd
   ```

3. Install `tree` (optional), `git`, and the `epel` packages:

   ```
   # yum install -y tree git epel-release
   ```

4. Add host information to the `/etc/hosts` file:

```
192.168.123.100 vsm-controller
192.168.123.101 vsm-node1
192.168.123.102 vsm-node2
192.168.123.103 vsm-node3
```

 These are some steps that we have automated using Vagrant, which uses the `post-deploy.sh` script. If you are using the specified GitHub `Ceph-Designing-and-Implementing-Scalable-Storage-Systems` repository that we have created for VSM, then you do not need to perform these four steps.

The following steps must be performed on the nodes as specified:

1. Log in to the `vsm-controller` node, and generate and share the SSH keys with other VSM nodes. During this step, you will need to input the `cephuser` password, which is `cephuser`:

```
# ssh cephuser@192.168.123.100
$ mkdir .ssh;ssh-keygen -f .ssh/id_rsa -t rsa -N ''
$ ssh-copy-id vsm-node1
$ ssh-copy-id vsm-node2
$ ssh-copy-id vsm-node3
```

2. Using Vagrant, we have attached three VirtualBox virtual disks on each `vsm-node1`, `vsm-node2`, `vsm-node3`, which will be used as Ceph OSD disks. We need to partition these disks manually for the Ceph OSD and Journal so that VSM can use them with Ceph. Execute the following commands on `vsm-node1`, `vsm-node2`, `vsm-node3`:

```
$ sudo parted /dev/sdb -- mklabel gpt
$ sudo parted -a optimal /dev/sdb -- mkpart primary 10% 100%
$ sudo parted -a optimal /dev/sdb -- mkpart primary 0 10%
$ sudo parted /dev/sdc -- mklabel gpt
$ sudo parted -a optimal /dev/sdc -- mkpart primary 10% 100%
$ sudo parted -a optimal /dev/sdc -- mkpart primary 0 10%
$ sudo parted /dev/sdd -- mklabel gpt
$ sudo parted -a optimal /dev/sdd -- mkpart primary 0 10%
$ sudo parted -a optimal /dev/sdd -- mkpart primary 10% 100%
```

```
[cephuser@vsm-node1 ~]$
[cephuser@vsm-node1 ~]$ sudo parted /dev/sdb -- mklabel gpt
Information: You may need to update /etc/fstab.

[cephuser@vsm-node1 ~]$ sudo parted -a optimal /dev/sdb -- mkpart primary 10% 100%
Information: You may need to update /etc/fstab.

[cephuser@vsm-node1 ~]$ sudo parted -a optimal /dev/sdb -- mkpart primary 0 10%
Warning: The resulting partition is not properly aligned for best performance.
Ignore/Cancel? Ignore
Information: You may need to update /etc/fstab.

[cephuser@vsm-node1 ~]$
```

3. Once you have created partitions on all disks, list block devices on these nodes to verify that the partitions look as shown here:

```
[cephuser@vsm-node1 ~]$
[cephuser@vsm-node1 ~]$ lsblk
NAME              MAJ:MIN RM   SIZE RO TYPE MOUNTPOINT
sda                   8:0   0    8G  0 disk
├─sda1                8:1   0  500M  0 part /boot
└─sda2                8:2   0  7.5G  0 part
  ├─centos-swap   253:0   0  820M  0 lvm  [SWAP]
  └─centos-root   253:1   0  6.7G  0 lvm  /
sdb                  8:16   0   20G  0 disk
├─sdb1               8:17   0   18G  0 part
└─sdb2               8:18   0    2G  0 part
sdc                  8:32   0   20G  0 disk
├─sdc1               8:33   0   18G  0 part
└─sdc2               8:34   0    2G  0 part
sdd                  8:48   0   20G  0 disk
├─sdd1               8:49   0   18G  0 part
└─sdd2               8:50   0    2G  0 part
sr0                 11:0   1 1024M  0 rom
[cephuser@vsm-node1 ~]$
```

4. At this stage, we have completed the prerequisites required for VSM:

```
[vumrao@ceph-jewel vsm]$
[vumrao@ceph-jewel vsm]$ for i in controller node1 node2 node3 ; do VBoxManage snapshot vsm-$i take good-state ; done
0%...10%...20%...30%...40%...50%...60%...70%...80%...90%...100%
Snapshot taken. UUID: ece2b285-6468-4897-9787-e37027e65d10
0%...10%...20%...30%...40%...50%...60%...70%...80%...90%...100%
Snapshot taken. UUID: 28abc511-357a-4333-94c3-e01a048a8ae5
0%...10%...20%...30%...40%...50%...60%...70%...80%...90%...100%
Snapshot taken. UUID: b24bffb5-50d6-4375-880a-4b9b9a323a3e
0%...10%...20%...30%...40%...50%...60%...70%...80%...90%...100%
Snapshot taken. UUID: 20469eef-ad7e-4bc8-b092-8b4b1793aa6a
[vumrao@ceph-jewel vsm]$ _
```

Installing VSM

In the last recipe, we made all the preparations required for deploying VSM. In this recipe, we will learn how to automatically deploy VSM on all the nodes.

How to do it...

We will be using the following steps to install the VSM software:

1. Before proceeding with VSM installation, let us upgrade all four VMs to the latest CentOS 7 packages and configuration:

   ```
   $ sudo yum update -y
   $ sudo reboot
   ```

2. Log in to all four VSM VMs and configure Ceph Jewel version repositories:

   ```
   sudo yum install -y http://download.ceph.com/rpm-jewel/el7/noarch/
                        ceph-release-1-1.el7.noarch.rpm
   ```

3. In this demonstration, we will use CentOS 7 as the base operating system; let's download the VSM repository for CentOS 7. Log in to the `vsm-controller` node as `cephuser` and get the VSM version 2.2.0:

   ```
   ssh cephuser@192.168.123.100
   $ wget https://github.com/01org/virtual-storage-
     manager/releases/download/v2.2.0/2.2.0-521-centos7.tar.gz
   ```

4. VSM is also available for the Ubuntu OS and can be downloaded from `https://` `github.com/01org/virtual-storage-manager`.

5. Extract VSM:

```
$ tar -xvf 2.2.0-521-centos7.tar.gz
$ cd  2.2.0-521
```

```
[cephuser@vsm-controller ~]$ cd 2.2.0-521
[cephuser@vsm-controller 2.2.0-521]$ ls -la
total 600
drwxr-xr-x 4 cephuser cephuser   4096 Jul 29  2016 .
drwx------ 4 cephuser cephuser    137 Aug  9 04:31 ..
-rw-r--r-- 1 cephuser cephuser  49343 Jul 29  2016 CHANGELOG.md
-rw-r--r-- 1 cephuser cephuser 195591 Jul 29  2016 CHANGELOG.pdf
-rwxr-xr-x 1 cephuser cephuser     94 Jul 29  2016 get_pass.sh
-rw-r--r-- 1 cephuser cephuser  30605 Jul 29  2016 INSTALL.md
-rw-r--r-- 1 cephuser cephuser 252953 Jul 29  2016 INSTALL.pdf
-rw-r--r-- 1 cephuser cephuser    739 Jul 29  2016 installrc
-rwxr-xr-x 1 cephuser cephuser  24629 Jul 29  2016 install.sh
-rw-r--r-- 1 cephuser cephuser    580 Jul 29  2016 LICENSE
drwxr-xr-x 2 cephuser cephuser     65 Jul 29  2016 manifest
-rw-r--r-- 1 cephuser cephuser    320 Jul 29  2016 NOTICE
-rwxr-xr-x 1 cephuser cephuser   1155 Jul 29  2016 prov_node.sh
-rw-r--r-- 1 cephuser cephuser   3121 Jul 29  2016 README.md
-rw-r--r-- 1 cephuser cephuser      4 Jul 29  2016 RELEASE
-rw-r--r-- 1 cephuser cephuser   1176 Jul 29  2016 rpms.lst
-rwxr-xr-x 1 cephuser cephuser   2569 Jul 29  2016 uninstall.sh
-rw-r--r-- 1 cephuser cephuser      6 Jul 29  2016 VERSION
drwxr-xr-x 3 cephuser cephuser   4096 Jul 29  2016 vsmrepo
[cephuser@vsm-controller 2.2.0-521]$
```

6. Set the controller node and agent node's address; add the following lines to the `installrc` file:

```
AGENT_ADDRESS_LIST="192.168.123.101 192.168.123.102
                    192.168.123.103"
CONTROLLER_ADDRESS="192.168.123.100"
```

7. Verify the `installrc` file:

```
$ cat installrc | egrep -v "#|^$"
```

```
[cephuser@vsm-controller 2.2.0-521]$
[cephuser@vsm-controller 2.2.0-521]$ cat installrc | egrep -v "#|^$"
AGENT_ADDRESS_LIST="192.168.123.101 192.168.123.102 192.168.123.103"
CONTROLLER_ADDRESS="192.168.123.100"
[cephuser@vsm-controller 2.2.0-521]$
```

8. In the `manifest` folder, create directories using the name of the management IP of the `vsm-controller` and `vsm-nodes`:

```
$ cd manifest
$ mkdir 192.168.123.100 192.168.123.101 192.168.123.102
        192.168.123.103
```

9. Copy the sample cluster manifest file to `192.168.123.100/cluster.manifest`, which is the `vsm-controller` node:

```
$ cp cluster.manifest.sample 192.168.123.100/cluster.manifest
```

10. Edit the `cluster.manifest` file that we added in the last step with the following changes:

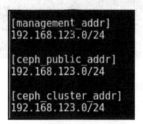

```
[management_addr]
192.168.123.0/24

[ceph_public_addr]
192.168.123.0/24

[ceph_cluster_addr]
192.168.123.0/24
```

You should know that in a production environment, it's recommended that you have separate networks for Ceph management, Ceph public, and Ceph cluster traffic. Using the `cluster.manifest` file, VSM can be instructed to use these different networks for your Ceph cluster.

11. Edit the `manifest/server.manifest.sample` file and make the following changes:

    1. Add the VSM controller IP, `192.168.123.100`, under the `[vsm_controller_ip]` section.

    2. Add a disk device name for `[sata_device]` and `[journal_device]`, as shown in the following screenshot. Make sure that the `sata_device` and `journal_device` names are separated by a space:

vim server.manifest.sample

```
[vsm_controller_ip]
192.168.123.100

[role]
#role can be storage, monitor, mds and rgw
storage
monitor

[auth_key]
token-tenant

[ssd]
#format [ssd_device]  [journal_device]

[7200_rpm_sata]
#format [sata_device]   [journal_device]
/dev/sdb1 /dev/sdb2
/dev/sdc1 /dev/sdc2
/dev/sdd1 /dev/sdd2

[10krpm_sas]
#format [sas_device]  [journal_device]
#%osd-by-path-1%   %journal-by-path-1%
#%osd-by-path-2%   %journal-by-path-2%
#%osd-by-path-3%   %journal-by-path-3%
#%osd-by-path-4%   %journal-by-path-4%
#%osd-by-path-5%   %journal-by-path-5%
#%osd-by-path-6%   %journal-by-path-6%
#%osd-by-path-7%   %journal-by-path-7%

[ssd_cached_7200rpm_sata]
#format [intel_cache_device]   [journal_device]

[ssd_cached_10krpm_sas]
#format [intel_cache_device]   [journal_device]
```

The `server.manifest` file provides several configuration options for different types of disks. In a production environment, it's recommended that you use the correct disk type based on your hardware.

12. Once you have made changes to the `manifest/server.manifest.sample` file, verify all the changes:

```
$ cat server.manifest.sample | egrep -v "#|^$"
```

```
[cephuser@vsm-controller manifest]$
[cephuser@vsm-controller manifest]$ cat server.manifest.sample | egrep -v "#|^$"
[vsm_controller_ip]
192.168.123.100
[role]
storage
monitor
[auth_key]
token-tenant
[ssd]
[7200_rpm_sata]
/dev/sdb1 /dev/sdb2
/dev/sdc1 /dev/sdc2
/dev/sdd1 /dev/sdd2
[10krpm_sas]
[ssd_cached_7200rpm_sata]
[ssd_cached_10krpm_sas]
[cephuser@vsm-controller manifest]$
```

13. Copy the `manifest/server.manifest.sample` file that we edited in the previous steps to all the VSM nodes, that is, `vsm-node1`, `vsm-node2`, and `vsm-node3`:

```
$ cp server.manifest.sample 192.168.123.101/server.manifest
$ cp server.manifest.sample 192.168.123.102/server.manifest
$ cp server.manifest.sample 192.168.123.103/server.manifest
```

14. Verify the manifest directory structure:

```
$ tree
```

```
[cephuser@vsm-controller manifest]$
[cephuser@vsm-controller manifest]$ tree
.
├── 192.168.123.100
│   └── cluster.manifest
├── 192.168.123.101
│   └── server.manifest
├── 192.168.123.102
│   └── server.manifest
├── 192.168.123.103
│   └── server.manifest
├── cluster.manifest.sample
└── server.manifest.sample

4 directories, 6 files
[cephuser@vsm-controller manifest]$
```

15. To begin the VSM installation, add the execute permission to the `install.sh` file:

    ```
    $ cd ..
    $ chmod +x install.sh
    ```

16. Finally, install VSM by running the `install.sh` file with the `--check-dependence-package` parameter, which downloads packages that are necessary for the VSM installation from `https//github.com/01org/vsm-dependencies`:

    ```
    $ ./install.sh -u cephuser -v 2.1 --check-dependence-package
    ```

    We need to use the version as 2.1 in the command line for resolving the dependencies. But the installed version will be 2.2.0. This book is targeted for Ceph version Jewel and VSM 2.2.0 is still in beta and has not released 2.2 dependencies, we need to use 2.1 released dependencies. VSM 2.2.0 beta is the only version which supports Jewel.

    The VSM installation will take several minutes. The installer process might require you to input the `cephuser` password for the `vsm-controller` node. In that case, please input `cephuser` as the password. In case you encounter any errors and wish to restart the VSM installation, it is recommended that you clean your system before you retry it. Execute the `uninstall.sh` script file for a system cleanup.

Once the installation is finished, you will have the following messages as shown in the screenshot:

```
Warning: Permanently added '192.168.123.103' (ECDSA) to the list of known hosts.
Restarting diamond (via systemctl):                          [  OK  ]
Connection to 192.168.123.103 closed.
+ ssh -t cephuser@192.168.123.103 'cd /etc/yum.repos.d; if [[ -d /tmp/backup ]]; then sudo -E mv /tmp/backup/* .; sudo -E rm -rf /tmp/backup; fi'
Warning: Permanently added '192.168.123.103' (ECDSA) to the list of known hosts.
Connection to 192.168.123.103 closed.
+  scp vsm_conf_to_agent_from_controller 192.168.123.103
+ [[ -n '' ]]
+ echo Finished.
Finished.
+ set +o xtrace
[cephuser@vsm-controller 2.2.0-521]$ █
```

17. Once the VSM installation is finished, extract the password for the admin user by executing `get_pass.sh` on the `vsm-controller` node:

    $ ./get_pass.sh

```
[cephuser@vsm-controller 2.2.0-521]$
[cephuser@vsm-controller 2.2.0-521]$ ./get_pass.sh
9f80e475f1e3f31dd442
[cephuser@vsm-controller 2.2.0-521]$
```

18. Finally, log in to the VSM dashboard, `https://192.168.123.100/dashboard/vsm`, with the user, `admin`, and password that we extracted in the last step.

Creating a Ceph cluster using VSM

In the last recipe, we just installed VSM; we do not yet have a Ceph cluster. In this recipe, we will create the Ceph cluster using VSM so that VSM can manage this cluster later. You will find that deploying the Ceph cluster is extremely easy with VSM.

How to do it...

To create the Ceph cluster from the VSM dashboard, navigate to **Cluster Management | Create Cluster**, and then click on the **Create Cluster** button.

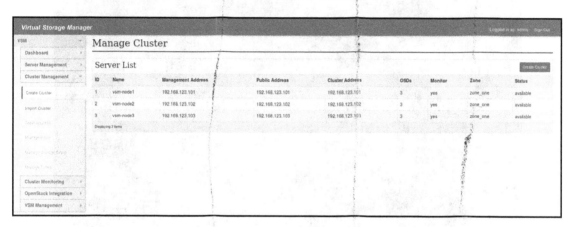

VSM Dashboard create cluster section

If you check preceding screenshot, version 2.2.0 has the **Import Cluster tab. As 2.20 is still in beta, we need to use a couple of hacks:**

1. Disable MDSs and RGWs and restart `vsm-api`.

   Open file `/usr/lib/python2.7/site-packages/vsm/api/v1/clusters.py`.

   The file can be found at `https://github.com/01org/virtual-storage-manager/blob/master/source/vsm/vsm/api/v1/clusters.py`.

RGW is already disabled, we need to do it for MDS also:

```
"""
# only and should only one mds
mds_count = 0
for server in server_list:
    if server['is_mds'] == False:
    #if server['is_mds'] == True:
        mds_count = mds_count + 1
if mds_count > 1:
    raise exc.HTTPBadRequest("More than one mds.")

"""


# RGW with simple configuration(one rgw instance)
# RGW with federated configuration(multiple rgw instances)

"""
# only and should only one rgw
rgw_count = 0
for server in server_list:
    if server['is_rgw'] == True:
        rgw_count = rgw_count + 1
if rgw_count > 1:
    raise exc.HTTPBadRequest("More than one rgw.")
"""
```

/etc/init.d/vsm-api restart

2. Disable MDSs and RGWs and restart `vsm-scheduler`:

Open file `/usr/lib/python2.7/site-packages/vsm/scheduler/manager.py`.

```
for ser in server_list:
    if ser['is_monitor'] == True:
        count += 1
    #if ser['is_mds'] == True:
    #    mds_node = ser
    #if ser['is_rgw'] == True:
    #    rgw_node.append(ser)
```

`/etc/init.d/vsm-scheduler restart`

3. Select all the nodes by clicking on the checkbox next to the ID, and finally, click on the **Create Cluster button:**

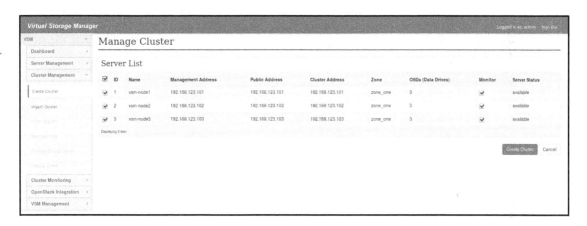

VSM Dashboard create cluster section after clicking on create cluster tab

The Ceph cluster's creation will take a few minutes. VSM will display very briefly what it's doing in the background under the status field of the dashboard as shown next:

Monitor	Zone	Status
yes	zone_one	Cleaning
yes	zone_one	Cleaning
yes	zone_one	Cleaning

After cleaning, it will mount disks, as shown under the status field of the dashboard in the following screenshot:

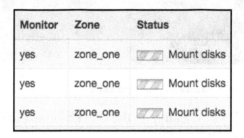

Once the Ceph cluster deployment is completed, VSM will display the node status as **Active. But only monitor daemons will be up and OSDs will not be started. VSM creates the OSD data path as** `/var/lib/ceph/osd/osd$id` **but Ceph Jewel version expects the OSD's data path as** `/var/lib/ceph/osd/$cluster-$id`:

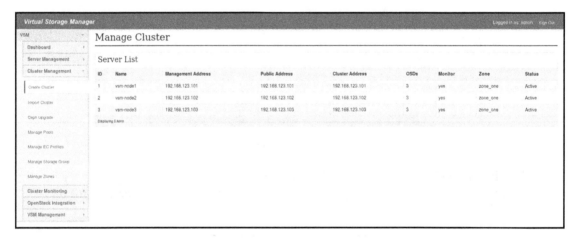

VSM Dashboard after cluster got created with status as active

4. We need to apply the following patch `/usr/lib/ceph/ceph-osd-prestart.sh` in all three VMs:

   ```
   data="/var/lib/ceph/osd/${cluster:-ceph}-$id"
   data="/var/lib/ceph/osd/osd$id"
   ```

5. Start the OSD's in all the three VM's one by one with the following command:

   ```
   $ systemctl start ceph-osd@$id
   ```

   This will bring all the OSDs up and in.

6. If PG's are stuck while creating, you might want to remove the default pool and recreate it:

```
[cephuser@vsm-node1 ~]$
[cephuser@vsm-node1 ~]$ ceph -s
    cluster 406d2572-7caf-11e7-9402-080027c5464e
     health HEALTH_OK
     monmap e1: 3 mons at {0=192.168.123.101:6789/0,1=192.168.123.102:6789/0,2=192.168.123.103:6789/0}
            election epoch 4, quorum 0,1,2 0,1,2
     osdmap e91: 9 osds: 9 up, 9 in
            flags sortbitwise,require_jewel_osds
      pgmap v246: 128 pgs, 1 pools, 0 bytes data, 0 objects
            306 MB used, 161 GB / 161 GB avail
                 128 active+clean
[cephuser@vsm-node1 ~]$ ceph osd tree
ID  WEIGHT  TYPE NAME                                UP/DOWN REWEIGHT PRIMARY-AFFINITY
-16 9.00000 root vsm
-15 9.00000     storage_group capacity
-12 9.00000         zone zone_one_capacity
 -3 3.00000             host vsm-node1_capacity_zone_one
  0 1.00000                 osd.0                         up  1.00000          1.00000
  1 1.00000                 osd.1                         up  1.00000          1.00000
  2 1.00000                 osd.2                         up  1.00000          1.00000
 -6 3.00000             host vsm-node2_capacity_zone_one
  3 1.00000                 osd.3                         up  1.00000          1.00000
  4 1.00000                 osd.4                         up  1.00000          1.00000
  5 1.00000                 osd.5                         up  1.00000          1.00000
 -9 3.00000             host vsm-node3_capacity_zone_one
  6 1.00000                 osd.6                         up  1.00000          1.00000
  7 1.00000                 osd.7                         up  1.00000          1.00000
  8 1.00000                 osd.8                         up  1.00000          1.00000
[cephuser@vsm-node1 ~]$
```

Installed Ceph Jewel version:

```
[root@vsm-node1 ~]#
[root@vsm-node1 ~]# ceph -v
ceph version 10.2.9 (2ee413f77150c0f375ff6f10edd6c8f9c7d060d0)
[root@vsm-node1 ~]# ceph daemon osd.0 version
{"version":"10.2.9"}
[root@vsm-node1 ~]#
```

7. Finally, check the cluster status from **Dashboard** | **Cluster Status:**

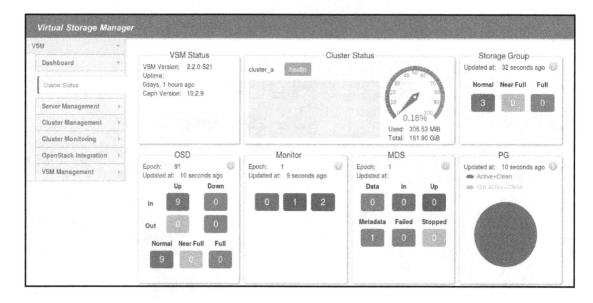

IOPS, Latency, Bandwidth, and CPU details are also available in the dashboard:

Exploring the VSM dashboard

The VSM dashboard makes most of the operations around the Ceph cluster extremely easy, whether it's deployment, server management, cluster management/monitoring, or even OpenStack integration. The VSM dashboard is very user-friendly and you can explore most of its features by yourself. The VSM dashboard provides the following options:

- **Dashboard: This provides the complete status of the system including the following:**
    - **VSM Status: This gives you the VSM version, uptime, Ceph version, and so on**
    - **Cluster Summary: This gives you the Ceph cluster status, similar to the** `ceph -s` **command output**
    - **Summary: OSD, Monitor, MDS, and PG summary gives performance metrics such as IOPS, Latency, Bandwidth, and CPU utilization for all Ceph nodes**

- **Server Management: This includes the following:**
  - **Manage Servers: The functions are described as follows:**
    - It provides lists of all servers with information such as **Management Address, Cluster Address and Public Address, Ceph Version, Status, and so on**
    - It provides options to `Add Servers` or `Remove Servers`, **Add Monitors, and Start Servers or Stop Servers:**

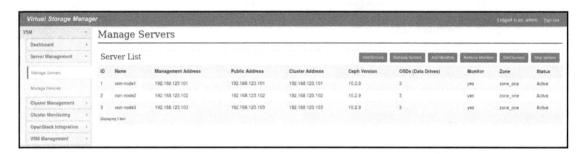

VSM Dashboard Manage Server section - server list tab

  - **Manage Devices: The functions are described as follows:**
    - This gives the list of all Ceph OSDs including their status, weight, server they are hosted on, as well as storage class
    - This allows the creation of new OSDs as well as the restarting, removing, and restoring of OSDs

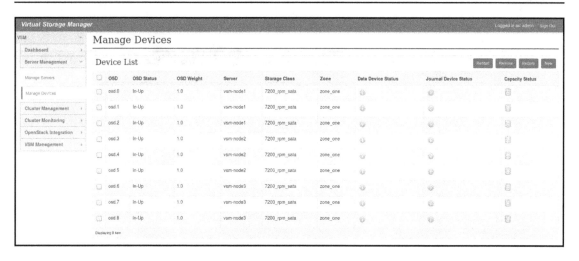

VSM Dashboard Manage Device section - device list tab

- **Cluster Management**: This section of the VSM dashboard provides several options to manage the Ceph cluster:
    - **Create Cluster, Upgrade Cluster, and Manage Pools** helps you to create replicated/erasure coded pools, add/remove cache tier, and so on
    - **Manage Storage Group** adds new storage groups
- **Cluster Monitoring**: This section of the VSM dashboard provides complete cluster monitoring, including all of its components:
    - **Storage Group Status**
    - **Pool Status**
    - **OSD Status**
    - **Monitor Status**
    - **MDS Status**
    - **PG Status**
    - **RBD Status**

The components can be seen in the following screenshot:

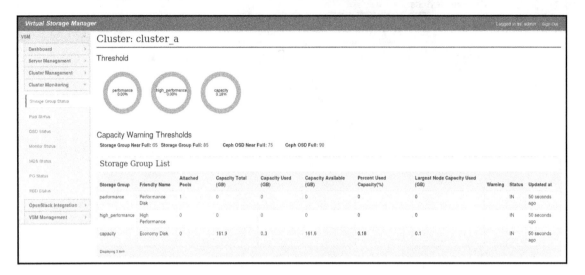

VSM Dashboad cluster storage group status

- **OpenStack Integration**: This section of the VSM dashboard allows us to integrate Ceph storage to the OpenStack by adding OpenStack endpoints and presenting RBD pools to OpenStack:

    - **Manage RBD Pools: Presents RBD Pools to OpenStack**
    - **OpenStack Access: Adds the OpenStack endpoint**

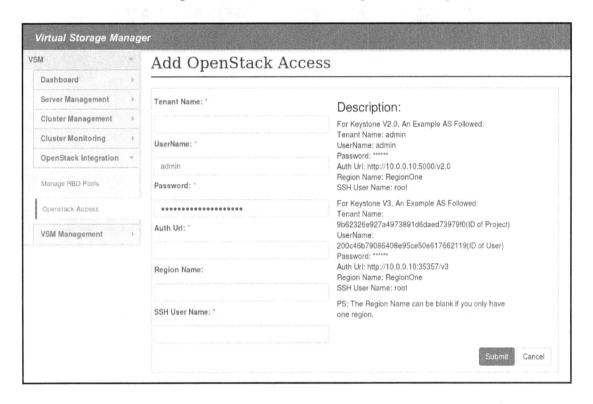

- **VSM Management: This section of the VSM dashboard allows us to manage settings related to the VSM dashboard itself:**
    - **Add/Remove User: Create or remove a user and change the password**
    - **Settings: Various settings related to Ceph**

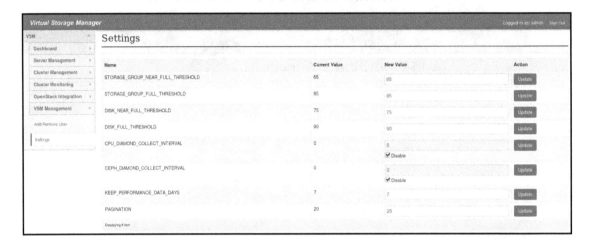

Upgrading the Ceph cluster using VSM

You are now quite familiar with VSM and know that it provides a nice dashboard that makes complicated Ceph related operations, such as Cluster creation, extremely easy. Another important aspect of VSM is that it automates the Ceph cluster upgrade process and simplifies it but as 2.2.0 is the latest beta release and it at the most, supports version Jewel and this Jewel version is already installed so we are not covering the upgrade to Kraken or Luminous release in this upgrade section.

VSM roadmap

The current stable version of VSM at the time of writing this book is 2.1. This is not the same version that we demonstrated in this chapter. In this chapter, we used 2.2 beta version because this is the version which supports Jewel. 2.2 supports cluster import and Ceph version Jewel.

VSM resources

In this chapter, we covered most of the important aspects of VSM. If you were planning to use VSM in your environment, I would recommend that you check out the following resources to get more information on VSM:

- The official source code repository can be found at: `https://github.com/01org/virtual-storage-manager`
- VSM Wiki can be found at: `https://github.com/01org/virtual-storage-manager/wiki`
- The VSM issue, development, and roadmap tracking can be found at: `https://01.org/jira/browse/VSM`
- The VSM mailing list can be found at: `http://vsm-discuss.33411.n7.nabble.com/`

As you already know that VSM is an open source project, it's worth mentioning that VSM's development efforts are being led by Intel with the help of its community.

We would like to thank Dan Ferber and Yaguang Wang from Intel, as well as the entire VSM community, for delivering to us a nice piece of software for deploying and managing the Ceph cluster. To help VSM develop further, please become an active member of the community and consider giving back by making meaningful contributions.

10
More on Ceph

In this chapter, we will cover the following recipes:

- Disk performance baseline
- Baseline network performance
- Ceph rados bench
- RADOS load-gen
- Benchmarking the Ceph Block Device
- Benchmarking Ceph RBD using FIO
- Ceph admin socket
- Using the ceph tell command
- Ceph REST API
- Profiling Ceph memory
- The ceph-objectstore-tool
- Using ceph-medic
- Deploying the experimental Ceph BlueStore

Introduction

In this chapter, we will cover benchmarking the Ceph cluster, which is a must-do thing before moving to production. We will also cover advanced methods of Ceph administration and troubleshooting using the admin socket, REST API, and the `ceph-objectstore-tool`. Finally, we will learn about Ceph memory profiling.

Benchmarking your Ceph cluster before using it for the production workload should be a priority. Benchmarking gives you approximate results on how your cluster will perform during read, write, latency, and other workloads.

Before doing the real benchmarking, it's a good idea to establish a baseline for the expected maximum performance by measuring the performance of the hardware connected to the cluster node, such as the disk and network.

Disk performance baseline

The disk performance baseline test will be done in two steps. First, we will measure the performance of a single disk, and after that, we will measure the performance of all the disks connected to one Ceph OSD node simultaneously.

 To get realistic results, I am running the benchmarking tests described in this recipe against a Ceph cluster deployed on physical hardware. We can also run these tests on the Ceph cluster, hosted on a virtual machine, but we might not get appealing results.

Single disk write performance

To get the disk read and write performance, we will use the `dd` command with `oflag` set to `direct` in order to bypass disk cache for realistic results.

How to do it...

Let's benchmark single disk write performance:

1. Drop caches:

   ```
   # echo 3 > /proc/sys/vm/drop_caches
   ```

2. Use `dd` to write a file named `deleteme` of the size `10G`, filled with zeros `/dev/zero` as the input file to the directory where Ceph OSD is mounted, that is, `/var/lib/ceph/osd/ceph-0/`:

   ```
   # dd if=/dev/zero of=/var/lib/ceph/osd/ceph-0/deleteme
     bs=10G count=1
     oflag=direct
   ```

Ideally, you should repeat step 1 and step 2 a few times and take the average value. In our case, the average value for write operations comes to be *121 MB/s*, as shown in the following screenshot:

```
[root@ceph4 ~]# dd if=/dev/zero of=/var/lib/ceph/osd/ceph-0/deleteme bs=10G count=1 oflag=
direct
0+1 records in
0+1 records out
2147479552 bytes (2.1 GB) copied, 17.81 s, 121 MB/s
[root@ceph4 ~]# dd if=/dev/zero of=/var/lib/ceph/osd/ceph-0/deleteme bs=10G count=1 oflag=
direct
0+1 records in
0+1 records out
2147479552 bytes (2.1 GB) copied, 17.7427 s, 121 MB/s
[root@ceph4 ~]# dd if=/dev/zero of=/var/lib/ceph/osd/ceph-0/deleteme bs=10G count=1 oflag=
direct
0+1 records in
0+1 records out
2147479552 bytes (2.1 GB) copied, 17.7595 s, 121 MB/s
[root@ceph4 ~]# dd if=/dev/zero of=/var/lib/ceph/osd/ceph-0/deleteme bs=10G count=1 oflag=
direct
0+1 records in
0+1 records out
2147479552 bytes (2.1 GB) copied, 17.8519 s, 120 MB/s
[root@ceph4 ~]# dd if=/dev/zero of=/var/lib/ceph/osd/ceph-0/deleteme bs=10G count=1 oflag=
direct
0+1 records in
0+1 records out
2147479552 bytes (2.1 GB) copied, 17.8278 s, 120 MB/s
[root@ceph4 ~]#
```

Multiple disk write performance

As the next step, we will run `dd` on all the OSD disks used by Ceph on the node, `ceph-node1`, to get the aggregated disk write performance out of a single node.

How to do it...

Let's benchmark multiple disk write performance:

1. Get the total number of disks in use with the Ceph OSD; in my case, it's three disks:

```
# mount | grep -i osd | wc -l
```

2. Drop caches:

```
# echo 3 > /proc/sys/vm/drop_caches
```

3. The following command will execute the dd command on all the Ceph OSD disks:

```
# for i in `mount | grep osd | awk '{print $3}'`;
  do (dd if=/dev/zero
  of=$i/deleteme bs=10G count=1 oflag=direct &) ; done
```

To get the aggregated disk write performance, take the average of all the write speeds. In my case, the average comes out to be *127 MB/s*:

```
[root@ceph4 ~]# for i in `mount | grep osd | awk '{print $3}'`; do (dd if=/dev/zero of=$i/
deleteme bs=10G count=1 oflag=direct &) ; done
[root@ceph4 ~]# 0+1 records in
0+1 records out
2147479552 bytes (2.1 GB) copied, 16.5385 s, 130 MB/s
0+1 records in
0+1 records out
2147479552 bytes (2.1 GB) copied, 16.8428 s, 128 MB/s
0+1 records in
0+1 records out
2147479552 bytes (2.1 GB) copied, 17.3382 s, 124 MB/s
```

Single disk read performance

To get the single disk read performance, we will again use the dd command.

How to do it...

Let's benchmark single disk read performance:

1. Drop caches:

```
# echo 3 > /proc/sys/vm/drop_caches
```

2. Use dd to read from the file, deleteme, which we created during the write test. We will read the deleteme file to /dev/null with iflag set to direct:

```
# dd if=/var/lib/ceph/osd/ceph-0/deleteme of=/dev/null bs=10G
  count=1 iflag=direct
```

Ideally, you should repeat step 1 and step 2 a few times and take the average value. In our case, the average value for read operations comes to be *133 MB/s*, as shown in the following screenshot:

Multiple disk read performance

Similar to the single disk read performance, we will use dd to get the aggregated multiple disk read performance.

How to do it...

Let's benchmark multiple disk read performance:

1. Get the total number of disks in use with the Ceph OSD; in my case, it's three disks:

```
# mount | grep -i osd | wc -l
```

2. Drop caches:

```
# echo 3 > /proc/sys/vm/drop_caches
```

3. The following command will execute the dd command on all the Ceph OSD disks:

```
# for i in `mount | grep osd | awk '{print $3}'`;
  do (dd if=$i/deleteme
of=/dev/null bs=10G count=1 iflag=direct &); done
```

To get the aggregated disk read performance, take the average of all the read speeds. In my case, the average comes out to be 137 MB/s:

```
[root@ceph4 ~]# dd if=/var/lib/ceph/osd/ceph-0/deleteme of=/dev/null bs=10G count=1 iflag=
direct
0+1 records in
0+1 records out
2147479552 bytes (2.1 GB) copied, 16.0875 s, 133 MB/s
[root@ceph4 ~]# dd if=/var/lib/ceph/osd/ceph-0/deleteme of=/dev/null bs=10G count=1 iflag=
direct
0+1 records in
0+1 records out
2147479552 bytes (2.1 GB) copied, 16.0845 s, 134 MB/s
[root@ceph4 ~]# dd if=/var/lib/ceph/osd/ceph-0/deleteme of=/dev/null bs=10G count=1 iflag=
direct
0+1 records in
0+1 records out
2147479552 bytes (2.1 GB) copied, 16.0866 s, 133 MB/s
```

Results

Based on the tests that we performed, the results will look like this. These results vary a lot from environment to environment; the hardware that you are using and the number of disks on the OSD node can play a big part:

Operation	Per Disk	Aggregate
Read	133 MB/s	137 MB/s
Write	121 MB/s	127 MB/s

Baseline network performance

In this recipe, we will perform tests to discover the baseline performance of the network between the Ceph OSD nodes. For this, we will be using the `iperf` utility. Make sure that the `iperf` package is installed on the Ceph nodes. `iperf` is a simple, point-to-point network bandwidth tester that works on the client-server model.

To start network benchmarking, execute `iperf` with the server option on the first Ceph node and with the client option on the second Ceph node.

How to do it...

Using `iperf`, let's get a baseline for our clusters' network performance:

1. Install `iperf` on the `ceph-node1` and `ceph-node2`:

   ```
   # sudo yum install iperf -y
   ```

2. On `ceph-node1`, execute `iperf` with `-s` for the server, and `-p` to listen on a specific port:

   ```
   # iperf -s -p 6900
   ```

```
[root@ceph-node1 vagrant]# iperf -s -p 6900
------------------------------------------------------------
Server listening on TCP port 6900
TCP window size: 85.3 KByte (default)
------------------------------------------------------------
[  4] local 10.19.1.101 port 6900 connected with 10.19.1.102
port 44198
[ ID] Interval       Transfer     Bandwidth
[  4]  0.0-10.0 sec  2.51 GBytes  2.15 Gbits/sec
```

You can skip the –p option if the TPC port 5201 is open, or you can choose any other port that is open and not in use.

3. On `ceph-node2`, execute `iperf` with the client option, `-c`:

```
# iperf -c ceph-node1 -p 6900
```

```
[root@ceph-node2 vagrant]# iperf -c ceph-node1 -p 6900
------------------------------------------------------------
Client connecting to ceph-node1, TCP port 6900
TCP window size: 85.0 KByte (default)
------------------------------------------------------------
[  3] local 10.19.1.102 port 44198 connected with 10.19.1.101
port 6900
[ ID] Interval        Transfer     Bandwidth
[  3]  0.0-10.0 sec  2.51 GBytes  2.15 Gbits/sec
```

You can also use the –p option with the `iperf` command to determine the number of parallel stream connections to make with the server. It will return a realistic result if you have a channel-bonding technique such as **LACP**.

This shows that we have network connectivity of ~2.15 Gbits/s between the Ceph nodes. Similarly, you can perform a network bandwidth check for the other nodes of your Ceph cluster. The network bandwidth really depends on the network infrastructure you are using between your Ceph nodes.

Ceph rados bench

Ceph ships with an inbuilt benchmarking tool known as the `rados bench`, which can be used to measure the performance of a Ceph cluster at the pool level. The `rados bench` tool supports write, sequential read, and random read benchmarking tests, and it also allows the cleaning of temporary benchmarking data, which is quite neat.

How to do it...

Let's try to run some tests using the `rados bench`:

1. To run a 10 second write test to the pool RDB without cleanup, use the following command:

    ```
    # rados bench -p rbd 10 write --no-cleanup
    ```

    We get the following screenshot after executing the command:

```
[root@ceph-node1 vagrant]# rados bench -p rbd 10 write --no-cleanup
Maintaining 16 concurrent writes of 4194304 bytes to objects of size 4194304 for up to 10 seconds or 0 o
bjects
Object prefix: benchmark_data_ceph-node1_4602
  sec Cur ops   started  finished  avg MB/s  cur MB/s last lat(s)  avg lat(s)
    0      16        16         0         0         0           -           0
    1      16        16         0         0         0           -           0
    2      16        17         1   1.99799         2     1.48653     1.48653
    3      16        17         1   1.33238         0                 1.48653
    4      16        22         6   5.99659        10     3.90358     3.21756
    5      16        24         8   6.39683         8     4.95659     3.61188
    6      16        26        10   6.66373         8     5.70409     3.96487
    7      16        30        14   7.99683        16     6.57053     4.62909
    8      16        33        17   8.49691        12     7.83897     5.07123
    9      16        34        18   7.99733         4     5.43368     5.09136
   10      16        34        18   7.19775         0                 5.09136
   11      16        35        19   6.90705         2       6.455     5.16313
   12      15        35        20   6.66479         4     8.45558     5.32776
   13      14        35        21   6.45977         4     7.69405     5.44044
   14      14        35        21   5.99841         0                 5.44044
   15      14        35        21   5.59856         0           -     5.44044
   16      14        35        21    5.2487         0           -     5.44044
   17       1        35        34   7.99808        13     8.64804     7.25059
Total time run:         17.098624
Total writes made:      35
Write size:             4194304
Object size:            4194304
Bandwidth (MB/sec):     8.18779
Stddev Bandwidth:       5.29011
Max bandwidth (MB/sec): 16
Min bandwidth (MB/sec): 0
Average IOPS:           2
Stddev IOPS:            1
Max IOPS:               4
Min IOPS:               0
Average Latency(s):     7.24247
Stddev Latency(s):      2.82164
Max latency(s):         12.7414
Min latency(s):         1.48653
```

You will notice my test actually ran for a total time of 17 seconds, this is due to running the test on VM's and extended time required to complete the write OPS for the test.

2. Similarly, to run a 10-second sequential read test on the RBD pool, run the following:

```
[root@ceph-node1 vagrant]# rados bench -p rbd 10 seq
  sec Cur ops   started  finished  avg MB/s  cur MB/s last lat(s)  avg lat(s)
    0      16        16         0         0         0          -            0
Total time run:         0.486342
Total reads made:       35
Read size:              4194304
Object size:            4194304
Bandwidth (MB/sec):     287.863
Average IOPS            71
Stddev IOPS:            0
Max IOPS:               0
Min IOPS:               2147483647
Average Latency(s):     0.210983
Max latency(s):         0.482909
Min latency(s):         0.00569763
[root@ceph-node1 vagrant]#
```

It might be interesting to know, in this case, why the read test finished in a few seconds, or why it didn't execute for the specified 10 seconds. It's because the read speed is faster than the write speed, and `rados bench` had finished reading all the data generated during the write test. However, this behavior depends highly on your hardware and software infrastructure.

3. Similar to running a random read test with the `rados bench`, execute the following:

```
# rados bench -p rbd 10 rand
```

```
[root@ceph-node1 vagrant]# rados bench -p rbd 10 rand
  sec Cur ops   started  finished  avg MB/s  cur MB/s last lat(s)  avg lat(s)
    0      16        16         0         0         0          -           0
    1      16        90        74   295.084       296   0.599054    0.163539
    2      16       167       151   301.505       308 0.00830807    0.174942
    3      16       256       240   319.497       356  0.0125922    0.178822
    4      16       339       323   322.601       332   0.985727    0.178563
    5      16       413       397   317.281       296   0.059229    0.189206
    6      16       492       476   317.058       316 0.00984665    0.191377
    7      16       575       559   319.178       332   0.729541    0.192266
    8      16       653       637   318.271       312   0.419988    0.195358
    9      16       741       725   321.953       352  0.0135654    0.192576
   10      16       824       808   322.952       332 0.00603637    0.192886
Total time run:        10.440927
Total reads made:      825
Read size:             4194304
Object size:           4194304
Bandwidth (MB/sec):    316.064
Average IOPS:          79
Stddev IOPS:           5
Max IOPS:              89
Min IOPS:              74
Average Latency(s):    0.200897
Max latency(s):        1.10138
Min latency(s):        0.00461121
[root@ceph-node1 vagrant]#
```

How it works...

The syntax for the `rados bench` is as follows:

```
# rados bench -p <pool_name> <seconds> <write|seq|rand> -b <block size> -t
--no-cleanup
```

The syntax can be explained as follows:

- `-p`: `-p` or `--pool` specifies the pool name.
- `<seconds>`: Tests the time in seconds.
- `<write|seq|rand>`: Is the type of test, for example, write, sequential read, or random read.
- `-b`: For the block size; by default, it's 4M.
- `-t`: Is the number of concurrent threads; the default is 16.
- `--no-cleanup`: Is the temporary data that is written to the pool by the `rados bench` that should not be cleaned. This data will be used for read operations when they are used with sequential reads or random reads. The default is cleaned up.

The `rados bench` is a pretty handy tool to quickly measure the raw performance of your Ceph cluster, and you can creatively design your test cases based on write, read, and random read profiles.

RADOS load-gen

A bit similar to the `rados bench`, RADOS `load-gen` is another interesting tool provided by Ceph, which runs out-of-the-box. As the name suggests, the RADOS `load-gen` tool can be used to generate load on a Ceph cluster and can be useful to simulate high load scenarios.

How to do it...

1. Let's try to generate some load on our Ceph cluster with the following command:

```
# rados -p rbd load-gen --num-objects 50 --min-object-size 4M
--max-object-size 4M --max-ops 16 --min-op-len 4M --max-op-len 4M
--percent 5 --target-throughput 2000 --run-length 60
```

How it works...

The syntax for RADOS `load-gen` is as follows:

```
# rados -p <pool-name> load-gen
```

Following is the detailed explanation of preceding command:

- `--num-objects`: The total number of objects
- `--min-object-size`: The minimum object size in bytes
- `--max-object-size`: The maximum object size in bytes
- `--min-ops`: The minimum number of operations
- `--max-ops`: The maximum number of operations
- `--min-op-len`: The minimum operation length
- `--max-op-len`: The maximum operation length
- `--max-backlog`: The maximum backlog (in MB)
- `--percent`: The percentage of read operations
- `--target-throughput`: The target throughput (in MB)
- `--run-length`: The total run time in seconds

This command will generate load on the Ceph cluster by writing 50 objects to the RBD pool. Each of these objects and operation lengths is 4 MB in size, with 5% of the read, and test runtime as 60 seconds:

```
run length 60 seconds
preparing 50 objects
load-gen will run 60 seconds
     1: throughput=0MB/sec pending data=0
WRITE : oid=obj-SqfntMlPcrX_W_y off=0 len=4194304
READ : oid=obj-jmZb2a7EqJe6qlo off=0 len=4194304
READ : oid=obj-gxoKhvVN1K4VmnS off=0 len=4194304
op 2 completed, throughput=3.81MB/sec
READ : oid=obj-jmZb2a7EqJe6qlo off=0 len=4194304
op 1 completed, throughput=7.49MB/sec
WRITE : oid=obj-a0Lw9lOomUmuCZG off=0 len=4194304
op 4 completed, throughput=10.1MB/sec
READ : oid=obj-NeakTvz7c-zK08V off=0 len=4194304
op 3 completed, throughput=13.4MB/sec
READ : oid=obj-IkIfJv8PmKrhdge off=0 len=4194304
op 6 completed, throughput=16.3MB/sec
READ : oid=obj-IkIfJv8PmKrhdge off=0 len=4194304
op 5 completed, throughput=19.1MB/sec
op 0 completed, throughput=22.3MB/sec
READ : oid=obj-hJWFhQhGCbw3-sZ off=0 len=4194304
READ : oid=obj-PzmOkKBWXHslN1A off=0 len=4194304
op 9 completed, throughput=25.4MB/sec
READ : oid=obj-uz6SrFQ-u35jFSU off=0 len=4194304
op 7 completed, throughput=28.3MB/sec
```

The output has been trimmed for brevity's sake. Once the `load-gen` command finishes, it cleans all the objects it has created during the test and shows the operation throughput:

```
WRITE : oid=obj-IkIfJv8PmKrhdge off=0 len=4194304
op 2195 completed, throughput=147MB/sec
READ : oid=obj-sEr26ImSkp19do9 off=0 len=4194304
op 2199 completed, throughput=147MB/sec
READ : oid=obj-L5-GOQshs9IdyaY off=0 len=4194304
op 2200 completed, throughput=147MB/sec
waiting for all operations to complete
op 2197 completed, throughput=147MB/sec
cleaning up objects
op 2198 completed, throughput=147MB/sec
```

There's more...

You can also monitor your cluster status for the read and write speed/operation using the watch `ceph -s` command or `ceph -w`; meanwhile, RADOS `load-gen` will be running, just to see how it goes.

Benchmarking the Ceph Block Device

The tools, `rados bench`, and RADOS `load-gen`, which we discussed in the last recipe, are used to benchmark the Ceph cluster pool. In this recipe, we will focus on benchmarking the Ceph Block Device with the `rbd bench-write` tool. The `ceph rbd` command-line interface provides an option known as `bench-write`, which is a tool to perform write benchmarking operations on the Ceph Rados Block Device.

How to do it...

To benchmark the Ceph Block Device, we need to create a block device and map it to the Ceph client node:

1. Create a Ceph Block Device named `block-device1`, of size 10 G, and map it:

   ```
   # rbd create block-device1 --size 10240 --image-feature layering
   # rbd info --image block-device1
   # rbd map block-device1
   # rbd showmapped
   ```

   ```
   [root@client-node1 ceph]# rbd create block-device1 --size 10240 --image-feature layering
   [root@client-node1 ceph]# rbd info --image block-device1
   rbd image 'block-device1':
           size 10240 MB in 2560 objects
           order 22 (4096 kB objects)
           block_name_prefix: rbd_data.d3982ae8944a
           format: 2
           features: layering
           flags:
   [root@client-node1 ceph]# rbd map block-device1
   /dev/rbd1
   [root@client-node1 ceph]# rbd showmapped
   id pool image         snap device
   0  rbd  rbd1          -    /dev/rbd0
   1  rbd  block-device1 -    /dev/rbd1
   [root@client-node1 ceph]#
   ```

2. Create a filesystem on the block device and mount it:

   ```
   # mkfs.xfs /dev/rbd1
   # mkdir -p /mnt/ceph-block-device1
   # mount /dev/rbd1 /mnt/ceph-block-device1
   # df -h /mnt/ceph-block-device1
   ```

   ```
   [root@client-node1 ceph]# mkfs.xfs /dev/rbd1
   meta-data=/dev/rbd1              isize=512    agcount=17, agsize=162816 blks
            =                       sectsz=512   attr=2, projid32bit=1
            =                       crc=1        finobt=0, sparse=0
   data     =                       bsize=4096   blocks=2621440, imaxpct=25
            =                       sunit=1024   swidth=1024 blks
   naming   =version 2              bsize=4096   ascii-ci=0 ftype=1
   log      =internal log           bsize=4096   blocks=2560, version=2
            =                       sectsz=512   sunit=8 blks, lazy-count=1
   realtime =none                   extsz=4096   blocks=0, rtextents=0
   [root@client-node1 ceph]# mkdir -p /mnt/ceph-block-device1
   [root@client-node1 ceph]# mount /dev/rbd1 /mnt/ceph-block-device1
   [root@client-node1 ceph]# df -h /mnt/ceph-block-device1
   Filesystem      Size  Used Avail Use% Mounted on
   /dev/rbd1        10G   33M   10G   1% /mnt/ceph-block-device1
   [root@client-node1 ceph]#
   ```

3. To benchmark `block-device1` for 5 GB of total write length, execute the following command:

   ```
   # rbd bench-write block-device1 --io-total 5368709200
   ```

```
[root@client-node1 ceph]# rbd bench-write block-device1 --io-total 5368709200
bench-write  io size 4096  io threads 16 bytes 5368709200 pattern sequential
  SEC      OPS     OPS/SEC    BYTES/SEC
    1     7712    7146.39   29271607.00
    2    10400    4772.22   19546995.12
    3    11984    3859.78   15809663.09
    4    13232    3208.56   13142247.04
    5    14304    2749.05   11260097.30
    6    16192    1713.59    7018868.12
    7    18000    1486.58    6089039.05
    8    19760    1584.64    6490679.38
    9    21920    1756.58    7194957.91
   10    22880    1788.79    7326901.81
   11    25776    1884.37    7718399.08
   12    28320    2168.06    8880367.34
   13    31536    2272.50    9308154.70
   14    32816    2212.22    9061271.50
   15    34288    2114.19    8659737.38
   16    35200    1707.37    6993367.68
   17    36624    1543.51    6322235.38
   18    37952    1316.11    5390785.79
   19    38400    1110.44    4548372.98
```

As you can see, the rbd bench-write outputs nicely formatted results.

How it works...

The syntax for the rbd bench-write looks like the following:

```
# rbd bench-write <RBD image name>
```

Following is the detailed explanation of preceding syntax:

- --io-size: The write size in bytes; the default is 4M
- --io-threads: The number of threads; the default is 16
- --io-total: The total bytes to write; the default is 1024M
- --io-pattern <seq|rand>: This is the write pattern, the default is seq

> You can use different options with the rbd bench-write tool to adjust the block size, number of threads, and IO pattern.

Benchmarking Ceph RBD using FIO

Flexible I/O (**FIO**); it's one of the most popular tools for generating I/O workload and benchmarking. FIO has recently added native support for RBD. FIO is highly customizable and can be used to simulate and benchmark almost all kinds of workloads. In this recipe, we will learn how FIO can be used to benchmark the Ceph RBD.

How to do it...

To benchmark the Ceph Block Device, we need to create a block device and map that to the Ceph client node:

1. Install the FIO package on the node where you mapped the Ceph RBD image. In our case, it's the `ceph-client1` node:

   ```
   # yum install fio -y
   ```

   Since FIO supports RBD ioengine, we do not need to mount the RBD image as a filesystem. To benchmark RBD, we simply need to provide the RBD image name, pool, and Ceph user that will be used to connect to the Ceph cluster. Create the FIO profile with the following content:

   ```
   [write-4M]
   description="write test with block size of 4M"
   ioengine=rbd
   clientname=admin
   pool=rbd
   rbdname=block-device1
   iodepth=32
   runtime=120
   rw=write
   bs=4M
   ```

```
[root@client-node1 ~]# vim write.fio
[root@client-node1 ~]# cat write.fio
[write-4M]
description="write test with block size of 4M"
ioengine=rbd
clientname=admin
pool=rbd
rbdname=block-device1
iodepth=32
runtime=120
rw=write
bs=4M
[root@client-node1 ~]#
```

2. To start FIO benchmarking, execute the following FIO command by providing
    the FIO profile file as an argument:

    ```
    # fio write.fio
    ```

```
[root@client-node1 ~]# fio write.fio
write-4M: (g=0): rw=write, bs=4M-4M/4M-4M/4M-4M, ioengine=rbd, iodepth=32
fio-2.2.8
Starting 1 process
rbd engine: RBD version: 0.1.11
Jobs: 1 (f=0): [W(1)] [6.6% done] [0KB/0KB/0KB /s] [0/0/0 iops] [eta 34m:37s]
write-4M: (groupid=0, jobs=1): err= 0: pid=3139: Sat Sep 23 20:17:49 2017
  Description  : ["write test with block size of 4M"]
  write: io=684032KB, bw=4903.2KB/s, iops=1, runt=139509msec
    slat (usec): min=0, max=4382.7K, avg=103019.13, stdev=507104.51
    clat (msec): min=1231, max=33203, avg=24763.43, stdev=5731.42
    lat (msec): min=1276, max=33204, avg=24866.45, stdev=5652.06
    clat percentiles (msec):
     |  1.00th=[ 1270],  5.00th=[16712], 10.00th=[16712], 20.00th=[16712],
     | 30.00th=[16712], 40.00th=[16712], 50.00th=[16712], 60.00th=[16712],
     | 70.00th=[16712], 80.00th=[16712], 90.00th=[16712], 95.00th=[16712],
     | 99.00th=[16712], 99.50th=[16712], 99.90th=[16712], 99.95th=[16712],
     | 99.99th=[16712]
    bw (KB  /s): min=  144, max=29708, per=100.00%, avg=7690.57, stdev=10365.12
    lat (msec): 2000=1.80%, >=2000=98.20%
  cpu          : usr=0.03%, sys=0.07%, ctx=1210, majf=1185, minf=35410
  IO depths    : 1=1.8%, 2=4.8%, 4=9.6%, 8=23.4%, 16=56.3%, 32=4.2%, >=64=0.0%
     submit    : 0=0.0%, 4=100.0%, 8=0.0%, 16=0.0%, 32=0.0%, 64=0.0%, >=64=0.0%
     complete  : 0=0.0%, 4=96.0%, 8=0.6%, 16=0.6%, 32=2.9%, 64=0.0%, >=64=0.0%
     issued    : total=r=0/w=167/d=0, short=r=0/w=0/d=0, drop=r=0/w=0/d=0
     latency   : target=0, window=0, percentile=100.00%, depth=32

Run status group 0 (all jobs):
  WRITE: io=684032KB, aggrb=4903KB/s, minb=4903KB/s, maxb=4903KB/s, mint=139509msec, maxt=139509msec

Disk stats (read/write):
  dm-1: ios=1912/9, merge=0/0, ticks=444228/31171, in_queue=475399, util=23.66%, aggrios=5946/943, aggrmerge=25595/91400, aggrticks=556744/5417170, aggrin_queue=5980030, aggrutil=54.83%
    sda: ios=5946/943, merge=25595/91400, ticks=556744/5417170, in_queue=5980030, util=54.83%
[root@client-node1 ~]#
```

On completion, FIO generates a lot of useful information that should be carefully observed.
However, at first glance, you might be interested mostly in IOPS and the aggregated
bandwidth, which are both highlighted in the previous screenshot.

Ceph admin socket

Ceph components are daemons and Unix-domain sockets. Ceph allows us to use these sockets to query its daemons. The Ceph admin socket is a powerful tool to get and set the Ceph daemon configurations at runtime. With this tool, changing the daemon configuration values becomes a lot easier, rather than changing the Ceph configuration file, which requires the daemon to restart.

To do this, you should log in to the node running the Ceph daemons and execute the `ceph daemon` commands.

How to do it...

There are two ways to access the admin socket:

1. Using the Ceph `daemon-name`:

   ```
   $ sudo ceph daemon {daemon-name} {option}
   ```

2. The default location is `/var/run/ceph`. Using the absolute path of the socket file:

   ```
   $ sudo ceph daemon {absolute path to socket file} {option}
   ```

We will now try to access the Ceph daemon using the admin socket:

1. List all the available admin socket commands for the OSD:

   ```
   # ceph daemon osd.0 help
   ```

2. Similarly, list all the available socket commands for MON:

   ```
   # ceph daemon mon.ceph-node1 help
   ```

3. Check the OSD configuration settings for `osd.0`:

```
# ceph daemon osd.0 config show
```

4. Check the MON configuration settings for `mon.ceph-node1`:

```
# ceph daemon mon.ceph-node1 config show
```

 The Ceph admin daemon allows you to change the daemon configuration settings at runtime. However, these changes are temporary. To permanently change the Ceph daemon configuration, update the Ceph configuration file.

5. To get the current config value for `osd`, use the `_recover_max_chunk` parameter for the `osd.0` daemon:

```
# ceph daemon osd.0 config get osd_recovery_max_chunk
```

6. To change the `osd_recovery_max_chunk` value for `osd.0`, execute the following command:

```
# ceph daemon osd.0 config set osd_recovery_max_chunk 1000000
```

```
[root@ceph-node3 ~]# ceph daemon osd.0 config get osd_recovery_max_chunk
{
    "osd_recovery_max_chunk": "8388608"
}

[root@ceph-node3 ~]#
[root@ceph-node3 ~]# ceph daemon osd.0 config set osd_recovery_max_chunk 1000000
{
    "success": "osd_recovery_max_chunk = '1000000' (unchangeable) "
}

[root@ceph-node3 ~]# ceph daemon osd.0 config get osd_recovery_max_chunk
{
    "osd_recovery_max_chunk": "1000000"
}

[root@ceph-node3 ~]# 
```

Using the ceph tell command

Another efficient way to change the runtime configuration for the Ceph daemon without the overhead of logging in to that node is to use the `ceph tell` command.

How to do it...

The `ceph tell` command saves you the effort of logging into the node where the daemon is running. This command goes through the monitor node, so you can execute it from any node in the cluster:

1. The syntax for the `ceph tell` command is as follows:

```
# ceph tell {daemon-type}.{id or *} injectargs
  --{config_setting_name} {value}
```

2. To change the `osd_recovery_threads` setting from `osd.0`, execute the following:

```
# ceph tell osd.0 injectargs '--osd_recovery_threads=2'
```

3. To change the same setting for all the OSDs across the cluster, execute the following:

```
# ceph tell osd.* injectargs '--osd_recovery_threads=2'
```

4. You can also change multiple settings as a one liner:

```
# ceph tell osd.* injectargs '--osd_recovery_max_active=1
  --osd_recovery_max_single_start=1 --osd_recovery_op_priority=50'
```

Ceph REST API

Ceph comes with powerful REST API interface access, which allows you to administer your cluster programmatically. It can run as a WSGI application or as a standalone server, listening on the default port `5000`. It provides a similar kind of functionality to that of the Ceph command-line tool through an HTTP-accessible interface. Commands are submitted as HTTP GET and PUT requests, and the results can be returned in the JSON, XML, and text formats. In this recipe, I will quickly show you how to set up the Ceph REST API and interact with it.

How to do it...

Let's configure and use the Ceph REST API to check some cluster states:

1. Create a user, `client.restapi`, on the Ceph cluster with appropriate access to mon, osd, and mds:

   ```
   # ceph auth get-or-create client.restapi
       mds 'allow *' osd 'allow *'
   mon 'allow *' > /etc/ceph/ceph.client.restapi.keyring
   ```

2. Add the following section to the `ceph.conf` file:

   ```
   [client.restapi]
   log file = /var/log/ceph/ceph.restapi.log
   keyring = /etc/ceph/ceph.client.restapi.keyring
   ```

3. Execute the following command to start the `ceph-rest-api` as a standalone web server in the background:

   ```
   # nohup ceph-rest-api > /var/log/ceph-rest-api &> /var/log/
   ceph-rest-api-error.log &
   ```

   You can also run the `ceph-rest-api` without `nohup`, suppressing it to the background.

4. The `ceph-rest-api` should now be listening on `0.0.0.0:5000`; use `curl` to query the `ceph-rest-api` for the cluster health:

   ```
   # curl localhost:5000/api/v0.1/health
   ```

5. Similarly, check the `osd` and `mon` status via `rest-api`:

   ```
   # curl localhost:5000/api/v0.1/osd/stat
   # curl localhost:5000/api/v0.1/mon/stat
   ```

```
[root@ceph-node1 ceph-ansible]# curl localhost:5000/api/v0.1/health
HEALTH_OK
[root@ceph-node1 ceph-ansible]# curl localhost:5000/api/v0.1/osd/stat
    osdmap e140: 9 osds: 9 up, 9 in
        flags sortbitwise,require_jewel_osds
[root@ceph-node1 ceph-ansible]# curl localhost:5000/api/v0.1/mon/stat
e1: 3 mons at {ceph-node1=10.19.1.101:6789/0,ceph-node2=10.19.1.102:6789/0,ceph-node3=10.19.1.103:6789/0}, election
 epoch 20, quorum 0,1,2 ceph-node1,ceph-node2,ceph-node3
[root@ceph-node1 ceph-ansible]#
```

6. The `ceph-rest-api` has support for most of the Ceph CLI commands. To check the list of available `ceph-rest-api` commands, execute the following:

```
# curl localhost:5000/api/v0.1
```

This command will return the output in HTML; it will be good if you visit `localhost:5000/api/v0.1` from a web browser to render the HTML for easier readability.

This is a basic implementation of the `ceph-rest-api`. To use it in a production environment, it's a good idea to deploy it in more than one instance with a WSGI application wrapped with a web server and frontend is done by load balancers. The `ceph-rest-api` is a scalable, lightweight service that allows you to administer your Ceph cluster like a pro.

Profiling Ceph memory

Memory profiling is the process of dynamic program analysis using *TCMalloc* to determine a program's memory consumption and identify ways to optimize it. In this recipe, we discuss how you can use memory profilers on the Ceph daemons for memory investigation.

How to do it...

Let's see how to profile memory use for the Ceph daemons running on our nodes:

1. Start the memory profiler on a specific daemon:

```
# ceph tell osd.2 heap start_profiler
```

To auto-start the profiler as soon as the Ceph `osd` daemon starts set the environment variable as `CEPH_HEAP_PROFILER_INIT=true`.

It's a good idea to keep the profiler running for a few hours so that it can collect as much information related to the memory footprint as possible. At the same time, you can also generate some load on the cluster.

2. Next, print heap statistics about the memory footprint that the profiler has collected:

```
# ceph tell osd.2 heap stats
```

```
[root@ceph-node1 group_vars]# ceph tell osd.2 heap start_profiler
osd.2 started profiler
[root@ceph-node1 group_vars]#
[root@ceph-node1 group_vars]# ceph tell osd.2 heap stats
osd.2 tcmalloc heap stats:------------------------------------------------
MALLOC:       12410568 (    11.8 MiB) Bytes in use by application
MALLOC: +            0 (     0.0 MiB) Bytes in page heap freelist
MALLOC: +      1626984 (     1.6 MiB) Bytes in central cache freelist
MALLOC: +       129536 (     0.1 MiB) Bytes in transfer cache freelist
MALLOC: +      5362640 (     5.1 MiB) Bytes in thread cache freelists
MALLOC: +      1421472 (     1.4 MiB) Bytes in malloc metadata
MALLOC:   ------------
MALLOC: =     20951200 (    20.0 MiB) Actual memory used (physical + swap)
MALLOC: +       393216 (     0.4 MiB) Bytes released to OS (aka unmapped)
MALLOC:   ------------
MALLOC: =     21344416 (    20.4 MiB) Virtual address space used
MALLOC:
MALLOC:           1080              Spans in use
MALLOC:            121              Thread heaps in use
MALLOC:           8192              Tcmalloc page size
------------------------------------------------
Call ReleaseFreeMemory() to release freelist memory to the OS (via madvise()).
Bytes released to the OS take up virtual address space but no physical memory.
[root@ceph-node1 group_vars]# ▉
```

3. You can also dump heap stats on a file that can be used later; by default, it will create the dump file as `/var/log/ceph/osd.2.profile.0001.heap`:

```
# ceph tell osd.2 heap dump
```

```
[root@ceph-node1 group_vars]# ceph tell osd.2 heap dump
osd.2 dumping heap profile now.
------------------------------------------
MALLOC:       12407576 (    11.8 MiB) Bytes in use by application
MALLOC: +            0 (     0.0 MiB) Bytes in page heap freelist
MALLOC: +      1686952 (     1.6 MiB) Bytes in central cache freelist
MALLOC: +       129536 (     0.1 MiB) Bytes in transfer cache freelist
MALLOC: +      5354816 (     5.1 MiB) Bytes in thread cache freelists
MALLOC: +      1421472 (     1.4 MiB) Bytes in malloc metadata
MALLOC:    ------------
MALLOC: =     21000352 (    20.0 MiB) Actual memory used (physical + swap)
MALLOC: +       344064 (     0.3 MiB) Bytes released to OS (aka unmapped)
MALLOC:    ------------
MALLOC: =     21344416 (    20.4 MiB) Virtual address space used
MALLOC:
MALLOC:           1083              Spans in use
MALLOC:            121              Thread heaps in use
MALLOC:           8192              Tcmalloc page size
------------------------------------------
Call ReleaseFreeMemory() to release freelist memory to the OS (via madvise()).
Bytes released to the OS take up virtual address space but no physical memory.
[root@ceph-node1 group_vars]#
```

4. To read this dump file, you will require `google-perftools`:

```
# yum install -y google-perftools
```

 Refer to `http://goog-perftools.sourceforge.net/doc/heap_profiler.`
`html` for additional details.

5. To view the profiler logs:

```
# pprof --text {path-to-daemon} {log-path/filename}
# pprof --text /usr/bin/ceph-osd
                /var/log/ceph/osd.2.profile.0001.heap
```

6. For granule comparison, generate several profile dump files for the same daemon, and use the Google profiler tool to compare it:

```
# pprof --text --base /var/log/ceph/osd.0.profile.0001.heap
/usr/bin/
ceph-osd /var/log/ceph/osd.2.profile.0002.heap
```

7. Release memory that TCMalloc has allocated but is not being used by Ceph:

```
# ceph tell osd.2 heap release
```

8. Once you are done, stop the profiler as you do not want to leave this running in a production cluster:

```
# ceph tell osd.2 heap stop_profiler
```

The Ceph daemons process has matured much, and you might not really need memory profilers for analysis unless you encounter a bug that's causing memory leaks. You can use the previously discussed procedure to figure out memory issues with the Ceph daemons.

The ceph-objectstore-tool

One of the key features of Ceph is its self-repairing and self-healing qualities. Ceph does this by keeping multiple copies of placement groups across different *OSDs* and ensures a very high probability that you will not lose your data. In very rare cases, you may see the failure of multiple *OSDs*, where one or more PG replicas are on a failed *OSD*, and the PG state becomes incomplete, which leads to errors in the cluster health. For granular recovery, Ceph provides a low-level PG and object data recovery tool known as `ceph-objectstore-tool`.

 The `ceph-objectstore-tool` can be a risky operation, and the command needs to be run either as root or sudo. **Do not attempt this on a production cluster without engaging the Red Hat Ceph Storage Support**, unless you are sure of what you are doing. It can cause irreversible data loss in your cluster.

How to do it...

Let's run through some example uses for the `ceph-objectstore-tool`:

1. Find incomplete PGs on your Ceph cluster. Using this command, you can get the PG ID and its acting set:

   ```
   # ceph health detail | grep incomplete
   ```

2. Using the acting set, you can locate the OSD host:

   ```
   # ceph osd find <osd_number>
   ```

3. Log in to the OSD node and stop the OSD that you intend to work on:

   ```
   # systemctl stop ceph-osd@<id>
   ```

The following sections describe the OSD and placement group functions that you can use with the `ceph-objectstore-tool`:

1. To identify the objects within an OSD, execute the following. The tool will output all objects, irrespective of their placement groups:

   ```
   # ceph-objectstore-tool --data-path </path/to/osd>
   --journal-path </path/to/journal> --op list
   ```

2. To identify the objects within a placement group, execute the following:

   ```
   # ceph-objectstore-tool --data-path </path/to/osd>
   --journal-path </path/to/journal> --pgid <pgid> --op list
   ```

3. To list the placement groups stored on an OSD, execute the following:

   ```
   # ceph-objectstore-tool --data-path </path/to/osd>
   --journal-path </path/to/journal> --op list-pgs
   ```

4. If you know the object ID that you are looking for, specify it to find the PG ID:

   ```
   # ceph-objectstore-tool --data-path </path/to/osd>
   --journal-path </path/to/journal> --op list <object-id>
   ```

5. Retrieve information about a particular placement group:

   ```
   # ceph-objectstore-tool --data-path </path/to/osd>
   --journal-path </path/to/journal> --pgid <pg-id> --op info
   ```

6. Retrieve a log of operations on a placement group:

   ```
   # ceph-objectstore-tool --data-path </path/to/osd>
   --journal-path </path/to/journal> --pgid <pg-id> --op log
   ```

Removing a placement group is a risky operation and may cause data loss; use this feature with caution. If you have a corrupt placement group on an OSD that prevents the peering or starting of the OSD service, before removing the placement group, ensure that you have a valid copy of the placement group on another OSD. As a precaution, before removing the PG, you can also take a backup of the PG by exporting it to a file:

1. To remove a placement group, execute the following command:

   ```
   # ceph-objectstore-tool --data-path </path/to/osd>
   --journal-path </path/to/journal> --pgid <pg-id> --op remove
   ```

2. To export a placement group to a file, execute the following:

```
# ceph-objectstore-tool --data-path </path/to/osd>
--journal-path </path/to/journal> --pgid <pg-id>
--file /path/to/file --op export
```

3. To import a placement group from a file, execute the following:

```
# ceph-objectstore-tool --data-path </path/to/osd>
--journal-path </path/to/journal> --file </path/to/file>
--op import
```

4. An OSD may have objects marked as `lost`. To list the `lost` or `unfound` objects, execute the following:

```
# ceph-objectstore-tool --data-path </path/to/osd>
--journal-path </path/to/journal> --op list-lost
```

5. To find objects marked as `lost` for a single placement group, specify `pgid`:

```
# ceph-objectstore-tool --data-path </path/to/osd>
--journal-path </path/to/journal> --pgid <pgid> --op list-lost
```

6. The `ceph-objectstore-tool` is purposely used to fix the PG's lost objects. An OSD may have objects marked `lost`. To remove the `lost` setting for the `lost` objects of a placement group, execute the following:

```
# ceph-objectstore-tool --data-path </path/to/osd>
--journal-path </path/to/journal> --op fix-lost
```

7. To fix `lost` objects for a particular placement group, specify `pgid`:

```
# ceph-objectstore-tool --data-path </path/to/osd>
--journal-path </path/to/journal> --pgid <pg-id> --op fix-lost
```

8. If you know the identity of the `lost` object you want to fix, specify the object ID:

```
# ceph-objectstore-tool --data-path </path/to/osd>
--journal-path </path/to/journal> --op fix-lost <object-id>
```

How it works...

The syntax for `ceph-objectstore-tool` is:

`ceph-objectstore-tool <options>`

The values for `<options>` can be as follows:

- `--data-path`: The path to the OSD
- `--journal-path`: The path to the journal
- `--op`: The operation
- `--pgid`: The placement group ID
- `--skip-journal-replay`: Use this when the journal is corrupted
- `--skip-mount-omap`: Use this when the LevelDB data store is corrupted and unable to mount
- `--file`: The path to the file, used with the import/export operation

To understand this tool better, let's take an example: a pool makes two copies of an object, and PGs are located on `osd.1` and `osd.2`. At this point, if failure happens, the following sequence will occur:

1. `osd.1` goes down.
2. `osd.2` handles all the write operations in a degraded state.
3. `osd.1` comes up and peers with `osd.2` for data replication.
4. Suddenly, `osd.2` goes down before replicating all the objects to `osd.1`.
5. At this point, you have data on `osd.1`, but it's stale.

After troubleshooting, you will find that you can read the `osd.2` data from the filesystem, but its `osd` service is not getting started. In such a situation, one should use the `ceph-objectstore-tool` to export/retrieve data from the failed `osd`. The `ceph-objectstore-tool` provides you with enough capability to examine, modify, and retrieve object data and metadata.

You should avoid using Linux tools such as `cp` and `rsync` for recovering data from a failed OSD, as these tools do not take all the necessary metadata into account, and the recovered object might be unusable!

Using ceph-medic

Since it's inception Ceph has lacked an overall health-check tool which would easily highlight an issue inside the Ceph cluster. The `ceph status` and `ceph health detail` commands exist and are good for providing overall cluster health details but do not point the user in any concrete direction if there is a more complex issue. The creation of the `ceph-medic` project enables running a single command to poll multiple predefined checks on a Ceph cluster. These checks range from best practice recommendations to validation of keyrings and directory ownership. The `ceph-medic` project continues to develop at a fast pace and new checks are added often.

 At the time of writing this book, only rpm repos built for centOS 7 are supported.

How to do it...

We will use the following steps to install and use `ceph-medic`:

1. Install the latest RPM repo:

   ```
   # wget http://download.ceph.com/ceph-medic/latest/rpm/el7/
       ceph-medic.repo
    -O /etc/yum.repos.d/ceph-medic.repo
   ```

2. Install `epel-release`:

   ```
   # yum install epel-release
   ```

3. Install the GPG key for `ceph-medic`:

   ```
   # wget https://download.ceph.com/keys/release.asc
   # rpm --import release.asc
   ```

4. Install `ceph-medic`:

   ```
   # yum install ceph-medic
   ```

5. Validate the install:

   ```
   # ceph-medic --help
   ```

6. Run `ceph-medic check` on your cluster:

```
# ceph-medic check
```

```
[root@ceph-node1 ~]# ceph-medic check
Host: ceph-node2            connection: [connected  ]
Host: client-node1          connection: [connected  ]
Host: ceph-node1            connection: [connected  ]
Host: ceph-node2            connection: [connected  ]
Host: ceph-node3            connection: [connected  ]
Host: ceph-node1            connection: [connected  ]
Host: ceph-node2            connection: [connected  ]
Host: ceph-node3            connection: [connected  ]
Collection completed!


==================== Starting remote check session ====================
Version: 1.0.2    Cluster Name: "ceph"
Total hosts: [8]
OSDs:    3    MONs:    3    Clients:    1
MDSs:    1    RGWs:    0    MGRs:    0


=======================================================================


---------- clients -----------
 client-node1

----------- osds ------------
 ceph-node1
 ceph-node3
 ceph-node2

----------- mons ------------
 ceph-node1
   WMON2: collocated OSDs found: ceph-5,ceph-7,ceph-2
 ceph-node3
   WMON2: collocated OSDs found: ceph-4,ceph-8,ceph-0
 ceph-node2
   WMON2: collocated OSDs found: ceph-6,ceph-1,ceph-3

-------------mdss-------------
 ceph-node2

49 passed, 3 failed, on 8 hosts
[root@ceph-node1 ~]# 
```

`ceph-medic` will output a complete log file to the current working directory where the command was issued. This log is much more verbose than the output the command sends to the terminal. This log location can be modified by utilizing the `--log-path` option in `~/.cephmedic.conf`.

How it works...

Since `ceph-medic` performs checks against the entire cluster it needs to know the nodes that exist in your cluster as well as have password-less SSH access to the nodes in your cluster. If your cluster is deployed via `ceph-ansible` then your nodes are already configured and this will not be required, if not, then you will need to point `ceph-medic` towards an inventory file and SSH config file.

The syntax for the `ceph-medic` command is as follows:

```
# ceph-medic --inventory /path/to/hosts
--ssh-config /path/to/ssh_config check
```

The `inventory` file is a typical Ansible `inventory` file and can be created in the current working directory where the `ceph-medic` check is run. The file must be called `hosts` and the following standard host groups are supported: `mons`, `osds`, `rgws`, `mdss`, `mgrs`, and clients. An example hosts file would look as follows:

```
[mons]
ceph-node1
ceph-node2
ceph-node3

[osds]
ceph-node1
ceph-node2
ceph-node3

[mdss]
ceph-node2
```

The SSH config file allows non-interactive SSH access to specific accounts that can sudo without a password prompt. This file can be created in the working directory where the `ceph-medic` check is run. An example SSH config file on a cluster of Vagrant VMs would look as follows:

```
Host ceph-node1
    HostName 127.0.0.1
    User vagrant
```

```
Port 2200
UserKnownHostsFile /dev/null
StrictHostKeyChecking no
PasswordAuthentication no
IdentityFile /Users/andrewschoen/.vagrant.d/insecure_private_key
IdentitiesOnly yes
LogLevel FATAL

Host ceph-node2
  HostName 127.0.0.1
  User vagrant
  Port 2201
  UserKnownHostsFile /dev/null
  StrictHostKeyChecking no
  PasswordAuthentication no
  IdentityFile /Users/andrewschoen/.vagrant.d/insecure_private_key
  IdentitiesOnly yes
  LogLevel FATAL
```

See also

- The upstream project page has details of the `ceph-medic` tool and it's various checks and is a good source of information as this tool develops further: `https://github.com/ceph/ceph-medic`.

Deploying the experimental Ceph BlueStore

BlueStore is a new backend for the Ceph OSD daemons. Its highlights are better performance (roughly 2x for writes), full data checksumming, and built-in compression. Compared to the currently used FileStore backend, BlueStore allows for storing objects directly on the Ceph Block Device without requiring any filesystem interface. BlueStore is the new default storage backend for the Luminous (12.2.z) release and will be used by default when provisioning new OSDs. BlueStore is *not* considered production ready in Jewel and it is not recommended to run any production Jewel clusters with BlueStore as a backend.

Some of BlueStore's features and enhancements are:

- **RocksDB backend**: Metadata is stored in a RocksDB backend as opposed to FileStore's current LevelDB. RocksDB is a multithreaded backend and is much more performant than the current LevelDB backend.
- **Multi-device support**: BlueStore can use multiple block devices for storing different data.
- **No large double-writes**: BlueStore will only fall back to typical write-ahead journaling scheme if write size is below a certain configurable threshold.
- **Efficient block device usage**: BlueStore doesn't use a filesystem so it minimizes the need to clear the storage device cache.
- **Flexible allocator**: BlueStore can implement different policies for different types of storage devices. Basically setting different behaviors between SSDs and HDDs.

How to do it...

OSD's can be deployed with the BlueStore backend via `ceph-ansible` and I encourage you to deploy a second Ceph cluster or an OSD node in your existing cluster with the BlueStore backend and compare the benchmark tests described earlier in this chapter on the Ceph cluster or OSD node backed by BlueStore, you will see a significant improvement on `rados bench` testing!

To install `ceph-node4` as an OSD node with BlueStore backend via `ceph-ansible`, you can do the following:

1. Add `ceph-node4` to the `/etc/ansible/hosts` file under `[osds]`:

```
###########ceph-cookbook###############
[mons]
ceph-node1
ceph-node2
ceph-node3

[osds]
ceph-node1
ceph-node2
ceph-node3
ceph-node4
```

2. In the `group_vars/all.yml` file on the `ceph-ansible` management node, `ceph-node1`, update the config overrides and `osd_objectsotre` settings:

```
osd_objectstore: bluestore

ceph_conf_overrides:
        global:
                        enable experimental unrecoverable data
                                                corrupting
                features: 'bluestore rocksdb'
```

```
ceph_conf_overrides:
  global:
    enable experimental unrecoverable data corrupting features: 'bluestore rocksdb'

osd_objectstore: bluestore
```

3. In the `group_vars/osds.yml` file on the `ceph-ansible` management node, `ceph-node1`, update the following settings:

```
bluestore: true
# journal colocation: true
```

```
#journal_collocation: true

bluestore: true
```

4. Rerun the Ansible playbook on `ceph-node1`:

```
root@ceph-node1 ceph-ansible # ansible-playbook site.yml
```

5. Check `ceph -s` command and note the new flags enabled in the cluster for the BlueStore experimental feature:

```
[root@ceph-node1 ceph-ansible]# ceph -s
2017-09-23 23:52:53.933048 7f93e1007700 -1 WARNING: the following dangerous and experimental features are enabled:
bluestore,rocksdb
2017-09-23 23:52:53.954601 7f93e1007700 -1 WARNING: the following dangerous and experimental features are enabled:
bluestore,rocksdb
    cluster d0195896-eb15-4ddc-8f6f-9387d381a886
    health HEALTH_OK
    monmap e1: 3 mons at {ceph-node1=10.19.1.101:6789/0,ceph-node2=10.19.1.102:6789/0,ceph-node3=10.19.1.103:6789/
0}
        election epoch 22, quorum 0,1,2 ceph-node1,ceph-node2,ceph-node3
    fsmap e25: 1/1/1 up {0=ceph-node2=up:active}
    osdmap e165: 12 osds: 12 up, 12 in
        flags sortbitwise,require_jewel_osds
    pgmap v7878: 144 pgs, 3 pools, 3193 MB data, 864 objects
        12902 MB used, 209 GB / 221 GB avail
            144 active+clean
```

6. Check the OSD data directory on one of the newly deployed OSDs backed by BlueStore and compared to a FileStore backed OSD. You can see the link directly on the block device on the BlueStore OSD. The output for FileStore is as follows:

```
[root@ceph-node3 ceph-0]# ll
total 56
-rw-r--r--   1 root root   496 Sep 15 20:18 activate.monmap
-rw-r--r--   1 ceph ceph     3 Sep 15 20:18 active
-rw-r--r--   1 ceph ceph    37 Sep 15 20:18 ceph_fsid
drwxr-xr-x 120 ceph ceph  4096 Sep 20 21:00 current
-rw-r--r--   1 ceph ceph    37 Sep 15 20:18 fsid
lrwxrwxrwx   1 ceph ceph    58 Sep 15 20:18 journal -> /dev/disk/by-partuuid/b1aec159-80ca-4f95-9d33-fbd535d09b89
-rw-r--r--   1 ceph ceph    37 Sep 15 20:18 journal_uuid
-rw-------   1 ceph ceph    56 Sep 15 20:18 keyring
-rw-r--r--   1 ceph ceph    21 Sep 15 20:18 magic
-rw-r--r--   1 ceph ceph     6 Sep 15 20:18 ready
-rw-r--r--   1 ceph ceph     4 Sep 15 20:18 store_version
-rw-r--r--   1 ceph ceph    53 Sep 15 20:18 superblock
-rw-r--r--   1 ceph ceph     0 Sep 23 17:38 systemd
-rw-r--r--   1 ceph ceph    10 Sep 15 20:18 type
-rw-r--r--   1 ceph ceph     2 Sep 15 20:18 whoami
[root@ceph-node3 ceph-0]#
```

The output for BlueStore is as follows:

```
[vagrant@ceph-node4 ceph-10]$ ll
total 52
-rw-r--r-- 1 root root 496 Sep 23 23:46 activate.monmap
-rw-r--r-- 1 ceph ceph   3 Sep 23 23:46 active
lrwxrwxrwx 1 ceph ceph  58 Sep 23 23:46 block -> /dev/disk/by-partuuid/494f2e6e-3630-4326-9319-
ad1e6dece2c7
-rw-r--r-- 1 ceph ceph  37 Sep 23 23:46 block_uuid
-rw-r--r-- 1 ceph ceph   2 Sep 23 23:46 bluefs
-rw-r--r-- 1 ceph ceph  37 Sep 23 23:46 ceph_fsid
-rw-r--r-- 1 ceph ceph  37 Sep 23 23:46 fsid
-rw------- 1 ceph ceph  57 Sep 23 23:46 keyring
-rw-r--r-- 1 ceph ceph   8 Sep 23 23:46 kv_backend
-rw-r--r-- 1 ceph ceph  21 Sep 23 23:46 magic
-rw-r--r-- 1 ceph ceph   4 Sep 23 23:46 mkfs_done
-rw-r--r-- 1 ceph ceph   6 Sep 23 23:46 ready
-rw-r--r-- 1 ceph ceph   0 Sep 23 23:46 systemd
-rw-r--r-- 1 ceph ceph  10 Sep 23 23:46 type
-rw-r--r-- 1 ceph ceph   3 Sep 23 23:46 whoami
[vagrant@ceph-node4 ceph-10]$
```

Ceph-node4 has now been successfully deployed with three OSDs with a BlueStore backend. The rest of the OSDs in the cluster remain with the Jewel default FileStore backend. Feel free to test performance comparisons between the BlueStore backend and FileStore backend with the tools provided in this chapter!

See Also

- For further details on Ceph BlueStore please see the recent upstream blog detailing this feature: `http://ceph.com/community/new-luminous-bluestore/`.

11
Deploying Ceph

This chapter will demonstrate how to quickly deploy test environments for testing and development by the use of Vagrant. It will also explain the reasons why you might want to consider using an orchestration tool to deploy Ceph rather than using the supplied Ceph tools. As a popular orchestration tool, Ansible will be used to show how quickly and reliably a Ceph cluster can be deployed and the advantages that using it can bring.

In this chapter, you will learn about the following topics:

- Preparing a testing environment with Vagrant and VirtualBox
- Learning about the differences between `ceph-deploy` and orchestration tools
- The advantages of using orchestration tools
- Installing and using Ansible
- Configuring the Ceph Ansible modules
- Deploying a test cluster with Vagrant and Ansible
- Ideas around how to manage your Ceph configuration

Preparing your environment with Vagrant and VirtualBox

Although a test cluster can be deployed on any hardware or **virtual machine** (**VM**), for the purposes of this book, a combination of Vagrant and VirtualBox will be used. This will allow rapid provisioning of the VMs and ensure a consistent environment.

VirtualBox is a free and open source *type 2* (hosted) hypervisor currently being developed by Oracle. Performance and features may be lacking compared with high-end hypervisors, but its lightweight approach, and multi-OS support lends itself to be a prime candidate for testing.

Vagrant helps allow an environment that may comprise many machines to be created quickly and efficiently. It works with the concepts of boxes, which are predefined templates for use with hypervisors and its **Vagrantfile**, which defines the environment to be built. It supports multiple hypervisors and allows a Vagrantfile to be portable across them.

System requirements

In order to be able to run the Ceph environment described later in this chapter, it's important that your computer meets a number of following requirements to ensure that the VM can be provided with sufficient resources:

- An **operating system** (**OS**) compatible with Vagrant and VirtualBox; this includes Linux, macOS, and Windows
- 2 Core CPU
- 8 GB RAM
- Virtualization instructions enabled in the bios

Obtaining and installing VirtualBox

Visit the VirtualBox web site at `https://www.virtualbox.org` and download the package that is appropriate with the OS you are using.

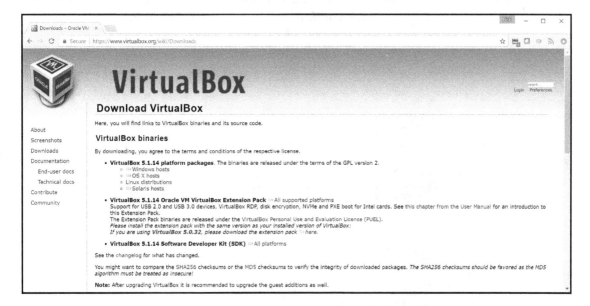

Setting up Vagrant

Perform the following steps in order to set up Vagrant:

1. Follow installation instructions from Vagrant's website https://www.vagrantup.com/downloads.html to get Vagrant installed on your chosen OS:

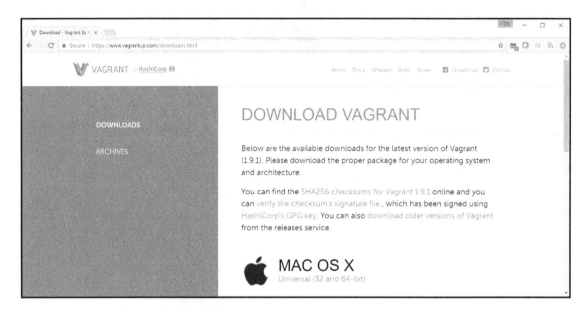

2. Create a new directory for your Vagrant project; for example, ceph-ansible.
3. Change to this directory and run the following commands:

```
C:\Users\nfisk\vagrant>cd ceph

C:\Users\nfisk\vagrant\ceph>
```

```
vagrant plugin install vagrant-hostmanager
```

The preceding command gives the following output:

```
Installing the 'vagrant-hostmanager' plugin. This can take a few minutes...
Fetching: vagrant-hostmanager-1.8.5.gem (100%)
Installed the plugin 'vagrant-hostmanager (1.8.5)'!
```

```
vagrant box add bento/ubuntu-16.04
```

The preceding command gives the following output:

```
==> box: Loading metadata for box 'bento/ubuntu-16.04'
    box: URL: https://atlas.hashicorp.com/bento/ubuntu-16.04
This box can work with multiple providers! The providers that it
can work with are listed below. Please review the list and choose
the provider you will be working with.

1) parallels
2) virtualbox
3) vmware_desktop

Enter your choice: 2
==> box: Adding box 'bento/ubuntu-16.04' (v2.3.1) for provider: virtualbox
    box: Downloading: https://atlas.hashicorp.com/bento/boxes/ubuntu-16.04/versions/2.3.1/providers/virtualbox.box
    box: Progress: 100% (Rate: 5257k/s, Estimated time remaining: --:--:--)
==> box: Successfully added box 'bento/ubuntu-16.04' (v2.3.1) for 'virtualbox'!
```

Now create an empty file named `Vagrantfile` and place the following into it:

```
nodes = [
  { :hostname => 'ansible', :ip => '192.168.0.40', :box => 'xenial64'
  },
  { :hostname => 'mon1', :ip => '192.168.0.41', :box => 'xenial64' },
  { :hostname => 'mon2', :ip => '192.168.0.42', :box => 'xenial64' },
  { :hostname => 'mon3', :ip => '192.168.0.43', :box => 'xenial64' },
  { :hostname => 'osd1', :ip => '192.168.0.51', :box => 'xenial64',
  :ram => 1024, :osd => 'yes' },
  { :hostname => 'osd2', :ip => '192.168.0.52', :box => 'xenial64',
  :ram => 1024, :osd => 'yes' },
  { :hostname => 'osd3', :ip => '192.168.0.53', :box => 'xenial64',
  :ram => 1024, :osd => 'yes' }
]

Vagrant.configure("2") do |config|
  nodes.each do |node|
    config.vm.define node[:hostname] do |nodeconfig|
      nodeconfig.vm.box = "bento/ubuntu-16.04"
      nodeconfig.vm.hostname = node[:hostname]
      nodeconfig.vm.network :private_network, ip: node[:ip]

      memory = node[:ram] ? node[:ram] : 512;
      nodeconfig.vm.provider :virtualbox do |vb|
        vb.customize [
          "modifyvm", :id,
          "--memory", memory.to_s,
        ]
        if node[:osd] == "yes"
          vb.customize [ "createhd", "--filename", "disk_osd-#
          {node[:hostname]}", "--size", "10000" ]
          vb.customize [ "storageattach", :id, "--storagectl", "SATA
```

```
        Controller", "--port", 3, "--device", 0, "--type", "hdd",
        "--medium", "disk_osd-#{node[:hostname]}.vdi" ]
      end
    end
  end
  config.hostmanager.enabled = true
  config.hostmanager.manage_guest = true
  end
end
```

 Just in case if you encounter error in this step, you need to disable Hyper-V.

Run `vagrant up` to bring up the VMs defined in `Vagrantfile`:

```
Bringing machine 'ansible' up with 'virtualbox' provider...
Bringing machine 'mon1' up with 'virtualbox' provider...
Bringing machine 'mon2' up with 'virtualbox' provider...
Bringing machine 'mon3' up with 'virtualbox' provider...
Bringing machine 'osd1' up with 'virtualbox' provider...
Bringing machine 'osd2' up with 'virtualbox' provider...
Bringing machine 'osd3' up with 'virtualbox' provider...
==> ansible: Importing base box 'bento/ubuntu-16.04'...
==> ansible: Matching MAC address for NAT networking...
==> ansible: Checking if box 'bento/ubuntu-16.04' is up to date...
==> ansible: Setting the name of the VM: ceph_ansible_1486503043550_56998
==> ansible: Clearing any previously set network interfaces...
==> ansible: Preparing network interfaces based on configuration...
    ansible: Adapter 1: nat
    ansible: Adapter 2: hostonly
==> ansible: Forwarding ports...
    ansible: 22 (guest) => 2222 (host) (adapter 1)
==> ansible: Running 'pre-boot' VM customizations...
==> ansible: Booting VM...
==> ansible: Waiting for machine to boot. This may take a few minutes...
```

Now let's connect to the `ansible` VM using `ssh`:

```
vagrant ssh ansible
```

The preceding command gives the following output:

```
`ssh` executable not found in any directories in the %PATH% variable. Is an
SSH client installed? Try installing Cygwin, MinGW or Git, all of which
contain an SSH client. Or use your favorite SSH client with the following
authentication information shown below:

Host: 127.0.0.1
Port: 2200
Username: vagrant
```

 If you are running Vagrant on Windows, the ssh command will inform you that you need to use an SSH client of your choice and provide the details to use it.

PuTTY would be a good suggestion for an SSH client. On Linux, the command will connect you straight onto the VM.

The username and password are both vagrant. After logging in, you should find yourself sitting at the Bash shell of the ansible VM:

```
login as: vagrant
vagrant@127.0.0.1's password:
Welcome to Ubuntu 16.04.1 LTS (GNU/Linux 4.4.0-51-generic x86_64)

 * Documentation:  https://help.ubuntu.com
 * Management:      https://landscape.canonical.com
 * Support:         https://ubuntu.com/advantage

0 packages can be updated.
0 updates are security updates.

vagrant@ansible:~$
```

Simply type exit to return to your host machine.

Congratulations! You have just deployed three servers for using as Ceph monitors, three servers for using as Ceph OSDs, and an Ansible server. Vagrantfile could have also contained extra steps to execute commands on the servers to configure them, but for now, let's shut down the servers using the following command; we can bring them back up for when needed by the examples later in this chapter:

```
vagrant destroy --force
```

The ceph-deploy tool

`ceph-deploy` is the official tool to deploy **Ceph clusters**. It works on the principle of having an admin node with SSH access (without password) to all machines in your Ceph cluster; it also holds a copy of the Ceph configuration file. Every time you carry out a deployment action, it uses SSH to connect to your Ceph nodes to carry out the necessary steps. Although the `ceph-deploy` tool is an entirely supported method, which will leave you with a perfectly functioning Ceph cluster, ongoing management of Ceph will not be as easy as desired. Larger scale Ceph clusters will also cause a lot of management overheads if `ceph-deploy` is to be used. For this reason, it is recommended that `ceph-deploy` is limited to test or small-scale production clusters, although as you will see, an orchestration tool allows the rapid deployment of Ceph and is probably better suited for test environments where you might need to continually build new Ceph clusters.

Orchestration

One solution to making the installation and management of Ceph easier is to use an orchestration tool. There are several tools available, such as Puppet, Chef, Salt, and Ansible, all of which have Ceph modules available. If you are already using an orchestration tool in your environment, then it would be recommended that you stick to using that tool. For the purposes of this book, Ansible will be used; this is for a number of reasons:

- It's the favored deployment method of Red Hat, who are the owners of both the Ceph and Ansible projects
- It has a well-developed and mature set of Ceph roles and playbooks
- Ansible tends to be easier to learn if you have never used an orchestration tool before
- It doesn't require a central server to be set up, which means demonstrations are more focused on using the tool rather than installing it

All tools follow the same principle of where you provide them with an inventory of hosts and a set of tasks to be carried out on the hosts. These tasks often reference variables that allows customization of the task at runtime. Orchestration tools are designed to be run on a schedule so that if for any reason the state or configuration of a host changes, it will be correctly changed back to the intended state during the next run.

Another advantage of using orchestration tools is documentation. Although they are not a replacement for good documentation, the fact that they clearly describe your environment including roles and configuration options means that your environment starts to become self-documenting. If you ensure that any installations or changes are carried out via your orchestration tool, then the configuration file of the orchestration tool will clearly describe the current state of your environment. If this is combined with something like a git repository to store the orchestration configuration, you have the makings of a change control system. This is covered in more detail later in this chapter. The only disadvantages are around the extra time it takes to carry out the initial setup and configuration of the tool.

So, using an orchestration tool, not only do you get a faster and less error-prone deployment, but you also get documentation and change management for free. If you haven't got the hint by now, this is something you should really be looking at.

Ansible

As mentioned, Ansible will be the orchestration tool of choice for this book, let's look at it in a bit more detail.

Ansible is an agentless orchestration tool written in Python, which uses SSH to carry out configuration tasks on remote nodes. It was first released in 2012 and has gained widespread adoption, and it is known for its ease of adoption and low learning curve. Red Hat purchased the commercial company Ansible, Inc. in 2015 and so has a very well-developed and close-knit integration for deploying Ceph.

Files named **playbooks** are used in Ansible to describe a list of commands, actions, and configurations to carry out on specified hosts or groups of hosts and are stored in a YAML file format. Instead of having large unmanageable playbooks, Ansible roles can be created that allow a playbook to contain a single task, which may then carry out a number of tasks associated with the role.

The use of SSH to connect to remote nodes and execute the playbooks means that it is very lightweight and does not require either an agent or a centralized server.

For testing Ansible also integrates well with Vagrant, an Ansible playbook can be specified as part of the Vagrant provisioning configuration and will automatically generate an inventory file from the VM's Vagrant created and run the playbook once the servers have booted. This allows a Ceph cluster including OS to be deployed via just a single command.

Installing Ansible

Bring your Vagrant environment back up that you created earlier on and SSH onto the Ansible server. For this example, only `ansible`, `mon1`, and `osd1` will be needed, as follows:

```
vagrant up ansible mon1 osd1
```

Add the Ansible `ppa`, as follows:

```
$ sudo apt-add-repository ppa:ansible/ansible
```

The preceding command gives the following output:

```
Ansible is a radically simple IT automation platform that makes your applications and systems easie
r to deploy. Avoid writing scripts or custom code to deploy and update your applications- automate i
n a language that approaches plain English, using SSH, with no agents to install on remote systems.

http://ansible.com/
 More info: https://launchpad.net/~ansible/+archive/ubuntu/ansible
Press [ENTER] to continue or ctrl-c to cancel adding it

gpg: keyring `/tmp/tmpt5a6qdao/secring.gpg' created
gpg: keyring `/tmp/tmpt5a6qdao/pubring.gpg' created
gpg: requesting key 7BB9C367 from hkp server keyserver.ubuntu.com
gpg: /tmp/tmpt5a6qdao/trustdb.gpg: trustdb created
gpg: key 7BB9C367: public key "Launchpad PPA for Ansible, Inc." imported
gpg: Total number processed: 1
gpg:               imported: 1  (RSA: 1)
OK
```

Update **Advanced Package Tool** (**APT**) sources and install Ansible:

```
$ sudo apt-get update && sudo apt-get install ansible -y
```

The preceding command gives the following output:

```
Setting up libyaml-0-2:amd64 (0.1.6-3) ...
Setting up python-markupsafe (0.23-2build2) ...
Setting up python-jinja2 (2.8-1) ...
Setting up python-yaml (3.11-3build1) ...
Setting up python-crypto (2.6.1-6build1) ...
Setting up python-six (1.10.0-3) ...
Setting up python-ecdsa (0.13-2) ...
Setting up python-paramiko (1.16.0-1) ...
Setting up python-httplib2 (0.9.1+dfsg-1) ...
Setting up python-pkg-resources (20.7.0-1) ...
Setting up python-setuptools (20.7.0-1) ...
Setting up sshpass (1.05-1) ...
Setting up ansible (2.2.1.0-1ppa~xenial) ...
Processing triggers for libc-bin (2.23-0ubuntu4) ...
vagrant@ansible:~$
```

Creating your inventory file

The Ansible inventory file is used by Ansible to reference all known hosts and to which group they belong. A group is defined by placing its name in square brackets, groups can be nested inside other groups by the use of the children definition.

Before we add hosts to the inventory file, we first need to configure the remote nodes for SSH (without password); otherwise, we will have to enter a password every time Ansible tries to connect to a remote machine.

Generate an SSH key as follows:

```
$ ssh-keygen
```

The preceding command gives the following output:

```
vagrant@ansible:~$ ssh-keygen
Generating public/private rsa key pair.
Enter file in which to save the key (/home/vagrant/.ssh/id_rsa):
Enter passphrase (empty for no passphrase):
Enter same passphrase again:
Your identification has been saved in /home/vagrant/.ssh/id_rsa.
Your public key has been saved in /home/vagrant/.ssh/id_rsa.pub.
The key fingerprint is:
SHA256:mdvKrx6ZG88AKQsFnaFpjKlPb8pmmnfqDiQPv4OQnpw vagrant@ansible
The key's randomart image is:
+----[RSA 2048]----+
|                  |
|                  |
|         .        |
| + + o . o        |
|=oB + o S         |
|*= + o . =        |
|*.* o   B .       |
|.E=oo   . O       |
|oBO*.   .*o+      |
+----[SHA256]----+
```

Copy the key to the remote hosts:

```
$ ssh-copy-id mon1
```

The preceding command gives the following output:

```
vagrant@ansible:~$ ssh-copy-id mon1
/usr/bin/ssh-copy-id: INFO: Source of key(s) to be installed: "/home/vagrant/.ssh/id_rsa.pub"
The authenticity of host 'mon1 (192.168.0.41)' can't be established.
ECDSA key fingerprint is SHA256:RI5/3ep65qXeDkZSACi/rN0hBxiLrBxMvcyk9CfLkyg.
Are you sure you want to continue connecting (yes/no)? yes
/usr/bin/ssh-copy-id: INFO: attempting to log in with the new key(s), to filter out any that are alr
eady installed
/usr/bin/ssh-copy-id: INFO: 1 key(s) remain to be installed -- if you are prompted now it is to inst
all the new keys
vagrant@mon1's password:

Number of key(s) added: 1

Now try logging into the machine, with:   "ssh 'mon1'"
and check to make sure that only the key(s) you wanted were added.
```

This will need to be repeated for each host. Normally, you would include this step in your Vagrant provisioning stage, but it is useful to carry out these tasks manually the first couple of times so that an understanding of the process is learned.

Now try logging into the machine using `ssh mon1`:

```
vagrant@ansible:~$ ssh mon1
Welcome to Ubuntu 16.04.1 LTS (GNU/Linux 4.4.0-51-generic x86_64)

 * Documentation:  https://help.ubuntu.com
 * Management:     https://landscape.canonical.com
 * Support:        https://ubuntu.com/advantage

0 packages can be updated.
0 updates are security updates.

vagrant@mon1:~$
```

Type `exit` to return to the Ansible VM.

Now, let's create the Ansible inventory file.

Edit the file named `hosts` in `/etc/ansible`:

```
$ sudo nano /etc/ansible/hosts
```

Create two groups named `osds` and `mons` and finally a third group named `ceph`. This third group will contain the `osds` and `mons` groups as children.

Enter a list of your hosts under the correct group, as follows:

```
[mons]
mon1
mon2
mon3

[osds]
osd1
osd2
osd3

[ceph:children]
mons
osds
```

Variables

Most playbooks and roles will make use of variables; these variables can be overridden in several ways. The simplest way is to create files in the host_vars and groups_vars folders, these allow you to override variables either based on the host or group membership, respectively. For this, perform the following steps:

1. Create a directory /etc/ansible/group_vars.
2. Create a file in group_vars named mons. Add the following in mons:

   ```
   a_variable: "foo"
   ```

3. Create a file in group_vars named osds. Add the following in osds:

   ```
   a_variable: "bar"
   ```

Variables follow a precedence order; you can also create an all file, which will apply to all groups. However, a variable of the same name that is in a more specific matching group will override it. The **Ceph Ansible modules** make use of this to allow you to have a set of default variables and then also allow you to specify different values for the specific roles.

Testing

To test that Ansible is working correctly and that we can successfully connect and run commands remotely, let's use the Ansible `ping` command to check one of our hosts. Note that this is not like a network ping, Ansible `ping` confirms that it can communicate via SSH and execute commands remotely:

```
$ ansible mon1 -m ping
```

The preceding command gives the following output:

```
vagrant@ansible:~$ ansible mon1 -m ping
mon1 | SUCCESS => {
    "changed": false,
    "ping": "pong"
}
vagrant@ansible:~$
```

Excellent, that worked, now let's run a simple command remotely to demonstrate the power of Ansible. The following command will retrieve the current running kernel version on the specified remote node:

```
$ ansible mon1 -a 'uname -r'
```

This is the desired result:

```
vagrant@ansible:~$ ansible mon1 -a 'uname -r'
mon1 | SUCCESS | rc=0 >>
4.4.0-51-generic

vagrant@ansible:~$
```

A very simple playbook

To demonstrate how playbooks work, the following example will show a small playbook that also makes use of the variables we configured earlier:

```
- hosts: mon1 osd1
tasks:
- name: Echo Variables
debug: msg="I am a {{ a_variable }}"
```

Now run the playbook. Note the command to run a playbook that differs from running ad hoc Ansible commands:

```
$ ansible-playbook /etc/ansible/playbook.yml
```

The preceding command gives the following output:

```
vagrant@ansible:~$ ansible-playbook /etc/ansible/playbook.yml

PLAY [mon1 osd1] ***********************************************************

TASK [setup] **************************************************************
ok: [mon1]
ok: [osd1]

TASK [Echo Variables] *****************************************************
ok: [mon1] => {
    "msg": "I am a foo"
}
ok: [osd1] => {
    "msg": "I am a bar"
}

PLAY RECAP ****************************************************************
mon1                       : ok=2    changed=0    unreachable=0    failed=0
osd1                       : ok=2    changed=0    unreachable=0    failed=0

vagrant@ansible:~$
```

The output shows the playbook being executed on both `mon1` and `osd1` as they are in groups, which are children of the parent group `ceph`. Also, note how the output is different between the two servers as they are picking up the variables that you set earlier in the `group_vars` directory.

Finally, the last couple of lines show the overall run status of the playbook run. You can now destroy your Vagrant environment again, ready for the next section:

```
vagrant destroy --force
```

This concludes the introduction to Ansible, but it is not a complete guide. It's recommended that you should explore other resources to gain a more in-depth knowledge of Ansible before using it in a production environment.

Adding the Ceph Ansible modules

We can use `git` to clone the Ceph Ansible repository:

```
git clone https://github.com/ceph/ceph-ansible.git

sudo cp -a ceph-ansible/* /etc/ansible/
```

The preceding commands gives the following output:

```
vagrant@ansible:~$ git clone https://github.com/ceph/ceph-ansible.git
Cloning into 'ceph-ansible'...
remote: Counting objects: 13875, done.
remote: Compressing objects: 100% (69/69), done.
remote: Total 13875 (delta 32), reused 0 (delta 0), pack-reused 13802
Receiving objects: 100% (13875/13875), 2.29 MiB | 1.94 MiB/s, done.
Resolving deltas: 100% (9234/9234), done.
Checking connectivity... done.
vagrant@ansible:~$ sudo cp -a ceph-ansible/* /etc/ansible/
vagrant@ansible:~$
```

Let's also explore some of the key folders in the git repository:

- `group_vars`: We've already covered what lives in here and will explore the possible configuration options in more detail later.
- `infrastructure-playbooks`: This directory contains prewritten playbooks to carry out some standard tasks, such as deploying cluster or adding OSDs to an existing one. The comments at the top of the playbooks give a good idea of what they do.
- `roles`: This directory contains all the roles that make up the Ceph Ansible modules. You will see that there is a role for each Ceph component, these are what are called via the playbooks to install, configure and maintain Ceph.

In order to be able to deploy a Ceph cluster with Ansible a number of key variables need to be set in the `group_vars` directory. The following variables either are required to set or are advised to be changed from their defaults. For the remaining variables, it is suggested that you read the comments in the variable files.

The following are the key variables from `global`:

```
#mon_group_name: mons
#osd_group_name: osds
#rgw_group_name: rgws
#mds_group_name: mdss
#nfs_group_name: nfss
...
#iscsi_group_name: iscsigws
```

These control what group name the modules use to identify the types of Ceph hosts. If you will be using Ansible in a wider setting, it might be advisable to prepend `ceph-` to the start to make it clear that these groups are related to Ceph:

```
#ceph_origin: 'upstream' # or 'distro' or 'local'
```

Set to `upstream` to use the packages generated by the Ceph team, or `distro` for packages generated by your distribution maintainer. Setting to `upstream` is recommended if you want to be able to upgrade Ceph independently of your distribution.

By default a fsid will be generated for your cluster and stored in a file where it can be referenced again:

```
#fsid: "{{ cluster_uuid.stdout }}"
#generate_fsid: true
```

You shouldn't need to touch this unless you want control over the fsid or you wish to hard code the fsid in the group variable file.

```
#monitor_interface: interface
#monitor_address: 0.0.0.0
```

One of these should be specified. If you are using a variable in group_vars then you probably want to use the `monitor_interface`, which is the interface name as seen by the OS, as they will probably be the same across all `mons` groups. Otherwise if you specify the `monitor_address` in host_vars, you can specify the IP of the interface, which obviously will be different across your three or more `mons` groups.

```
#ceph_conf_overrides: {}
```

Not every Ceph variable is directly managed by Ansible, but the preceding variable is provided to allow you to pass any extra variables through to the `ceph.conf` file and its corresponding sections. An example of how this would look is (notice the indentation):

```
ceph_conf_overrides:
  global:
```

```
    variable1: value
  mon:
    variable2: value
  osd:
    variable3: value
```

Key variables from OSD variable file:

```
#copy_admin_key: false
```

If you want to be able to manage your cluster from your OSD nodes instead of just your monitors, set this to true, which will copy the admin key to your OSD nodes:

```
#devices: [] #osd_auto_discovery: false #journal_collocation:
false #raw_multi_journal: false #raw_journal_devices: []
```

These are probably the most crucial set of variables in the whole configuration of Ansible. They control what disks get used as OSDs and how the journals are placed. You can either manually specify the devices that you wish to use as OSDs or you can use auto discovery. The examples in this book will use the static device configuration.

The journal_collocation variable sets whether you want to store the journal on the same disk as the OSD data; a separate partition will be created for it.

raw_journal_devices allows you to specify the devices you wish to use for journals. Quite often a single SSD will be a journal for several OSDs, in this case, enable raw_multi_journal and simply specify the journal device multiple times, no partition numbers are needed if you want Ansible to instruct ceph-disk to create them for you.

These are the main variables that you should need to consider. It is recommended that you read the comments in the variable files to see if there are any others you may need to modify for your environment.

Deploying a test cluster with Ansible

There are several examples on the Internet which contain a fully configured Vagrantfile and associated Ansible playbooks which allows you to bring up a fully functional Ceph environment with just one command. As handy as this may be it doesn't help to learn how to correctly configure and use the Ceph Ansible modules as you would if you were deploying a Ceph cluster on real hardware in a production environment. As such, this book will guide you through configuring Ansible from the scratch, although running on Vagrant provisioned servers.

At this point your Vagrant environment should be up and running, and Ansible should be able to connect to all six of your Ceph servers. You should also have a cloned copy of the Ceph Ansible module:

1. Create a file called /etc/ansible/group_vars/ceph:

```
ceph_origin: 'upstream'
ceph_stable: true # use ceph stable branch
ceph_stable_key: https://download.ceph.com/keys/release.asc
ceph_stable_release: jewel # ceph stable release
ceph_stable_repo: "http://download.ceph.com/debian-{{
ceph_stable_release }}"monitor_interface: enp0s8 #Check ifconfig
public_network: 192.168.0.0/24
journal_size: 1024
```

2. Create a file called /etc/ansible/group_vars/osds:

```
devices:
  - /dev/sdb
journal_collocation: true
```

3. Create a fetch folder and change the owner to the vagrant user:

```
sudo mkdir /etc/ansible/fetch
sudo chown vagrant /etc/ansible/fetch
```

4. Run the Ceph cluster deployment playbook:

```
cd /etc/ansible
sudo mv site.yml.sample site.yml
ansible-playbook -K site.yml
```

The K parameter tells Ansible that it should ask you for the sudo password.

Now sit back and watch Ansible deploy your cluster:

```
PLAY RECAP *********************************************************************
mon1                       : ok=57    changed=15    unreachable=0    failed=0
mon2                       : ok=51    changed=12    unreachable=0    failed=0
mon3                       : ok=51    changed=12    unreachable=0    failed=0
osd1                       : ok=59    changed=11    unreachable=0    failed=0
osd2                       : ok=57    changed=11    unreachable=0    failed=0
osd3                       : ok=57    changed=11    unreachable=0    failed=0
```

Once done, assuming Ansible completed without errors, SSH into `mon1` and run the following code. If Ansible did encounter errors, scroll up and look for the part which errored, the error text should give you a clue as to why it failed.

```
vagrant@mon1:~$ sudo ceph -s:
```

```
vagrant@ansible:/etc/ansible$ ssh mon1
Welcome to Ubuntu 16.04.1 LTS (GNU/Linux 4.4.0-51-generic x86_64)

 * Documentation:  https://help.ubuntu.com
 * Management:      https://landscape.canonical.com
 * Support:         https://ubuntu.com/advantage

93 packages can be updated.
28 updates are security updates.


Last login: Tue Feb  7 22:08:42 2017 from 192.168.0.40
vagrant@mon1:~$ sudo ceph -s
    cluster d9f58afd-3e62-4493-ba80-0356290b3d9f
     health HEALTH_OK
     monmap e1: 3 mons at {mon1=192.168.0.41:6789/0,mon2=192.168.0.42:6789/0,mon3=192.168.0.43:6789/0}
            election epoch 6, quorum 0,1,2 mon1,mon2,mon3
     osdmap e8: 3 osds: 3 up, 3 in
            flags sortbitwise,require_jewel_osds
      pgmap v15: 64 pgs, 1 pools, 0 bytes data, 0 objects
            100 MB used, 26794 MB / 26894 MB avail
                  64 active+clean
```

And that concludes the deployment of a fully functional Ceph cluster via Ansible.

If you want to be able to stop the Vagrant Ceph cluster without losing your work so far, you can run the following command:

vagrant suspend

This will pause all the VMs in their current state.

The following command will power the VMs on and resume running at the state you left them:

vagrant resume

Change and configuration management

If you deploy your infrastructure with an orchestration tool such as Ansible, managing the Ansible playbooks becomes important. As we have seen Ansible allows you to rapidly deploy both the initial Ceph cluster but also configuration updates further down the line. It must be appreciated that this power can also have devastating effects if incorrect configuration or operations are deployed. By implementing some form of configuration management, Ceph administrators will clearly be able to see what changes have been made to the Ansible playbooks before running them.

A recommended approach would be to store your Ceph Ansible configuration in a git repository, this will allow you to track changes and gives the ability to implement some form of change control either by monitoring git commits or by forcing people to submit merge requests into the master branch.

Summary

In this chapter, you will have learned about the various deployment methods of Ceph that are available and the differences between them. You will now also have a basic understanding of how Ansible works and how to deploy a Ceph cluster with it. It would be advisable at this point to continue investigating and practicing deployment and configuration of Ceph with Ansible so that you are confident to use it in production environments.

12
BlueStore

In this chapter, you will learn about BlueStore, the new object store in Ceph designed to replace the existing filestore. Its increased performance and enhanced feature set are designed to allow Ceph to continue to grow and provide a resilient high-performance distributed storage system for the future.

You will learn the following topics:

- What is BlueStore?
- The limitations with filestore
- What problems BlueStore overcomes
- The components of BlueStore and how it works
- How to deploy BlueStore OSDs

What is BlueStore?

BlueStore is a Ceph object store that is primarily designed to address the limitations of filestore, which, as of the **Kraken** release, is the current object store. Initially, a new object store was being developed to replace filestore, with a highly original name of **NewStore**. NewStore was a combination of **RocksDB**, a key value store to store metadata and a standard **portable operating system interface** (**POSIX**) filesystem for the actual objects. However, it quickly became apparent that using a POSIX filesystem still introduced high overheads, which was one of the key reasons from trying to move away from filestore.

Thus, BlueStore was born; using raw block devices in combination with RocksDB, a number of problems were solved that had stunted NewStore. The name *BlueStore* was a reflection of the combination of the words *Block* and *NewStore*:

Block+NewStore=BlewStore=BlueStore

BlueStore is designed to remove the double write penalty associated with filestore and improve performance. Also, with the ability to now have more control over the way objects are stored on disk, additional features, such as checksums and compression, can be implemented.

Why was it needed?

The current object store in Ceph, Filestore, has a number of limitations which have started to limit the scale at which Ceph can operate and features that it can offer. Following are some of the main reasons why Bluestore was needed.

Ceph's requirements

An object in Ceph along with its data also has certain metadata associated with it, and it's crucial that both the data and metadata are updated atomically. If either of this metadata or data is updated without the other, the whole consistency model of Ceph is at risk. To ensure that these updates occur atomically, they need to be carried out in a single transaction.

Filestore limitations

Filestore was originally designed as an object store to enable developers to test Ceph on their local machines. Due to its stability, it quickly became the standard object store and found itself in use in production clusters throughout the world.

Initially, the thought behind filestore was that the upcoming **B-tree file system** (**btrfs**), which offered transaction support, would allow Ceph to offload the atomic requirements to btrfs. Transactions allow an application to send a series of requests to btrfs and only receive acknowledgement once all have been committed to stable storage. Without a transaction support, if there is an interruption halfway through a Ceph write operation, either the data or metadata could be missing or one out of sync with the other.

Unfortunately, the reliance on btrfs to solve these problems turned out to be a false hope, and several limitations were discovered. btrfs can still be used with filestore, but there are numerous known issues that can affect the stability of Ceph.

In the end, it turned out that **XFS** was the best choice to use with filestore, but XFS had the major limitation that it didn't support transactions, meaning that there was no way for Ceph to guarantee atomicity of its writes. The solution to this was the write-ahead journal. All writes including data and metadata would first be written into a journal, residing on a raw block device. Once the filesystem containing the data and metadata confirmed that all data had been safely flushed to disk, the journal entries could be flushed. A beneficial side effect of this is that when using a SSD to hold the journal for a spinning disk, it acts like a write back cache, lowering the latency of writes to the speed of the SSD. However, if the filestore journal resides on the same storage device as the data partition, then throughput will be at least halved. In the case of spinning disk OSDs, this can lead to very poor performance as the disk heads are constantly moving between two areas of the disks, even for sequential operations. Although filestore on SSD-based OSDs don't suffer nearly the same performance penalty, their throughput is still effectively halved due to double the amount of data required to be written. In either case, this loss of performance is very undesirable and in the case of flash, also wears the device faster, requiring more expensive write endurance flash. The following diagram shows how Filestore and its journal interacts with a block device, you can see that all data operations have to go through the Filestore journal and the filesystems journal.

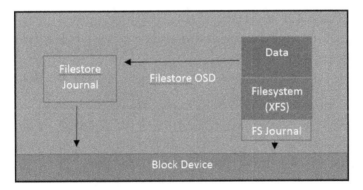

Additional challenges with filestore were around trying to control the actions of the underlying POSIX filesystem to perform and behave in a way that Ceph required. Large amounts of work has been done over the years by filesystem developers to try and make filesystems intelligent and to predict how an application might submit I/O. In the case of Ceph, a lot of these optimizations interfere with what it's trying to instruct the filesystem to do, requiring more work around and complexity.

Object metadata is stored in combinations of filesystem attributes named **Extended Attributes (XATTRs)** and in a **LevelDB** key value store, which also resides on the OSD disk. LevelDB was chosen at the time of filestore's creation rather than RocksDB, as RocksDB was not available and LevelDB suited a lot of Ceph's requirements.

Ceph is designed to scale to petabytes of data and store billions of objects. However, due to limitations around the number of files you can reasonably store in a directory, further workarounds to help limit this were introduced. Objects are stored in a hierarchy of hashed directory names; when the number of files in one of these folders reaches the set limit, the directory is split into a further level and the objects moved. However, there is a trade-off to improving the speed of object enumeration, when these directory splits occur they impact performance as the objects are moved into the correct directories. On larger disks, the increased number of directories puts additional pressure on the VFS cache and can lead to additional performance penalties for infrequently accessed objects.

For scenarios where there are a large number of objects stored per OSD, there is currently no real solution to this problem, and it's quite common to observe that the Ceph cluster gradually starts to slow down as it fills up.

Moving away from storing objects on a POSIX filesystem is really the only way to solve most of these problems.

Why is BlueStore the solution?

BlueStore was designed to address these limitations. From the development of NewStore, it was obvious that trying to use a POSIX filesystem as the underlying storage layer in any approach would introduce a number of issues that were also present in filestore. In order for Ceph to be able to get the guarantees, it not only needed from the storage but also without the overheads of a filesystem, Ceph needed to have direct block level access to the storage devices. By storing metadata in RocksDB and the actual object data directly on block devices, Ceph can leverage much better control over the underlying storage and at the same time, also provide better performance.

How BlueStore works

The following diagram shows how Bluestore interacts with a block device. Unlike filestore, data is directly written to the block device and metadata operations are handled by RocksDB.

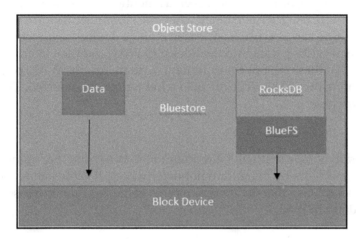

RocksDB

RocksDB is a high-performance key value store, which was originally forked from LevelDB, but after development, Facebook went on to offer significant performance improvements suited for multiprocessor servers with low latency storage devices. It has also had numerous feature enhancements, some of which are used in BlueStore.

RocksDB is used to store metadata about the stored objects, which was previously handled by a combination of LevelDB and XATTRs in filestore.

A feature of RocksDB, which BlueStore takes advantage of, is the ability to store the WAL on a faster storage device, which can help to lower latency of RocksDB operations. This also hopefully improves Ceph's performance, particularly for smaller I/Os. This gives a number of possible storage layout configurations, where the WAL, DB, and data can be placed on different storage devices. Three examples are given here:

- WAL, DB, and data all on spinning disk
- WAL and DB on SSD, data on spinning disk
- WAL on NVMe, DB on SSD, and data on spinning disk

Deferred writes

Unlike in filestore where every write is written in its entirely to both the journal and finally to disk, in BlueStore, the data part of the write in most cases is written directly to the block device. This removes the double write penalty and on pure spinning disk OSDs dramatically improves performance. However, as mentioned previously, this double write has a side effect of decreasing write latency when the spinning disks are combined with SSD journals. BlueStore can also use flash-based storage devices to lower write latency by deferring writes, first writing data into the RocksDB WAL and then later flushing these entries to disk. Unlike filestore, not every write is written into the WAL, configuration parameters determine the I/O size cut-off as to what writes are deferred. The configuration parameter is shown here:

```
bluestore_prefer_deferred_size
```

This controls the size of I/Os that will be written to the WAL first. For spinning disks, this defaults to 32 KB, and SSDs by default do not defer writes. If write latency is important and your SSD is sufficiently fast, then by increasing this value, you can increase the size of I/Os that you wish to defer to WAL.

BlueFS

Although the main driver of BlueStore was not to use an underlying filesystem, BlueStore still needs a method to store RocksDB and the data on the OSD disk. BlueFS was developed, which is an extremely cut down filesystem that provides just the minimal set of features that BlueStore requires. It also means that it has been designed to operate in a dependable manner for the slim set of operations that Ceph submits. It also removes the overhead of the double journal write impact that would be present when using a standard POSIX filesystem.

How to use BlueStore

To create a BlueStore OSD, you can use ceph-disk that fully supports creating BlueStore OSDs with either the RocksDB data and WAL collocated or stored on separate disks. The operation is similar to when creating a filestore OSD except instead of specifying a device for use as the filestore journal, you specify devices for the RocksDB data. As previously mentioned, you can separate the DB and WAL parts of RocksDB if you so wish:

```
ceph-disk prepare --bluestore /dev/sda --block.wal /dev/sdb --block.db
/dev/sdb
```

The preceding code assumes that your data disk is /dev/sda. For this example, assume a spinning disk and you have a faster device such as SSD as /dev/sdb. Ceph-disk would create two partitions on the data disk: one for storing the actual Ceph objects and another small XFS partition for storing details about the OSD. It would also create two partitions for SSD for the DB and WAL. You can create multiple OSDs sharing the same SSD for DB and WAL without fear of overwriting previous OSDs; ceph-disk is smart enough to create new partitions without having to specify them.

However, as we discovered in Chapter 11, *Deploying Ceph* using a proper deployment tool for your Ceph cluster helps to reduce deployment time and ensures consistent configuration across the cluster. Although the Ceph Ansible modules also support deploying BlueStore OSDs, at the time of publication of this book, it did not currently support deploying separate DB and WAL partitions. For the basis of demonstrating BlueStore, we will use ceph-disk to non-disruptively manually upgrade our test cluster's OSDs from filestore to BlueStore.

Upgrading an OSD in your test cluster

Make sure that your Ceph cluster is in full health by checking with the ceph -s command. We will be upgrading OSD by first removing it from the cluster and then letting Ceph recover the data onto the new BlueStore OSD. By taking advantage of this hot maintenance capability in Ceph, you can repeat this procedure across all the OSDs in your cluster.

In this example, we will remove osd.2, which is residing on the /dev/sdb disk on the OSD node, by performing the following steps:

1. Use the following command:

   ```
   sudo ceph osd out 2
   ```

   The preceding command gives the following output:

   ```
   vagrant@mon1:~$ sudo ceph osd out 2
   marked out osd.2.
   ```

2. Log into the OSD node that contains the OSD you wish to recreate. We will stop the service and unmount the XFS partition:

   ```
   systemctl stop ceph-osd@2
   umount /dev/sdb1
   ```

3. Go back to one of your monitors and now remove the OSD using the following commands:

```
sudo ceph osd crush remove osd.2
```

The preceding command gives the following output:

```
vagrant@mon1:~$ sudo ceph osd crush remove osd.2
removed item id 2 name 'osd.2' from crush map
```

```
sudo ceph auth del osd.2
```

The preceding command gives the following output:

```
vagrant@mon1:~$ sudo ceph auth del osd.2
updated
```

```
sudo ceph osd rm osd.2
```

The preceding command gives the following output:

```
vagrant@mon1:~$ sudo ceph osd rm osd.2
removed osd.2
```

4. Check the status of your Ceph cluster with the ceph -s command. You should now see that the OSD has been removed. Once recovery has completed, you can now recreate the disk as a BlueStore OSD.
5. Go back to your OSD node and run the following ceph-disk command to wipe the partition details from the disk:

```
sudo ceph-disk zap /dev/sdb
```

The preceding command gives the following output:

```
vagrant@osd3:~$ sudo ceph-disk zap /dev/sdb
Caution: invalid backup GPT header, but valid main header; regenerating
backup header from main header.

Warning! Main and backup partition tables differ! Use the 'c' and 'e' options
on the recovery & transformation menu to examine the two tables.

Warning! One or more CRCs don't match. You should repair the disk!

*****************************************************************************
Caution: Found protective or hybrid MBR and corrupt GPT. Using GPT, but disk
verification and recovery are STRONGLY recommended.
*****************************************************************************
GPT data structures destroyed! You may now partition the disk using fdisk or
other utilities.
Creating new GPT entries.
The operation has completed successfully.
```

6. Now issue the `ceph-disk` command to create the `bluestore` OSD. In this example, we will not be storing the WAL and DB on separate disks, so we do not need to specify those options:

```
ceph-disk prepare --bluestore /dev/sdb
```

The preceding command gives the following output:

```
vagrant@osd3:~$ sudo ceph-disk prepare --bluestore /dev/sdb
Setting name!
partNum is 0
REALLY setting name!
The operation has completed successfully.
Setting name!
partNum is 1
REALLY setting name!
The operation has completed successfully.
The operation has completed successfully.
meta-data=/dev/sdb1              isize=2048   agcount=4, agsize=6400 blks
         =                       sectsz=512   attr=2, projid32bit=1
         =                       crc=1        finobt=1, sparse=0
data     =                       bsize=4096   blocks=25600, imaxpct=25
         =                       sunit=0      swidth=0 blks
naming   =version 2              bsize=4096   ascii-ci=0 ftype=1
log      =internal log           bsize=4096   blocks=864, version=2
         =                       sectsz=512   sunit=0 blks, lazy-count=1
realtime =none                   extsz=4096   blocks=0, rtextents=0
The operation has completed successfully.
```

7. And finally activate OSD:

```
ceph-disk activate /dev/sdb1
```

Returning to our monitor node, we can now run another `ceph -s` and see that a new OSD has been created and data is starting to be backfilled to it.

As you can see, the overall procedure is very simple and is identical to the steps required to replace a failed disk.

Summary

In this chapter, you learned about the new object store in Ceph named BlueStore. Hopefully, you have a better understanding of why it was needed and the limitations in the existing filestore design. You should also have a basic understanding of the inner workings of BlueStore and feel confident in how to upgrade your OSDs to BlueStore.

13
Erasure Coding for Better Storage Efficiency

Ceph's default replication level provides excellent protection against data loss by storing three copies of your data on different OSDs. The chance of losing all three disks that contain the same objects, within the period that it takes Ceph to rebuild from a failed disk, is verging on the extreme edge of probability. However, storing three copies of data vastly increases both the purchase cost of the hardware and also associated operational costs such as power and cooling. Furthermore, storing copies also means that for every client write, the backend storage must write three times the amount of data. In some scenarios, either of these drawbacks may mean that Ceph is not a viable option.

Erasure codes are designed to offer a solution. Much like how RAID 5 and 6 offer increased usable storage capacity over RAID 1, erasure coding allows Ceph to provide more usable storage from the same raw capacity. However, also like the parity-based RAID levels, erasure coding brings its own set of disadvantages.

In this chapter you will learn the following:

- What is erasure coding and how does it work?
- Details around Ceph's implementation of erasure coding
- How to create and tune an erasure-coded RADOS pool
- A look into the future features of erasure coding with the Ceph Kraken release

What is erasure coding?

Erasure coding allows Ceph to achieve either greater usable storage capacity or increase resilience to disk failure for the same number of disks versus the standard replica method. Erasure coding achieves this by splitting up the object into a number of parts and then also calculating a type of **cyclic redundancy check** (**CRC**), the erasure code, and then storing the results in one or more extra parts. Each part is then stored on a separate OSD. These parts are referred to as K and M chunks, where K refers to the number of data shards and M refers to the number of erasure code shards. As in RAID, these can often be expressed in the form **K+M**, or 4+2, for example.

In the event of an OSD failure which contains an object's shard which is one of the calculated erasure codes, data is read from the remaining OSDs that store data with no impact. However, in the event of an OSD failure which contains the data shards of an object, Ceph can use the erasure codes to mathematically recreate the data from a combination of the remaining data and erasure code shards.

K+M

The more erasure code shards you have, the more OSD failures you can tolerate and still successfully read data. Likewise, the ratio of K to M shards each object is split into has a direct effect on the percentage of raw storage that is required for each object.

A *3+1* configuration will give you 75% usable capacity but only allows for a single OSD failure, and so would not be recommended. In comparison, a three-way replica pool only gives you 33% usable capacity.

4+2 configurations would give you 66% usable capacity and allows for two OSD failures. This is probably a good configuration for most people to use.

At the other end of the scale, *18+2* would give you 90% usable capacity and still allows for two OSD failures. On the surface this sounds like an ideal option, but the greater total number of shards comes at a cost. A higher number of total shards has a negative impact on performance and also an increased CPU demand. The same 4 MB object that would be stored as a whole single object in a replicated pool would now be split into 20x200 KB chunks, which have to be tracked and written to 20 different OSDs. Spinning disks will exhibit faster bandwidth, measured in MBps with larger I/O sizes, but bandwidth drastically tails off at smaller I/O sizes. These smaller shards will generate a large amount of small I/O and cause additional load on some clusters.

Also, it's important not to forget that these shards need to be spread across different hosts according to the CRUSH map rules: no shard belonging to the same object can be stored on the same host as another shard from the same object. Some clusters may not have a sufficient number of hosts to satisfy this requirement.

Reading back from these high chunk pools is also a problem. Unlike in a replica pool where Ceph can read just the requested data from any offset in an object, in an erasure pool, all shards from all OSDs have to be read before the read request can be satisfied. In the *18+2* example, this can massively amplify the amount of required disk read ops and average latency will increase as a result. This behavior is a side effect which tends to only cause a performance impact with pools that use a large number of shards. A 4+2 configuration in some instances will get a performance gain compared to a replica pool, from the result of splitting an object into shards. As the data is effectively striped over a number of OSDs, each OSD has to write less data and there are no secondary and tertiary replicas to write.

How does erasure coding work in Ceph?

As with replication, Ceph has a concept of a primary OSD, which also exists when using erasure-coded pools. The primary OSD has the responsibility of communicating with the client, calculating the erasure shards, and sending them out to the remaining OSDs in the PG set. This is illustrated in the following diagram:

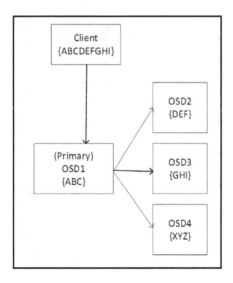

If an OSD in the set is down, the primary OSD can use the remaining data and erasure shards to reconstruct the data, before sending it back to the client. During read operations, the primary OSD requests all OSDs in the PG set to send their shards. The primary OSD uses data from the data shards to construct the requested data, and the erasure shards are discarded. There is a fast read option that can be enabled on erasure pools, which allows the primary OSD to reconstruct the data from erasure shards if they return quicker than data shards. This can help to lower average latency at the cost of a slightly higher CPU usage. The following diagram shows how Ceph reads from an erasure-coded pool:

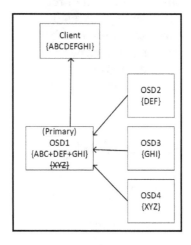

The following diagram shows how Ceph reads from an erasure pool when one of the data shards is unavailable. Data is reconstructed by reversing the erasure algorithm using the remaining data and erasure shards:

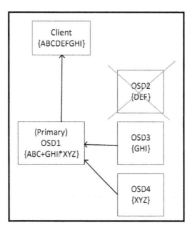

Algorithms and profiles

There are a number of different erasure plugins you can use to create your erasure-coded pool.

Jerasure

The default erasure plugin in Ceph is the **Jerasure** plugin, which is a highly optimized open source erasure coding library. The library has a number of different techniques that can be used to calculate the erasure codes. The default is **Reed-Solomon** and provides good performance on modern processors which can accelerate the instructions that the technique uses. **Cauchy** is another technique in the library; it is a good alternative to Reed- Solomon and tends to perform slightly better. As always, benchmarks should be conducted before storing any production data on an erasure-coded pool to identify which technique best suits your workload.

There are also a number of other techniques that can be used which all have a fixed number of *M* shards. If you are intending on only having two *M* shards, then they can be a good candidate as their fixed size means that optimizations are possible, lending to increased performance.

In general, the Jerasure profile should be preferred in most cases unless another profile has a major advantage, as it offers well-balanced performance and is well-tested.

ISA

The **ISA library** is designed to work with Intel processors and offers enhanced performance. It too supports both Reed-Solomon and Cauchy techniques.

LRC

One of the disadvantages of using erasure coding in a distributed storage system is that recovery can be very intensive on networking between hosts. As each shard is stored on a separate host, recovery operations require multiple hosts to participate in the process. When the CRUSH topology spans multiple racks, this can put pressure on the inter-rack networking links. The **Locally Repairable erasure Code** (**LRC**) erasure plugin adds an additional parity shard, which is local to each OSD node. This allows recovery operations to remain local to the node where an OSD has failed and remove the need for nodes to receive data from all other remaining shard-holding nodes.

However, the addition of these local recovery codes does impact the amount of usable storage for a given number of disks. In the event of multiple disk failures, the LRC plugin has to resort to using global recovery, as would happen with the Jerasure plugin.

SHEC

The **Shingled Erasure Coding** (**SHEC**) profile is designed with similar goals to the LRC plugin, in that it reduces the networking requirements during recovery. However, instead of creating extra parity shards on each node, SHEC shingles the shards across OSDs in an overlapping fashion. The shingle part of the plugin name represents the way the data distribution resembles shingled tiles on a roof of a house. By overlapping the parity shards across OSDs, the SHEC plugin reduces recovery resource requirements for both single and multiple disk failures.

Where can I use erasure coding?

Since the **Firefly** release of Ceph in 2014, there has been the ability to create a RADOS pool using erasure coding. There is one major thing that you should be aware of: the erasure coding support in RADOS does not allow an object to be partially updated. You can write to an object in an erasure pool, read it back, and even overwrite it whole, but you cannot update a partial section of it. This means that erasure-coded pools can't be used for RBD and CephFS workloads and are limited to providing pure object storage either via the RADOS gateway or applications written to use librados.

The solution at the time was to use the cache tiering ability which was released around the same time, to act as a layer above an erasure-coded pool so that RBD could be used. In theory this was a great idea; in practice, performance was extremely poor. Every time an object was required to be written to, the whole object first had to be promoted into the cache tier. This act of promotion probably also meant that another object somewhere in the cache pool was evicted. Finally, the object now in the cache tier could be written to. This whole process of constantly reading and writing data between the two pools meant that performance was unacceptable, unless a very high percentage of the data was idle.

During the development cycle of the Kraken release, an initial implementation for support for direct overwrites on an erasure-coded pool was introduced. As of the final Kraken release, support is marked as experimental and is expected to be marked as stable in the following release. Testing of this feature will be covered later in this chapter.

Creating an erasure-coded pool

Let's bring our test cluster up again and switch into **superuser** mode in Linux, so we don't have to keep prepending `sudo` to our commands.

Erasure-coded pools are controlled by the use of erasure profiles; these controls how many shards each object is broken up into including the split between data and erasure shards. The profiles also include configuration to determine what erasure code plugin is used to calculate the hashes.

The following plugins are available to use:

- Jerasure
- ISA
- LRC
- SHEC

To see a list of the erasure profiles, run the following command:

```
# ceph osd erasure-code-profile ls
```

You can see there is a `default` profile in a fresh installation of Ceph:

```
vagrant@mon1:~$ sudo ceph osd erasure-code-profile ls
default
```

Let's see what configuration options it contains using the following command:

```
# ceph osd erasure-code-profile get default
```

The `default` profile specifies that it will use the Jerasure plugin with the Reed-Solomon error-correcting codes and will split objects into 2 data shards and 1 erasure shard:

```
vagrant@mon1:~$ sudo ceph osd erasure-code-profile get default
k=2
m=1
plugin=jerasure
technique=reed_sol_van
```

This is almost perfect for our test cluster; however, for the purpose of this exercise, we will create a new profile using the following commands:

```
# ceph osd erasure-code-profile set example_profile k=2 m=1
plugin=jerasure technique=reed_sol_van
# ceph osd erasure-code-profile ls
```

You can see our new `example_profile` has been created:

```
vagrant@mon1:~$ sudo ceph osd erasure-code-profile ls
default
example_profile
```

Now, let's create our erasure-coded pool with this profile:

```
# ceph osd pool create ecpool 128 128 erasure example_profile
```

The preceding command gives the following output:

```
vagrant@mon1:~$ sudo ceph osd pool create ecpool 128 128 erasure example_profile
pool 'ecpool' created
```

The preceding command instructs Ceph to create a new pool called `ecpool` with 128 PGs. It should be an erasure-coded pool and should use the `example_profile` we previously created.

Let's create an object with a small text string inside it and then prove the data has been stored by reading it back:

```
# echo "I am test data for a test object" | rados --pool
ecpool put Test1 -
# rados --pool ecpool get Test1 -
```

That proves that the erasure-coded pool is working, but it's hardly the most exciting of discoveries:

```
root@mon1:/home/vagrant# echo "I am test data for a test object" | rados --pool ecpool put Test1 -
root@mon1:/home/vagrant# rados --pool ecpool get Test1 -
I am test data for a test object
```

Let's have a look to see if we can see what's happening at a lower level.

First, find out what PG is holding the object we just created:

```
# ceph osd map ecpool Test1
```

The result of the preceding command tells us that the object is stored in PG 3.40 on OSDs 1, 2, and 0 in this example Ceph cluster. That's pretty obvious as we only have three OSDs, but in larger clusters that is a very useful piece of information:

```
root@mon1:/home/vagrant# ceph osd map ecpool Test1
osdmap e114 pool 'ecpool' (3) object 'Test1' -> pg 3.ae48bdc0 (3.40) -> up ([1,2,0], p1) acting ([1,2,0], p1)
```

The PGs will likely be different on your test cluster, so make sure the PG folder structure matches the output of the preceding `ceph osd map` command.

We can now look at the folder structure of the OSDs and see how the object has been split using the following commands:

```
ls -l /var/lib/ceph/osd/ceph-2/current/1.40s0_head/
```

The preceding command gives the following output:

```
root@osd1:/home/vagrant# ls -l /var/lib/ceph/osd/ceph-0/current/3.40s2_head/
total 4
-rw-r--r-- 1 ceph ceph    0 Feb 12 19:53  head_00000040__3_ffffffffffffffff_2
-rw-r--r-- 1 ceph ceph 2048 Feb 12 19:56 Test1__head_AE48BDC0__3_ffffffffffffffff_2
```

```
# ls -l /var/lib/ceph/osd/ceph-1/current/1.40s1_head/
```

The preceding command gives the following output:

```
root@osd2:/home/vagrant# ls -l /var/lib/ceph/osd/ceph-2/current/3.40s1_head/
total 4
-rw-r--r-- 1 ceph ceph    0 Feb 12 19:53  head_00000040__3_ffffffffffffffff_1
-rw-r--r-- 1 ceph ceph 2048 Feb 12 19:56 Test1__head_AE48BDC0__3_ffffffffffffffff_1
```

```
# ls -l /var/lib/ceph/osd/ceph-0/current/1.40s2_head/
total 4
```

The preceding command gives the following output:

```
root@osd3:/home/vagrant# ls -l /var/lib/ceph/osd/ceph-1/current/3.40s0_head/
total 4
-rw-r--r-- 1 ceph ceph    0 Feb 12 19:53 __head_00000040__3_ffffffffffffffff_0
-rw-r--r-- 1 ceph ceph 2048 Feb 12 19:56 Test1__head_AE48BDC0__3_ffffffffffffffff_0
```

Notice how the PG directory names have been appended with the shard number and replicated pools just have the PG number as their directory name. If you examine the contents of the object files, you will see our text string that we entered into the object when we created it. However, due to the small size of the text string, Ceph has padded out the second shard with null characters and the erasure shard, hence it will contain the same as the first. You can repeat this example with a new object containing larger amounts of text to see how Ceph splits the text into the shards and calculates the erasure code.

Overwrites on erasure code pools with Kraken

Introduced for the first time in the Kraken release of Ceph as an experimental feature was the ability to allow partial overwrites on erasure-coded pools. **Partial overwrite** support allows RBD volumes to be created on erasure-coded pools, making better use of the raw capacity of the Ceph cluster.

In parity RAID, where a write request doesn't span the entire stripe, a read-modify-write operation is required. This is needed as the modified data chunks will mean the parity chunk is now incorrect. The RAID controller has to read all the current chunks in the stripe, modify them in memory, calculate the new parity chunk, and finally write this back out to the disk.

Ceph is also required to perform this read-modify-write operation, however the distributed model of Ceph increases the complexity of this operation. When the primary OSD for a PG receives a write request that will partially overwrite an existing object, it first works out which shards will not be fully modified by the request and contacts the relevant OSDs to request a copy of these shards. The primary OSD then combines these received shards with the new data and calculates the erasure shards. Finally, the modified shards are sent out to the respective OSDs to be committed. This entire operation needs to conform to the other consistency requirements Ceph enforces; this entails the use of temporary objects on the OSD, should a condition arise that Ceph needs to roll back a write operation.

This partial overwrite operation, as can be expected, has a performance impact. In general, the smaller the write I/Os, the greater the apparent impact. The performance impact is a result of the I/O path now being longer, requiring more disk I/Os, and extra network hops. However, it should be noted that due to the striping effect of erasure-coded pools, in the scenario where full stripe writes occur, performance will normally exceed that of a replication-based pool. This is simply down to there being less write amplification due to the effect of striping. If the performance of an erasure pool is not suitable, consider placing it behind a cache tier made up of a replicated pool.

Despite partial overwrite support coming to erasure-coded pools in Ceph, not every operation is supported. In order to store RBD data on an erasure-coded pool, a replicated pool is still required to hold key metadata about the RBD. This configuration is enabled by using the –data-pool option with the **rbd utility**. Partial overwrite is also not recommended to be used with filestore. Filestore lacks several features that partial overwrites on erasure-coded pools use; without these features, extremely poor performance is experienced.

Demonstration

This feature requires the Kraken release or newer of Ceph. If you have deployed your test cluster with the Ansible and the configuration provided, you will be running Ceph Jewel release. The following steps show how to use Ansible to perform a rolling upgrade of your cluster to the Kraken release. We will also enable options to enable experimental options such as BlueStore and support for partial overwrites on erasure-coded pools.

Edit your group_vars/ceph variable file and change the release version from Jewel to Kraken.

Also, add the following:

```
ceph_conf_overrides:
  global:
    enable_experimental_unrecoverable_data_corrupting_features:
    "debug_white_box_testing_ec_overwrites bluestore"

And to correct a small bug when using Ansible to deploy Ceph Kraken, add
debian_ceph_packages:
  - ceph
  - ceph-common
  - ceph-fuse
```

To the bottom of the file, run the following Ansible playbook:

```
ansible-playbook -K infrastructure-playbooks/rolling_update.yml
```

The preceding command gives the following output:

```
vagrant@ansible:/etc/ansible$ ansible-playbook -K infrastructure-playbooks/rolling_update.yml
SUDO password:
[DEPRECATION WARNING]: docker is kept for backwards compatibility but usage is discouraged. The module
documentation details page may explain more about this rationale..
This feature will be removed in a
future release. Deprecation warnings can be disabled by setting deprecation_warnings=False in
ansible.cfg.
Are you sure you want to upgrade the cluster? [no]: yes
```

Ansible will prompt you to make sure that you want to carry out the upgrade. Once you confirm by entering yes, the upgrade process will begin.

Once Ansible has finished, all the stages should be successful, as shown in the following screenshot:

```
PLAY RECAP ***********************************************************************
localhost                  : ok=1    changed=0    unreachable=0    failed=0
mon1                       : ok=73   changed=13   unreachable=0    failed=0
mon2                       : ok=68   changed=7    unreachable=0    failed=0
mon3                       : ok=68   changed=7    unreachable=0    failed=0
osd1                       : ok=69   changed=9    unreachable=0    failed=0
osd2                       : ok=69   changed=9    unreachable=0    failed=0
osd3                       : ok=69   changed=9    unreachable=0    failed=0
```

Your cluster has now been upgraded to Kraken and can be confirmed by running ceph -v on one of your VMs running Ceph:

```
vagrant@mon1:~$ ceph -v
ceph version 11.2.0 (f223e27eeb35991352ebc1f67423d4ebc252adb7)
```

As a result of enabling the experimental options in the configuration file, every time you now run a Ceph command, you will be presented with the following warning:

```
vagrant@mon1:~$ sudo ceph -s
2017-02-10 20:56:29.825996 7f6f18fc9700 -1 WARNING: the following dangerous and experimental features are enabled: bluestor
e,debug_white_box_testing_ec_overwrites
2017-02-10 20:56:29.831159 7f6f18fc9700 -1 WARNING: the following dangerous and experimental features are enabled: bluestor
e,debug_white_box_testing_ec_overwrites
    cluster d9f58afd-3e62-4493-ba80-0356290b3d9f
     health HEALTH_WARN
            all OSDs are running kraken or later but the 'require_kraken_osds' osdmap flag is not set
     monmap e2: 3 mons at {mon1=192.168.0.41:6789/0,mon2=192.168.0.42:6789/0,mon3=192.168.0.43:6789/0}
            election epoch 46, quorum 0,1,2 mon1,mon2,mon3
        mgr active: mon1 standbys: mon2, mon3
     osdmap e74: 3 osds: 3 up, 3 in
            flags sortbitwise,require_jewel_osds
      pgmap v600: 64 pgs, 1 pools, 3920 bytes data, 2 objects
            107 MB used, 26787 MB / 26894 MB avail
                  64 active+clean
```

This is designed as a safety warning to stop you running these options in a live environment, as they may cause irreversible data loss. As we are doing this on a test cluster, it is fine to ignore, but it should be a stark warning not to run this anywhere near live data.

The next command that is required to be run is to enable the experimental flag, which allows partial overwrites on erasure-coded pools:

```
ceph osd pool get ecpool debug_white_box_testing_ec_overwrites
true
```

Do not run this on production clusters.

Double check you still have your erasure pool called `ecpool` and the default `rbd` pool:

```
# ceph osd lspools
0 rbd,1 ecpool,
```

Now, create `rbd`. Notice that the actual RBD header object still has to live on a replica pool, but by providing an additional parameter, we can tell Ceph to store data for this RBD on an erasure-coded pool:

```
rbd create Test_On_EC --data-pool=ecpool --size=1G
```

The command should return without error and you now have an erasure-coded backed RBD image. You should now be able to use this image with any **librbd application**.

Partial overwrites on erasure pools require BlueStore to operate efficiently. Whilst filestore will work, performance will be extremely poor.

Troubleshooting the 2147483647 error

This small section is included within the erasure coding chapter rather than the troubleshooting section of this book, as it's commonly seen with erasure-coded pools and so is very relevant to this chapter. An example of this error is shown in the following screenshot, when running the `ceph health detail` command:

```
pg 2.7a is creating+incomplete, acting [0,2,1,2147483647] (reducing pool broken_ecpool min_size from 4
may help; search ceph.com/docs for 'incomplete')
pg 2.79 is creating+incomplete, acting [1,0,2,2147483647] (reducing pool broken_ecpool min_size from 4
may help; search ceph.com/docs for 'incomplete')
pg 2.78 is creating+incomplete, acting [1,0,2147483647,2] (reducing pool broken_ecpool min_size from 4
may help; search ceph.com/docs for 'incomplete')
pg 2.7f is creating+incomplete, acting [0,2,1,2147483647] (reducing pool broken_ecpool min_size from 4
may help; search ceph.com/docs for 'incomplete')
```

If you see `2147483647` listed as one of the OSDs for an erasure-coded pool, this normally means that CRUSH was unable to find a sufficient number of OSDs to complete the PG peering process. This is normally due to the number of K+M shards being larger than the number of hosts in the CRUSH topology. However, in some cases this error can still occur even when the number of hosts is equal to or greater than the number of shards. In this scenario it's important to understand how CRUSH picks OSDs as candidates for data placement. When CRUSH is used to find a candidate OSD for a PG, it applies the CRUSH map to find an appropriate location in the CRUSH topology. If the result comes back as the same as a previously selected OSD, Ceph will retry to generate another mapping by passing slightly different values into the CRUSH algorithm. In some cases, if there is a similar number of hosts to the number of erasure shards, CRUSH may run out of attempts before it can suitably find the correct OSD mappings for all the shards. Newer versions of Ceph have mostly fixed these problems by increasing the CRUSH tunable `choose_total_tries`.

Reproducing the problem

In order to aid understanding of the problem in more detail, the following steps will demonstrate how to create an erasure-coded profile that will require more shards than our three node cluster can support.

Firstly, like earlier in the chapter, create a new erasure profile but modify the K/M parameters to be k=3 and m=1:

```
$ ceph osd erasure-code-profile set broken_profile k=3 m=1
plugin=jerasure technique=reed_sol_van
```

Now, create a pool with it:

```
$ ceph osd pool create broken_ecpool 128 128 erasure broken_profile
```

The preceding command gives the following result:

```
vagrant@mon1:~$ sudo ceph osd pool create broken_ecpool 128 128 erasure broken_profile
2017-02-12 19:25:55.660243 7f3c6b74e700 -1 WARNING: the following dangerous and experimental features a
re enabled: bluestore,debug_white_box_testing_ec_overwrites
2017-02-12 19:25:55.671201 7f3c6b74e700 -1 WARNING: the following dangerous and experimental features a
re enabled: bluestore,debug_white_box_testing_ec_overwrites
pool 'broken_ecpool' created
```

If we look at the output from ceph -s, we will see that the PGs for this new pool are stuck in the creating state:

```
    cluster d9f58afd-3e62-4493-ba80-0356290b3d9f
     health HEALTH_ERR
            128 pgs are stuck inactive for more than 300 seconds
            128 pgs incomplete
            128 pgs stuck inactive
            128 pgs stuck unclean
            all OSDs are running kraken or later but the 'require_kraken_osds' osdmap flag is not set
     monmap e2: 3 mons at {mon1=192.168.0.41:6789/0,mon2=192.168.0.42:6789/0,mon3=192.168.0.43:6789/0}
            election epoch 64, quorum 0,1,2 mon1,mon2,mon3
        mgr active: mon1 standbys: mon2, mon3
     osdmap e98: 3 osds: 3 up, 3 in
            flags sortbitwise,require_jewel_osds
      pgmap v695: 192 pgs, 2 pools, 3920 bytes data, 2 objects
            112 MB used, 26782 MB / 26894 MB avail
                 128 creating+incomplete
                  64 active+clean
```

The output of ceph health detail shows the reason why, and we see the 2147483647 error:

```
pg 2.7a is creating+incomplete, acting [0,2,1,2147483647] (reducing pool broken_ecpool min_size from 4
may help; search ceph.com/docs for 'incomplete')
pg 2.79 is creating+incomplete, acting [1,0,2,2147483647] (reducing pool broken_ecpool min_size from 4
may help; search ceph.com/docs for 'incomplete')
pg 2.78 is creating+incomplete, acting [1,0,2147483647,2] (reducing pool broken_ecpool min_size from 4
may help; search ceph.com/docs for 'incomplete')
pg 2.7f is creating+incomplete, acting [0,2,1,2147483647] (reducing pool broken_ecpool min_size from 4
may help; search ceph.com/docs for 'incomplete')
```

If you encounter this error and it is a result of your erasure profile being larger than your number of hosts or racks, depending on how you have designed your CRUSH map, then the only real solution is to either drop the number of shards or increase the number of hosts.

Summary

In this chapter you have learnt what erasure coding is and how it is implemented in Ceph. You should also have an understanding of the different configuration options possible when creating erasure-coded pools and their suitability for different types of scenarios and workloads.

14
Developing with Librados

Ceph provides block, file, and object storage via the built-in interfaces which will meet the requirements of a large number of users. However, in some scenarios where an application is developed internally, there may be benefits to directly interfacing it into Ceph via the use of librados. Librados is the Ceph library that allows applications to directly read and write objects to the RADOS layer in Ceph.

We will cover the following topics in this chapter:

- What is librados?
- How to use librados and what languages it supports
- How to write an example librados application
- How to write a librados application that stores image files in Ceph using Python
- How to write a librados application using atomic operations using C++

What is librados?

Librados is the Ceph library which you can include in your own applications to allow you to directly talk to a Ceph cluster using the native protocols. As librados communicates with Ceph using its native communication protocols, it allows your application to harness the full power, speed, and flexibility of Ceph, instead of having to make use of high-level protocols like Amazon S3. A vast array of functions allows your application to read and write simple objects all the way to advanced operations, where you might want to wrap several operations in a transaction or run them asynchronously. Librados is available for several languages, including C, C++, Python, PHP, and Java.

How to use librados?

To get started with librados, a development environment is needed. For the examples in this chapter, one of the monitor nodes can be used to act as both the development environment and the client to run the developed application. The examples in this book assume you are using a Debian based distribution:

1. Firstly, install the base build tools for the operating system:

   ```
   $ sudo apt-get install build-essential
   ```

   The preceding command gives the following output:

   ```
   vagrant@mon1:~$ sudo apt-get install build-essential
   Reading package lists... Done
   Building dependency tree
   Reading state information... Done
   The following additional packages will be installed:
     dpkg-dev g++ g++-5 libalgorithm-diff-perl libalgorithm-diff-xs-perl libalgorithm-merge-perl
     libstdc++-5-dev
   Suggested packages:
     debian-keyring g++-multilib g++-5-multilib gcc-5-doc libstdc++6-5-dbg libstdc++-5-doc
   The following NEW packages will be installed:
     build-essential dpkg-dev g++ g++-5 libalgorithm-diff-perl libalgorithm-diff-xs-perl
     libalgorithm-merge-perl libstdc++-5-dev
   0 upgraded, 8 newly installed, 0 to remove and 93 not upgraded.
   Need to get 10.4 MB of archives.
   After this operation, 41.0 MB of additional disk space will be used.
   Do you want to continue? [Y/n]
   ```

2. Install the librados development library:

   ```
   $ sudo apt-get install librados-dev
   ```

   The preceding command gives the following output:

   ```
   vagrant@mon1:~$ sudo apt-get install librados-dev
   Reading package lists... Done
   Building dependency tree
   Reading state information... Done
   The following NEW packages will be installed:
     librados-dev
   0 upgraded, 1 newly installed, 0 to remove and 93 not upgraded.
   Need to get 42.0 MB of archives.
   After this operation, 358 MB of additional disk space will be used.
   Get:1 http://download.ceph.com/debian-jewel xenial/main amd64 librados-dev amd64 10.2.5-1xenial [42.0 MB]
   Fetched 42.0 MB in 30s (1,359 kB/s)
   Selecting previously unselected package librados-dev.
   (Reading database ... 40080 files and directories currently installed.)
   Preparing to unpack .../librados-dev_10.2.5-1xenial_amd64.deb ...
   Unpacking librados-dev (10.2.5-1xenial) ...
   Processing triggers for man-db (2.7.5-1) ...
   Setting up librados-dev (10.2.5-1xenial) ...
   ```

3. Now that your environment is complete, let's create a quick application written in C to establish a connection to the test Ceph cluster:

```
$ mkdir test_app
$ cd test_app
```

4. Create a file called `test_app.c` with your favorite text editor and place the following in it:

```c
#include <rados/librados.h>
#include <stdio.h>
#include <stdlib.h>

rados_t rados = NULL;

int exit_func();


int main(int argc, const char **argv)
{
  int ret = 0;
  ret = rados_create(&rados, "admin"); // Use the
  client.admin keyring
  if (ret < 0) { // Check that the rados object was created
    printf("couldn't initialize rados! error %d\n", ret);
    ret = EXIT_FAILURE;
    exit_func;
  }
  else
    printf("RADOS initialized\n");

  ret = rados_conf_read_file(rados, "/etc/ceph/ceph.conf");
  if (ret < 0) { //Parse the ceph.conf to obtain cluster details
    printf("failed to parse config options! error %d\n", ret);
    ret = EXIT_FAILURE;
    exit_func();
  }
  else
    printf("Ceph config parsed\n");

  ret = rados_connect(rados); //Initiate connection to the
  Ceph cluster
  if (ret < 0) {
    printf("couldn't connect to cluster! error %d\n", ret);
    ret = EXIT_FAILURE;
    exit_func;
  } else {
    printf("Connected to the rados cluster\n");
```

```
    }

    exit_func(); //End of example, call exit_func to clean
    up and finish

}


int exit_func ()
{
    rados_shutdown(rados); //Destroy connection to the
    Ceph cluster
    printf("RADOS connection destroyed\n");
    printf("The END\n");
    exit(0);
}
```

5. Compile the test application, by running the following command:

   $ gcc test_app.c -o test_app -lrados

   It's important to note that you need to tell gcc to link to the librados
   library to make use of its functions.

6. Then, test that the app works by running it. Don't forget to run it as root or use
   sudo, otherwise you won't have access to the Ceph keyring:

   sudo ./test_app

   The preceding command gives the following output:

```
vagrant@mon1:~/test_app$ sudo ./test_app
RADOS initialised
Ceph config parsed
Connected to the rados cluster
RADOS connection destroyed
The END
```

The test application simply reads your `ceph.conf` configuration, uses it to establish a connection to your Ceph cluster, and then disconnects. It's hardly the most exciting of applications but it tests that the basic infrastructure is in place and is working and establishes a foundation for the rest of the examples in this chapter.

Example librados application

We will now go through some example librados applications which use librados to get a better understanding of what you can accomplish with the library.

The following example will take you through the steps to create an application which, when given an image file as a parameter, will store the image as an object in a Ceph cluster and store various attributes about the image file as object attributes. The application will also allow you to retrieve the object and export it as an image file. This example will be written in Python, which is also supported by librados. The following example also uses the **Python Imaging Library** (**PIL**) to read an image's size and the **Argument Parser library** to read command-line parameters:

1. We first need to install the librados Python bindings and image manipulation libraries:

   ```
   $ sudo apt-get install python-rados python-imaging
   ```

   The preceding command gives the following output:

   ```
   Reading package lists... Done
   Building dependency tree
   Reading state information... Done
   python-rados is already the newest version (10.2.5-1xenial).
   python-rados set to manually installed.
   The following additional packages will be installed:
     libjbig0 libjpeg-turbo8 libjpeg8 liblcms2-2 libtiff5 libwebp5 libwebpmux1 python-pil
   Suggested packages:
     liblcms2-utils python-pil-doc python-pil-dbg
   The following NEW packages will be installed:
     libjbig0 libjpeg-turbo8 libjpeg8 liblcms2-2 libtiff5 libwebp5 libwebpmux1 python-imaging python-pil
   0 upgraded, 9 newly installed, 0 to remove and 93 not upgraded.
   Need to get 916 kB of archives.
   After this operation, 3,303 kB of additional disk space will be used.
   Do you want to continue? [Y/n] y
   ```

2. Create a new file for your Python application ending with the extension `.py` and enter the following into it:

   ```
   import rados, sys, argparse
   from PIL import Image
   ```

```
#Argument Parser used to read parameters and generate --help
parser = argparse.ArgumentParser(description='Image to RADOS
Object Utility')
parser.add_argument('--action', dest='action', action='store',
required=True, help='Either upload or download image to/from
Ceph')
parser.add_argument('--image-file', dest='imagefile',
action='store', required=True, help='The image file to
upload to RADOS')
parser.add_argument('--object-name', dest='objectname',
action='store', required=True, help='The name of the
RADOS object')
parser.add_argument('--pool', dest='pool', action='store',
required=True, help='The name of the RADOS pool to store
the object')
parser.add_argument('--comment', dest='comment', action=
'store', help='A comment to store with the object')


args = parser.parse_args()

try: #Read ceph.conf config file to obtain monitors
  cluster = rados.Rados(conffile='/etc/ceph/ceph.conf')
except:
  print "Error reading Ceph configuration"
  sys.exit(1)

try: #Connect to the Ceph cluster
  cluster.connect()
except:
  print "Error connecting to Ceph Cluster"
  sys.exit(1)

try: #Open specified RADOS pool
  ioctx = cluster.open_ioctx(args.pool)
except:
  print "Error opening pool: " + args.pool
  cluster.shutdown()
  sys.exit(1)

if args.action == 'upload': #If action is to upload
  try: #Open image file in read binary mode
    image=open(args.imagefile,'rb')
    im=Image.open(args.imagefile)
  except:
    print "Error opening image file"
    ioctx.close()
    cluster.shutdown()
```

```
      sys.exit(1)
    print "Image size is x=" + str(im.size[0]) + " y=" +
    str(im.size[1])
    try: #Write the contents of image file to object and add
    attributes
      ioctx.write_full(args.objectname,image.read())
      ioctx.set_xattr(args.objectname,'xres',str(im.size[0])
      +"\n")
      ioctx.set_xattr(args.objectname,'yres',str(im.size[1])
      +"\n")
      im.close()
      if args.comment:
        ioctx.set_xattr(args.objectname,'comment',args.comment
        +"\n")
    except:
      print "Error writing object or attributes"
      ioctx.close()
      cluster.shutdown()
      sys.exit(1)
    image.close()
  elif args.action == 'download':
    try: #Open image file in write binary mode
      image=open(args.imagefile,'wb')
    except:
      print "Error opening image file"
      ioctx.close()
      cluster.shutdown()
      sys.exit(1)
    try: #Write object to image file
      image.write(ioctx.read(args.objectname))
    except:
      print "Error writing object to image file"
      ioctx.close()
      cluster.shutdown()
      sys.exit(1)
    image.close()
  else:
    print "Please specify --action as either upload or download"
  ioctx.close() #Close connection to pool
  cluster.shutdown() #Close connection to Ceph
  #The End
```

3. Test the `help` functionality generated by the Argument Parser library:

```
$ sudo python app1.py --help
```

The preceding command gives the following output:

```
vagrant@mon1:~$ sudo python app1.py --help
usage: app1.py [-h] --action ACTION --image-file IMAGEFILE --object-name
               OBJECTNAME --pool POOL [--comment COMMENT]

Image to RADOS Object Utility

optional arguments:
  -h, --help            show this help message and exit
  --action ACTION       Either upload or download image to/from Ceph
  --image-file IMAGEFILE
                        The image file to upload to RADOS
  --object-name OBJECTNAME
                        The name of the RADOS object
  --pool POOL           The name of the RADOS pool to store the object
  --comment COMMENT     A comment to store with the object
```

4. Download the Ceph logo to use as a test image:

```
wget http://docs.ceph.com/docs/master/_static/logo.png
```

The preceding command gives the following output:

```
vagrant@mon1:~$ wget http://docs.ceph.com/docs/master/_static/logo.png
--2017-02-08 20:37:01--  http://docs.ceph.com/docs/master/_static/logo.png
Resolving docs.ceph.com (docs.ceph.com)... 158.69.67.53
Connecting to docs.ceph.com (docs.ceph.com)|158.69.67.53|:80... connected.
HTTP request sent, awaiting response... 200 OK
Length: 3898 (3.8K) [image/png]
Saving to: 'logo.png'

logo.png            100%[===================================>]   3.81K  --.-KB/s    in 0s

2017-02-08 20:37:01 (106 MB/s) - 'logo.png' saved [3898/3898]
```

5. Run our Python application to read an image file and upload it to Ceph as an object:

```
$ sudo python app1.py --action=upload --image-file=test1.png
--object-name=image_test --pool=rbd --comment="Ceph Logo"
```

The preceding command gives the following output:

```
vagrant@mon1:~$ sudo python appl.py --action=upload --image-file=logo.png --object-name=image_test --pool=rbd --comment="Ceph Logo"
Image size is x=140 y=38
```

6. Verify that the object has been created:

```
$ sudo rados -p rbd ls
```

The preceding command gives the following output:

```
vagrant@mon1:~$ sudo rados -p rbd ls
image_test
```

7. Use `rados` to verify that the attributes have been added to the object:

```
$ sudo rados -p rbd listxattr image_test
```

The preceding command gives the following output:

```
vagrant@mon1:~$ sudo rados -p rbd ls
image_test
vagrant@mon1:~$ sudo rados -p rbd listxattr image_test
comment
xres
yres
```

8. Use `rados` to verify the attributes' contents, as shown in the following screenshot:

```
vagrant@mon1:~$ sudo rados -p rbd getxattr image_test comment
Ceph Logo
vagrant@mon1:~$ sudo rados -p rbd getxattr image_test xres
140
vagrant@mon1:~$ sudo rados -p rbd getxattr image_test yres
38
```

Example of the librados application with atomic operations

In the previous librados application example, an object was created on the Ceph cluster and then the object's attributes were added. In most cases, this two-stage operation may be fine, however, some applications might require that the creation of the object and its attributes are atomic. That is to say, that if there was an interruption of service, the object should only exist if it has all its attributes set, otherwise the Ceph cluster should roll back the transaction. The following example, written in C++, shows how to use librados atomic operations to ensure transaction consistency across multiple operations. The example will write an object and then prompt the user if they wish to abort the transaction. If they choose to abort then the object writes operation will be rolled back. If they choose to continue then the attributes will be written and the whole transaction will be committed. Perform the following steps:

1. Create a new file with a `.cc` extension and place the following into it:

```
#include <cctype>
#include <rados/librados.hpp>
#include <iostream>
#include <string>

void exit_func(int ret);

librados::Rados rados;

int main(int argc, const char **argv)
{
  int ret = 0;

  // Define variables
  const char *pool_name = "rbd";
  std::string object_string("I am an atomic object\n");
  std::string attribute_string("I am an atomic attribute\n");
  std::string object_name("atomic_object");
  librados::IoCtx io_ctx;

  // Create the Rados object and initialize it
  {
    ret = rados.init("admin"); // Use the default client.admin
    keyring
    if (ret < 0) {
      std::cerr << "Failed to initialize rados! error " << ret
      << std::endl;
      ret = EXIT_FAILURE;
```

```
  }
}

// Read the ceph config file in its default location
ret = rados.conf_read_file("/etc/ceph/ceph.conf");
if (ret < 0) {
  std::cerr << "Failed to parse config file "
            << "! Error" << ret << std::endl;
  ret = EXIT_FAILURE;
}

// Connect to the Ceph cluster
ret = rados.connect();
if (ret < 0) {
  std::cerr << "Failed to connect to cluster! Error " << ret
  << std::endl;
  ret = EXIT_FAILURE;
} else {
  std::cout << "Connected to the Ceph cluster" << std::endl;
}

// Create connection to the Rados pool
ret = rados.ioctx_create(pool_name, io_ctx);
if (ret < 0) {
  std::cerr << "Failed to connect to pool! Error: " << ret <<
  std::endl;
  ret = EXIT_FAILURE;
} else {
  std::cout << "Connected to pool: " << pool_name <<
  std::endl;
}

librados::bufferlist object_bl; // Initialize a bufferlist
object_bl.append(object_string); // Add our object text
string to the bufferlist
librados::ObjectWriteOperation write_op; // Create a write
transaction
write_op.write_full(object_bl); // Write our bufferlist to the
transaction
std::cout << "Object: " << object_name << " has been written
to transaction" << std::endl;
char c;
std::cout << "Would you like to abort transaction? (Y/N)? ";
std::cin >> c;
if (toupper( c ) == 'Y') {
  std::cout << "Transaction has been aborted, so object will
  not actually be written" << std::endl;
  exit_func(99);
```

```
  }
  librados::bufferlist attr_bl; // Initialize another bufferlist
  attr_bl.append(attribute_string); // Add our attribute to the
  bufferlist
  write_op.setxattr("atomic_attribute", attr_bl); // Write our
  attribute to our transaction
  std::cout << "Attribute has been written to transaction" <<
  std::endl;
  ret = io_ctx.operate(object_name, &write_op); // Commit the
  transaction
  if (ret < 0) {
    std::cerr << "failed to do compound write! error " << ret <<
    std::endl;
    ret = EXIT_FAILURE;
  } else {
    std::cout << "We wrote the transaction containing our object
    and attribute" << object_name << std::endl;
  }

}

void exit_func(int ret)
{
  // Clean up and exit
  rados.shutdown();
  exit(ret);
}
```

2. Compile the source using g++:

   ```
   g++ atomic.cc -o atomic -lrados -std=c++11
   ```

3. We can now run the application. First, let's run through it and abort the transaction:

```
vagrant@mon1:~$ sudo ./atomic
Connected to the rados cluster
Connected to pool: rbd
Object: atomic_object has been written to transaction
Would you like to abort transaction? (Y/N)? y
Transaction has been aborted, so object will not actually be written
vagrant@mon1:~$ sudo rados -p rbd ls
```

The preceding screenshot shows that, even though we sent a write object command, as the transaction was not committed, the object was never actually written to the Ceph cluster.

4. Now let's run the application again and, this time, let it continue the transaction:

```
vagrant@mon1:~$ sudo ./atomic
Connected to the rados cluster
Connected to pool: rbd
Object: atomic_object has been written to transaction
Would you like to abort transaction? (Y/N)? n
Attribute has been written to transaction
We wrote the transaction containing our object and attributeatomic_object
vagrant@mon1:~$ sudo rados -p rbd ls
atomic_object
vagrant@mon1:~$ sudo rados -p rbd getxattr atomic_object atomic_attribute
I am an atomic attribute
```

As you can see, this time the object was written along with its attribute.

Example of the librados application that uses watchers and notifiers

The following librados application is written in C and shows how to use the `watch` or `notify` functionality in RADOS. Ceph enables a client to create a watcher on an object and receive notifications from a completely separate client connected to the same cluster.

The watcher functionality is implemented via callback functions. When you call the librados function to create the watcher, two of the arguments are for callback functions, one is for what to do when a notification is received and another is for what to do if the watcher loses contact or encounters an error with the object. These callback functions then contain the code you want to run when a notification or error occurs.

This simple form of messaging is commonly used to instruct a client that has an RBD in use that a snapshot is wished to be taken. The client who wishes to take a snapshot sends a notification to all clients that may be watching the RBD object so that it can flush its cache and possibly make sure the filesystem is in a consistent state.

The following example creates a watcher on an object named `my_object` and then waits. When it receives a notification, it will display the payload and then send a received message back to the notifier.

1. Create a new file with a `.c` extension and place the following into it:

```c
#include <stdio.h>
#include <stdlib.h>
#include <string.h>
#include <syslog.h>

#include <rados/librados.h>
#include <rados/rados_types.h>

uint64_t cookie;
rados_ioctx_t io;
rados_t cluster;
char cluster_name[] = "ceph";
char user_name[] = "client.admin";
char object[] = "my_object";
char pool[] = "rbd";

/* Watcher callback function - called when watcher receives a
notification */
void watch_notify2_cb(void *arg, uint64_t notify_id, uint64_t
cookie, uint64_t notifier_gid, void *data, size_t data_len)
{
  const char *notify_oid = 0;
  char *temp = (char*)data+4;
  int ret;
  printf("Message from Notifier: %s\n",temp);
  rados_notify_ack(io, object, notify_id, cookie, "Received", 8);
}

/* Watcher error callback function - called if watcher encounters
an error */
void watch_notify2_errcb(void *arg, uint64_t cookie, int err)
{
  printf("Removing Watcher on object %s\n",object);
  err = rados_unwatch2(io,cookie);
  printf("Creating Watcher on object %s\n",object);
  err = rados_watch2(io,object,&cookie,watch_notify2_cb,
  watch_notify2_errcb,NULL);
  if (err < 0) {
    fprintf(stderr, "Cannot create watcher on %s/%s: %s\n", object,
    pool, strerror(-err));
    rados_ioctx_destroy(io);
    rados_shutdown(cluster);
```

```
      exit(1);
   }
}

int main (int argc, char **argv)
{
   int err;
   uint64_t flags;

   /* Create Rados object */
   err = rados_create2(&cluster, cluster_name, user_name, flags);
   if (err < 0) {
     fprintf(stderr, "Couldn't create the cluster object!: %s\n",
     strerror(-err));
     exit(EXIT_FAILURE);
   } else {
     printf("Created the rados object.\n");
   }


   /* Read a Ceph configuration file to configure the cluster
   handle. */
   err = rados_conf_read_file(cluster, "/etc/ceph/ceph.conf");
   if (err < 0) {
     fprintf(stderr, "Cannot read config file: %s\n",
     strerror(-err));
     exit(EXIT_FAILURE);
   } else {
     printf("Read the config file.\n");
   }
   /* Connect to the cluster */
   err = rados_connect(cluster);
   if (err < 0) {
     fprintf(stderr, "Cannot connect to cluster: %s\n",
     strerror(-err));
     exit(EXIT_FAILURE);
   } else {
     printf("\n Connected to the cluster.\n");
   }

   /* Create connection to the Rados pool */
   err = rados_ioctx_create(cluster, pool, &io);
   if (err < 0) {
     fprintf(stderr, "Cannot open rados pool %s: %s\n", pool,
     strerror(-err));
     rados_shutdown(cluster);
     exit(1);
   }
```

```
/* Create the Rados Watcher */
printf("Creating Watcher on object %s/%s\n",pool,object);
err = rados_watch2(io,object,&cookie,watch_notify2_cb,
watch_notify2_errcb,NULL);
if (err < 0) {
  fprintf(stderr, "Cannot create watcher on object %s/%s: %s\n",
  pool, object, strerror(-err));
  rados_ioctx_destroy(io);
  rados_shutdown(cluster);
  exit(1);
}

/* Loop whilst waiting for notifier */
while(1){
  sleep(1);
}
/* Clean up */
rados_ioctx_destroy(io);
rados_shutdown(cluster);
}
```

2. Compile the watcher example code:

   $ gcc watcher.c -o watcher -lrados

3. Run the watcher example application:

```
vagrant@mon1:~$ sudo ./watcher
Created the rados object.
Read the config file.

Connected to the cluster.
Creating Watcher on object rbd/my_object
```

4. The watcher is now waiting for a notification. In another Terminal window, using rados, send a notification to the my_object object which is being watched:

```
vagrant@mon1:~$ sudo rados -p rbd notify my_object "Hello There!"
reply client.24135 cookie 29079312 : 8 bytes
00000000  52 65 63 69 65 76 65 64                           |Recieved|
00000008
```

5. You can see that the notification was sent and an acknowledgment notification has been received back. If we look at the first Terminal window again, we can see the message from the notifier:

```
vagrant@mon1:~$ sudo ./watcher
Created the rados object.
Read the config file.

Connected to the cluster.
Creating Watcher on object rbd/my_object
Message from Notifier: Hello There!
```

Summary

This concludes the chapter on developing applications with librados. You should now feel comfortable with the basic concepts of how to include librados functionality in your application and how to read and write objects to your Ceph cluster. It would be recommended to read the official librados documentation in more detail if you intend to develop an application with librados, so that you can gain a better understanding of the full range of functions that are available.

Distributed Computation with Ceph RADOS Classes

15

An often overlooked feature of Ceph is the ability to load custom code directly into OSD, which can then be executed from within a librados application. This allows you to take advantage of the large distributed scale of Ceph to not only provide high-performance scale-out storage but also distribute computational tasks over OSDs to achieve mass parallel computing. This ability is realized by dynamically loading in RADOS classes to each OSD.

In this chapter you will learn the following topics:

- Example applications and benefits of using RADOS classes
- Writing a simple RADOS class in Lua
- Writing a RADOS class that simulates distributed computing

Example applications and the benefits of using RADOS classes

As mentioned earlier, with RADOS classes, code is executed directly inside the OSD code base and so can harness the combined power of all of the OSD nodes. With a typical client application approach, where the client would have to read the object from the Ceph cluster, run computations on it, and then write it back, there is a large amount of round trip overheads. Using RADOS classes dramatically reduces the amount of round trips to and from OSDs, and also the available compute power is much higher than that single client could provide. Offloading operations directly to the OSDs therefore enables a single client to dramatically increase its processing rate.

A simple example of where RADOS classes could be used is where you need to calculate a hash of every object in a RADOS pool and store each objects hash as an attribute. Having a client perform this would highlight the bottlenecks and extra latency introduced by having the client perform these operations remotely from the cluster. With a RADOS class that contains the required code to read the object calculate the hash and store it as an attribute, all that the client would need to do is send the command to OSD to execute the RADOS class.

Writing a simple RADOS class in Lua

One of the default RADOS classes in Ceph from the Kraken release onward is one that can run Lua scripts. The Lua script is dynamically passed to the Lua RADOS object class, which then executes the contents of the script. The scripts are typically passed in a JSON-formatted string to the object class. Although this brings advantages over the traditional RADOS object classes, which need to be compiled before they can be used, it also limits the complexity of what the Lua scripts can accomplish and as such thought should be given as to what method is appropriate for the task you wish to accomplish.

The following Python code example demonstrates how to create and pass a Lua script to be executed on an OSD. The Lua scripts reads the contents of the specified object and returns the string of text back in upper case, all processing is done on the remote OSD, which holds the object; the original object contents are never sent to the client.

Place the following into a file named `rados_lua.py`:

```python
import rados, json, sys

try: #Read ceph.conf config file to obtain monitors
  cluster = rados.Rados(conffile='/etc/ceph/ceph.conf')
except:
  print "Error reading Ceph configuration"
  exit(1)

try: #Connect to the Ceph cluster
  cluster.connect()
except:
  print "Error connecting to Ceph Cluster"
  exit(1)

try: #Open specified RADOS pool
  ioctx = cluster.open_ioctx("rbd")
except:
  print "Error opening pool"
```

```
    cluster.shutdown()
    exit(1)

cmd = {
  "script": """
      function upper(input, output)
        size = objclass.stat()
        data = objclass.read(0, size)
        upper_str = string.upper(data:str())
        output:append(upper_str)
      end
      objclass.register(upper)
  """,
  "handler": "upper",
}

ret, data = ioctx.execute(str(sys.argv[1]), 'lua', 'eval_json',
json.dumps(cmd))
print data[:ret]

ioctx.close() #Close connection to pool
cluster.shutdown() #Close connection to Ceph
```

Let's now create a test object with all lowercase characters:

echo this string was in lowercase | sudo rados -p rbd put LowerObject -

The Lua object class by default is not allowed to be called by OSDs; we need to add the following to all the OSDs in their ceph.conf:

```
[osd]
osd class load list = *
osd class default list = *
```

And now run our Python librados application:

sudo python rados_lua.py LowerObject

The preceding command gives the following output:

```
vagrant@mon1:~$ sudo python rados_lua.py LowerObject
THIS STRING WAS IN LOWERCASE
```

You should see that the text from our object has been converted all into uppercase. You can see from the Python code earlier that we are not doing any of the conversion in the local Python code and it's all being done remotely on OSD.

Writing a RADOS class that simulates distributed computing

As mentioned in the example given earlier, although using the Lua object class reduces the complexity to use RADOS object classes, there is a limit to what you can currently achieve. In order to write a class that is capable of performing more advanced processing, we need to fall back to writing the class in C. We will then need to compile the new class into the Ceph source.

To demonstrate this, we will write a new RADOS object class that will calculate the MD5 hash of the specified object and then store it as an attribute of the object. This process will be repeated 1000 times to simulate a busy environment and also to make the runtime easier to measure. We will then compare the operating speed of doing this via the object class versus calculating the MD5 hash on the client. Although this is still a fairly basic task, it will allow us to produce a controlled repeatable scenario and will allow us to compare the speed of completing a task client side versus doing it directly on the OSD via a RADOS class. It will also serve as a good foundation to enable understanding on how to build more advanced applications.

Preparing the build environment

Use the following command to clone the Ceph git repository:

```
git clone https://github.com/ceph/ceph.git
```

The preceding command will give the following output:

```
vagrant@ansible:~$ git clone https://github.com/ceph/ceph.git
Cloning into 'ceph'...
remote: Counting objects: 500133, done.
remote: Compressing objects: 100% (21/21), done.
remote: Total 500133 (delta 12), reused 2 (delta 2), pack-reused 500110
Receiving objects: 100% (500133/500133), 203.37 MiB | 2.38 MiB/s, done.
Resolving deltas: 100% (394234/394234), done.
Checking connectivity... done.
```

Once we have cloned the Ceph git repository, we need to edit the CMakeLists.txt file and add in a section for our new class that we are going to write.

Edit the following file in the source tree:

~/ceph/src/cls/CMakeLists.txt

Also, place the following in the file:

```
# cls_md5
set(cls_md5_srcs md5/cls_md5.cc)
add_library(cls_md5 SHARED ${cls_md5_srcs})
set_target_properties(cls_md5 PROPERTIES
  VERSION "1.0.0"
  SOVERSION "1"
  INSTALL_RPATH "")
install(TARGETS cls_md5 DESTINATION ${cls_dir})
target_link_libraries(cls_md5 crypto)
list(APPEND cls_embedded_srcs ${cls_md5_srcs})
```

Once the `cmakelist.txt` file is updated, we can get `cmake` to make the build environment by running the following command:

do_cmake.sh

The preceding command will give the following output:

```
-- Configuring done
-- Generating done
-- Build files have been written to: /home/vagrant/ceph/build
+ cat
+ echo 40000
+ echo done.
done.
```

This will create a `build` directory in the source tree.

In order for us to build the RADOS class, we need to install the required packages that contains the `make` command:

sudo apt-get install build-essentials

There is also a `install-deps.sh` file in the Ceph source tree, which will install the remaining required packages when run.

RADOS class

The following code sample is a RADOS class which when executed reads the object, calculates the MD5 hash, and then writes it as an attribute to the object without any client involvement. Each time this class is called, it repeats this operation a 1000 times locally to OSD and only notifies the client at the end of this processing. We have the following steps to perform:

1. Create the directory for our new RADOS class:

   mkdir ~/ceph/src/cls/md5

2. Now create the C++ source file:

   ~/ceph/src/cls/md5/cls_md5.cc

3. Place the following code into it:

```
#include "objclass/objclass.h"
#include <openssl/md5.h>

CLS_VER(1,0)
CLS_NAME(md5)

cls_handle_t h_class;
cls_method_handle_t h_calc_md5;

static int calc_md5(cls_method_context_t hctx, bufferlist *in,
bufferlist *out)
{
  char md5string[33];

  for(int i = 0; i < 1000; ++i)
  {
    size_t size;
    int ret = cls_cxx_stat(hctx, &size, NULL);
    if (ret < 0)
      return ret;

    bufferlist data;
    ret = cls_cxx_read(hctx, 0, size, &data);
    if (ret < 0)
      return ret;
    unsigned char md5out[16];
    MD5((unsigned char*)data.c_str(), data.length(), md5out);
    for(int i = 0; i < 16; ++i)
      sprintf(&md5string[i*2], "%02x", (unsigned int)md5out[i]);
```

```
CLS_LOG(0,"Loop:%d - %s",i,md5string);
bufferlist attrbl;
attrbl.append(md5string);
ret = cls_cxx_setxattr(hctx, "MD5", &attrbl);
if (ret < 0)
{
  CLS_LOG(0, "Error setting attribute");
  return ret;
}
}
out->append((const char*)md5string, sizeof(md5string));
return 0;
}

void __cls_init()
{
  CLS_LOG(0, "loading cls_md5");
  cls_register("md5", &h_class);
  cls_register_cxx_method(h_class, "calc_md5", CLS_METHOD_RD |
  CLS_METHOD_WR, calc_md5, &h_calc_md5)
}
```

4. Change into the `build` directory created previously and create our new RADOS class using `make`:

   cd ~/ceph/build
   make cls_md5

   The preceding commands will give the following output:

```
vagrant@ansible:~/ceph/build$ make cls_md5
Scanning dependencies of target cls_md5
[  0%] Building CXX object src/cls/CMakeFiles/cls_md5.dir/md5/cls_md5.cc.o
[100%] Linking CXX shared library ../../lib/libcls_md5.so
[100%] Built target cls_md5
```

5. We now need to copy our new class to OSDs in our cluster:

   sudo scp vagrant@ansible:/home/vagrant/ceph/build/lib/libcls_md5.so*
   /usr/lib/rados-classes/

   The preceding command will give the following output:

```
vagrant@osd2:~$ sudo scp vagrant@ansible:/home/vagrant/ceph/build/lib/libcls_md5.so* /usr/lib/rados-classes/
vagrant@ansible's password:
libcls_md5.so                                               100%  155KB 155.0KB/s   00:00
libcls_md5.so.1                                             100%  155KB 155.0KB/s   00:00
libcls_md5.so.1.0.0                                         100%  155KB 155.0KB/s   00:00
```

Also, restart the OSD for it to load the class.

You will now see in the Ceph OSD log that it is loading our new class:

```
2017-05-10 19:47:57.251739 7fdb99ca2700  1 leveldb: Compacting 400 + 401 files
2017-05-10 19:47:57.260570 7fdba409fa40  1 journal _open /var/lib/ceph/osd/ceph-1/journal fd 28: 1073741824 bytes, bl
ock size 4096 bytes, directio = 1, aio = 1
2017-05-10 19:47:57.280605 7fdba409fa40  1 journal _open /var/lib/ceph/osd/ceph-1/journal fd 28: 1073741824 bytes, bl
ock size 4096 bytes, directio = 1, aio = 1
2017-05-10 19:47:57.283291 7fdba409fa40  1 filestore(/var/lib/ceph/osd/ceph-1) upgrade
2017-05-10 19:47:57.300701 7fdba409fa40  0 <cls> /home/vagrant/ceph/src/cls/md5/cls_md5.cc:46: loading cls_md5
2017-05-10 19:47:57.301246 7fdba409fa40  0 <cls> /tmp/buildd/ceph-11.2.0/src/cls/cephfs/cls_cephfs.cc:198: loading ce
phfs
2017-05-10 19:47:57.308766 7fdba409fa40  0 <cls> /tmp/buildd/ceph-11.2.0/src/cls/hello/cls_hello.cc:296: loading cls_
hello
2017-05-10 19:47:57.318132 7fdba409fa40  0 osd.1 279 crush map has features 2200130813952, adjusting msgr requires fo
r clients
2017-05-10 19:47:57.318940 7fdba409fa40  0 osd.1 279 crush map has features 2200130813952 was 8705, adjusting msgr re
quires for mons
2017-05-10 19:47:57.318966 7fdba409fa40  0 osd.1 279 crush map has features 2200130813952, adjusting msgr requires fo
r osds
```

This needs to be repeated for all OSD nodes in the cluster.

Client librados applications

As mentioned earlier, we will use two librados applications, one to calculate the MD5 hash directly on the client and another to call our RADOS class and have it calculate the MD5 hash. The two applications both need to be run from the monitor nodes in the test cluster, but can be compiled on any node and copied across if desired. For the purpose of this example, we will compile the applications directly on the monitor nodes.

Before we start, let's make sure that the build environment is present on the monitor node:

```
apt-get install build-essential librados-dev
```

Calculating MD5 on the client

The following code sample is the librados client-side application, which will read the object from the OSD, calculate the MD5 hash of the object on the client, and write it back as an attribute to the object. This is doing the calculation and storage in the same way as the RADOS class, with the only difference being the location of the processing.

Create a new file named `rados_md5.cc` and place the following into it:

```
#include <cctype>
#include <rados/librados.hpp>
#include <iostream>
#include <string>
#include <openssl/md5.h>
```

```
void exit_func(int ret);

librados::Rados rados;

int main(int argc, const char **argv)
{
  int ret = 0;

  // Define variables
  const char *pool_name = "rbd";
  std::string object_name("LowerObject");
  librados::IoCtx io_ctx;

  // Create the Rados object and initialize it
  {
    ret = rados.init("admin"); // Use the default client.admin keyring
    if (ret < 0) {
      std::cerr << "Failed to initialize rados! error " << ret <<
      std::endl;
      ret = EXIT_FAILURE;
    }
  }

  // Read the ceph config file in its default location
  ret = rados.conf_read_file("/etc/ceph/ceph.conf");
  if (ret < 0) {
    std::cerr << "Failed to parse config file "
              << "! Error" << ret << std::endl;
    ret = EXIT_FAILURE;
  }

  // Connect to the Ceph cluster
  ret = rados.connect();
  if (ret < 0) {
    std::cerr << "Failed to connect to cluster! Error " << ret <<
    std::endl;
    ret = EXIT_FAILURE;
  } else {
    std::cout << "Connected to the Ceph cluster" << std::endl;
  }

  // Create connection to the Rados pool
  ret = rados.ioctx_create(pool_name, io_ctx);
  if (ret < 0) {
    std::cerr << "Failed to connect to pool! Error: " << ret <<
    std::endl;
    ret = EXIT_FAILURE;
  } else {
```

```
      std::cout << "Connected to pool: " << pool_name << std::endl;
    }
    for(int i = 0; i < 1000; ++i)
    {
      size_t size;
      int ret = io_ctx.stat(object_name, &size, NULL);
      if (ret < 0)
        return ret;

      librados::bufferlist data;
      ret = io_ctx.read(object_name, data, size, 0);
      if (ret < 0)
        return ret;
      unsigned char md5out[16];
      MD5((unsigned char*)data.c_str(), data.length(), md5out);
      char md5string[33];
      for(int i = 0; i < 16; ++i)
        sprintf(&md5string[i*2], "%02x", (unsigned int)md5out[i]);
      librados::bufferlist attrbl;
      attrbl.append(md5string);
      ret = io_ctx.setxattr(object_name, "MD5", attrbl);
      if (ret < 0)
      {
        exit_func(1);
      }
    }
    exit_func(0);
}

void exit_func(int ret)
{
  // Clean up and exit
  rados.shutdown();
  exit(ret);
}
```

Calculating MD5 on the OSD via RADOS class

Finally, the last code sample is the librados application, which instructs OSD to calculate the MD5 hash locally without transferring any data to or from the client. You will note that the code given later has no librados read or write statements and relies purely on the `exec` function to trigger the MD5 hash creation.

Create a new file named `rados_class_md5.cc` and place the following into it:

```
#include <cctype>
#include <rados/librados.hpp>
#include <iostream>
#include <string>

void exit_func(int ret);

librados::Rados rados;

int main(int argc, const char **argv)
{
  int ret = 0;

  // Define variables
  const char *pool_name = "rbd";
  std::string object_name("LowerObject");
  librados::IoCtx io_ctx;
  // Create the Rados object and initialize it
  {
    ret = rados.init("admin"); // Use the default client.admin keyring
    if (ret < 0) {
      std::cerr << "Failed to initialize rados! error " << ret <<
      std::endl;
      ret = EXIT_FAILURE;
    }
  }

  // Read the ceph config file in its default location
  ret = rados.conf_read_file("/etc/ceph/ceph.conf");
  if (ret < 0) {
    std::cerr << "Failed to parse config file "
              << "! Error" << ret << std::endl;
    ret = EXIT_FAILURE;
  }

  // Connect to the Ceph cluster
  ret = rados.connect();
  if (ret < 0) {
    std::cerr << "Failed to connect to cluster! Error " << ret <<
    std::endl;
    ret = EXIT_FAILURE;
  } else {
    std::cout << "Connected to the Ceph cluster" << std::endl;
  }

  // Create connection to the Rados pool
```

```
    ret = rados.ioctx_create(pool_name, io_ctx);
    if (ret < 0) {
      std::cerr << "Failed to connect to pool! Error: " << ret <<
      std::endl;
      ret = EXIT_FAILURE;
    } else {
      std::cout << "Connected to pool: " << pool_name <<
      std::endl;
    }
    librados::bufferlist in, out;
    io_ctx.exec(object_name, "md5", "calc_md5", in, out);
    exit_func(0);

}
void exit_func(int ret)
{
  // Clean up and exit
  rados.shutdown();
  exit(ret);
}
```

We can now compile both applications:

```
vagrant@mon1:~$ g++ rados_class_md5.cc -o rados_class_md5 -lrados -std=c++11
vagrant@mon1:~$ g++ rados_md5.cc -o rados_md5 -lrados -lcrypto -std=c++11
```

If the applications compile successfully, there will be no output.

Testing

We will run the two librados applications using the standard Linux `time` utility to measure how long each run takes:

```
time sudo ./rados_md5
```

The preceding command will give the following output:

```
vagrant@mon1:~$ time sudo ./rados_md5
Connected to the Ceph cluster
Connected to pool: rbd

real    0m4.708s
user    0m0.084s
sys     0m1.008s
```

Let's make sure that the attribute was actually created:

```
sudo rados -p rbd getxattr LowerObject MD5
```

The preceding command will give the following output:

```
vagrant@mon1:~$ sudo rados -p rbd getxattr LowerObject MD5
9d40bae4ff2032c9eff59806298a95bdvagrant@mon1:~$
```

Let's delete the object attribute, so we can be certain that the RADOS class correctly creates it when it runs:

```
sudo rados -p rbd rmxattr LowerObject MD5
```

And now run the application that performs the MD5 calculation via the RADOS class:

```
time sudo ./rados_class_md5
```

The preceding command will give the following output:

```
vagrant@mon1:~$ time sudo ./rados_class_md5
Connected to the Ceph cluster
Connected to pool: rbd

real    0m0.038s
user    0m0.004s
sys     0m0.012s
```

As you can see, using the RADOS class method is a lot faster, in fact almost two orders of magnitude faster.

However, let's also confirm that the attribute was created and that the code ran a thousand times:

```
sudo rados -p rbd getxattr LowerObject MD5
```

The preceding command will give the following output:

```
vagrant@mon1:~$ sudo rados -p rbd getxattr LowerObject MD5
9d40bae4ff2032c9eff59806298a95bdvagrant@mon1:~$
```

Due to the logging we inserted in the RADOS class, we can also check OSD logs to confirm that the RADOS class did run a thousand times:

```
0 <cls> /home/vagrant/ceph/src/cls/md5/cls_md5.cc:30: Loop:984 - 9d40bae4ff2032c9eff59806298a95bd
0 <cls> /home/vagrant/ceph/src/cls/md5/cls_md5.cc:30: Loop:985 - 9d40bae4ff2032c9eff59806298a95bd
0 <cls> /home/vagrant/ceph/src/cls/md5/cls_md5.cc:30: Loop:986 - 9d40bae4ff2032c9eff59806298a95bd
0 <cls> /home/vagrant/ceph/src/cls/md5/cls_md5.cc:30: Loop:987 - 9d40bae4ff2032c9eff59806298a95bd
0 <cls> /home/vagrant/ceph/src/cls/md5/cls_md5.cc:30: Loop:988 - 9d40bae4ff2032c9eff59806298a95bd
0 <cls> /home/vagrant/ceph/src/cls/md5/cls_md5.cc:30: Loop:989 - 9d40bae4ff2032c9eff59806298a95bd
0 <cls> /home/vagrant/ceph/src/cls/md5/cls_md5.cc:30: Loop:990 - 9d40bae4ff2032c9eff59806298a95bd
0 <cls> /home/vagrant/ceph/src/cls/md5/cls_md5.cc:30: Loop:991 - 9d40bae4ff2032c9eff59806298a95bd
0 <cls> /home/vagrant/ceph/src/cls/md5/cls_md5.cc:30: Loop:992 - 9d40bae4ff2032c9eff59806298a95bd
0 <cls> /home/vagrant/ceph/src/cls/md5/cls_md5.cc:30: Loop:993 - 9d40bae4ff2032c9eff59806298a95bd
0 <cls> /home/vagrant/ceph/src/cls/md5/cls_md5.cc:30: Loop:994 - 9d40bae4ff2032c9eff59806298a95bd
0 <cls> /home/vagrant/ceph/src/cls/md5/cls_md5.cc:30: Loop:995 - 9d40bae4ff2032c9eff59806298a95bd
0 <cls> /home/vagrant/ceph/src/cls/md5/cls_md5.cc:30: Loop:996 - 9d40bae4ff2032c9eff59806298a95bd
0 <cls> /home/vagrant/ceph/src/cls/md5/cls_md5.cc:30: Loop:997 - 9d40bae4ff2032c9eff59806298a95bd
0 <cls> /home/vagrant/ceph/src/cls/md5/cls_md5.cc:30: Loop:998 - 9d40bae4ff2032c9eff59806298a95bd
0 <cls> /home/vagrant/ceph/src/cls/md5/cls_md5.cc:30: Loop:999 - 9d40bae4ff2032c9eff59806298a95bd
```

When repeating small tasks, the overhead of communication between the client and OSDs really adds up. By moving processing directly to OSD, we can eliminate this.

RADOS class caveats

Although we have seen the power that can be harnessed using Ceph's RADOS classes, it's important to note that this is achieved by calling your own customized code from deep inside OSDs. As a consequence, great care needs to be taken that your RADOS class is bug free. A RADOS class has the ability to modify any data on your Ceph cluster, and so accidental data corruption is easily possible. It is also possible for the RADOS class to crash the OSD process. If the class is used in large-scale cluster operations, this has the ability to affect all OSDs in the cluster and so great care should be taken to ensure that error handling is properly done to avoid errors.

Summary

You should now have an understanding on what RADOS classes are and how they can be used to speed up processing by moving tasks directly to OSD. From building simple classes via Lua to developing classes in the Ceph source tree via C++, you should now have the knowledge to build a RADOS class for whatever problem you are trying to solve. By building on this concept, there is nothing stopping you from building a larger application that can take advantage of the scale-out nature of a Ceph cluster to provide large amounts of storage and compute resource.

For more examples of how to use RADOS object classes, please consult the hello object class in the Ceph source tree found at `https://github.com/ceph/ceph/blob/master/src/cls/hello/cls_hello.cc`.

16
Tiering with Ceph

The tiering functionality in Ceph allows you to overlay one RADOS pool over another and let Ceph intelligently promote and evict objects between them. In most configurations, the top-level pool will be comprised of fast storage devices like **Solid State Drives (SSDs)** and the base pool will be comprised of the slower storage devices like **Serial ATA (SATA)** or **Serial Attached SCSI (SAS)** disks. If the working set of your data is of a comparatively small percentage, then this allows you to use Ceph to provide high capacity storage but yet still maintain a good level of performance of frequently accessed data.

In this chapter, we will cover the following topics:

- How Cephs tiering functionality works
- What are good use cases for tiering
- How to configure two pools into a tier
- Cover various tuning options available for tiering

 It's recommended that you should be running at least the Jewel release of Ceph if you wish to use the tiering functionality. Previous releases were lacking a lot of required features that made tiering usable.

Tiering versus caching

Although often described as **cache tiering**, it's better to think of the functionality in Ceph as a tiering technology rather than a cache. It's important that you take this into consideration before reading any further as it's vital to understand the difference between the two.

A cache is typically designed to accelerate access to a set of data unless it's a writeback cache; it will not hold the only copy of the data, and normally there is little overhead to promoting data to cache. Cache tends to operate over a shorter timeframe, quite often everything that is accessed is promoted into cache.

A tiering solution is also designed to accelerate access to a set of data; however, it's promotion strategy normally works over a longer period of time and is more selective about what data is promoted, mainly due to the promotion action having a small impact on overall storage performance. Also, it is quite common with tiering technologies that only a single tier may hold the valid state of the data, and so all tiers in the system need equal protection against data loss.

How Cephs tiering functionality works

Once you have configured a RADOS pool to be an overlay of another RADOS pool, Cephs tiering functionality works on the basic principal that if an object does not exist in the top-level tier, then it must exist in the base tier. All object requests from clients are sent to the top tier; if the OSD does not have the requested object, then depending on the tiering mode, it may either proxy the read or write request down to the base tier or force a promotion. The base tier then proxies the request back through the top tier to the client. It's important to note that the tiering functionality is transparent to clients, and there is no specific client configuration needed.

There are three main actions in tiering that move objects between tiers. **Promotions** copy objects from the base tier up to the top tier. If tiering is configured in writeback mode, the **flushing** action is used to update the contents of the base tier object from the top tier. Finally, when the top tier pool reaches capacity, objects are evicted by the **eviction** action.

In order to be able to make decisions on what objects to move between the two tiers, Ceph uses HitSets to track accesses to objects. A **HitSet** is a collection of all object access requests and is consulted to determine if an object has had either a read or write request since that HitSet was created. The HitSets use a **bloom filter** to statistically track object accesses rather than storing every access to every object, which would generate large overheads. The bloom filter only stores binary states; an object can only be marked as accessed or not; and there is no concept of storing the number of accesses to an object in a single HitSet. If an object appears in a number of the most recent HitSets and is in the base pool, then it will be promoted.

Likewise, objects that no longer appear in recent HitSets will become candidates for flushing or eviction if the top tier comes under pressure. The number of HitSets and how often a new one gets created can be configured, along with the required number of recent HitSets a write or read I/O must appear in, in order for a promotion to take place. The size of the top-level tier can also be configured and is disconnected from the available capacity of the RADOSpool it sits on.

There are a number of configuration and tuning options that define how Ceph reacts to the generated HitSets and the thresholds at which promotions, flushes, and evictions occur. These will be covered in more detail later in the chapter.

What is a bloom filter

A bloom filter is used in Ceph to provide an efficient way of tracking whether an object is a member of a HitSet without having to individually store the access status of each object. It is probabilistic in nature, and although it can return **false positives**, it will never return as **false negative**. This means that when querying a bloom filter, it may report that an item is present when it is not, but it will never report that an item is not present when it is.

Ceph's use of bloom filters allows it to efficiently track the accesses of millions of objects without the overhead of storing every single access. In the event of a false positive, it could mean that an object is incorrectly promoted; however, the probability of this happening combined with the minimal impact is of little concern.

Tiering modes

There are a number of tiering modes that determine the precise actions of how Ceph reacts to the contents of the HitSets. However, in most cases, the writeback mode will be used. The available modes for use in tiering are **writeback**, **forward**, **read-forward**, **proxy**, and **read-proxy**. There are brief descriptions of the available modes and how they act.

Writeback

In writeback mode, data is promoted to the top-level tier by both reads and writes depending on how frequently accessed the object are. Objects in the top-level tier can be modified, and dirty objects will be flushed to the pool at a later date. If an object needs to be read or written to in the bottom tier and the bottom pool supports it, then Ceph will try and directly proxy the operation that has a minimal impact on latency.

Forward

The forward mode simply forwards all requests from the top tier to the base tier without doing any promotions. It should be noted that a forward causes OSD to tell the client to resend the request to the correct OSD and so has a greater impact on latency than just simply proxying it.

Read-forward

Read-forward mode forces a promotion on every write and like the forward mode earlier, redirects the client for all reads to the base pool. This can be useful if you wish to only use the top-tier pool for write acceleration. Using write intensive SSDs overlayed over read intensive SSDs is one such example.

Proxy

Similar to forward mode, except proxy all reads and writes without promoting anything. By proxying the request, OSD itself retrieves data from the base tier OSD and then passes it back to the client. This reduces the overhead compared with using forwarding.

Read-proxy

Similar to read-forward mode, except that it proxies reads and always promote on writes requests. It should be noted that the writeback and read-proxy modes are the only modes that receive rigorous testing, and so care should be taken when using the other modes. Also, there is probably little gain from using the other modes, and they will likely be phased out in future releases.

Uses cases

As mentioned at the start of the chapter, the tiering functionality should be thought of as tiering and not a cache. The reason behind this statement is that the act of promotions has a detrimental effect to cluster performance when compared with most caching solutions, which do normally not degrade performance if enabled on noncacheable workloads. The performance impact of promotions are caused by two main reasons. First, the promotion happens in the I/O path, the entire object to be promoted needs to be read from the base tier and then written into the top tier before the I/O is returned to the client.

Second, this promotion action will likely also cause a flush and an eviction, which cause even more reads and writes to both tiers. If both tiers are using 3x replication, this starts to cause a large amount of write amplification for even just a single promotion. In the worse case scenario, a single 4 KB access that causes a promotion could cause 8 MB of read I/O and 24 MB of write I/O across the two tiers. This increased I/O will cause an increase in latency; for this reason, promotions should be considered expensive, and tuning should be done to minimize them.

With that in mind, Ceph tiering should only be used where the hot or active part of the data will fit into the top tier. Workloads that are uniformly random will likely see no benefit and in many cases may actually cause performance degradation, either due to no suitable objects being available to promote, or too many promotions occurring.

Most workloads that involve providing storage for generic virtual machines tend to be good candidates as normally only a small percentage of VM tends to be accessed.

Online transaction processing (OLTP) databases, will normally show improvements when used with either caching or tiering as their hot set of data is relatively small and data patterns are reasonably consistent. However, reporting or batch processing database are generally not a good fit as they can quite often require a large range of the data to be accessed without any prior warm-up period.

RADOS Block Devices (RBD) workloads that involve random access with no specific pattern or workloads that involve large read or write streaming should be avoided and will likely suffer from the addition of a cache tier.

Creating tiers in Ceph

To test Ceph tiering functionality, two RADOS pools are required. If you are running these examples on a laptop or desktop hardware, although spinning disk-based OSDs can be used to create the pools; SSDs are highly recommended if there is any intention to read and write data. If you have multiple disk types available in your testing hardware, then the base tier can exist on spinning disks and the top tier can be placed on SSDs.

Let's create tiers using the following commands, all of which make use of the Ceph `tier` command:

1. Create two RADOS pools:

   ceph osd pool create base 64 64 replicated

   ceph osd pool create top 64 64 replicated

   The preceding commands give the following output:

   ```
   root@mon1:/home/vagrant# ceph osd pool create base 64 64 replicated
   pool 'base' created
   root@mon1:/home/vagrant# ceph osd pool create top 64 64 replicated
   pool 'top' created
   ```

2. Create a tier consisting of the two pools:

   ceph osd tier add base top

   The preceding command gives the following output:

   ```
   root@mon1:/home/vagrant# ceph osd tier add base top
   pool 'top' is now (or already was) a tier of 'base'
   ```

3. Configure the cache mode:

   ceph osd tier cache-mode top writeback

   The preceding command gives the following output:

   ```
   root@mon1:/home/vagrant# ceph osd tier cache-mode top writeback
   set cache-mode for pool 'top' to writeback
   ```

4. Make the top tier and overlay of the base tier:

   ceph osd tier set-overlay base top

   The preceding command gives the following output:

   ```
   root@mon1:/home/vagrant# ceph osd tier set-overlay base top
   overlay for 'base' is now (or already was) 'top'
   ```

5. Now that the tiering is configured, we need to set some simple values to make sure that the tiering agent can function. Without these, the tiering mechanism will not work properly. Note that these commands are just setting variables on the pool:

```
ceph osd pool set top hit_set_type bloom

ceph osd pool set top hit_set_count 10

ceph osd pool set top hit_set_period 60

ceph osd pool set top target_max_bytes 100000000
```

The preceding commands give the following output:

```
root@mon1:/home/vagrant# ceph osd pool set top hit_set_type bloom
set pool 5 hit_set_type to bloom
root@mon1:/home/vagrant# ceph osd pool set top hit_set_count 10
set pool 5 hit_set_count to 10
root@mon1:/home/vagrant# ceph osd pool set top hit_set_period 60
set pool 5 hit_set_period to 60
root@mon1:/home/vagrant# ceph osd pool set top target_max_bytes 100000000
set pool 5 target_max_bytes to 100000000
```

The earlier-mentioned commands are simply telling Ceph that the HitSets should be created using the bloom filter. It should create a new HitSet every 60 seconds and that it should keep 10 of them before discarding the oldest one. Finally, the top tier pool should hold no more than 100 MB; if it reaches this limit, I/O operations will block. More detailed explanations of these settings will follow in the next section.

6. Next, we need to configure the various options that control how Ceph flushes and evicts objects from the top to the base tier:

```
ceph osd pool set top cache_target_dirty_ratio 0.4

ceph osd pool set top cache_target_full_ratio 0.8
```

The preceding commands give the following output:

```
root@mon1:/home/vagrant# ceph osd pool set top cache_target_dirty_ratio 0.4
set pool 5 cache_target_dirty_ratio to 0.4
root@mon1:/home/vagrant# ceph osd pool set top cache_target_full_ratio 0.8
set pool 5 cache_target_full_ratio to 0.8
```

The earlier example tells Ceph that it should start flushing dirty objects in the top tier down to the base tier when the top tier is 40% full. And that objects should be evicted from the top tier when the top tier is 80% full.

7. And finally, the last two commands instruct Ceph that any object should have been in the top tier for at least 60 seconds before it can be considered for flushing or eviction:

```
ceph osd pool set top cache_min_flush_age 60

ceph osd pool set top cache_min_evict_age 60
```

The preceding commands give the following output:

```
root@mon1:/home/vagrant# ceph osd pool set top cache_min_flush_age 60
set pool 5 cache_min_flush_age to 60
root@mon1:/home/vagrant# ceph osd pool set top cache_min_evict_age 60
set pool 5 cache_min_evict_age to 60
```

Tuning tiering

Unlike the majority of Cephs features, which by default perform well for a large number of workloads, Cephs tiering functionality requires careful configuration of its various parameters to ensure good performance. You should also have a basic understanding of your workloads I/O profile; tiering will only work well if your data has a small percentage of hot data. Workloads that are uniformly random or involve lots of sequential access patterns will either show no improvement or in some cases may actually be slower.

Flushing and eviction

The main tuning options should be looked at first are the ones that define the size limit to the top tier, when it should flush and when it should evict.

The following two configuration options configure the maximum size of the data to be stored in the top tier pool:

```
target_max_bytes

target_max_objects
```

The size is either specified in bytes or number objects and does not have to be the same size as the actual pool, but it cannot be larger. The size is also based on the available capacity after replication of the RADOS pool, so for a 3x replica pool, this will be a one-third of your raw capacity. If the number of bytes or objects in this pool goes above this limit, I/O will block; therefore, it's important that thought is given to the other config options later so that this limit is not reached. It's also important that this value is set, as without it, no flushing or evictions will occur and the pool will simply fill up OSDs to their full limit and then block I/O.

The reason that this setting exists instead of Ceph just using the size of the underlying capacity of the disks in the RADOS pool is that by specifying the size, you could if you desire, have multiple top-level tier pools on the same set of disks.

As you have learned earlier, `target_max_bytes` sets the maximum size of the tiered data on the pool and if this limit is reached, I/O will block. In order to make sure that the RADOS pool does not reach this limit, `cache_target_full_ratio` instructs Ceph to try and keep the pool at a percentage of `target_max_bytes` by evicting objects when this target is breached. Unlike promotions and flushes, evictions are fairly low-cost operations:

cache_target_full_ratio

The value is specified as a value between 0 and 1 and works like a percentage. It should be noted that although `target_max_bytes` and `cache_target_full_ratio` are set against the pool, internally Ceph uses these values to calculate per PG limits instead. This can mean that in certain circumstances, some PGs may reach the calculated maximum limit before others and can sometimes lead to unexpected results. For this reason, it is recommended not to set `cache_target_full_ratio` to high and leave some headroom; a value of 0.8 normally works well. We have the following code:

cache_target_dirty_ratio

cache_target_dirty_high_ratio

These two configuration options control when Ceph flushes dirty objects from the top tier to the base tier if the tiering has been configured in writeback mode. An object is considered dirty if it has been modified while being in the top tier, objects modified in the base tier do not get marked as dirty. Flushing involves copying the object out of the top tier and into the base tier, as this is a full object write, the base tier can be an erasure-coded pool. The behavior is asynchronous and aside from increasing I/O on the RADOS pools, is not directly linked to any impact on the client I/O. Objects are typically flushed at a lower speed than what they can be evicted at. As flushing is an expensive operation compared with eviction, this means that if required, large amounts of objects can be evicted quickly if needed.

The two ratios control what speed of flushing OSD allows, by restricting the number of parallel flushing threads that are allowed to run at once. These can be controlled by the OSD configuration options `osd_agent_max_ops` and `osd_agent_max_high_ops`, respectively. By default, these are set to 2 and 4 parallel threads.

In theory, the percentage of dirty objects should hover around the low dirty ratio during normal cluster usage. This will mean that objects are flushed with low parallelism of flushing to minimize the impact on cluster latency. As normal bursts of writes hit the cluster, the number of dirty objects may rise, but over time, these writes are flushed down to the base tier.

However, if there are periods of sustained writes that outstrip the low-speed flushing's capability, then the number of dirty objects will start to rise. Hopefully, this period of high write I/O will not go on for long enough to fill the tier with dirty objects and thus will gradually reduce back down to the low threshold. However, if the number of dirty objects continues to increase and reaches the high ratio, then the flushing parallelism gets increased and will hopefully be able to stop the number of dirty objects from increasing any further. Once the write traffic reduces, the number of dirty objects will be brought back down the low ratio again. These sequence of events are illustrated in the following graph:

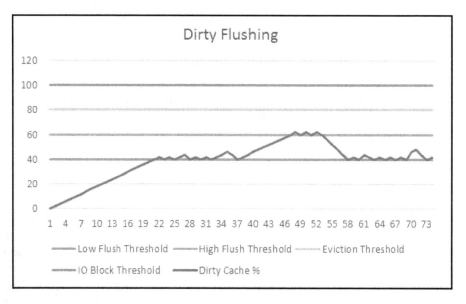

The two dirty ratios should have sufficient difference between them that normal bursts of writes can be absorbed, without the high ratio kicking in. The high ratio should be thought of as an emergency limit. A good value to start with is 0.4 for the low ratio and 0.6 for the high ratio.

The `osd_agent_max_ops` configuration settings should be adjusted so that in normal operating conditions, the number of dirty objects is hovering around or just over the low dirty ratio. It's not easy to recommend a value for these settings as they will largely depend on the ratio of the size and performance of the top tier to the base tier. However, start with setting `osd_agent_max_ops` to 1 and increase as necessary and set `osd_agent_max_high_ops` to at least double.

If you see status messages in the Ceph status screen indicating that high-speed flushing is occurring, then you will want to increase `osd_agent_max_ops`. If you ever see the top tier getting full and blocking I/O, then you either need to consider lowering the `cache_target_dirty_high_ratio` variable or increase the `osd_agent_max_high_ops` setting to stop the tier filling up with dirty objects.

Promotions

The next tuning options that should be looked at are the ones that define the HitSets and the required recency to trigger a promotion:

hitset_count

hitset_period

The `hitset_count` setting controls how many HitSets can exist before the oldest one starts getting trimmed. The `hitset_period` setting controls how often a HitSet should be created. If you are testing tiering in a laboratory environment, it should be noted that I/O to the PG needs to be occurring in order for a HitSet to be created; on an idle cluster, no HitSets will be created or trimmed.

Having the correct number and controlling how often HitSets are created is a key to being able to reliably control when objects get promoted. Remember that HitSets only contain data about whether an object has been accessed or not; they don't contain a count of the number of times an object was accessed. If `hitset_period` is too large, then even relatively low-accessed objects will appear in the majority of the HitSets. For example, with a `hitset_period` of 2 minutes, an RBD object containing the disk block where a log file is updated once a minute would be in all the same HitSets as an object getting access 100 times a second.

Conversely, if the period is too low, then even hot objects may fail to appear in enough HitSets to make them candidates for promotion and your top tier will likely not be fully used. By finding the correct HitSet period, you should be able to capture the right view of your I/O that a suitable sized proportion of hot objects are candidates for promotion:

```
min_read_recency_for_promote
```

```
min_write_recency_for_promote
```

These two settings define how many of the last recent HitSets an object must appear in to be promoted. Due to the effect of probability, the relationship between semi-hot objects and recency setting is not linear. Once the recency settings are set past about 3 or 4, the number of eligible objects for promotion drops off in a logarithmic fashion. It should be noted that while promotion decisions can be made on reads or writes separately, they both reference the same HitSet data, which has no way of determining access from being either a read or a write. As a handy feature, if you set the recency higher than the `hitset_count` setting, then it will never promote. This can be used for example to make sure that a write I/O will never cause an object to be promoted, by setting the write recency higher than the `hitset_count` setting.

Promotion throttling

As has been covered earlier, promotions are very expensive operations in tiering and care should be taken to make sure that they only happen when necessary. A large part of this is done by carefully tuning the HitSet and recency settings. However, in order to limit the impact of promotions, there is an additional throttle that restricts the number of promotions to a certain speed. This limit can either be specified as number of bytes or objects per second via two OSD configuration options:

```
osd_tier_promote_max_bytes_sec
```

```
osd_tier_promote_max_objects_sec
```

The default limits are 4 MBps or five objects a second. While these figures may sound low, especially when compared with the performance of the latest SSDs, their primary goal is to minimize the impact of promotions on latency. Careful tuning should be done to find a good balance on your cluster. It should be noted that this value is configured per OSD, and so the total promotion speed will be a sum across all OSDs.

Finally, the following configuration options allow tuning of the selection process for flushing objects:

`hit_set_grade_search_last_n`

This controls how may HitSets are queried in order to determine object temperature, with the the temperature of an object reflects how often it is accessed. A cold object is rarely accessed, with a hot object being accessed far more frequently being candidates for eviction. Setting this to a similar figure as the recency settings is recommended. We have the following code:

`hit_set_grade_decay_rate`

This works in combination with the `hit_set_grade_search_last_n` setting and decays the HitSet results the older they become. Objects that have been accessed more frequently than others have a hotter rating and will make sure that objects that are more frequently accessed are not incorrectly flushed. It should be noted that the `min_flush` and `evict_age` settings may override the temperature of an object when it comes to being flushed or evicted:

`cache_min_flush_age`

`cache_min_evict_age`

The `cache_min_evict_age` and `cache_min_flush_age` settings simply define how long an object must have not been modified for before it is allowed to be flushed or evicted. These can be used to stop objects that are only just not enough to be promoted, from continually being stuck in a cycle of moving between tiers. Setting them between 10 and 30 minutes is probably a good approach although care needs to be taken that the top tier does not fill up, in the case where there are no eligible objects to be flushed or evicted.

Monitoring parameters

In order to monitor the performance and characteristics of a cache tier in a Ceph cluster, there are a number of performance counters you can monitor. We will assume for the moment that you are already collecting the Ceph performance counters from the admin socket as discussed in the next chapter.

The most important thing to remember when looking at the performance counters is that once you configure a tier in Ceph all client requests, go through the top-level tier. Therefore, only read and write operation counters on OSDs that make up your top-level tier will show any requests, assuming that the base tier OSDs are not used for any other pools. To understand the number of requests handled by the base tier, there are proxy operation counters, which will show this number. These proxy operation counters are also calculated on the top-level OSDs, and so to monitor the throughput of a Ceph cluster with tiering, only the top-level OSDs need to be included in the calculations.

The following counters can be used to monitor tiering in Ceph, all are to be monitored on the top-level OSDs:

Counter	Description
op_r	Read operations handled by the OSD
op_w	Write operations handled by the OSD
tier_proxy_read	Read operations that were proxied to the base tier
tier_proxy_write	Write operations that were proxied to the base tier
tier_promote	The number of promotions from base to top-level tier
tier_try_flush	The number of flushes from the top-level to the base tier
tier_evict	The number of evictions from the top-level to the base tier

Tiering with erasure-coded pools

At the current time, Ceph doesn't support overwrite operations on erasure-coded pools and so cannot be directly used for storing RBD images. However, by the use of tiering, an erasure-coded pool can be used as the base pool and a 3x replica pool used as the top level. This allows the hot active dataset which will comprise of frequently accessed data, to sit in the top tier and any infrequently accessed cold data to reside in the base erasure-coded tier.

Care should be taken with this approach; although in theory, it sounds like a brilliant idea, it shouldn't be forgotten that in this configuration proxy writes are not supported to the base erasure-coded pool. All write operations to the base tier, therefore, have to be promoted up to the top tier first. If even a small percentage write operations start targeting your base tier, then performance will quickly fall off a cliff as the constant promotion and flushing operations overwhelm the disks in your cluster. This approach is only recommended for use cases where write operations are infrequent or are contained to a small number of objects.

Alternative caching mechanisms

While the native RADOS tiering functionality provides numerous benefits around flexibility and allows management by the same Ceph toolset. However, it cannot be denied that for pure performance RADOS tiering lags behind other caching technologies that typically function at the block device level.

 Bcache is a block device cache in the Linux kernel, which can use an SSD to cache a slower block device such as a spinning disk.

Bcache is one example of a popular way of increasing the performance of Ceph with SSDs. Unlike RADOS tiering, which you can choose which pool you wish to cache, with bcache the entire OSD is cached. This method of caching brings a number of advantages around performance. The first is that the OSD itself has a much more consistent latency response due to the SSD caching. Filestore adds an increased amount of random I/O to every Ceph request regardless of whether the Ceph request is random of sequential in nature. Bcache can absorb these random I/Os and allow the spinning disk to perform a larger amount of sequential I/O. This can be very helpful during high periods of utilization where normal spinning disk OSDs would start to exhibit high latency. Second, where RADOS tiering operates at the size of the object stored in the pool, which is 4 MB by default for RBD workloads. Bcache caches data in much smaller blocks; this allows it to make better use of available SSD space and also suffer less from promotion overheads.

The SSD capacity assigned to bcache will also be used as a read cache for hot data; this will improve read performance as well as writes. Since bcache will only be using this capacity for read caching, it will only store one copy of the data and so will have 3x more read cache capacity than compared with using the same SSD in a RADOS-tiered pool.

However, there are a number of disadvantages to using bcache that make using RADOS cache pools still look attractive. As mentioned earlier, bcache will cache the entire OSD, in some cases where multiple pools may reside on the same OSDs, this behavior may be undesirable. Also, once bcache has been configured with SSD and HDD, it is harder to expand the amount of cache if needed in the future. This also applies if your cluster does not currently have any form of caching; in this scenario, introducing bcache would be very disruptive. With RADOS tiering, you can simply add additional SSDs or specifically designed SSD nodes to add or expand the top tier as and when needed.

Another approach is to place the spinning disk OSDs behind a RAID controller with battery backed write back cache. The RAID controller performs a similar role to bcache and absorbs a lot of the random write I/O relating to filestore's extra metadata. Both latency and sequential write performance will increase as a result, read performance will unlikely increase however due to the relatively small size of the RAID controllers cache. Using a RAID controller, the OSD's journal can also be placed directly on the disk instead of using a separate SSD. By doing this, journal writes are absorbed by the RAID controllers cache and will improve the random performance of the journal, as likely most of the time, the journals contents will just be sitting in the controllers cache. Care does need to be taken though as if the incoming write traffic exceeds the capacity of the controllers cache, journal contents will start being flushed to disk, and performance will degrade. For best performance, a separate SSD or NVMe should be used for the filestore journal although attention should be paid to the cost of using both a RAID controller with sufficient performance and cache, in addition to the cost of the SSDs.

Both methods have their merits and should be considered before implementing caching in your cluster.

Summary

In this chapter, we have covered the theory behind Cephs RADOS tiering functionality and looked at the configuration and tuning operations available to best make it work for your workload. It should not be forgotten that the most important aspect is to understand your workload and be confident that its I/O pattern and distribution is cache friendly. By following the examples in this chapter, you should also now understand the required steps to implement tiered pools and how to apply the configuration options.

17
Troubleshooting

Ceph is largely autonomous in taking care of itself and recovering from failure scenarios, but in some cases human intervention is required. This chapter will look at such common errors and failure scenarios and how to bring Ceph back to working by troubleshooting them. You will learn the following topics:

- How to correctly repair inconsistent objects
- How to solve problems with the help of peering
- How to deal with `near_full` and `too_full` OSDs
- How to investigate errors via Ceph logging
- How to investigate poor performance
- How to investigate PGs in a down state

Repairing inconsistent objects

We will now see how we can correctly repair inconsistent objects.

1. To be able to recreate an inconsistent scenario, create an RBD, and later we'll make a file system on it:

```
vagrant@mon1:~$ sudo rbd create test --size=1G
vagrant@mon1:~$ sudo rbd feature disable test exclusive-lock object-map fast-diff deep-flatten
vagrant@mon1:~$ sudo rbd map test
/dev/rbd0
vagrant@mon1:~$ sudo mkfs.ext4 /dev/rbd0
mke2fs 1.42.13 (17-May-2015)
Discarding device blocks: done
Creating filesystem with 262144 4k blocks and 65536 inodes
Filesystem UUID: a95d7f60-3be3-4c15-bafd-9d37559174db
Superblock backups stored on blocks:
        32768, 98304, 163840, 229376

Allocating group tables: done
Writing inode tables: done
Creating journal (8192 blocks): done
Writing superblocks and filesystem accounting information: done
```

2. Now, check to see which objects have been created by formatting the RBD with a file system:

```
root@mon1:/home/vagrant# rados -p rbd ls
rbd_data.1e502238e1f29.0000000000000086
rbd_data.1e502238e1f29.0000000000000000
rbd_data.1e502238e1f29.0000000000000083
rbd_data.1e502238e1f29.0000000000000060
rbd_data.1e502238e1f29.0000000000000004
```

3. Pick one object at random and use the `osd map` command to find out which PG the object is stored in:

```
root@mon1:/home/vagrant# ceph osd map rbd rbd_data.1e502238e1f29.0000000000000086
osdmap e234 pool 'rbd' (0) object 'rbd_data.1e502238e1f29.0000000000000086' -> pg 0.5ee4eb42 (0.2)
> up ([1,0,2], p1) acting ([1,0,2], p1)
```

4. Find this object on the disk on one of the OSD nodes; in this case, it is OSD.0 on OSD1:

```
vagrant@osd1:~$ sudo ls -l /var/lib/ceph/osd/ceph-0/current/0.5_head/
total 4096
-rw-r--r-- 1 ceph ceph       0 Feb  7 22:07 __head_00000005__0
-rw-r--r-- 1 ceph ceph 4194304 Mar 17 21:28 rbd\udata.1e502238e1f29.0000000000000083__head_327C8305__0
```

5. Corrupt it by echoing garbage over the top of it:

```
root@osd1:/home/vagrant# echo blah > /var/lib/ceph/osd/ceph-0/current/0.5_head/rbd\udata.1e502238e1f29.
0000000000000083__head_327C8305__0
```

6. Now, tell Ceph to do a scrub on the PG that contains the object that we corrupted:

```
root@mon1:/home/vagrant# ceph pg deep-scrub 0.5
instructing pg 0.5 on osd.2 to deep-scrub
```

7. If you check the Ceph status, you will see that Ceph has detected the corrupted object and marked the PG as inconsistent. From this point onward, forget that we corrupted the object manually and work through the process as if it were for real:

```
root@mon1:/home/vagrant# ceph -s
    cluster d9f58afd-3e62-4493-ba80-0356290b3d9f
     health HEALTH_ERR
            1 pgs inconsistent
            3 scrub errors
            too many PGs per OSD (320 > max 300)
            all OSDs are running kraken or later but the 'require_kraken_osds' osdmap flag is not set
     monmap e2: 3 mons at {mon1=192.168.0.41:6789/0,mon2=192.168.0.42:6789/0,mon3=192.168.0.43:6789/0}
            election epoch 158, quorum 0,1,2 mon1,mon2,mon3
        mgr active: mon2 standbys: mon3, mon1
     osdmap e234: 3 osds: 3 up, 3 in
            flags sortbitwise,require_jewel_osds
      pgmap v3879: 320 pgs, 4 pools, 37575 kB data, 23 objects
            229 MB used, 26665 MB / 26894 MB avail
                 319 active+clean
                   1 active+clean+inconsistent
```

By looking at the detailed health report, we can find the PG that contains the corrupted object. We could just tell Ceph to repair the PG now; however, if the primary OSD is the one that holds the corrupted object, it will overwrite the remaining good copies. This would be bad; thus in order to make sure this doesn't happen, before running the repair command we will confirm which OSD holds the corrupt object.

```
root@mon1:/home/vagrant# ceph health detail
HEALTH_ERR 1 pgs inconsistent; 3 scrub errors; too many PGs per OSD (320 > max 300); all OSDs are running kr
aken or later but the 'require_kraken_osds' osdmap flag is not set
pg 0.5 is active+clean+inconsistent, acting [2,0,1]
3 scrub errors
```

By looking at the health report we can see the three OSD's which hold a copy of the object; the first OSD is the primary.

8. Log onto the primary OSD node and open the log file for the primary OSD. You should be able to find the log entry where it indicates what object was flagged up by the PG scrub.

9. Now by logging on to each OSD and navigating through the PG structure, find the object mentioned in the log file and calculate a md5sum of each copy.

```
root@osd1:/var/lib/ceph/osd/ceph-0/current/0.5_head# md5sum rbd\\udata.1e502238e1f29.0000000000000083__head_327C8305__0
\0d599f0ec05c3bda8c3b8a68c32a1b47  rbd\\udata.1e502238e1f29.0000000000000083__head_327C8305__0
```

md5sum of object on osd node one

```
root@osd2:/home/vagrant# cd /var/lib/ceph/osd/ceph-2/current/0.5_head/
root@osd2:/var/lib/ceph/osd/ceph-2/current/0.5_head# md5sum rbd\\udata.1e502238e1f29.0000000000000083__
head_327C8305__0
\b5cfa9d6c8febd618f91ac2843d50a1c  rbd\\udata.1e502238e1f29.0000000000000083__head_327C8305__0
```

md5sum of object on osd node two

```
root@osd3:/home/vagrant# cd /var/lib/ceph/osd/ceph-1/current/0.5_head/
root@osd3:/var/lib/ceph/osd/ceph-1/current/0.5_head# md5sum rbd\\udata.1e502238e1f29.0000000000000083__
head_327C8305__0
\b5cfa9d6c8febd618f91ac2843d50a1c  rbd\\udata.1e502238e1f29.0000000000000083__head_327C8305__0
```

md5sum of object on osd node three.

We can see that the object on OSD.0 has a different md5sum, and so we know that it is the corrupt object.

```
OSD.0 = \0d599f0ec05c3bda8c3b8a68c32a1b47
OSD.2 = \b5cfa9d6c8febd618f91ac2843d50a1c
OSD.3 = \b5cfa9d6c8febd618f91ac2843d50a1c
```

Although we already know which copy of the object was corrupted as we manually corrupted the object on OSD.0, let's pretend we hadn't done it, and this corruption was caused by some random cosmic ray. We now have the md5sum of the three replica copies and can clearly see that the copy on OSD.0 is wrong. This is a big reason why a 2x replication scheme is bad; if a PG becomes inconsistent, you can't figure out which one is the bad one. As the primary OSD for this PG is 2, as can be seen in both the Ceph health details and the Ceph OSD map commands, we can safely run the ceph pg repair command without the fear of copying the bad object over the top of the remaining good copies.

```
root@mon1:/home/vagrant# ceph pg repair 0.5
instructing pg 0.5 on osd.2 to repair
```

We can see that the inconsistent PG has repaired itself:

```
root@mon1:/home/vagrant# ceph -s
    cluster d9f58afd-3e62-4493-ba80-0356290b3d9f
     health HEALTH_WARN
            too many PGs per OSD (320 > max 300)
            all OSDs are running kraken or later but the 'require_kraken_osds' osdmap flag is not
    monmap e2: 3 mons at {mon1=192.168.0.41:6789/0,mon2=192.168.0.42:6789/0,mon3=192.168.0.43:67
            election epoch 158, quorum 0,1,2 mon1,mon2,mon3
       mgr active: mon2 standbys: mon3, mon1
    osdmap e234: 3 osds: 3 up, 3 in
            flags sortbitwise,require_jewel_osds
     pgmap v3900: 320 pgs, 4 pools, 37575 kB data, 23 objects
            229 MB used, 26665 MB / 26894 MB avail
                 320 active+clean
```

In the event that the copy is corrupt on the primary OSD, then the following steps should be taken:

1. Stop the primary OSD.
2. Delete the object from the PG directory.
3. Restart the OSD.
4. Instruct Ceph to repair the PG.

Full OSDs

By default, Ceph will warn when OSD utilization approaches 85%, and it will stop write I/O to the OSD when it reaches 95%. If, for some reason, the OSD completely fills up to 100%, then the OSD is likely to crash and will refuse to come back online. An OSD that is above the 85% warning level will also refuse to participate in backfilling, so the recovery of the cluster may be impacted when OSDs are in a near full state.

Before covering the troubleshooting steps around full OSDs, it is highly recommended that you monitor the capacity utilization of your OSDs, as described in the monitoring chapter. This will give you advanced warning as OSDs approach the near_full warning threshold.

If you find yourself in a situation where your cluster is above the near full warning state, you have two main options:

1. Add some more OSDs.
2. Delete some data.

However, in the real world, both of these are either impossible or will take time, in which case the situation can deteriorate. If the OSD is only at the `near_full` threshold, then you can probably get things back on track by checking whether your OSD utilization is balanced, and then you can perform PG balancing if not. This was covered in more detail in the tuning chapter. The same applies to the `too_full` OSDs as well; although you are unlikely going to get them back below 85%, at least you can resume write operations.

If your OSDs have completely filled up, then they are in an offline state and will refuse to start. Now, you have an additional problem. If the OSDs will not start, then no matter what rebalancing or deletion of data you carry out, it will not be reflected on the full OSDs as they are offline. The only way to recover from this situation is to manually delete some PGs from the disk's file system to let the OSD start.

The following steps should be undertaken for this:

1. Make sure the OSD process is not running.
2. Set `nobackfill` on the cluster, to stop the recovery from happening when the OSD comes back online.
3. Find a PG that is in an active, clean, and remapped state and exists on the offline OSD.
4. Delete this PG from the offline OSD.
5. Hopefully you should now be able to restart the OSD.
6. Delete data from the Ceph cluster or rebalance PG's.
7. Remove nobackfill.
8. Run a scrub and repair the PG you just deleted.

Ceph logging

When investigating errors, it is very handy to be able to look through the Ceph log files to get a better idea of what is going on. By default, the logging levels are set so that only the important events are logged. During troubleshooting the logging levels may need to be increased in order to reveal the cause of the error. To increase the logging level, you can either edit `ceph.conf`, add the new logging level, and then restart the component, or, if you don't wish to restart the Ceph daemons, you can inject the new configuration parameter into the live running daemon. To inject parameters, use the ceph `tell` command:

```
ceph tell osd.0 injectargs --debug-osd 0/5
```

Then, set the logging level for the OSD log on `osd.0` to `0/5`. The number 0 is the disk logging level, and the number 5 is the in memory logging level.

 At a logging level of 20, the logs are extremely verbose and will grow quickly. Do not keep high verbosity logging enabled for too long. Higher logging levels will also have an impact on performance.

Slow performance

Slow performance is defined when the cluster is actively processing IO requests, but it appears to be operating at a lower performance level than what is expected. Generally, slow performance is caused by a component of your Ceph cluster reaching saturation and becoming a bottleneck. This maybe due to an increased number of client requests or a component failure that is causing Ceph to perform recovery.

Causes

Although there are many things which may cause Ceph to experience slow performance, here are some of the most likely causes.

Increased client workload

Sometimes, slow performance may not be due to an underlying fault; it may just be that the number and the type of client requests may have exceeded the capability of the hardware. Whether this is due to a number of separate workloads all running at the same time, or just a slow general increase over a period of time, if you are capturing the number of client requests across your cluster, this should be easy to trend. If the increased workload looks like it's permanent, then the only solution is to add some additional hardware.

Down OSDs

If a significant number of OSDs are marked down in a cluster, perhaps due to a whole OSD node going offline, although recovery will not start until the OSD's are marked out, the performance will be affected, as the number of IOPs available to service the client IO will now be lower. Your monitoring solution should alert you if this is happening and allow you to take action.

Recovery and backfilling

When an OSD is marked out, the affected PGs will re-peer with new OSDs and start the process of recovering and backfilling data across the cluster. This process can put strain on the disks in a Ceph cluster and lead to higher latencies for client requests. There are several tuning options that can reduce the impact of backfilling by reducing the rate and priority. These should be evaluated against the impact of slower recovery from failed disks, which may reduce the durability of the cluster.

Scrubbing

When Ceph performs deep scrubbing to check your data for any inconsistencies, it has to read all the objects from the OSD; this can be a very IO-intensive task, and on large drives, the process can take a long time. Scrubbing is vital to protect against data loss and therefore should not be disabled. By tweaking these settings, a lot of the performance impact on client workloads from scrubbing can be avoided.

Snaptrimming

When you remove a snapshot, Ceph has to delete all the objects which have been created due to the copy on write nature of the snapshot process. From Ceph 10.2.8 onward, there is an improved OSD setting called `osd_snap_trim_sleep`, which makes Ceph wait for the specified number of settings between the trimming of each snapshot object. This ensures that the backing object store does not become overloaded.

 Although this setting was available in previous jewel releases, its behavior was not the same and should not be used.

Hardware or driver issues

If you have recently introduced new hardware into your Ceph cluster and, after backfilling has rebalanced your data, you start experiencing slow performance, check for firmware or driver updates relating to your hardware, as newer drivers may require a newer kernel. If you have only introduced a small amount of hardware, then you can temporarily mark the OSDs out on it without going below your pool's `min_size`; this can be a good way to rule out hardware issues.

Monitoring

This is where the monitoring you configured in Chapter 16, *Tiering with Ceph* can really come in useful, as it will allow you to compare long-term trends with current metric readings and see if there are any clear anomalies.

It is recommended you first look at the disk performance as, in most cases of poor performance, the underlying disks are normally the components that become the bottleneck.

If you do not have monitoring configured or wish to manually drill deeper into the performance metrics, then there are a number of tools you can use to accomplish this.

iostat

iostat can be used to get a running overview of the performance and latency of all the disks running in your OSD nodes. Run `iostat` with the following command:

```
iostat -d 1 -x
```

You will get a display similar to this, which will refresh once a second:

Device:	rrqm/s	wrqm/s	r/s	w/s	rkB/s	wkB/s	avgrq-sz	avgqu-sz	await	r_await	w_await	svctm	%util
sda	0.00	4.00	2.00	24.00	68.00	9396.00	728.00	0.34	12.92	12.00	13.00	8.77	22.80
sdc	0.00	9.00	17.00	42.00	548.00	20468.00	712.41	1.11	18.71	27.76	15.05	10.17	60.00
sdd	0.00	8.00	9.00	51.00	36.00	20888.00	697.47	1.61	26.93	27.56	26.82	8.53	51.20
sdb	0.00	2.00	10.00	18.00	416.00	8108.00	608.86	0.43	15.29	16.00	14.89	5.57	15.60
nvme0n1	0.00	0.00	0.00	1254.00	0.00	126556.00	201.84	1.66	1.32	0.00	1.32	0.06	8.00
sde	0.00	2.00	10.00	9.00	416.00	3304.00	391.58	0.26	12.84	12.40	13.33	12.42	23.60
sdf	1.00	1.00	78.00	9.00	20492.00	3820.00	558.90	1.05	12.09	9.03	38.67	4.87	42.40
sdg	0.00	18.00	117.00	108.00	29600.00	47020.00	681.07	14.59	55.38	8.17	106.52	3.70	83.20
sdh	0.00	3.00	2.00	35.00	384.00	15816.00	875.68	0.38	10.38	10.00	10.40	5.41	20.00
sdi	0.00	1.00	83.00	15.00	20508.00	7024.00	561.88	1.56	15.96	7.57	62.40	3.59	35.20
sdj	0.00	5.00	87.00	52.00	14740.00	18760.00	482.01	2.78	25.84	11.77	49.38	7.19	100.00
sdk	0.00	0.00	3.00	160.00	12.00	5748.00	70.67	11.08	350.06	17.33	356.30	1.84	30.00
sdl	0.00	0.00	6.00	0.00	24.00	0.00	8.00	0.07	11.33	11.33	0.00	9.33	5.60

As a rule of thumb, if a large number of your disks are showing a high % util over a period of time, it is likely that your disks are being saturated. It may also be worth looking at the `r_await` time to see if read requests are taking longer than what should be expected for the type of disk in your OSD nodes. As mentioned earlier, if you find that high disk utilization is the cause of slow performance and the triggering factor is unlikely to dissipate soon, then extra disks are the only solution.

htop

Like the standard top utility, htop provides a live view of the CPU and the memory consumption of the host. However, it also produces a more intuitive display that may make judging overall system resource use easier, especially with the rapidly changing resource usage of Ceph.

```
 1  [||||||                          8.9%]    5  [|||||                          9.5%]
 2  [|||||||||||                    25.6%]    6  [||||                           8.0%]
 3  [|||||||||                      20.0%]    7  [|||||||||                     14.9%]
 4  [|||||||||                      16.7%]    8  [||                             4.4%]
Mem[||||||||||||||||||||||||||||||||||23.8G/62.7G]    Tasks: 49,  7845 thr;  1 running
Swp[|                          88.2M/9.31G]    Load average: 6.46 6.33 6.09
                                               Uptime: 7 days, 08:32:23

   PID USER      PRI  NI  VIRT   RES   SHR S CPU% MEM%   TIME+  Command
  7308 ceph       20   0 2662M 1045M  6788 S 11.9  1.6 13h51:18 /usr/bin/ceph-osd -f --cluster ceph
  3945 ceph       20   0 2778M 1059M  7996 S 11.9  1.7 14h12:58 /usr/bin/ceph-osd -f --cluster ceph
```

atop

atop is another useful tool; it captures performance metrics for CPU, RAM, disk, network, and can present this all in one view; this makes it very easy to get a complete overview of the system resource usage.

Diagnostics

There are a number of internal Ceph tools that can be used to help diagnose a slow performance. The most useful command for investigating slow performance is dumping current in-flight operations, which can be done with a command such as the following:

```
sudo ceph daemon osd.x dump_ops_in_flight
```

This will dump all current operations for the specified OSD and break down all the various timings for each step of the operation. Here is an example of an inflight IO:

```
            "description": "osd_op(client.29342781.1:262455793 17.768b3a6 rb.0.4d983.238e1
f29.000000001988 [set-alloc-hint object_size 4194304 write_size 4194304,write 1318912~1228
8] snapc 0=[] ondisk+write e98614)",
            "initiated_at": "2017-04-21 22:23:11.401997",
            "age": 0.000626,
            "duration": 0.000704,
            "type_data": [
                "waiting for sub ops",
                {
                    "client": "client.29342781",
                    "tid": 262455793
                },
                [
                    {
                        "time": "2017-04-21 22:23:11.401997",
                        "event": "initiated"
                    },
                    {
                        "time": "2017-04-21 22:23:11.402107",
                        "event": "queued_for_pg"
                    },
                    {
                        "time": "2017-04-21 22:23:11.402122",
                        "event": "reached_pg"
                    },
                    {
                        "time": "2017-04-21 22:23:11.402146",
                        "event": "started"
                    },
                    {
                        "time": "2017-04-21 22:23:11.402177",
                        "event": "waiting for subops from 14,37"
                    },
                    {
                        "time": "2017-04-21 22:23:11.402368",
                        "event": "commit_queued_for_journal_write"
                    },
                    {
                        "time": "2017-04-21 22:23:11.402379",
                        "event": "write_thread_in_journal_buffer"
                    },
                    {
                        "time": "2017-04-21 22:23:11.402585",
                        "event": "journaled_completion_queued"
                    },
                    {
                        "time": "2017-04-21 22:23:11.402598",
                        "event": "op_commit"
                    }
```

From the previous example IO, we can see all the stages that are logged for each operation; it is clear that this operation is running without any performance problems. However, in the event of slow performance, you may see a large delay between two steps, and directing your investigation into this area may lead you to the route cause.

Extremely slow performance or no IO

If your cluster is performing really slowly, to the point that it is barely servicing IO requests, then there is probably an underlying fault or configuration issue. These slow requests will likely be highlighted on the Ceph status display with a counter for how long the request has been blocked. There are a number of things to check in this case.

Flapping OSDs

Check `ceph.log` on the monitors, and see whether it looks like any OSDs are flapping up and down. When an OSD joins a cluster, its PGs begin peering. During this peering process, IO is temporarily halted, so in the event of a number of OSD's flapping, the client IO can be severely impacted. If there is evidence of flapping OSDs, the next step is to go through the logs for the OSDs that are flapping and see whether there are any clues as to what is causing them to flap. Flapping OSDs can be tough to track down as there can be several different causes, and the problem can be widespread.

Jumbo frames

Check that a network change hasn't caused problems with jumbo frames if in use. If jumbo frames are not working correctly, smaller packets will most likely be successfully getting through to other OSDs and MONs, but larger packets will be dropped. This will result in OSDs that appear to be half functioning, and it can be very difficult to find an obvious cause. If something odd seems to be happening, always check that jumbo frames are being allowed across your network using ping.

Failing disks

As Ceph stripes data across all disks in the cluster, a single disk, which is in the process of failing but has not yet completely failed, may start to cause slow or blocked IO across the cluster. Often, this will be caused by a disk that is suffering from a large number of read errors, but it is not severe enough for the disk to completely fail. Normally, a disk will only reallocate sectors when a bad sector is written to. Monitoring the SMART stats from the disks will normally pick up conditions such as these and allow you to take action.

Slow OSDs

Sometimes an OSD may start performing very poorly for no apparent reason. If there is nothing obvious being revealed by your monitoring tools, consult `ceph.log` and the Ceph health detail output. You can also run Ceph `osd perf`, which will list all the commit and apply latencies of all your OSDs and may also help you identify a problematic OSD.
If there is a common pattern of OSDs referenced in the slow requests, then there is a good chance that the mentioned OSD is the cause of the problems. It is probably worth restarting the OSD in case that resolves the issue; if the OSD is still problematic, it would be advisable to mark it out and then replace the OSD.

Investigating PGs in a down state

A PG in a down state will not service any client operations, and any object contained within the PG will be unavailable. This will cause slow requests to build up across the cluster as clients try to access these objects. The most common reason for a PG to be in a down state is when a number of OSDs are offline, which means that there are no valid copies of the PGs on any active OSDs. However, to find out why a PG is down, you can run the following command:

```
ceph pg x.y query
```

This will produce a large amount of output; the section we are interested in shows the peering status. The example here was taken from a PG whose pool was set to `min_size 1` and had data written to it when only OSD 0 was up and running. OSD 0 was then stopped and OSDs 1 and 2 were started.

```
    "probing_osds": [
        "1",
        "2"
    ],
    "blocked": "peering is blocked due to down osds",
    "down_osds_we_would_probe": [
        0
    ],
    "peering_blocked_by": [
        {
            "osd": 0,
            "current_lost_at": 0,
            "comment": "starting or marking this osd lost may let us proceed"
        }
    ]
},
```

We can see that the peering process is being blocked, as Ceph knows that the PG has newer data written to OSD 0. It has probed OSDs 1 and 2 for the data, which means that it didn't find anything it needed. It wants to try and pol OSD 0, but it can't because the OSD is down, hence the message **starting or marking this osd lost may let us proceed** appeared.

Large monitor databases

Ceph monitors use `leveldb` to store all of the required monitor data for your cluster. This includes things such as the monitor map, OSD map, and PG map, which OSDs and clients pull from the monitors to be able to locate objects in the RADOS cluster. One particular feature that one should be aware of is that during a period where the health of the cluster doesn't equal `HEALTH_OK`, the monitors do not discard any of the older cluster maps from its database. If the cluster is in a degraded state for an extended period of time and/or the cluster has a large number of OSDs, the monitor database can grow very large.

In normal operating conditions, the monitors are very lightweight on resource consumption; because of this, it's quite common for smaller disk sizes to be used for the monitors. In the scenario where a degraded condition continues for an extended period, it's possible for the disk holding the monitor database to fill up, which, if it occurs across all your monitor nodes, will take down the entire cluster.

To guard against this behavior, it may be worth deploying your monitor nodes using LVM so that, in the event, the disks need to be expanded, this can be done a lot more easily. When you get into this situation, adding disk space is the only solution, until you can get the rest of your cluster into a `HEALTH_OK` state.

If your cluster is in a `HEALTH_OK` state, but the monitor database is still large, you can compact it by running the following command:

```
sudo ceph tell mon.{id} compact
```

However, this will only work if your cluster is in a `HEALTH_OK` state; the cluster will not discard old cluster maps, which can be compacted until it's in a `HEALTH_OK` state.

Summary

In this chapter, you learned how to deal with problems that Ceph is not able to solve by itself. You now understand the necessary steps to troubleshoot a variety of issues that, if left unhandled, could escalate into bigger problems. Furthermore, you also have a good idea of the key areas to look at when your Ceph cluster is not performing as expected. You should feel confident that you are now in a much better place to handle Ceph-related issues whenever they appear.

18
Disaster Recovery

In the previous chapter, you learned how to troubleshoot common Ceph problems, which, although may be affecting the operation of the cluster, weren't likely to cause a total outage or data loss. This chapter will cover more serious scenarios where the Ceph cluster is down or unresponsive. It will also cover various techniques to recover from data loss. It is to be understood that these techniques are more than capable of causing severe data loss themselves and should only be attempted as a last resort. If you have a support contract with your Ceph vendor or have a relationship with Red Hat, it is highly advisable to consult them first before carrying out any of the recovery techniques listed in this chapter.

In this chapter, you will learn the following:

- How to avoid data loss
- How to use RBD mirroring to provide highly available block storage
- How to investigate asserts
- How to rebuild monitor dbs from OSDs
- How to extract PGs from a dead OSD
- How to recover from lost objects or inactive PGs
- How to rebuild a RBD from dead OSDs

What is a disaster?

To be able to recover from a disaster, you first have to understand and be able to recognize one. For the purpose of this chapter, we will work with the assumption that anything that leads to a sustained period of downtime is classed as a disaster. This will not cover scenarios where a failure happens that Ceph is actively working to recover from, or where it is believed that the cause is likely to be short lived. The other type of disaster is one that leads to a permanent loss of data unless recovery of the Ceph cluster is possible. Data loss is probably the most serious issue as the data may be irreplaceable or can cause serious harm to the future of the business.

Avoiding data loss

Firstly, make sure you have working and tested backups of your data; in the event of an outage you will feel a million times more relaxed if you know that in the worst cases, you can fall back to backups. While an outage may cause discomfort for your users or customers, informing them that their data, which they had entrusted you with, is now gone and is far worse. Also, just because you have a backup system in place, do not blindly put your trust in it. Regular test restores will mean that you will be able to rely on them when needed.

Don't use configuration options, such as `nobarrier`, and strongly consider the replication level you use with in Ceph to protect your data. The chances of data loss are strongly linked to the redundancy level configured in Ceph, so careful planning is advised here.

What can cause an outage or data loss?

The majority of outages and cases of data loss will be directly caused by the loss of a number of OSDs that exceed the replication level in a short period of time. If these OSDs do not come back online, be it due to a software or hardware failure and Ceph was not able to recover objects in-between OSD failures, then these objects are now lost.

If an OSD has failed due to a failed disk, then it is unlikely that recovery will be possible unless costly disk recovery services are utilized, and there is no guarantee that any recovered data will be in a consistent state. This chapter will not cover recovering from physical disk failures and will simply suggest that the default replication level of 3 should be used to protect you against multiple disk failures.

If an OSD has failed due to a software bug, the outcome is possibly a lot more positive, but the process is complex and time-consuming. Usually, an OSD, which, although the physical disk is in a good condition is unable to start, is normally linked to either a software bug or some form of corruption. A software bug may be triggered by an uncaught exception that leaves the OSD in a state that it cannot recover from. Corruption may occur after an unexpected loss of power where the hardware or software was not correctly configured to maintain data consistency. In both cases, the outlook for the OSD itself is probably terminal, and if the cluster has managed to recover from the lost OSDs, it's best just to erase and reintroduce the OSD as an empty disk.

If the number of offline OSDs has meant that all copies of an object are offline, then recovery procedures should be attempted to try and extract the objects from the failed OSDs, and insert them back into the cluster.

RBD mirroring

As mentioned previously, working backups are a key strategy in ensuring that a failure does not result in the loss of data. Starting with the Jewel release, Ceph introduced RBD mirroring, which allows you to asynchronously mirror an RBD from one cluster to another. Note the difference between Cephs native replication, which is synchronous, and RBD mirroring. With synchronous replication, low latency between peers is essential, and asynchronous replication allows the two Ceph clusters to be geographically remote, as latency is no longer a factor.

By having a replicated copy of your RBD images on a separate cluster, you can dramatically reduce both your **Recovery Time Objective (RTO)** and **Recovery Point Objective (RPO)**. The RTO is a measure of how long it takes from initiating recovery to when the data is usable. It is the worst case measurement of time between each data point and describes the expected data loss. A daily backup would have an RPO of 24 hours; for example, potentially, any data written up to 24 hours since the last backup would be lost if you had to restore from a backup.

With RBD mirroring, data is asynchronously replicated to the target RBD, and so, in most cases, the RPO should be under a minute. As the target RBD is also a replica and not a backup that would require to be first restored, the RTO is also likely going to be extremely low. Additionally, as the target RBD is stored on a separate Ceph cluster, it offers additional protection over snapshots, which could also be impacted if the Ceph cluster itself experiences issues. At first glance, this makes RBD mirroring seem like the perfect tool to protect against data loss, and in most cases, it is a very useful tool. RBD mirroring is not a replacement for a proper backup routine though. In the cases where data loss is caused by actions internal to the RBD, such as file system corruption or user error, these changes will be replicated to the target RBD. A separate isolated copy of your data is vital.

With that said, let's take a closer look into how RBD mirroring works.

The journal

One of the key components in RBD mirroring is the journal. The RBD mirroring journal stores all writes to the RBD and acknowledges to the client once they have been written. These writes are then written to the primary RBD image. The journal itself is stored as RADOS objects, prefixed similarly to how RBD images are. Separately, the remote `rbd-mirror` daemon polls the configured RBD mirrors and pulls the newly written journal objects across to the target cluster and replays them into the target RBD.

The rbd-mirror daemon

The `rbd-mirror` daemon is responsible for replaying the contents of the journal to a target RBD in another Ceph cluster. The `rbd-mirror` daemon only needs to run on the target cluster, unless you wish to replicate both ways, in which case, it will need to run on both clusters.

Configuring RBD mirroring

In order to use the RBD mirroring functionality, we will require two Ceph clusters. We could deploy two identical clusters we have been using previously, but the number of VMs involved may exceed the capabilities of what most people's personal machines can run. Therefore, we will modify our vagrant and ansible configuration files to deploy two separate Ceph clusters each with a single monitor and an OSD node.

The hosts part at the top should now look like this:

```
nodes = [
  { :hostname => 'ansible', :ip => '192.168.0.40', :box => 'xenial64' },
    { :hostname => 'site1-mon1', :ip => '192.168.0.41', :box => 'xenial64' },
    { :hostname => 'site2-mon1', :ip => '192.168.0.42', :box => 'xenial64' },
    { :hostname => 'site1-osd1', :ip => '192.168.0.51', :box => 'xenial64',
  :ram => 1024, :osd => 'yes' },
    { :hostname => 'site2-osd1', :ip => '192.168.0.52', :box => 'xenial64',
  :ram => 1024, :osd => 'yes' }
  ]
```

For the anisble configuration, we will maintain two separate ansible configuration instances so that each cluster can be deployed seperately. We will then maintain separate hosts files per instance, which we will specify when we run the playbook. To do this, we will not copy the ceph-ansible files into /etc/ansible, but keep them in the home directory.

git clone https://github.com/ceph/ceph-ansible.git

```
cp -a ceph-ansible ~/ceph-ansible2
```

Create the same two files called all and Ceph, in the group_vars directory. This needs to be done in both copies of ceph-ansible:

1. Create a hosts file in each ansible directory, and place the two hosts in each:

```
vagrant@ansible:~/ceph-ansible$ cat hosts
[mons]
site1-mon1

[osds]
site1-osd1

[ceph:children]
mons
osds
```

The above image is for host one and the below image is for the second host

```
vagrant@ansible:~/ceph-ansible2$ cat hosts
[mons]
site2-mon1

[osds]
site2-osd1

[ceph:children]
mons
osds
```

2. Then, run the `site.yml` playbook under each `ceph-ansible` instance to deploy our two Ceph clusters:

```
ansible-playbook -K -i hosts site.yml
```

3. Before we can continue with the configuration of the RBD mirroring, we need to adjust the replication level of the default pools to 1, as our clusters only have 1 OSD. Run these commands on both the clusters:

```
vagrant@site1-mon1:~$ sudo ceph osd pool set rbd size 1
set pool 0 size to 1
vagrant@site1-mon1:~$ sudo ceph osd pool set rbd min_size 1
set pool 0 min_size to 1
```

4. Now, install the RBD mirroring daemon on both the clusters:

```
sudo apt-get install rbd-mirror
```

```
vagrant@mon1:~$ sudo apt-get install rbd-mirror
Reading package lists... Done
Building dependency tree
Reading state information... Done
The following NEW packages will be installed:
  rbd-mirror
0 upgraded, 1 newly installed, 0 to remove and 121 not upgraded.
Need to get 1,726 kB of archives.
After this operation, 7,240 kB of additional disk space will be used.
Get:1 http://download.ceph.com/debian-kraken xenial/main amd64 rbd-mirror amd64 11.2.0-1xenial [1,726 kB]
Fetched 1,726 kB in 1s (1,289 kB/s)
Selecting previously unselected package rbd-mirror.
(Reading database ... 54945 files and directories currently installed.)
Preparing to unpack .../rbd-mirror_11.2.0-1xenial_amd64.deb ...
Unpacking rbd-mirror (11.2.0-1xenial) ...
Processing triggers for ureadahead (0.100.0-19) ...
Processing triggers for man-db (2.7.5-1) ...
Setting up rbd-mirror (11.2.0-1xenial) ...
ceph-rbd-mirror.target is a disabled or a static unit, not starting it.
Processing triggers for ureadahead (0.100.0-19) ...
```

5. In order for the `rbd-mirror` daemon to be able to communicate with both clusters, we need to copy `ceph.conf` and the `keyring` from both the clusters to each other:

6. Copy `ceph.conf` from `site1-mon1` to `site2-mon1` and call it `remote.conf`:

7. Copy `ceph.client.admin.keyring` from `site1-mon1` to `site2-mon1` and call it `remote.client.admin.keyring`:

8. Repeat these two steps but this time copy the files from `site2-mon1` to `site1-mon1`:

9. Remember to make sure the keyrings are owned by `ceph:ceph`:

```
sudo chown ceph:ceph /etc/ceph/remote.client.admin.keyring
```

10. Now, we need to tell Ceph that the pool called rbd should have the mirroring function enabled:

```
sudo rbd --cluster ceph mirror pool enable rbd image
```

11. Repeat this for the target cluster:

```
sudo rbd --cluster remote mirror pool enable rbd image
```

12. Add the target cluster as a peer of the pool mirroring configuration:

```
sudo rbd --cluster ceph mirror pool peer add rbd
client.admin@remote
```

13. Run the same command locally on the second Ceph cluster as well:

```
sudo rbd --cluster ceph mirror pool peer add rbd
client.admin@remote
```

14. Back on the first cluster, let's create a test RBD to use with our mirroring lab:

```
sudo rbd create mirror_test --size=1G
```

15. Enable the journaling feature on the RBD image:

```
sudo rbd feature enable rbd/mirror_test journaling
```

16. Finally, enable mirroring for the RBD:

```
sudo rbd mirror image enable rbd/mirror_test
```

```
vagrant@site1-mon1:~$ sudo rbd mirror image enable rbd/mirror_test
Mirroring enabled
```

It's important to note that RBD mirroring works via a pull system. The `rbd-mirror` daemon needs to run on the cluster that you wish to mirror the RBDs to; it then connects to the source cluster and pulls the RBDs across. If you were intending to implement a two-way replication where each Ceph cluster replicates with each other, then you would run the `rbd-mirror` daemon on both the clusters. With this in mind, let's enable and start the systemd service for `rbd-mirror` on your target host:

```
sudo systemctl enable ceph-rbd-mirror@admin
sudo systemctl start ceph-rbd-mirror@admin
```

The `rbd-mirror` daemon will now start processing all the RBD images configured for mirroring on your primary cluster.

We can confirm that everything is working as expected by running the following command on the target cluster:

```
sudo rbd --cluster remote mirror pool status rbd -verbose
```

```
vagrant@site1-mon1:~$ sudo rbd --cluster remote mirror pool status rbd --verbose
health: OK
images: 1 total
    1 replaying

mirror_test:
  global_id:    a90b307a-98ec-4835-9ea8-fc2f91b4ae37
  state:        up+replaying
  description:  replaying, master_position=[object_number=3, tag_tid=1, entry_tid=2607], mirror_position=
[object_number=3, tag_tid=1, entry_tid=2607], entries_behind_master=0
  last_update: 2017-04-17 14:37:09
```

In the previous screenshot, we can see that our `mirror_test` RBD is in a **up+replaying** state; this means that mirroring is in progress, and we can see via `entries_behind_master` that it is currently up-to-date.

Also, note the difference in the output of the RBD `info` commands on either of the clusters. On the source cluster, the primary status is true, which allows you to determine which cluster the RBD is the master state and can be used by clients. This also confirms that although we only created the RBD on the primary cluster, it has been replicated to the secondary one.

The source cluster is shown here:

```
rbd image 'mirror_test':
        size 1024 MB in 256 objects
        order 22 (4096 kB objects)
        block_name_prefix: rbd_data.374b74b0dc51
        format: 2
        features: layering, exclusive-lock, object-map, fast-diff, deep-flatten, journaling
        flags:
        journal: 374b74b0dc51
        mirroring state: enabled
        mirroring global id: a90b307a-98ec-4835-9ea8-fc2f91b4ae37
        mirroring primary: true
```

The target cluster is shown here:

```
rbd image 'mirror_test':
        size 1024 MB in 256 objects
        order 22 (4096 kB objects)
        block_name_prefix: rbd_data.377d2eb141f2
        format: 2
        features: layering, exclusive-lock, object-map, fast-diff, deep-flatten, journaling
        flags:
        journal: 377d2eb141f2
        mirroring state: enabled
        mirroring global id: a90b307a-98ec-4835-9ea8-fc2f91b4ae37
        mirroring primary: false
```

Performing RBD failover

Before we failover the RBD to the secondary cluster, let's map it, create a file system, and place a file on it, so we can confirm that the mirroring is working correctly. As of Linux kernel 4.11, the kernel RBD driver does not support the RBD journaling feature required for RBD mirroring; this means you cannot map the RBD using the kernel RBD client. As such, we will need to use the rbd-nbd utility, which uses the librbd driver in combination with Linux nbd devices to map RBDs via user space. Although there are many things which may cause Ceph to experience slow performance, here are some of the most likely causes.

```
sudo rbd-nbd map mirror_test
```

```
vagrant@site1-mon1:~$ sudo rbd-nbd map mirror_test
/dev/nbd0
```

```
sudo mkfs.ext4 /dev/nbd0
```

```
vagrant@site1-mon1:~$ sudo mkfs.ext4 /dev/nbd0
mke2fs 1.42.13 (17-May-2015)
Discarding device blocks: done
Creating filesystem with 262144 4k blocks and 65536 inodes
Filesystem UUID: d4ff2036-a10b-4003-8a0a-144b0863b55a
Superblock backups stored on blocks:
        32768, 98304, 163840, 229376

Allocating group tables: done
Writing inode tables: done
Creating journal (8192 blocks): done
Writing superblocks and filesystem accounting information: done
```

```
sudo mount /dev/nbd0 /mnt
echo This is a test | sudo tee /mnt/test.txt
sudo umount /mnt
sudo rbd-nbd unmap /dev/nbd0
Now lets demote the RBD on the primary cluster and promote it on the
secondary
sudo rbd --cluster ceph mirror image demote rbd/mirror_test
sudo rbd --cluster remote mirror image promote rbd/mirror_test
```

Now, map and mount the RBD on the secondary cluster, and you should be able to read the test text file that you created on the primary cluster:

```
vagrant@site2-mon1:~$ sudo rbd-nbd map mirror_test
/dev/nbd0
vagrant@site2-mon1:~$ sudo mount /dev/nbd0 /mnt
vagrant@site2-mon1:~$ cat /mnt/test.txt
This is a test
```

We can clearly see that the RBD has successfully been mirrored to the secondary cluster, and the file system content is just as we left it on the primary cluster.

 If you try and map and mount the RBD on the cluster where the RBD is not in the primary state, the operation will just hang, as Ceph will not permit IO to an RBD image in a non-master state.

This concludes the section on RBD mirroring.

RBD recovery

In the event that a number of OSDs have failed, and you are unable to recover them via the `ceph-object-store` tool, your cluster will most likely be in a state where most, if not all, RBD images are inaccessible. However, there is still a chance that you may be able to recover RBD data from the disks in your Ceph cluster. There are tools that can search through the OSD data structure, find the object files relating to RBDs, and then assemble these objects back into a disk image, resembling the original RBD image.

In this section, we will focus on a tool by *Lennart Bader* to recover a test RBD image from our test Ceph cluster. The tool allows the recovery of RBD images from the contents of Ceph OSDs, without any requirement that the OSD is in a running or usable state. It should be noted that if the OSD has been corrupted due to an underlying file system corruption, the contents of the RBD image may still be corrupt.The RBD recovery tool can be found in the following GitHub repository:

```
https://gitlab.lbader.de/kryptur/ceph-recovery
```

Before we start, make sure you have a small test RBD with a valid file system created on your Ceph cluster. Due to the size of the disks in the test environment that we created, it is recommended that the RBD is only a gigabyte in size.

We will perform the recovery on one of the monitor nodes, but in practice, this recovery procedure can be done from any node that can access the Ceph OSD disks. To access the disks, we need to make sure that the recovery server has sufficient space to recover the data.

In this example, we will mount the remote OSDs contents via `sshfs`, which allows you to mount remote directories over `ssh`. However in real life, there is nothing to stop you from physically inserting disks into another server or whatever method is required. The tool only requires to see the OSDs data directories:

1. First, we need to clone the Ceph recovery tool from the Git repository.

git clone `https://gitlab.lbader.de/kryptur/ceph-recovery.git`

```
vagrant@mon1:~$ git clone https://gitlab.lbader.de/kryptur/ceph-recovery.git
Cloning into 'ceph-recovery'...
remote: Counting objects: 18, done.
remote: Compressing objects: 100% (18/18), done.
remote: Total 18 (delta 6), reused 0 (delta 0)
Unpacking objects: 100% (18/18), done.
Checking connectivity... done.
```

2. Also, make sure you have `sshfs` installed:

```
sudo apt-get install sshfs
```

```
vagrant@mon1:~$ sudo apt-get install sshfs
Reading package lists... Done
Building dependency tree
Reading state information... Done
The following packages were automatically installed and are no longer required:
  libboost-iostreams1.58.0 libboost-program-options1.58.0 libboost-random1.58.0 libboost-regex1.58.0 libboost-system1.58.0
  libboost-thread1.58.0 libcephfs1 libfcgi0ldbl
Use 'sudo apt autoremove' to remove them.
The following NEW packages will be installed:
  sshfs
0 upgraded, 1 newly installed, 0 to remove and 103 not upgraded.
Need to get 41.7 kB of archives.
After this operation, 138 kB of additional disk space will be used.
Get:1 http://us.archive.ubuntu.com/ubuntu xenial/universe amd64 sshfs amd64 2.5-1ubuntu1 [41.7 kB]
Fetched 41.7 kB in 0s (109 kB/s)
Selecting previously unselected package sshfs.
(Reading database ... 40714 files and directories currently installed.)
Preparing to unpack .../sshfs_2.5-1ubuntu1_amd64.deb ...
Unpacking sshfs (2.5-1ubuntu1) ...
Processing triggers for man-db (2.7.5-1) ...
Setting up sshfs (2.5-1ubuntu1) ...
```

3. Change into the cloned tool directory, and create the empty directories for each of the OSDs:

```
cd ceph-recovery

sudo mkdir osds

sudo mkdir osds/ceph-0

sudo mkdir osds/ceph-1

sudo mkdir osds/ceph-2
```

Now, mount each remote OSD to the directories that we have just created. Note that you need to make sure your OSD directories match your actual test cluster:

```
sudo sshfs vagrant@osd1:/var/lib/ceph/osd/ceph-0 osds/ceph-0

sudo sshfs vagrant@osd2:/var/lib/ceph/osd/ceph-2 osds/ceph-2

sudo sshfs vagrant@osd3:/var/lib/ceph/osd/ceph-1 osds/ceph-1
```

Now, we can use the tool to scan the OSD directories and compile a list of the RBDs that are available. The only parameter needed for this command is the location where the OSDs are mounted. In this case, it is in a directory called `osds`. The results will be listed in the VM directory:

```
sudo ./collect_files.sh osds
```

```
vagrant@mon1:~/ceph-recovery$ sudo ./collect_files.sh osds
Scanning ceph-0
Scanning ceph-1
Scanning ceph-2
Preparing UDATA files
UDATA files ready
Extracting VM IDs
VM IDs extracted
```

If we look inside the VM directory, we can see that the tool has found our test RBD image. Now that we have located the image, the next step is to assemble various objects located on the OSDs. The three parameters for this command are the name of the RBD image found in the previous step, the size of the image, and the destination for the recovered image file. The size of the image is specified in bytes, and it is important that it is at least as big as the original image; it can be bigger, but the RBD will not recover if the size is smaller:

```
sudo ./assemble.sh vms/test.id 1073741824 .
```

```
vagrant@mon1:~/ceph-recovery$ sudo ./assemble.sh vms/test.id 1073741824 .
1e502238e1f29
test
file_lists/1e502238e1f29.files

CEPH RECOVERY
Assemble test with ID 1e502238e1f29

Searching file list
file_lists/1e502238e1f29.files found

Output Image will be ./test.raw

There are 15 blocks found
The output file will be created as a file of size 1073741824 Bytes
The blocksize is 512

Creating Image file...
Starting reassembly...
100% [###################################################################################################_]
Image written to ./test.raw
```

The RBD will now be recovered from the mounted OSD contents to the specified image file. Depending on the size of the image, it may take a while, and a progress bar will show you its progress.

Once completed, we can run a file system called `fsck` on the image to make sure that it has been recovered correctly. In this case, the RBD was formatted with `ext4`, so we can use the `e2fsck` tool to check the image:

```
sudo e2fsck test.raw
```

```
vagrant@mon1:~/ceph-recovery$ sudo e2fsck test.raw
e2fsck 1.42.13 (17-May-2015)
test.raw: clean, 11/65536 files, 12635/262144 blocks
```

Excellent, the image file is clean, which means that there is now a very high chance that all our data has been recovered successfully.

Now, we can finally mount the image as a loopback device to access our data. If the command returns no output, then we have successfully mounted it:

```
sudo mount -o loop test.raw /mnt
```

You can see that the image is successfully mounted as a loop device:

```
vagrant@mon1:~/ceph-recovery$ df -h
Filesystem                   Size  Used Avail Use% Mounted on
udev                         225M     0  225M   0% /dev
tmpfs                         49M  5.7M   44M  12% /run
/dev/mapper/vagrant--vg-root  38G  2.6G   34G   8% /
tmpfs                        245M     0  245M   0% /dev/shm
tmpfs                        5.0M     0  5.0M   0% /run/lock
tmpfs                        245M     0  245M   0% /sys/fs/cgroup
/dev/sda1                    472M   57M  391M  13% /boot
vagrant                      238G   95G  144G  40% /vagrant
tmpfs                         49M     0   49M   0% /run/user/1000
/dev/loop0                   976M  1.3M  908M   1% /mnt
```

This concludes the process for recovering RBD images from dead Ceph OSDs.

Lost objects and inactive PGs

This section of the chapter will cover the scenario where a number of OSDs may have gone offline in a short period of time, leaving some objects with no valid replica copies. It's important to note that there is a difference between an object that has no remaining copies and an object that has a remaining copy, but it is known that another copy has had more recent writes. The latter is normally seen when running the cluster with `min_size` set to 1.

To demonstrate how to recover an object that has an out-of-date copy of data, let's perform a series of steps to break the cluster:

1. First, let's set `min_size` to 1; hopefully, by the end of this example, you will see why you don't ever want to do this in real life:

   ```
   sudo ceph osd pool set rbd min_size 1
   ```

   ```
   vagrant@mon1:~/ceph-recovery$ sudo ceph osd pool set rbd min_size 1
   set pool 0 min_size to 1
   ```

2. Create a test object that we will make later make Ceph believe is lost:

   ```
   sudo rados -p rbd put lost_object logo.png
   sudo ceph osd set norecover
   sudo ceph osd set nobackfill
   ```

   These two flags make sure that when the OSDS come back online after making the write to a single OSD, the changes are not recovered. Since we are only testing with a single option, we need these flags to simulate the condition in real life, where it's likely that not all objects can be recovered in sufficient time before the OSD, when the only copy goes offline for whatever reason.

3. Shut down two of the OSD nodes, so only one OSD is remaining. Since we have set `min_size` to 1, we will still be able to write data to the cluster. You can see that the Ceph status shows that the two OSDS are now down:

   ```
       cluster d9f58afd-3e62-4493-ba80-0356290b3d9f
        health HEALTH_WARN
               64 pgs degraded
               26 pgs stuck unclean
               64 pgs undersized
               recovery 46/69 objects degraded (66.667%)
               too few PGs per OSD (21 < min 30)
               2/3 in osds are down
               nobackfill,norecover flag(s) set
               all OSDs are running kraken or later but the 'require_kraken_osds' osdmap flag is not set
        monmap e2: 3 mons at {mon1=192.168.0.41:6789/0,mon2=192.168.0.42:6789/0,mon3=192.168.0.43:6789/0}
               election epoch 258, quorum 0,1,2 mon1,mon2,mon3
           mgr active: mon1 standbys: mon2, mon3
        osdmap e398: 3 osds: 1 up, 3 in; 64 remapped pgs
               flags nobackfill,norecover,sortbitwise,require_jewel_osds
         pgmap v5286: 64 pgs, 1 pools, 37579 kB data, 23 objects
               226 MB used, 26668 MB / 26894 MB avail
               46/69 objects degraded (66.667%)
                     64 active+undersized+degraded
   ```

4. Now, write to the object again, the write will go to the remaining OSD:

   ```
   sudo rados -p rbd put lost_object logo.png
   ```

5. Now, shut down the remaining OSDS; once it has gone offline, power back the remaining 2 OSDS:

```
cluster d9f58afd-3e62-4493-ba80-0356290b3d9f
 health HEALTH_WARN
        64 pgs degraded
        1 pgs recovering
        64 pgs stuck unclean
        64 pgs undersized
        recovery 25/69 objects degraded (36.232%)
        recovery 1/23 unfound (4.348%)
        1/3 in osds are down
        all OSDs are running kraken or later but the 'require_kraken_osds' osdmap flag is not set
 monmap e2: 3 mons at {mon1=192.168.0.41:6789/0,mon2=192.168.0.42:6789/0,mon3=192.168.0.43:6789/0}
        election epoch 258, quorum 0,1,2 mon1,mon2,mon3
    mgr active: mon1 standbys: mon2, mon3
 osdmap e409: 3 osds: 2 up, 3 in; 64 remapped pgs
        flags sortbitwise,require_jewel_osds
  pgmap v5319: 64 pgs, 1 pools, 37579 kB data, 23 objects
        220 MB used, 26674 MB / 26894 MB avail
        25/69 objects degraded (36.232%)
        1/23 unfound (4.348%)
              63 active+undersized+degraded
               1 active+recovering+undersized+degraded
```

You can see that Ceph knows that it already has an unfound object even before the recovery process has started. This is because, during the peering phase, the PG containing the modified object knows that the only valid copy is on osd.0,which is now offline.

6. Remove the nobackfill and norecover flags, and let the cluster try and perform recovery. You will see that even after the recovery has progressed, there will be 1 PG in a degraded state, and the unfound object warning will still be present. This is a good thing, as Ceph is protecting your data from corruption. Imagine what would happen if a 4 MB chunk of an RBD containing a database suddenly went back in time!

If you try and read or write to our test object, you will notice the request will just hang; this is Ceph again protecting your data. There are three ways to fix this problem. The first solution and the most ideal one is to get a valid copy of this object back online; this could either be done by bringing osd.0 online, or by using the objectstore tool to export and import this object into a healthy OSD. But for the purpose of this section, let's assume that neither of those options is possible. Before we cover the remaining two options, let's investigate further to try and uncover what is going on under-the-hood.

Run the Ceph health detail to find out which PG is having the problem:

```
vagrant@mon1:~$ sudo ceph health detail
HEALTH_WARN 1 pgs degraded; 1 pgs stuck unclean; recovery 2/46 objects degraded (4.348%); recovery 1/
 are running kraken or later but the 'require_kraken_osds' osdmap flag is not set
pg 0.31 is stuck unclean for 1370.786568, current state active+degraded, last acting [2,1]
pg 0.31 is active+degraded, acting [2,1], 1 unfound
recovery 2/46 objects degraded (4.348%)
recovery 1/23 unfound (4.348%)
```

In this case, it's pg 0.31, which is in a degraded state, because it has an unfound object. Let's query the pg:

```
ceph pg 0.31 query
```

Look for the recovery section; we can see that Ceph has tried to probe "osd": "0" for the object, but it is down. It has tried to probe "osd": "1" for the object, but for whatever reason, it was of no use, we know the reason is that it is an out-of-date copy.

Now, let's look into some more detail on the missing object:

```
sudo ceph pg 0.31 list_missing
```

The need and have lines reveal the reason. We have `epoch 383'5`, but the valid copy of the object exists in `398'6`; this is why `min_size=1` is bad. You might be in a situation where you only have a single valid copy of an object. If this was caused by a disk failure, you would have bigger problems.

To recover from this, we have two options: we can either choose to use the older copy of the object or simply delete it. It should be noted that if this object is new and an older copy does not exist on the remaining OSDS, then it will also delete the object.

To delete the object, run this:

```
ceph pg 0.31 mark_unfound_lost delete
```

To revert it, run this:

```
ceph pg 0.31 mark_unfound_lost revert
```

This concludes recovering from unfound objects.

Recovering from a complete monitor failure

In the unlikely event that you lose all of your monitors, all is not lost. You can rebuild the monitor database from the contents of the OSDs by the use of the `ceph-objectstore` tool.

To set the scenario, we will assume that an event has occurred and has corrupted all three monitors, effectively leaving the Ceph cluster inaccessible. To recover the cluster, we will shut down two of the monitors and leave a single failed monitor running. We will then rebuild the monitor database, overwrite the corrupted copy, and then restart the monitor to bring the Ceph cluster back online.

The `objectstore` tool needs to be able to access every OSD in the cluster to rebuild the monitor database; in this example, we will use a script, which will connect via `ssh` to access the OSD data. As the OSD data is not accessible by every user, we will use the root user to log in to the OSD hosts. By default, most Linux distributions will not allow remote, password-based root logins, so ensure you have copied your public `ssh` key to the root users on some remote OSD nodes.

The following script will connect to each of the OSD nodes specified in the hosts variable, and it will extract the data required to build the monitor database:

```
#!/bin/bash
hosts="osd1 osd2 osd3"
ms=/tmp/mon-store/
mkdir $ms
# collect the cluster map from OSDs
for host in $hosts; do
  echo $host
  rsync -avz $ms root@$host:$ms
  rm -rf $ms
  ssh root@$host <<EOF
    for osd in /var/lib/ceph/osd/ceph-*; do
      ceph-objectstore-tool --data-path \$osd --op update-mon-db --mon-store-path $ms
    done
EOF
  rsync -avz root@$host:$ms $ms
done
```

This will generate the following contents in the `/tmp/mon-store` directory:

```
vagrant@mon1:~$ ls /tmp/mon-store/
kv_backend  store.db
```

We also need to assign new permissions via the `keyring`:

```
sudo ceph-authtool /etc/ceph/ceph.client.admin.keyring --create-keyring --
gen-key -n client.admin --cap mon 'allow *' --cap osd 'allow *' --cap mds
'allow *'
```

```
vagrant@mon1:~$ sudo ceph-authtool /etc/ceph/ceph.client.admin.keyring --create-keyring --gen-key -n client.admin --cap mon 'allow *' --cap
osd 'allow *' --cap mds 'allow *'
creating /etc/ceph/ceph.client.admin.keyring
```

```
sudo ceph-authtool /etc/ceph/ceph.client.admin.keyring --gen-key -n mon. --
cap mon 'allow *'
```

```
sudo cat /etc/ceph/ceph.client.admin.keyring
```

```
vagrant@mon1:~$ sudo cat /etc/ceph/ceph.client.admin.keyring
[mon.]
        key = AQBODeBYfJFeIRAALrllDmvSO16983LxfCsDpA==
        caps mon = "allow *"
[client.admin]
        key = AQAzDeBYbuP+IRAA4milZnbZW41v4F8taiRPHg==
        caps mds = "allow *"
        caps mon = "allow *"
        caps osd = "allow *"
```

Now that the monitor database is rebuilt, we can copy it to the monitor directory, but before we do so, let's take a backup of the existing database:

```
sudo mv /var/lib/ceph/mon/ceph-mon1/store.db /var/lib/ceph/mon/ceph-mon1/store.bak
```

Now, copy the rebuilt version:

```
sudo mv /tmp/mon-store/store.db /var/lib/ceph/mon/ceph-mon1/store.db
sudo chown -R ceph:ceph /var/lib/ceph/mon/ceph-mon1
```

If you try and start the monitor now, it will get stuck in a probing state, as it tries to probe for other monitors. This is Ceph trying to avoid a split-brain scenario; however, in this case, we want to force it to form a quorum and go fully online. To do this, we need to edit monmap, remove the other monitors, and then inject it back into the monitors database:

```
sudo ceph-mon -i mon1 --extract-monmap /tmp/monmap
```

Check the contents of the monmap:

```
sudo monmaptool /tmp/monmap -print
```

```
vagrant@mon1:~$ sudo monmaptool /tmp/monmap --print
monmaptool: monmap file /tmp/monmap
epoch 0
fsid d9f58afd-3e62-4493-ba80-0356290b3d9f
last_changed 2017-03-29 21:14:32.762117
created 2017-03-29 21:14:32.762117
0: 192.168.0.41:6789/0 mon.noname-a
1: 192.168.0.42:6789/0 mon.noname-b
2: 192.168.0.43:6789/0 mon.noname-c
```

You will see that there are three mons present, so let's remove two of them:

```
sudo monmaptool /tmp/monmap --rm noname-b
```

```
sudo monmaptool /tmp/monmap --rm noname-c
```

Now, check again to make sure they are completely gone:

```
sudo monmaptool /tmp/monmap -print
```

```
vagrant@mon1:~$ sudo monmaptool /tmp/monmap --print
monmaptool: monmap file /tmp/monmap
epoch 0
fsid d9f58afd-3e62-4493-ba80-0356290b3d9f
last_changed 2017-03-29 21:14:32.762117
created 2017-03-29 21:14:32.762117
0: 192.168.0.41:6789/0 mon.noname-a
```

```
sudo ceph-mon -i mon1 --inject-monmap /tmp/monmap
```

Restart all your OSDs, so they rejoin the cluster; then you will be able to successfully query the cluster status and see that your data is still there:

```
vagrant@mon1:~$ sudo ceph -s
    cluster d9f58afd-3e62-4493-ba80-0356290b3d9f
     health HEALTH_WARN
            all OSDs are running kraken or later but the 'require_kraken_osds' osdmap flag is not set
     monmap e2: 1 mons at {mon1=192.168.0.41:6789/0}
            election epoch 3, quorum 0 mon1
        mgr no daemons active
     osdmap e460: 3 osds: 3 up, 3 in
            flags sortbitwise,require_jewel_osds
      pgmap v90: 64 pgs, 1 pools, 37579 kB data, 23 objects
            174 MB used, 26720 MB / 26894 MB avail
                  64 active+clean
recovery io 199 kB/s, 0 objects/s
vagrant@mon1:~$ sudo rbd ls
test
```

This concludes the section of this chapter on how to recover from a complete monitor failure.

Using the Cephs object store tool

Hopefully, if you have followed best practice, your cluster is running with three replicas and is not configured with any dangerous configuration options. Ceph, in most cases, should be able to recover from any failure.

However, in the scenario where a number of OSDs go offline, a number of PGs and/or objects may become unavailable. If you are unable to reintroduce these OSDs back into the cluster to allow Ceph to recover them gracefully, then the data in those PGs is effectively lost. However, there is a possibility that the OSD is still readable to use the objectstore tool to recover the PGs contents. The process involves exporting the PGs from the failed OSDs and then importing the PGs back into the cluster. The objectstore tool does require that the OSDs internal metadata is still in a consistent state, so a full recovery is not guaranteed.

In order to demonstrate the use of the objectstore tool, we will shut down two of our three test cluster OSDs, and then recover the missing PGs back into the cluster. In real life, its unlikely you would be facing a situation where every single PG from the failed OSDs is missing, but for demonstration purposes, the required steps are the same:

1. First, let's set the pool size to 2, so we can make sure that we lose all the copies of some PGs when we stop the OSD service:

```
vagrant@mon1:~$ sudo ceph osd pool set rbd size 2
set pool 0 size to 2
```

2. Now, shut down two of the OSD services, and you will see from the Ceph status screen that the number of PGs will go offline:

```
vagrant@mon1:~$ sudo ceph -s
    cluster d9f58afd-3e62-4493-ba80-0356290b3d9f
     health HEALTH_ERR
            27 pgs are stuck inactive for more than 300 seconds
            64 pgs degraded
            23 pgs stale
            27 pgs stuck inactive
            27 pgs stuck unclean
            64 pgs undersized
            recovery 18/36 objects degraded (50.000%)
            too few PGs per OSD (21 < min 30)
            2/3 in osds are down
     monmap e2: 3 mons at {mon1=192.168.0.41:6789/0,mon2=192.168.0.42:6789/0,mon3=192.168.0.43:6789/0}
            election epoch 10, quorum 0,1,2 mon1,mon2,mon3
        mgr active: mon2 standbys: mon3, mon1
     osdmap e22: 3 osds: 1 up, 3 in; 41 remapped pgs
            flags sortbitwise,require_jewel_osds,require_kraken_osds
      pgmap v105: 64 pgs, 1 pools, 37572 kB data, 18 objects
            233 MB used, 26661 MB / 26894 MB avail
            18/36 objects degraded (50.000%)
                41 undersized+degraded+peered
                23 stale+undersized+degraded+peered
```

3. Running a Ceph health detail will also show which PGs are in a degraded state:

```
pg 0.21 is stale+undersized+degraded+peered, acting [2]
pg 0.22 is stale+undersized+degraded+peered, acting [2]
pg 0.23 is stale+undersized+degraded+peered, acting [2]
pg 0.24 is undersized+degraded+peered, acting [0]
pg 0.25 is undersized+degraded+peered, acting [0]
pg 0.26 is undersized+degraded+peered, acting [0]
pg 0.27 is undersized+degraded+peered, acting [0]
pg 0.28 is undersized+degraded+peered, acting [0]
pg 0.29 is undersized+degraded+peered, acting [0]
pg 0.2a is stale+undersized+degraded+peered, acting [2]
pg 0.2b is stale+undersized+degraded+peered, acting [2]
pg 0.2c is undersized+degraded+peered, acting [0]
pg 0.2d is stale+undersized+degraded+peered, acting [2]
```

The stale PGs are the ones that no longer have a surviving copy, and it can be seen that the acting OSD is the one that was shut down.

If we use `grep` to filter out just the stale PGs, we can use the resulting list to work out what PGs we need to recover. If the OSDs have actually been removed from the cluster, then the PGs will be listed as incomplete rather than stale.

4. Check the OSD to make sure the PG exists in it:

```
vagrant@osd3:~$ sudo ls -l /var/lib/ceph/osd/ceph-2/current/0.2d_head
total 0
-rw-r--r-- 1 ceph ceph 0 Apr  2 20:13 __head_0000002D__0
```

5. We will now use the `objectstore` tool to export the pg to a file. As the amount of data in our test cluster is small, we can just export the data to the OS disk. In real life, you probably want to consider connecting additional storage to the server. USB disks are ideal for this, as they can easily be moved between servers as part of the recovery process:

```
sudo ceph-objectstore-tool --op export --pgid 0.2a --data-path
/var/lib/ceph/osd/ceph-2 --file 0.2a_export
```

```
vagrant@osd3:~$ sudo ceph-objectstore-tool --op export --pgid 0.2a --data-path /var/lib/ceph/osd/ceph-2 --file 0.2a_export
Exporting 0.2a
Read #0:54d415a2:::rbd_data.fa68238e1f29.0000000000000060:head#
Export successful
```

If you experience an assert while running the tool, you can try running it with the `--skip-journal-replay` flag, which will skip replaying the journal into the OSD. If there was any outstanding data in the journal, it will be lost. But this may allow you to recover the bulk of the missing PGs that would have otherwise been impossible. And repeat this until you have exported all the missing PGs.

6. Now, we can import the missing PGs back into an operating OSD; while we could import the PGs into an existing OSD, it is much safer to perform the import on a new OSD, so we don't risk further data loss. For this demonstration, we will create a directory-based OSD on the disk used by the failed OSD. It's highly recommended in a real disaster scenario that the data would be inserted into an OSD running on a separate disk, rather than using an existing OSD. This is done so that there is no further risk to any data in the Ceph cluster.

Also, it doesn't matter that the PGs that are being imported are all inserted into the same temporary OSD. As soon as Ceph discovers the objects, it will recover them to the correct location in the cluster.

7. Create a new empty folder for the OSD:

```
sudo mkdir /var/lib/ceph/osd/ceph-2/tmposd/
```

8. Use `ceph-disk` to prepare the directory for Ceph:

```
sudo ceph-disk prepare  /var/lib/ceph/osd/ceph-2/tmposd/
```

9. Change the ownership of the folder to the ceph user and the group:

```
sudo chown -R ceph:ceph /var/lib/ceph/osd/ceph-2/tmposd/
```

10. Activate the OSD to bring it online:

```
sudo ceph-disk activate  /var/lib/ceph/osd/ceph-2/tmposd/
```

11. Set the weight of the OSD to stop any objects from being backfilled into it:

```
sudo ceph osd crush reweight osd.3 0
```

12. Now, we can proceed with the PG import, specifying the temporary OSD location and the PG files that we exported earlier:

```
sudo ceph-objectstore-tool --op import --data-path
/var/lib/ceph/osd/ceph-3 --file 0.2a_export
```

```
vagrant@osd3:~$ sudo ceph-objectstore-tool --op import --data-path /var/lib/ceph/osd/ceph-3 --file 0.2a_export
Importing pgid 0.2a
Write #0:54d415a2:::rbd_data.fa68238e1f29.0000000000000060:head#
Import successful
```

13. Repeat this for every PG that you exported previously. Once complete, reset file onwership and restart the new temp OSD:

```
sudo chown -R ceph:ceph /var/lib/ceph/osd/ceph-2/tmposd/
sudo systemctl start ceph-osd@3
```

14. After checking the Ceph status output, you will see that your PGs are now active, but in a degraded state. In the case of our test cluster, there are not sufficient OSDs to allow the objects to recover to the correct amount of copies. If there were more OSDs in the cluster, the objects would then be backfilled around the cluster and would recover to full health with the correct number of copies.

```
vagrant@mon1:~$ sudo ceph -s
    cluster d9f58afd-3e62-4493-ba80-0356290b3d9f
     health HEALTH_WARN
            clock skew detected on mon.mon2
            41 pgs degraded
            64 pgs stuck unclean
            41 pgs undersized
            recovery 13/36 objects degraded (36.111%)
            recovery 5/36 objects misplaced (13.889%)
            Monitor clock skew detected
     monmap e2: 3 mons at {mon1=192.168.0.41:6789/0,mon2=192.168.0.42:6789/0,mon3=192.168.0.43:6789/0}
            election epoch 10, quorum 0,1,2 mon1,mon2,mon3
        mgr active: mon2 standbys: mon3, mon1
     osdmap e48: 4 osds: 2 up, 2 in; 23 remapped pgs
            flags sortbitwise,require_jewel_osds,require_kraken_osds
      pgmap v182: 64 pgs, 1 pools, 37572 kB data, 18 objects
            1184 MB used, 16744 MB / 17929 MB avail
            13/36 objects degraded (36.111%)
            5/36 objects misplaced (13.889%)
                  41 active+undersized+degraded
                  23 active+remapped
```

Investigating asserts

Assertions are used in Ceph to ensure that during the execution of the code any assumptions that have been made about the operating environment remain true. These assertions are scattered throughout the Ceph code and are designed to catch any conditions that may go on to cause further problems if the code is not stopped.

If you trigger an assertion in Ceph, it's likely that some form of data has a value that is unexpected. This may be caused by some form or corruption or unhandled bug.

If an OSD causes an assert and refuses to start anymore, the usual recommended approach would be to destroy the OSD, recreate it, and then let Ceph backfill objects back to it. If you have a reproducible failure scenario, then it is probably also worth filing a bug in the Ceph bug tracker.

As mentioned several times in this chapter, OSDs can fail either due to hardware faults or soft faults in either the stored data or OSD code. Soft faults are much more likely to affect multiple OSDs at once; if your OSDs have become corrupted due to a power outage, then it's highly likely that more than once OSD will be affected. In the case, where multiple OSDs are failing with asserts and they are causing one or more PG's in the cluster to be offline, simply recreating the OSDs is not an option. The OSDs that are offline contain all the three copies of the PG, and so, recreating the OSDs would make any form of recovery impossible and result in permanent data loss.

First, before attempting the recovery techniques in this chapter, such as exporting and importing PGs, investigation into the asserts should be done. Depending on your technical ability and how much downtime you can tolerate before you need to start focusing on other recovery steps, investigating the asserts may not result in any success. By investigating the assert and looking through the Ceph source referenced by the assert, it may be possible to identify the cause of the assert. If this is possible then a fix can be implemented in the Ceph code to avoid the OSD asserting. Don't be afraid to reach out to the community for help on these matters.

In some cases, the OSD corruption may be so severe that even the `objectstore` tool may itself assert when trying to read from the OSD. This will limit the recovery steps outlined in this chapter, and trying to fix the reason behind the assert might be the only option. Although by this point, it is likely that the OSD has sustained heavy corruption, and recovery may not be possible.

Example assert

The following assert was taken from the Ceph user's mailing list:

```
2017-03-02 22:41:32.338290 7f8bfd6d7700 -1 osd/ReplicatedPG.cc: In function
'void ReplicatedPG::hit_set_trim(ReplicatedPG::RepGather*, unsigned int)'
thread 7f8bfd6d7700 time 2017-03-02 22:41:32.335020

osd/ReplicatedPG.cc: 10514: FAILED assert(obc)


ceph version 0.94.7 (d56bdf93ced6b80b07397d57e3fa68fe68304432)
 1: (ceph::__ceph_assert_fail(char const*, char const*, int, char
const*)+0x85) [0xbddac5]
 2: (ReplicatedPG::hit_set_trim(ReplicatedPG::RepGather*, unsigned
int)+0x75f) [0x87e48f]
 3: (ReplicatedPG::hit_set_persist()+0xedb) [0x87f4ab]
 4: (ReplicatedPG::do_op(std::tr1::shared_ptr<OpRequest>&)+0xe3a)
[0x8a0d1a]
 5: (ReplicatedPG::do_request(std::tr1::shared_ptr<OpRequest>&,
ThreadPool::TPHandle&)+0x68a) [0x83be4a]
 6: (OSD::dequeue_op(boost::intrusive_ptr<PG>,
std::tr1::shared_ptr<OpRequest>, ThreadPool::TPHandle&)+0x405) [0x69a5c5]
 7: (OSD::ShardedOpWQ::_process(unsigned int,
ceph::heartbeat_handle_d*)+0x333) [0x69ab33]
 8: (ShardedThreadPool::shardedthreadpool_worker(unsigned int)+0x86f)
[0xbcd1cf]
 9: (ShardedThreadPool::WorkThreadSharded::entry()+0x10) [0xbcf300]
 10: (()+0x7dc5) [0x7f8c1c209dc5]
 11: (clone()+0x6d) [0x7f8c1aceaced]
```

The top part of the assert shows the function from where the assert was triggered and also the line number and file where the assert can be found. In this example, the `hit_set_trim` function is apparently the cause of the assert. We can look into the `ReplicatePG.cc` file around line 10514 to try and understand what might have happened. Note the version of the Ceph release (0.94.7), as the line number in GitHub will only match if you are looking at the same version.

From looking at the code, it appears that the returned value from the `get_object_context` function call is directly passed to the `assert` function. If the value is zero, indicating the object containing the hitset to be trimmed could not be found, then the OSD will assert. From this information, there is a chance that an investigation could be done to work out why the object is missing and recover it. Or the `assert` command could be commented out to see if it allows the OSD to continue functioning. In this example, allowing the OSD to continue processing will likely not cause an issue, but in other cases, an assert may be the only thing stopping more serious corruption from occurring. If you don't understand 100% why something is causing an assert, and the impact of any potential change you might make, seek help before continuing.

Summary

In this chapter, you have learned how to troubleshoot Ceph when all looks lost. In the event that Ceph is unable to recover PGs itself, you now understand how to manually rebuild PGs from failed OSDs. You can also rebuild the monitor's database in the event that you lose all of your monitor nodes but still have access to your OSDs. In the event of a complete cluster failure that you are unable to recover from, you also have gone through the process of recreating RBDs from the raw data remaining on your OSDs. Finally, you have configured two separate Ceph clusters and configured replication between them using RBD mirroring to provide a failover option, should you encounter a complete Ceph cluster failure.

19
Operations and Maintenance

In this chapter, we explore the panoply of day-to-day tasks for maintaining your Ceph clusters. The topics covered include:

- Topology
- Configuration
- Common tasks
- Scrubs
- Logs
- Working with remote hands

We'll cover a lot of ground in this chapter. Be sure to take periodic breaks to refuel with garlic fries.

Topology

In this section, we'll describe commands to explore the logical layout of an example Ceph cluster. Before we go changing anything, we need to know exactly what we have first.

The 40,000 foot view

To visually see the overall topology of a Ceph cluster, run `ceph osd tree`. This will show us at once the hierarchy of CRUSH buckets, including the name of each bucket, the weight, whether it is marked up or down, a weight adjustment, and an advanced attribute of `primary affinity`. This cluster was provisioned initially with 3 racks each housing 4 hosts for a total of 12 OSD nodes. Each OSD node (also known as host, also known as server) in turn houses 24 OSD drives.

```
# ceph osd tree
ID   WEIGHT     TYPE NAME         UP/DOWN  REWEIGHT  PRIMARY-AFFINITY
-1   974.89661  root default
-14  330.76886      rack r1
-2   83.56099           host data001
 0    3.48199               osd.0      up   1.00000        1.00000
...
23    3.48199               osd.23     up   1.00000        1.00000
-3   80.08588           host data002
24    3.48199               osd.24     up   1.00000        1.00000
25    3.48199               osd.25     up   1.00000        1.00000
26    3.48199               osd.26     up   1.00000        1.00000
27    3.48199               osd.27     up   1.00000        1.00000
28    3.48199               osd.28     up   1.00000        1.00000
29    3.48199               osd.29     up   1.00000        1.00000
30    3.48199               osd.30     up   1.00000        1.00000
31    3.48199               osd.31     up   1.00000        1.00000
32    3.48199               osd.32     up   1.00000        1.00000
34    3.48199               osd.34     up   1.00000        1.00000
35    3.48199               osd.35     up   1.00000        1.00000
36    3.48199               osd.36     up   1.00000        1.00000
37    3.48199               osd.37     up   1.00000        1.00000
38    3.48199               osd.38     up   1.00000        1.00000
39    3.48199               osd.39     down        0        1.00000
40    3.48199               osd.40     up   1.00000        1.00000
41    3.48199               osd.41     up   1.00000        1.00000
42    3.48199               osd.42     up   1.00000        1.00000
43    3.48199               osd.43     up   1.00000        1.00000
44    3.48199               osd.44     up   1.00000        1.00000
45    3.48199               osd.45     up   1.00000        1.00000
46    3.48199               osd.46     up   1.00000        1.00000
47    3.48199               osd.47     up   1.00000        1.00000
-4   83.56099           host data003
48    3.48199               osd.48     up   1.00000        1.00000
...
-5   83.56099           host data004
72    3.48199               osd.72     up   1.00000        1.00000
...
```

```
 95    3.48199              osd.95      up  1.00000        1.00000
-15  330.76810      rack r2
 -6   83.56099          host data005
 96    3.48199              osd.96      up  1.00000        1.00000
...
 -7   80.08557          host data006
120    3.48199              osd.120     up  1.00000        1.00000
...
 -8   83.56055          host data007
 33    3.48169              osd.33      up  1.00000        1.00000
144    3.48169              osd.144     up  1.00000        1.00000
...
232    3.48169              osd.232     up  1.00000        1.00000
 -9   83.56099          host data008
168    3.48199              osd.168     up  1.00000        1.00000
-16  313.35965      rack r3
-10   83.56099          host data009
192    3.48199              osd.192     up  1.00000        1.00000
...
-11   69.63379          host data010
133    3.48169              osd.133     up  1.00000        1.00000
...
-12   83.56099          host data011
239    3.48199              osd.239     up  1.00000        1.00000
...
-13   76.60388          host data012
...
286    3.48199              osd.286     up  1.00000        1.00000
```

Let's go over what this tree is telling us. Note that a number of similar lines have been replaced with ellipses for brevity, a practice we will continue throughout this and following chapters.

After the column headers the first data line is:

```
-1 974.89661 root default
```

The first column is an ID number that Ceph uses internally, and with which we rarely need to concern ourselves. The second column under the WEIGHT heading is the *CRUSH weight*. By default, the CRUSH weight of any bucket corresponds to its raw capacity in TB; in this case we have a bit shy of a **petabyte** (**PB**) of raw space. We'll see that this weight is the sum of the weights of the buckets under the root in the tree.

Since this cluster utilizes the conventional replication factor of 3, roughly 324 TB of usable space is currently available in this cluster. The balance of the line is `root default`, which tells us that this CRUSH bucket is of the `root` type, and that it's name is `default`. Complex Ceph clusters can contain multiple roots, but most need only one.

The next line is as follows:

```
-14 330.76886     rack r1
```

It shows a bucket of type rack, with a weight of roughly 330 TB. Skipping ahead a bit we see two more rack buckets with weights 330 and 313 each. Their sum gets us to the roughly 974 TB capacity (weight) of the root bucket. When the rack weights are not equal, as in our example, usually either they contain different numbers of host buckets (or simply *hosts*), or more often their underlying hosts have unequal weights.

Next we see the following:

```
-2  83.56099         host data001
```

This indicates a bucket of type `host`, with the name `data001`. As with `root` and `rack` buckets, the weight reflects the raw capacity (before replication) of the underlying buckets in the hierarchy. Below `rack1` in our hierarchy we see hosts named `data001`, `data002`, `data003`, and `data004`. In our example, we see that host `data002` presents a somewhat lower weight than the other three racks. This may mean that a mixture of drive sizes has been deployed or that some drives were missed during initial deployment. In our example, though, the host only contains 23 OSD buckets (or simply OSDs) instead of the expected 24. This reflects a drive that has failed and been removed entirely, or one that was not deployed in the first place.

Under each `host` bucket we see a number of OSD entries.

```
24 3.48199 osd.24 up 1.00000 1.00000
```

In our example, these drives are SAS SSDs each nominally 3840 GB in size, which we describe as the *marketing* capacity. The discrepancy between that figure and the 3.48199 TB weight presented here is due to multiple factors:

- The marketing capacity is expressed in base 10 units; everything else uses base 2 units
- Each drive carves out 10 GB for journal use
- XFS filesystem overhead

Note also that one OSD under `data002` is marked down. This could be a question of the process having been killed or a hardware failure. The CRUSH weight is unchanged, but the weight adjustment is set to 0, which means that data previously allocated to this drive has been directed elsewhere. When we restart the OSD process successfully, the weight adjustment returns to one and data backfills to the drive.

Note also that while many Ceph commands will present OSDs and other items sorted, the IDs (or names) of OSDs on a given host or rack are a function of the cluster's history. When deployed sequentially the numbers will increment neatly, but over time as OSDs and hosts are added and removed discontinuities will accrue. In the above example, note that OSD 33 (also known as `osd.33`) currently lives on host `data007` instead of data002 as one might expect from the present pattern. This reflects the sequence of events:

- Drive failed on `data002` and was removed
- Drive failed on `data007` and was removed
- The replacement drive on `data007` was deployed as a new OSD

When deploying OSDs, Ceph generally picks the lowest unused number; in our case that was 33. It is futile to try to maintain any given OSD number arrangement; it will change over time as drives and host come and go, and the cluster is expanded.

A number of Ceph status commands accept an optional `-f` json or `-fjson –pretty` switch, which results in output in a form less readable by humans, but more readily parsed by code. The format of default format commands may change between releases, but the JSON output formats are mostly constant. For this reason management and monitoring scripts are encouraged to use the `-f json` output format to ensure continued proper operation when Ceph itself is upgraded.

```
    # ceph osd tree -f json
{"nodes":[{"id":-1,"name":"default","type":"root","type_id":10,"children":[
-16,-15,-14]},{"id":-14,"name":"r1","type":"rack","type_id":3,"children":[-
5,-4,-3,-2]},{"id":-2,"name":"data001","type":"host","type_id":1,"children"
:
[23,22,21,20,19,18,17,16,15,14,13,12,11,10,9,8,7,6,5,4,3,2,1,0]},{"id":0,"n
ame":"osd.0","type":"osd","type_id":0,"crush_weight":3.481995,"depth":3,"ex
ists":1,"status":"up","reweight":1.000000,"primary_affinity":1.000000},{"id
":1,"name":"osd
.1","type":"osd","type_id":0,"crush_weight":3.481995,"depth":3,"exists":1,"
status":"up","reweight":1.000000,"primary_affinity":1.000000},{"id":2,"name
":"osd.2","type":"osd","type_id":0,"crush_weight":3.481995,"depth":3,"exist
s":1,"status":"
up","reweight":1.000000,"primary_affinity":1.000000},{"id":3,"name":"osd.3"
,"type":"osd","type_id":0,"crush_weight":3.481995,"depth":3,"exists":1,"sta
tus":"up","reweight":1.000000,"primary_affinity":1.000000},{"id":4,"name":"
```

```
osd.4","type":"
    ...
```

The `-f json-pretty` output format is something of a compromise: it includes structure to aid programmatic parsing, but also uses whitespace to allow humans to readily inspect visually.

```
# ceph osd tree -f json-pretty
{
    "nodes": [
        {
            "id": -1,
            "name": "default",
            "type": "root",
            "type_id": 10,
            "children": [
                -16,
                -15,
                -14
            ]
        },
        {
            "id": -14,
            "name": "1",
            "type": "rack",
            "type_id": 3,
            "children": [
                -5,
                -4,
                -3,
                -2
            ]
        },
        {
            "id": -2,
            "name": "data001",
            "type": "host",
            "type_id": 1,
            "children": [
                23,
                22,
                21,
                ...
```

One may for example extract a list of OSDs that have a non-default reweight adjustment value, using the `jq` utility. This approach saves a lot of tedious and error-prone coding with `awk` or `perl`.

```
# ceph osd tree -f json | jq \
  '.nodes[]|select(.type=="osd")|select(.reweight != 1)|.id'
11
66
```

Some commands in Ceph that show a detailed status emit hundreds or thousands of lines of output. It is strongly suggested you to enable unlimited scroll back in your terminal application and to pipe such commands through a pager, for example, `less`.

iTerm2 is a free package for macOS that offers a wealth of features not found in Apple's bundled Terminal.app. It can be downloaded from https://www.iterm2.com/.

Drilling down

Next we'll explore a number of commands that can help us collect specific information about the logical units within our topology.

OSD dump

The ceph osd dump command shows a wealth of lower-level information about our clusters. This includes a list of pools with their attributes and a list of OSDs each including reweight adjustment, up/in status, and more. This command is mostly used in unusual troubleshooting situations.

```
# ceph osd dump | head
epoch 33291
fsid 3369c9c6-bfaf-4114-9c31-ncc17014d0fe
created 2017-09-06 20:21:06.448220
modified 2017-09-17 21:38:44.530321
flags sortbitwise,require_jewel_osds
pool 1 'rbd' replicated size 3 min_size 2 crush_ruleset 0 object_hash
rjenkins pg_num 16384 pgp_num 16384 last_change 31616 flags
hashpspool,nodelete,nopgchange,nosizechange stripe_width 0
        removed_snaps [1~3]
max_osd 287
    osd.0 up   in  weight 1 up_from 31886 up_thru 33113 down_at 31884
last_clean_interval [4,31884) 10.8.45.15:6800/116320
```

```
10.24.49.15:6828/1116320 10.24.49.15:6829/1116320 10.8.45.15:6829/1116
    320 exists,up 34a68621-b8dc-4c3a-b47e-26acaacfc838
    osd.1 up   in   weight 1 up_from 8 up_thru 33108 down_at 0
last_clean_interval [0,0) 10.8.45.15:6802/117132 10.24.49.15:6802/117132
10.24.49.15:6803/117132 10.8.45.15:6803/117132 exists,up
f5a3a635-4058-4499-99af-1b340192e321
    . . .
```

OSD list

The ceph osd ls command simply returns a list of the OSD numbers currently deployed within the cluster.

```
# ceph osd ls | head -3
0
1
2
# ceph osd ls |wc
    280     280     1010
#
```

This information could be derived by processing the output of ceph osd tree, but this is a convenient way to drive all in a single command

OSD find

To locate the host on which a given OSD lives, the ceph osd find command is invaluable.

```
# ceph osd find 66 { "osd": 66, "ip": "10.8.45.17:6836\/130331",
"crush_location": { "host": "data003", "rack": "r1", "root": "default" } }
```

This is especially useful when monitoring detects that an OSD is down; the first step is typically to locate the host that houses it so that one may check it out, for example, by inspecting Ceph OSD and syslog files. In older Ceph releases, this command omitted the last newline, which was a bit awkward. As of the Ceph Jewel release this has been fixed.

CRUSH dump

This command presents much the same information as ceph osd tree, though in a different, JSON, format. Note a peek into the additional bucket types that Ceph predefines for large and complex deployments. As before many of the 2899 lines of output this command yielded on the author's reference cluster are cropped for brevity.

```
# ceph osd crush dump | more
{
    "devices": [
        {
            "id": 0,
            "name": "osd.0"
        },
        {
            "id": 1,
            "name": "osd.1"
        },
        ...
        {
            "id": 286,
            "name": "osd.286"
        }
    ],
    "types": [
        {
            "type_id": 0,
            "name": "osd"
        },
        {
            "type_id": 1,
            "name": "host"
        },
        {
            "type_id": 2,
            "name": "chassis"
        },
        {
            "type_id": 3,
            "name": "rack"
        },
        {
            "type_id": 4,
            "name": "row"
        },
        {
            "type_id": 5,
```

```
                    "name": "pdu"
            },
            {
                    "type_id": 6,
                    "name": "pod"
            },
            {
                    "type_id": 7,
                    "name": "room"
            },
            {
                    "type_id": 8,
                    "name": "datacenter"
            },
            {
                    "type_id": 9,
                    "name": "region"
            },
            {
                    "type_id": 10,
                    "name": "root"
            }
    ],
    "buckets": [
            {
                    "id": -1,
                    "name": "default",
                    "type_id": 10,
                    "type_name": "root",
                    "weight": 63890823,
                    "alg": "straw",
                    "hash": "rjenkins1",
                    "items": [
                            {
                                    "id": -14,
                                    "weight": 21677267,
                                    "pos": 0
                            },
                            {
                                    "id": -15,
                                    "weight": 21677218,
                                    "pos": 1
                            },
                            {
                                    "id": -16,
                                    "weight": 20536338,
                                    "pos": 2
                            }
```

```
            ]
    },
    {
        "id": -2,
        "name": "data001",
        "type_id": 1,
        "type_name": "host",
        "weight": 5476704,
        "alg": "straw",
        "hash": "rjenkins1",
        "items": [
            {
                "id": 0,
                "weight": 228196,
                "pos": 0
            },
            {
                "id": 1,
                "weight": 228196,
                "pos": 1
            },
            . . .
```

Pools

Ceph allows us to create multiple pools of storage, with sizes and attributes specified according to the unique needs of each. For example, in an OpenStack deployment one will typically find a large Cinder pool, a medium to large Glance pool, and perhaps a number of pools for the RGW service. Here we'll succinctly show you a number of commands for managing them.

To simply list the pools provisioned:

```
# rados lspools
rbd
# ceph osd lspools
1 rbd,
```

There are sometimes multiple ways to accomplish a given task within Ceph. Here's another, showing the larger constellation of pools provisioned for OpenStack and the RADOS GateWay service using the Ceph Firefly release. This same information can also be displayed with ceph osd pool ls detail.

```
# ceph osd dump | grep pool
pool 3 'csi-a-cinder-volume-1' replicated size 3 min_size 2
```

```
crush_ruleset 0 object_hash rjenkins pg_num 16384 pgp_num 16384 last_change
261136 stripe_width 0
    pool 4 csi-a-glance-image-1' replicated size 3 min_size 2 crush_ruleset
0 object_hash rjenkins pg_num 16384 pgp_num 16384 last_change 261134
stripe_width 0
    pool 5 '.rgw' replicated size 3 min_size 2 crush_ruleset 0 object_hash
rjenkins pg_num 1024 pgp_num 1024 last_change 882 stripe_width 0
    pool 6 '.rgw.control' replicated size 3 min_size 2 crush_ruleset 0
object_hash rjenkins pg_num 1024 pgp_num 1024 last_change 884 stripe_width
0
    pool 7 '.rgw.gc' replicated size 3 min_size 2 crush_ruleset 0
object_hash rjenkins pg_num 1024 pgp_num 1024 last_change 886 stripe_width
0
    pool 8 '.log' replicated size 3 min_size 2 crush_ruleset 0 object_hash
rjenkins pg_num 1024 pgp_num 1024 last_change 888 stripe_width 0
    pool 9 '.intent-log' replicated size 3 min_size 2 crush_ruleset 0
object_hash rjenkins pg_num 1024 pgp_num 1024 last_change 890 stripe_width
0
    pool 10 '.usage' replicated size 3 min_size 2 crush_ruleset 0
object_hash rjenkins pg_num 1024 pgp_num 1024 last_change 892 stripe_width
0
    pool 11 '.users' replicated size 3 min_size 2 crush_ruleset 0
object_hash rjenkins pg_num 1024 pgp_num 1024 last_change 894 stripe_width
0
    pool 12 '.users.email' replicated size 3 min_size 2 crush_ruleset 0
object_hash rjenkins pg_num 1024 pgp_num 1024 last_change 896 stripe_width
0
    pool 13 '.users.swift' replicated size 3 min_size 2 crush_ruleset 0
object_hash rjenkins pg_num 1024 pgp_num 1024 last_change 898 stripe_width
0
 pool 14 '.users.uid' replicated size 3 min_size 2 crush_ruleset 0
object_hash rjenkins pg_num 1024 pgp_num 1024 last_change 165075
stripe_width 0
    pool 15 '.rgw.buckets' replicated size 3 min_size 2 crush_ruleset 0
object_hash rjenkins pg_num 16384 pgp_num 16384 last_change 902
stripe_width 0
    pool 17 'css-a-glance-image-1' replicated size 3 min_size 2
crush_ruleset 0 object_hash rjenkins pg_num 16384 pgp_num 16384 last_change
906 stripe_width 0
    pool 18 '.rgw.root' replicated size 3 min_size 2 crush_ruleset 0
object_hash rjenkins pg_num 8 pgp_num 8 last_change 908 stripe_width 0
    pool 19 '.rgw.buckets.index' replicated size 3 min_size 2 crush_ruleset
0 object_hash rjenkins pg_num 1024 pgp_num 1024 last_change 261117
stripe_width 0
    pool 20 '' replicated size 3 min_size 2 crush_ruleset 0 object_hash
rjenkins pg_num 8 pgp_num 8 last_change 7282 stripe_width 0
```

We see that each pool is configured to maintain three copies of data and to still service operations if only two are active. The CRUSH ruleset is specified; here all pools use the same ruleset as is fairly common for Ceph deployments. The three largest pools each contain 16,384 placement groups.

Yes, there's a pool with a null name, which is an artifact of an automation inventory misconfiguration. If this ever happens to you, use the following command to clean up:

```
# rados rmpool "" "" --yes-i-really-really-mean-it
successfully deleted pool
```

Ceph really really wants to be sure that we want to delete that pool, so it makes us enter the name twice and a strongly affirmative switch as well. With the Jewel and later releases, there is another step yet we can take to really, really, REALLY make sure we don't accidentally delete a production pool (and with it our jobs).

```
# ceph osd pool set csi-a-cinder-volume-1 nodelete true
```

Monitors

We discuss Ceph Monitors (also known as MONs or mons) in other chapters in detail, but we'll describe them a bit here as well for context. Ceph MONs maintain and serves a wealth of information about cluster topology and status. In this way they are a clearinghouse of sorts, accepting connections and updates from other Ceph daemons including other MONs, OSDs, and MDS instances.

Ceph MONs operate as a cluster, exploiting the Paxos consensus algorithm to ensure reliable and consistent operation as a quorum. The vital information collected and distributed by MONs includes:

- The mon map, which includes names, addresses, state, epoch, and so on for all MONs in the cluster. The mon map is vital for quorum maintenance and client connections.
- The CRUSH map, which includes similar information for the collection of OSDs holding Ceph's payload data. The CRUSH map is also the source of the information displayed by `ceph osd tree` as shown earlier.

- The MDS map of CephFS MetaData Servers.
- The PG map of which OSDs house each PG.
- Cluster flags.
- Cluster health.
- Authentication keys and client capabilities.

The mon map and quorum status information can be displayed by the `ceph mon stat` and `ceph mon dump` commands.

```
# ceph mon stat
e2: 5 mons at
{mon001=10.8.45.10:6789/0,mon002=10.8.45.11:6789/0,mon003=10.8.45.143:6789/
0,mon004=10.8.46.10:6789/0,mon005=10.8.46.11:6789/0}, election epoch 24,
quorum 0,1,2,3,4 mon001,mon002,mon003,mon004,mon005
# ceph mon dump
dumped monmap epoch 2
epoch 2
fsid 3369c9c6-bfaf-4114-9c31-576afa64d0fe
last_changed 2017-09-06 20:21:09.396928
created 2017-09-06 20:20:42.336193
0: 10.8.45.10:6789/0 mon.mon001
1: 10.8.45.11:6789/0 mon.mon002
2: 10.8.45.143:6789/0 mon.mon003
3: 10.8.46.10:6789/0 mon.mon004
4: 10.8.46.11:6789/0 mon.mon05
```

The output of `ceph mon stat` may look familiar: the `ceph status` command we'll explore later in this chapter includes this very information.

CephFS

To check the status of Ceph's MDS, run `ceph mds stat` or `ceph mds dump`.

```
# ceph mds stat
e85: 1/1/1 up {0=ceph-mds001=up:active}
# ceph mds dump
dumped mdsmap epoch 85
epoch     85
flags     0
created 2017-10-20 11:11:11.1138
modified 2017-10-22 13:13:13.1701
tableserver     0
root      0
session_timeout 60
```

```
session_autoclose          300
max_file_size    1099511627776
last_failure     0
last_failure_osd_epoch    666
compat  compat={},rocompat={},incompat={1=base v0.20,2=client writeable
ranges,3=default file layouts on dirs,4=dir inode in separate object,5=mds
uses versioned encoding,6=dirfrag is stored in omap}
max_mds    1
in         0
up         {0=1138}
failed
stopped
data_pools      0
metadta_pool    1
inline_data     disabled
1138:  196.168.1.1:6800/2046 'ceph-mds001' mds.0 13 up; active seq 4252
```

Configuration

Ceph's behavior is highly configurable and tunable via settings, which allow us to control Ceph's behavior and performance. Ceph daemons and clients at startup read /etc/ceph/ceph.conf to load configuration settings and other cluster information for the cluster named ceph. There are hundreds of values that can be set, but fortunately, we mostly need to concern ourselves with only a much smaller subset.

Cluster naming and configuration

The startup configuration file defines values that Ceph components need to start up and find each other. Many Ceph admins think of the file as always being named /etc/ceph/ceph.conf, but other names are possible. The directory /etc/ceph is the default location, but the filename's base is actually the name of a given cluster, which itself defaults to Ceph. Many installations, especially those with a single cluster, leave this defaulted, but custom names are becoming increasingly popular.

Throughout this book, we write in terms of the default cluster name `ceph`, but let's say we wish our cluster to be known as `cephelmerman`. Our configuration file will then be found at `/etc/ceph/cephelmerman.conf`. Most Ceph commands default to operating on a cluster named `ceph`, but now we would need to add the `--cluster cephelmerman` switch so that they find the proper cluster components. This quickly becomes cumbersome, but Ceph gives us a shortcut -- the contents of the `CEPH_ARGS` environment variable are appended to core commands. So in our example instead of typing the following:

```
# ceph status --cluster cephelmerman
# ceph -s --cluster cephelmerman
# ceph osd tree --cluster cephelmerman
```

We can instead issue (using the bash shell):

```
# export CEPH_ARGS="--cluster cephelmerman"
# ceph status
# ceph -s
# ceph osd tree
```

We do recommend using the default cluster name of ceph unless you have a compelling reason to vary it. As of the Jewel release, Ceph still suffers a few gotchas with non-default names, and the `ceph-deploy` utility we will explore later in this chapter does not yet honor `CEPH_ARGS`.

It is possible—though very uncommon—to run more than one Ceph logical cluster on the same set of hardware. At system startup Ceph will attempt to start daemons for any config file it files in `/etc/ceph`, that is, any file matching the pattern `/etc/ceph/*.conf`. Thus in this uncommon situation, we might see something like:

```
# ls -1 /etc/ceph
ceph.conf
cephelmerman.conf
music.conf
rhythm.conf
```

This is important to remember even for default, single-cluster deployments because it might seem convenient to stash backup copies when changes are made.

```
# ls -1 /etc/ceph
ceph.CR1138.conf
ceph.OLD.conf
ceph.conf
ceph.conf.old
ceph.old.conf
ceph.firefly.conf
```

In this example, when the system boots Ceph will most likely not behave as expected. For this reason, if you elect to keep backup copies of `ceph.conf`, it is vital that their filenames not end in `.conf`.

The Ceph configuration file

Ceph's config files comprise multiple sections, one global and one for each core Ceph component daemon. A few entries are mandatory; many are optional. Each section begins with a bracketed name, a convention that is often called the INI format, after its widespread use in MS-DOS. Let's go through these sections with some examples of their contents.

```
# cat /etc/ceph/ceph.conf
[global]
fsid = 5591400a-6868-447f-be89-thx1138656b6
max open files = 131072
mon initial members = ceph-mon0
mon host = 192.168.42.10
public network = 192.168.42.0/24
cluster network = 192.168.43.0/24
[client.libvirt]
admin socket = /var/run/ceph/$cluster-$type.$id.$pid.$cctid.asok
log file = /var/log/ceph/qemu-guest-$pid.log
[osd]
osd mkfs type = xfs
osd mkfs options xfs = -f -i size=2048
osd mount options xfs = noatime,largeio,inode64,swalloc
osd journal size = 100
[client.restapi]
public addr = 192.168.42.10:5000
keyring = /var/lib/ceph/restapi/ceph-restapi/keyring
log file = /var/log/ceph/ceph-restapi.log
```

The `[global]` section contains settings that are common to all components of a Ceph deployment. Settings entered here will apply to all Ceph components unless overridden in a later, component-specific section.

We discuss `fsid` a bit in other chapters; briefly, it is a unique identifier for a given cluster and must be present.

The `mon initial members` and `mon host` lines, however, are required; they enable Ceph Monitors to find each other. These lines also help Ceph OSD, RADOS Gateway, and other daemons find the cluster's MONs.

The `public network` definition is also required; it defines a network address range for Ceph's Monitor cluster. If `cluster network` is present it defines a dedicated IP network for Ceph's replication traffic. If no `cluster network` is defined, all traffic will share the `public network`.

The `[client.libvirt]` section includes settings appropriate for virtualization clients such as QEMU. Here the client is expected to be named `client.libvirt` and should possess the corresponding keyring to successfully authenticate to the cluster. Note that this section need not be present at all in `ceph.conf` files for MON, OSD, and RGW nodes, but it doesn't hurt to have it there. It may be convenient to include all sections in the `ceph.conf` file located on each Ceph node type; this can ease configuration management. In this example, we specify an `admin socket` to which one may connect to query the state of client library running within the hypervisor. We'll discuss admin sockets later in this chapter. The second line defines a `log file` to which the client should write events and other messages.

The `[osd]` section often garners the most attention from Ceph admins. In our example, `osd mkfs type` directs that FileStore OSDs should provision an XFS filesystem, vs EXT4, or btrfs.

The following `osd mkfs options xfs` line lists options to be specified on the command line when the OSD provisioning process invokes `mkfs.xfs`. The options in our example duplicate the defaults compiled into Ceph, but it can be useful to have them explicitly configured so that the parameters for new OSDs are very clear. One occasionally finds advice to add `-n size=65536` here, in an attempt to save CPU cycles. Don't do it. Ceph's use-case does not benefit from a non-default setting here, and this author has witnessed it precipitating untold grief. The defaults are best for almost everybody. Other options are possible if you *really* know what you are doing and understand that going back requires destroying and reprovisioning every OSD created by them.

Next we see the associated `osd mount options xfs` entry. Here again Ceph's defaults work well for most applications; change them only with careful study. Unlike `mkfs` options, mount options are only applied as each FileStore OSD is mounted at system startup, so changes here can be applied by stopping the OSD processes, unmounting their filesystems, and restarting. A somewhat more nuclear but entirely reasonable alternative is to temporarily set the `noout` flag and simply reboot the server.

 The `osd mount options xfs` shown above is taken straight from our sandbox, which sets non-default values. The default option list as of Jewel is `rw,noatime,inode64`; please do not take the above excerpt as a recommendation.

Last in our example's `[osd]` section is `osd journal size`. Our sandbox does not serve a real workload so the value is unusually small so as to not strain desktop virtualization. The suggested value in production is `10240` which provisions a 10 GB partition when colocating FileStore journals. This value is recommended as a safe one-size-fits-all. You may never fill a 10 GB journal before it flushes, but the safety margin is an easy tradeoff against saving a few trivial GBs for the FileStore filesystem.

The last section in our example is `[client.restapi]`. This section is only required when using the REST API for interrogating and managing Ceph clusters externally.

When the RGW service is used, an additional section is required for it as well.

Sharp-eyed readers may notice that ceph configuration settings are sometimes written with spaces in their names, and sometimes with underscores. For example:

`osd journal size = 10240`

and

`osd_journal_size = 10240`

are both valid. We recommend sticking with the underscore form for ease of selection with mouse/pointer clicks and tools like grep. This can also simplify management within scripts and other places where space characters might need to be escaped or quoted.

Admin sockets

Each Ceph daemon (and client if so enabled) listens on an *admin socket* for requests to get or set information or to perform certain actions. We can see these sockets in `/var/run/ceph`; here are examples from both OSD and MON nodes.

```
osd-1701# ls /var/run/ceph
ceph-osd.0.asok      ceph-osd.10.asok      ceph-osd.11.asok
ceph-osd.12.asok     ceph-osd.13.asok      ceph-osd.14.asok
ceph-osd.15.asok     ceph-osd.16.asok      ceph-osd.17.asok
ceph-osd.18.asok     ceph-osd.19.asok      ceph-osd.1.asok
ceph-osd.20.asok     ceph-osd.21.asok      ceph-osd.22.asok
ceph-osd.23.asok     ceph-osd.2.asok       ceph-osd.3.asok
ceph-osd.4.asok      ceph-osd.5.asok       ceph-osd.69.asok
ceph-osd.7.asok      ceph-osd.8.asok       ceph-osd.9.asok
mon-05# ls /var/run/ceph
ceph-mon.mon05.asok
```

To interact with `osd.69` we first ssh into the `osd-1701` system. We can then ask `osd.69` machine admin socket what it can do for us.

```
# ceph daemon osd.69 help
{
"config diff": "dump diff of current config and default config",
"config get": "config get <field>: get the config value",
"config set": "config set <field> <val> [<val> ...]: set a config
variable",
"config show": "dump current config settings",
"dump_blacklist": "dump blacklisted clients and times",
"dump_blocked_ops": "show the blocked ops currently in flight",
"dump_historic_ops": "show slowest recent ops",
"dump_op_pq_state": "dump op priority queue state",
"dump_ops_in_flight": "show the ops currently in flight",
"dump_reservations": "show recovery reservations",
"dump_watchers": "show clients which have active watches, and on which
objects",
"flush_journal": "flush the journal to permanent store",
"get_command_descriptions": "list available commands",
"get_heap_property": "get malloc extension heap property",
"get_latest_osdmap": "force osd to update the latest map from the mon",
"getomap": "output entire object map",
"git_version": "get git sha1",
"help": "list available commands",
"injectdataerr": "inject data error to an object",
"injectmdataerr": "inject metadata error to an object",
"log dump": "dump recent log entries to log file",
"log flush": "flush log entries to log file",
"log reopen": "reopen log file",
"objecter_requests": "show in-progress osd requests",
"ops": "show the ops currently in flight",
"perf dump": "dump perfcounters value",
"perf reset": "perf reset <name>: perf reset all or one perfcounter name",
"perf schema": "dump perfcounters schema",
"rmomapkey": "remove omap key",
"set_heap_property": "update malloc extension heap property",
"set_recovery_delay": "Delay osd recovery by specified seconds",
"setomapheader": "set omap header",
"setomapval": "set omap key",
"status": "high-level status of OSD",
"truncobj": "truncate object to length","version": "get ceph version"
}
```

Holy options, Batman! For day-to-day operations we need not become immediately or intimately familiar with all of these commands; many of them are useful primarily for arcane troubleshooting and development tasks. The most frequently used commands are near the top of the list.

In this chapter, we discuss a number of Ceph's configuration settings. The config commands presented by the admin socket allow us to extract the current settings from within a given OSD or MON. Just for a laugh, let's see how many of those there are, this time on a Ceph Jewel system:

```
# ceph daemon osd.1701 config show | wc -l
1116
```

Yikes! Over a thousand settings. How could we ever hope to understand and tune them all? As we'll explore more in the next section, for the most part we don't need to. Each Ceph release increasingly improves behavior and setting defaults; the vast majority of these settings are best left alone unless we have a compelling reason and really know what we're doing. Among the more frequently adjusted settings are ones that affect backfill and recovery.

```
# ceph daemon osd.1701 config show | egrep backfill\|recovery
  "osd_max_backfills": "3",
  "osd_min_recovery_priority": "0",
  "osd_backfill_full_ratio": "0.9",
  "osd_backfill_retry_interval": "10",
  "osd_allow_recovery_below_min_size": "true",
  "osd_recovery_threads": "1",
  "osd_backfill_scan_min": "64",
  "osd_backfill_scan_max": "512",
  "osd_recovery_thread_timeout": "30",
  "osd_recovery_thread_suicide_timeout": "300",
  "osd_recovery_sleep": "0",
  "osd_recovery_delay_start": "0",
  "osd_recovery_max_active": "3",
  "osd_recovery_max_single_start": "1",
  "osd_recovery_max_chunk": "8388608",
  "osd_recovery_max_omap_entries_per_chunk": "64000",
  "osd_recovery_forget_lost_objects": "false",
  "osd_scrub_during_recovery": "true",
  "osd_kill_backfill_at": "0",
  "osd_debug_skip_full_check_in_backfill_reservation": "false",
  "osd_debug_reject_backfill_probability": "0",
  "osd_recovery_op_priority": "3",
  "osd_recovery_op_warn_multiple": "16"
```

Yikes again! Twenty-three settings just for recovery and backfill! Again, many of these are best left alone, but as we'll discuss below several of them are commonly adjusted. Best practice for knowing what to tweak and what to leave be is to err on the side of defaults unless research, professional advice, and/or thorough testing support changes.

> The `dump_historic_ops` and `dump_ops_in_flight` commands to the admin socket are also invaluable when troubleshooting complex issues. Interpretation of this information can require advanced knowledge of Ceph's innards and protocols.

Another method of extracting information from running Ceph daemons is the `ceph tell` command issued from a MON or admin node.

```
# ceph tell osd.* version
osd.0: {
    "version": "ceph version 10.2.6
(656b5b63ed7c43bd014bcafd81b001959d5f089f)"
}
osd.1: {
    "version": "ceph version 10.2.6
(656b5b63ed7c43bd014bcafd81b001959d5f089f)"
}
osd.2: {
    "version": "ceph version 10.2.6
(656b5b63ed7c43bd014bcafd81b001959d5f089f)"
}
...
```

This offers a more limited set of functionality compared to that provided through admin sockets, but the version command is very useful when ensuring that all components of a cluster are running the desired (and usually same) release versions.

Ceph's Luminous release adds additional and quite handy ways to survey cluster components.

- `ceph versions`
- `ceph {mon,mds,osd,mgr}`
  Summarize the running versions of each type of daemon
- `ceph {mon,mds,osd,mgr} metadata`
- `ceph {mon,mds,osd,mgr}count-metadata <property>`
  Gather other daemon metadata

- `ceph features`

  Reports features supported by both daemons and clients connected to the cluster. This is priceless when ensuring that planned Ceph upgrades and certain cluster map changes will not break existing clients.

Injection

Earlier in this chapter we discussed Ceph settings defined in the `ceph.conf` config file. When present as each Ceph daemon starts up, these settings override compiled-in defaults. To borrow a term from the network router world, `ceph.conf` is an example of *stored, startup* or *saved config*. As circumstances cause us to adjust or augment these explicit file-based settings we can effect them by rolling restarts of Ceph daemon processes or even server reboots.

While Ceph's resilient and fault-tolerant architecture affords us the flexibility to carefully apply configuration changes by service restarts, there is faster and less disruptive method: **injection**.

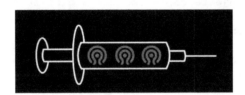

Ceph's injection mechanism is a handy and nearly immediate way to affect Ceph's *running config*, which is the set of values that each running daemon process holds within its memory address space. When we inject changes, we avoid the time and potential disruption that a sequential rolling restart of hundreds or thousands of Ceph daemons would entail.

Let's explore some real-world examples of the value of injection, and cover two important caveats as well.

One common use-case for injection is to adjust settings that affect the rate and distribution of backfill and recovery operations. Ceph initiates these as required to maintain data replication as OSDs come up and down or are added or removed from the cluster. It is natural to wish this process to complete as quickly as possible so that the cluster enjoys optimal resilience. Recovery operations, however, can contend with a client I/O; during heavy recovery, users may notice significant performance degradation or even failed operations.

When we anticipate heavy recovery traffic, say if we plan to remove an entire OSD node from service, we can use injection to temporarily throttle recovery to ensure that it does not overwhelm routine operations. First, let's consider the following set of Ceph settings and their default values as of Ceph's Hammer release

osd_recovery_max_single_start (this setting may be undocumented for Hammer)	5
osd_max_backfills	10
osd_recovery_op_priority	10
osd_recovery_max_active	15

For many Hammer clusters, these default values are overly aggressive and can precipitate user impact and even dreaded *slow requests*. We can lower (or increase) them on a temporary or experimental basis to accommodate planned maintenance or to converge on an optimal balance between recovery speed and client impact. Each Ceph OSD daemon maintains its own running state, and we can inject new values into one or all of them with a single command issued from an admin or MON node.

```
# ceph tell osd.\* injectargs '--osd_max_backfills 1 --
osd_recovery_max_active 1 --osd_recovery_max_single_start 1 --
osd_recovery_op_priority 1'
osd.0: osd_max_backfills = '1' osd_recovery_max_active = '1' (unchangeable)
osd_recovery_max_single_start = '1' (unchangeable) osd_recovery_op_priority
= '1' (unchangeable)
osd.1: osd_max_backfills = '1' osd_recovery_max_active = '1' (unchangeable)
osd_recovery_max_single_start = '1' (unchangeable) osd_recovery_op_priority
= '1' (unchangeable)
    . . .
```

Note the (unchangeable) tags appended to the results for three out of our four variables. This is intended to alert us to values that we can inject, but which do not take effect immediately. Not all values change behavior when injected, some may not be injected at all. In the above example, these messages would lead us to believe that our efforts are in vain and that we must change ceph.conf and restart all OSDs to effect the new values. As of Ceph's Jewel release, though, the code that issues these warnings does not always accurately determine the effectiveness of injection for certain values, including those above.

Experience tells us that these particular values do in fact take effect immediately. Until the code is improved, unfortunately, one must either determine the truth via tests or by researching the experiences of others within the community. Other values known to this author to be effective when injected include

- `osd_scrub_max_interval`
- `osd_deep_scrub_interval`
- `mon_pg_warn_max_per_osd`

Alert readers may infer from the third setting above that one can also successfully inject values into not only OSDs but also Ceph MONs.

An important limitation of injection is that since it modifies only the running config and not the stored config, changes are lost when each Ceph daemon or server is restarted or reboots. Configuration via injection is invaluable for effecting immediate change with minimal disruption, especially when testing the efficacy of a given set of values. Injection helps us respond quickly to incidents within our clusters, and also to temporarily optimize behavior profiles during maintenance operations. Settings that we wish to persist permanently must be also be written to the stored config in `ceph.conf` or they will be lost in the future as servers are restarted.

> *Merci beaucoup* to Sébastien Han for his gracious permission to use the delightful syringe graphic above.
>
> Additional information regarding Ceph's myriad and subtle configuration settings may be found here `http://docs.ceph.com/docs/master/rados/configuration/ceph-conf`.

> Ceph's vast array of settings changes somewhat with each release; values for earlier versions are available under release-specific URL paths, for example, for Hammer consult `http://docs.ceph.com/docs/hammer/rados/configuration/osd-config-ref/`.
>
> The authoritative source for settings and their defaults is, of course, the source. For Luminous their definitions may be found here: `https://github.com/ceph/ceph/blob/luminous/src/common/options.cc`
>
> `Older Ceph source releases define defaults in config_opts.h`

Configuration management

Many Ceph admins exploit *configuration management* software to ensure correct and consistent application of packages and config files. Popular systems include Puppet, Chef, Ansible, and cfengine. Such systems are invaluable for ensuring that all systems remain consistent and up to date throughout their life cycle, especially when configuration settings are changed and hosts come and go.

Typical configuration management systems allow one to distribute an entire file to multiple managed systems. It is also usually possible to employ *templating*, a scheme by which a skeleton outline of a file is distributed to remote systems with embedded markup that allows variable interpolation, conditional inclusion of text, iterators, and even calculation of values for the destination file. This allows one to centrally and at scale manage files that may contain both invariant text and system-specific values.

Details of managing Ceph with each configuration management tool are beyond the scope of this book, but many resources are available online. Your natural choice may be a system already implemented by your organization.

One Ceph-specific management system that is rapidly maturing and gaining popularity is `ceph-ansible`, which as you might guess is built upon the popular Ansible configuration and orchestration tool. We employed `ceph-ansible` in the previous chapter for effortless provisioning of our sandbox cluster and suggest its use for those starting out with Ceph, or those fed up with doing everything by hand, iteratively.

`Ceph-ansible` may be found here:
`http://docs.ceph.com/ceph-ansible/master/`

Scrubs

Data corruption is rare but it does happen, a phenomenon described scientifically as *bit-rot*. Sometimes we write to a drive, and a surface or cell failure results in reads failing or returning something other than what we wrote. HBA misconfiguration, SAS expander flakes, firmware design flaws, drive electronics errors, and medium failures can also corrupt data. Surface errors affect between 1 in 10^{16} to as many as 1 in 10^{14} bits stored on HDDs. Drives can also become unseated due to human error or even a truck rumbling by. This author has also seen literal cosmic rays flip bits.

Ceph lives for strong data integrity and has a mechanism to alert us of this situation: *scrubs*. Scrubs are somewhat analogous to `fsck` on a filesystem and the *patrol reads* or *surface scans* that many HBAs run. The idea is to check each replicated copy of data to ensure that they're mutually consistent. Since copies of data are distributed throughout the cluster this is done at **Placement Group** (**PG**) granularity. Each PG's objects reside together on the same set of OSDs so it is natural and efficient to scrub them together.

When a given PG is scrubbed, the primary OSD for that PG calculates a checksum of data and requests that the other OSDs in the PG's Acting Set do the same. The checksums are compared; if they agree, all is well. If they do not agree, Ceph flags the PG in question with the `inconsistent` state, and its complement of data becomes inaccessible.

Ceph scrubs, like dark glasses, come in two classes: *light* and *deep*.

Light scrubs are also known as *shallow* scrubs or simply *scrubs* and are, well, lightweight and by default are performed for every PG every day. They checksum and compare only object metadata (such as size, XATTR, and omap data) and completely quickly and without taking much in the way of resources. Filesystem errors and rare Ceph bugs can be caught by light scrubs.

Deep scrubs read and checksum all of the PG's objects payload data. Since each replica of a PG may hold multiple gigabytes of data, these require substantially more resources than light scrubs. Large reads from media take a much longer time to complete and contend with ongoing client operations, so deep scrubs are spread across a longer period of time, by default, this is one week.

Many Ceph operators find that even weekly runs result in unacceptable impact and use the `osd_deep_scrub_interval` setting in `ceph.conf` to spread them out over a longer period. There are also options to align deep scrubs with off-hours or other times of lessened client workload. One may also prevent deep scrubs from slowing recovery (as Ceph scrambles to restore data replication) by configuring `osd_scrub_during_recovery` with a value of `false`. This applies at PG granularity, not across the entire cluster, and helps avoid the dreaded blocked requests that can result when scrub and recovery operations align to disrupt pesky user traffic.

Scrub settings can be dynamically adjusted throughout the cluster through the injection mechanism we explored earlier in this chapter, with the requisite caveat regarding permanence. Say as our awesome cluster has become a victim of its own success we find that deep scrubs are becoming too aggressive and we want to space them out over four weeks instead of cramming into just one but don't want to serially restart hundreds of OSD daemons. We can stage the change in `ceph.conf` and also immediately update the running config (Note: the value is specified in seconds; 4 weeks x 7 days x 24 hours x 60 minutes x 60 seconds = 2419200).

```
# ceph tell osd.* injectargs '--osd_deep_scrub_interval 2419200'
```

We can also exploit flags to turn scrubs off and on completely throughout the cluster if say they are getting in the way of a deep dive into cluster protocol dynamics or if one wishes to test or refute an assertion that they are responsible for poor performance. Leaving deep scrubs disabled for a long period of time can result in a thundering herd phenomenon, especially in Ceph's Hammer and earlier releases, so it is wise to not forget to re-enable them.

A well-engineered cluster does just fine with scrubs running even during rolling reboots, so you are encouraged to resist the urge to disable them for the duration of maintenance. Ceph Jewel and later releases leverage the `osd_scrub_interval_randomize_ratio` to mitigate this effect by slewing scrub scheduling to distribute them evenly, which additionally helps prevent them from clumping up. Remember that light scrubs consume little in the way of resources, so it even more rarely makes sense to disable them.

```
# ceph osd set noscrub
set noscrub
# ceph osd set nodeep-scrub
set nodeep-scrub
...
# ceph osd unset noscrub
# ceph osd unset nodeep-scrub
```

Bit-flips affecting stored data can remain latent for some time until a user thinks to read the affected object and gets back an error -- or worse, something different from what she wrote. Ceph stores multiple replicas of data to ensure data durability and accessibility, but serves reads only from the lead OSD in each placement group's Acting Set. This means that errors in the other replicas may be unnoticed until overwritten or when peering results in a change in lead OSD designation. This is why we actively seek them out with deep scrubs, to find and address them before they can impair client operations.

Here's an example of HDD errors due to a drive firmware design flaw precipitating an inconsistent PG. The format of such errors varies depending on drive type, Linux distribution, and kernel version, but they're similar with respect to the data presented.

```
Dec 15 10:55:44 csx-ceph1-020 kernel: end_request: I/O error, dev
  sdh, sector 1996791104
Dec 15 10:55:44 csx-ceph1-020 kernel: end_request: I/O error, dev
. sdh, sector 3936989616
Dec 15 10:55:44 csx-ceph1-020 kernel: end_request: I/O error, dev
  sdh, sector 4001236872
Dec 15 13:00:18 csx-ceph1-020 kernel: XFS (sdh1): xfs_log_force:
    error 5 returned.
Dec 15 13:00:48 csx-ceph1-020 kernel: XFS (sdh1): xfs_log_force:
    error 5 returned.
    . . .
```

Here we see the common pattern where drive errors result in large numbers of filesystem errors.

The server in the above example uses an HBA that we can manage with LSI's `storcli` utility, so let's see what we can discover about what happened.

```
[root@csx-ceph1-020 ~]# /opt/MegaRAID/storcli/storcli64 /c0 /eall
/s9 show all | grep Error
Media Error Count = 66
Other Error Count = 1
```

On these HBAs `Media Error Count` typically reflects surface (medium) errors and `Other Error Count` reflects something more systemic like drive electronics failure or accidental unseating.

Here's a log excerpt that shows Ceph's diligent deep scrubbing discovering the affected data replica.

```
2015-12-19 09:10:30.403351 osd.121 10.203.1.22:6815/3987 10429 :
[ERR] 20.376b shard 121: soid
a0c2f76b/rbd_data.5134a9222632125.0000000000000001/head//20
candidate had a read error
2015-12-19 09:10:33.224777 osd.121 10.203.1.22:6815/3987 10430 :
[ERR] 20.376b deep-scrub 0 missing, 1 inconsistent objects
2015-12-19 09:10:33.224834 osd.121 10.203.1.22:6815/3987 10431 :
[ERR] 20.376b deep-scrub 1 errors
```

This is then reflected in the output of `ceph health` or `ceph status`.

```
root@csx-a-ceph1-001:~# ceph status
   cluster ab84e9c8-e141-4f41-aa3f-bfe66707f388
    health HEALTH_ERR 1 pgs inconsistent; 1 scrub errors
    osdmap e46754: 416 osds: 416 up, 416 in
    pgmap v7734947: 59416 pgs: 59409 active+clean, 1
    active+clean+inconsistent, 6 active+clean+scrubbing+deep
root@csx-a-ceph1-001:~# ceph health detail
HEALTH_ERR 1 pgs inconsistent; 1 scrub errors
pg 20.376b is active+clean+inconsistent, acting [11,38,121]
1 scrub errors
```

The affected placement group has been flagged as inconsistent. Since this state impacts the availability of even a fraction of a percent of the cluster's data, the overall cluster health is set to `HEALTH_ERR`, which alerts us to a situation that must be addressed immediately.

Remediation of an inconsistent PG generally begins with identifying the ailing OSD; the log messages above direct us to `osd.121`. We use the procedure described later in this chapter to remove the OSD from service. The removal itself may clear the inconsistent state of the PG, or we may need to manually repair it.

```
root@csx-a-ceph1-001:~# ceph pg repair 20.376b
```

This directs Ceph to replace the faulty replicas of data by reading clean, authoritative copies from the OSDs in the balance of the Active Set.

Logs

Ceph performs extensive logging. Ceph can be configured to log directly through the central `syslog` or `rsyslog` service, but by default, it writes to local files. These are managed by the stock Linux `logrotate` facility. Here's the default rotation stanza that the Ceph Jewel release installs.

```
# cat /etc/logrotate.d/ceph.logrotate
/var/log/ceph/*.log {
    rotate 7
    daily
    compress
    sharedscripts
    postrotate
        killall -q -1 ceph-mon ceph-mds ceph-osd ceph-fuse radosgw
            || true
    endscript
```

```
    missingok
    notifempty
    su root ceph
}
```

The default retention is 7 days, which this author at times finds to be too short. To increase to four weeks, replace the 7 with 30, but be careful that the filesystem where /var/log lives has adequate free space. As we note later in this chapter, Ceph logs can become quite large at times, and modestly-provisioned systems experience filled filesystems. To mitigate the risk of logjams (clogged logs?) it may be expedient to also add a maxsize directive to rotate and compress logs sooner than daily if their sizes surge. The tradeoff is that logged messages will not always be neatly partitioned into roughly 24-hour chunks, but zcat and zgrep will quickly become your best friends.

MON logs

Ceph MONs by default write logs to /var/log/ceph/ceph-mon.hostname.log. On each MON server, there is also a global cluster log written by default to /var/log/ceph/ceph.log. The combined information in the latter can help correlate activity among the constellation of Ceph daemons one has deployed, so in this chapter, we will focus on it. These default filenames are a function of the default cluster name, which as you may have deduced is ceph. Tricky, isn't it? One may configure a cluster to use a non-default name; we discuss that briefly below in the context of configuration file naming. It reduces clutter in text boxes that may already be awkwardly wrapped. Most Ceph admins roll with the default name and as of the Jewel LTS release support for custom, names is still incomplete in certain utilities.

OSDs log into a file with a name that includes their ID number. The National Creature Consortium, for example, might boldly run a Ceph cluster with a non-default name whose OSD log files are named for example /var/log/ceph/ncc-osd.1701.log. Let's peek at the entries one finds in each.

```
2017-09-15 00:16:55.398807 osd.83 10.8.45.18:6822/127973 788 :
cluster [INF] 0.26c5 deep-scrub starts
2017-09-15 00:16:56.800561 osd.177 10.8.45.148:6818/129314 572 :
cluster [INF] 0.691 deep-scrub ok
2017-09-15 00:17:02.032534 mon.0 10.8.45.10:6789/0 418279 : cluster
[INF] pgmap v372250: 16384 pgs: 2 active+clean+scrubbing, 3
active+clean+scrubbing+deep, 16379 active+clean; 77786 GB data, 228
TB used, 596 TB / 825 TB avail
2017-09-15 00:16:55.958743 osd.142 10.8.45.146:6844/137783 793 :
cluster [INF] 0.3833 scrub starts
2017-09-15 00:17:00.607877 osd.83 10.8.45.18:6822/127973 789 :
```

```
cluster [INF] 0.26c5 deep-scrub ok
2017-09-15 00:17:01.329174 osd.88 10.8.45.18:6832/132624 918 :
cluster [INF] 0.19bb scrub ok
```

Business as usual for a healthy Ceph cluster. We see OSDs reporting successful light and deep scrubs, and the lead MON summarized the `pgmap` and cluster utilization.

```
2017-09-15 19:23:52.733080 mon.0 10.8.45.10:6789/0 473491 : cluster [INF]
pgmap v419600: 16384 pgs: 1 active+clean+scrubbing, 16383 active+clean;
77786 GB data, 228 TB used, 596 TB / 825 TB avail
2017-09-15 19:23:52.749005 mon.0 10.8.45.10:6789/0 473493 : cluster [INF]
osdmap e19228: 238 osds: 237 up, 238 in
```

Here are entries from later the same day show a summary of the `osdmap`, with one OSD down.

```
2017-09-15 19:24:00.513677 osd.16 10.8.45.15:6832/131296 808 :
cluster [INF] 0.b0 starting backfill to osd.33 from (0'0,0'0] MAX
to 7447'3975
2017-09-15 19:24:32.733030 mon.0 10.8.45.10:6789/0 473556 : cluster
[INF] HEALTH_WARN; 331 pgs backfill_wait; 93 pgs backfilling; 132
pgs stuck unclean; recovery 1115024/60328695 objects misplaced (1.848%)
2017-09-15 19:24:32.889755 mon.0 10.8.45.10:6789/0 473557 : cluster
[INF] pgmap v419645: 16384 pgs: 331 active+remapped+wait_backfill,
93 active+remapped+backfilling, 15960 active+clean; 77786 GB data,
228 TB used, 599 TB / 828 TB avail; 1113183/60328695 objects
misplaced (1.845%); 15548 MB/s, 3887 objects/s recovering
2017-09-15 19:24:33.922688 mon.0 10.8.45.10:6789/0 473558 : cluster
[INF] osdmap e19237: 238 osds: 238 up, 238 in
2017-09-15 19:24:33.937792 mon.0 10.8.45.10:6789/0 473559 : cluster
[INF] pgmap v419647: 16384 pgs: 331 active+remapped+wait_backfill,
93 active+remapped+backfilling, 15960 active+clean; 77786 GB data,
228 TB used, 599 TB / 828 TB avail; 1112020/60328695 objects
misplaced (1.843%); 8404 MB/s, 2101 objects/s recovering
```

Here the `osdmap` shows that the down OSD has now come back up, and data has been remapped to utilize it. Note the pgmap entries. They show 93 separate PGs are actively backfilling, with 331 waiting their turn. In the Configuration section above we touched on Ceph's settings that limit how much backfill/recovery can run at any given time. This spreads out the impact in order to protect user operations.

```
2017-09-16 00:16:56.093643 mon.0 10.8.45.10:6789/0 511866 : cluster [INF]
pgmap v441064: 16384 pgs: 16384 active+clean; 44667 MB data, 1197 GB used,
963 TB / 964 TB avail; 4316 kB/s rd, 10278 kB/s wr, 5991 op/s
```

OSD logs

Next, let's check out entries from osd.8's log. Since Ceph OSDs are more numerous than MONs and process a larger rate of transactions we find that they grow much more quickly. Be sure to allocate ample space for them. As above, this cluster is running Ceph's Jewel release.

```
2017-09-18 00:19:08.268212 7fe07b990700  1 leveldb: Compacting 4@0
+ 5@1 files
2017-09-18 00:19:08.327958 7fe07b990700  1 leveldb: Generated table
#14159: 55666 keys, 2129686 bytes
2017-09-18 00:19:08.382062 7fe07b990700  1 leveldb: Generated table
#14160: 52973 keys, 2129584 bytes
2017-09-18 00:19:08.434451 7fe07b990700  1 leveldb: Generated table
#14161: 54404 keys, 2129467 bytes
2017-09-18 00:19:08.488200 7fe07b990700  1 leveldb: Generated table
#14162: 54929 keys, 2129347 bytes
2017-09-18 00:19:08.553861 7fe07b990700  1 leveldb: Generated table
#14163: 53000 keys, 2129511 bytes
2017-09-18 00:19:08.570029 7fe07b990700  1 leveldb: Generated table
#14164: 14956 keys, 600195 bytes
2017-09-18 00:19:08.594003 7fe07b990700  1 leveldb: Generated table
#14165: 17061 keys, 710889 bytes
2017-09-18 00:19:08.594016 7fe07b990700  1 leveldb: Compacted 4@0 +
5@1 files => 11958679 bytes
2017-09-18 00:19:08.595153 7fe07b990700  1 leveldb: compacted to:
files[ 0 7 17 0 0 0 0 ]
2017-09-18 00:19:08.595317 7fe07b990700  1 leveldb: Delete type=2
#14154
```

This is normal housekeeping. The OSD maintains an internal metadata database that it periodically redds up.

```
2017-09-18 00:19:53.953129 7fe0b5c2f700  0 --
10.24.49.15:6816/123339 >> 10.24.49.147:6834/1012539
pipe(0x557b7551b400 sd=83 :6816 s=0 pgs=0 cs=0 l=0
c=0x557b76a0ea80).accept connect_seq 15 vs existing 15 state
standby
2017-09-18 00:19:53.953290 7fe0b5c2f700  0 --
10.24.49.15:6816/123339 >> 10.24.49.147:6834/1012539
pipe(0x557b7551b400 sd=83 :6816 s=0 pgs=0 cs=0 l=0
c=0x557b76a0ea80).accept connect_seq 16 vs existing 15 state
standby
2017-09-18 00:19:54.933317 7fe0b07db700  0 --
10.24.49.15:6816/123339 >> 10.24.50.15:6844/135559
pipe(0x557b7f57e000 sd=38 :6816 s=0 pgs=0 cs=0 l=0
c=0x557b7fb54700).accept connect_seq 57 vs existing 57 state
standby
2017-09-18 00:19:54.933774 7fe0b07db700  0 --
10.24.49.15:6816/123339 >> 10.24.50.15:6844/135559
pipe(0x557b7f57e000 sd=38 :6816 s=0 pgs=0 cs=0 l=0
c=0x557b7fb54700).accept connect_seq 58 vs existing 57 state
standby
```

The OSD has decided to relieve its boredom by accepting some connection requests.

```
2017-09-18 00:34:54.052375 7fe0b5c2f700  0 --
10.240.49.15:6816/123339 >> 10.240.49.147:6834/1012539
pipe(0x557b7551b400 sd=83 :6816 s=2 pgs=1045 cs=17 l=0
c=0x557b86d4e600).fault with nothing to send, going to standby
2017-09-18 00:34:55.031169 7fe0b07db700  0 --
10.240.49.15:6816/123339 >> 10.240.50.15:6844/135559
pipe(0x557b7f57e000 sd=38 :6816 s=2 pgs=3948 cs=59 l=0
c=0x557b76c85e00).fault with nothing to send, going to standby
```

The word `fault` in these messages is scary, but they're a normal part of the OSD request lifecycle.

```
2017-09-18 02:08:51.710567 7fe0e466f700  0 log_channel(cluster) log
[INF] : 1.35da deep-scrub starts
2017-09-18 02:08:52.040149 7fe0e466f700  0 log_channel(cluster) log
[INF] : 1.35da deep-scrub ok
```

Here a deep scrub started and completed successfully. We love it when that happens.

```
2017-09-18 02:27:44.036497 7fe0926fc700  0 --
10.240.49.15:6816/123339 >> 10.240.50.17:6834/1124935
pipe(0x557b95384800 sd=34 :6816 s=0 pgs=0 cs=0 l=0
c=0x557b80759200).accept connect_seq 4 vs existing 3 state standby
2017-09-18 02:39:53.195393 7fe118064700 -1 osd.8 33380
heartbeat_check: no reply from 0x557b91ccd390 osd.272 since back
2017-09-18 02:39:32.671169 front 2017-09-18 02:39:32.671169 (cutoff
2017-09-18 02:39:33.195374)
2017-09-18 02:39:54.195516 7fe118064700 -1 osd.8 33380
heartbeat_check: no reply from 0x557b91ccd390 osd.272 since back
2017-09-18 02:39:32.671169 front 2017-09-18 02:39:32.671169 (cutoff
2017-09-18 02:39:34.195502)
```

Ugh!!! The OSD with the ID number 272 has gone incommunicado. These entries may indicate a network problem, exhaustion of the `nf_conntrack` table, or that `osd.272` machine's daemon process has given up the ghost. Go ahead and take a garlic fries break. You don't want to tackle this next block on an empty stomach. Ellipses indicate spots that have been edited for relative brevity.

```
-4> 2017-09-15 21:58:20.149473 7f158d64f700  0
    filestore(/var/lib/ceph/osd/ceph-231) write couldn't open
    meta/#-1:97b6cd72:::osdmap.25489:0#: (117) Structure needs
    cleaning
-3> 2017-09-15 21:58:20.149536 7f158d64f700  0
    filestore(/var/lib/ceph/osd/ceph-231)  error (117) Structure
    needs cleaning not handled on operation 0x55a18d942b88
    (17413.0.1, or op 1, counting from 0)
-2> 2017-09-15 21:58:20.149544 7f158d64f700  0
    filestore(/var/lib/ceph/osd/ceph-231) unexpected error code
-1> 2017-09-15 21:58:20.149545 7f158d64f700  0
    filestore(/var/lib/ceph/osd/ceph-231)  transaction dump:
    {
      "ops": [
          {
              "op_num": 0,
              "op_name": "write",
              "collection": "meta",
              "oid": "#-1:725cc562:::inc_osdmap.25489:0#",
              "length": 203,
              "offset": 0,
              "bufferlist length": 203
          },
          {
              "op_num": 1,
              "op_name": "write",
```

```
                "collection": "meta",
                "oid": "#-1:97b6cd72:::osdmap.25489:0#",
                "length": 404169,
                "offset": 0,
                "bufferlist length": 404169
          },
          {

                "op_num": 2,
                "op_name": "write",
                "collection": "meta",
                "oid": "#-1:7b3f43c4:::osd_superblock:0#",
                "length": 417,
                "offset": 0,
                "bufferlist length": 417
          }
      ]
  }
      0> 2017-09-15 21:58:20.152050 7f158d64f700 -1
      os/filestore/FileStore.cc: In function 'void
      FileStore::_do_transaction(ObjectStore::Transaction&,
      uint64_t, int, ThreadPool::TPHandle*)' thread 7f158d64f700
      time 2017-09-15 21:58:20.149608
      os/filestore/FileStore.cc: 2920: FAILED assert(0 ==
      "unexpected error")
      ceph version 10.2.6
      (656b5b63ed7c43bd014bcafd81b001959d5f089f)
  1: (ceph::__ceph_assert_fail(char const*, char const*, int,
      char const*)+0x8b) [0x55a1826b007b]
  2: (FileStore::_do_transaction(ObjectStore::Transaction&,
      unsigned long, int, ThreadPool::TPHandle*)+0xefd)
      [0x55a1823a26ed]
  3: (FileStore::_do_transactions
                  (std::vector<ObjectStore::Transaction,
      std::allocator<ObjectStore::Transaction> >&, unsigned long,
      ThreadPool::TPHandle*)+0x3b) [0x55a1823a842b]
  4:  (FileStore::_do_op(FileStore::OpSequencer*,
      ThreadPool::TPHandle&)+0x2b5) [0x55a1823a8715]
  5:  (ThreadPool::worker(ThreadPool::WorkThread*)+0xa6e)
      [0x55a1826a145e]
  6: (ThreadPool::WorkThread::entry()+0x10) [0x55a1826a2340]
  7: (()+0x8184) [0x7f159bbff184]
  8: (clone()+0x6d)  [0x7f1599d28ffd]  NOTE: a copy of the
      executable, or `objdump -rdS <executable>` is needed to
      interpret this. --- logging levels --- 0/ 5 none  0/ 0
      lockdep  0/ 0 context  0/ 0 crush  0/ 0 mds  0/ 1 optracker
  ...
log_file /var/log/ceph/ceph-osd.231.log
--- end dump of recent events --- 2017-09-15 21:58:20.155893 7f158d64f700
```

```
-1 *** Caught signal (Aborted) **  in thread 7f158d64f700
thread_name:tp_fstore_op  ceph version 10.2.6
(656b5b63ed7c43bd014bcafd81b001959d5f089f)
     1: (()+0x8f3942) [0x55a1825bb942]
     2: (()+0x10330) [0x7f159bc07330]
     3: (gsignal()+0x37) [0x7f1599c61c37]
     4: (abort()+0x148) [0x7f1599c65028]
     5: (ceph::__ceph_assert_fail(char const*, char const*, int,
        char const*)+0x265) [0x55a1826b0255]
     6: (FileStore::_do_transaction(ObjectStore::Transaction&,
        unsigned long, int, ThreadPool::TPHandle*)+0xefd)
        [0x55a1823a26ed]
...
```

Yikes! This definitely does not serve Vaal. Here the Ceph OSD code has encountered an error it can't cope with. Backtraces and information about ops that were being processed are dumped for forensics. We've highlighted two lines out of the dozens above to discuss specifically.

The first highlighted line shows a failed code assertion. These often afford a quick stab at the general cause of the problem. In this case, the OSD formerly known as 231 has encountered a problem in FileStore code. These almost always reflect a problem with the underlying hardware, or at the very least an XFS filesystem that has gone astray for another reason.

```
os/filestore/FileStore.cc: 2920: FAILED assert(0 == "unexpected error")
```

In this specific case, the kernel log shows I/O errors on the underlying SSD drive.

Skipping down to the second highlighted line we see

```
2017-09-15 21:58:20.155893 7f158d64f700 -1 *** Caught signal (Aborted) **
in thread 7f158d64f700 thread_name:tp_fstore_op
```

When grepping (or groping) through voluminous OSD logs to discern failure causes it can be handy to search for the word *signal* in order to quickly zero in on the region of interest. Note though that Ceph daemons also log signal messages when they are shut down normally, say for a server reboot.

Debug levels

The constellation of messages that Ceph OSDs can log is huge and changes with each release. Full interpretation of logs could easily itself fill a book, but we'll end this section with a brief note regarding the logging levels summary within the above excerpt.

```
--- logging levels ---
0/ 5 none
0/ 0 lockdep
0/ 0 context
```

Ceph's allows us to finely control the verbosity with which it logs events, status, and errors. Levels may be independently set for each subsystem to control verbosity. Moreover, each subsystem has separate verbosity levels for information kept in process memory and for messages sent to log files or the `syslog` service. Higher numbers increase verbosity. The output and memory levels can be set independently, or separately. For example, if our MONs are proving unruly, we might add lines like the below to `ceph.conf`.

```
[global]
debug ms = 1
[mon]
debug mon = 15/20
debug paxos = 20
debug auth = 20
```

Note how for the mon subsystem we have specified different levels for output and memory logs by separating the two values with a slash character. If only a single value is given, Ceph applies it to both.

Recall from earlier in this chapter that Ceph daemons only read configuration files at startup. This means that to effect the above changes, one would need to make them on each MON node and perform a rolling restart of all MON daemons. This is tedious and awkward; in times of crisis, it can also be precarious to stir the pot by bouncing services.

This is a perfect example of how the admin socket and injection mechanisms described earlier in this chapter earn their keep.

Say yesterday `osd.666` and `osd.1701` were being squirrelly, so we elevated the logging levels of the `filestore` and `osd` modules. Today we find that the increased log flow has half-filled the OSD node's `/var/log` filesystem and need to back off on the verbosity. After logging into osd.666's node we check the settings that are currently active in the daemon's running config.

```
# ceph daemon osd.666 config show | grep debug
    "debug_none": "0\/5",
    "debug_lockdep": "0\/0",
    "debug_context": "0\/0",
    "debug_crush": "0\/0",
    "debug_mds": "1\/5",
...

    "debug_osd": "10\/10",
    "debug_optracker": "0\/0",
    "debug_objclass": "0\/0",
    "debug_filestore": "10\/10",
...
```

On Ceph's Jewel 10.2.6 release this matches no fewer than *98* individual settings, hence the ellipses for brevity. Now log into an admin or mon node and inject those puppies into submission.

```
# ceph tell osd.666 injectargs '--debug-filestore 0/0 --debug-osd
0/0'debug_filestore=0/0 debug_osd=0/0
```

Boom. Instant satisfaction. Since we can inject these values on the fly, we can set them low in `ceph.conf` and inject temporary increases on the fly, followed by decreases when we're through. In fact if the log file has grown so large that there isn't even space to compress it we can truncate and reopen it without having to restart the OSD daemon.

```
# rm /var/log/ceph/ceph-osd.666.log
# ceph daemon osd.666 log reopen
```

To quote my high school chemistry teacher, *Isn't this FUN!? NOW we're cooking with gas!*

Oh wait, we forgot about `osd.1701`. And maybe we also elevated `osd.1864` and ... we don't remember. It was late and we were groggy due to garlic fries deprivation. This morning after a waking up with a soy chai we remember that we can inject values into the running state of all OSDs with a single command.

```
# ceph tell osd.* injectargs '--debug-filestore 0/0 --debug-osd 0/0'
osd.0: debug_filestore=0/0 debug_osd=0/0
osd.1: debug_filestore=0/0 debug_osd=0/0
osd.2: debug_filestore=0/0 debug_osd=0/0
```

...

Better safe than sorry; we're best off being sure. Injecting values that may be identical to those already set is safe and idempotent, and sure beats nuking the site from orbit.

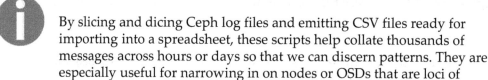

> Analysis of Ceph logs can involve lots of time and gnarly awk/sed pipelines. A singularly useful set of tools for identifying patterns in log files can be found here:
> `https://github.com/linuxkidd/ceph-log-parsers`
>
> By slicing and dicing Ceph log files and emitting CSV files ready for importing into a spreadsheet, these scripts help collate thousands of messages across hours or days so that we can discern patterns. They are especially useful for narrowing in on nodes or OSDs that are loci of chronic slow / blocked requests.

Common tasks

In this section, we cover procedures for a number of common tasks that Ceph admins execute as needed. These include managing flags and services, dealing with component failures, cluster expansion, and balancing OSD utilization. We'll also touch on upgrades between Ceph releases.

Installation

Here we will summarize the bootstrapping of Ceph on bare metal utilizing the same `ceph-ansible` tools but without Vagrant orchestrating. If you're using `for` loops, like Jack Butler you're doing it wrong.

First, clone the ceph-ansible GitHub repo onto a system or VM that will serve as your admin node.

```
$ git clone https://github.com/ceph/ceph-ansible/
```

Next install Ansible via your Linux distribution's package manager, `pip`, or download from `http://docs.ansible.com/ansible/latest/intro_installation.html` . The latest stable release is suggested.

Next populate Ansible's inventory file with hosts and host groups using `/etc/ansible/hosts` as a starting point. You'll end up with a file resembling this example:

```
[mons]
ceph-mon01
ceph-mon02
ceph-mon03

[osds]
ceph-osd001
ceph-osd002
ceph-osd003
ceph-osd004
ceph-osd005
ceph-osd006

[rgws]
ceph-rgw01

[clients]
ceph-client-01
```

Next, follow your organization's usual process to populate SSH keys then use Ansible's handy `ping` module to verify that you can connect to each system without supplying a password.

```
$ ansible all -m ping
10.10.17.01 | success >> {
   "changed": false,
   "ping": "pong"
}
10.10.11.38 | success >> {
   "changed": false,
   "ping": "pong"
}
...
```

If you experience difficulty with the above test, check the permissions on your .ssh directory and examine /etc/ansible/ansible.cfg.

Next customize the group_vars and site.yml files, just like we did in the previous chapter.

```
$ cp group_vars/all.yml.sample group_vars/all.yml
$ cp group_vars/mons.yml.sample group_vars/mons.yml
$ cp group_vars/osds.yml.sample group_vars/osds.yml
$ cp site.yml.sample site.yml
```

As you might surmise, next we must edit the group_vars/all.yml file to reflect our local conditions.

First, edit the entries for public_nework and monitor_interface as appropriate to your systems. Next consider where you wish to snag Ceph's installation package and configure the familiar ceph_origin line with distro, upstream, or local. When choosing the upstream package source you must designate how far upstream you wish to swim. The safe choice is ceph_stable, though ceph_rhcs is valid for RHEL deployments and the adventurous may skate with ceph_dev.

Our sandbox deployment did not touch on customization of OSD creation details, but for bare metal deployment you must edit group_vars/osds.yml and edit at the very least the osd_scenario line to select a strategy from among those presented: journal_collocation, bluestore, osd_directory, raw_multi_journal, dmcrypt_journal_collocation, dmcrypt_dedicated_journal. Note the spelling, collocation not colocation. It is worth reading through this entire file before proceeding. Note that osd_directory has been problematic in some ways and may be removed in the future.

Also, edit the devices and raw_journal_devices entries as appropriate for your deployment.

You're ready! Light the fuse by invoking

```
$ ansible-playbook site.yml
```

and enjoy the show as ceph-ansible does what in the bad old days we needed dozens of for loops and individual commands to accomplish. Remember earlier in this chapter when we advised unlimited scrollback history for your terminal application? And garlic fries? This is the time for both.

Ceph-deploy

Alternately, one may use the `ceph-deploy` tool to perform Ceph management tasks at a smaller granularity. If your Ceph infrastructure does not already have `ceph-deploy` enabled, below are succinct instructions on installation and configuration. We discuss the actions to be taken; you will need to apply them across your Ceph nodes via your usual server management practices.

First, create a dedicated user for `ceph-deploy` on all systems to be managed. Popular documentation creates the `ceph-server` user for this task, though you may choose a different name.

```
$ sudo useradd -d /home/ceph-server -m ceph
$ sudo passwd ceph-server
```

Installation of software packages, access to devices, and management of system services require root privileges. `Ceph-deploy` runs and connects to remote systems as our new dedicated user and escalates via `sudo` as it needs to, an approach that avoids having to enable password-less SSH trusts on your cluster nodes. We next enable password-less `sudo` for the unprivileged `ceph-server` user on all nodes to be managed.

```
$ echo "ceph-server ALL = (ALL) NOPASSWD: ALL" | sudo tee
    /etc/sudoers.d/ceph-server
$ sudo chmod 0440 /etc/sudoers.d/ceph-server
```

Next set up password-less SSH trust from your admin host to each of your Ceph production systems for the `ceph-server` user.

```
$ sudo -i -u ceph-server
ceph-server$ ssh-keygen
Generating public/private key pair.
Enter file in which to save the key (/home/ceph-server/.ssh/id_rsa):
Enter passphrase (empty for no passphrase):
Enter same passphrase again:
Your identification has been saved in /home/ceph-server/.ssh/id_rsa.
Your public key has been saved in /home/ceph-server/.ssh/id_rsa.pub.
```

Distribute the new key to each production node (or use your usual method).

```
$ ssh-copy-id ceph-server@some.node
# apt-get install -y ceph-deploy
```

Now install `ceph-deploy` itself on your admin node. Your Linux distribution may already provide this package, or you can download prebuilt packages from `https://download.ceph.com/`. Those so inclined can use the source at `https://github.com/ceph/ceph-deploy`.

```
# yum install -y ceph-deploy
```

That's all it takes! Remember that it is customary to sudo to the `ceph-server` user before running `ceph-deploy`, rather than running as the `root` user.

TIP

When invoking `ceph-deploy`, especially when creating OSDs, it's important to have an up-to-date copy of your `ceph.conf` configuration file in the `ceph-server` user's home directory. `ceph-deploy` will compare this to that present on the other side, and if differences are found may require the `--override-conf` flag to continue, which will overwrite `ceph.conf` on the remote system. This is handy when deploying the first OSD on a new node if `ceph.conf` is not distributed via other means. Be sure that if you automate the distribution of `ceph.conf` to your cluster nodes you must maintain the ceph-server user's copy as well.

Flags

Ceph has a number of *flags* that are usually applied across the cluster as a whole. These flags direct Ceph's behavior in a number of ways and when set are reported by `ceph status`.

The most commonly utilized flag is `noout`, which directs Ceph to not automatically mark out any OSDs that enter the down state. Since OSDs will not be marked out while the flag is set, the cluster will not start the backfill/recovery process to ensure optimal replication. This is most useful when performing maintenance, including simple reboots. By telling Ceph *Hold on, we'll be right back* we save the overhead and churn of automatically-triggered data movement.

Here's an example of rebooting an OSD node within a Jewel cluster. First, we run `ceph -s` to check the overall status of the cluster. This is an excellent habit to get into before, during, and after even the simplest of maintenance; if something is amiss it is almost always best to restore full health before stirring the pot.

```
# ceph -s
    cluster 3369c9c6-bfaf-4114-9c31-576afa64d0fe
       health HEALTH_OK
       monmap e2: 5 mons at
```

```
{mon001=10.8.45.10:6789/0,mon002=10.8.45.11:6789/0,mon003=10.8.45.143:6789/
0,mon004=10.80.46.10:6789/0,mon005=10.80.46.11:6789/0}
            election epoch 24, quorum 0,1,2,3,4
mon001,mon002,mon003,mon004,mon005
        osdmap e33039: 280 osds: 280 up, 280 in
            flags sortbitwise,require_jewel_osds
        pgmap v725092: 16384 pgs, 1 pools, 0 bytes data, 1 objects
            58364 MB used, 974 TB / 974 TB avail
                16384 active+clean
```

Here we see that the cluster health is HEALTH_OK, and that all 280 OSDs are both up and in. Squeaky clean healthy cluster. Note that two flags are already set: sortbitwise and require_jewel_osds. The sortbitwise flag denotes an internal sorting change required for certain new features. The require_jewel_osds flag avoids compatibility problems by preventing pre-Jewel OSDs from joining the cluster. Both should always be set on clusters running Jewel or later releases, and you will not need to mess with either directly unless you're upgrading from an earlier release.

```
# ceph osd set noout
set noout
```

Now that we've ensured that the cluster is healthy going into our maintenance, we set the noout flag to forestall unwarranted recovery. Note that the cluster health immediately becomes HEALTH_WARN and that a line is added by ceph status showing the reason for the warning state.

```
# ceph status
    cluster 3369c9c6-bfaf-4114-9c31-576afa64d0fe
        health HEALTH_WARN
                noout flag(s) set
        monmap e2: 5 mons at
{mon001=10.8.45.10:6789/0,mon002=10.8.45.11:6789/0,mon003=10.8.45.143:6789/
0,mon004=10.80.46.10:6789/0,mon005=10.80.46.11:6789/0}
            election epoch 24, quorum 0,1,2,3,4
mon001,mon002,mon003,mon004,mon005
        osdmap e33050: 280 osds: 280 up, 280 in
            flags noout,sortbitwise,require_jewel_osds
        pgmap v725101: 16384 pgs, 1 pools, 0 bytes data, 1 objects
            58364 MB used, 974 TB / 974 TB avail
                16384 active+clean
```

At this point we still have all OSDs up and in; we're good to proceed.

```
# ssh osd013 shutdown -r now
```

We've rebooted a specific OSD node, say to effect a new kernel or to straighten out a confused HBA. Ceph quickly marks the OSDs on this system down; 20 currently are provisioned on this particular node. Note a new line in the status output below calling out these down OSDs with a corresponding adjustment to the number of up OSDs on the osdmap line. It's easy to gloss over disparities in the osdmap entry, especially when using fonts where values like 260 and 280 are visually similar, so we're pleased that Ceph explicitly alerts us to the situation.

This cluster has CRUSH rules that require copies of data to be in disjoint racks. With the default replicated pool size and min_size settings of three and two respectively all placement groups (PGs) whose acting sets include one of these OSDs are marked undersized and degraded. With only one replica out of service, Ceph continues serving data without missing a beat. This example cluster is idle, but in production when we do this there will be operations that come in while the host is down. These operations will manifest in the output of ceph status as additional lines listing PGs in the state backfill_wait. This indicates that Ceph has data that yearns to be written to the OSDs that are (temporarily) down.

If we had not set the noout flag, after a short grace period Ceph would have proceeded to map that new data (and the existing data allocated to the down OSDs) to other OSDs in the same failure domain. Since a multi-rack replicated pool usually specifies the failure domain as the rack, that would mean that each of the surviving three hosts in the same rack as osd013 would receive a share. Then when the host (and its OSDs) comes back up, Ceph would map that data to its original locations, and lots of recovery would ensue to move it back. This double movement of data is superfluous so long as we get the OSDs back up within a reasonable amount of time.

```
# ceph status
    cluster 3369c9c6-bfaf-4114-9c31-576afa64d0fe
     health HEALTH_WARN
            3563 pgs degraded
            3261 pgs stuck unclean
            3563 pgs undersized
            20/280 in osds are down
            noout flag(s) set
     monmap e2: 5 mons at
{mon001=10.8.45.10:6789/0,mon002=10.8.45.11:6789/0,mon003=10.8.45.143:6789/
0,mon004=10.80.46.10:6789/0,mon005=10.80.46.11:6789/0}
            election epoch 24, quorum 0,1,2,3,4
mon001,mon002,mon003,mon004,mon005
     osdmap e33187: 280 osds: 260 up, 280 in; 3563 remapped pgs
            flags noout,sortbitwise,require_jewel_osds
      pgmap v725174: 16384 pgs, 1 pools, 0 bytes data, 1 objects
            70498 MB used, 974 TB / 974 TB avail
```

```
12821 active+clean
3563 active+undersized+degraded
```

Note also that the tail end of this output tallies PGs that are in certain combinations of states. Here 3563 PGs are noted again as undersized but also active, since they are still available for client operations. The balance of the cluster's PGs are reported as active+clean. Sum the two numbers and we get 16384, as reported on the pgmap line.

We can exploit these PG state sums as a handy programmatic test for cluster health. During operations like rolling reboots, it is prudent to ensure complete cluster health between iterations. One way to do that is to compare the total PG count with the active number. Since PGs can have other states at the same time as active, such as active+scrubbing and active+scrubbing+deep, we need to sum all such combinations. Here is a simple Ansible play that implements this check.

```
- name: wait until clean PG == total PG
  shell: "ceph -s | awk '/active\+clean/ { total += $1 }; END { print total
}'"
  register:    clean_PG
  until:       total_PG.stdout|int == clean_PG.stdout|int
  retries:     20
  delay:       20
  delegate_to: "{{ ceph_primary_mon }}"
  run_once:    true
```

There is room for improvement: we should use the more surgical ceph pg stat as input, and we should use the safer -f json or -f json-pretty output formats along with the jq utility to guard against inter-release changes. This is, as they say, left as an exercise for the reader.

While we were diverted to the above tip the OSD node we rebooted came back up and the cluster again became healthy. Note that the warning that 20 out of 280 OSDs are down is gone, reflected on the osdmap line as well. The health status, however, remains at HEALTH_WARN so long as we have a flag set that limits cluster behavior. This helps us remember to remove temporary flags when we no longer need their specific behavior modification.

```
# ceph status
  cluster 3369c9c6-bfaf-4114-9c31-576afa64d0fe
  health HEALTH_WARN
  noout flag(s) set
  monmap e2: 5 mons at
{mon001=10.8.45.10:6789/0,mon002=10.8.45.11:6789/0,mon003=10.8.45.143:6789/
0,mon004=10.80.46.10:6789/0,mon005=10.80.46.11:6789/0}
          election epoch 24, quorum 0,1,2,3,4
```

```
mon001,mon002,mon003,mon004,mon005
    osdmap e33239: 280 osds: 280 up, 280 in
          flags noout,sortbitwise,require_jewel_osds
    pgmap v725292: 16384 pgs, 1 pools, 0 bytes data, 1 objects
          58364 MB used, 974 TB / 974 TB avail
          16384 active+clean
```

We'll proceed to remove that flag. This double-negative command would irk your high school grammar teacher, but here it makes total sense in the context of a flag setting.

```
# ceph osd unset noout
unset noout
```

Now that we have no longer tied Ceph's hands the cluster's health status has returned to HEALTH_OK and our exercise is complete.

```
# ceph status
    cluster 3369c9c6-bfaf-4114-9c31-576afa64d0fe
    health HEALTH_OK
    monmap e2: 5 mons at
{mon001=10.8.45.10:6789/0,mon002=10.8.45.11:6789/0,mon003=10.8.45.143:6789/
0,mon004=10.80.46.10:6789/0,mon005=10.80.46.11:6789/0}
          election epoch 24, quorum 0,1,2,3,4
mon001,mon002,mon003,mon004,mon005
    osdmap e33259: 280 osds: 280 up, 280 in
          flags noout,sortbitwise,require_jewel_osds
    pgmap v725392: 16384 pgs, 1 pools, 0 bytes data, 1 objects
          58364 MB used, 974 TB / 974 TB avail
          16384 active+clean
```

With the Luminous release, the plain format output of ceph status has changed quite a bit, showing the value of using the -f json output format for scripting tasks.

```
# ceph -s
  cluster:
  id: 2afa26cb-95e0-4830-94q4-5195beakba930c
  health: HEALTH_OK

    services:
      mon: 5 daemons, quorum mon01,mon02,mon03,mon04,mon05
      mgr: mon04(active), standbys: mon05
      osd: 282 osds: 282 up, 282 in

    data:
      pools: 1 pools, 16384 pgs
      objects: 6125k objects, 24502 GB
      usage: 73955 GB used, 912 TB / 985 TB avail
      pgs: 16384 active+clean
```

```
# ceph -s
  cluster:
    id: 2af1107b-9950-4800-94a4-51951701a02a930c
    health: HEALTH_WARN
            noout flag(s) set
            48 osds down
            2 hosts (48 osds) down
            Degraded data redundancy: 3130612/18817908 objects degraded
(16.636%), 8171 pgs unclean, 8172 pgs degraded, 4071 pgs undersized

  services:
    mon: 5 daemons, quorum mon01,mon02,mon03,mon04,mon05
    mgr: mon04(active), standbys: mon05
    osd: 282 osds: 234 up, 282 in
         flags noout

  data:
    pools:   1 pools, 16384 pgs
    objects: 6125k objects, 24502 GB
    usage:   73941 GB used, 912 TB / 985 TB avail
    pgs:     3130612/18817908 objects degraded (16.636%)
             8212 active+clean
             8172 active+undersized+degraded

  io:
    client:  8010 MB/s wr, 0 op/s rd, 4007 op/s wr

# ceph status
  cluster:
    id: 2afa26cb-95e0-4830-94q4-5195beakba930c
    health: HEALTH_WARN
            Degraded data redundancy: 289727/18817908 objects degraded
(1.540%), 414 pgs unclean, 414 pgs degraded

  services:
    mon: 5 daemons, quorum mon01,mon02,mon03,mon04,mon05
    mgr: mon04(active), standbys: mon05
    osd: 283 osds: 283 up, 283 in

  data:
    pools:   1 pools, 16384 pgs
    objects: 6125k objects, 24502 GB
    usage:   73996 GB used, 916 TB / 988 TB avail
    pgs:     289727/18817908 objects degraded (1.540%)
             15970 active+clean
             363 active+recovery_wait+degraded
             51 active+recovering+degraded
```

```
io:
    recovery: 1031 MB/s, 258 objects/s
```

Other flags include `noin`, `norecover`, `nobackfill`, and `norebalance`. Their effects are nuanced and use-cases are few. It is possible to shoot oneself in the foot, so it is suggested to research them and experiment in a busy but non-production cluster to gain a full understanding of their dynamics before messing with them.

Later in this chapter, we'll touch on the `noscrub` and `nodeepscrub` flags.

Service management

Each Ceph MON, OSD, RGW, MDS, and in recent releases Manager (`ceph-mgr`) daemon is structured as a Linux *service*. Starting and stopping these are at times necessary. The mechanics for doing so differ among Linux distributions, and even among releases of a given distribution.

Systemd: the wave (tsunami?) of the future

Let's first explore Ceph service management on `systemd`—based Linux releases. Loved, hated, but never ignored, `systemd` is becoming increasingly prevalent within major Linux distributions. These include the Red Hat family: RHEL 7 and later, CentOS 7 and later, and Fedora 15 and later. Debian adopted `systemd` with version 8 (Jessie), Ubuntu as of 16.04 (Xenial), and SUSE as of SLES 12.

Installation of Ceph packages leverages `udev` rules and the native service management system to start configured services at boot time. We may also list and manage them individually or on a host-wide basis.

`systemd` organizes services as *units*, which we manage as the root user with the `systemctl` command. To show all the Ceph units configured on a host we issue:

```
# systemctl status ceph.target
```

To stop all running Ceph daemons of any type on a node:

And to start them all back up:

```
# systemctl stop ceph.target
# systemctl start ceph.target
```

Sometimes we need to manage services more precisely, especially on converged (AIO) deployments. We can manage classes of individual Ceph component daemons by specifying their names:

```
# systemctl stop ceph-osd.target
# systemctl start ceph-osd.target
# systemctl stop ceph-mon.target
# systemctl start ceph-mon.target
# systemctl stop ceph-mds.target
# systemctl start ceph-mds.target
# systemctl stop ceph-radosgw.target
# systemctl start ceph-radsogw.target
```

As Ceph's OSDs are both the most numerous and most volatile components of any cluster, we often find ourselves needing to surgically manage individual OSDs without disturbing others on the same server. This applies to other daemons as well, so we can issue the above commands with a more narrow focus on an individual *instance*.

```
# systemctl stop ceph-osd@instance
# systemctl start ceph-osd@instance

# systemctl stop ceph-mds@instance
# systemctl start ceph-mds@instance
# systemctl stop ceph-mon@instance
# systemctl start ceph-mon@instance
# systemctl stop ceph-radosgw@instance
# systemctl start ceph-radosgw@instance
```

For OSDs the *instance* is simply the OSD's number; for other services we use the hostname.

```
# systemctl stop ceph-osd@11
# systemctl start ceph-osd@11
# systemctl stop ceph-mds@monhost-003
# systemctl start ceph-mds@monhost-003
# systemctl stop ceph-mon@monhost-002
# systemctl start ceph-mon@monhost-002
# systemctl stop ceph-radosgw@rgwhost-001
# systemctl start ceph-radosgw@rgwhost-001
```

If one wishes to be very sure or is impatient, one may of course simply reboot the entire host to restart all services. Each reboot, however, takes considerably longer and holds a slight but nonzero risk of something going wrong, so it is advised to manage services surgically.

 An exhaustive dive into `systemd` is beyond the scope of this book, but an excellent resource for learning more is here:
`https://www.digitalocean.com/community/tutorials/systemd-essentials-working-with-services-units-and-the-journal`

Upstart

Ubuntu releases earlier than Xenial (such as Trusty) use the Upstart service management system, which is almost, but not entirely unlike `systemd`. Here we'll list analogous Upstart commands for each task explored above.

Showing all Upstart jobs and instances on a given system:

```
# initctl list | grep ceph
```

Stopping and starting all Ceph daemons on a host:

```
# stop ceph-all
# start ceph-all
```

To stop and start all instances of a particular Ceph component on a given host:

```
# stop ceph-osd-all
# start ceph-osd-all
# stop ceph-mon-all
# start ceph-mon-all
# stop ceph-mds-all
# start ceph-mds-all
```

To stop and start individual instances:

```
# stop ceph-osd id=11
# start ceph-osd id=11
# stop ceph-mon id=monhost-005
# start ceph-mon id=monhost-005
# stop ceph-mds id=mdshost-001
# stop ceph-mds id=mdshost-001
# stop ceph-radosgw id=rgwhost-003
# start ceph-radosgw id=rgwhost-003
```

sysvinit

Older releases of Ceph on older Linux releases, such as Firefly on CentOS 6, use traditional *sysvinit* service management with scripts located under /etc/init.d. Below are the analogous service management commands.

```
# /etc/init.d/ceph stop
# /etc/init.d/ceph start
# /etc/init.d/ceph stop mon
# /etc/init.d/ceph start mon
# /etc/init.d/ceph stop osd.69
# /etc/init.d/ceph start osd.69
```

On some systems, you may also use the service command.

```
# service ceph start
# service ceph stop mon
# service ceph start osd.69
```

Component failures

Hardware failures are a fact of life. The larger your cluster grows, the more frequently you'll see failures. Fortunately, Ceph goes to great lengths to ensure the durability and availability of your precious data.

With proper deployment and consideration of fault domains, your Ceph cluster will cruise right through common hardware failures. It is, however, essential to integrate Ceph into your organization's monitoring framework so that you can address failed components before they pile up. Earlier in this chapter we introduced Ceph's logging strategies and showed some examples; in the next chapter, we'll focus on monitoring. At the very least you will want to frequently consult your MON or admin node for cluster status, and alert on these conditions:

- One or more OSDs are down
- Cluster health is HEALTH_ERR
- Inconsistent PGs are reported

Hardware failures are by far the most common causes of these problems. Given the myriad choices of systems and components one may encounter as well as space constraints it would be impractical to cover the details of hardware diagnosis. Chances are that your organization already has mechanisms for checking for drive health, PSU status, HBA faults, memory errors, and dangerous environmental conditions. If your NICs are bonded, you should also ensure that both ports in each bond are up. Your Ceph servers are no less susceptible to these than others, and comprehensive monitoring can often alert you to problems before they become dire.

Probably the most common errors are OSD drive failures; these are the most heavily exercised drives in your deployment. Your servers' management controllers may offer drive error logging, but watching for Linux syslog messages may be more expedient and less hardware-specific. For example on Ubuntu 14.04 with a 3.19 kernel drive errors look like this:

```
2017-09-11T20:21:30 jank11 kernel: [965236] sd 0:0:9:0: [sdk]
FAILED Result: hostbyte=DID_OK driverbyte=DRIVER_SENSE
2017-09-11T20:21:30 jank11 kernel: [965236] sd 0:0:9:0: [sdk] Sense
Key : Medium Error [current] [descriptor]
2017-09-11T20:21:30 jank11 kernel: [965236] sd 0:0:9:0: [sdk] Add.
Sense: Unrecovered read error
2017-09-11T20:21:30 jank11 kernel: [965236] sd 0:0:9:0: [sdk] CDB:
2017-09-11T20:21:30 jank11 kernel: [965236] Read(16): 88 00 00 00
00 01 33 c9 bf 93 00 00 00 01 00 00
2017-09-11T20:21:30 jank11 kernel: [965236] blk_update_request:
critical medium error, dev sdk, sector 5163827091
2017-09-11T20:21:30 jank11 kernel: [965236] XFS (dm-18): metadata
I/O error: block 0x132895793 ("xfs_trans_read_buf_map") error 61
numblks 1
2017-09-11T20:21:30 jank11 kernel: [965236] XFS (dm-18): page
discard on page ffffea002c9b8340, inode 0x580008bc, offset 0.
```

In this case, the drive slot number is right there in the messages -- slot #9. It is common for drive errors to be followed by XFS errors when using FileStore. In most cases, this type of error will not cause the associated OSD to crash, but it may continue in a degraded state.

When a hardware error is clearly identified, it's usually best to remove the affected OSD from the cluster, replace the drive, then redeploy. To remove an OSD from service, follow these steps:

- Positively identify the affected OSD, which may or may not showdown in `ceph osd tree`.
- Use `ceph osd find` or `ceph osd tree` to find the host that serves that OSD.

- On the OSD host, stop the specific OSD's service instance as we described earlier in this chapter if it has not already crashed. Back on the admin node, ceph status will report the OSD going down.
- Unmount the OSD filesystem, for example,

```
# umount /var/lib/ceph/osd/ceph-1138 &
```

The backgrounding of this command is deliberate. Drive and filesystem errors may result in this hanging.

- Using `sgdisk` or other tools, wipe the partitions from the drive if possible. Again it is prudent to background this in case it blocks.
- Back on your admin node, `ceph status` may already show the cluster recovering from the OSD going down.
- Remove the OSD from the CRUSH map, from the cluster roster, and from the MONs' auth list. Mark it out first for good measure; there are race conditions that this can help avoid.

```
# ceph osd out 1138
# ceph osd crush remove osd.1138
# ceph osd rm osd.1138
# ceph auth del osd.1138
```

- You will now for sure see `ceph status` reporting recovery as the cluster heals, with the health status `HEALTH_WARN`. Once backfill/recovery completes status will return to `HEALTH_OK`.
- After replacing the drive, you can deploy a fresh OSD on it with ceph-deploy using the technique shown in the next section. For a single OSD deploy you most likely do not need to worry about the incremental weighting that we perform below when adding a large number of OSDs at once. If you don't see persistent `slow request` or users with torches and pitchforks most likely this goes unnoticed.

   A proof of concept script to automate OSD removal, including additional housekeeping, may be retrieved from Digital Ocean's *Spaces* service: https://nyc3.digitaloceanspaces.com/learningceph2ed/remove_osd

Expansion

In this section, we'll cover strategies for growing capacity to meet your users' never-ending thirst for storage. Below we'll summarize the process for adding a new OSD host to an existing Ceph cluster in a more manual, hands-on fashion. It is strongly encouraged that you practice this process with lab or pre-production. Another flexible strategy is to practice on virtualized systems, be they in-house or from a cloud provider such as Digital Ocean.

Visit `https://github.com/cernceph/ceph-scripts`. Here can be found a wealth of useful Ceph tools from the fine folks at CERN. Here we need to download `tools/ceph-gentle-reweight` onto our admin node. Around line 63 is a line that looks like the below; comment it out by adding a # at the beginning.

```
# latency = measure_latency(test_pool)
```

In a dedicated window run `watch ceph -s` to keep an eye on cluster status.

Now install Ceph packages on your new systems. This may be done with `eph-ansible`, with locally-appropriate invocations of `yum`, `apt-get`, or other package management tools. To install, say, the latest Jewel release of Ceph with the `ceph-deploy` utility, invoke

```
$ ceph-deploy install --release jewel mynewhostname
```

Add the new host(s) to our CRUSH topology. Our cluster for this example is spread across 12 existing hosts located in 4 sturdy metal racks named `rack1-iommi`, `rack2-butler`, `rack3-ward`, and `rack4-dio`. In order to maintain balance, we're adding 1 host to the 3 in each existing rack. First, we create `host` buckets.

```
$ ceph osd crush add-bucket newhost13 host
$ ceph osd crush add-bucket newhost14 host
$ ceph osd crush add-bucket newhost15 host
$ ceph osd crush add-bucket newhost16 host
```

For now, our new host buckets live outside of our cluster's default root bucket, so they are not allocated any data. This is deliberate so that we can set them up fully and bring them into service carefully and on our own terms.

Our `ceph -s` window shows us the OSD population.

```
osdmap e33981: 279 osds: 279 up, 279 in
flags sortbitwise,require_jewel_osds
```

Our new OSD drives may have been previously used for other purposes, and they may even come fresh from your system vendor with an unpredictable yet bizarre set of partitions on them. Our next step will be to survey drives on each remote system then wipe any such partitions from the drives so that they don't confuse our deployment tools. We can use ceph-deploy to show us the status of existing drives and to zap them clean.

```
$ ceph-deploy disk list newhost13 newhost14 newhost15 newhost16
[newhost13][DEBUG ]/dev/sda :
[newhost13][DEBUG ] /dev/sda1 other, linux_raid_member
[newhost13][DEBUG ] /dev/sda2 other, linux_raid_member
[newhost13][DEBUG ]/dev/sdb other, unknown
[newhost13][DEBUG ]/dev/sdc :
[newhost13][DEBUG ] /dev/sdc1 other, unknown
[newhost13][DEBUG ] /dev/sdc2 other, unknown
[...]
```

The `lsblk` utility is also handy for identifying the partitioning and mounts of each drive.

```
# lsblk
NAME   MAJ:MIN RM    SIZE RO TYPE   MOUNTPOINT
sda            8:0   0 223.6G  0 disk
├─sda1         8:1   0   243M  0 part
│ └─md0        9:0   0 242.8M  0 raid1 /boot
├─sda2         8:2   0 223.3G  0 part
└─md1          9:1   0 223.2G  0 raid1
  └─vg0-root (dm-0) 252:0 0 223.2G  0 lvm   /
sdb           8:16   0   3.5T  0 disk
├─sdb1        8:17   0   3.5T  0 part /var/lib/ceph/osd/ceph-0
└─sdb2        8:18   0    10G  0 part
sdc           8:32   0   3.5T  0 disk
```

After verifying that the boot drives are the ones we think they are, zap the rest.

```
$ for i in {b..i} ; do ceph-deploy disk zap newhost13:$i ; ceph-
deploy disk zap newhost14:$i ; ceph-deploy disk zap newhost15:
$i; ceph-deploy disk zap newhost16:$i ; done
```

This will take a while but when finished we'll know that all of our drives are ready for deployment. When creating a new OSD, if `ceph-deploy` runs into any existing partitions, it will complain and fail.

Now we create an OSD on each of our new drives. These will automatically be placed inside the appropriate `host` buckets we created above. Since the new host buckets are still located outside of our CRUSH root, these OSDs will not yet receive any new data. If we would prefer to use dmcrypt encryption or the new BlueStore back end we could add `--dmcrypt` and `--bluestore` flags, but let's keep it simple for now.

```
$ ceph-deploy osd create newhost13:sd{b..i}
[ceph_deploy.cli][INFO  ] Invoked (1.5.37): /usr/bin/ceph-deploy osd
create newhost13:sdb
[ceph_deploy.cli][INFO  ] ceph-deploy options:
[ceph_deploy.cli][INFO  ]  username                : None
[ceph_deploy.cli][INFO  ]  disk                    : [('newhost13',
'/dev/sdb', None)]
[ceph_deploy.cli][INFO  ]  dmcrypt                 : False
[ceph_deploy.cli][INFO  ]  verbose                 : False
[ceph_deploy.cli][INFO  ]  bluestore               : None
[ceph_deploy.cli][INFO  ]  overwrite_conf          : False
[ceph_deploy.cli][INFO  ]  subcommand              : create
[ceph_deploy.cli][INFO  ]  dmcrypt_key_dir         : /etc/ceph/dmcrypt-keys
[ceph_deploy.cli][INFO  ]  quiet                   : False
[ceph_deploy.cli][INFO  ]  cd_conf                 :
<ceph_deploy.conf.cephdeploy.Conf instance at 0x7feeb5599998>
[ceph_deploy.cli][INFO  ]  cluster                 : ceph
[ceph_deploy.cli][INFO  ]  fs_type                 : xfs
[ceph_deploy.cli][INFO  ]  func                    : <function osd at
0x7feeb5e641b8>
[ceph_deploy.cli][INFO  ]  ceph_conf               : None
[ceph_deploy.cli][INFO  ]  default_release         : False
[ceph_deploy.cli][INFO  ]  zap_disk                : False
[ceph_deploy.osd][DEBUG ] Preparing cluster ceph disks
newhost13:/dev/sdb:
[newhost13][DEBUG ] connection detected need for sudo
[newhost13][DEBUG ] connected to host: newhost13
[newhost13][DEBUG ] detect platform information from remote host
[newhost13][DEBUG ] detect machine type
[newhost13][DEBUG ] find the location of an executable
[newhost13][INFO  ] Running command: sudo /sbin/initctl version
[newhost13][DEBUG ] find the location of an executable
[ceph_deploy.osd][INFO  ] Distro info: Ubuntu 14.04 trusty
[ceph_deploy.osd][DEBUG ] Deploying osd to newhost13
[newhost13][DEBUG ] write cluster configuration to
/etc/ceph/{cluster}.conf
[ceph_deploy.osd][DEBUG ] Preparing host newhost13 disk /dev/sdb
```

```
journal None activate True
[newhost13][DEBUG ] find the location of an executable
[newhost13][INFO  ] Running command: sudo /usr/sbin/ceph-disk -v
prepare --fs-type xfs -- /dev/sdb
[newhost13][WARNIN] command: Running command: /usr/bin/ceph-osd --show-
config-value=fsid
[newhost13][WARNIN] command: Running command: /usr/bin/ceph-osd --
check-allows-journal -i 0 --setuser ceph --setgroup ceph
[newhost13][WARNIN] command: Running command: /usr/bin/ceph-osd --
check-wants-journal -i 0 --setuser ceph --setgroup ceph
[newhost13][WARNIN] command: Running command: /usr/bin/ceph-osd --
check-needs-journal -i 0 --setuser ceph --setgroup ceph
[newhost13][WARNIN] get_dm_uuid: get_dm_uuid /dev/sdb uuid path is
/sys/dev/block/8:16/dm/uuid
[newhost13][WARNIN] set_type: Will colocate journal with data on
/dev/sdb
[newhost13][WARNIN] command: Running command: /usr/bin/ceph-osd --show-
config-value=osd_journal_size
[newhost13][WARNIN] get_dm_uuid: get_dm_uuid /dev/sdb uuid path is
/sys/dev/block/8:16/dm/uuid
[newhost13][WARNIN] get_dm_uuid: get_dm_uuid /dev/sdb uuid path is
/sys/dev/block/8:16/dm/uuid
[newhost13][WARNIN] get_dm_uuid: get_dm_uuid /dev/sdb uuid path is
/sys/dev/block/8:16/dm/uuid
[newhost13][WARNIN] command: Running command: /usr/bin/ceph-conf --
name=osd. --lookup osd_mkfs_options_xfs
[newhost13][WARNIN] command: Running command: /usr/bin/ceph-conf --
name=osd. --lookup osd_mount_options_xfs
[newhost13][WARNIN] get_dm_uuid: get_dm_uuid /dev/sdb uuid path is
/sys/dev/block/8:16/dm/uuid
[newhost13][WARNIN] get_dm_uuid: get_dm_uuid /dev/sdb uuid path is
/sys/dev/block/8:16/dm/uuid
[newhost13][WARNIN] ptype_tobe_for_name: name = journal
newhost13][WARNIN] get_dm_uuid: get_dm_uuid /dev/sdb uuid path is
/sys/dev/block/8:16/dm/uuid
[newhost13][WARNIN] create_partition: Creating journal partition num 2
size 10240 on /dev/sdb
newhost13][WARNIN] command_check_call: Running command: /sbin/sgdisk --
new=2:0:+10240M --change-name=2:ceph journal --partition-
guid=2:8733d257-5b21-4574-8537-95a040ae5929 --
typecode=2:45b0969e-9b03-4f30-b4c6-b4b80ceff106 --mbrtogpt -- /dev/sdb
[newhost13][DEBUG ] Creating new GPT entries.
[newhost13][DEBUG ] The operation has completed successfully.
[newhost13][WARNIN] update_partition: Calling partprobe on created
device /dev/sdb
[newhost13][WARNIN] command_check_call: Running command: /sbin/udevadm
settle --timeout=600
[newhost13][WARNIN] command: Running command: /usr/bin/flock -s
```

```
/dev/sdb /sbin/partprobe /dev/sdb
[newhost13][WARNIN] command_check_call: Running command: /sbin/udevadm
settle --timeout=600
[newhost13][WARNIN] get_dm_uuid: get_dm_uuid /dev/sdb uuid path is
/sys/dev/block/8:16/dm/uuid
newhost13][WARNIN] get_dm_uuid: get_dm_uuid /dev/sdb uuid path is
/sys/dev/block/8:16/dm/uuid
newhost13][WARNIN] get_dm_uuid: get_dm_uuid /dev/sdb2 uuid path is
/sys/dev/block/8:18/dm/uuid
[newhost13][WARNIN] prepare_device: Journal is GPT partition
/dev/disk/by-partuuid/8733d257-5b21-4574-8537-95a040ae5929
[newhost13][WARNIN] prepare_device: Journal is GPT partition
/dev/disk/by-partuuid/8733d257-5b21-4574-8537-95a040ae5929
[newhost13][WARNIN] get_dm_uuid: get_dm_uuid /dev/sdb uuid path is
/sys/dev/block/8:16/dm/uuid
[newhost13][WARNIN] set_data_partition: Creating osd partition on
/dev/sdb
[newhost13][WARNIN] get_dm_uuid: get_dm_uuid /dev/sdb uuid path is
/sys/dev/block/8:16/dm/uuid
[newhost13][WARNIN] ptype_tobe_for_name: name = data
[newhost13][WARNIN] get_dm_uuid: get_dm_uuid /dev/sdb uuid path is
/sys/dev/block/8:16/dm/uuid
[newhost13][WARNIN] create_partition: Creating data partition num 1
size 0 on /dev/sdb
[newhost13][WARNIN] command_check_call: Running comma_partition:
Calling partprobe on created device /dev/sdb
[newhost13][WARNIN] command_check_call: Running command: /sbin/udevadm
settle --timeout=600
[newhost13][WARNIN] command: Running command: /usr/bin/flock -s
/dev/sdb /sbin/partprobe /dev/sdb
[newhost13][WARNIN] command_check_call: Running command: /sbin/udevadm
settle --timeout=600
[newhost13][WARNIN] get_dm_uuid: get_dm_uuid /dev/sdb uuid path is
/sys/dev/block/8:16/dm/uuid
[newhost13][WARNIN] get_dm_uuid:size 8192
[newhost13][WARNIN] switching to logical sector size 512
[newhost13][DEBUG ] meta-data=/dev/sdb1 isize=2048
agcount=32,agsize=29220715 blks
[newhost13][DEBUG ]          =          sectsz=512 attr=2, projid32bit=0
[newhost13][DEBUG ] data =          bsize=4096 blocks=935062865,imaxpct=5
[newhost13][DEBUG ]          =          sunit=0time,
nodiratime,inode64,logbsize=256k,delaylog
[newhost13][WARNIN] command_check_call: Running command: /bin/mount
   -t xfs -o rw,noatime,nodiratime,inode64,logbsize=256k,delaylog --
   /dev/sdb1 /var/lib/ceph/tmp/mnt.LjUwTs
[newhost13][WARNIN] populate_data_path: Preparing osd data dir
   /var/lib/ceph/tmp/mnt.LjUwTs
[newhost13][WARNIN] command: Running command: /bin/chown -R
```

```
          ceph:ceph /var/lib/ceph/tmp/mnt.LjUwTs/ceph_fsid.44648.tmp
     [newhost13][WARNIN7-95a040ae5929
     [newhost13][WARNIN] command: Running command: /bin/chown -R
          ceph:ceph /var/lib/ceph/tmp/mnt.LjUwTs
     [newhost13][WARNIN] unmount: Unmounting /var/lib/ceph/tmp/mnt.LjUwTs
     [newhost13][WARNIN] command_check_call: Running command_check_call:
     Running command: /sbin/udevadm settle --timeout=600
     [newhost13][WARNIN] command_check_call: Running command:
          /sbin/udevadm trigger --action=add --sysname-match sdb1
     [newhost13][INFO  ] checking OSD status...
     [newhost13][DEBUG ] find the location of an executable
     [newhost13][INFO  ] Running command: sudo /usr/bin/ceph osd stat --
          format=json
     [newhost13][WARNIN] there is 1 OSD down
     [newhost13][DEBUG ] Host newhost13 is now ready for osd use.
          . . .
     $ ceph-deploy osd create newhost14:sd{b..i}
     $ ceph-deploy osd create newhost15:sd{b..i}
     $ ceph-deploy osd create newhost16:sd{b..i}
```

Wow, a lot went on there. You can see the value of using a tool like ceph-deploy to do the heavy lifting for you. We won't go over every line of output above, but in summary, ceph-deploy ensures proper partitioning on the drive, creates an XFS filesystem, populates it with the wherewithal for OSD service, and invokes Ceph-specific udev rules that mount and start the OSD. The there is 1 OSD down message looks alarming, but it's harmless: OSDs can take a minute or two to fully boot and register themselves with the MONs

In our ceph -s window we see the new OSD added to the family, with the up, in, and osds numbers increment as the process progresses.

```
     osdmap e33999: 97 osds: 97 up, 97 in
     flags sortbitwise, require_jewel_osds
```

We can run ceph osd tree to see the new OSDs on our new host. With the addition of our nominal 3.84 TB drive, the output is something like this.

```
       . . .
     -18   3.48199          host
      0    3.48199          osd.96       up  1.00000 1.00000
```

Once all our new OSDs are successfully provisioned, we still haven't moved data onto them. First, we'll temporarily set their CRUSH weights to 0 to prevent a flood of data rushing in before we're ready.

First be sure that you've captured the CRUSH weights displayed by `ceph osd tree`, as we'll need them later. On an admin or MON node as root execute this command with the ID of each of the new OSDs.

```
# ceph osd crush reweight osd.id 0
```

Now it's safe to move the new hosts with their flock of OSDs into their racks. Since the host and OSD weights are now 0, no new data will be allocated to them yet.

```
# ceph osd crush move newhost13 rack=rack1-iommi
# ceph osd crush move newhost14 rack=rack2-butler
# ceph osd crush move newhost15 rack=rack3-ward
# ceph osd crush move newhost16 rack=rack4-dio
```

Running `ceph osd tree` now will show the new hosts and OSDs under each rack.

Now we'll ever so gradually increase the CRUSH weights on our new OSDs so that Ceph will begin to add data. By going in small steps of a few PGs each, we avoid causing a bunch of churn and potential user impact from an avalanche of data flooding onto the new OSDs. Fill in the list of new OSD numbers shown by `ceph osd tree`, being very careful to get the numbers of all (and only) the new OSDs that are currently weighted to 0. For brevity, we'll only list three here, but you should list all. Our new OSDs should return to weight 3.48199 but you must be careful to specify the proper number for yours. The -r flag indicates a trial run; when you are satisfied that the script's plan is sound, execute again without it.

```
# ceph-gentle-reweight -b 10 -d 0.01 -t 3.48199 -i 10 -r -o
osd.96,osd.97,osd.98
. . .
# ceph-gentle-reweight -b 10 -d 0.01 -t 3.48199 -i 10 -o
osd.96,osd.97,osd.98
```

While you watch this invaluable utility safely weight your OSDs up into full service, let's briefly discuss what's happening. This script checks the current CRUSH weights of the OSDs in question and keeps an eye on cluster health. When it's safe, each OSD's CRUSH weight is incremented by the -d absolute amount and the script watches as the cluster rebalances. No additional steps will be taken until the number of PGs backfilling drops below 10, as specified by the -b argument. By setting this to a small but nonzero number we save a bit of time that would otherwise be spent waiting for the last bits of rebalancing to proceed. When backfilling is this light, it's OK to pile on more. The -t argument specifies the final CRUSH weight we want our OSDs to reach. In our case nearly 350 steps will be taken to get us there, a la the Tortoise and the Hare. Finally the -i argument asks the script to rest for an additional 10 seconds between steps, just for good measure.

You may, of course, adjust these settings to your local conditions, but these are a good starting point. Depending on how full your cluster is and especially the size of your new OSDs this may take a few hours to a few days. Consider running within a tmux session.

As it runs, and especially after it completes, you can invoke `ceph df`; `ceph osd tree` in a separate window to see the cluster's capacity and the OSD's CRUSH weights slowly but steadily increase. The capacity will also be reflected in your `ceph -s` window. When the script exits you may see a very very slightly different target weight than you had initially. Ceph has a way of truncating or rounding the last significant digit or two. This difference is insignificant and can be disregarded.

Now we've successfully expanded your cluster's capacity by 33% -- possibly more if the new OSD drives are larger than the originals. Your users did not even notice this was going on. Ceph FTW.

Balancing

In this section, we'll explore what to do about it. The larger a cluster's OSD count grows, the wider the variance can become, approximating a bell curve. The `ceph osd df` utility can be used to summarize the utilization of each OSD along with an indication of how much it varies from the overall average. Here's an example of a cluster's distribution before and after we take action. Here our least full OSD is 29% full, just 80% of the cluster's mean, and the most full is over 44% full, 124% of the cluster's mean.

```
# ceph status
    cluster ce2bcf60-efd0-1138-bxc5-936beak1s9a7
      health HEALTH_OK
      monmap e1: 5 mons at
{mon01=10.7.4.4:6789/0,mon02=10.7.4.5:6789/0,mon03=10.7.4.132:6789/0,mon04=
10.7.4.133:6789/0,mon05=10.7.5.4:6789/0}
             election epoch 10, quorum 0,1,2,3,4
mon01,mon02,mon03,mon04,mon05
      osdmap e14922: 285 osds: 285 up, 285 in
          flags sortbitwise,require_jewel_osds
       pgmap v18454754: 16384 pgs, 1 pools, 119 TB data, 32487 kobjects
             353 TB used, 638 TB / 992 TB avail
                 16364 active+clean
                    14 active+clean+scrubbing+deep
                     6 active+clean+scrubbing
    client io 814 MB/s rd, 537 MB/s wr, 18375 op/s rd, 7170 op/s wr
# ceph osd df | head -3
ID  WEIGHT  REWEIGHT SIZE  USE   AVAIL %USE  VAR  PGS
 0 3.48199  1.00000 3565G 1250G 2314G 35.08 0.98 169
 1 3.48199  1.00000 3565G 1377G 2187G 38.64 1.08 186
```

```
# ceph osd df | sort -n -k 7 | head -6
ID  WEIGHT  REWEIGHT SIZE  USE    AVAIL %USE  VAR  PGS
MIN/MAX VAR: 0.80/1.24  STDDEV: 2.90
                 TOTAL  992T  355T  636T 35.85
253 3.48199 1.00000 3565G 1028G 2536G 28.85 0.80 139
208 3.48199 1.00000 3565G 1046G 2518G 29.36 0.82 141
124 3.48199 1.00000 3565G 1051G 2514G 29.48 0.82 142
# ceph osd df | sort -n -k 7 |tail -3
176 3.48199 1.00000 3565G 1542G 2022G 43.27 1.21 208
241 3.48199 1.00000 3565G 1565G 1999G 43.92 1.22 211
283 3.48199 1.00000 3565G 1589G 1975G 44.58 1.24 214
```

This tabular data shows us what's going on in the cluster, but it can be helpful to visualize the distribution of data as well. Use a wide terminal window; you can see how the longer bars wrap in this rendering.

```
    # ceph osd df | egrep -v WEIGHT\|TOTAL\|MIN\|ID | awk '{print 1,
int($7)}' |   ./histogram.py -a -b 100 -m 0 -x 100 -p 1
    # NumSamples = 285; Min = 0.00; Max = 100.00
    # Mean = 35.385965; Variance = 8.587873; SD = 2.930507; Median
35.000000
    # each ▌ represents a count of 1
        0.0000 -     1.0000 [     0]:  (0.00%)
        1.0000 -     2.0000 [     0]:  (0.00%)
        2.0000 -     3.0000 [     0]:  (0.00%)
    . . .
       26.0000 -    27.0000 [     0]:  (0.00%)
       27.0000 -    28.0000 [     1]: ▌ (0.35%)
       28.0000 -    29.0000 [     3]: ▌▌▌ (1.05%)
       29.0000 -    30.0000 [     6]: ▌▌▌▌▌▌ (2.11%)
       30.0000 -    31.0000 [    13]: ▌▌▌▌▌▌▌▌▌▌▌▌▌ (4.56%)
       31.0000 -    32.0000 [    29]:
▌▌▌▌▌▌▌▌▌▌▌▌▌▌▌▌▌▌▌▌▌▌▌▌▌▌▌▌▌ (10.18%)
       32.0000 -    33.0000 [    30]:
▌▌▌▌▌▌▌▌▌▌▌▌▌▌▌▌▌▌▌▌▌▌▌▌▌▌▌▌▌▌▌ (10.53%)
       33.0000 -    34.0000 [    25]:
▌▌▌▌▌▌▌▌▌▌▌▌▌▌▌▌▌▌▌▌▌▌▌▌▌ (8.77%)
       34.0000 -    35.0000 [    37]:
▌▌▌▌▌▌▌▌▌▌▌▌▌▌▌▌▌▌▌▌▌▌▌▌▌▌▌▌▌▌▌▌▌▌▌▌▌▌▌ (12.98%)
       35.0000 -    36.0000 [    46]:
▌▌▌▌▌▌▌▌▌▌▌▌▌▌▌▌▌▌▌▌▌▌▌▌▌▌▌▌▌▌▌▌▌▌▌▌▌▌▌▌▌▌▌▌▌▌
                                                         (16.14%)
       36.0000 -    37.0000 [    32]:
▌▌▌▌▌▌▌▌▌▌▌▌▌▌▌▌▌▌▌▌▌▌▌▌▌▌▌▌▌▌▌▌▌▌ (11.23%)
       37.0000 -    38.0000 [    21]: ▌▌▌▌▌▌▌▌▌▌▌▌▌▌▌▌▌▌▌▌▌
                                      (7.37%)
       38.0000 -    39.0000 [    22]: ▌▌▌▌▌▌▌▌▌▌▌▌▌▌▌▌▌▌▌▌▌▌
                                      (7.72%)
```

```
39.0000 -    40.0000 [    7]: ███████ (2.46%)
40.0000 -    41.0000 [    5]: █████ (1.75%)
41.0000 -    42.0000 [    2]: ██ (0.70%)
42.0000 -    43.0000 [    5]: █████ (1.75%)
43.0000 -    44.0000 [    1]: █ (0.35%)
44.0000 -    45.0000 [    0]:   (0.00%)
45.0000 -    46.0000 [    0]:   (0.00%)
46.0000 -    47.0000 [    0]:   (0.00%)
```

OSDs that are significantly underweight do not shoulder their share of the cluster's iops; OSDs that are overweight get more than their share and risk an outage when they fill prematurely.

We can squeeze this distribution into a narrower range by adjusting the reweight value of individual OSDs to cause them to receive more (or less) data. In the above example, we might attack the worst offender:

```
# ceph osd reweight 283 .98000
```

This will adjust osd.283's data allocation by a small amount; data will move off of it onto other OSDs. Runs of `ceph status` will show PGs in the `remapped` state while the cluster performs *recovery* to converge on the new data distribution. The reweight value must be between `0.0` and `1.0` so, unfortunately, we cannot assign a reweight greater than 1 to increase utilization of under full OSDs. Thus we work down from the top; overfull OSD's are the real danger.

We chose to decrement the reweight value only slightly. The greater the change, the more data moves with more potential impact to the cluster. The wise course is slow and steady to avoid disruption and so that we don't overshoot and turn our overfull OSD into an underfull OSD.

We may continue this process iteratively, pushing down the worst offenders, allowing the cluster to rebalance, then pushing down the new worst offender. Rinse, lather, repeat. This becomes something of a Whack-a-Mole game, though, or like squeezing a balloon. A more effective and faster process is to reweight multiple OSDs at once.

This is where Ceph's `ceph osd reweight-by-utilization` tool comes in. This was introduced in the Hammer release, though documentation remains incomplete. One invokes with three arguments:

- A cutoff percentage (or *overload*) threshold; OSDs more full than this value are targeted for deweighting.
- The largest weight change permitted
- The maximal number of PG's to change

This process was initially a stab in the dark; it was difficult to predict how much data would move, and thus rightsizing parameters was a shot in the dark. Jewel introduced a `test-reweight-by-utilization` command to model sets of parameters with a dry run; this was also backported into later dot releases of Hammer.

Here are some example dry runs on the above cluster. We choose a conservative maximum weight change to take and a cap on the number of OSD's to tweak based on the total number in our cluster. It would be nice to add an option to specify this as a percentage versus an absolute number, but we don't have that today. We choose a conservative starting point for the cutoff percentage threshold based on the *overload* that `ceph osd df` shows for our most full OSD. Below we'll try increasingly aggressive thresholds; note that as we approach the mean value of 100% (roughly 35% full as per `ceph df`) the number of PGs affect grows. Once we find a set of parameters that results in a significant but tolerable degree of adjustment we fire it off for real.

```
# ceph osd test-reweight-by-utilization 120 0.01 30
no change
moved 7 / 49152 (0.0142415%)
avg 172.463
stddev 13.9391 -> 13.8722 (expected baseline 13.1095)
min osd.253 with 139 -> 139 pgs (0.805969 -> 0.805969 * mean)
max osd.283 with 214 -> 212 pgs (1.24084 -> 1.22925 * mean)
oload 120
max_change 0.01
max_change_osds 30
average 0.358507
overload 0.430208
osd.283 weight 1.000000 -> 0.990005
osd.241 weight 1.000000 -> 0.990005
osd.176 weight 1.000000 -> 0.990005
osd.144 weight 1.000000 -> 0.990005
osd.19 weight 1.000000 -> 0.990005
osd.158 weight 1.000000 -> 0.990005
```

The above parameters only move 7 PGs, that isn't much of a change. Let's dial down down the threshold value to grab more of the high end of the distribution's tail.

```
# ceph osd test-reweight-by-utilization 117 0.01 30
no change
moved 10 / 49152 (0.0203451%)
avg 172.463
stddev 13.9391 -> 13.8395 (expected baseline 13.1095)
min osd.253 with 139 -> 139 pgs (0.805969 -> 0.805969 * mean)
max osd.283 with 214 -> 212 pgs (1.24084 -> 1.22925 * mean)
oload 117
max_change 0.01
max_change_osds 30
average 0.358474
overload 0.419415
osd.283 weight 1.000000 -> 0.990005
osd.241 weight 1.000000 -> 0.990005
osd.176 weight 1.000000 -> 0.990005
osd.144 weight 1.000000 -> 0.990005
osd.19 weight 1.000000 -> 0.990005
osd.158 weight 1.000000 -> 0.990005
osd.128 weight 1.000000 -> 0.990005
osd.257 weight 1.000000 -> 0.990005
```

A bit better, but we can be more aggressive.

```
# ceph osd test-reweight-by-utilization 114 0.01 30
no change
moved 24 / 49152 (0.0488281%)
avg 172.463
stddev 13.9391 -> 13.7556 (expected baseline 13.1095)
min osd.253 with 139 -> 139 pgs (0.805969 -> 0.805969 * mean)
max osd.283 with 214 -> 212 pgs (1.24084 -> 1.22925 * mean)
oload 114
max_change 0.01
max_change_osds 30
average 0.358479
overload 0.408666
osd.283 weight 1.000000 -> 0.990005
osd.241 weight 1.000000 -> 0.990005
osd.176 weight 1.000000 -> 0.990005
osd.144 weight 1.000000 -> 0.990005
osd.19 weight 1.000000 -> 0.990005
osd.158 weight 1.000000 -> 0.990005
osd.128 weight 1.000000 -> 0.990005
osd.257 weight 1.000000 -> 0.990005
osd.171 weight 1.000000 -> 0.990005
osd.179 weight 1.000000 -> 0.990005
```

```
osd.149 weight 1.000000 -> 0.990005
osd.97 weight 1.000000 -> 0.990005
osd.37 weight 1.000000 -> 0.990005
osd.304 weight 1.000000 -> 0.990005
# ceph osd test-reweight-by-utilization 112 0.01 30
no change
moved 28 / 49152 (0.0569661%)
avg 172.463
stddev 13.9391 -> 13.7446 (expected baseline 13.1095)
min osd.253 with 139 -> 139 pgs (0.805969 -> 0.805969 * mean)
max osd.283 with 214 -> 212 pgs (1.24084 -> 1.22925 * mean)
oload 112
max_change 0.01
max_change_osds 30
average 0.358480
overload 0.401497
. . .
```

Better still, but on this all-SSD cluster, we can afford to bite off more.

```
# ceph osd test-reweight-by-utilization 110 0.01 30
no change
moved 44 / 49152 (0.0895182%)
avg 172.463
stddev 13.9391 -> 13.6904 (expected baseline 13.1095)
min osd.253 with 139 -> 139 pgs (0.805969 -> 0.805969 * mean)
max osd.283 with 214 -> 212 pgs (1.24084 -> 1.22925 * mean)
oload 110
max_change 0.01
max_change_osds 30
average 0.358480
overload 0.394328
osd.283 weight 1.000000 -> 0.990005
osd.241 weight 1.000000 -> 0.990005
osd.176 weight 1.000000 -> 0.990005
. . .
```

You can see that as we enter the thicker part of the histogram each step adjusts increasingly more PGs. These parameters seem like a pretty good choice; prudent values for each cluster are unique and must be determined by careful testing and simulation.

Let's go ahead and invoke the process with these parameters.

```
# ceph osd reweight-by-utilization 110 0.01 30
moved 44 / 49152 (0.0895182%)
avg 172.463
stddev 13.9391 -> 13.6904 (expected baseline 13.1095)
min osd.253 with 139 -> 139 pgs (0.805969 -> 0.805969 * mean)
max osd.283 with 214 -> 212 pgs (1.24084 -> 1.22925 * mean)
oload 110
max_change 0.01
max_change_osds 30
average 0.358437
overload 0.394280
osd.283 weight 1.000000 -> 0.990005
osd.241 weight 1.000000 -> 0.990005
osd.176 weight 1.000000 -> 0.990005
osd.144 weight 1.000000 -> 0.990005
osd.19 weight 1.000000 -> 0.990005
```

As the reweight values are changed the cluster shifts data to converge onto the new CRUSH mappings. This is equivalent to issuing 30 separate `ceph osd reweight` commands or with Luminous a single `ceph osd reweightn` invocation acting on all at once.

The cluster now enters a period of backfill/recovery. In your trusty `watch ceph status` window, you will see the number and percentage of degraded/misplaced objects increase as the PGs plan their adjustments. These values will then progressively decrease as PGs enter the backfilling state where they are actively moving data reflecting our changes to their Acting Sets.

```
cluster cef00bar40-efd0-11e6-bcc5-936eieiob9a7
     health HEALTH_WARN
             44 pgs backfilling
             recovery 8/100169721 objects degraded (0.000%)
             recovery 157792/100169721 objects misplaced (0.158%)
     monmap e1: 5 mons at
{mon01=10.7.4.4:6789/0,mon02=10.7.4.5:6789/0,mon03=10.7.4.132:6789/0,mo
    n04=10.7.4.133:6789/0,mon05=10.7.5.4:6789/0}
             election epoch 10, quorum 0,1,2,3,4
     mon01,mon02,mon03,mon04,mon05
     osdmap e15516: 285 osds: 285 up, 285 in; 44 remapped pgs
             flags sortbitwise,require_jewel_osds
      pgmap v18489106: 16384 pgs, 1 pools, 120 TB data, 32578
     kobjects
             355 TB used, 636 TB / 992 TB avail
             8/100169721 objects degraded (0.000%)
             157792/100169721 objects misplaced (0.158%)
```

```
               16313 active+clean
                  44 active+remapped+backfilling
                  18 active+clean+scrubbing+deep
                   9 active+clean+scrubbing
      recovery io 7568 MB/s, 2 keys/s, 2018 objects/s
        client io 1080 MB/s rd, 574 MB/s wr, 27120 op/s rd, 11987 op/s wr
```

When this process completes the cluster returns to HEALTH_OK and a histogram refresh shows that we have ever so gently squeezed down the most full OSDs.

```
# ceph osd df | sort -n -k 7 | tail -3
128 3.48199  0.99001 3565G 1541G 2023G 43.23 1.21 208
241 3.48199  0.99001 3565G 1565G 1999G 43.92 1.22 211
283 3.48199  0.99001 3565G 1574G 1990G 44.17 1.23 212
```

Above we see that the most full osd is now only 44.17% full and its variance from the mean has decreased to 123%. osd.283 now holds 15 GB less data than it did before.

```
    cluster cef00bar40-efd0-11e6-bcc5-936eieiob9a7
        health HEALTH_OK
        monmap e1: 5 mons at
{mon01=10.7.4.4:6789/0,mon02=10.7.4.5:6789/0,mon03=10.7.4.132:6789/0,mo
  n04=10.7.4.133:6789/0,mon05=10.76.50.4:6789/0}
             election epoch 10, quorum 0,1,2,3,4
  mon01,mon02,mon03,mon04,mon05
        osdmap e15559: 285 osds: 285 up, 285 in
             flags sortbitwise,require_jewel_osds
        pgmap v18492138: 16384 pgs, 1 pools, 120 TB data, 32592 kobjects
             355 TB used, 636 TB / 992 TB avail
               16361 active+clean
                  17 active+clean+scrubbing+deep
                   6 active+clean+scrubbing
      client io 996 MB/s rd, 573 MB/s wr, 29542 op/s rd, 14264 op/s wr
    # ceph osd df | egrep -v WEIGHT\|TOTAL\|MIN\|ID | awk '{print 1,
int($7)}' | ./histogram.py -a -b 100 -m 0 -x 100 -p 1
    # NumSamples = 285; Min = 0.00; Max = 100.00
    # Mean = 35.392982; Variance = 8.182407; SD = 2.860491; Median
35.000000
    # each ▌ represents a count of 1
       0.0000 -    1.0000 [    0]:  (0.00%)
    ...
      26.0000 -   27.0000 [    0]:  (0.00%)
      27.0000 -   28.0000 [    1]: ▌ (0.35%)
      28.0000 -   29.0000 [    2]: ▌▌ (0.70%)
      29.0000 -   30.0000 [    6]: ▌▌▌▌▌▌ (2.11%)
      30.0000 -   31.0000 [   14]: ▌▌▌▌▌▌▌▌▌▌▌▌▌▌ (4.91%)
      31.0000 -   32.0000 [   26]: ▌▌▌▌▌▌▌▌▌▌▌▌▌▌▌▌▌▌▌▌▌▌▌▌▌▌ (9.12%)
      32.0000 -   33.0000 [   32]: ▌▌▌▌▌▌▌▌▌▌▌▌▌▌▌▌▌▌▌▌▌▌▌▌▌▌▌▌▌▌▌▌▌▌ (11.23%)
```

```
        33.0000 -      34.0000 [     26]: ■■■■■■■■■■■■■■■■■■■■■■■■■■ (9.12%)
        34.0000 -      35.0000 [     36]: ■■■■■■■■■■■■■■■■■■■■■■■■■■■■■■■■■■■■■■
 (12.63%)
        35.0000 -      36.0000 [     45]: ■■■■■■■■■■■■■■■■■■■■■■■■■■■■■■■■■■■■■■■■■■■■■■■■■
 (15.79%)
        36.0000 -      37.0000 [     33]: ■■■■■■■■■■■■■■■■■■■■■■■■■■■■■■■■■■■ (11.58%)
        37.0000 -      38.0000 [     22]: ■■■■■■■■■■■■■■■■■■■■■■ (7.72%)
        38.0000 -      39.0000 [     25]: ■■■■■■■■■■■■■■■■■■■■■■■■■ (8.77%)
        39.0000 -      40.0000 [      7]: ■■■■■■■ (2.46%)
        40.0000 -      41.0000 [      3]: ■■■ (1.05%)
        41.0000 -      42.0000 [      2]: ■■ (0.70%)
        42.0000 -      43.0000 [      4]: ■■■■ (1.40%)
        43.0000 -      44.0000 [      1]: ■ (0.35%)
        44.0000 -      45.0000 [      0]:    (0.00%)
```

The post-reweight histogram reflects a modest improvement in variance and standard deviation. We actually made more of a difference than the absolute values reported by ceph df indicate; in the time between our first look at distribution and our post-adjustment survey the cluster gained roughly 2TB of data, which pushes up the percentage fullness of all OSD's a bit as each accepts new data.

In production, we would repeat this process with an incrementally larger threshold and/or OSD count values to put the squeeze on the distribution curve, which will become flat on the high end and more narrow toward the low end. This ensures that our cluster can accept more data and be more fully utilized before most-full OSDs cross our warning and error thresholds described in the next chapter.

The `histogram.py` filter and other useful tools can be retrieved from: https://gitlab.cern.ch/ceph/ceph-scripts

Upgrades

Upgrading an existing, production Ceph cluster can be both straightforward and tricky. It is best to not leapfrog LTS releases when upgrading. For example, if you're still running Firefly, instead of upgrading directly to Luminous you should consider upgrading first to Hammer, then to Jewel, and only then to Luminous. This strategy considers that the constellation of old and new versions is as large as the resources to test all combinations are limited.

Each Ceph release is accompanied by release notes that detail the best process for upgrades. In some cases, there are crucial gotchas that must be considered. For example, by default daemons in Jewel and later releases run as the ceph user, instead of root. When upgrading to Jewel from an earlier release one must carefully change the ownership of all files within each OSD's filesystem. Bear in mind as well that downgrading to an earlier major release of Ceph is generally not supported. Try out a new version in a test cluster before you commit it to production.

The logistics of upgrades include many variables, including your management tools, package management strategy, and the components one has deployed. In at least one case package names changed between releases, complicating their management. In general terms an upgrade follows this path:

- Upgrade the `ceph`, `ceph-common`, `librbd`, etc. packages with `yum`, `apt-get`, etc. This can be performed in parallel and without taking down servers, though you do not want to do this too far in advance. Validate the successful and full installation of all packages on every system.
- Sequentially restart the MONs, allowing each to boot and fully rejoin the quorum before proceeding to the next.
- Sequentially restart the OSDs. You may do them individually, or an entire host at a time. Don't forget the `noout` flag! Before proceeding to the next server and especially before crossing failure domains it is critical to ensure that all OSDs are up and in, that backfill/recovery has completed, and that all PGs are active+clean.
- Sequentially restart any RGW and MDS servers. Allow each to fully start and become active before proceeding.

That said, some major Ceph releases, or even dot releases within a major version, may require different ordering, say OSD nodes first then MONs. Read the release notes carefully.

Above we mentioned the need for pervasive file ownership permission changes on FileStore OSDs when one upgrades to Jewel. This adds up to considerable elapsed time even if one runs all OSDs on each host in parallel. There's a clever trick that allows us to perform this transition task incrementally. In `ceph.conf` one can configure

`setuser match path = /var/lib/ceph/$type/$cluster-$id`

This will direct daemons to run as the user who owns each individual data directory root. In this way one may then proceed at relative leisure to iterate across the OSD complement halting each individual OSD in sequence, `chown -R`, start the OSD anew, and remove the noout flag. Don't forget to bracket each set of OSDs with the `noout` flag!

Linux kernel or even whole operating system upgrades are often more straightforward than Ceph release upgrades. One can typically install updated packages in advance, effect any necessary configuration file changes, then sequentially reboot Ceph servers, again ensuring that they come back up fully and the cluster heals between each. Ordering is usually not important here, though it is not uncommon to follow the same MON=>OSD=>RGW=>MDS sequence as above.

> An excellent summary of many of the commands described in this chapter may be found here:
> `https://sabaini.at/pages/ceph-cheatsheet.html`
> The `ceph-ansible` project mentioned in this and other chapters offers convenient tools for Ceph release upgrades and other management tasks. See `http://ceph.com/geen-categorie/ceph-rolling-upgrades-with-ansible/` for details.

Working with remote hands

Practices for the actual physical management of servers and components vary by organization. In smaller settings especially Ceph admins may site near the datacenters in which production systems are housed, and be responsible for hardware installation and management. In other and larger organizations, especially those with multiple datacenters within a country or around the world, there may be a dedicated DC Ops team or contracted third party.

We often refer to anyone who performs physical server installation and maintenance tasks as *remote hands* or simply *hands*, referring to the fact that they are able to lay literal hands on the systems that a distant admin cannot.

Whichever arrangement floats your organization's boat, there are a number of practices that can optimize hardware management logistics. Some of us may work in a busy, loud, shared office spaces, but datacenters are a whole new level of loud and cold. Careful co-ordination can save time and avoid mistakes when performing maintenance tasks, especially when replacing failed components. This topic may seem trivial and out of scope, but Ceph clusters comprise large numbers of twisty servers, all alike, and this author has seen this aspect of server management time and again fail horribly.

Here's a litany of best practices for working with datacenter hands.

- **Lose your voice**

  DCs house hundreds or thousands of spinning fans and cacophonous air handlers. They are *LOUD* and your hands folks should be wearing hearing protection. Fancy noise-canceling headsets if available can vary in their effectiveness. But even in a silent room voice is a flawed way to communicate with DC hands. Like luggage at an airport, many names and digits do sound alike, and transcription errors are all too common. Was that serial number was 83423NCC1701 or A3423NEE1701? Should I yank drive twenty or twenty-one? The only way to win is not to play. Calls are fine for discussing logistics, but not for exchanging precise data.

- **Real-time digital communication**

  It's vital for admins and hands to be able to communicate digitally. Ideal is a laptop or tablet with instant messaging or collaboration tools like Jabber, Slack, or Cisco Spark. In a pinch, you can use a smartphone or even the chat pane of a Zoom, Cisco WebEx, Google Hangout conference. These media allow one to cut/paste information, avoiding transcription errors. Email is not the best medium here given propagation delays, but it can be useful when nothing else is available.

- **Network access**

  It's best for the DC hands to have network access, to the Internet at large or at least to your internal network. This allows them to retrieve firmware files and diagrams, and to send you photos and screen captures.

- **Just the right tool**

  Software and hardware: This author once worked with an excellent node engineer who was employed by a different and rather parsimonious business unit. They had him using hand tools for hundreds of fasteners every day. The gift of a $30 electric screwdriver was invaluable for efficiency and made me his new best friend.

  Simple hand tools also have a way of walking away even from a locked DC hall, and among the worst frustrations is discovering only after you take a system down that your system vendor uses T10 Torx screws but the tech has only a stripped Phillips driver.

- **Verify server identity**
  Adhesive stickers can be handy for visually locating a server, but they can just as easily be deadly. Don't rely on them. They can fade, fall off, be reattached to the wrong server, or be written incorrectly in the first place. Repurposed systems may not get a new and unique label. A different department's server in the next rack may have a name that varies from yours only by a hyphen. This author has been bit by all of these and has learned to not trust them. Modern systems often don't even have a space to attach a label given the desire to pack the front panel with as many connectors, indicator lights, and drive bays as possible.

  There are several better methods for ensuring that hands unplug and work on the proper server. Use them together when possible.

  - Indicator lights: tools like ipmitool, storcli, and hpssacli allow one to flash LED's for visual identification of desired servers
  - Serial numbers: Always refer to servers and drives by their serial numbers and never transcribe them. Cut/paste or extract digitally. The facter utility is great for this on a variety of hardware. Run facter hostname serialnumber productname and paste the results to your tech for multiple levels of identification. Utilities like hpssacli, dmidecode, facter, and storcli also help with component serials
  - Power: modern servers often have sophisticated BMCs or other ACPI power management systems. The last step of preparing a system for maintenance can be to run shutdown -P now; this will power down most server components, lights, and fans. The subject server is thus visually and audibly distinct.
  - Lockstep check-in
    Ensure that remote hands verify with you that your server is ready for them to tear into, that they have located the proper serial number, and that you're ready for them to reconnect power and network connections and boot it on up. Most importantly of all, make sure that they don't leave for the day until you both agree that the task is complete and the server is functional.

Summary

In this chapter, we covered a wide variety of operational and maintenance tasks that are part of a Ceph cluster's lifecycle. We explored cluster topology, a topic we'll continue in `Chapter 20`, *Monitoring Ceph*, as well as Ceph's logging system. We also delved into `ceph.conf` for startup configuration, injection for dynamic runtime configuration, and admin sockets for harvesting a wealth of status and configuration detail. Also touched upon was the value of a formal configuration management system such as `ceph-ansible`.

We also expanded on the topics of adding and replacing failed drives that were touched upon in the previous chapter and offered strategies for the oft-overlooked nuances of working effectively with remote hands.

It may seem odd that we have not devoted an entire chapter to the step by step initial deployment of production Ceph clusters. There are readily available automation tools and resources to help with this process. Duplicating their multivariate minutia here or cutting and pasting large swaths of ceph.com would leave less space to focus on the insights and wisdom the authors strive to share.

For initial cluster bootstrapping we recommend the excellent ceph-ansible project available here:

```
https://github.com/ceph/ceph-ansible/wiki
```

A useful blog post detailing one admin's experience using ceph-ansible to bootstrap a cluster can be read here:

```
http://egonzalez.org/ceph-ansible-baremetal-deployment/
```

Those wishing a more hands-on, under-the-hood bootstrap experience will enjoy the reference site:

```
http://docs.ceph.com/docs/master/rados/deployment/
```

In the next chapter, we will explore the monitoring of your Ceph clusters' well-being.

20
Monitoring Ceph

In this chapter, we will cover the following topics.

- Monitoring Ceph clusters
- Monitoring Ceph MONs
- Monitoring Ceph OSDs
- Monitoring Ceph PGs
- Monitoring Ceph MDS
- Open source dashboards and tools

Monitoring Ceph clusters

Monitoring is the process of gathering, aggregating, and processing important quantifiable information about a given system. It enables us to understand the health of the system and its components and provides information necessary to take steps to troubleshoot problems that arise. A well-monitored system will let us know when something is broken or is about to break. Deploying a Ceph cluster involves an orchestration dance among hundreds, thousands, or even tens of thousands of interconnected components including variety of kernels, processes, storage drives, controllers (HBAs), network cards (NICs), chassis, switches, PSUs,and so on. Each of these components can fail or degrade in its own unique way.

External monitoring of a complex system is itself a significant endeavor and is best worked right into the architecture and deployment model. When monitoring is an afterthought (*we'll get to it in phase 2*) it tends to be less effective and less pervasively implemented.

Ceph is in many ways a self-monitoring and self-healing system. It is however valuable to integrate with external monitoring and trending tools so that we can address hardware faults and ensure optimal performance and capacity. Identifying and fixing the root causes of hardware or non-Ceph process failures is beyond the scope of this chapter, so we will focus on the overall functionality and performance of Ceph clusters.

Third party components or services often provide their own monitoring interfaces. Production Ceph clusters typically serve a large set of clients. The types of those clients vary depending on whether a cluster is used for RBD images, CephFS volumes, as an Object Storage backend, or all of the above. Each deployment environment has different requirements for reliability that depend primarily on the use-case. Some Ceph clusters are used predominantly for internal clients and a **Service Level Agreement** (**SLA**) of less than 99% uptime suffices. Others serve users who are external actors/customers that pay for higher reliability and uptime guarantees. There are also clusters deployed with a mixed client population with separate tiers of SLAs. There are all sorts of use-cases for Ceph on varied types of client systems, too many to cover in this chapter so we will not dive into the details of client-side monitoring here.

When monitoring a Ceph system we will primary exploit native CLI tools that are provided by the ceph-common package. These tools are available as subcommands of the ceph utility and output reports on their standard output (stdout). These reports can offer a great deal of detail and usually provide ample information to help diagnose issues is and locate the where the problem lies. These tools provide invaluable information regarding the state of the cluster but do not always provide everything required for a thorough **root-cause analysis** (**RCA**).

For this reason it is recommended to rely on other diagnostic utilities that your Linux distribution or hardware manufacturer provides. We touched upon some of these Ceph commands and external utilities in previous chapters. It is vital that in addition to the Ceph-specific monitoring that we monitor basic hardware state -- CPUs, memory modules, NICs, drive controllers, power supplies, and so on. We can do so either through the operating system with tools including mcelog, rsyslog, and ipmitool or directly leveraging a server's management controller (BMC) using network IPMI, Redfish, or SNMP traps. Some platforms offer rich proprietary tools as well, including the XML API to Cisco's UCS. Your existing infrastructure no doubt already exploits one or more of these hardware monitoring approaches, and your Ceph systems should slot right in.

Ceph cluster health

The health check is one of the most common and important commands that a Ceph system administrator will employ frequently to stay aware of any major issues. The output of the health check gives a quick 40,000 ft. view of whether the cluster is performing normally or if it is degraded. If a cluster is unhealthy, we can use the same command to get a detailed view of where the problem lies. Even though it might not always be able tell us what the exact problem is, we can use it in almost every case to narrow our scope and focus our investigation to a very specific area.

To check the health of the cluster, we will use the health subcommand of the ceph utility.

```
root@ceph-client0:~# ceph health
HEALTH_OK
```

When Ceph cluster is healthy the status will be HEALTH_OK. In all other cases, it will present a status of HEALTH_WARN or HEALTH_ERR followed by a short summary of the major problems the cluster is undergoing. There is talk of introducing additional states with future versions of Ceph, but as we write these are the only three.

It is useful to note that all Ceph commands emit output in a plain format that is easily readable by humans. There isn't always a human parsing the output, though: sometimes code may invoke commands for monitoring, to display in a dashboard, or to derive additional results based on analysis. In such cases we can use the --format switch to emit output in an appropriate format. This is especially useful for monitoring systems, as the plain, human-oriented formatting tends to change between releases, but the computer-oriented formats are largely invariant.
For instance if we desire the health output in JSON format we can invoke:

```
root@ceph-client0:~# ceph health --format json
```

```
{"health":{"health_services":[{"mons":[{"name":"ceph-
mon0","kb_total":306935960,"kb_used":2815616,"kb_avail":2
88505780,"avail_percent":93,"last_updated":"2017-09-17
19:07:59.682571","store_stats":{"bytes_total":98218171,"b
ytes_sst":0,"bytes_log":938237,"bytes_misc":97279934,"las
t_updated":"0.000000"},"health":"HEALTH_OK"}]}]},"timeche
cks":{"epoch":6,"round":0,"round_status":"finished"},"sum
mary":[],"overall_status":"HEALTH_OK","detail":[]}
```

The --format json switch emits output in JSON format. The details of plain and other formats may differ, so make sure to understand the output before sending to a parser.

Ceph currently avails us of following output formats:

- plain (default)
- xml
- xml-pretty (both parser and human friendly)
- json
- json-pretty (both parser and human friendly)

An unhealthy cluster, for example, can look as follows:

```
root@ceph-client0:~# ceph health
HEALTH_WARN 71 pgs degraded; 67 pgs stuck unclean; 71 pgs undersized;
recovery 57/573 objects degraded (9.948%); mds cluster is degraded; 1/6 in
osds are down
```

The first word in the output (HEALTH_WARN) indicates the current health of the cluster. As of Ceph's Jewel release, the health of a Ceph cluster can only be in 3 states:

1. HEALTH_OK: The cluster is healthy and client I/O is serviced as expected.
2. HEALTH_WARN: The cluster is degraded but there is a (possibly) minor problem. A host may have died or a rack may have lost power, but client I/O continues.
3. HEALTH_ERR: The cluster is unhealthy and there is major impact to some or all client I/O. This can be triggered by large scale degradation when multiple racks or hosts across multiple racks go down simultaneously.

Let's examine about the output of the above command in slightly more detail, splitting the output into distinct symptoms. Each symptom is separated by a semicolon (";").

- HEALTH_WARN: The cluster is degraded.
- 71 PGs degraded: A total of 71 PGs are affected, possibly because one or more of OSDs have gone down.
- 67 pgs stuck unclean: Out of a total of 71 affected PGs, 67 are in the unclean state. PGs that do not have their all the OSDs in their acting set completely up to date are marked unclean.
- 71 pgs undersized: There are 71 PGs which have fewer copies than configured as the replication size of the their pool.

- `Recovery 57/573 objects degraded (9.948%)`: The recovery process has begun and presently 53 RADOS objects are marked degraded and queued for recovery. The cluster holds a total of 573 RADOS objects, thus the fraction in the degraded state is 53 / 573 = 9.948%.

- `mds cluster is degraded`: The MDS cluster deployed for CephFS is degraded as well. This could be because one or more of MDS daemons are not started yet or not functioning as expected.

- `1/6 osds are down`: 1 OSD is down in our cluster out of a total of 6. The degradation of 67 PGs (across 53 objects) may have been a result of the OSD going down.

Every cluster is built and configured differently, with a different number of OSDs and unique pool settings. Thus all the above issues might not translate 1-to-1 to your setup; we provide them here as a reference example. However, if your cluster is showing HEALTH_WARN that does mean you might need to take a look even if the problem seems transient in nature.

There are other subcommands we can use to display the current state of a Ceph cluster, notably status (-s). The output of this command during the above degradation is shown in the following:

```
root@ceph-client0:~# ceph status
cluster e6d4e4ab-f59f-470d-bb76-511deebc8de3
health HEALTH_WARN
71 pgs degraded
67 pgs stuck unclean
71 pgs undersized
recovery 57/573 objects degraded (9.948%)
1/6 in osds are down
monmap e1: 1 mons at {ceph-mon0=192.168.42.10:6789/0}
election epoch 5, quorum 0 ceph-mon0
fsmap e10989: 1/1/1 up {0=ceph-mds0=up:active}
osdmap e4165: 6 osds: 5 up, 6 in; 71 remapped pgs
flags sortbitwise,require_jewel_osds
pgmap v10881: 128 pgs, 9 pools, 3656 bytes data, 191 objects
1570 MB used, 63763 MB / 65333 MB avail
57/573 objects degraded (9.948%)
71 active+undersized+degraded
57 active+clean
client io 15433 B/s rd, 14 op/s rd, 0 op/s wr
```

We will talk about the output of status command in detail further in this chapter.

Sometimes it is useful to pull detailed information about cluster health. We can pass in the detail flag to see a comprehensive report about degradation. This is especially useful when ceph status reports slow/blocked requests, as at a glance we can see if they are systemic or limited to a specific OSD:

```
root@ceph-client0:~# ceph health detail
HEALTH_WARN 71 pgs degraded; 67 pgs stuck unclean; 71 pgs undersized;
recovery 57/573 objects degraded (9.948%); 1/6 in osds are down
pg 0.f is stuck unclean for 358.447499, current
stateactive+undersized+degraded, last acting [3,2]
pg 8.7 is stuck unclean for 514634.143404, current state
active+undersized+degraded, last acting [2,3]
pg 8.6 is stuck unclean for 358.625153, current state
active+undersized+degraded, last acting [2,3]
pg 0.d is stuck unclean for 362.888847, current state
active+undersized+degraded, last acting [4,3]
pg 8.5 is stuck unclean for 358.446944, current state
active+undersized+degraded, last acting [3,2]
pg 0.a is stuck unclean for 362.888290, current state
active+undersized+degraded, last acting [4,3]
. . .
pg 0.38 is active+undersized+degraded, acting [0,4]
pg 0.37 is active+undersized+degraded, acting [3,2]
pg 0.34 is active+undersized+degraded, acting [4,3]pg 0.33 is
active+undersized+degraded, acting [4,0]
pg 7.4 is active+undersized+degraded, acting [0,4]
. . .
recovery 57/573 objects degraded (9.948%)
osd.1 is down since epoch 4160, last address 192.168.42.100:6800/11356
```

We have already discussed the summary at the top of this example output. We will now explore the balance of the output by breaking it down into the following segments.

- `pg X is stuck unclean for T, current state Y, last acting Z`

  This message is printed for each PG that is degraded (mainly in the stuck unclean state). The X indicates the ID of the PG, T shows the duration it has been degraded, the current state of the PG is Y, and Z denotes the acting set of OSDs that were last serving the I/O.

- `pg X is Y, acting Z`

  Building on what we learned about the above pattern, we can see that the ID (pgid) of the subject PG is X, the state is Y, and Z is the acting set of OSDs.

- `recovery A/B objects degraded (C%)`

These messages tell us that `A` number of Ceph objects are being recovered, out of a total of `B` objects in the cluster. `C`'s value is `A` divided by `B`, expressed as a percentage, and thus shows the fraction of data within the cluster that is not optimally replicated.

- `osd.X is down since epoch Y, last address Z`

These entries list any Ceph OSDs that are marked with the down state. `X` is the numeric ID of the subject OSD. `Y` is the integer epoch of the cluster's OSD map. `Z` is the most recent IP address: the port pair from which the OSD last communicated to the MONs. There may also be a process ID appended to the `ip:port` pair separated by a slash character (`/`), which is 11,356 in the preceding example.

Watching cluster events

We can specify the `-w` switch in the ceph utility to watch the cluster for events in real time. We can watch for all types of messages including **debug (DBG)**, **info (INF)**, **warn (WRN)**, **error, (ERR)**, and **security (SEC)**. Output will be continually printed as events occur until we terminate the process.

```
root@ceph-client0:~# ceph -w
cluster e6d4e4ab-f59f-470d-bb76-511deebc8de3
health HEALTH_OK
monmap e1: 1 mons at {ceph-mon0=192.168.42.10:6789/0}
election epoch 5, quorum 0 ceph-mon0
fsmap e15527: 1/1/1 up {0=ceph-mds0=up:active}
osdmap e6264: 6 osds: 6 up, 6 in
flags sortbitwise,require_jewel_osds
pgmap v16377: 128 pgs, 9 pools, 3656 bytes data, 191 objects
2102 MB used, 63231 MB / 65333 MB avail
128 active+clean
2017-09-16 23:39:10.225183 mon.0 [INF] pgmap v16377: 128 pgs: 128
active+clean; 3656 bytes data, 2102 MB used, 63231 MB / 65333 MB avail
2017-09-16 23:40:28.009152 mon.0 [INF] osd.1 marked itself down
2017-09-16 23:40:28.087948 mon.0 [INF] osdmap e6265: 6 osds: 5 up, 6 in
2017-09-16 23:40:28.101414 mon.0 [INF] pgmap v16378: 128 pgs: 128
active+clean; 3656 bytes data, 2102 MB used, 63231 MB / 65333 MB avail
2017-09-16 23:40:29.111695 mon.0 [INF] osdmap e6266: 6 osds: 5 up, 6 in
2017-09-16 23:40:32.152057 mon.0 [INF] pgmap v16381: 128 pgs: 71
active+undersized+degraded, 67 active+clean; 3656 bytes data, 2100 MB used,
63233 MB / 65333 MB avail; 57/573 objects degraded (9.948%) ...
```

The severity for events will be familiar to those who have worked with syslog. The DBG severity is at the lowest level and ERR is at the highest. If we specify the DBG level (and implicitly all higher levels) while watching events, we will track everything happening on the cluster. By default the event level is INF, which is one level higher than DBG, and thus we see everything in the event stream with the exception of debug entries.

The following are the levels we can add to constrain event reporting:

- `--watch-debug`: Watch all events, including debug events. This is the most verbose level.
- `--watch-info`: Watch info and all events at higher levels. Debug events won't be visible.
- `--watch-sec`: Watch security and higher level events.
- `--watch-warn`: Watch warning events and the ones at a higher level.
- `--watch-error`: Watch only error events. No other events will be visible.

You may recognize the preamble of the output of ceph -w as identical to that of the ceph status command.

Utilizing your cluster

Your awesome Ceph clusters will find themselves increasingly full of user data. It will be necessary to track and anticipate utilization over time to plan future cluster expansion. It's important to plan ahead: acquiring and provisioning new servers can take months. Your users will be doubly unhappy if the cluster runs out of space before you can expand. Ceph provides tools that show the overall cluster utilization as well as the distribution per Ceph pool. We will use the df subcommand of the ceph utility to display the current stats.

```
root@ceph-client0:~# ceph df
GLOBAL:
SIZE AVAIL RAW USED %RAW USED
65333M 63376M 1957M 3.00
POOLS:
NAME ID USED %USED MAX AVAIL OBJECTS
rbd 0 0 0 21113M 0
cephfs_data 1 0 0 21113M 0
cephfs_metadata 2 2068 0 21113M 20
.rgw.root 3 1588 0 21113M 4
default.rgw.control 4 0 0 21113M 8
default.rgw.data.root 5 0 0 21113M 0
```

```
default.rgw.gc 6 0 0 21113M 32
default.rgw.log 7 0 0 21113M 127
default.rgw.users.uid 8 0 0 21113M 0
```

The df subcommand presents utilization stats in two sections, global and per-pool. A single Ceph cluster may have multiple pools for RBD, RGW, and CephFS services, each with their own level of utilization.

The columns in GLOBAL section present the following:

- SIZE: The total usable capacity in bytes of the Ceph cluster, accounting for replication.
- AVAIL: The amount of total capacity that is yet to be utilized, that is available for user data. This value is equal to total capacity of the pool subtracted from Raw Used.
- RAW USED: The total number of bytes that have already been allocated on the cluster.
- %RAW USED: This value is denoted by the percentage of utilized space on the cluster. This value is calculated by *(Raw Used / Size) * 100*.

The columns in the POOLS section present the following:

- NAME: The name of the pool.
- ID: The unique integer identifier of the pool. The ID of the pool prefixes the placement group pgids of all PGs belonging to that pool. This ensures that the pgid of a PG is unique across the entire cluster.
- Used: Size in amount of bytes allocated within the pool.
- %Used: Total percentage utilized to be allocated capacity within the pool.
- Max Avail: The capacity available to be allocated within the pool. Note that this value is a function of the replication size of the pool, a topic we'll cover in more detail in the next chapter. We can see from the preceding example that for each of our example's pools Max Avail is 21 GB. Each of our pools is configured with a replication size of three and thus their total raw unused is equal to 63 GB raw (which is the capacity of the cluster). Also note that this value is shared across all pools and is calculated relative to the total capacity of the cluster. This distinction can be tricky: PGs themselves belong strictly to a given pool, but when multiple pools share the same OSDs their PGs all contend for the same available drive space.
- objects: The count of Ceph objects within each pool.

The holistic view is quite useful, especially while forecasting growth for the entire cluster and planning for expansion. At times we may also want to check how evenly the data is internally distributed within the cluster and how much each OSD holds. Ceph releases starting with Hammer provide the invaluable osd df subcommand to display the internal distribution, allowing us to see if any one or more OSDs are taking on more capacity, and thus workload, than they should. This is similar to the Linux df command used for traditional filesystem statistics.

```
root@ceph-client0:~# ceph osd df
ID WEIGHT REWEIGHT SIZE USE AVAIL %USE VAR PGS
0 0.01039 1.00000 10888M 325M 10563M 2.99 1.00 57
3 0.01039 1.00000 10888M 323M 10565M 2.97 0.99 71
1 0.01039 1.00000 10888M 332M 10556M 3.05 1.02 71
5 0.01039 1.00000 10888M 325M 10563M 2.99 1.00 57
2 0.01039 1.00000 10888M 326M 10562M 3.00 1.00 71
4 0.01039 1.00000 10888M 326M 10562M 3.00 1.00 57
TOTAL 65333M 1959M 63374M 3.00
MIN/MAX VAR: 0.99/1.02 STDDEV: 0.03
```

We can see that the OSDs are barely utilized (at approximately 1% each) and to nearly equal degrees. Let's discuss the columns shown in the output below:

- ID: The unique OSD identifier.
- WEIGHT: The CRUSH weight of the OSD. This should be equal to the size of your disk expressed usually in tebibytes (2^30).
- REWEIGHT: An adjustment factor that is applied to the CRUSH weight of an OSD to determine the final weight of the OSD. This defaults to 1.0, which makes no adjustment. Occasionally the placement of PGs in your cluster might not distribute data in a balanced manner and some OSDs might end up with more or less than their share. Applying an adjustment to the CRUSH weight helps rebalance this data by moving the objects from incongruously heavier OSDs to lighter OSDs. Refer to the OSD variance section below for more details on this problem. This REWEIGHT is often used instead of changing the CRUSH weight, so that the CRUSH weight remains an accurate indicator of the size of the underlying storage drive.
- SIZE: The size of your disk in bytes.
- USE: The capacity of your disk that is already utilized for data.
- AVAIL: The unused capacity of your disk in bytes.
- %USE: The percentage of disk that is used.

- VAR: Variance of data distribution relative to the overall mean. The CRUSH algorithm that Ceph uses for data placement attempts to achieve equal distribution by allocating PGs to OSDs in a pseudo-random manner. Not all OSDs get exactly the same number of PGs, and thus depending on how those PGs are utilized, the variance can change. OSDs mapped to PGs that have undergone more allocations relative to others will show a higher variance.
- PGs: The count of PGs located on a given OSD.

The last row summarizes the variance among OSDs. Values of minimum and maximum variance as well as the standard deviation are printed.

OSD variance and fillage

The variance in OSD utilization is crucial in determining whether one or more OSDs need to be reweighted to even out the workload. A reasonably uniform distribution of PGs, and thus of data, among OSDs is also important so that outliers allocated significantly more than their share do not become full. In this section, we'll explore this phenomenon and how to watch for it. In Chapter 19, *Operations and Maintenance*, we described a strategy for mitigating uneven distribution; here we explore why it happens and how to adjust thresholds to meet your local needs.

The variance for some OSDs can increase when objects are not allocated in a balanced manner across all PGs. The CRUSH algorithm is designed to treat every PG as equal and thus distributes based on PG count and OSD weight, but usually, this does not match real-world demands. Client-side workloads are not aware of PGs or their distribution in the cluster; they only know about S3 objects or RBD image blocks. Thus, depending on the name of the underlying RADOS objects that comprise the higher level S3 objects or RBD image blocks, these objects may get mapped to a small set of PGs that are colocated a small set of OSDs. If this occurs, the OSDs in which those PGs are housed will show a higher variance and hence are likely to reach capacity sooner than others. Thus we need to watch out for the OSDs that show higher utilization variance. Similarly, we also need to watch out for OSDs that show significantly lower variance for a long period of time. This means that these OSDs are not pulling their weight and should be examined to determine why. OSDs that have variance equal or close to 1.0 can be considered to be in their optimal state.

CRUSH weights reflect disk capacity, while the OSD reweight mentioned in the previous chapter acts as an override (or fudge factor) to ensure balanced PG distribution. Ceph has configurable limits that allow us to control the amount of space being utilized within an OSD and take actions when those limits are reached. The two main configuration options are `mon_osd_nearfull_ratio` and `mon_osd_full_ratio`. The near-full ratio acts as a warning; OSDs that exceed this threshold results in the overall Ceph cluster status changing to `HEALTH_WARN` from `HEALTH_OK`. The full ratio provides a hard threshold above which client I/O cannot complete on the disk until the usage drops below the threshold. These values default to 85% and 95% respectively, of the total disk capacity.

It is vital to note that unlike most Ceph settings, the compiled-in defaults and any changes in `ceph.conf` provide initial values. Once a cluster goes through multiple OSD map updates, however, the near-full and full ratio from the PG map override the initial values. In order to ensure that the thresholds we set are always respected for all drives within the cluster, we should ensure that the values that we configure for the near-full and full ratio match those in the PG map. We can set the PG map values as below:

```
root@ceph-client0:~# ceph pg set_nearfull_ratio 0.85
root@ceph-client0:~# ceph pg set_full_ratio 0.95
```

These commands may be used to raise the thresholds in an emergency, in order to restore cluster operation until the situation can be addressed properly, but be warned that these thresholds are there for a reason and it is vital for the continued well-being of your cluster to promptly address very full OSDs.

Cluster status

Cluster status checks are among the most frequent tasks of any Ceph administrator; indeed like driving a manual transmission car they quickly become reflexive. These dovetail with the health check we discussed above. The overall status of the cluster can be checked by using the ceph status subcommand or the -s switch.

```
root@ceph-client0:~# ceph status
cluster e6d4e4ab-f59f-470d-bb76-511deebc8de3
health HEALTH_OK
monmap e1: 1 mons at {ceph-mon0=192.168.42.10:6789/0}
election epoch 5, quorum 0 ceph-mon0
fsmap e15527: 1/1/1 up {0=ceph-mds0=up:active}
osdmap e6279: 6 osds: 6 up, 6 in
flags sortbitwise,require_jewel_osds
pgmap v16658: 128 pgs, 9 pools, 3656 bytes data, 191 objects
1962 MB used, 63371 MB / 65333 MB avail
128 active+clean
```

The output of the ceph status is split into two columns. The first column on the left side displays each key and its value is displayed to the right. The keys are always single words but the values can occupy multiple lines.

- `cluster`: The unique identifier for a given cluster, also known as `fsid`.
- `health`: The present state of cluster health.
- `monmap`: This value summarizes the output of the cluster MON map. It shows the epoch version of the MON map, a list of Ceph MONs with their IP addresses and ports the, election epoch version, and quorum members with their IDs.
- `fsmap`: Displays the values from MDS map (in older versions of Ceph this was keyed with `mdsmap`). This includes the latest epoch version, total MDSs that are up, and their sync status.
- `osdmap`: This represents the cluster OSD map including the most recent epoch version, the total number of provisioned OSDs, and the number of OSDs that are marked up and in. When OSDs go down, the up count reduces, but it stays the same until they are removed from the OSD map. The flags entry shows any cluster flags applied to the OSD map.
- `pgmap`: This contains the epoch version of the cluster's PG map, total counts of PGs and pools, bytes allocated for data, and the total count of objects within the cluster. The next line shows the amount of data the cluster holds and the balance available out of the total cluster capacity. The last line shows the count of PGs that are inactive and clean states. If the cluster has degraded PGs, there will be additional lines summarizing the numbers of PGs in each state.

If the cluster has ongoing recovery or client I/O, that will be displayed as two more lines at the end.

We typically use the status command to observe PG state transitions when we are performing changes within the cluster like reweighting OSDs during maintenance or adding new OSDs or hosts. In such scenarios, it best to open a dedicated window that continually updates this crucial status information instead of us repeatedly issuing this command manually. We can leverage the Linux watch command to periodically update the display of changes in cluster state. By default, the watch will run the command every 2 seconds, displaying a timestamp at the upper right. This timestamp itself is valuable. If we notice that the value is not updating as expected, it's likely that our cluster's Monitor nodes are experiencing problems.

```
$ watch ceph status
```

Cluster authentication

Ceph provides Kerberos-type authentication for all clients and daemons of the cluster using the cephx protocol. Each entity that communicates with other cluster components needs to communicate using their respective keys. Any MON can authenticate a client based on the key it provides, then send it a session key to use when talking to other processes within the cluster, such as OSDs. Once the session expires the clients need to authenticate to the cluster again before they can resume talking to OSDs. The list of keys that authorized clients can use is retrieved from the auth list subcommand.

```
root@ceph-client0:~# ceph auth list
installed auth entries:
client.admin
key: AQBSdLVZN8DNDBAAIwIhHp/np5uUk9Rftzb5kg==
caps: [mds] allow *
caps: [mon] allow *
caps: [osd] allow *
client.bootstrap-mds
key: AQBSdLVZIC0yMhAAmRka3/+OpszwNPNSXuY5nQ==
caps: [mon] allow profile bootstrap-mds
client.bootstrap-osd
key: AQBSdLVZ99T2FxAAIj54OM3qAVxeLz+ECF3CyA==
caps: [mon] allow profile bootstrap-osd
client.bootstrap-rgw
key: AQBSdLVZPUiDIhAAAPCNfNceDU3eGSvrwYNQUg==
caps: [mon] allow profile bootstrap-rgw
client.restapi
key: AQBUdLVZFVdQLhAA/PxeXrWDHP9c8dtY3Mu2sA==
caps: [mon] allow *
caps: [osd] allow *
client.rgw.ceph-rgw0
key: AQB1drVZ8OmfBhAAw8Uxu3tKJ2uz5OvdR8nu/A==
caps: [mon] allow rw
caps: [osd] allow rwx
```

Monitoring Ceph MONs

A proper Ceph cluster comprises three or more Monitor daemons, ideally situated on distinct physical servers. If a cluster's MONs cannot form a quorum, which happens if not enough of the provisioned MONs are up, then new clients won't be able to connect to the system. Worse yet, existing clients will no longer be able to perform operations once their sessions expire. It is paramount for cluster health to have a majority of MONs up and able to fulfill their quorum duties.

MON status

We can retrieve basic information about all MONs in the cluster by running the ceph utility's mon stat subcommand. If our clusters contain MONs that are down or unavailable and thus have been temporarily kicked out of quorum, this command will alert us to the situation so that we can address it.

```
root@ceph-client0:~# ceph mon stat
e1: 1 mons at {ceph-mon0=192.168.42.10:6789/0}, election epoch 5, quorum 0
ceph-mon0
```

If we need detailed information about the state of the entire cluster MON map, we can use the mon dump subcommand.

```
root@ceph-client0:~# ceph mon dump
dumped monmap epoch 1
epoch 1
fsid e6d4e4ab-f59f-470d-bb76-511deebc8de3
last_changed 2017-09-10 20:20:16.458985
created 2017-09-10 20:20:16.458985
0: 192.168.42.10:6789/0 mon.ceph-mon0
```

Most of this information is also present in the Ceph health status summary, but it is sometimes useful to detect issues when we are adding new MONs to an existing cluster if they are not making themselves a part of the quorum. Examining the MON map dumps on the new MONs and comparing them with those of the existing MONs might help point a finger towards the problem.

MON quorum status

The concept of *quorum* is fundamental to all consensus algorithms that are designed to access information in a fault-tolerant distributed system. The minimum number of votes necessary to achieve consensus among a set of nodes is called a quorum. In Ceph's case, MONs are exploited to persist operations that result in a change of the cluster state. They need to agree to the global order of operations and register them synchronously. Hence, an active quorum of MON nodes is important in order to make progress. To keep a cluster operational, the quorum (or majority) of MON nodes needs to be available at all times. Mathematically, it means we need (n/2)+1 MON nodes available at all times, where n is the total number of MONs provisioned. For example, if we have 5 MONs, we need at least (5/2)+1 = 3 MONs available at all times. Ceph considers all MONs equal when testing for a majority, and thus any three working MONs in the above example will qualify to be within the quorum.

We can obtain the cluster quorum status by using the `quorum_status` subcommand of our trusty Swiss Army Knife—like the Ceph utility.

```
root@ceph-client0:~# ceph quorum_status
{
"election_epoch": 6,
"quorum": [
0
],
"quorum_names": [
"ceph-mon0"
],
"quorum_leader_name": "ceph-mon0",
"monmap": {
"epoch": 1,
"fsid": "e6d4e4ab-f59f-470d-bb76-511deebc8de3",
"modified": "2017-09-10 20:20:16.458985",
"created": "2017-09-10 20:20:16.458985",
"mons": [
{
"rank": 0,
"name": "ceph-mon0",
"addr": "192.168.42.10:6789/0"
}
]
}
}
```

The output is displayed in JSON format. Let's discuss the fields below:

- `election_epoch`: A counter that indications the number of re-elections that have been proposed and completed to date.
- `quorum`: A list of the *ranks* of MON nodes. Each active MON is associated with a unique rank value within the cluster. The value is an integer and starts at zero.
- `quorum_names`: The unique identifier of each MON process.
- `quorum_leader_name`: The identifier of a MON that is elected to be the leader of the ensemble. When a client first talks to the cluster, it acquires all the necessary information and cluster maps from the current or acting leader node.
- `monmap`: The dump of the cluster's MON map.

A MON leader acts as an arbiter to ensure that writes are applied to all nodes and in the proper order. In Ceph versions up to and including Jewel, the leader of MON nodes was selected based on the advertised IP address. The MON node with the lowest IP address (*lowest* is calculated by transforming the IP address from a quad-dotted notation to a 32-bit integer value) was picked as the leader. If it was unavailable, then the one with the next highest IP address was selected, and so on. Once the unavailable, MON came back up, assuming that it still had the lowest IP address of all MONs, it would be re-elected the leader.

Ceph's Luminous release adds a new configuration setting called `mon priority` that lets us adjust priorities of MONs regardless of the values of their IP addresses. This helps us apply custom ordering to all MONs that we want to act as temporary leaders when the previous leader dies. It also allows us to change the existing leader dynamically and in a controlled manner. We might, for example, switch the leader a day before performing firmware upgrades or a disk/chassis replacement, so that the former lead server going down does not trigger an election at a time when we need to concentrate on other priorities.

Monitoring Ceph OSDs

OSDs are the workhorses within a Ceph cluster; they are responsible for performing all the work to store and manage client data. Monitoring OSDs is crucial, though complex because they are typically present in large numbers. This task is relatively trivial but even more critical in very small clusters with only 5 to 10 OSDs, especially if high availability and durability guarantees are required. We will take a look at the Ceph commands available for monitoring OSDs.

OSD tree lookup

If we need a quick view into the state and availability of all OSDs, we will use the OSD tree subcommand. This command is usually the second-most used (or abused) after the Ceph status command.

```
root@ceph-client0:~# ceph osd tree
ID WEIGHT TYPE NAME UP/DOWN REWEIGHT PRIMARY-AFFINITY
-1 0.06235 root default
-2 0.02078 host ceph-osd1
```

```
0 0.01039 osd.0 up 1.00000 1.00000
3 0.01039 osd.3 up 1.00000 1.00000
-3 0.02078 host ceph-osd0
1 0.01039 osd.1 up 1.00000 1.00000
5 0.01039 osd.5 up 1.00000 1.00000
-4 0.02078 host ceph-osd2
2 0.01039 osd.2 up 1.00000 1.00000
4 0.01039 osd.4 up 1.00000 1.00000
```

Let's dive into the columns of the preceding output and their particulars a little more in the following:

- `ID`: The unique identifier of each bucket. All buckets that are not leaf nodes or devices always have negative values and all devices or OSDs have positive values. The IDs for OSDs are prefixed by osd to form their names. These values are pulled directly from the CRUSH map.
- `WEIGHT`: This value shows the weight of a bucket in tebibytes (i.e. 2^30). The weight of each bucket is a critical input to the CRUSH placement algorithm, and thus for the balanced placement of data across the cluster.
- `TYPE`: This field shows the bucket type. Valid default types include device, host, chassis, rack, row, pdu, pod, room, datacenter, region, and root. We can create custom types if desired, but it is recommended to employ the predefined types in most cases. This helps Ceph's CRUSH map accurately mimic your physical topology. The root bucket, as its name implies, is at the root of the hierarchical map of buckets, and all the rulesets (replicated or erasure coded) for a pool will be applied to a given root.
- `NAME`: The name of each bucket. In the above example, we have one root bucket named default, three host buckets named `ceph-osd1`, `ceph-osd2`, and `ceph-osd3`, and six device or OSD buckets.
- `UP`/`DOWN`: This column displays the state of the OSD devices. Up means, the OSD is actively communicating with other OSDs in the cluster and readily accepting the client I/O. Down indicates that the OSD is unavailable. It may be running slowly or its process is dead and thus unable to communicate with the cluster. This OSD should be looked at and fixed.
- `REWEIGHT`: If we have applied an override weight to an existing OSD, that will show up here. The floating point values for overrides lie between zero and one.

- PRIMARY AFFINITY: This value controls the probability of an OSD being elected as a primary. Changing this value to zero will ensure that the corresponding OSD is never elected primarily for any PGs that are stored on it. This is sometimes useful when you are deploying a hybrid SSD-HDD cluster and want all your primary OSDs to be on SSD nodes to maximize performance, especially for reads. Tread carefully when changing those values because they do add limitations to how well Ceph can handle failures when the primaries go down.

It might be easy in a small cluster to determine by inspection which OSD belongs to which host. Within a large cluster comprising hundreds or thousands of OSDs located in tens of servers, it is distinctly harder to quickly isolate a problem to a specific host when an OSD fails and thus is marked down. Ceph provides us with the osd find subcommand that makes it really easy to identify which host a broken OSD belongs to.

```
root@ceph-client0:~# ceph osd find 1
{
"osd": 1,
"ip": "192.168.42.100:6802\/4104",
"crush_location": {
"host": "ceph-osd0",
"root": "default"
}
}
```

The command takes the numeric OSD ID in as an input and prints a list of important fields as JSON output.

- osd: The numeric ID of an OSD.
- ip: The IP address, port of the OSD host and PID of the OSD process running on that host.
- crush_location: This prints the hostname and also the root which the OSD is part of.

OSD statistics

The counts of provisioned, up, and down OSDs is available via the osd stat subcommand as shown in the following:

```
root@ceph-client0:~# ceph osd stat
osdmap e7785: 6 osds: 6 up, 6 in
flags sortbitwise,require_jewel_osds
```

Note that the above information is exactly the same as the information present in the Ceph health status we described earlier in this chapter. The output of Ceph status is useful when watching problems visually, but if you want to isolate only the basic OSD stats, `osd stat` may be convenient.

OSD CRUSH map

The CRUSH map holds a variety of information necessary for Ceph to distribute and place objects. Sometimes it is useful to find out if this distribution isn't working properly because of a wrong value in the CRUSH map. The CRUSH map can be downloaded as a file in a binary format that we decompile locally for viewing. It is also possible to dump the CRUSH map and rules directly from the command line, which is expedient for a quick check.

We can use osd crush dump to display the entire CRUSH map.

```
root@ceph-client0:~# ceph osd crush dump
{
"devices": [
{
"id": 0,
"name": "osd.0"
},
. . .
"rules": [
{
"rule_id": 0,
"rule_name": "replicated_ruleset",
"ruleset": 0,
. . .
"tunables": {
"choose_local_tries": 0,
"choose_local_fallback_tries": 0,
"choose_total_tries": 50,
"chooseleaf_descend_once": 1,
. . .
```

This might not always be useful depending on the information sought. A better way to dump individual rules is by using the osd crush rule dump subcommand.

We first list the CRUSH rules currently defined within our cluster:

```
root@ceph-client0:~# ceph osd crush rule ls
[
"replicated_ruleset"
]
```

Here we only have one rule, and it is named `replicated_ruleset`. Let's see what it does.

```
root@ceph-client0:~# ceph osd crush rule dump replicated_ruleset
{
"rule_id": 0,
"rule_name": "replicated_ruleset",
"ruleset": 0,
"type": 1,
"min_size": 1,
"max_size": 10,
"steps": [
{
"op": "take",
"item": -1,
"item_name": "default"
},
{
"op": "chooseleaf_firstn",
"num": 0,
"type": "host"
},
{
"op": "emit"
}
]
}
```

This rule is applied to replicated pools and distributes one copy of all objects to separate hosts.

Monitoring Ceph placement groups

Ceph objects are mapped to distinct and unique **placement groups** (**PGs**) that are stored by OSDs. The health of the cluster depends on the state and health of the placement groups, both individually and collectively. If a placement group is degraded then the health of the cluster is impacted, even though the rest of the PGs may be healthy and do not experience issues with a client I/O. The cluster status will be HEALTH_OK only when all placement groups are in active and clean states. An unhealthy cluster manifests PGs that may be either in the active or clean state but not both—and possibly neither. The active state is required to serve client I/O, while clean indicates that the PG is not only serving I/O but also meeting other necessary requirements including replication.

PG states

We can divide PG states into three categories: Critical, Warning, and Info. PG states in the *Critical* category indicate severe damage to the cluster and immediate action should be taken to resolve their issues. For example, if we are running out of space on an OSD, we will see the backfill-toofull state being applied. If a PG has lost all OSDs assigned to hold its replicas, then it will be marked as inactive and the client I/O grinds to a halt. PGs in the *Warning* category indicate that something is wrong with the cluster that needs to be fixed, but there most likely is not a major impact to client I/O that would lead to its complete stoppage. PGs in the *Info* category do not indicate an issue with the cluster, but rather convey routine information regarding the state of PGs.

Category	PG States
Critical	inactive, backfill-toofull
Warning	down, degraded, inconsistent, repair, recovering, backfill, backfill-wait, incomplete, stale, remapped, undersized
Info	peering, scrubbing, scrubbing+deep, active, clean

The state of placement groups can be monitored via the Ceph health status check described in the sections above. To display the just summary information about our collection of PGs and extract specific stats, we can use the ceph utility's `pg stat` subcommand.

```
root@ceph-client0:~# ceph pg stat
v40524: 128 pgs: 128 active+clean; 3656 bytes data, 1736 MB used, 63597 MB
/ 65333 MB avail
```

There may be a desire, at times, to view the state and the history of all PGs in your cluster. It is possible to dump complete state information of all PGs including the total count of objects, the total bytes they hold, the up and acting sets, the primaries of both those sets of OSDs, and the timestamps of the most recent shallow and deep scrubs. This extensive information can be overwhelming for humans, so it is recommended to filter it through a parser or script that transforms it to supply answers to the questions that humans pose. We can extract this data by using the ceph subcommand `pg dump`.

```
root@ceph-client0:~# ceph pg dump
dumped all in format plain
version 40582
stamp 2017-09-18 00:39:21.452578
last_osdmap_epoch 15487
last_pg_scan 15487
full_ratio 0.95
nearfull_ratio 0.85
pg_stat objects mip degr misp unf bytes log disklog state state_stamp v
```

```
reported up up_primary acting acting_primary last_scrub scrub_stamp
last_deep_scrub deep_scrub_stamp
0.39 0 0 0 0 0 0 0 0 active+clean 2017-09-17 17:52:23.574152 0'0 15424:130
[5,3,4] 5 [5,3,4] 5 0'0 2017-09-17 17:52:23.574107 0'0 2017-09-16
16:32:04.037088
0.38 0 0 0 0 0 0 0 0 active+clean 2017-09-17 22:29:40.588864 0'0 15439:183
[1,0,4] 1 [1,0,4] 1 0'0 2017-09-17 22:29:40.588828 0'0 2017-09-17
22:29:40.588828
0.37 0 0 0 0 0 0 0 0 active+clean 2017-09-17 17:52:41.700284 0'0 15425:178
[1,3,2] 1 [1,3,2] 1 0'0 2017-09-17 17:52:41.700258 0'0 2017-09-10
20:20:17.163705
. . .
```

Sometimes we might want to know the details of just a specific PG. This can be achieved by issuing ceph pg <pgid> query. The pgid string is the PG identifier of the placement group we wish to query. For instance:

```
root@ceph-client0:~# ceph pg 0.39 query
{
"state": "active+clean",
"snap_trimq": "[]",
"epoch": 15502,
"up": [
5,
3,
4
],
"acting": [
5,
3,
4
],
"actingbackfill": [
"3",
"4",
"5"
],
"info": {
"pgid": "0.39",
"last_update": "0'0",
"last_complete": "0'0",
. . .
```

Querying PGs is useful for troubleshooting potential issues with them. Sometimes PGs can degrade due to issues with the scrubbing process that can case blocks for extreme amounts of time. In such cases, querying the PG can provide enlightening information about why the scrub is blocked and on which OSD. If we deem it to be a bug with Ceph as opposed to a hardware fault, we can easily restart the OSD to resolve the issue.

Ceph also allows us to list all PGs that are marked unclean, inactive, degraded, undersized, or stale. The subcommand we use for this operation is `dump_stuck`.

```
root@ceph-client0:~# ceph pg dump_stuck undersized
pg_stat state up up_primary acting acting_primary
0.f active+undersized+degraded [3,2] 3 [3,2] 3
8.7 active+undersized+degraded [2,3] 2 [2,3] 2
8.6 active+undersized+degraded [2,3] 2 [2,3] 2
...
```

Monitoring Ceph MDS

Ceph MDS servers manage CephFS filesystems. A Ceph MDS server can be in various states including up, down, active, and inactive. An MDS server should always be up and active when it is in a correct and functioning state.

There are two main commands we can use to monitor an operational MDS cluster. We use `mds stat` to get a quick insight into the present state of MDSs. You might recognize this output format as the same one presented by the Ceph status `fsmap` key.

```
root@ceph-client0:~# ceph mds stat
e38611: 1/1/1 up {0=ceph-mds0=up:active}
```

If we would like the detailed output of the MDS map of a given cluster, we can use the `mds dump` subcommand. Like all other subcommands containing dump, it prints the entire MDS map, which contains detailed information about active MDS daemons as well as other stats.

```
root@ceph-client0:~# ceph mds dump
dumped fsmap epoch 38611
fs_name cephfs
epoch 38611
flags 0
created 2017-09-10 20:20:28.275607
modified 2017-09-10 20:20:28.275607
tableserver 0
root 0
session_timeout 60
session_autoclose 300
```

```
max_file_size 1099511627776
last_failure 0
last_failure_osd_epoch 15221
compat compat={},rocompat={},incompat={1=base v0.20,2=client writeable
ranges,3=default file layouts on dirs,4=dir inode in separate object,5=mds
uses versioned encoding,6=dirfrag is stored in omap,8=file layout v2}
max_mds 1
in 0
up {0=38784}
failed
damaged
stopped
data_pools 1
metadata_pool 2
inline_data disabled
38784: 192.168.42.70:6800/1630589528 'ceph-mds0' mds.0.38608 up:active seq
5
```

Open source dashboards and tools

Ceph storage administrators can perform most cluster monitoring and management with the CLI commands provided by Ceph. Ceph also provides a rich admin API that can be used to monitor and visualize the entire Ceph cluster. There are several open source projects that make use of Ceph's REST admin API and present a GUI dashboard for a visual overview of your entire cluster. Some tools focus on monitoring; others have more expansive scopes and include orchestration and lifecycle management features as well.

Kraken

Kraken is an open source Ceph dashboard written in Python. Initial development was by Don Talton, who was later joined by David Moreau Simard. Don has over twenty years of experience with prominent companies and runs Merrymack, an IT consulting company.

The development of Kraken came about because, at the time, Ceph's Calamari tool was only available to commercial customers of Inktank. Don believed that it was desirable to have a good open source dashboard for monitoring Ceph clusters and components from a single window. This would enable better management and the adoption of Ceph proper. Don utilized Ceph's RESTful API to extract necessary cluster data for monitoring and reporting.

While Kraken has not received updates in two years as we write, you may still find it useful. You can find Kraken's GitHub page at `https://github.com/ krakendash/krakendash`. Kraken is fully open source with BSD licensing. Kraken leverages several other open source projects; details can be found at the above GitHub page.

Ceph-dash

The ceph-dash project is another free open source dashboard/monitoring dashboard, developed by Christian Eichelmann, at 1&1 Internet AG in Germany as a senior software developer. As Don did with Kraken, Christian began this project at a time when there were very few open source dashboards available for Ceph. Moreover, the other available dashboards had complex architectures and did not work well with large clusters. The home of ceph-dash may be found at `https://github.com/Crapworks/ceph-dash`.

Decapod

Another interesting Ceph management tool is Decapod from Mirantis. Decapod builds on the popular Ansible-based ceph-ansible management framework. One can read all about it here:

`https://www.mirantis.com/blog/introducing-decapod-easier-way-manage-ceph/`

Rook

Rook is a young but promising open source tool for distributed storage management in cloud-native environments. As with some of the other tools we describe here, Rook does more than just monitoring; it is a full-blown orchestration tool. You can read all about it on Rook's GitHub page, maintained by an active contributing community.

`https://github.com/rook/rook`

Calamari

Calamari is a management platform for Ceph, an attractive dashboard to monitor and manage your Ceph cluster. It was initially developed by Inktank as proprietary software that shipped with Inktank's Ceph Enterprise product. After Inktank was acquired by Red Hat, Calamari was open sourced and has received additional development. The Calamari back end leverages Python, SaltStack, ZeroRPC, Graphite, Django, and gevent. The Calamari backend has been open sourced with the LGPL2+ license; you can find the repository and ample information at `https://github.com/ceph/calamari`.

Excellent Calamari documentation is available at `http://calamari.readthedocs.org`.

Ceph-mgr

New with the Luminous release is the core `ceph-mgr` daemon, which offers a promising dashboard plugin that is bound to receive considerable attention from the community.

Enabling this dashboard is straightforward:

Edit `ceph.conf` on each node that runs the `ceph-mgr` daemon; these are usually the MONs. Add the following section:

```
[mgr]
mgr_modules = dashboard
```

Next configure IP addressing on each `ceph-mgr` server:

```
# ceph config-key put mgr/dashboard/server_addr ::
```

The value `::` enables the dashboard on port `7000` of each system.

Next restart the `ceph-mgr` daemon. On systemd-centric distributions this is done with:

```
$ systemctl restart ceph-mgr@
```

You should now be able to browse to the dashboard on the active ceph-mgr server's 7000/tcp port.

Prometheus and Grafana

The last two tools we'll discuss in this chapter are excellent general purpose monitoring and trending solutions. Prometheus is a flexible monitoring and time-series tool for alerting and trending all manner of system data. While the standalone operation is possible, linkage with the Grafana visualization dashboard provides a visually appealing and user-friendly experience. Prometheus enables flexible and powerful analysis of data from a variety of sources. Ceph integration is done through the sophisticated Ceph Exporter data collector.

You can discover each of these tools at their respective links:

Grafana: `https://github.com/grafana/grafana`

Prometheus: `https://prometheus.io/`

Ceph Exporter: `https://github.com/digitalocean/ceph_exporter`

Summary

In this chapter, we covered Ceph's monitoring needs and utilities. This included overall cluster states as well as individual Ceph components including MONs, OSDs, and MDS. We also investigated placement groups. The states of placement groups can change dynamically and they require close monitoring. Most of the changes that happen in a Ceph cluster are visibly surfaced from changes to placement groups. This chapter also covered several open source GUI monitoring dashboard projects. Some of these are managed and developed outside of Ceph proper, but they are also open source, so you can contribute to and benefit from these projects freely. We also covered an overview of Calamari and the new ceph-mgr dashboard.

21
Performance and Stability Tuning

In this chapter, we look at getting the most out of your Ceph cluster. There are operating systems as well as Ceph settings, that we should look at to ensure smooth and performant operation.

Topics covered include:

- Kernel settings
- Network settings
- Ceph settings
- Ceph daemon osd | mon | radosgw perf dump
- Benchmarking

Ceph performance overview

It has long been said that data expands to fill available space, a phenomenon quite familiar to Ceph admins. As your constellation of Ceph clients continues to change and grow, it becomes increasingly vital to plan for sustained performance. Many factors at the operating system and Ceph architectural levels become increasingly important as Ceph clusters grow in capacity and workload.

Fortunately, Ceph is up to the challenge, and we will explore a number of ways to measure and optimize your deployments in this final chapter.

As we've explored in earlier chapters, many traditional and commercial storage systems exhibit performance that is limited by a single SAS, Fiber Channel, or network interface. As they are scaled for capacity, throughput may remain constant, or at best grow at a lower rate than capacity. Among Ceph's strengths is the ability to avoid data-plane choke points so that we are able to scale capacity and throughput together as we add additional storage nodes and take advantage of improved networking technologies.

Kernel settings

The Linux kernel adapts to the system on which it runs in a number of ways, scaling buffers and pools according to the number of CPU cores present and the amount of RAM provisioned. However, since the kernel and other operating system components must be usable on both heavily-equipped servers and modest consumer systems, there's only so much it can do out of the box.

Experience with Ceph has taught us a number of ways to ensure operational stability and continued performance as the workload grows. Some are common to most systems; others are highly dependent on your individual hardware and situation.

Many Linux kernel settings are persistently configured via the `sysctl` framework when the system boots. Historically, additions or changes were made within the `/etc/sysctl.conf` file, but with modern distributions it is advisable to instead exploit the drop-in directory `/etc/sysctl.d`. We can group related settings into individual files that can be conveniently managed separately within this directory. By convention Ceph-related settings would be entered in a file named something like `/etc/sysctl.d/60-ceph.conf`.

pid_max

Your Linux kernel manages traditional processes as threads and has a setting that limits how high a thread's numerical identifier may grow, and thus indirectly limits how many may exist system-wide at any given time. This `pid_max` setting defaults to `32768` as of the 3.19 kernel, a value more than sufficient for desktops or systems that host traditionally-architected applications. Ceph's daemons, however, are multi-threaded and can spawn thousands of threads, especially during heavy recovery. As clusters become larger and busier, OSD nodes with multiple OSDs running can easily exceed this limit. If your OSD or system logs contain messages like *unable to fork* or *thread_create failed*, this is likely what's going on.

Since we know that Ceph behaves this way, we need to increase the limit. This can be done at boot time in the appropriate `sysctl` file:

```
kernel.pid_max = 4194303
```

It can also be done in the running state:

```
$ echo 4194303 > /proc/sys/kernel/pid_max
```

This value should suffice for even very dense OSD nodes. When deciding on values for this and other settings related to scale, consider that in the future your systems will be busier, more numerous, and likely denser. It pays to anticipate future resource needs to avoid service issues before they happen.

kernel.threads-max, vm.max_map_count

Space does not permit detailed descriptions of all settings, but we'll note here that raising these also helps to avoid thread/process creation problems.

```
kernel.threads-max=2097152
vm.max_map_count=524288
```

XFS filesystem settings

Busy XFS-based FileStore OSDs may find that these settings optimize performance, especially if you have the luxury of using SSDs. The XFS metadata sync operations have traditionally been intrusive and somewhat painful. When the sync thread awakens it may pre-empt the writes of all other processes (threads), which can interfere with Ceph's journal and data flushes. The `fs.xfs` settings here help to mitigate that effect.

The `fs.aio-max-nr` setting expands the queue for disk operations. Modest to moderate OSD nodes say those with fewer than 20 OSDs, may do fine with the default value. As the per-host OSD density increases, it increasingly becomes a limiting factor. Throughput benefits from scaling this value proportionally to drive count; this value of 50 million should be ample for even the densest Ceph OSD nodes:

```
fs.xfs.xfssyncd_centisecs=720000
fs.xfs.xfsbufd_centisecs=3000          # pre-4.0 kernels only
fs.xfs.age_buffer_centisecs=720000     # pre-4.0 kernels only
fs.aio-max-nr=50000000
```

Virtual memory settings

These are perhaps the most controversial of the settings we list in this chapter: ones that affect the kernel's management of virtual memory. Research the latter five on the net before setting; your kernel and situation may have dynamics that favor different or default settings.

`vm.min_free_kbytes` sizes a pool of free memory that the kernel tries to maintain in order to service allocation requests. By raising the value, we can speed up memory allocation and avoid fragmentation that confounds larger request sizes.

At the very least, though, we recommend setting `vm.min_free_kbytes` to `1048576`, or even `2097152` unless your systems are provisioned with limited memory, in which case you should really consider getting more. Modern RAM is affordable, especially on the open market:

```
vm.min_free_kbytes=1048576
vm.vfs_cache_pressure=10
vm.zone_reclaim_mode=0
vm.dirty_ratio=80
vm.dirty_background_ratio=3
```

Network settings

Most operating systems are not prepared to efficiently handle very heavy network traffic out of the box. You will need to consult with your networking team in the right settings for your infrastructure and adapt to your kernel, Linux distribution, and network environment. In this section, we'll discuss several common changes that can benefit Ceph deployments.

Jumbo frames

We've mentioned before the value of Jumbo frames to increase performance by increasing network and protocol efficiency. A common raised MTU size is 9,000 bytes; this must be configured within your network infrastructure as well as your system's interface configuration. Depending on your distribution, you may configure this in `/etc/network/interfaces` or, interface-specific files like `/etc/sysconfig/network-scripts/ifcfg-eth0`.

TIP

To dive more deeply into Linux network optimization, including topics like increasing NIC ring buffers, we suggest this document:
https://access.redhat.com/sites/default/files/attachments/
20150325_network_performance_tuning.pdf

TCP and network core

Space does not allow us to discuss this group of settings in detail. Consider them food for thought and online research. Most mainstream Linux distributions come out of the box tuned to run on even modest hardware. Systems like Ceph that do heavy network traffic can benefit considerably from tuning.

```
net.ipv4.tcp_timestamps=0
net.ipv4.tcp_sack=1
net.core.netdev_max_backlog=250000
net.ipv4.tcp_max_syn_backlog=100000
net.ipv4.tcp_max_tw_buckets=2000000
net.ipv4.tcp_tw_reuse=1
net.core.rmem_max=4194304
net.core.wmem_max=4194304
net.core.rmem_default=4194304
net.core.wmem_default=4194304
net.core.optmem_max=4194304
net.ipv4.tcp_rmem="4096 87380 4194304"
net.ipv4.tcp_wmem="4096 65536 4194304"
net.ipv4.tcp_low_latency=1
net.ipv4.tcp_adv_win_scale=1
net.ipv4.tcp_slow_start_after_idle=0
net.ipv4.tcp_no_metrics_save=1
net.ipv4.tcp_syncookies=0
net.core.somaxconn=5000
net.ipv4.tcp_ecn=0
net.ipv4.conf.all.send_redirects=0
net.ipv4.conf.all.accept_source_route=0
net.ipv4.icmp_echo_ignore_broadcasts=1
net.ipv4.tcp_no_metrics_save=1
net.ipv4.tcp_slow_start_after_idle=0
net.ipv4.tcp_fin_timeout=10
```

iptables and nf_conntrack

These kernel modules are used to enhance network security by implementing a flexible kernel-level firewall. As with other aspects of the Linux kernel, default settings are often insufficient for a busy Ceph cluster. If your organization's policies permit it, you may blacklist these all together to keep them from loading. It's still prudent to raise their limits as a fallback option, as even blacklisted modules have a way of slipping back in. There is a connection table maintained by `nf_conntrack` that may default to as low as 65536. We suggest half a million as an ample value for OSD nodes hosting 24 4TB OSDs. Extremely dense nodes may require an even larger setting:

```
net.netfilter.nf_conntrack_max=524288
net.nf_conntrack_max=524288
```

Your kernel may use one or both of these names. Raising these will consume megabytes of additional kernel memory; on modern systems, this is trivial.

Below is an Ansible playbook to unload and remove `iptables` and `nf_conntrack` along with their dependencies.

```
# Unload and blacklist kernel modules related to iptables and nf_conntrack
# ref: https://goo.gl/aQFI8d
#
# Usage: ansible-playbook -e target=hostname rmmod.yml
# It is ok for some of the modules to fail during removal if
# they are not loaded. these are ignored.
- name: ensure we are applying to ceph server nodes
  assert:
    that: "'ceph_mon' in group_names or 'ceph_osd' in group_names or
'ceph_rgw' in group_names or 'ceph_aio' in group_names"
- name: stop and disable iptables
  service:
    name: iptables
    enabled: no
    state: stopped
- name: remove nat, conntrack modules. order here is important.
  command: rmmod {{ item }}
  with_items:
    - iptable_nat- nf_nat_ipv4
    - nf_nat
    - nf_conntrack_ipv4
    - nf_defrag_ipv4
    - nf_conntrack_proto_gre
    - xt_CT
    - nf_conntrack
    - iptable_filter
```

```
        - iptable_raw
        - ip_tables
      ignore_errors: true
    - name: do not load conntrack on boot
      file: path=/etc/sysconfig/modules/ip_conntrack.modules state=absent
    - name: do not load conntrack_proto_gre on boot
      file: path=/etc/sysconfig/modules/nf_conntrack_proto_gre.modules
state=absent
    - name: blacklist the modules to ensure they are not loaded on reboot
      copy:
        owner: root
        mode: 0644
        dest: /etc/modprobe.d/conntrack.conf
        content: |
          blacklist nf_conntrack
          blacklist nf_conntrack_ipv6
          blacklist xt_conntrack
          blacklist nf_conntrack_ftp
          blacklist xt_state
          blacklist iptable_nat
          blacklist ipt_REDIRECT
          blacklist nf_nat
          blacklist nf_conntrack_ipv4
          blacklist nf_conntrack_proto_gre
          blacklist xt_CT
          blacklist iptable_raw
          blacklist ip_tables
```

This playbook was designed for RHEL7.2 systems using an Ansible inventory file with certain hostgroup definitions. Your site practices, Linux distribution, and kernel release version will require adjustments to the inventory file and the lists of modules.

 This file may be downloaded from:
`https://learningceph2ed.nyc3.digitaloceanspaces.com/rmmod.yml`

Every Ceph admin (and every sysadmin) has a favorite set of tunables and values to set, and there can be controversy over best practice. The names and effects of settings, as well as their defaults vary by kernel and Linux distribution release. Those we present here are based on our experiences. Your mileage, as they say, may vary, and you are encouraged to research what's right for you. The archives of the `ceph-users` mailing list are an especially rich hunting ground.

ceph-users archives may be found at
http://lists.ceph.com/pipermail/ceph-users-ceph.com.

In Chapter 19, *Operations and Maintenance,* we learned mechanisms to configure myriad Ceph behavioral and tuning settings. We changed values both in the configuration file read at startup and dynamically in running daemons by injection. Those settings dovetail into those we describe in this chapter to maximize the stability and performance of your Ceph deployments.

Ceph settings

In earlier chapters, we discussed the hundreds of internal settings that may be tweaked to optimize Ceph performance or adapt to local needs. The vast majority of these are eldritch and arcane; you're likely to shoot yourself in the foot by tweaking them. In this section, we will discuss a number that are conceptually accessible and which have clear benefits.

max_open_files

Earlier in this chapter, we discussed Ceph daemons' thirst for threads. On busy systems, they can also run out of file handles. The proper way to increase this limit varies by operating system and Ceph release. Suggested values are a minimum of 131072, and potentially as high as 524288 on dense, busy servers. Recent versions of Ceph allow one to set this in ceph.conf and will raise it on your behalf. Yes, this an OS setting, but Ceph can manage it for us now:

```
[global]
max_open_files = 131072
```

If your system has /etc/init/ceph-osd.conf, you may raise the value, which may be as low as 32768 there. On other systems you may need to use sysctl:

```
fs.file-max=524288
```

Recovery

Among the most tweaked Ceph settings are those that limit the behavior of backfill and recovery. We explored these in Chapter 19, *Operations and Maintenance*. In summary: one trades off the speed of healing against disruption to ongoing client operations. Through the Hammer LTS release, the defaults were too aggressive for many deployments, especially those running on relatively slow LFF HDDs with colocated journals. The Jewel release brought significantly more conservative defaults; if you're running Jewel or later, you may do well without tweaks. If you're on an earlier release, revisit Chapter 19, *Operations and Maintenance*, and consider throttling these down.

OSD and FileStore settings

There are quite a few settings that may be tweaked for OSDs; optimal values vary depending on the speeds of your OSD and journal drives, your workload, and the number of CPU cores available. The suggestions here must be researched and tested in the context of your unique deployment:

```
[osd]
filestore_queue_max_bytes = 1048576000
filestore_queue_max_ops = 50000
```

The above settings work well for the authors to enhance the performance of FileStore OSDs deployed on fast SSDs. Your mileage may vary, especially on HDD OSDs:

```
[osd]
osd_op_threads = 16
osd_disk_threads = 4
```

These thread settings are sometimes controversial; some hold that increasing them can benefit performance, others that they increase contention and can lead to thrashing. Their effects vary by Ceph release, internal management of work queues has evolved. Kernel versions and I/O scheduler settings also affect what's best here. Tweak these carefully and benchmark before and after. If your systems have a larger number of OSD daemons but a small number of CPU cores, you may experience context switching overhead by setting them too high.

We discussed scrub settings in Chapter 19, *Operations and Maintenance* as well; you may wish to consider lengthening your osd_deep_scrub_interval to minimize contention, especially on HDD systems.

MON settings

In Ceph releases beginning with Jewel, the MONs do a pretty good job at managing their databases. This was not necessarily the case in older releases. MON DB size is a function of both the numbers of OSDs and PGs in your cluster and of how much topology churn is going on. During periods of heavy recovery or node maintenance, the `/var/lib/ceph/mon` DB can grow to tens of GBs. This can become problematic on systems that provision meager filesystem space, and in some cases, it can impact MON responsiveness and thus overall cluster snappiness.

Even on Jewel and later releases, this setting is recommended; it directs MON daemons to sweep stale entries from their DBs at startup-time:

```
[mon]
mon_compact_on_start = true
```

Another valuable setting is the mouthful `mon_osd_down_out_subtree_limit`. This affects how Ceph behaves when components go down:

```
[mon]
mon_osd_down_out_subtree_limit = host
```

This behavior, like the name, is tricky. This is defined as the smallest CRUSH bucket type that will not automatically be marked out. What this means is that if everything underneath a CRUSH bucket of the specified type fails at once, those items will not have the out state applied to them. With the default value of rack, hosts and OSD buckets will be marked out if they enter the down state due to failure and the cluster will begin recovery to ensure replication policy.

If we change the value to host, this means that if an entire OSD node suddenly bites the dust, Ceph will not mark its OSDs down. If we have a replicated cluster with a failure domain of rack, the loss of an entire host at once will no longer trigger recovery. The idea is that most of the time a host can be brought back up quickly, say by a hard reset because it wedged during reboot. Or maybe we installed a bad kernel that we need to remove before a second reboot.

If the host is legitimately dead, then we have the ability to run backfill/recovery on our own terms at our own rate, say with the `ceph-gentle-reweight` script we used in Chapter 19, *Operations and Maintenance*.

This option is tricky and can be difficult to understand. If you aren't really sure it's right for you, you should stick with the default.

Many other settings are possible and may benefit your deployment. We do not want to overwhelm you with a raft of settings that you aren't comfortable with and which may not be right for your installation's unique mix of hardware, versions, and use-cases. Once you are conversant with Ceph's components and the dynamics of your clusters, we suggest perusing the larger set of settings detailed at `http://docs.ceph.com` and the `ceph-users` mailing list archives.

Client settings

Ceph's RBD block service is heavily utilized by cloud platforms like OpenStack and other virtualization solutions. Effective caching in memory on the client side can significantly improve the performance that users experience:

```
[client.yourclientname]
rbd_cache = true
rbd_cache_size = 67108864
rbd_cache_max_dirty = 50331648
rbd_cache_target_dirty = 33554432
```

These values of 64MB, 48MB, and 32MB are double the default numerical values as of Luminous.

Settings must be selected so that `rbd_cache_size` > `rbd_cache_max_dirty` > `rbd_cache_target_dirty`.

Some references suggest larger values but consider that these cache buffers are allocated per attached volume. Consider a dense hypervisor node hosting 100 smaller VM instances, each mapping an RBD volume for its boot drive. With these values, the hypervisor node will dedicate more than 6 GB of RAM just for caching guest boot drives. You may be able to spare that much, but hypervisors are often limited by RAM, and this should be considered carefully within the context of the overall server memory budget and the capacity configured for scheduling.

Benchmarking

There are utilities built into Ceph to measure performance, as well as valuable external tools. We'll discuss both. It's important to remember that workloads that issue smaller requests will yield much lower numbers than those issuing larger requests.

RADOS bench

To use Ceph's built-in tool, first create a dedicated, disposable pool to scribble into. For this to be a legitimate test, it must have the same attributes as your production pool: PG count, replication factor, CRUSH rules, etc.

Options to rados bench include:

- -p: The name of our dedicated test pool
- seconds: Number of seconds the test should run
- write|seq|rand: Type of workload to present: write, sequential read, random read
- -t: Number of concurrent operations; the default is 16
- --no-cleanup: Don't clean up the objects created during the run

Let's run a 60-second write test against a small cluster with a pool named data. A dedicated pool should be used to ensure that user data is not clobbered. Longer tests are better than shorter, as they ensure that caching effects do not overly skew the results:

```
# rados bench -p data 60 write
Maintaining 16 concurrent writes of 4194304 bytes for up to 60 seconds or 0
objects
Object prefix: benchmark_data_ncc_1701
sec Cur ops started finished avg MB/s cur MB/s last lat avg lat
0 0 0 0 0 0 - 0
1 16 39 23 92.9777 93 0.627 0.56
2 16 67 50 98.853 109 0.523 0.59
3 16 97 80 105.234 119 0.267 0.55
4 16 126 109 107.843 114 0.231 0.54
5 16 152 135 106.111 103 0.301 0.52
6 16 181 164 108.334 114 0.714 0.56
7 16 209 192 108.945 110 0.843 0.59
8 16 237 220 108.238 111 0.133 0.53
9 16 266 249 109.934 113 0.780 0.53
10 15 292 276 109.364 111 0.822 0.51
. . .
```

Tests should be run multiple times and for longer periods and the results compared and averaged to validate the method.

CBT

The Ceph Benchmarking Tool is a sophisticated test harness that can leverage multiple data collection methods. Space does not permit a full exploration in this book. Those interested in serious repeatable quantitative data, say for testing different EC profiles or FileStore settings, will find this invaluable.

CBT can be found at `https://github.com/ceph/cbt`.

FIO

The Flexible I/O Tester is what it says: a highly configurable tool for testing a variety of storage systems. Many Linux distributions provide bundled `fio` packages for easy installation.

> One may visit `https://github.com/axboe/fio` to grok all things FIO.
> Especially useful is the collection of example profiles at `https://github.com/axboe/fio/tree/master/examples` .
> The FIO examples boxed below may be downloaded with these URLs:
> `https://learningceph2ed.nyc3.digitaloceanspaces.com/random.1m.fio`
> `https://learningceph2ed.nyc3.digitaloceanspaces.com/mix.fio`
> `https://learningceph2ed.nyc3.digitaloceanspaces.com/random.small.fio`

Here are some example FIO profiles that the authors find useful for benchmarking Ceph RBD clusters. Instances are run from several virtual machine clients in parallel.

Fill volume, then random 1M writes for 96 hours, no read verification:

```
[global]
ioengine=libaio
direct=1
group_reporting
filename=/dev/sda
[sequential-fill]
description=Sequential fill phase
```

```
rw=write
iodepth=16
bs=4M
random-write-steady]
stonewall
description=Random write steady state phase
rw=randwrite
bs=1M
iodepth=32
numjobs=4
time_based
runtime=345600
write_bw_log=fio-write-bw
write_lat_log=fio-write-lat
write_iops_log=fio-write-iops
log_avg_msec=1000
```

Fill volume, then small block writes for 96 hours, no read verification:

```
[global]
ioengine=libaio
direct=1
group_reporting
filename=/dev/sda[sequential-fill]
description=Sequential fill phase
rw=write
iodepth=16
bs=4M
[random-write-steady]
stonewall
description=Random write steady state phase
rw=randwrite
bssplit=512b/10:1k/3:2k/3:4k/45:8k/15:16k/7:32k/5:64k/5:128k/7
time_based
runtime=345600
iodepth=32
numjobs=4
write_bw_log=fio-write-bw
write_lat_log=fio-write-lat
write_iops_log=fio-write-iops
log_avg_msec=1000
```

Fill volume, then 4k random writes for 96 hours, occasional read verification:

```
[global]
ioengine=libaio
direct=1group_reporting
filename=/dev/sda
[sequential-fill]
description=Sequential fill phase
rw=write
iodepth=16
bs=4M
[random-write-steady]
stonewall
description=Random write steady state with verification
rw=randwrite
bssplit=512b/10:4k/80:64k/5:1M/5
time_based
runtime=345600
iodepth=32
numjobs=4
write_bw_log=fio-write-bw
write_lat_log=fio-write-lat
write_iops_log=fio-write-iops
log_avg_msec=1000
verify=crc32c-intel
verify_dump=1
verify_backlog=1000000
```

Summary

The learning does not stop here; not for you, and not for your humble authors. Several companies in the Ceph community offer interactive classes and professional services. Ceph topics are popular at conferences, including the semiannual OpenStack Summits.

Other Books You May Enjoy

If you enjoyed this book, you may be interested in these other books by Packt:

Mastering Kubernetes

Gigi Sayfan

ISBN: 9781788999786

- Architect a robust Kubernetes cluster for long-time operation
- Discover the advantages of running Kubernetes on GCE, AWS, Azure, and bare metal
- Understand the identity model of Kubernetes, along with the options for cluster federation
- Monitor and troubleshoot Kubernetes clusters and run a highly available Kubernetes
- Create and configure custom Kubernetes resources and use third-party resources in your automation workflows
- Enjoy the art of running complex stateful applications in your container environment
- Deliver applications as standard packages

DevOps with Kubernetes

Hideto Saito, Hui-Chuan Chloe Lee and Cheng-Yang Wu

ISBN: 9781788396646

- Learn fundamental and advanced DevOps skills and tools
- Get a comprehensive understanding for container
- Learn how to move your application to container world
- Learn how to manipulate your application by Kubernetes
- Learn how to work with Kubernetes in popular public cloud
- Improve time to market with Kubernetes and Continuous Delivery
- Learn how to monitor, log, and troubleshoot your application with Kubernetes

Software-Defined Networking (SDN) with OpenStack

Sriram Subramanian and Sreenivas Voruganti

ISBN: 9781786465993

- Understand how OVS is used for Overlay networks
- Get familiar with SDN Controllers with Architectural details and functionalities
- Create core ODL services and understand how OpenDaylight integrates with OpenStack to provide SDN capabilities
- Understand OpenContrail architecture and how it supports key SDN functionality such as Service Function Chaining (SFC) along with OpenStack
- Explore Open Network Operating System (ONOS) – a carrier grade SDN platform embraced by the biggest telecom service providers
- Learn about upcoming SDN technologies in OpenStack such as Dragonflow and OVN

Leave a review - let other readers know what you think

Please share your thoughts on this book with others by leaving a review on the site that you bought it from. If you purchased the book from Amazon, please leave us an honest review on this book's Amazon page. This is vital so that other potential readers can see and use your unbiased opinion to make purchasing decisions, we can understand what our customers think about our products, and our authors can see your feedback on the title that they have worked with Packt to create. It will only take a few minutes of your time but is valuable to other potential customers, our authors, and Packt. Thank you!

Index

www.ingramcontent.com/pod-product-compliance
Lightning Source LLC
Chambersburg PA
CBHW060635060326
40690CB00020B/4407